Panama

THE BRADT TRAVEL GUIDE

THE BRADT STORY

The first Bradt travel guide was written in 1974 by George and Hilary Bradt on a river barge floating down a tributary of the Amazon. In the 1980s and '90s the focus shifted away from hiking to broader-based guides covering new destinations – usually the first to be published about these places. In the 21st century Bradt continues to publish such ground-breaking guides, as well as others to established holiday destinations, incorporating in-depth information on culture and natural history with the nuts and bolts of where to stay and what to see.

Bradt authors support responsible travel, and provide advice not only on minimum impact but also on how to give something back through local charities. In this way a true synergy is achieved between the traveller and local communities.

*

I have a special affection for any country that featured in the early Bradt guides. In 1978 George and I entered Panama on foot from Colombia via The Darién Gap (no longer feasible for security reasons) and were entranced. We were fascinated by the costume and culture of the Kuna Indians in whose villages we stayed, and by the Embera, whose simple lifestyle seemed so idyllic. And all this in wonderful virgin rainforest! It hasn't changed – much. Sarah tells me that what she loves most about Panama is that she can buy designer clothes at the city's top department store in the morning, and in the afternoon be taken gently down a river by a man wearing a loin-cloth who points out the imprint of a jaguar's paw on the sandy shore. I don't think I'd recognise Panama City these days, but the jungle sounds just the same. It makes me long to go back – and next time I shall include Sarah's favourite place, Bocas del Toro, for a bit of beach relaxation.

Hilary Bradt

19 High Street, Chalfont St Peter, Bucks SL9 9QE, England
Tel: 01753 893444   Fax: 01753 892333
Email: info@bradtguides.com   www.bradtguides.com

Panama

THE BRADT TRAVEL GUIDE

Sarah Woods

Bradt Travel Guides Ltd, UK
The Globe Pequot Press Inc, USA

First published in March 2005

Bradt Travel Guides Ltd,
19 High Street, Chalfont St Peter, Bucks SL9 9QE, England
www.bradtguides.com
Published in the USA by The Globe Pequot Press Inc, 246 Goose Lane,
PO Box 480, Guilford, Connecticut 06437-0480

British Library Cataloguing in Publication Data
A catalogue record for this book is available from the British Library

ISBN-10: 1 84162 117 X
ISBN-13: 978 1 84162 117 3

Photographs
Front cover: Resplendent quetzal (Michael and Patricia Fogden)
Text: David Short (DS), Chris Talbot (CT)

Illustrations Carole Vincer
Maps Alan Whitaker. Regional maps based on ITM *Panamá*

Typeset from the author's disc by Wakewing, High Wycombe
Printed and bound in Italy by Legoprint SpA

Author

Travel writer **Sarah Woods** has been crisscrossing the globe since the early 1980s, clocking up more than 500,000km and visiting around 50 countries along the way. She discovered Panama in the wake of the Canal handover and set about travelling its length and breadth. Ask her what is so great about the home of the world's greatest short cut and Sarah is unequivocal, citing wild untrodden jungle, extraordinary wildlife and a mix of cultures at its heart. A veteran of volunteering, she has worked on projects in Bocas del Toro and Panama City. Today Sarah supports an SOS village for abandoned and orphaned children in David, and writes about her Panama experiences for magazines and newspapers worldwide.

Contributor **Heloise Crowther** is a specialist writer on Latin America and has travelled extensively in the region. She lives in Panama and London.

DEDICATION
For David

Contents

LIST OF MAPS

Golden frog

Acknowledgements

I'd like to extend my enormous gratitude to every Panamanian who lent their support to this project, from the Kuna womenfolk who surprised me with songs and lobster on my birthday, to the potter who shared his life story whilst at the wheel in Herrera. It's impossible to list everyone who helped me along the way, but a special mention goes to Feleciano González in Chiriqui, Claudio Atencio in Los Santos, Anibal Murillo and Leonel F Moreno in Coiba, Leonel E Vega in Veraguas, Jeronimo de la Ossa in Kuna Yala, and Educardo Moscoso on Isla Iguana, and to every single person I met in the isthmus who felt inspired to share their thoughts.

I owe heartfelt thanks to Mario Bernal who accompanied me for much of my last trip. He was generous with his time and also with his patience and I defy anyone not to feel enlivened by his infectious enthusiasm for everything that lives and breathes around him. Also Tammy Liu and Gustavo Chan who joined me through the central provinces and provided an ultra-efficient back-up system during my journey. I would surely have missed my 05.00 *cayaco* without their excellent knowledge of Panama's back roads and I applaud their ability to remain cheerful despite downpours and mechanical failure.

I owe extra special thanks to Heloise Crowther, whose professionalism and good humour made her an invaluable contributor to this project. Thanks also to Captain Joanne for her insight on diving in the Bocas del Toro archipelago; Kevin Mellinger who helped no end on rafting and kayaking in Chiriqui; and Michael Richlen and Liz Spencer who provided considerable assistance on marine life and coastal habitat. A debt of gratitude too to Raichel Rickels and Helen Ponting simply for being prepared to lend a hand and get stuck in.

As usual not a chapter would have been typed without the constant encouragement of travel photographer David Short. His great photos, bad jokes and keen interest in this project were a tremendous boost. Thank you.

KEY TO STANDARD SYMBOLS

Bradt

—·—·—	International boundary	𝒊	Tourist information
------	District boundary	🏺	Museum
	National park or reserve	∴	Archaeological or historic site
	Forest park or reserve	🏛	Historic building
✈	Airport (international)	🏰	Castle/fortress
✈	Airport (other)	✝	Church or cathedral
✛	Airstrip	🛕	Hindu temple
⭢	Helicopter service	▶	Golf course
▭▭▭	Railway	🏃	Stadium
----------	Featured footpath/trek	●	Other place of interest
----------	Other footpath	▲	Summit/peak name height (in metres)
--⛴--	Car ferry	△	Water depth
--⛴--	Passenger ferry	⤛	Border post
⛽	Petrol station or garage	⌂	Cave/rock shelter
🅿	Car park		Cable car, funicular
🚌	Bus station etc	)))	Waterfall
🚲	Cycle hire	※	Scenic viewpoint
⌂	Hotel, inn etc	❋	Botanical site
⛺	Campsite	♣	Specific woodland feature
⬤	Hut	⚘	Lighthouse
♈	Wine bar	---	Marsh
✕	Restaurant, café etc	🌳	Mangrove
☆	Night club	➤	Bird watching/nesting site
⊠	Post office		Coral reef
ℓ	Telephone		Sandy beach (extensive)
e	Internet access	➤	Sandy beach
✚	Hospital, clinic etc	✓	Scuba diving
✚	Pharmacy/health centre	⤚	Fishing sites
$	Bank		
⬤	Statue or monument		

Other map symbols are sometimes shown in separate key boxes with individual explanations for their meanings.

Introduction

Why Panama?

For me, Panama is without doubt one of the most misunderstood countries in Central America: a skinny squiggle of land overshadowed by high-profile neighbours and largely ignored by tourists. Dismissed for years by an international travel press that favoured the gloss and glamour of Costa Rica, Panama's fledgling tourism industry has been slow to gain strength. Yet things are changing for Panama – a country on the up – and while it still relies a little too heavily on its appeal as 'the Costa Rica of yesteryear', visitor numbers in 2004 showed a significant rise. Many arrive as sceptics and leave as converts, helping to disprove that Panama is 'where the worst of North America and Central America meet', as the British tabloid newspaper the *Sun* once declared in caustic tones.

As an inquisitive traveller in search of untrodden land, I found these misconceptions made Panama all the more inviting. Wild, tangled jungles, riverbank Indian villages, alpine-sloped volcanoes and golden islands aroused my curiosity, whilst the prospect of getting to know a nation much maligned appealed to my sense of fair play. Despite an infamous former dictator and a landmark canal, Panama is something of an enigma – a secret in waiting. For me, few lands are more exciting than those that beg to be discovered, as travellers in Panama soon find to their delight.

Proud, diverse and extraordinary, Panama is a pleasing mishmash of cultures, a land of opportunity and scenic splendour that boasts rainforests, beaches, valleys and mountains dotted with waterfalls, hot springs, caves and petroglyphs. Home to 940 bird species, 1,500 islands, 480 rivers, 125 unique species of wildlife and 40 conservation areas, more than a third of Panama's land is protected, with surrounding off-shore waters rich in marine life. Vast expanses of wilderness support a biodiversity attributable to Panama's crossroads location, a land bridge linking North and Central America, comprising wetlands, grasslands, forests and coastal plains. More fishing records have been broken here than anywhere else on the planet, while Panama's turtle nesting sites are some of the most important in the world. Festivals, parades and rituals celebrate Panama's seven indigenous peoples, Spanish heritage and mixed ethnicities with gusto. From masked parades and Congo drumming to carnival floats and puberty rites, it's a riot of colour, noise and pride. Puma prowl and giant harpy eagles roost just 45 minutes from the capital's gleaming financial district, while at just 50km wide at its narrowest point Panama's land mass is easily traversable in a day. Dip a toe in the Caribbean Sea in the morning sun and be on the Pacific coast by lunchtime – much like a transiting vessel on the Panama Canal.

Like most places on earth Panama is no flawless travel brochure cliché and, as a tourist destination in its infancy, the isthmus is far from perfect. Pristine in parts and decaying in others, Panama is awe-inspiring, humbling and maddening all in one day. Travel here requires patience, a skill for second-guessing and an acceptance that things will change in an instant without warning. Timetables are unpredictable. Working hours are open to loose interpretation. Maps are inaccurate. Public holidays occur without notice. Places have at least three names spelt at least four ways. Roads terminate unannounced. And even some of Panama's medium-sized towns see no need for street names. Consequently, having a Plan B in Panama is as essential as having had a Plan A in the first place. Expect to resort to C, D or E in remote spots (I've even pulled out F on occasions) and attempt to view these characteristics as much a part of Panama's appeal as its coralline coastline and deserted, palm-fringed islands. Foreign visitors, a new phenomenon in many rural areas, should expect a gamut of reactions from Panamanians, ranging from welcoming smiles to open-mouthed stares at you, an alien species on an intergalactic jaunt. Of one thing I'm sure; Panama is never dull; and I intend to relish the foibles of this country while I can, in case they are dutifully 'ironed out' by the state-run tourism machine in time.

Most of the legwork for this guide took place at the end of 2003 (with a considerable amount of research before and after). Once back at my desk in a leafy British village I began to wonder if I'd be able to capture Panama accurately in 140,000 words. The pace at which the isthmus is changing is staggering; this is a period of immense adjustment for Panama, and it didn't take long for me to realise that this rapidity of growth makes it impossible for any guidebook to be 100% reliable, however dogged its author. Oversights, amendments and errors are inevitable, prices will change, places will close and open, and new roads and airports will be built. With this in mind I've included as many online resources as possible to enable a double-checking of detail. While all times, schedules, opening hours, distances and durations have been listed in good faith, I recommend factoring in a contingency for the quirks of Panamanian bureaucracy, and a transportation system that likes to depart as and when, on a whim.

So, it just leaves me to say, 'enjoy Panama' – a land synonymous with straw hats, dictators, cigars and the Canal (the 'Big Ditch'), but with much, much more to offer. If you pick up any great tips or discover new places, please pass them on. Your experiences will help to make the next Bradt Guide to Panama even better. Drop me a line by email to sarah.woods@dial.pipex.com or write c/o Bradt Guides 19 High Street, Chalfont St Peter, Bucks SL9 9QE, UK. There's also an online feedback form at www.bradtguides.com.

Part One

General Information

PANAMA AT A GLANCE

Location Panama is the southernmost of the Central American countries, bordered by Costa Rica on the west and Colombia on the east
Area 78,046 km²
Relief Alpine peaks and volcanic crags in the west give way to the dusty savannas of the interior, while the thousands of islands that flank the coastlines are surrounded by coral reefs
Highest point Volcán Barú (3,475m), a dormant volcano in the Chiriquí province
Climate Warm and tropical, with a wet and dry season, and constant temperatures
Average temperatures 29°C
Government Constitutional democracy
Population 3.1 million, of which 65% are mestizo (mixed Indian-Spanish descent), 15% English-speaking Antilleans, and 8% indigenous Indians
Capital Panama City
Language Spanish
Religion Roman Catholicism is the dominant faith, with Islamic, Jewish and Protestant minorities
National flag Divided into four rectangles (clockwise from top left): white with blue star motif; red; white with red star motif; blue
National anthem *Himno Istemño* ('Isthmus Hymn')
Public holidays Wise Men Day (January 6), Martyrs' Day (January 9), Carnaval (Tuesday before Ash Wednesday), Good Friday (April 9), All Saints Day, Independence Day (from Colombia) and Flag Day (November 2–4), Independence Day (from Spain) (November 28), Christmas (December 24–25), New Year's Eve (December 31)
Tourist season Peak season runs from mid-December to mid-April
Entry regulations Every visitor needs a valid passport and an onward ticket
Health No special vaccination requirements
Air access Via Tocumen International Airport near Panama City
Road links Via any of Panama's three border posts with Costa Rica; road access from Colombia is not possible
Currency Panama uses the US$ as its legal tender. Domestic currency is found only in coinage (balboa) and is used in conjunction with the US$
Weights and measures Although metric is the official system, imperial measurements are common
Electricity Voltages vary, but 110 volts is the norm with some sockets 220
Time Unlike the rest of Central America, Panama is five hours behind GMT
Internet domain .pa
International dialling code +507

Background Information

LOCATION
Located in the middle of the American continent, the Republic of Panama is the southernmost of the Central American countries; bordered on the east by Colombia and on the west by Costa Rica, between the Caribbean Sea to the north and the Pacific Ocean to the south. At just 50km in width at its narrowest point, this S-shaped isthmus can be traversed in a day, a bridge of land linking Central and South America. Stand at a lofty point on the continental divide to see the Atlantic and the Pacific in one magnificent view.

TOPOGRAPHY
Some 30% of Panama's landscape has been set aside for conservation, more than in any other country in Central America. Yet this pleasing figure hides the gloomy reality that more than 75% of its forests have already been lost. However, large swathes of jungle remain, much of it wild and unexplored, particularly in the east. Alpine peaks and volcanic crags in the west give way to the dusty savannahs of the interior. Rugged headlands, sandy coves and lush plains in the south edge the mountains that split the isthmus along its spine, while the thousands of islands that flank each coastline are surrounded by coral reefs.

POPULATION
In 1987 demographers estimated the population of Panama at 2.3 million, with 40% under the age of 15. Today, according to UN figures, the number exceeds 3.1 million, with a predicted continued growth rate of 1.6% per annum. The highest population density is found in and around Panama City at 704,000 according to the 2000 census. Despite being one of the least populated countries in Central America, Panama has a population of great ethnic diversity.

PEOPLE
Panamanians view their society as being composed of three principal groups: the Spanish-speaking Roman Catholic Mestizo (mixed Indian–Spanish descent) majority (65%); English-speaking Protestant Antilleans (15%); and indigenous Indians (8%). Panama also has a large Chinese population and a growing number of American expatriates.

Indigenous Indians
Pre-Columbian Panama was home to numerous Indian communities, many of whom were migratory settlers. In the 16th century the Conquistador invasion resulted in the disappearance of a number of tribes, not only in battle but also due to the arrival of foreign diseases that the Indians had no resistance to. In fact so many were lost in Panama that colonial European settlers later chose to import Indian slaves from other areas of the Americas.

Five major Indian communities in Panama comprise the 8% indigenous population of 200,000 (Smithsonian Tropical Research Institute). The Emberá and Wounaan, together numbering approximately 20,000, originated from the Choco area of Colombia and now populate villages throughout Panama's Darién rainforest. In recent years they have collectively campaigned for land rights, which were finally recognised in 1983 when the government named 300,000ha of jungle the Comarca Emberá–Drua. They continue to petition against plans to join the Pan-American Highway between Panama and Colombia, a measure they feel would seriously threaten their future.

Both the Emberá and Wounaan live, hunt and gather as their ancestors did, in thick jungle surroundings, utilising forest plants for medicines. The Darién's natural system of jungle canals is vital to trade, which they traverse using dugout *cayucos* to buy and sell with other communities. Customs such as painting their bodies with plant dyes and hunting with poison-tipped blowgun darts are still widely practised. However, the Emberá and Wounaan are struggling to continue this ancient way of life, primarily due to deforestation and aggressive farming in the region. Individuals are gradually turning to cash crops to support themselves and their families. The style of native Indian craft is unique to each culture; the weaving of the Emberá and Wounaan is so distinctive that it is now exported to North America. The intricately patterned baskets and jugs woven from palm fibres are first dyed with natural colour compounds from roots and plants, and can even be watertight. These now fetch high prices abroad and are sold with pride throughout Panama. Other crafts include pottery, and animals carved from the forest seed tagua, which is remarkably similar to ivory in colour consistency.

The Kuna culture, also known as Tule, is a tight community now legendary among native Latin American Indians. Like the Emberá and Wounaan, they are believed to have migrated north from Colombia. The Spanish documented them in the Darién on their arrival and later during the 19th century the Kuna moved to the islands of the San Blas archipelago. The Kuna are well known as an outstanding Indian community and have fought hard to achieve what they have today – political and social autonomy. In 1925 continual pressure from the Panamanian government to assimilate Kuna people into modern mainstream culture concluded in a violent Kuna revolution. A US Navy vessel stationed in nearby waters stepped in on behalf of the Indians, an act that has kept the US in favour with the Kuna to this day. In fact, in 1932 the Kuna signed an agreement with the US that allowed Kuna men to work on military bases in the Canal Zone. Panamanian governments backed down under US threat and in 1938 the Kuna were finally granted autonomous rule as a comarca. Currently, the Kuna General Congress is comprised of local governments and is presided over by three national chiefs.

The Kuna are deeply respectful of their natural environment and as such have strict laws concerning tourism. You may hear tourists grumbling about what they are and are not allowed to do on the islands of Kuna Yala, as dictated by the Kuna. This, to me, stands as testimony to the lengths most Kuna are willing to go to protect their environment, and not waver over a quick buck. In 1985 they established an internationally recognised rainforest reserve measuring 60,000ha within their comarca, and went on to develop a learning centre for rainforest management.

The Kuna economy is now mainly dependent upon tourism, handmade crafts and small-scale farming and fishing. Kuna women are instantly recognisable from their colourful headscarves and hand-stitched molas that make up the bodice of their dress. Jewellery consists of heavy gold ear and nose rings, and strings of tiny coloured beads that adorn their arms and legs in elaborate wave-like patterns.

A much less populous community is the Buglé (or Bokota) culture, many of whom have now mixed with the Ngwobe or Ngöbe. Hence these peoples are now collectively known as Ngöbe Buglé. There is added confusion over their name as Ngöbe Buglé are widely known within the country as Guaymi, a name that does not exist in their language. A local in the Bocas del Toro province once told me a sad tale of its origin. During slavery years these Indians used to cry out 'Why me, why me?' which later became Guaymi. Whatever the history, it has stuck and Guaymi is used more often than Ngöbe Buglé.

One of the fastest-growing native communities of the Americas, Ngöbe Buglé now number around 125,000 in Panama. Inhabiting the western provinces of Chiriquí, Bocas del Toro and Veraguas, they are also fighting for a comarca. They wish to protect traditional laws and their own language and have reportedly requested to be shielded from missionary sects. Ngöbe Buglé people are also suffering integration with expanding urban sprawl. Alarming amounts of land have been cleared encroaching on their space, including slash-and-burn areas and new paved roads. Although many traditions are retained in their communities, the economy is now mainly down to poorly paid farming, and many are joining the banana and coffee plantation workforce. Ngöbe Buglé dress for women consists of long smock-like garments, with hand-stitched coloured triangles and edging. Men wear a tiny beaded necklace known as *chaquira*.

Other Indians in the region include small numbers of Bribri that have, over generations, crossed the Costa Rican border from Talamanca. Along with the Teribe (or Tiribe), a larger group that have settled on the Teribe River near Changuinola, they now neighbour the Ngöbe Buglé.

Despite a hard fight by the Kuna and Ngöbe Buglé for their rights to an equal existence in the country, increasing deforestation and mass farming is forcing Indians out of their native environment. The Teribe, remaining original Buglé, and Bribri are expected to assimilate into modern Panamanian culture, or at worst face extinction. Along with communities, languages, customs and wisdom concerning Panama's natural habitat will be lost. Even the Kuna language is predicted not to last.

Antilleans

The majority of Panama's West Indian population are descendants of the 19th-century workforce shipped over from Jamaica and Trinidad as cheap labour. Most worked on the Canal, the banana plantations of Bocas del Toro or the transisthmian railway.

RACISM

This diverse ethnic mix is not without its tensions yet there are fewer racial frictions in Panama than in most developed nations. The country has no organised racist groups and hate crimes are few and far between. Distinct cultures exist within each racial group yet Panama's diversity is such that these often combine to create new ethnicity. However, you don't need to look very hard in Panamanian society to see racism in its most common form, from jobs-for-the-boys to private member clubs that preclude certain ethnic groups. As a Kuna friend said, 'The ugliness of racism is here but is outweighed by Panama's beauty, in its people and the wildlife and plants.'

RELIGION

The freedom to practice any religion is a constitutional right in Panama although Roman Catholicism is the dominant faith. In Panama City (home to a sizeable immigrant population) beliefs are mixed and Jewish synagogues, Muslim mosques, Hindu temples and a large number of Catholic and Protestant churches are found throughout the capital. Official figures cite Panama's religious make-up as Roman Catholicism (85%), Protestantism (5%) and Islam (5%). Each of the seven Indian communities has its own belief system.

LANGUAGE

Panama's seven Indian tribes speak eight different languages, including a unique Kuna variant found only in the east. Arabic, Chinese (both Cantonese and Hakka), Hebrew, San Miguel Creole French and Western Caribbean Creole English are all spoken in Panama, although Spanish is the official and dominant language. English is the second language but is a rarity away from the capital and mastering a few Spanish basics is essential for those heading to the interior provinces. Americanisms and slang have infiltrated the language to a large extent and *Streetwise Spanish* (McGraw-Hill, US$14.95), a guide to Latin American Spanish, is especially useful in the isthmus.

ECONOMY

Disparity between rich and poor is all too evident in Panama, which is fast becoming a country of haves and have-nots. Although its per-capita income (US$3,070) is the highest in Central America, a third of the population remain poverty-stricken and unemployment sits at around 13%. In slums close to the capital's Porsche showrooms and luminous designer stores, the poor of Panama City lack basic everyday needs. Begging and street crime are the survival tools in these districts just a few blocks away from skyscraper banks and the Canal Zone, the very symbol of Panama's prosperity.

Despite a rousing presidential speech, Mireya Moscoso's pledge in 1999 to 'wipe out poverty' in Panama was little more than a crowd pleaser. The refusal by her administration to address the money gap, or even acknowledge it, was a genuine disappointment to those who voted for social change. Pleas by labour unions to increase the minimum wage to US$500 per month also fell on deaf ears. At the time of writing President Torrijos is in the early stages of his tenure so it's a case of wait and see and fingers crossed.

Service industries account for approximately 75% of Panama's GNP, an economic characteristic that bolstered its financial system after the political turmoil of the late 1980s. Panama's exclusive right to use the US dollar as its par-value currency has also strengthened its economy as many of its Latin American neighbours struggle. Textiles, tobacco, construction, brewing, cement and agriculture are all key industries, yet it is Panama's location as a transit and transportation hub that forms its pecuniary backbone. America's recent economic slow-down has hampered Panama's economic expansion (the US is its largest commercial partner), yet GDP achieved a 2.1% growth to US$8.8 billion in 2004, strengthened by trade with Europe, Central America, the Caribbean and Japan.

Contacts

American Chamber of Commerce & Industry in Panama Estafeta Balboa, Apartado 168, Panama; tel: (507) 269 3881; fax: (507) 223 3508; email: amcham@pan.gbm.net; www.panamcham.com

US Department of Commerce International Trade Administration, Office of Latin America and the Caribbean, 14th and Constitution Av, NW, Washington, DC 20230; tel: (202) 482 0057/800 (USA trade); fax: (202) 482 0464; www.ita.doc.gov

EDUCATION

The education system in Panama is made up of three levels: primary, secondary and university, each lasting six years. Enrolment in primary school is high at more than 90% as, officially, education is compulsory for six years between the ages of six and 15. However, only about half of these students continue to secondary school despite education being free to university level. The pledge by President Moscoso to address education as a 'national priority' in 2001 was followed by a US$545 million injection of funds, a sizeable budget but one that only scratched the surface.

Panamanians attend school for an average of seven years although children in indigenous communities (especially girls) are schooled for as few as three. The national illiteracy rate of 2.7% also fails to reflect the educational needs of the indigenous population. A third of the Indian groups are illiterate and in the Ngöbe Buglé communities 50% of women are unable to read or write.

GEOGRAPHY AND CLIMATE
Geography

At three to four million years of age, the Central American continent is a relatively new part of the world, geologically speaking. Twenty million years ago, the Cocos Plate slid eastward, colliding with the Antilles Plate and becoming hidden underneath it. When these plates moved, volcanic activity became pronounced, forming new land that created a bridge between two continents that had separated. The Cocas Plate continues to slide over the Antilles Plate at a rate of 10cm each year, a geological rapidity that creates friction in the form of earthquakes and volcanic activity.

On a map the Republic of Panama looks rather insignificant compared with neighbouring Colombia; a vast spread of land that overshadows Panama's narrow squiggle. Yet few stretches of land are more important in strategic terms: a bridge that connects South and Central America and the Atlantic and Pacific Oceans; a unique landmass in every sense. At 716km at its widest point and 50km at the narrowest, the isthmus extends east from Costa Rica for 1,699km, with more than 1,000 islands on its southern coastline and 600 islands to the north. At 78,046km^2 Panama is triple the size of Belize yet barely the size of Ireland.

Much of Panama's territory is at less than 915m (3,000ft). The Cordillera Central, the most dominant mountain range, originates in Costa Rica and pushes eastward out to the Coclé Province. Panama's highest elevation is Volcán Barú, a dormant volcano in the Chiriquí Province at 3,475m (1,140ft). More than 2,200km^2 of Panama's landscape comprises water, with 500 rivers and the freshwater Panama Canal. One hundred and fifty rivers flow into the Caribbean Sea and more than 300 into the Pacific Ocean; the Changuinola (140km), the Indio (99km), the Chagres (92km), the Bayano (280km), the Chucunaque (242km) and the Tuira (230km) are the most important.

In geographic and administrative terms Panama is divided into nine provinces. Chiriquí and Bocas del Toro border Costa Rica; Veraguas, Herrera and Los Santos form the interior regions; Coclé and Colón edge the province of Panama; while Darién in the east forms a boundary with Colombia. Kuna Yala (formerly Comarca de San Blas), a self-governing territory of Kuna Indians, occupies a sliver of mainland and an archipelago on the Caribbean coastline above Panama Province and Darién.

Panamanian terrain was wholly intact until the US construction of the Canal in the early 20th century. Splitting the isthmus became one of the world's greatest feats of engineering, creating a freedom of transit that revolutionised international shipping and transport, but interrupted the path of migrating wildlife.

Climate

Panama lies below the hurricane route and suffers from few adverse weather conditions apart from an occasional tropical depression from the Caribbean. The country enjoys a warm, wet tropical climate north of the Equator in a humid tropical zone. Two seasons, wet and dry, maintain uniform year-round high temperatures. The highlands are steady at 19–21°C while elsewhere 28–31°C is the norm. The dry season (Panamanians call this *verano*, meaning summer) runs from mid-December to mid-April. March and April are generally the hottest months when several successive weeks will experience little or no rainfall. The wet season (*invierno*, meaning winter) is from mid-April to November and brings high humidity and the risk of heavy rains. October, November and the beginning of December are the wettest months of the year, although constant rain is rare on the southern coast. Rainfall generally arrives in short, torrential downpours – but not always. Predicting the amount of rain is impossible in Panama, especially on the Caribbean coastline. Rainfall varies dramatically from province to province (see *Climatic Charts*) and visitors to Bocas del Toro should expect a downpour at least once a week.

NATURAL HISTORY AND CONSERVATION

The recent increase in revenue generated from eco-tourism has encouraged the Panamanian government to shift its focus from consumption to preservation. Today a third of all land in Panama has been set aside for protection, more than in any of its Central American neighbours, although a continued problem with illegal logging and hunting suggests the state-owned environmental authority, ANAM (Autoridad Nacional del Ambiente), is managing these protected areas with mixed success.

According to the World Conservation Monitoring Centre at least 600 plant and 300 wildlife species in Panama are on the endangered list. American crocodile, five species of turtle, Central American tapir, jaguar, spectacled bear and dozens of birds including scarlet macaw are under threat. Panama's marine environment, the lifeblood of indigenous communities, are in danger as a result of direct and indirect human activity. The link between terrestrial and marine ecosystems is an intimate one, and Panama is slowly waking up to the repercussions of damage from one to the other.

At the time of writing the International Whaling Commission is set to meet Panama, which has no whaling and just the beginnings of whale-watching tourism, is a key swing vote for Japan's move to expand whaling. The Moscoso government (1999–2004) voted with the Japanese, Norwegians and other pro-whaling nations, a decision that became an issue in the 2004 election battle. The Torrijos administration (2004–08) has promised that Panama will be a solid anti-whaling vote, and conservationists are keen to see if this promise is kept.

Another environmental concern is Panama's cruise-ship tourism, a market that IPAT, Panama's tourist board, has earmarked for significant growth. Raw sewage and toxic chemicals dumped directly into ocean waters pose a grave threat to Panama's marine habitat. However, with the cruise-ship industry growing by an average of 10% per annum, Panama is keen for a slice of the action.

Deforestation, a major threat to Panama's ecosystem, continues to affect the country's river systems and wildlife. More than 75% of natural forest has been destroyed. Soil erosion and loss of flora and fauna have impacted large areas of Panama threatening the biodiversity at an alarming rate. In 1997 forest cover totalled 70% of the land yet today just 38% of rainforest remains (*EarthTrends*; see *Appendix 1, Websites*). Should deforestation continue at the current rate of 58,000ha

CLIMATIC CHARTS

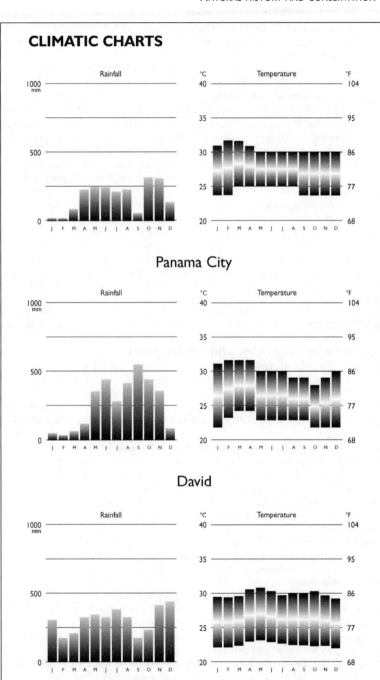

Panama City

David

Bocas del Toro

a year, the national parks will be the only rainforest cover left in 20 years, according to ANAM. Tropical hardwood forests cannot be replaced and 208 tree species are already under serious threat.

Deforestation surrounding the Panama Canal has affected the famous waterway itself. The forested watershed basin around the canal has halved since the 1970s and without roots to provide a drainage filter for three manmade lakes, mud and debris lead to silting and blockage. Establishing Soberanía and Chagres national parks has offered some protection to the canal watershed although the proposed Plan Puebla Panama Highway places other large areas of forest in jeopardy. Other plans include an extension of the Interamericana across the 'Darién Gap' to reach the Colombian border. This will cut through the Parque Nacional Darién, a UNESCO biosphere reserve, which comprises 20,000km^2 of dense primary rainforest.

Numerous non-profit organisations are proactive in research, education and enactment policies in a bid to restore natural habitats in Panama. The National Association for the Conservation of Nature (ANCON, Associación Nacional para la Conservación de la Naturaleza) is a privately funded conservation organisation founded by Panamanian academics, whose budget props up ANAM's cash-stretched efforts. ANCON's sister organisation, Ancon Expeditions, employs many of the country's leading naturalists as tour guides. The number of local conservation groups emerging has been especially encouraging to environmentalists. Many require volunteer resources (see *Giving Something Back*).

Conservation agencies and associations

Autorídad Nacional de Ambiente (ANAM) Tel: 315 0855/315 0903; www.anam.gob.pa. Panama's state-run National Environment Authority manages all national parks and protected areas, about a third of Panama's land.

Panama Verde Tel: 236 5619/626 2621/620 1965; email: Panamaverde@Panamaverde.org; www.Panamaverde.org. Vocal, well-organised student conservation group with a lobbying arm.

Associación Nacional para la Conservación de la Naturaleza (ANCON) Tel: 314 0600; fax: 314 0061; email: ancon@ancon.com; www.ancon.org. Panama's largest private conservation group, founded in 1985 by Panamanian business leaders and academics.

Panama Audubon Society Tel: 224 9371; fax: 224 4740; email: info@Panamaaudubon.org; www.Panamaaudubon.org. The conservation arm of the Panama Audubon Society runs community education projects to encourage preservation of habitat and species.

ConserVA Tel: 693 8213; email: mariobernalg@hotmail.com. Regional conservation group led by naturalist and birding guide Mario Bernal. Education and preservation focus in El Valle and surrounding areas, working with indigenous and local communities.

La Fundación Natura Tel: 232 7615/7616/7617; fax: 232 7613; email: info@naturaPanama.org; www.naturaPanama.org. A private, non-profit organization founded in Panama in 1991. Promotes sustainable development projects and the strengthening of the environmental sector of civil society in Panama. Since 1995, Fundación Natura' s principal activity has been the administration of funds originating from the Ecological Trust Fund of Panama (FIDECO).

Proyecto de Estudio para el Manejo de Areas Silvestres de Kuna Yala (PEMASKY) Tel/fax: (507) 225 7603; email: aekpemase@pty.com). Kuna-run NGO established to protect, study and manage the conservation efforts in Kuna Yala. Set up by the Kuna General Congress to prevent 'back door deforestation' from the Pan-American Highway and adjacent roads, aided by the MacArthur Foundation and the WWF.

Conservation through Research Education and Action (CREA) (UK office) Woodlawn, Heanton, Devon EX31 4DG; tel: +44 (0)1271 812937; email: admin@crea-Panama.org; (Panama office) PO Box 2704, Ancon, Balboa, Panama City; tel: 317 6635; email: admin@crea-Panama.org ; www.crea-Panama.org. UK-registered charity with volunteer staff dedicated to the conservation of tropical environments. Undertakes field study in Panama and funds reforestation and research projects. Currently working with the City of Trees (a Panamanian NGO) and local communities to design a buffer zone for human resource extraction and wildlife habitat, between the Chagres National Park and local communities.

The Peregrine Fund Neotropical Conservation Project 5668 West Flying Hawk Lane, Boise, Idaho 83709, USA; tel: (208) 362 3716; fax: (208) 362 2376; email: tpf@peregrinefund.org; www.peregrinefund.org. Run year-round educational programmes to further conservation efforts of the endangered harpy eagle, targeting release sites in the Panama Canal watershed and within the communities of Darién.

Autoridad de la Region Interoceanica (ARI) www.ari.gob.pa. The state-run Regional Inter-Oceanic Authority manages the development of the areas adjacent to the Panama Canal, planning, coordinating and managing projects for the sustainable use and preservation of the land.

The Primate Refuge and Sanctuary of Panama (PRSP) Email: DRR@PrimatesofPanama.org; www.PrimatesofPanama.org. This education, research and conservation group is focused on nonhuman primates in Panama and since being established in the early 1980s has become the second-largest primate sanctuary in the world. Comprises over 150 monkeys with a refuge, research study programme and community project on a 33ha site on Isla Tigre, Gatún Lake.

American Birding Association Inc PO Box 6599, Colorado Springs, CO 80934-6599, USA; tel: (719) 578 9703; fax: (719) 578 1480; email: member@aba.org; www.americanbirding.org. Run a Birder Conservationist programme and a Birder Exchange scheme in Panama, working with young wildlife enthusiasts in village communities.

The IUCN (Unión Mundial para la Naturaleza) IUCN Program for Wetlands & Coastal Zones Conservation in Mesoamerica, PO Box 1160-2150, Moravia, Costa Rica; email: nestor.windevoxhel@orma.iucn.org. Costa Rican-registered wetlands conservation group established in 1989, specialising in the coastal zones of Mesoamerica. Key projects in Panama include the wetlands of the Gulf of Montijo.

Sea Turtle Restoration Project PO Box 400, Forrest Knolls, CA 94933, USA; tel: (415) 488 0370; www.seaturtles.org. California-based turtle conservation project with programmes throughout Central America, including research programmes and sustainable fisheries and safe shrimping initiatives.

Smithsonian Tropical Research Institute Tupper Building, Roosevelt Av, Ancon, Balboa; tel: 212 8000; www.stri.org. Pioneering institute engaged in the study of tropical flora and fauna to further conservation efforts in Panama, working with NGOs and government bodies.

DOING YOUR BIT

Iguanas, monkeys, ocelots and sea turtles are poached for their meat, pelts, eggs and shells, an illegal trade that threatens these species. Widespread poverty encourages the trade in these animals countrywide and goods are often sold to tourists. Visitors who are offered such items or witness a threat to an endangered wildlife species should report it immediately to ANCON; tel: 314 0060 or ANAM; tel: 315 0855.

PANAMÁ: ABUNDANCE OF FISH

Panamá means 'abundance of fish' and according to archaeologists the Pacific coastline of Panama was fished by settlers as early as 1500BC. Moving between rivers, mangroves and ocean as the seasons dictated, these ancient fishermen began to look further afield in search of different species, when they began to actively trade. By AD1600 European colonists had begun to influence fishing methods, although not enough to erode traditional fishing forever. Many ancient practices are still favoured by Indian tribesmen today and in Kuna Yala and the fishing villages of the Darién, spears are used.

Flowers, trees and plants

Panama boasts 10,000 plant species (practically eight different species per km^2) and ranks fourth in terms of flora in North and Central America. Some 687 species of fern and more than 1,000 different tree types have been recorded. The country is mainly tropical rainforest of cedar, jacaranda, anonaceae, 'espave' anacardiaceae and palm. Buttressed trunks are common, their lower trunks spreading in wide flanks and often interlinking with other trees. Spiny cedar (*Bombacopsis quinata*) can reach a height of 40m and is covered in small sharp spikes. It is found in the canal area, Darién, Bocas del Toro and Coclé provinces.

Produce grown in Panama includes whitecane, coffee, cashews, almonds, oranges, grapefruit, lime, melon, papaya, passion fruit and pineapple. Mango trees are abundant throughout the country, even in Panama City, where they grow wild near shopping centres and major highways.

There are approximately 1,200 varieties of orchids in Panama, including *Laelia purpurata, Epidendrum ibaguense, Ionopsis utricularioides, Encyclia cordigere* and *Brassavola cucullata*. Each has a unique colour and shape and can be found at sea level, in elevated areas, dense jungle and mountain valleys. Epiphytic orchids live on trees and rocks and often grow with other plants, such as creepers, ferns and bromeliads. In the town of Boquete (see *Chiriquí Province* chapter) residents celebrate the orchid each spring with a fair in the park.

Other tropical flowers include the dramatic pink and yellow, rubber-like fronds of heliconia (a relative of the banana family), which grow at a low level in rainforest and jungle verges. The bright orange bird-of-paradise can also be found in these areas. Numerous vibrant varieties of hibiscus are found in Panama as well as orange ixora (or flame of wood, a common plant with striking star-shaped blossoms), oleanders, lantanas and wild lilies.

Wildlife

Despite its relatively small size Panama is home to a staggering array of wildlife, a biodiversity that is attributable to its bridging position between two vast continents. A large number of species from North and South America form one of the largest and most diverse collections of wildlife in the world. Two hundred types of mammal can be found in Panama, including jaguars, pumas, monkeys and tapirs, with 125 species that are unique to the isthmus.

That Panama is still relatively undiscovered and undeveloped allows a greater chance to observe wildlife in a variety of habitats. Crocodiles, iguana, agouti and sloth can easily be spotted even in urban neighbourhoods. A stroll up Cerro Ancon (Ancon Hill) in Panama City leads to toucan and monkey, minutes from major roads. Visit one of Panama's 12 national parks (see *National parks*) for rich natural habitat via umpteen tours and trails. Twenty-five protected areas of marine, forest and wetland habitat also provide ample opportunity to see Panama's wildlife in its natural surroundings.

Insects and spiders

The tiny **fire ant** (*Solenopsis sp.*), found throughout the country in gardens, old houses and even sandy areas, is an unassuming species with a nasty sting: apply vinegar to the bite to ease the pain. **Leaf-cutters** *(Atta cephalotus)*, a hardworking species found in rural areas, vary in size. Processions make these ants distinctive and it is not uncommon to see large convoys on the forest floor carrying tiny leaf pieces from trees, shrubs and other plants. At a central nest these shreds are chewed to a pulp and added to 'fungus gardens', a cultivated mulch of nourishing nodules on which the ants feed.

According to the Smithsonian Tropical Research Institute, Panama has 16,000 varieties of lepidopteron (butterflies and moths) and more than 1,600 of these are thought to be butterflies. No exact figure exists as surveys are still under way but Panama is an important crossway for migrating lepidopteron species. The brown-coloured **anartia fatima** is by far the most common butterfly in Panama, and sports a thick white stripe on each wing. **Swallowtails** (papilionidae family) can also be easily found as can the **heliconius,** distinctive for tribal-looking red or blue markings and yellow blotches on black wings. The migrating **urania fulgens** (uraniidae) is a black day-flying moth with distinctive electric green stripes. Eighty varieties have been reported of the electric-blue **morpho** (*Genus morpho*) butterfly and common species the size of a human hand can be seen in the Parque Natural Metropolitano. The **Cream Owl** has wings with markings that resemble the eyes of its namesake and is one of the largest butterflies in the world.

The notorious **African honeybee** (*Apis mellifera*) is common to coffee-producing regions where it is credited with enhancing the quality of beans. Its second name, killer bee, reflects its tendency to sting, delivering the same kind and amount of venom as the common honey bee, but it is more easily provoked and attacks in large numbers.

Arthropod and member of the arachnid family, the **scorpion** (*Centruroides sp.*) is commonly found in most regions of the isthmus. Locally known as **alacran**, this oldest surviving arachnid is a nocturnal creature that will sting only in self-defence (biggest threat when camping, so shake clothing and shoes).

Of the numerous spider species in Central America none poses a serious threat to visitors. The **black tarantula** (*Sericopelma rubronitens*) is found throughout Panama, a chunky-bodied species that inhabits hollow logs and dark spots and feeds on insects and small rodents at night. This spider rarely bites humans unless aggravated and is not considered life-threatening. The **black widow** (*Latrodectus mactans*) also occurs throughout the Americas, a spider with a distinctive red hourglass marking on its underside that lives low, under stones, loose bark, woodpiles and in dark corners in buildings and outdoor toilets. Complications from a bite of the female can be fatal, but are extremely rare.

Reptiles and amphibians

Humid rainforest, rivers and marshes set in tropical climes are the perfect environment for reptiles. Panama is home to the **American crocodile** (*Crocodylus acutus*) and the **common caiman** (*Caiman crocodiles*). The American crocodile is one of the world's largest living reptiles, reaching up to 3.5m in length and inhabiting fresh water, reservoirs and lakes as well as coastal waters, tidal estuaries and mangrove swamps. During Panama's early colonial years, Chagres River was nicknamed 'crocodile river' due to the numbers living there, and remains a good place to spot them today, as do the lakes and swamps of the national parks and inland canals. The American crocodile is now listed as vulnerable on the endangered species list. Caiman (the Spanish term for alligator), the smallest and most abundant crocodile in the Western hemisphere, are found in lowland swamps, ponds and lakeshore inlets throughout the tropics. Two species are recognised in Panama with little difference between them. The **spectacled caiman** (*Caiman crocodilus crocodilus*) and the **brown caiman** (*Caiman crocodiles fuscus*) are both identifiable by a long, thin snout. An adaptable predator, it lies open-mouthed waiting for dinner to arrive, relaxing as fish drift into its open jaws.

Two types of iguana are found throughout Panama, the **green** or **common iguana** *(Iguana iguana)*, a lime-coloured species; and the brown-coloured **land iguana** (*Conolophus subcristatus*). Both sport large flaps of skin (dewlaps) at the throat and are ridged with scales along the back and tail. Iguanas spend a great deal of time lying motionless and camouflaged on tree branches and favour areas near water where they can leap for cover from predators. Humans are their main enemy; despite being a protected species in Panama they are illegally poached for their meat and skin and preserved with their front feet tied behind their backs using their own tendons, cut and pulled from their middle front claws while they are still alive. The **basilisk** lizard (*Basiliscus basiliscus*) is widespread in humid marshy and wetland areas and nicknamed 'Jesús lizard' for its practice of walking (or rather, running) on water. It manages this miracle thanks to thin flaps of skin on large hind feet that act as paddles to distribute weight evenly across the surface. Basilisks are slim, sit almost upright and have distinctive crests on their backs and tails. The male has a larger fan on the back of the head than the female.

There are more than 130 snakes in Panama, but only 20 or so are poisonous, and there is a less than 10% mortality rate among bite victims in Central America. Snakes in the region feed well and do not hibernate, two factors that reduce the potency of the venom. The only endangered snake is the **boa** or **red tailed boa constrictor** *(Boa constrictor)*, a species hunted for its skin. Sharp inward-pointing teeth are used to kill birds and rodents, but are not poisonous. The **vine snake** is long, thin and grey, and has mild venom in its rear fangs. One of the most feared venomous snakes is the **fer de lance** (*Bothrops asper*), a species that varies in colour and can be grey to olive, brown or even red, with dark, light-edged cross-bands or triangles along its length. Vipers include the **eyelash viper** or **palm viper** (*Bothriechis bothrops schlegelii*) and the **pacific hog-nosed pit viper** (*Porthidium bothrops lansbergii*). The **bushmaster** (*Lachesis muta*) is the one of the largest vipers and is the second-largest poisonous snake, reaching 3.5m in length. The **coral snake** (*Micrurus nigrocinctus*) can be highly venomous and is characterised by its bright red body with yellow-trimmed black bands.

In Soberanía National Park alone there are 59 different species of frogs and toads. The brown and white striped **lowland dart frog** (*Colosthetus flotator*) has a loud call that is easily heard in forested areas. It is hard to miss the **marine toad** (*Bufo marinus*), the biggest amphibian in Central America, commonly found in rural back yards looking for insects to eat. Another common species is the **leaf-litter toad** (*Bufo haematiticus*), a small brownish-yellow amphibian that camouflages against fallen leaves. Panama hosts the largest diversity of **coloured dart frogs** (*Dendrobates pumilio*) in Central America. Averaging only a centimetre in size, dendrobates vary dramatically in colour depending on their location, inhabiting lowland rainforested slopes in Chiriquí and the tropical jungles of Bocas del Toro. Glands in the skin secrete powerful toxins that were once used on spearheads by Indians but are now being researched by biochemists for possible uses in human medicine. Epabatidine (derived from the frog **epipedobates tricolor** by chemical manipulation) has been converted into a painkiller 200 times more powerful than morphine. There is no conclusive evidence explaining the variety of colours and patterns found in this frog species. In the Bocas region alone many colours are found: green on Isla Popa, dark blue in Cerro Brujo, orange in Cayo Nancy, yellow with black dots on Bocas island. The **red frog** (*Dendrobates pumilio*) or strawberry poison dart frog is unique to Isla Bastimentos where a beach has been named in its honour. The plight of the threatened **golden frog** (*Atelopus zateki*) has worsened due to deforestation and poaching for the exotic pet trade. These yellow frogs, found only on the Central Cordillera of west central Panama, are known to communicate through semaphore and have been revered for centuries. Believed to represent fertility and luck, they became a model for the golden huacas of pre-Columbian society in Panama. According to Ngöbe Buglé legend, the chieftains' annual sacred rite of climbing the mountains of El Valle de Anton is to search for golden frogs that turn to gold upon death.

Mammals

Bats thrive in tropical temperatures and Panama hosts a variety of species, from humble fruit eaters to vampires. These nocturnal creatures use echolocation, emitting high-frequency sounds to navigate and find food. The returning echoes of its squeaks allow the bat to recognise movement, direction and distance of insects. In Bocas del Toro (and throughout Central and South America) **fishing bats** (*Noctilio leporinus*) can be sighted as with sharp claws they snatch tiny fish from the water and look like birds with a 51cm wingspan. The **white bat** (*Ectophylla alba*) is endemic to Central American lowlands and has soft white hair on its body. This small fruit-eating species belongs to the 'tent making' family that make nests from torn foliage leaves that accommodate as many as 12 bats. Contrary to myths and movies, the incidence of human attack by the **vampire bat** (*Desmodus rotundus*) is rare. Vampire bats feed off mammals, mainly cattle, and rarely cause the animal's death as only a small amount of blood (one tablespoon) is licked from the flesh wound. Hundreds of bats can be seen in their natural environment at La Gruta on the road to Bocas del Drago on Isla Colón (see *Bocas del Toro Province* chapter).

Once found in abundance throughout areas of North America, the **jaguar** (*Panthera onca*) is now severely threatened and inhabits only Mexico and selected parts of Central and South America. Pre-Columbian civilisations worshipped the animal as a god. A mature jaguar can measure from 1.5m to 2.6m including its tail, stands 61cm high at the shoulder and weighs 68–136kg. It is therefore the largest, most powerful cat in the Western hemisphere. Demand for the jaguar's rich-yellow to rust-coloured coat spotted with black rosettes has extensively threatened its existence. An adept climber and an excellent swimmer, the jaguar feeds at night on deer, fish, wild pigs, turtles and rodents. It inhabits jungle, forest and shrubby grasslands but specifically areas where it feels camouflaged. Panama's vast national parks provide these magnificent creatures with sufficient space to roam uninterrupted (Parque Nacional Darién alone covers 576,000ha), yet deforestation continues to encroach upon protected space and threaten the future of big cats. The **puma** (*Felis concolor*), also known as the mountain lion (a name given by American settlers), is common in Central and South America. Coats can be grey or tawny; in some areas, specifically South America, pumas are solid black. Fully grown pumas measure around 1.9m in length, have a long, slender body and a small, round head. The cry of a puma is terrifying and resembles a human screaming in pain. The wild **ocelot** (*Felis pardalis*) is found in national parks throughout the country. This small wild cat inhabits jungle and forest areas and measures between 1m and 1.2m long. An agile climber, it feeds at night on small rodents, birds and reptiles and is especially fond of agoutis. Ocelot fur can vary in colour from light pearl to reddish yellow and like the jaguar it is hunted for its attractive black markings. A small sanctuary for confiscated 'pet' ocelots has been set up in the Metropolitan Park.

The favourite food of the ocelot, the timid **agouti** (*Dasyprocta punctata*), common throughout Panama, is an odd-looking short and reddish-brown rodent with unusually long legs for its size. Agoutis feed on grasses, roots, leaves and fallen fruit and are hunted for their meat. A larger version of the agouti, **pacas** (*Agouti paca*) are nocturnal and rarely seen; distinguishable by protuberant eyes and rows of white spots along their flanks, this species are also good swimmers. The **collared peccary** (*Tayassu tajacu*) is a distant relative of the wild hog and its name refers to a white band around the neck. These blackish-grey creatures are covered with coarse hairs and release small amounts of heavy-smelling musk when excited. Peccaries travel in large groups and are very shy creatures, avoiding danger at all costs. However, they are capable of fighting and carry strong grinding jaws and sharp canines. They are widely hunted for meat, with skin that is used as pigskin. The **white-lipped peccary** (*Tayassu peccary*) can also be found in Panama. **Baird's tapir** (*Tapiridae bairdi*), another pig-like creature and the smallest of the tapir family, is found throughout Central America. Related to the horse and rhinoceros, these short, stocky brown animals have long noses, four toes on their front feet and three on their hind. They inhabit thickly forested areas and eat twigs, fallen fruits and shrubs.

Monkeys

All New World monkeys live in trees, and of the seven varieties in Panama the most likely to be seen are tamarins, capuchins and howlers. The most widespread are **tamarins** (*Saguinus geoffroyi*), also known as the Panamanian tamarin, red-crested tamarin, rufous-naped or mono titis. These mottled white monkeys, identifiable by a russet-coloured crest on the nape of the neck, can be spotted in Parque Nacional Soberanía and the forests around Lake Gatún. Tamarins live in mixed groups and prefer the tangled vines and dense plant material of second-growth forest as it protects them from predators and is rich in insects important to their diet. **White-faced capuchins** (*Cebus capucinus*) are the species once trailed around by organ grinders and are considered the most intelligent of all New World monkeys. The face, chest and shoulders are distinctly white to yellow in colour while the rest of the body is black. Their name derives from the dark patch on the head that resembles a hood or capuche (monk's hood). These black-and-white features make them quite easy to spot in jungle canopies. Mostly omnivorous, they spend on average 70% of their day travelling and foraging for invertebrates and fruit. The **mantled howler** (*Alouatta paliatta*), a herbivore in Panama, is renowned for its low bellowing howl, produced by the extended hyoid bone of the male, at dawn and dusk and when changing location. Despite being passive creatures, groups of howlers strongly dislike each other, and males make this resonating call in unison to keep neighbouring groups at bay. Howler monkeys, now listed as endangered, have a distinctive mantle of golden fur above the mid thorax and are among the largest of the neo-tropical primates. Other species include the **black handed spider monkey** (*Ateles geoffroyi*), now listed as critically endangered, and the **lemurine night monkey** (*Aotus lemurinus*) listed as vulnerable.

Known locally as the slow monkey, the sloth is perhaps one of the humblest, least disturbing creatures of the tropical wilderness. Two types are found in

Panama, the **common two-toed sloth** (*Choloepus hoffmanni*) and the **common three-toed sloth** (*Bradypus tridactylus*), whose claws distinguish each type as the names suggest. Using its claws to suspend upside down from branches the sloth spends most of its time hanging from boughs of trees, its legs and face turned upward and its back downward. The sloth tends to sleep and eat in a small area, often one tree. It climbs down once each week in order to defecate and urinate, a process that gives the host tree 50% of its nutritional needs.

Panama's marine life
by Michael Richlen, a marine scientist and conservationist whose main areas of interest are behavioural ecology and marine mammal bioacoustics
Panama offers an abundance of shoreline on both the Pacific Ocean and the Caribbean Sea and sea-bound trips provide opportunities for remarkable wildlife encounters. Completely different spectrums of resident and migratory marine species can be commonly observed. Taking advantage of scuba, snorkelling, deep-sea fishing and boating is a great way to discover a diversity of marine life and turtles, sharks, dolphins and large whales can all be seen regularly. Panama's waters are unique and understanding the background of this marine ecosystem, and the life it supports, will help you to experience and appreciate marine life with a new perspective.

The oceanic environment
Panama's proximity to Pacific equatorial currents and Atlantic boundary currents results in considerable upwelling of oceanic nutrients; consequently Panamanian waters support a diverse array of marine life, including deep-diving marine mammal species, large fish, birds and countless pelagic invertebrates. A great spot to view marine life is where the continental shelf drops quickly into deep waters.

In Panama, travellers can expect to encounter cetaceans and one sirenian species, the West Indian manatee. This was not always the case. One pinniped species, the Caribbean monk seal (*Monachus tropicalis*), did naturally occur here but has not been seen since the 1950s and is now considered extinct.

Species
Spotted dolphin *(Stenella attenuata)* Spotted dolphins are one of the more frequently encountered species in Panamanian waters. Investigations have led taxonomists to create new species designations for highly differentiated spotted dolphin populations.

Coastal spotted dolphin *(Stenella attenuata graffmani)* Coastal spotted dolphins are found in the Pacific Ocean and occur relatively close to the shore. They are approximately 1.5–2.4m in length and are dark grey with falcate dorsal fins and a pronounced rostrum. They can be distinguished from their offshore counterparts by their larger size and the greater amount of large white spots on their dorsum. Spotting patterns differ and the amount of spotting on individuals increases with age.

Offshore spotted dolphin *(Stenella attenuata attenuata)* Offshore spotted dolphins are widely distributed throughout the tropical Pacific. They are a little smaller than their pantropical spotted counterparts, the coastal spotted and Atlantic spotted. While not as heavily spotted they do gain more with age and are typically found in larger aggregations and are commonly associated with spinner dolphins. The easiest way to locate this species at sea is to look for large feeding bird flocks.

Atlantic spotted dolphin *(Stenella frontalis)* Atlantic spotted dolphins are found throughout tropical Atlantic waters and are more robust than Pantropical coastal spotted dolphins. They have an easily distinguishable spotting pattern, again acquiring more spots with age. Their rostrum is longer and more slender than the bottlenose and their spotting is much more diffuse compared with Atlantic spotted dolphins. The species is encountered frequently in the Caribbean and can be found in large familial aggregations but are more commonly seen in groups of 5–15 in coastal areas. They are social animals, are active at the surface and can be inquisitive when boats or people are nearby.

Bottlenose dolphin *(Tursiops truncatus)* Bottlenose dolphins are perhaps the most recognised dolphin species in the world and are fairly robust and typically much larger than most dolphin species at up to 4m. Bottlenose dolphins are varying shades of grey and have extremely variable colour patterns.

Rough-toothed dolphin *(Steno bredanensis)* Rough-toothed dolphins, or steno dolphins, are widely distributed in tropical waters but are not commonly encountered and as a result very little is known about them.

Short-beaked common dolphin *(Delphinus delphis)* Common dolphins have recently been separated into different subspecies but the only one encountered in Panamanian waters is the subspecies short-beaked morph. Their colour pattern is unique; major colouration includes a dark dorsum, yellowish flanks, white undersides, and light grey sweeps extending backwards on their tail stalk. They are slender and social animals, often encountered in large groups, and can be very acrobatic.

Striped dolphin *(Stenella coeruleoalba)* Striped dolphins are perhaps the most commonly encountered species in deep ocean waters and travel in large schools. Although evasive and difficult to approach, they are easily identifiable and are slender, between 1.8m and 2.5m in size. A dark dorsum, light-grey blaze pattern extending from behind their eye to their tail stalk, a white underside, and a dark stripe from their eye to separate white and grey colour patterns make these distinctive.

Long-snouted spinner dolphin *(Stenella longirostris)* Spinner dolphins have become a diverse group and are encountered in Panama farther offshore in large groups. They are very social and can be seen breaching and leaping at the surface and have a distinct spinning leap and long and narrow rostrum.

Short-snouted spinner dolphin *(Stenella clymene)* Short-snouted spinner dolphins are found only in the Atlantic and differ from their long-snouted counterparts. Although there is overlap between the two species, short-snouted spinner dolphins were given separate species status in 1981. These dolphins are a little bit more robust, have a less triangular dorsal fin, are tripartite in colouration, and as their name suggests have a much shorter and broad rostrum.

Risso's dolphin *(Grampus griseus)* These unique species are encountered throughout the tropics and range into colder temperate waters. They are easily identifiable at sea and have a taller, more erect, narrow dorsal fin (highly variable) and are grey in colouration, between 2.6m and 3.8m.

Fraser's dolphin *(Lagenodelphis hosei)* Fraser's dolphins are a unique species that was not actually observed in the wild until the 1970s despite their scientific classification in 1956. Found sporadically in open ocean habitats very near the Equator and rarely seen in the Atlantic, they are between 2m and 2.6m with a much reduced and almost triangular dorsal fin.

Killer whale *(Orcinus orca)* Perhaps one of the most diversified species and the most recognisable of all the dolphins, killer whales are a dynamic species that, despite copious research, is yet to be fully discovered. They are the largest of the dolphins and males can be as large as 10m with a distinctive large triangular dorsal fin that begins to 'sprout' in adolescence. Killer whales are black with white eye-patches, white belly patterns, and a variable white 'saddle patch' located just behind the dorsal fin. In Panamanian waters they are hunting marine-mammal prey; large cetaceans migrating to warm waters for calving present predictable feeding opportunities for killer whales.

False killer whale *(Psuedorca crassidens)* This medium-sized black dolphin has a dorsal fin that often resembles that of a killer whale's, hence their name. Reaching a maximum length of 6m, they can easily be distinguished from other dolphins, as they are black and do not have a pronounced rostrum. Their heads are rounded and blunt in appearance and their dorsal fins are falcate, more elongated and typically rounded at the tip. False killer whales are a gregarious species and are distributed throughout tropical waters.

Pygmy killer whale *(Feresa attenuata)* These are the smallest of the 'blackfish,' reaching 2.5m with a medium-sized falcate dorsal fin and a rounded head with no beak. They are all black with a darker cape pattern, white undersides and distinctive white colouration on their 'lips' and chin. They are aggressive towards humans and other cetaceans and there is evidence from wild populations that they prey on dolphins.

Melon-headed whale *(Peponocephala electra)* Commonly mistaken for pygmy killer whales, these are only slightly larger and have similar colouration and dorsal fins. They too have white around their 'lips' but do not have the white on their chins and travel in larger schools throughout the tropics.

Short-finned pilot whale *(Globicephala macrorhynchus)* Short-finned pilot whales are found throughout the tropics and can be as large as 6.5m. They are social animals and can be approached in the wild, but are typically not very active at the surface and, due to foraging at greater depths, have longer dive times.

Sperm whale *(Physeter macrocephalus)* This unique species is named after the copious amount of spermaceti oil in their extremely large melon. They were hunted extensively for this valuable commodity as well as for their ambergris (used to slow down the rate of evaporation in perfumes). Male sperm whales can be as large as 18m; females are smaller at up to 11m. They are brown, have a wrinkled appearance, a square head, and are slender with no significant dorsal fin. They are easily seen in the wild with tall blows at a 45° angle from their left nasal opening.

Pygmy sperm whale *(Kogia breviceps)* **and dwarf sperm whale** *(Kogia sima)* Kogia are difficult to see in the wild and are only conspicuous in extremely calm waters. These small dark animals are usually seen 'logging' at the surface and will simply sink below the water before a dive. Roughly between 2.7m and 3.4m they can be seen leaping at the surface, although surface behaviour is not common, and discharge a reddish-brown intestinal fluid when startled.

Beaked whales *(Ziphiidae)* The beaked whale family is an incredibly diverse group of animals and the least-known of all cetaceans. They are deep divers and very inconspicuous while at the surface, ranging in size from 3.5m to 13m. Of the 20 possible species, only four may be encountered in Panamanian waters and will only be seen in deep waters farther offshore.

Humpback whale *(Megaptera novaeangliae)* Migrating populations of humpback can be seen in the Atlantic and the Pacific Panamanian waters. Identified by pigmentation patterns, scarring, and notches on their flukes, humpbacks can reach lengths up to 15m. They have extremely long pectoral fins, the longest relative to body size of any cetacean, and this has led to their scientific name *Megaptera novaeangliae*, which means 'big wings of New England'. Dark with white on their undersides and pectoral fins, with small humped dorsal fins and bumps on their rostrum, commonly humpbacks have barnacles and lice located in clumps on the underside of their jaws.

Bryde's whale *(Balaenoptera edeni)* Bryde's (pronounced 'broodus') whales are commonly seen throughout the tropics and can be seen breaching but are not the most surface-active species. They do not fluke up when they dive and may raise their chin when surfacing after a longer dive. They are dark in colour with small falcate dorsal fins and measure up to 15.5m.

Sei whale *(Balaenoptera borealis)* Sei whales occur in both tropical and temperate waters and despite their wide distribution are likely the least well known of all the rorquals. They are not surface active, do not fluke up prior to a dive, and rarely breach.

Fin whale *(Balaenoptera physalus)* The second-largest cetacean reaches maximum lengths of 22m and are sleek (often referred to as 'greyhounds of the sea') and fast, reaching speeds as high as 30km/h. They are dark brown or grey with unique colour patterns including a white band on their pectoral fins, a white underside with white streaks from the dorsum, and white on the right side of their jaw. Fin whales can be found in small groups and appear to be indifferent to the presence of boats, neither approaching nor avoiding them.

Blue whale *(Balaenoptera musculus)* The largest animal ever to live on the planet has reached a maximum recorded length of 34m and a weight of 190 tonnes. However, due to intense hunting, blue whales today typically reach 27m in length (between 110 and 140 tonnes). Despite their size and regular occurrence in certain geographic areas, little is known about their population status and behaviour. They are a migratory species, feeding in Antarctic waters and nursing calves in warmer tropical latitudes, but their breeding grounds are uncertain. Blue whales are actually a mottled grey colour but have a blue appearance underwater. They are easy to locate at sea due to their tall columnar blow, which reaches up to 9m.

West Indian manatee *(Trichechus manatus)* Manatees are easy to identify in the wild and cannot be mistaken for other marine mammal species. They are large (reaching 3m and 1 tonne), round, grey in colouration, have no dorsal fin, and a round flattened tail. They are encountered in shallow warm water habitats and are the only vegetarian marine mammal. Manatees use large palpable lips to graze on sea grasses and other algae, consuming up to 15% of their body weight daily. Due to their foraging behaviour (subsurface in coastal areas) they are at risk from collision with marine vessels and are the subject of significant conservation efforts.

Sea turtles
by Elizabeth Spencer, a conservationist with a passion for sea turtles

For many people, the closest they will ever get to a sea turtle is the creature gliding through a tank in their local aquarium. Adult sea turtles are elusive at best, and the majority of hatchlings crawl from their beaches and into the surf, disappearing from human radar. Adult sea turtles spend the majority of their lives in the water migrating, foraging or mating. Females will return to the beach in order to lay eggs, and males will occasionally leave the water to 'bask', raising their body temperature by sitting in the sun. With the use of radio-tracking devices and a multitude of international tagging projects, researchers have created a map of migration routes, and we now have a concept of a sea turtle's life at sea. Sea turtles are reptiles, and even though they spend most of their lives at sea, they still demonstrate reptilian characteristics, such as cold-blooded body temperatures, and laying their eggs on land.

Marine turtles can be traced back to the Jurassic era, over 150 million years ago, evolving and adapting to include modifications to the forelimbs, shell and rear limbs for swimming. Of the surviving seven species four are found in Panama, namely hawksbill (*Eretmochelys imbricata*), leatherback (*Dermochelys coriacae*), green turtle (*Chelonia mydas*) and olive ridley (*Lepidochelys olivacea*).

Hawksbill *(Eretmochelys imbricata)* Hatchling hawksbill turtles emerge at night and immediately move to the water. Many researchers believe that during the 'lost year', these hatchlings are in deep-ocean water habitats. Hawksbills move to their juvenile foraging grounds at a very small size, averaging approximately 20–25cm (length of carapace only), when the turtles are probably between one to three years old. Age and growth rates have not been defined for sea turtles, so the age estimate is just that. Hawksbills forage in coral reefs and rocky habitats, feeding primarily on sponges. The females nest at night, taking an average of 60 to 90 minutes, and generally nest once every 12 to 15 days during the season. They are easily recognisable because of their smaller size, vibrant carapace and unique beak.

Leatherback *(Dermochelys coriacea)* Leatherbacks swim proactively for longer periods of time than many other species, up to six days and nights. Juvenile leatherbacks need to consume food equal to their body mass every day in order to survive and their juvenile foraging grounds are still not completely identified. Adult leatherbacks will forage close to shore and in shallow habitats, but are known for their ability to make deep dives. The females nest at night, taking an average of 90 minutes. They lay approximately once every nine to ten days.

Green *(Chelonia mydas)* In their juvenile stages, green turtles tend to be more carnivorous, although as they mature, they become omnivorous and feed predominantly on sea grasses and algae. They also commonly eat jellyfish, sponges and other animal matter. Green turtles move to their juvenile foraging grounds at approximately 30–40cm. Females nest at night, taking an average of two to three

TURTLES IN BOCAS DEL TORO

Bocas del Toro is one of the biggest nesting grounds for leatherback turtles in Central America. In fact, four out of the seven marine turtle species worldwide visit Panama's shores. Turtles migrate thousands of miles through warm-water oceans and, according to experts, cry real tears. In Bocas del Toro you will hear stories of when beaches were so full of turtles, men could not manoeuvre their boats out to sea. Today, marine turtles face extinction in Panama, and conservation groups now use volunteers to walk the beaches each night during the season in order to protect, tag and monitor those that arrive. Conservation groups in Bocas del Toro and throughout Central America are now collaborating on their recorded data, a vital move as turtles vary in their nesting destinations over the years. Marine turtles are also threatened by fishing wire and nets, which cause many to drown, as like all reptiles they need to breathe air. Visitors can help stop the illegal poaching of turtles by refusing to buy eggs, meat or shell, if offered it. Sadly tourists are still tempted by claims that the eggs act as an aphrodisiac and while locals are slowly responding to new education, many believe that the turtles will simply never die out (see *Giving something back*).

hours, although nesting can take seven or more hours. They lay approximately once every 10 to 14 days during the season. They are recognisable from their unique green colour, which can vary by individual. This colouration is from plasma absorption of plant pigmentation.

Olive ridley *(Lepidochelys olivacea)* Very little is known about the juvenile olive ridley habitat, besides the probability that juveniles are able to forage both in near-shore and open-ocean habitats. Olive ridleys are some of the smallest turtles, averaging approximately 30cm. They are omnivorous and their diets include fish, molluscs, algae, jellyfish and other marine invertebrates. Females nest in extremely large groups called *arribadas*. These nesting events occur on specific beaches, two of which are on the Pacific coast of Costa Rica and smaller ones on the coast of Nicaragua. This accounts for the prevalence of olive ridleys in Panamanian waters. The nesting process averages an hour in length, and occurs approximately every 17 to 30 days.

From beaches and beyond

Female sea turtles lay their nests in sand and never return, leaving their offspring to hatch, evacuate the nest, avoid predation and find the ocean all by themselves. Once the hatchlings emerge, they instinctively move into the water as quickly as possible. After the initial arduous journey ends, the turtles become very passive, drifting in the water instead of actively swimming. Juvenile hatchlings are a feast of the seas, as their carapaces (shells) are still quiet soft, leaving them defenceless. Hatchlings become a snack for a variety of predators, including sharks, large fish and sea birds. This time of mystery, labelled by noted researcher Archie Carr as 'the lost year', can eventually be reconstructed – in a very general sense. The hatchlings are floating in deep water, and eventually reappear as much larger juvenile sea turtles in their juvenile foraging habitat. With an idea of the location of this habitat, a typical hatchling's path can be recreated by paying attention to ocean currents, gyres and other hydrographic features.

In their first nesting season, sexually mature sea turtles migrate into poorly defined courtship/mating areas, which are generally much closer to the nesting beaches. After insemination male turtles return to their foraging areas and females move into nesting sites in the same region as their birth. The belief that a turtle has an uncanny ability to return to the exact beach where it was born is an exaggeration. Sea turtles do in fact return to the region of their birth (impressive considering their foraging habitats could easily be 1,000km away) but not necessarily the beach where they hatched. Within their birthing region, female turtles select a nesting beach (utilising an unknown selection process) and return to that very precise area for their successive nesting seasons approximately every three to five years.

Nesting and hatching

Sea turtles nest at night, although there are specific exceptions to that rule including, but not limited to, arribadas. However, it is still important to note that as cold-blooded reptiles, the majority of turtles nest during the cooler night-time hours, due to a decreased risk of overheating under the hot sun. The female crawls ashore, a laborious process during which she may change her mind and return to sea for no apparent reason. She may also select a nesting site (habitat choice is varied by species – green turtles and leatherback turtles lay nests in open sandy areas, while hawksbills often lay under trees and shrub cover), often facing away or parallel to the water. After selecting a site, she clears a surprisingly deep body pit with long, sweeping movements of her front flippers. When the pit is cleared sufficiently, the turtle begins digging her nest hole. This amazing process begins by her first easing one rear flipper into the sand, scooping up a 'flipper-full', and tossing it off to the side. Then she immediately places the flipper on top of the loose sand, effectively keeping it from sliding back into the nest. This process is continued as she alternates flippers while digging. This is a lengthy procedure that eventually results in a flask-shaped nest. The turtle will keep digging until her flippers cannot reach any more sand, and she never turns around to check on the progress of her nest.

When the turtle is ready to lay her eggs she positions herself directly over the top of the nest chamber. It is at this point in her nesting process that most permitted researchers will tag, measure and gather data since the turtles become much more tolerant of noise, light and other distractions. Once all of her eggs are deposited, the turtle begins a methodical process of covering them. She scoops up sand with one rear flipper, places it on top of the eggs, and taps it down. This continues until the eggs are totally covered.

Although her eggs are covered, she is not yet ready to return to the sea. As she moves forward slowly, she will stop and use her front flippers to sling massive quantities of sand behind her before advancing. This returns the beach environment surrounding the nest to its original condition, and, as researchers late in marking their nests have found out, it also serves as an effective camouflage. She then slowly makes her way back to the sea. Females create nests, deposit their eggs and return to sea multiple times in a single nesting season. Although it is extremely variable among and between species, this process is commonly completed as often as every two weeks but usually no more than four times in total.

Six to 13 weeks after laying, the hatchlings begin to emerge in a brief period of intense activity, termed 'a hatchling frenzy'. The hatchling frenzy consumes most of the resources provided by the egg yolk and their instinct is to immediately get to the water. Environmental cues, such as sand temperature, light reflection and the slope of the beach are significant tools that prompt ascending from the nest and aid in orienting their advancement towards the ocean.

Birds

Panama is a birdwatcher's dream, home to 950 recorded species (more than the combined amount in the whole of North America and Europe), of which 94 have a global range of less than 50,000km² and 12 are found nowhere else in the world. Some 600 species have been spotted in Parque Internacional La Amistad (see *Bocas del Toro Province* chapter) alone, where birders can expect to see hummingbirds, yellow-headed amazons (parrot), anis, fly catchers, tanagers, motmots and crimson crested woodpeckers during a short stroll. Enthusiasts visit the country to observe annual neo-migrants: 122 varieties cross Panama including swallows, warblers, buntings and orioles. The most spectacular migrations occur during October when thousands of raptors and shorebirds break their journey south to congregate in Panama. The best places to spot these are the Bay of Panama, Coste del Este, Panama Viejo and Playa El Rompio in the Azuero region. For migrating hawks and vultures simply look skyward during the peak of migration (November) to witness the passing black clouds of birds, especially over the capital.

The **harpy eagle** (*Harpia harpyja*), Panama's national bird, was once widespread in Central American tropical forests and central areas of South America, but numbers have been decimated due to extensive forest clearing, shooting and poaching. Harpies are the strongest of all eagles and weigh more than 4.5kg, stand 91cm tall and have a wingspread of 2m. Apart from a characteristic black crest of feathers on the back of the head, their bodies are predominantly grey with a white chest and slate-black markings. Harpy eagles mate for life; the female (sometimes weighing 50% more than the male) lays one or two eggs every two years in stick nests in high treetops. They use their long talons to capture arboreal mammals such as monkey and sloth straight from the tree. Harpies can be spotted in the bigger national parks, particularly Parque Nacional Darién, a vast dense primary forest that supports this now critically endangered species.

Another bird known for its size is the **resplendent quetzal** (*Pharomachrus mocinno*), one of the world's most spectacular birds. Panama is one of the best locations to spot this magnificent shimmering green bird that has a red underbelly and elongated tail feathers that can reach 60cm in length. These frugivorous birds build nests in holes in trees and are particular keen on wild avocados. Seeds are dispersed at great distances and help to spread new growth. The Chiriquí highlands are the place to sight this bird, especially at the Parque Nacional Volcán Barú. Many guides organise trips specifically to spot quetzals and know how to call the birds (see *Bird spotting* below).

All five species of **macaw** in Panama – the blue-and-yellow, the chestnut-fronted, the great green, the red-and-green and the scarlet – are considered greatly endangered, due to habitat loss and poaching for the pet market. There are stable populations in national parks but many predict this may not last. The **scarlet macaw** (*Ara macao*) is thought most at risk and now only inhabits Coiba and Cerro Hoya national parks (see *Veraguas Province* chapter). Guacamayos, as they are commonly known, have also been hunted for their long tail feathers for use in folkloric ceremonies, a tradition that Panama's leading ornithologists are keen to discourage (see *Giving something back*). A more common parrot in Panama is the **red-lored Amazon** (*Amazona autumnalis*). These birds are predominantly green, but have a distinctive crimson patch on their foreheads, and have a loud, sharp call that can be heard in the early morning. They are usually spotted in pairs and have a distinctive heavy flapping movement as they fly.

Panama's 55 species of hummingbird rotate their wings 180° and beat them up to 80 times per second, hovering in front of open flowers using their long thin bills to suck nectar. There are many variations of this tiny bird and not all are a glittery, oily green in colour. In Panama, the easiest to spot are the **garden emerald** (*Chlorostilbon assimilis*) and the **sapphire-throated** (*Lepidopyga coeruleogularis*), two species that provide an excellent illustration of how Panama acts as a land bridge between continents. The garden emerald is restricted to the lowlands between Costa Rica (Central America) and Panama, whereas the sapphire-throated is found only in Panama and Colombia (South America). The **rufous-tailed** (*Amazilia tzacatl*) is also very common throughout the country, particularly in local gardens.

There are a few species of toucan in Panama, but the **keel-billed toucan** (*Ramphastos sulfuratus*) is the most distinct due to its vibrantly coloured beak. Toucans are not easy to observe close up but can be glimpsed flying by. The body of the keel-billed toucan is mostly black with a bright yellow neck and breast and a white patch at the rump and red under-tail feathers. The magnificent bill is lime green, red tipped, with a blue-marked lower mandible and an orange mark on the upper mandible.

It has a bad reputation as a garbage eater and the **black vulture** (*Coragyps atratus*) waddles and hops on the ground but glides gracefully in flight. Almost entirely black in colouration as the name suggests, the bird has white patches on the tips of each wing. Among sea birds found in Panama, such as cormorants, waders and boobies, the **magnificent frigate bird** (*Fregata magnificens*) is commonly seen. Easy to spot, they are instantly recognisable by their pointed thin black wings and long, split black tail. The **brown pelican** (*Pelecanus occidentalis*), like the frigate, is found commonly on both oceans. The Amador Causeway (see *Panama City* chapter) is a great place to watch pelicans dive-bombing into the Pacific for fish.

Bird spotting

The country's hot birding spots are the Pipeline Road in Parque Nacional Soberanía, Parque Nacional Volcán Barú, Parque Nacional Darién, Parque Internacional La Amistad, Swans Key (Isla de los Pájaros) in Bocas del Toro, Isla de Coiba and Barro Colorado. In the province of Herrera, the Cienaga de las Macanas (Las Macanas Marshes) is also recommended as thousands of waterfowl pass through the nature preserve's marshlands during migratory months.

Undoubtedly the best way to see the most variety of birds is with a professional guide. There are many excellent guides in the country (see *Panama guides* for details). Ancon Expeditions is well renowned for the guides on its books (see *Tour operators, Panama* for contact details).

Further information

www.birdtours.co.uk
www.birdlife.org.uk
www.guidedbirding.com
Panama Audubon Society Sociedad Audubon de Panama, Apartado 2026, Balboa, Panama; tel: 224 9371; fax: 224 4740; email: info@Panamaaudubon.org; www.Panamaaudubon.org
Gamboa Resort www.gamboaresort.com. Offers specialised birdwatching expeditions (see *Panama Province* chapter).
Canopy Tower www.canopytower.com. An exceptional place to stay with accommodation at jungle canopy level and bilingual birding guides and birdwatching tours in national parks. The predicted list visitors may see is endless, and includes owls, hawks, blue cotingas, toucans, green shrike vireos, bats, butterflies, howler monkeys and iguanas (see *Panama Province* chapter)

Panama guides

The following natural history, adventure and birding guides come highly recommended by travellers to Panama.

Mario Bernal An avid naturalist and birder Bernal has spent his life studying the flora and fauna of Panama. He worked for many years for the Smithsonian Tropical Research Institute on Barro Colorado Island and leads environmental organisation ConserVA in his native El Valle region (tel: 693 8213; email: mariobernalg@hotamail.com or book via Panoramic Panama; www.panoramicPanama.com).

Hernan Arauz One of the first professional natural history guides in Panama, Hernan Arauz comes from a family of explorers and field scientists and is the son of Reina Torres de Arauz, Panama´s leading anthropologist and Amado Arauz, legendary explorer of the Darién (Ancon Expeditions, www.anconexpeditions.com).

Guido C Berguido Certified through the National Association for Interpretation (USA) and with a degree in biology, Berguido has worked as a guide in Panama for over seven years. He has worked with the Smithsonian Tropical Research Institute and is on the local Panama Audubon Society panel. He also runs academic programmes for US and Canadian schools and universities. Guido has a passion for Panama's birds and wildlife and guides groups anywhere in the country (PO Box 69, Ancon, Balboa, Panama; email: gcberguido@hotmail.com and info@advantagePanama.com).

Rich Cahill An experienced guide and tour leader specialising in eco-tourism expeditions, Rich's American mother is a direct descendant of Sir Francis Drake, whose lead coffin lies offshore of Portobelo. He is a veteran of Trans Darién Expeditions, where he has been bitten by a vampire bat, and has led over 250 tours to Barro Colorado Nature Monument (Ancon Expeditions; www.anconexpeditions.com).

Gilberto Alemancia This guide from Kuna Yala (San Blas) leads a wide range of natural history and adventure tours throughout Panama, including overnight beach camping in Kuna Yala. He has worked with ANCON, National Geographic and the BBC and specialises in one-to-one and small groups (tel: 691 2506 or book via Panoramic Panama; www.panoramicPanama.com).

Ivan Hoyos This graduate of the University of Maryland–Munich is an avid birder, speaks fluent German, Spanish and English and has led 100+ tours to Barro Colorado Nature Monument as well as trans Darién expeditions, Darién explorer treks, and countless adventures in Panama's wilderness (Ancon Expeditions; www.anconexpeditions.com).

FIRES, EARTHQUAKES AND OTHER NATURAL DISASTERS

While Panama isn't on the hurricane route it does not escape natural disaster entirely. History books are littered with tragic tales of fire and tremors on the isthmus, the most famous of which occurred during Henry Morgan's looting of Panama City (now Panama La Vieja) in 1671. Fire engulfed the entire municipality and destroyed the city beyond repair. Later, in 1737, another fire hit Panama's second city, Casco Viejo, destroying two-thirds of the area. A smaller fire in 1756 was fortunately much less severe, destroying just 90 houses. On May 5 1914, a large fire spread through a gunpowder factory, El Polovorin, in Avenida Nacional in the Calidonia area of Panama City. Six *bomberos* (firefighters) died attempting to control the blaze and in 1916 a monument and fountain was erected in their memory in Plaza Cinco de Mayo, which at the time was the centre of the city.

Outside of the capital there have been a number of significant fires in the provinces. On March 30 1885, most of the City of Colón on the Atlantic was lost to fire, reportedly begun by revolutionary Pedro Prestan from Colombia. The only buildings that survived were Panama's railroad office, the French Canal Company and the Pacific Mail Steamship Line. The estimated loss to the city was around US$6 million with 10,000 homeless and 18 deaths.

On Isla Colón, the city of Bocas del Toro is traditionally built from wood, although a tourist boom has seen concrete construction over the last decade. Local history has been sporadically interrupted with fires that have consumed its wooden buildings. A great fire destroyed 160 houses in March 1904, and further parts of the city were ruined by fire in 1907, 1918 and 1929.

Due to its location outside the major quake zone, Panama has escaped some vicious natural disasters experienced by its Central American neighbours. Annual small tremors occur, however, some of which result in loss of life. The largest earthquake in Panama in recent years hit Bocas del Toro on April 22 1991. Named Valle de la Estrella (Valley of the Star) the quake reached 150km along the Caribbean coast, measuring 7.4 on the Richter scale, a stronger reading than was thought possible in the province. Almirante and Changuinola suffered the greatest damage, with 30 reported dead, around 500 injured, 7,000 homeless and 1,120 buildings lost. Later that year the province suffered floods and landslides, killing two people.

On July 18 1934 a small tsunami was recorded in Bahía Honda in the Gulf of Chiriquí registering 7.6 on the Richter scale. There were no injuries but an earthquake three days later caused extensive damage to Puerto Armuelles on the southeast cost. In November 1988 Hurricane Joan killed seven in the capital as she passed through and in 1992 Panama City was hit by a tornado that caused 12 deaths. An earthquake in July 2000 measured 5.2 on the Richter scale in Pedasí, Los Santos, but nobody was hurt.

UNESCO IN PANAMA

Panama was ratified with the convention of United Nations Educational, Scientific and Cultural Organisation (UNESCO) in 1978. From this time UNESCO and, since 1997, the World Heritage Fund have recognised and helped fund four of Panama's National Heritage sites.

In 1980 UNESCO designated the entire site of San Lorenzo (see *Colón Province* chapter) as a World Cultural Monument. During 1997–98 the sites were added to the World Monuments Fund list of Endangered Monuments. These historic ruins were used by the US Defense Department for 46 years as a jungle training base for military troops. In July 2003 the archaeological ruins of Panama La Vieja – the oldest European settlement on the Pacific – and the historic district of Panama (Casco Viejo) were inscribed World Heritage Sites and added to UNESCO's list of protected cultural properties (see *Panama City* chapter).

UNESCO's 'Man and the Biosphere' programme was launched in 1970 to ensure the future of global biodiversity with sustainable use. Biosphere areas contain representative ecosystems that not only need to be protected, but researched, monitored and learnt from. A network of reserves has been created worldwide that are now regarded as living laboratories. The Biosphere project helps fund both conservation and education. Parque Nacional Darién, the vast jungle that spreads to the east and forms a border with Colombia, was added to the World Heritage List in 1981 (see *Darién Province* chapter). In 1983 the Darién was internationally recognised as a Biosphere Reserve due to its rich history and anthropology. On the western border with Costa Rica Parque Internacional La Amistad (see *Bocas del Toro Province* chapter) became a World Heritage Site in 1983 and was recognised as a Biosphere Reserve in 2000. On April 4 2003 Panama was the first of 14 member countries to ratify the Convention on the Protection of

Underwater Cultural Heritage, a legal strategy now owned by UNESCO. This will help to protect the numerous shipwrecks, treasures and sunken gold that surround Panama's coastal regions.

HISTORY

Evidence of human settlement in Panama has been traced as far back as 12000BC and some of the finest examples of pre-Columbian pottery, adorned with animals and elaborate patterns, have been found in the central interior. Archaeologists believe ceremonial artefacts such as impressive near-life-size statues and elongated ritual tables cast from volcanic stone date back to the 5th century AD and the Barriles culture in the Chiriquí region. Metal artefacts, including gold, demonstrate trade with Mexico and South America. Exquisitely moulded golden animals and jewellery were placed in burial tombs with Indian chiefs, many of which were later looted by foreign invaders. The Conquistadors also brought with them common illnesses that proved deadly to native Indians. Several tribes believed to belong to the Chibchan language found in Colombia and Costa Rica became extinct after the 16th century.

In 1501 Rodrigo de Bastidas, the first European on Panamanian soil, passed the Caribbean shoreline on a quest for gold. A year later Columbus arrived on Panama's Atlantic coast determined to find a waterway through to Asia, while Spanish explorer Vasco Núñez de Balboa crossed the isthmus in 1513 to proclaim the Pacific the Mar del Sur (South Sea). The country was taken for the Spanish crown and Panama City (now the ruins of Panama La Vieja) became the first European settlement on the Pacific coast. Peru's Inca gold was transported across the isthmus on the Camino Real, the first path to cross the country, to the Atlantic port of Nombre de Dios where it was shipped to Spain. Later the Camino de Cruces was constructed, a route that connected to the Chagres River and halved the overland distance to become the most important trade trail in the Americas. An inter-oceanic canal would have quickened shipments, but Spain never achieved this, and in 1821 when Panama gained independence from Spain as part of Gran Colombia, it was the Colombian authorities that first investigated the possibilities. In 1850 Panama was granted the US rights to construct a transcontinental railroad. This proved invaluable for thousands heading from the east coast of North America to the San Francisco gold rush on the west coast. In 1880 canal rights were finally sold to the French Compagnie Universelle du Canal Interocanique, which attempted to construct a canal at sea level, engineered by Ferdinand de Lesseps. The project was abandoned in 1889 due to mismanagement and bankruptcy, and thousands of workers lost their lives to tropical diseases during the attempt. In the hope of salvaging lost assets, French engineer Phillippe Bunau-Varilla encouraged a deal with Panamanian revolutionaries in return for a US canal treaty and in 1903 Panama gained independence at a high price. America defended the country's revolution against Colombian military for which they demanded full canal rights along with the go-ahead to intervene in Panama's internal affairs.

Thus the volatile relationship between Panama and America began and in ten years the Panama Canal was completed. Immigrant workers from West Indies arrived and helped shape Panama's now diverse mix of cultures. In 1936 the canal treaty was rewritten and US intervention rights relaxed. The Panamanian military, the Guardia Nacional, expanded leading to the ousting of twice-elected president Dr Arnulfo Arias Madrid. Omar Torrijos took office, a dictator though his social and land reforms won him the respect from the people, and in 1977 he signed a treaty with US President Jimmy Carter ensuring complete hand-over of the Canal to Panama within 20 years. When Torrijos died in a plane crash in 1981 Noriega took his place as head of the military, renaming it the Panama Defense Forces (PDF). Despite his history as an employee of the CIA, Noriega's involvement in corruption, drugs and arms trafficking sparked a political disaster, and in May 1989 Guillermo Endara rightfully won the presidential elections, a result annulled by the Noriega regime. Noriega installed himself as president, fuelling the US invasion, Operation Just Cause, in December 1989 (see *General Manuel Noriega*), and he was later charged in the US and jailed for drug-trafficking crimes.

During the invasion Guillermo Endara was reinstalled as president and pledged to improve the suffering economy. He also promised to transform the PDF, promises that were not quite realised in his five-year term. In 1994 Ernesto Perez Balladares of the Democratic Revolutionary Party (PRD) was sworn in as President followed by Mireya Moscoso, the widow of former President Arnulfo Arias Madrid, who won elections in 1999. Although she pledged to strengthen social programmes, accusations of corruption continued and general unrest still exists among many Panamanians when it comes to politics. The Canal, banking, commerce and, more recently, tourism generate revenue, but more than a third of the population remains below the poverty line.

The Panama Canal was handed over to Panamanian rule on December 31 1999 and, at the end of Moscoso's term in May 2004, PRD candidate Martín Torrijos (Omar's son) was elected. His defeat in 1999 was soon forgotten when he won 47% of the vote. More than 80% of the population polled that day, proving that Panamanians have not given up their voice.

Christopher Columbus

Columbus dedicated his life to the discovery of Asia and the mysteries of the Far East, a dream he never realised. Instead, unaware of its future importance, he founded South and Central America, the Western hemisphere, which he named the New World.

In 1502, after three unsuccessful attempts, he embarked on his final journey to discover Asia. He named the expedition the High Voyage and determined to find a channel from the Atlantic to the mainland of Asia. Convinced this was the route to the region of Cathay, he left Spain with a small, but fully prepared fleet of four ships.

Arriving on the shores of Nicaragua and Honduras, Columbus sailed south searching for the strait he was convinced existed. No such waterway appeared, but the convoy later came across a canoe of Mayan traders. Believing the exotic artefacts they were carrying were a sign that he was on the right track and also nearing gold, Columbus took one Mayan trader to guide him. At the Cape of Honduras his interpreter asked the Mayan from which direction the gold originated. Fearing the worst, the Mayan lied and pointed away from his gold-rich Yucatan homelands, to the east. Historians today consider Columbus far more diplomatic than Cortez, who later barbarically invaded Mayan Mexico and Guatemala. Many speculate that if the Mayan guide had pointed in the true direction, history could have been very different.

Freeing the Mayan, Columbus continued to sail in the indicated direction, east-southeast, along the coast of Honduras. On October 5 1502, he dropped anchor in the Bocas del Toro Province and was so overcome with its beauty he began to put his name to the islands and mainland: Bahía Almirante (Admiral's Bay), Isla Cristobel (Christopher Island) and Isla Colón (Columbus Island – Genoan-born Columbus called himself Christopher Colón after settling in Spain).

As the first white man to land on Panama's Caribbean shores, Columbus wanted no hostility with its people. He gave strict orders that his men could not trade with or harm them, but he later traded with those that accepted him.

As he entered the channel to what was locally named as Alburema (now known as Chiriquí Lagoon) Columbus saw Indians with solid gold medals and plates, and became convinced he was entering the final passage to China. The population of Ngöbe Buglé were friendly people who were willing not only to trade but also to share their knowledge of the area. When Columbus learnt of a land called Ciguare (Chiriquí) and its great body of water several days' march over the cordillera he was frustrated that he had not discovered a water passageway. Still convinced he was on the right track, Columbus was keen to learn more about the area and, importantly, the search for gold. In February 1503 he took his fleet 80km west of Colón, to a river mouth he called Belen. His plan was to initiate a colony there between Veraguas (the name comes from Verdes Aguas – green waters) and Colón. His hopes did not last. The local people, the Quibian, did not accept the Spaniards and attacked and massacred many of the troops. Fearing further attack and suffering from malaria, Columbus retreated. He set sail with his fleet for Hispaniola, his High Voyage defeated.

Columbus died in Valladolid, Spain, in 1506, reputedly of Reiter's disease. Although he died believing falsely that he had discovered Asia, he is now held as an outstanding navigator, the first man to introduce the Europeans and peoples of the Americas to each other.

Sir Henry Morgan

In the 17th century no Spanish strongholds were as tempting to buccaneers as those in Panama, a central route for treasures of the New World. Solid gold and silver bars, diamonds and other riches from Chile, Peru and lower California were carried from Panama City to waiting Spanish ships at Puerto Bello (now Portobelo). Welshman Henry Morgan was the first and only pirate to succeed in sacking both these principal cities.

In fact Morgan roamed Central American waters not as an illegal pirate, but as a privateer authorised by British powers to keep check on colonial assets. However, his first Panamanian attack, on Puerto Bello in May 1668, was so gruesome – in addition to rape, torture and murder, he had used Catholic priests and nuns as human shields against Spanish fire – that the English authorities denied all knowledge of it.

Nevertheless, Morgan returned to Jamaica with so many pieces of eight after plundering Puerto Bello that they became legal tender in Jamaica. Henceforth Morgan's name became revered as the pirate king – the greatest buccaneer in history. However, he was not satisfied with Puerto Bello and believed Panama City (now Panama Vieja) held far more riches. Although partly surrounded by sea the city was not fortified and that was enough to encourage Morgan to cross the isthmus.

On January 12 1671, he led 1,200 men on a journey inland by boat from the mouth of the Chagres River. Morgan made the mistake of leaving behind food and provisions, believing he would loot villages along the way. The villagers, however, warned of the pirates' progress, had fled, burning everything they could not carry. Morgan's troops trekked for over a week eating little more than leather, bark and leaves. However, as they neared the city environs, the Spanish chose not to immediately attack these advancing weak and famished men, something that still puzzles historians. Had they done so the pirates would have been scuppered before glimpsing the Pacific Ocean.

Stranger still, the starved pirates emerged from the jungle to a feast; the Spaniards had left their cattle grazing on the hillside. The next morning, after refuelling on the meat, Morgan and his troops descended on the city. Again to the perplexity of today's historians, Panama City's Governor de Guzman was not well prepared. With the Spaniards having positioned their largest, immovable guns along the main road leading into the city, the buccaneers simply approached from the opposite direction; the heavy guns were utterly useless.

The Spanish then chose an exposed block formation in rural fields surrounding the city. The pirates hid among scrub and ditches and waited until the Spanish were in such close range they could hardly miss them. Morgan's troops opened musket fire and a bloody carnage ensued. The Spanish made a series of retreats and re-advances, efforts that remained useless due to their adherence to strict formation. The pirates were scarcely touched.

At the sight of such slaughter de Guzman embarked on his second plan and released 2,000 wild bulls. This also proved fruitless. Whilst Morgan's crew fired on cowboys herding the bulls, the Spanish recognised impending defeat and fled. In less than eight hours Morgan had taken Panama City. Amid the ensuing chaos a fire broke out, ravaging splendid cedar-wood homes and denying Morgan many items of loot such as spices, silks, rugs and tapestries. There has been some historical dispute over responsibility for the fire. More than likely it was simply an accident.

Morgan returned with 600 slaves and 175 mules to carry his bounty across the isthmus. He and his troops were disappointed the raid was not the financial success for which they had hoped. Interestingly, when Morgan returned to England, which was no longer at war with Spain, he was thrown in jail for his piracy. However, some time later Charles II knighted Morgan for his deeds and returned him to Jamaica as lieutenant governor.

At the time Panama Vieja burnt down there were around 5,200 homes, a cathedral, a government building and eight convents and churches. With the town in ruins, the remaining Spaniards rebuilt a fortified city a few miles west in the present-day area of San Félipe.

Sir Francis Drake

An ambitious rogue of the sea and the first man to circumnavigate the world, Sir Francis Drake (1540–96) was greatly feared by the Spanish and nicknamed el draque (the dragon). In May 1572 Drake arrived on a deserted island off the Atlantic coast of Panama and planned a surprise attack on the Spanish city of Nombre de Dios. He and his crew sailed to the sleeping city at night on small pinnaces (shallow boats) loaded with muskets and gunpowder. Although the Spanish retaliated, they soon fled after realising the size of Drake's army. However, the treasure fleet Drake was after had already departed to Spain and the attackers returned empty handed.

Still determined to loot the South American gold transported through Panama, Drake took refuge in the Gulf of Darién, naming his small settlement Port Pheasant. He and his troops met with bands of escaped slaves, known as Cimaroons, who traded information for weapons and clothing. The Cimaroons informed Drake when the seasonal silver-train would journey from Panama City and Drake determined to wait for it. When the time came he forced his men through the jungle across the isthmus to the outskirts of Panama, with promises of great riches. Unfortunately for the pirates, the Spanish heard of their presence and sent instead a train full of clothing, pots and pans. Drake and his men had to retreat for fear of attack and they returned once again empty handed.

Still not deterred, Drake moved to the abandoned Nombre de Dios (after the attack the Spanish relocated to Puerto Bello, now Portobelo) to wait for the next silver-train. When it arrived the following year, Drake and his men finally got their loot, successfully attacking the train just outside Puerto Bello and saving on a long walk inland. There was too much loot to carry and many items were buried in the surrounding jungle, which the Spanish found soon after. But in August Drake and his crew returned as wealthy men to England where he was later knighted.

Drake returned in order to sack Panama City. He was unsuccessful and later died of fever. He was buried at sea by what is now known as Drake's Island, near Puerto Bello, in a lead coffin (see *Colón Province* chapter).

General Manuel Noriega

Born in Panama City in 1934, Manuel Noriega attended military academy in Peru before joining the infamous School of Americas located in the Canal Zone. This US training establishment taught Latin American armies and police officers counterinsurgency techniques and anticommunist programmes.

After enrolling in Panama's military, Noriega was rapidly promoted though the ranks to lieutenant and in 1970 he became commander of Panama's military intelligence agency. During these years he was highly regarded by the CIA, Washington and the Pentagon, and became an important informant.

In 1968 a successful coup led by populist military leader Omar Torrijos (General of the Guardia Nacional and father of Martín Torrijos, Panama's present president) began 21 years of military rule. Although Torrijos was a dictator in Panama, he supported racial equality, accomplished important land and labour reforms and achieved a new Canal treaty with US President Jimmy Carter that ensured America's hand-over of the canal.

In 1981 Torrijos was killed in a plane crash and is fondly remembered in Panama to this day. Noriega took control in 1983 when he was officially made Commander of the Guardia Nacional. Until this point, the Guardia Nacional, Panama's only armed force, had been responsible for acting as both civil police and a military front. Noriega expanded this force and created a new protectorate, renamed the Panamanian Defense Forces (PDF). Within the PDF the Guardia Nacional numbered around 11,000; Panama's army numbered 4,400.

Since Noriega's post in the intelligence agency, and throughout his years as a Commander, suspicions surrounded his involvement in drugs and arms trafficking and supplying information on US activities to Cuba. These concerns were continually ignored by the US and today evidence surrounding arms deals documented in the Iran–Contra investigations suggest links between Noriega and the US. The CIA considered Noriega an invaluable employee; he was an important spy in a strategic position. Additionally, the US had a number of military bases in Panama, which would be vital if America decided to attack Nicaragua or El Salvador (countries they were heavily involved with at the time). Speculation suggests Washington believed the stability of US control in Panama would suffer under friction between political relations.

Noriega continued his course of corruption in Panama, fraudulently installing Nicolás Ardito Barletta as President in 1984, the first presidential elections for 16 years. The Reagan administration welcomed the move.

In 1985 the tortured and decapitated body of former vice Health minister, Hugo Spadafora, was discovered on the border of Costa Rica. This was to become a major factor in Noriega's downfall, as Spadafora, a member of the opposition who was actively involved with the Contras, had been openly accusing Noriega of drug-trafficking activities. Accusations over the murder began to focus on Noriega and later that year Barletta commissioned a full investigation of the murder. In September 1985 Barletta resigned and was replaced by Noriega with Vice President Eric Arturo Delvalle, this time to the displeasure of the Reagan administration. In

December US National Security Adviser Admiral John Poindexter met with Noriega in Panama, and while stories abound concerning what was discussed, the outcome initiated Washington's bid to destroy the Panamanian dictator.

On a visit to the US in June 1986, suspicions connecting Noriega with drugs and arms trafficking were reported in the *New York Times*. The following year Noriega ousted his second in command, Roberto Diaz Herrera, who promptly launched a public attack. He charged Noriega's government with electoral fraud (1984); responsibility for the assassination of Spadafora; drug and arms trafficking; and plotting with the US Southern Command to kill Torrijos. Diaz was arrested and withdrew his charge, yet the situation was fast becoming one of the biggest political scandals in Panama's history.

These events were met with public outrage and Panamanians took to the streets demanding Noriega's resignation. Riots spread through Panama City, causing chaos and serious injuries over three days. The Civic Crusade, a group of professional civilians backed by the Catholic Church, provided a political platform against the government. This did not wholly work and was reportedly linked to US organisations, and a state of emergency was soon declared.

Noriega had now lost all support from Washington, who determined to bring him down. The US applied economic sanctions, halted Canal payments and withheld currency from 106 of Panama City's 120 banks, crippling the economy and sparking further strikes and riots. The US Embassy was pelted with rubble and red paint by more than 15,000 protesters and the situation became critical. Poorer Panamanians were beginning to starve and protests continued for over a month, while the opposition, dressed in white, filled the city streets demanding free elections and Noriega's resignation. The Panamanian national newspaper, *La Prensa*, accused Noriega of state terrorism and its offices were set alight. Dignity Battalions (nicknamed 'ding bats') were formed alongside the notorious Dobermans (the PDF's anti-riot squads) and employed violent measures to disperse angry crowds.

Guillermo Endara won the Panamanian presidential election in May 1989 with 62% of the vote, but Noriega, who led a failed military coup attempt against him, flexed his muscles to nullify the victory. In December the National Assembly elected Noriega head of government and in the same month an unarmed US Marine in civilian dress was shot by a member of the PDR. Four days later, on December 20 1989, the US launched Operation Just Cause.

US President George Bush cited his attack for 'the protection of American lives', the defence of the canal, restoration of democracy and extradition of Noriega to the US to face drug-trafficking charges. During the first 13 hours 442 bombs were dropped, mainly around El Chorrillo where Noriega's office was situated. Approximately 27,000 American troops attacked a country with a deployable army of just 4,000. The United Nations and the Organization of American States condemned the operation as a violation of international law and demanded the immediate withdrawal of US troops. While the effects of war engulfed the Panamanian people, the US installed Endara as President.

While there appears to be no certified Panamanian death toll, US counts suggest several hundred. Independent organisations estimate the number at over 2,000. Twenty-three US soldiers were killed.

Noriega stayed in hiding until Christmas Day when he sought refuge in the Vatican nunciature (embassy) in Panama City. Much to the amusement of the media, US troops blasted rock music through huge loudspeakers to hound him out. On January 3 1990, he surrendered.

Noriega, who was nicknamed 'Pineapple Face' by Panamanians because of his pockmarked complexion, was put on trial in Miami, Florida. Much of the evidence against him was taken from convicted drug traffickers, reputedly lured to testify with offers of early release. Judge Hoeveler sentenced him in 1992 to 40 years in prison for drug-trafficking offences, a sentence that has since been reduced to 30 years for good behaviour. Whilst serving his time, Noriega has joined the Baptist religion and has recently applied for early release.

The Panama Canal

> Whoever you are, if you are doing your duty, the balance of the country is placed under obligation to you, just as it is to a soldier in a great war. As I have looked at you, and seen you work, seen what you have done and are doing, I have felt just exactly as I would feel to see the big men of our country carrying on a great war. ...This is one of the great works of the world. It is a greater work than you yourselves at the moment realise.
>
> US President Theodore Roosevelt
> Speech to American canal workers, including John Stevens,
> the Canal's Chief Engineer up to 1907.

When the Isthmus of Panama was created between two continents four million years ago, it blocked a convenient pathway between the Atlantic and the Pacific Ocean.

As early as 1514, just a year after Vasco Núñez de Balboa had discovered the Pacific, Spain began to search for a suitable area for a waterway to speed trade between the oceans. Conquests in South America had amassed gold and other treasures for Spain. Pedrarias Dávila, the first governor of Panama City, failed to find a location for such a channel and instead built a road overland named the Camino Real. Vast amounts of South American gold passed along this infamous route to Spanish ships waiting at Puerto Bello (Beautiful Port, now Portobelo) on the Atlantic. Some time later, Spanish sailors Hernando de la Serna and Pablo Corzo found a 50km navigable area in the Chagres River and the river port of Cruces was established. The port joined a 30km road to Panama City, which became the central trade route on the American continent.

By 1524, King Charles V had decided to connect the Chagres River with the Pacific. During the centuries following this, the Spanish crown tried in vain to unite the two oceans, not only in Panama but in other areas of Central America, most notably Lake Nicaragua. From 1835, Colombia – of which Panama became part, after having gained independence from Spain in 1821 – talked to several candidates regarding building rights, but nothing materialised. International treaties were also signed with the US and the UK regarding the neutrality of any future Central American waterway.

While powerful countries continued to argue over an inter-oceanic canal, Colombia granted the US a concession to build a transcontinental railway. It was completed in 1855. Thousands used this railroad to join the San Francisco gold rush. Finally, in 1878, Colombia signed the Salgar–Wyse Agreement that gave Lucien Napoleon Bonaparte Wyse a 99-year concession for the construction and operation of a canal across Panama. Wyse promptly sold the rights to Ferdinand de Lesseps, who had successfully and spectacularly engineered the Suez Canal. De Lesseps' original plan was to construct a canal at sea level, therefore not requiring locks, as he had done with the Suez. However, this proved immensely problematic and he later changed his plans. But the initiative failed. The French were poorly prepared for the climate, ignorant of tropical diseases, and lacked materials and tools. The tropical conditions of Panama rendered weeks of work useless, as the ground would slide back to its former position after heavy rain. Tragically,

FROM CANAL LABOURER TO ARTIST

Life is merely a fraction of a second.
An infinitely small amount of time to fulfil
our desires, our dreams, our passions.

Paul Gauguin

Born on June 7 1848 in Paris, Paul (Eugéne-Henri) Gauguin is renowned for his celebrated post-Impressionist works of art, yet his career was as a stockbroker. Gauguin realised his passion for painting while attending an exhibition of impressionist art in 1874, purchasing works by Monet, Pissarro and Renoir with great enthusiasm. His collection spurred his desire to become an artist and when his employer experienced financial difficulties in 1883 Gauguin found himself free to paint full-time. His work was vivid and inspiring, but there was no financial success to match his growing confidence and in the winter of 1886 Gauguin was penniless and slowly starving to death. Poverty-stricken and disillusioned he decided to move to Panama, taking work as a labourer for the Panama Canal Company in 1887. 'Paris,' he wrote, 'is a desert for a poor man. I must get my energy back, so I'm going to Panama to live like a native.' Within a few months Gauguin had earned enough money to set up an art studio on Isla Taboga. Here he lived the simple life before moving to French Martinique, then on to Tahiti where he achieved international critical acclaim.

hundreds of workers (many of whom were brought in from the Caribbean) were struck with malaria and yellow fever. These setbacks broke budgets and de Lesseps was bankrupt within five years of starting construction. Since 1884 the French effort had removed over 60 million m³ of earth, constructed navigation channels at both entrances to the canal, and built bridges, ports and hospitals. By 1903 there were barely 700 workers left. More than 22,000 labourers were believed to have died.

The American Canal

The US also wanted an inter-oceanic route in Central America. This became even more desirable in 1898 when an important marine vessel stationed in the Pacific had been needed to help the Spanish–American War in Cuba. When the vessel in question finally reached Cuba, after sailing round Cape Horn, the war was over. The US Congress considered a route through Nicaragua, which was nearer to the USA and could be built entirely by US citizens, creating an all-American masterpiece. However, French lobbyist Philippe Bunau-Varilla, desperate for a return on his country's lost assets, reminded the US that Nicaragua lay in a volcanic zone. The asking price was dropped from US$102 million to just US$40 million and in 1902 Washington negotiated a treaty with Colombian minister Thomas Herran. The new treaty incorporated a US-controlled zone 10km in width, 5km either side of a strip of land allocated for a canal, with a 99-year lease. For this the US would pay US$10 million up front and US$250,000 per annum in rent. However, the Colombian Senate rejected the price, for such a valuable route was less than the French were asking for their assets.

Bunau-Varilla, determined not to lose out, seized on the opportunity offered by Panama's long-standing aspiration to gain independence. He met Panamanian nationalist Manuel Amador in New York and agreed to fund a Panamanian revolution on the condition he would become Panama's first foreign minister with

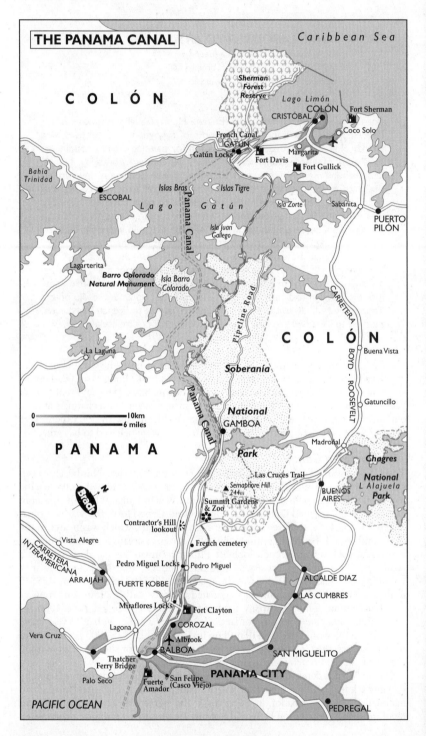

THE PANAMA CANAL

Caribbean Sea

C O L Ó N

Sherman Forest Reserve

Lago Limón
COLÓN
CRISTÓBAL
Fort Sherman
Coco Solo

French Canal
GATÚN
Gatún Locks
Fort Davis
Margarita
Fort Gullick

Bahía Trinidad

ESCOBAL

Islas Bras
Islas Tigre

L a g o   G a t ú n

Isla Zorte
Sabanita
PUERTO PILÓN

Isla Juan Gallego

Lagarterita

Barro Colorado Natural Monument
Isla Barro Colorado

Pipeline Road

C O L Ó N

Buena Vista

La Laguna

Soberanía

Gatuncillo

0 ____ 10km
0 ____ 6 miles

P A N A M A

National
GAMBOA

Madroñal

Chagres
National
L Alajuela
Park

Park

Las Cruces Trail

▲ *Semaphore Hill*
244m

BUENOS AIRES

Summit Gardens & Zoo

Contractor's Hill
lookout

Vista Alegre

French cemetery

CARRETERA INTERAMERICANA
ARRAIJÁN

Pedro Miguel Locks
Pedro Miguel

ALCALDE DIAZ

LAS CUMBRES

FUERTE KOBBE

Miraflores Locks
Fort Clayton

Vera Cruz

Lagona

COROZAL
Albrook
BALBOA

SAN MIGUELITO

Thatcher
Ferry Bridge

Palo Seco

Fuerte
Amador
San Felipe
(Casco Viejo)
PANAMA CITY

PACIFIC OCEAN

PEDREGAL

the right to negotiate a US canal treaty. On November 3 1903, the revolution was carried out successfully. Colombian troops were bribed with Bunau-Varilla's money and later held back with the help of the US Navy. On November 5 the US government officially recognised the independent republic of Panama. Before Amador had a chance to return for canal negotiations, the Hay–Bunau-Varilla treaty was signed in New York. The new treaty, extending the proposed US controlled zone to ten miles, gave the US a lease in perpetuity and the right to intervene in Panamanian politics. Panama furiously objected but the US threatened to withdraw its recognition and support unless the treaty was ratified. The treaty was approved.

The Isthmian Canal Commission, headed by John G Walker, supervised the construction of the new Panama Canal. The US decided on a canal with locks and Colonel George W Goethals was installed as chief engineer in 1907. It took ten years to complete. Gatún Dam was built at the mouth of the Chagres River to create Gatún Lake and locks were constructed in three places. The Gaillard Cut was the most arduous and 161m^3 of volcanic earth and rock were removed. Workers were spared the yellow fever and malaria that had so decimated the French by William Gorgas' successful methods of sanitation control, and both diseases remain effectively eradicated in the region to this day.

Initially 31,000 men and women workers were bought from the West Indies and throughout the years of construction, workers arrived on their own initiative. It has been estimated that as many as 150,000 to 200,000 immigrants joined in the building of the canal. There were racial tensions – trade unions barred black people from membership and paid them less than white people for the same work. That cultural mix contributed to the present rich culture of Panama.

The Panama Canal was completed on August 16 1914. With the outbreak of World War I, American officials took a hard line on their newest asset. President Wilson sent the Marine Corps and the Army into Panama on various pretexts and in 1918–19 the US pressed Panama to restructure its police force in order to avoid further intervention. Over the following decades Panama pushed for further rights to the Canal. In 1936 America surrendered rights to use US troops outside the Canal Zone, in the General Treaty of Friendship. But it was the treaty between Omar Torrijos and US President Jimmy Carter, in 1977, that finalised a date for the Canal's handover to Panama.

The treaty gave complete control of the Canal to Panama from noon on December 31 1999. In 1978, the US Senate had ratified the treaty, with a provision allowing US intervention should the Canal's operation be interrupted. On October 1 1979, US control officially ended. The Panama Canal Commission was created as a general management agency until the handover. A further treaty gave the US the right to defend the Canal's neutrality.

Canal date chart

1789   Alexander von Humbolt finds nine suitable locations for a canal on the American continents.

1821   Panama gains independence from Spain and joins Colombia.

1849   People from around the globe cross the Isthmus of Panama by rail during the San Francisco gold rush.

1878   The French Universal Canal Company purchases rights to the construction of a canal in Panama.

1884   The French begin the construction of the canal. The attempt failed due to severe work conditions and economic problems. Up to 22,000 workers died, many from yellow fever and malaria.

1903   Panama gains independence from Colombia at the cost of the new American-controlled canal treaty. The US take full rights within a ten-mile 'zone' at either side of the canal area and may intervene with Panamanian internal affairs.

1914   Panama Canal is completed.

1936   A new canal treaty is drawn between US President Franklin D Roosevelt and Harmodio Arias Madrid asserting the US will surrender their rights to intervene in Panama's politics.

1939   Washington ratifies the 1936 treaty and Panama ceases to be a US protectorate.

1968   General Omar Torrijos, chief of the National Guard, overthrows the elected president Arnulfo Arias and enforces a dictatorship.

1977   September 7, the Panama Canal Treaty is signed between Omar Torrijos and US President Jimmy Carter, observed by 28 governments and 19 heads of state at the site of the Organization of American States. The treaty guarantees the Canal will be transferred to the Republic of Panama, with full responsibility on December 31 1999.

1979   Canal treaties go into effect and US control of the Panama Canal officially ends.

1981   Torrijos dies in plane crash.

1997   The new Panama Canal Interoceanic Museum opens its doors. The Panama Canal Authority is created.

1999   December 31, Republic of Panama takes full control of the Panama Canal, ending nearly a century of American control.

GOVERNMENT AND POLITICS

The Republic of Panama is governed as a constitutional democracy, split into a central government and decentralised government entities. The central government is led by the cabinet, which is in turn led by a president that has been elected by popular vote to a five-year term in office. The executive branch comprises the president, vice-presidents and ministers of state. The first and second vice-presidents are elected by popular vote while the president chooses ministers. The legislative assembly has 72 members, also elected by popular vote to a five-year term. The judiciary consists of a supreme court, appointed to a ten-year term by the president and ratified by the legislature in various lower courts. Panama's nine provinces are divided into municipal districts. Each province has a governor appointed by the president and each municipality has a council of elected representatives. An autonomous Electroral Tribunal supervises voter registration, the election process, and the activities of political parties. Everyone over the age of 18 is required to vote in presidential elections, although those who fail to do so are not penalised.

President Martín Torrijos Espino was elected to office on May 2 2004 as candidate of the Partido Revolucionario Democrático (PRD, Democratic Revolutionary Party) in a Patria Nueva alliance with the support of the smaller People's Party (PP). His closest challenger, former President Guilemo Endara of the Solidarity Party, conceded defeat after polling 17% less votes that Torrijos. The result was widely expected and followed an impassioned campaign during which Torrijos capitalised on the legacy of his father Omar Torrijos, a former president of Panama who died in a plane crash in 1981. He repeatedly reminded audiences that it was his father who persuaded Jimmy Carter to return the Panama Canal to Panamanian ownership and control. Forty-year-old Torrijos, who was born an illegitimate child of the Panamanian dictator, studied political science and economics at Texas A&M University. He returned to Panama to serve as deputy minister for the interior and

A FEMALE FIRST

Since gaining independence from Colombia in 1903, Panama has had 55 presidents, but only one of them has been a woman. The election of Mireya Moscoso on May 2 1999 to the highest office in the land wasn't just a significant moment in Panama's history – it was a first for Central America as a whole. As the widow of former president Arnulfo Arias, who held three terms of office 1940–41, 1949–51 and 1968, Mireya Moscoso was no stranger to Panama's political echelons, but had limited personal experience. Her tenure, plagued by allegations of corruption and unfulfilled election promises, ended in 2004. Martín Torrijos, son of Omar Torrijos, a former president who deposed her husband in a coup in 1968, replaced her. He won 47% of the vote for the Partido Revolucionario Democrático (PRD), a party founded by his father.

justice during the presidency of Ernesto Pérez Balladares (1994–99) before running as the PRD candidate in the 1999 Presidential election. He was beaten into second place by Mireya Moscoso (see *A Female First*) of the Arnulfista Party whose husband had been deposed by Torrijos' father in 1968. President Martín Torrijos (www.martin2004.com), who is married with three children, says he's a man of the people, and once worked in McDonald's in Chicago.

CUSTOMS AND ETIQUETTE

Providing a standard set of dos and don'ts in Panama is not simple. So diverse is Panama's cultural make-up, that what may be deemed acceptable in one community may easily be wholly abhorrent in another. In general terms Panama is a conservative country with an underlying formality, where people view respect for one another as paramount and are suspicious of those who appear inconsiderate. They are fiercely nationalistic and enjoy having this pride and enthusiasm for their country endorsed by visitors. Underneath this culture of conservatism, Panamanians are relaxed and easy-going, although less gregarious than many of their Latin American neighbours. Gracious hosts who pride themselves on good humour and warmth, Panamanian people expect visitors to respect their country and its peoples. That they are less prone to obvious displays of exuberance is a sensible behavioural benchmark for visitors to adopt. Treat the people you meet as they treat you and you'll not go far wrong.

Panama's relaxed attitude to punctuality even extends to its business world and being 30 or 40 minutes late for an appointment is still considered to be 'on time'. Travellers will find this characteristic frustrating if on a tight schedule. To meet that deadline, catch that last boat home or hit the road before sunrise, factor in at least an hour contingency and make use of the phrase '*en punto*' (on the dot).

Many of the cultural considerations to observe in Panama relate to the indigenous Indian culture. The Ngöbe-Buglé, Emberá, Wounaan, Bokata, Bribri and Teribe (or Tiribe, Naso) tribes have their own distinct cultures with individual rules, traditions and tolerances. While a growing number of Panama's indigenous communities welcome tourists in controlled numbers, many don't. Each also has entirely separate views on what it expects from its visitors in financial, cultural and behavioural terms.

Photography remains the most contentious issue and Panama's indigenous people ask that permission be sought (often with a US$1 fee) prior to a photograph being taken.

Practical Information

WHEN TO VISIT (AND WHY)

Peak tourist season in Panama runs from mid-December to mid-April, in correlation with the dry season on the Pacific side. Land north of the continental divide will still experience downpours during this period but as a rule the driest months on the Caribbean coast are February, March, September and October (see *Climate* in *Chapter 1* for details). Crowds swell in the Bocas del Toro Province during these drier months when a mixed bunch from Costa Rica, America and Europe descend on the archipelago.

Choosing when to visit depends on what you plan to do. Hiking, walking or camping in the jungle is more accessible, less muddy and a good deal safer in the dry season. Getting around is also easier during this time as even major roads are prone to flood damage during or immediately after the rains. Assume that most of Panama's craterous dusty dirt tracks require a 4WD year-round and turn into glue-like mud during the wettest months.

Opinions differ on the prime snorkel months but visibility is often improved in Panamanian waters with a little light rain. Strong, gusty trade winds can stir up sediment to make conditions cloudy, yet much of Panama's coastline benefits from shelter from outlying islands. Birders visit Panama all year round, spoilt for choice by a large number of endemic and migratory species. Just 150 of 950 are migrants and only seen in Panama from September to April. Visiting one of the country's famous fiestas requires a bit of pre-planning. Hotel rooms are scarce, flights fully booked and shops, roads and banks close without warning. Panama's fondness for national holidays can see days added to the calendar unannounced, especially around both Independence Days (from Colombia, November 3, and from Spain, November 28). Prolonged Carnaval (Mardi Gras) celebrations reach their peak in the four days before Ash Wednesday with hotels at bursting point in towns countrywide. One, in the Chiriquí Province, claims to be pre-booked for Carnaval until 2007, while in Bocas del Toro the only available option is likely to be a hammock on the beach.

HIGHLIGHTS AND ITINERARIES

First-time travellers in Panama will find that many of its highlights are given pretty scant coverage in literature produced by IPAT, the national tourist board. As a result deciding 'where' in Panama relies on the ability of its visitors to seek out areas of particular interest, a mission helped by the fact that this small, squiggle of land is an easily navigable size. However, Panama's diminutive proportions are not an indication of its attractions, and even a month is barely long enough to see everything the country has to offer. Itineraries are best planned according to what it is you want to see and do – and the level of comfort you want to see and do it in. However no trip to the isthmus is complete without a decent amount of time spent exploring its fine national parks and reserves.

Highlights
Wildlife

Panama's most accessible reserves and national parks are the Parque Internacional La Amistad (Chiriquí), Parque Nacional Volcán Barú (Chiriquí), Parque Nacional Chagres and Parque Nacional Soberanía (Panama Province), Parque Nacional Camino de Cruces (Panama Province) and Parque Nacional Portobelo (Colón). Parque Nacional Darién, the largest reserve in Panama at 579,000ha, is not easily accessible and is unsafe to explore without a guide due to its impregnable jungle and cross-border paramilitary incursions from Colombia. A visit to Parque Nacional Coiba and its 216,543ha of marine habitat (Veraguas) requires a two- to four-hour boat journey from the mainland, as do the key islands in the Parque Nacional Marino Isla Bastimentos in Bocas del Toro.

Scenery

The finest scenery is in the highlands around Parque Nacional Volcán Barú, Boquete, Guadalupe, Bambito and Cerro Punta, the Las Perlas archipelago, the islands of Kuna Yala, the jungle in Darién and the lush green valleys of El Valle.

Beaches and watersports

Sportfishing is superb along both coastlines but it is a pretty little bay off of Punta Patina near to Jaqué in the Darién that has broken more International Game Fish Association (IGFA) world records than anywhere else – 170 at last count. Expect to find black marlin, blue marlin, Pacific sailfish, dorado, yellowfin tuna, grouper, roosterfish, snapper and amberjack here just 8–20km offshore. Strong currents mean that many of Panama's several hundred beaches are only for sunbathing, camping and beachcombing. The exceptions are those without fine, white sand on the Pacific side, the islands of the Nacional Parque de Coiba, some of the beaches on Isla Bastimentos in Bocas del Toro, and the islets of Kuna Yala. Divers will find plenty of sites in Bocas del Toro and around Portobelo in Colón. For world-class surf head to Santa Catalina and Playa Venao on the Pacific side, both venues for international surfing competitions and popular surfing hangouts. Bocas del Toro also has some excellent breaks, as do some of the many beaches in Los Santos and Veraguas.

Fun times

The archipelago of Bocas del Toro and the Isla Grande in Colón both boast a laid back Caribbean-style atmosphere and are home to the most outgoing people in Panama. Bocas del Toro's growing international expatriate population has spawned bars and restaurants aplenty. Like Isla Grande it also has a lively year-round festival calendar and attracts a mixed party crowd, from fresh-faced backpackers to salty old seadogs.

Museums

Despite a severe shortage of state funding, Panama's museums are well cared for and diverse. Apart from small collections found in the regions, the finest museums are all in Panama City, where institutions are indebted to generous benefactors. The Museo de Arte Contemporáneo is an excellent example of private funding, exhibiting fine works by Latin American artists year-round and hosting a month long art exhibition of Panamanian art.

Handicrafts

Head to the markets of El Valle and Panama City, the street stalls and festival vendors in Bocas del Toro, the mola makers in Kuna Yala, and the Ngöbe Buglé villages of Chiriquí.

People
All tour operators will be able to organise a visit to one of Panama's indigenous communities where interaction of varying degrees is possible with Kuna, Emberá and Ngöbe Buglé Indians. All three tribes have settlements throughout Panama but only a fraction of them are open to tourists – and then only by arrangement. The largest concentration of Kuna is found in Kuna Yala, while the Ngöbe Buglé predominantly live in Chiriquí, Bocas del Toro and Veraguas. Emberá are found in the Panama Province and along the Chagres River in the Darién.

Itineraries
Panama luxury
Away from the top-class hotels of Panama City there are only a handful of places that offer anything approaching real luxury. Doing Panama in style could involve travelling by private plane or helicopter out to an exclusive five-star resort on a privately owned island – but even this wouldn't guarantee hot running water or a bed free from creepy-crawlies.

The following hotels are in Panama's very good to luxury class: Punta Caracol Acqua-Lodge in Bocas del Toro, Al Natural in Bocas del Toro, Hacienda del Mar on San José in Las Perlas, Tropic Star Lodge in the Bahía Piña, Darién, Crater Valley Hotel & Spa and La Casa De Lourdes in El Valle, and the Islas Secas Resort on Islas Secas. Los Quetzales in Cerro Punta, Chiriquí, and the Gran Hotel Nacional and Las Olas Resort in David are also very good. The author's tip for Panama City is the excellent La Estancia.

Reliability and comfort
Choose the following accommodation for fuss-free, dependable options with good facilities. La Casa de Carmen (relaxed, central) and Hotel Continental (metro, central): Panama City. Cocomo by the Sea (cosy, waterfront) and Hotel Angela (breezy, waterfront): Bocas del Toro. Isla Verde (cabañas, garden setting), Cabañas La Vía Lactea (riverside, out of town) and Momentum (out of town, cabañas): Boquete, Chiriquí. Cerro Bruja (arty, hillside): Volcán, Chiriquí. Las Plumas Guesthouse (cabaña, garden setting): Paso Ancho, Chiriquí. Hostal Cielito Sur (village cabañas): Bambito, Chiriquí. Hotel La Hacienda (stylish, out of town): Santiago, Veraguas. Hotel Santa Fe (charming, rural): Santa Fé, Veraguas. The Hotel Versalles and Hotel Barcelo Guayacanes (both large, modern): Chitré, Herrera. In Los Santos: Hotel Kevin (roadside motel). In Pedasi, Los Santos: Dim's Hostel (room in a family home). Hotel la Pradera (large, modern): Penonomé, Coclé. Posada Ecológica (hilltop retreat): Chiguiri Arriba, Coclé. Residential El Valle, Hotel Campestre and Hotel Don Pepe (all comfy): El Vale, Coclé. Las Veraneras and Las Sirenas (both near-beach cabañas): Santa Clara, Coclé. Davis Suites and Melia Panama Canal (modern): Colón. Dolphin Lodge (island cabañas): Kuna Yala.

Nature reserves with accommodation and camping
Accomodation at the **Altos de Campana National Park** (Panama Province) is basic, but sought-after with six refugios (basic, covered areas) and several camping options (US$5 per night), which ANAM rangers will point out on arrival. The closest refugio is 15 minutes from the start of the trails and has no beds, but a dry roof and toilets. Options at **La Amistad** (Chiriquí) are more varied from camping and a ranger station to Visitors to an overnight stay at the Teribe Indian village for US$12 per person. At the **Humedal de San-San Pond Sak** (Bocas del Toro) camping is US$5 as is a bed at the ANAM ranger station, a place with few facilities other than a toilet but fine for those used to roughing it.

There are plenty of camping options in the **National Park Omar Torrijos-El Copé** (Coclé) where a dorm bed in the ANAM ranger station is US$5 (US$3 for camping) and rangers will guide for a tip. It's US$10 a night to stay on **Isla Coiba** in a rustic wooden hut with dorm beds on the beach, while at Cerro Hoya National Park a bed in a refuge near the ranger station is US$5 per night with camping for US$3 throughout the park. An overnight stay at **Isla Iguana** (Veraguas) costs US$3 for a permit plus US$5 to camp overnight, while a dorm bed at the ANAM ranger station is US$5 per person. To stay at **Isla Cana** (Veraguas) during turtle nesting season the cost is US$8–10 for a rustic cabaña with a fan and an outside bathroom. Camp on the beach for US$5 but allow for US$3 permit. Visitors to the **Parque Nacional Marino Golfo de Chiriquí** can lodge at the **ANAM Ranger Station** on Isla Parida. Accommodation is basic dormitory-style with cold-water taps (US$5 per person) or camping with few facilities for US$5 a tent.

A last word...

It's become something of a cliché to say that Panama is 'much more than just a canal' – but it is. Visiting the Canal isn't compulsory: in fact I travelled through Panama three times before I found the time to take a peek at the world's most famous shortcut. Did I feel guilty? Not a bit, as I'd done what I always do when I travel – I pleased myself. Your itinerary should reflect *your* interests not those of your tour operator. After all, you're in Panama to enjoy yourself and an important part of ensuring this is doing what *you* want to do – whatever and wherever that may be!

Enjoy your travels.

MAPS

Finding a decent map of Panama isn't easy. Good, accurate maps are scarce and few towns and islands have been properly charted. Many are wholly inaccurate, omitting entire settlements and roads and misspelling place names. The only reliable map of the country is produced by International Travel Maps, a 1:800,000 that charts geographical features, cities, airports, towns and national parks in colour. Order it ahead of arrival in Panama, as it is notoriously difficult to get one there. Those that are available are triple the usual sales price of US$12.95 for soft cover/US$13.95 hardcover from ITMB direct or £6.25 from UK stockists.

International Travel Maps 530 Broadway, Vancouver, BC VSZ 1E9, Canada; tel: (604) 879 3621; fax: (604) 879 4521; email: itmb@itmb.com; www.itmb.com

Although the National Geographic Institute in Panama City is renowned for its range of topographical, nautical, provincial, city and regional maps, poor stock control makes this option unreliable. Maps also vary enormously in quality (many are only suitable for wall mounting and are out of date). Taxi drivers know this place as 'Tommy Guardia', after the Institute's founder, and it's a US$2 trip across town.

Stanfords carry maps of Panama and all three UK branches hold a full stock. Order online at www.stanfords.co.uk.

Stanfords Covent Garden 12–14 Long Acre, Covent Garden, London WC2E 9LP; tel: 020 7836 1321; fax: 020 7632 8928

Stanfords Bristol 29 Corn St, Bristol BS1 1HT; tel: 0117 929 9966; fax: 0117 927 7232

Stanfords Manchester 39 Spring Gardens, Manchester M2 2BG; tel: 0161 831 0250; fax: 0161 831 0257

RED TAPE

While there are currently no dedicated Panamanian tourist board offices outside of Panama itself, some consulate offices fulfil a partial role and provide a fairly rudimentary information service. In London, the Panamanian Consulate is predominantly concerned with shipping, trade and commerce, but will tackle individual travel queries within reason. A Panamanian Consulate website for the UK (see below) provides some standard answers to basic travel questions relating to visa requirements, for UK and non-UK residents.

Every visitor entering Panama needs a valid passport and an onward ticket. After that requirements vary from country to country, and change, often without warning. A telephone call to the embassy or consulate to check the state of play is a sensible precaution.

At the time of writing citizens of the following countries with a valid passport can enter Panama without a visa: Argentina, Austria, Belgium, Chile, Costa Rica, El Salvador, Finland, France, Germany, Great Britain, Guatemala, Honduras, Hungary, Israel, Italy, Lichtenstein, Luxembourg, the Netherlands, Nicaragua, Paraguay, Poland, Portugal, Singapore, Spain, Sweden, Switzerland and Uruguay.

The following need a Panamanian tourist card or a visa, plus a valid passport: Antigua & Barbuda, Aruba, Australia, Bahamas, Barbados, Belize, Bermuda, Bolivia, Brazil, Canada, Colombia, Curacao, Ecuador, Granada, Greece, Guyana, Jamaica, Japan, Malta, Mexico, Monaco, New Zealand, Norway, Saint Lucia, Saint Vincent & Grenadines, Samoa Occidental, San Cristobal & Nevis, San Marino, San Tome & Principe, South Korea, Surinam, Sweden, Taiwan, Trinidad & Tobago, USA, Vatican City and Venezuela.

If you are a citizen of a country not included in the above lists then it is worth visiting the consulate website: www.Panamaconsul.com or telephoning for advice.

At the time of writing visitors are given a 90-day visa, although there were widespread, but unsubstantiated rumours of the introduction of a 60-day limit in 2005. After that given period, it is possible to extend your stay at the immigration office. There is an office, or representative office, in the administrative capital of each province. In bureaucratic Panama it is important to have every bit of paperwork in order. Proof of sufficient funds to stay in Panama may be required (US$500 a month is the norm), also a return ticket and reference from a Panamanian national vouching for your good character. This sponsor may also be required to prove their financial solvency. A *prologa de turista* should be obtained from an immigration office where you will need to officially register, for a nominal fee.

Staying in Panama after the 90-day period without the proper paperwork isn't without risk, following a concerted effort by the Panamanian government to toughen up on border controls. In the past passport control has always been more about contraband than bureaucracy, so visa dodgers have had an easy time. Not any more. Travellers with an expired visa face a fine, possible detention and even deportation.

GETTING THERE, AWAY AND AROUND

Panama can rightly claim to be one of the world's great crossroads, a transit hub of extraordinary magnitude wedged between two vast continents and oceans. More than 10,500 vessels transit the Panama Canal each year, saving some 12,669km on a journey from New York to San Francisco via the most famous shortcut on the planet. Then there are the cruise ships (more than 300 a year at last count) and hundreds of international flights to and from Tocumen International, one of the busiest airports in Central America. Overlanders arrive in Panama via the vast Interamericana, which stretches from the Tex–Mex border through Mexico, Guatemala, El Salvador, Honduras, Nicaragua and Costa Rica before dissolving in an expanse of swamp and jungle, Panama's untamed Darién Gap.

By air
International flights

Since the indefinite suspension of flights to and from Costa Rica to Enrique Malek Airport in David in 2003, all international flights arrive and depart from Tocumen International Airport, 35km from downtown Panama City.

Flights to and from Panama are pretty straightforward via North America. There are also connections with all other Central American countries, South America and much of the Caribbean. The main connection point for North America is Miami, but there are also flights out of Houston, New York, Washington DC, Dallas and Los Angeles. American Airlines (tel: 1 800 433 7300 (US); tel: 08457 789 789 (UK); www.aa.com) have a regular schedule from Miami. Continental Airlines (tel: 1 800 523 3273 (US); tel: 0845 607 6760 (UK); www.continental.com) have a daily direct flight from New York (Newark) and Houston. Iberia (tel: 1 800 772 4642 (US); tel: 0845 850 9000 (UK); www.iberia.com) and COPA Air (tel: 1 800 FLY COPA (US); tel: 0870 241 4126 (UK); www.copaair.com) fly from Miami daily, while Delta Airlines operate daily direct flights from Atlanta and Cincinnati (tel: 1 800 221 1212 (US); tel: 0800 414 767 (UK); www.delta.com). At the time of writing there

CLOTS AND DVT
Dr Jane Wilson-Howarth

Long-haul air travel increases the risk of deep vein thrombosis. This has been understood since 1946 when a doctor reported his own thrombosis after a 14 hours non-stop flight. Fortunately he survived, as do the vast majority of people who develop clots in their leg veins. Indeed recent research has suggested that most of us develop clots when immobilised but nearly all of them resolve without us ever having been aware of them. In certain susceptible individuals, though, large clots form and these can break away and lodge in the lungs. This is dangerous but happens in a tiny minority of passengers. Several conditions make the problem more likely. Immobility is the key, and factors like reduced oxygen in cabin air and dehydration may also contribute. Moving about the cabin hourly should help avoid the problem and abstaining from excessive alcohol will prevent sedation and also dehydration which both exacerbate the situation. Taking sleeping pills on long flights is also unwise.

Studies have shown that flights of over five-and-a-half-hours are significant; also people who take lots of shorter flights over a short space of time form clots. People at highest risk are:

- Those who have had a clot before – unless they are now taking warfarin
- People over 80 years of age
- Anyone who has recently undergone a major operation or surgery for varicose veins
- Someone who has had a hip or knee replacement in the last three months
- Cancer sufferers
- Those who have ever had a stroke
- People with heart disease
- Those with a close blood relative who has had a clot – they may have an inherited tendency to clot because of LeidenV factor.

Those with a slightly increased risk:

- People over 40

are no direct flights from mainland Europe.

Given Panama's status as a major business hub in the Latin American banking and finance sector, a regular schedule connects Panama City with Central American capitals, including Lacsa, Mexicana and TACA. COPA, the Panamanian airline, offers flights between Panama City and Colombia, Costa Rica, Cuba, the Dominican Republic, Ecuador, El Salvador, Guatemala, Haiti, Jamaica, Mexico, Peru, Nicaragua, Puerto Rico, Honduras, Chile, Brazil and Venezuela. Avianca, Lacsa, Varig, American Airlines, Continental Airlines and Delta Airlines all connect Panama City with South America, although not all with direct flights.

Tickets from the US to Panama City range in price from US$400 to US$700 depending on the schedule and time of year, although flights to and from Miami are generally the cheapest. From the UK tickets cost between £450 and £650 with flights from Birmingham, Gatwick and Heathrow.

Domestic flights

All domestic flights from Panama City operate out of Albrook Airport, a former military facility, less commonly referred to as Marcos A Gelabert. Small domestic

- Women who are pregnant or have had a baby in the last couple of weeks
- People taking female hormones or on other oestrogen therapy
- Heavy smokers
- Those who have very severe varicose veins
- The very obese
- People who are very tall (over 6ft/1.8m) or short (under 5ft/1.5m)

A deep vein thrombosis (DVT) is a clot of blood that forms in the deep leg veins. This is very different from irritating but harmless superficial phlebitis. DVT causes swelling and redness of one leg and there is usually heat and pain in one calf and sometimes the thigh. A DVT is only dangerous if a clot breaks away and travel to the lungs (pulmonary embolus). Symptoms of a pulmonary embolus (PE) include chest pain which is worse on breathing in deeply, shortness of breath and sometimes coughing up small amounts of blood. The symptoms commonly start three to ten days after a long flight. Anyone who thinks that they might have a DVT needs to see a doctor who will arrange a scan. Treatment is usually warfarin to thin the blood for six months or more.

Prevention of DVT

To reduce the risk of thrombosis on a long journey:

- Take a meal of oily fish in the 24 hours before departure
- Exercise before and after the flight
- Keep mobile before and during the flight; move around every couple of hours
- During the flight drink plenty of water or juices
- Avoid taking sleeping pills and excessive tea, coffee and alcohol
- Perform exercises that mimic walking and tense the calf muscles
- Consider wearing flight socks or support stockings (see www.legshealth.com)

The jury is still out on whether it is wise to take aspirin. If you think you are at increased risk of a clot ask your doctor if it is safe to travel.

airlines come and go in Panama but Aeroperlas and Maipex-Aero are the largest and most reliable. Aeroperlas (tel: 210 9500; fax: 210 9582; www.aeroperlas.com) is the larger of the two and serves every regional airport in Panama. Maipex-Aero (tel: 315 0888; fax: 315 0289) has a less extensive schedule, serving David, Bocas del Toro, Changuinola and Colón from the capital. Turismo Aereo (tel: 315 0279; www.turismoaereo.com) launched in 2004 and flies to Kuna Yala, Darién, Contadora and Chitré.

Chartered airlines
An increasing number of chartered airlines and helicopters serve Panama City to and from Albrook Airport. Prices vary according to distances. Try Helix Craft Corporation (tel: 269 4028/315 0153; fax: 269 4032; email: helix@helixcraft.com); Helipan (tel: 315 0452; www.helipan.com); Arrendamientos Aereos (tel: 315 0478); or Aero Ejecutivo (tel: 315 0439/0279).

By road
Panama's three border posts with Costa Rica are accessible by road but not the one with Colombia. The Interamericana fizzles out at the town of Yaviza in the Darién Province more than 260km from Panama City. A large expanse of jungle separates Yaviza from the Colombian border. It's known as the Darién Gap, a swathe of lush rainforest that forms a natural and almost impenetrable border. Talk by the Moscoso administration of extending the Interamericana was met with alarm in 2003. Since his election in 2004 President Torrijos has remained tight-lipped on the subject, but conservationists and Darién's indigenous communities have made no secret of their vehement opposition to the plans. Apart from the highway's environmental impact there are also concerns about opening up the Colombian border. Rebel incursions and drug traffickers make this area a dangerous prospect for tourists. British Foreign Office advice remains unequivocal (see *Darién Province* chapter), advising that travellers 'should not attempt to travel to Colombia by transiting the Isthmus of Darién as the border area is unsafe'. For up-to-date information visit the Foreign Office website: www.fco.gov.uk, see BBC Ceefax page 470 onwards, or contact the following:

Travel Advice Unit Consular Directorate, Foreign & Commonwealth Office, Old Admiralty Building, London SW1A 2PA; tel: 0870 6060290; fax: 020 7008 0155; email: consular.fco@gtnet.gov.uk

Border crossings with Costa Rica
The three road border crossings between Costa Rica and Panama are Paso Canoas, Sixaola/Guabito and Río Sereno. To enter Panama from Costa Rica you'll need a passport and possibly a tourist card and/or visa (see *Red tape*). The tourist card can be purchased at the border for US$5. Visitors who are carrying more than US$4,999 in cash will need to declare it and pay a tax of 5% on the amount. Travellers can catch

WHAT'S IN A NAME?
The highway that runs almost the entire length of Panama is known under a variety of names. Depending on whom you're talking to this 266km road, stretching from Costa Rica to Yaviza ahead of the Darién Gap, is referred to as the Pan-American, the Interamerican Highway or Carretera Interamericana, or the Interamericana – simply take your pick.

TEX–MEX TO PANAMA BY BUS

Travellers from the US can travel to Panama overland from North America, a big road-trip adventure of some 5,000km. Those that have done it report that it's expensive (all those bus tickets soon add up) but the border permits were not as much of a headache as they had imagined. The trip itself is a substantial appetiser to the Panama entrée, taking in Mexico, Belize, Guatemala, El Salvador, Honduras, Nicaragua and Costa Rica on the way.

Brownsville on the Tex–Mex border makes a pretty good departure base and is served by Houston International Airport (six hours' drive away) via Continental Airline flights into Brownsville-South Padre Island International Airport. Non-US citizens keen to embark on the great US–Panama road-trip will need to sort visa paperwork ahead of leaving their respective countries. To check out visa requirements (both US and non-US nationals) and for some practical help with accommodation planning in Mexico, call toll free in the US on tel: 1 800 626 2639; email: visinfo@brownsville.org; www.brownsville.org. According to the worldwide public transport portal, Bus Station, it is possible to travel from Canada to Panama by bus; visit www.bustation.net for details.

a local bus to the border, hop off to take care of paperwork, cross the border and then catch another bus on the other side to continue on their way.

The **Paso Canoas** crossing is by far the most commonly used exit and entry point, sitting midway in the city of Paso Canoas and neatly divided between Costa Rica and Panama. Although officials will swear to the contrary, it is almost impossible to provide a definitive guide to border opening times. They seem to chop and change on a daily basis, reliant on all manner of unknown influences. However, travellers who arrive between 08.00 and 22.00 are sure to find it open for business. It is often open a good hour earlier and later for no obvious reason. A bank just beyond the immigration booth on the Panamanian side is open 08.00–15.00, but it doesn't change Costa Rican colones into US dollars so make alternative plans. A frequent bus service connects Paso Canoas with David between 05.00 and 21.45. The journey takes about 1½ hours, departs every 10–15 minutes and costs a couple of dollars. Reaching Panama City from Paso Canoas by bus is a bit of a slog with four departures daily between 08.00 and 22.00. The trip can take anything up to ten hours depending on the number of stops it makes along the way. Ticket prices vary on each of the four scheduled services, but expect to pay US$20 on the overnight journey, which departs at 22.00. Taxis sit in a line near the station 24 hours a day. Most are willing to do the drive to David for US$30 per trip, regardless of the number of passengers, although many fresh arrivals can be stung for considerably more.

The **Sixaola–Guabito** crossing is split between Sixaola on the Costa Rica side and Guabito on the Caribbean coast of Panama. While its opening hours are listed as 07.00–23.00 it is frequently closed earlier than this, often by 20.00. The transport system that serves the crossing mirrors these business hours with a minibus service at backpacker rates that links Guabito with Changuinola, 18km away. The town of Changuinola has banks, shops, hotels, buses, taxis and an airport with daily flights to David and Bocas Town (Isla Colón). Travellers who arrive in Guabito with a pocket full of Costa Rican colones will find that vendors throughout the town accept them as a matter of course.

Río Sereno is little more than a pinprick of a town, located on the Concepción–Volcán road in Chiriquí. It provides no real physical border between Panama and Costa Rica, just a small immigration booth. Yet what Río Sereno may lack in stature it more than makes up for in officialdom, and its bureaucratic nitpicking is infamous with travellers throughout Panama. Opening hours are 07.30 to 17.00 and officials are sticklers for punctuality. This is not the crossing to choose for those without extraordinary levels of patience. Immigration officials make travellers jump through hoops so the process takes some time. There is a bank in Río Sereno with an ATM but no foreign currency exchange service. Buses leave hourly from 05.00 to 17.00 each day from a terminal nearby, stopping at Volcán for a couple of dollars and continuing on to David for less than US$5.

Driving in Panama

Visitors can drive on a foreign licence for up to 90 days. Car hire requires a passport, and driving licence. Seat belts must be worn by drivers and front-seat passengers but are not required by passengers in the rear. Children aged five and under must travel in fitted child seats in rear seats only. All drivers in Panama should carry insurance paperwork, ownership documents and ID at all times. Most hire agreements are for drivers aged 25 and require credit card payment.

Panama's main highway, the Interamericana, stretches almost its entire length and is, by and large, in pretty good shape, albeit mainly single-lane. Pot-holes, flooding, livestock and mudslides are part and parcel of life on the Interamericana. Yet the journey west to east offers plenty of great views from behind the wheel along a patchwork route of geographic diversities.

Risks to tourists on the road are low, although caution should be taken when driving through some areas in Panama City and Colón City, even in daylight. Panama's US-style road system makes getting from A to B easier than in most Latin American countries, although back roads are poorly maintained. Many are unlit, unpaved and uneven, requiring extreme care after dark. Fallen branches, spilt loads, sharp bends, burst riverbanks and an absence of road signs are hazardous, yet it is excess speed that poses the biggest threat to safety. However, roads are generally quiet as just 97 in 1,000 Panamanians own a car (just 5.59 vehicles per km^2) but are served by at least one petrol station per town – and often more.

Police roadblocks are common along the Interamericana and slow traffic to enable a cursory checking of ID. While police corruption is not as big a problem as it is in other Central America countries, it does exist. This is targeted at tourists and usually amounts to little more than a demand for an on-the-spot fine for an unspecified violation of the law. Make a fuss or feign poverty and the fine can be quickly forgotten. If it isn't, try negotiating it down to a nominal amount. On the single occasion that this happened to me, I ended up paying a quarter of the original US$20 fine. It was money well spent as I received a hand-drawn map in return that enabled me to bypass 2km of congestion.

By sea

During the months of January, February and March Panama welcomes hundreds of cruise ships to its shores. Most arrive via the Caribbean from North America, and are so vast that they need to inch their way slowly along the Panama Canal to avoid scraping the sides of the locks. Liners carry up to 2,000 cruise-goers at a time and the spending power of these captive visitors hasn't been lost on the Panamanian government. A growing menu of onshore excursions is geared entirely towards the needs of this cruise market. The Panama Canal remains the number one destination for cruise-ship passengers. Other popular options include the following:

Panama Canal

Up to 14,000 vessels annually transit the Canal, representing approximately 5% of world trade. Viewing platforms at Miraflores, Gatún and Pedro Miguel locks allow spectator views of transits (see *The Panama Canal* in the *Panama Province* chapter) and an option for a partial transit.

Kuna Yala (the San Blas Islands)

Attractions include Kuna villages, deserted islands, snorkeling and traditional handicrafts (including molas, a reverse-appliqué blouse panel depicting Kuna beliefs), flora and fauna and local customs (see *Kuna Yala* chapter).

Panama City

Four different tour options are cruise ship staples in Panama City, including a 20-minute helicopter flight over the city and a trip along the Chagres River in search of howler monkeys, toucan, kingfisher, blue heron, sloths and iguanas. Others include a trip to Amador Causeway and a walking tour of the Old Quarter, Casco Viejo (San Félipe) (see *Panama City* chapter).

Colón Free Trade Zone and Colón 2000

Tax-free goods and designer brands, restaurants and bars offer cruise passengers plenty of opportunity to part with their cash. Electrical items, perfumes and computer equipment are especially keenly priced (see *Colón Province* chapter).

Transisthmus Train Journey

This wonderful journey at a sedate pace takes in beautiful scenery from an old red and yellow train. Trains depart Monday to Friday at 07.15 from Corozal Passenger Station in Panama City (taxi from Panama City centre US$2.75) and return from Colón Passenger Station at 17.15. The trip takes just under an hour (one-way US$20, return US$35) and reservations are not always necessary. Since cruise lines have started arriving in Colón to see the Canal and the Colón Free Zone, the city has made efforts to improve its appearance but is still very run-down. However, because it is adjacent to such tourist attractions as Gatún Locks, Fort Lorenzo, the Free Zone and Portobelo, the train from Panama to Colón is well served by taxis that whisk visitors off to a more scenic environment in a trice (see *Colón Province* chapter).

Portobelo and Fort Lorenzo

Attractions include historical forts, cannon-topped hillsides and Atlanic coastline views with a protected area of 9,653ha of forests and wetlands, coast and rivers (see *Colón Province* chapter). Discovered and named by Christopher Columbus when, in 1502, his ships sought refuge from a great storm, Portobelo was once one of the more heavily fortified harbours on earth. For more than a century, it was a trans-shipping point for tonnes of gold and silver looted from Incan mines by the Conquistadors. The riches were trekked by donkey caravans from the Pacific side of the Isthmus of Panama to Portobelo on the Caribbean side, en route to the Spanish king.

Emberá Indian Village

Visits to Emberá Indian tribes in the Panama Province have a good take-up from cruise passengers arriving in Panama. Most live by the same traditions and maintain the same lifestyle as before the Spaniards colonised Panama. Reaching the Emberá, who are keepers of the rainforest and Chagres River, is possible by dugout canoe along the vine-tangled river teeming with birds (see *Panama Province* chapter).

Cruise operators

Princess Cruise Line Tel: 1 800 PRINCESS (US); tel: 020 7800 2222 (UK); www.princess.com

Carnival Tel: 1 888 CARNIVAL (US); tel: 0207 940 4466 (UK); www.carnival.com (US); www.carnivalcruise.co.uk

P&O Cruises Tel: 0845 3 555 333 (UK); www.pocruises.com

Fred Olsen Cruise Line Tel: 1 612 822 4640 (travel agent: Borton Overseas); tel: 01473 742424 (UK); www.fredolsen.co.uk

Celebrity Tel: 1 800 280 3423 (US); tel: 0800 018 2525 (UK); www.celebrity.com

Holland America Tel: 1 877 SAIL HAL (US); tel: 020 7940 4477 (UK); www.hollandamerica.com

Departure tax

Visitors are required to pay a US$20 departure tax.

TOUR OPERATORS
Panama

Ancon Expeditions Calle Elvira Mendez, Edificio El Dorado 3, Bella Vista, Panama City; tel: 269 9415; fax: 264 3713; email: info@anconexpeditions.com; www.anconexpeditions.com. A long-established company in Panama who offer an extensive variety of cultural, adventure and natural history trips. It employs some of the finest guides in Panama and is the commercial arm of ANCON, the largest private conservation group in the country. Associated with Journey Latin America in the UK (see *Tour operators, UK*).

Panoramic Panama Tel/fax: 314 1417; email: enquiry@panoramicPanama.com; www.panoramicPanama.com. Tailor-made tours for independent travellers and small groups. All areas of Panama covered and every type of trip catered for, from adventure treks and fishing to real estate and culture. Personal service and professional standards.

Adventures in Panama Av La Amistad, Plaza Psari, Local 1; tel: 236 8146; email: contact@adventuresinpanama.com; www.adventuresinpanama.com. UK office: Frederick Street, Aldershot, Hants GU11 1 LQ; tel +44 (0)1252 760200; email: ops@exploreworldwide.com. A respected tour operator in Panama that caters for adventure-loving travellers and offers a variety of packages from white-water rafting and repelling to hiking and mountain biking.

Ecocircuitos Panama, SA Hotel Country Inn & Suites, Ground Floor, Pelican Av, Amador Causeway, Panama City; tel/fax: 314 1586; US fax: +1 (708) 810 9350; email: annie@ecocircuitos.com; www.ecocircuitos.com. Birding, hiking, national parks, indigenous-cultural encounters and diving. Customised packages for individuals, seniors, families and couples.

Extreme Panama Bd El Dorado, Centro Comercial Camino de Cruces, No 10, Panama City; tel: 269 7326; fax: 360 2035; email: info@extremePanama.com; www.extremePanama.com. Great range of adventure packages, including hiking, trekking, mountain biking, camping, caving and island excursions.

Aventuras Panama Tel: 260 0044/236 5814; fax: 260 7535; email: info@aventurasPanama.com; www.aventurasPanama.com. White-water rafting, kayaking, hiking, climbing and camping trips with a website in Spanish, English, Portuguese, German and Italian.

Experience Panama PO Box 0832-1437, World Trade Centre, Panama City; tel: 214 2030; fax: 214 2033; email: info@experiencePanama.com; www.experiencePanama.com. US office: 1602 NW 97th Av, Miami, FL 33102-5207. Broad range of travel options including a variety of general sightseeing tours, wildlife holidays and business incentive travel.

Panama Jones tel: toll free 1 888 726 2621 (Panama); tel: (580) 428 3476, ext 12 (US); www.Panamacanal.com. Canal cruises, cultural tours, island hopping, walking and birding.

PTY Marine Adventures Tel: 226 8917; fax: 226 6088; email: info@ptymarineadventures.com; www.ptymarineadventures.com. Full and partial transits of the Canal in the restored *Pacific Queen*, a Hansaline ship.

Panama Star Tours Tel: 265 7970; fax: 265 7980; email: info@Panamastar.com; www.Panamastar.com. Canal tours, and other excursions throughout Panama, including shopping trips in Panama City and the Colón Free Zone.

Panama Motorcycle Tours Tel: 236 7232; fax: 694 8226; email: info@ace-panama.com; www.acs-Panama.com. Exhilarating tours of Panama by motorbike along the Interamericana and back roads, including trips to the Darién.

Scuba Panama Tel: 261 3841/4064; email: info@scubapanama.com; www.scubaPanama.com. A wide range of beginner, advanced and certified diving courses in various locations on both the Pacific and Atlantic coastlines.

Panama Rafters Boquete; tel: 720 2712; email: reservations@Panamarafters.com; www.Panamarafters.com. Independent rafting specialist with white-water rafting, kayaking and river rafting for every standard, and tailor-made and tuition options.

Chiriquí River Rafting Boquete; tel: 720 1505; fax: 720 1506; email: rafting@Panama-rafting.com; www.Panama-rafting.com. White-water rafting, kayaking and river rafting tours with runs to suit novices and experts alike.

Europe/Australia
UK

Journey Latin America 12 & 13 Heathfield Terrace, Chiswick, London W4 4JE; tel: 020 8747 3108/8747 8315; fax: 020 8747 1312; email: flights@journeylatinamerica.co.uk or for tours: tours@journeylatinamerica.co.uk; for escorted groups: groups@journeylatinamerica.co.uk; www.journeylatinamerica.co.uk. Long-established specialist operator offering flights, package and tailor-made holidays for individuals and escorted groups. JLA work with Ancon Expeditions of Panama (see *Tour operators, Panama*).

Explore Worldwide 1 Frederick St, Aldershot, Hants GU11 1LQ; tel: 01252 760 200; fax: 01252 760 201; email: info@exploreworldwide.com; www.exploreworldwide.com. Adventure tours including biking, hiking, river tubing, cultural expeditions and whale watching. Associated with Adventures in Panama (see *Tour operators, Panama*).

South American Experience 47 Causton St, Pimlico, London SW1P 4AT; tel: 020 7976 5511; fax: 020 7976 6908; email: info@southamericanexperience.co.uk; www.southamericanexperience.co.uk. Tailor-made trips to Panama including the Canal Zone, full and partial transits of the canal, hotel reservations and transfers.

Global Travel Club 1 Kiln Shaw, Langdon Hills, Basildon, Essex SS16 6LE; tel: 01268 541 732; fax: 01268 541 363; email: info@global-travel.co.uk; www.global-travel.co.uk. Small-group tours including Panama Canal, Anton Valley, Portobelo, Bocas del Toro, and 'Survivor II film locations'. A company passionate about Central America and happy to tweak packages to suit.

Trips Worldwide 14 Frederick Pl, Clifton, Bristol BS8 1AS; tel: 0117 311 4400; fax: 0117 311 4401; email: info@tripsworldwide.co.uk; www.tripsworldwide.co.uk. Latin American Travel Writer of the Year Howard Marx and AITO Travel Writer of the Year Peter Hughes both won their awards for articles in Panama on trips organised by this tailor-made holiday specialist.

STA Travel 86 Old Brompton Rd, South Kensington, London SW7 3LQ; tel: 0870 1600 599; www.statravel.com. Student flights and some accommodation with several branches in London and others throughout the world.

Trailfinders 194 Kensington High St, London W8 7RG and 215 Kensington High St, London W8 6BD; tel: 020 7938 3939; tel: 020 7938 3444 (first and business class); tel: 0845 0505 905 (visa and passport service); tel: 020 7938 3999 (travel clinic); www.trailfinders.com. Flights only, visa and travel health advice, some accommodation.

Belgium

Discovery Expeditions Acacialaan 29 2460, Kasterlee, Belgium; tel: 1423 2424; fax: 1423 2423; email: info@discovery-expeditions.com; www.discovery-expeditions.com. Associated with Adventures in Panama (see *Tour operators, Panama*).

Germany

Gamboa Tours Mollstr 43, D-68165, Mannheim; tel: 621 3247880; fax: 621 3247881; email: info@gamboatours.de; www.gamboatours.de. Associated with Adventures in Panama (see *Tour operators, Panama*).

Aventoura Reise & Begegnung Rehlingstr 17, D-79100 Freiburg; tel: 761 2116990; email: heike.alter@aventoura.de; www.aventoura.de. Associated with Ecocircuitus, Panama (see *Tour operators, Panama*).

Switzerland

Nouveaux Mondes SA 9 Route Suisse, 1295 Mies; tel: 22 950 9660; fax: 22 950 9666; email: info@nouveauxmondes.com; www.nouveauxmondes.com. Associated with Ecocircuitus, Panama (see *Tour operators, Panama*).

Australia and New Zealand

South American Travel Centre 104 Hardware St, Melbourne; tel: (03) 9642 5353 or tel: toll free 1800 655 051; www.satc.com.au. Numerous package options including Kuna Yala, Contadora Island and the Panama Canal.

STA Travel Australia 260 Hoddle St, Abbotsford VIC 3067; tel: (03) 84176911; www.statravel.com. Student flights and some accommodation with branches throughout Australia.

STA Travel New Zealand Level 8, 229 Queen St, Auckland; tel: 9309 9723; fax: 9309 9829; www.statravel.co.nz. Student flights and some accommodation with branches throughout New Zealand.

Travel Makers Level 1, Baileys Corner Arcade, Canberra City; tel: (02) 6247 4444; fax: (02) 2 6257 6452; email: travmake@travelmakers.com.au; www.travelmakers.com.au. Flights and accommodation in Panama.

USA

Adventures in Panama 1700 17th St, # B10, Boulder, CO 80302; tel: (303) 728 9701; fax: (303) 728 9701; email: contact@adventuresinPanama.com; www.adventuresinPanama.com. Adventure tours including biking, hiking, river tubing, cultural expeditions and whale watching with a main office in Panama (see *Tour operators, Panama*).

Toto Tours 1326 West Albion Av, Chicago, IL 60626-4753; tel: toll free 1 800 565 1241 (US only); tel: (773) 274 8686; fax: (773) 274 8695; email: info@tototours.com; www.tototours.com. Specialist adventure travel operator for gay male travellers, associated with Adventures in Panama (see *Tour operators, Panama*).

TourTech International 3100 Airway Av, Suite 131, Costa Mesa, CA 92626; tel: toll free 800 882 2636 (US only); tel: (714) 436 6561; fax: (714) 435 4069; email: info@tourtech.net; www.tourtech.net. Multi-day packages, customised options, trips to Gamboa rainforest, Panama Canal, Bocas del Toro, San Blas, Coronado beach resort, highland retreats.

iExplore Tel: toll free 1 800 iExplore; tel: 1 312 492 9443; www.adventure.iexplore.com. iExplore are associated with National Geographic and offer various travel packages to Panama.

Latin American Escapes, Inc PMB#421/712 Bancroft Av, Walnut Creek, CA 94598; tel: toll free 1 800 510 5999; fax: (925) 945 0154; email: travel@latinamericanescapes.com;

www.latinamericanescapes.com. Escorted programmes and numerous adventure, historical and cultural packages; happy to customise.

Coral Star Tours M/V Coral Star, 5150 Hwy 22 Suite C10, Mandeville, LA 70471; tel: toll free (866) 924 2837; fax: (985) 845 4939; email: sherri@coralstar.com; www.coralstar.com

Coral Star Florida 94220 Overseas Hwy, Unit 4-B, Tavernier, FL 33070; tel: toll free: (877) 835 3474; email: joan@coralstar.com; www.coralstar.com. Diving, fishing and sailing tours around the islands of Panama.

Adventure Life Journeys 1655 S 3rd St West, Suite 1, Missoula, MT 59801; tel: toll free 1 800 344 6118; tel: (406) 541 2677; fax: (406) 541 2676; www.adventure-life.com. Various adventure trips and tours including the Panama Canal.

Lindblad Expeditions 96 Morton St, 9th Floor, New York, NY 10014; tel: toll free 1 800 Expedition; www.expeditions.com. Twin-centre adventure packages in Panama and Costa Rica.

Canada

STA Travel Canada 200 Bloor St West, Toronto, Ontario M5S 1T8; tel: (416) 925 5800; fax: (416) 925 6300; www.statravel.ca. Student flights and some accommodation with branches throughout Canada.

Costa Rica

Fly Latin America San José; tel: 256 3222; tel: toll free 1 888 246 1431 (flights); tel: toll free 1 888 246 1431 (tours and hotels); www.flylatinamerica.com

Escapes Ecológicos Barrio Amon, San José; tel: 257 4566; fax: 257 1489; email: info@escapesecologicos.com; www.escapesecologicos.com

HEALTH

A wide variety of health topics are relevant to travel in Panama. Factors such as geography, climate, culture and food present travellers with a range of health considerations, as do Panama's many outdoor pursuits. First-aid preparation and understanding common ailments will help to prevent a health crisis. For suggestions on additional material on travel health in Panama see *Appendix 3*.

Before you go
Immunisations

Panama does not require visitors to have any specific vaccinations prior to entry. Neither does it insist on an up-to-date international vaccination or immunisation card. However, travellers that enter Panama from a country that has experienced high incidences of malaria or yellow fever may be asked to present proof that they have been vaccinated, or are taking anti-malarial precautions. Recent reports suggest that dengue fever, a mosquito-spread disease, and leishmaniasis, a disease carried by sand flies, are on the increase in Panama. This has done much to reinforce the message that a good mosquito repellent is essential. Pack plenty, should space allow, as it can be scarce outside the main cities, or exorbitantly priced.

Both the Center for Disease Control and Prevention (CDC), a US government agency, and the UK Department of Health (DoH) offer similar advice to travellers, despite Panama's entry stipulations. The DoH recommends that visitors immunise against hepatitis A and typhoid, plus yellow fever if travel plans include Chepo Darién or San Blas. Malaria prophylaxis is also advised for those travelling to Bocas Del Toro in the west or Darién and San Blas in the east. The following are also worthwhile precautions: vaccination against tetanus and diphtheria (a combined vaccine that protects for ten years), rabies (for those visitors who are likely to spend time in the backcountry away from medical help for 24 hours or more), and hepatitis B (a good idea for those travellers who are embarking on longer trips or who may come into contact with blood or who are working with children). Both hepatitis B and rabies vaccinations consist of three injections and can be given over as short a time as 21 days. If time permits then the longer course given over eight weeks should be used.

Travel insurance
Before travelling to Panama check any pre-existing travel insurance to ensure it covers your trip. If it does then check what the cover includes. White-water rafting in Chiriquí, jet skiing in Bocas del Toro or a hike through the Darién may all be activities that are exempt from a standard policy. IAMAT is a good source of advice on insurance topics. It should also be able to provide a list of recommended doctors in Panama (see Travel clinics for details). Scuba divers should consider the specialist insurance plan offered by the Divers Alert Network (DAN). This non-profit organisation was founded in 1990 and now has 200,000 members, providing medical R&D services and health and safety support to recreational scuba divers in association with Duke University Medical Center. The organisation offers two plans that cover emergency air evacuation to hyperbaric chamber treatment, plus a wide range of equipment and medical safety aspects. DAN The Peter B Bennett Center, 6 West Colony Pl, Durham, NC 27705, USA; tel: 1 800 443 2671; email: dan@diversnetwork.org; www.diversalertnetwork.org.

Travel clinics
UK
British Airways Travel Clinic and Immunisation Service
There are currently two BA clinics, both London based, containing a Stanfords concession as well as a decent stock of travel essentials, guidebooks and travel-health leaflets. At the time of writing, BA has ceased all of its clinic franchise operations internationally, including those in South Africa. For an update on new clinics in the UK, tel: 01276 685040; www.britishairways.com.

BA Clinic 213 Piccadilly, London W1J 9HQ; tel: 0845 600 2236. Walk-in service, Mon–Fri 09.30–18.00, appointments also available. Sat 10.00 16.00 (walk-in only).
BA Clinic 101 Cheapside, London EC2V 6DT; tel: 0845 600 2236. Appointment-only service, Mon–Fri 09.00–16.30.

Nomad Travel Vaccination Centres
There are four Nomad Travel Vaccination Centres, three in London and one in Bristol. For preliminary advice travellers can also call the Travel Health Line on 09068 633414. Calls are charged at 60p per minute and are answered during office hours only. There is also some basic travel health information on the website: www.nomadtravel.co.uk.

Nomad Travel 40 Bernard St, Russell Sq, London WC1H 1LJ; tel: 020 7833 4114
Nomad Travel 3–4 Wellington Terrace, Turnpike La, London N8 0PX; tel: 020 8889 7014
Nomad Travel Terminal House, 52 Grosvenor Gdns, London SW1W 0AG; tel: 0207 823 5823
Nomad Travel 43 Queens Rd, Clifton, Bristol BS8 1QH; tel: 0117 922 6567

Others
Interhealth 157 Waterloo Rd, London SE1 8US; tel: 020 7902 9000; fax: 020 7928 0927; email: info@interhealth.org.uk; www.interhealth.org.uk. Interhealth was founded as a

charity in 1989 to provide health care and support services to mission organisations and voluntary agencies. Today it continues to provide travel health advice to some 150 voluntary organisations and also offers a service to business travellers and holidaymakers, although these do not qualify for discounted rates. Open Mon–Fri 09.00–17.00, on an appointment basis.

The Health Station 21 Brand St, Hitchin, Herts SG5 1JE; tel: 01462 459595; fax 01462 435373; email: main@thehealthstation.co.uk; www.thehealthstation.co.uk. This travel health clinic has a comprehensive vaccination menu and stocks a number of travel products and supplies, including tropical travel health kits. Open Tue 09.00–19.00, Wed 09.00–13.00, Thu 09.00–19.00, Fri 09.00–17.00, Sat 09.00–13.00 and Sun by appointment only. Closed Mon.

Medical Advisory Service for Travellers Abroad (MASTA) Tel: 09068 224100; www.masta.org. Online travel health information, including news on outbreaks, travel chat rooms, immunisation updates and a travel clinic portal. Premium-line advice service for travel-health queries, charged at 50p per minute.

Trailfinders Travel Clinic 194 Kensington High St, London W8 7RG; tel: 020 7938 3999; www.trailfinders.com. This place has a full range of travel vaccines and plenty of practical information on disease prevention for travellers. It also stocks mosquito nets, insect repellents and needle and syringe packs, as well as basic first-aid travel kits. No appointment is necessary. Open Mon–Fri 09.00–17.00, Thu 09.00–18.00, Sat 10.00–17.15, closed Sun.

Australia

Travel Clinics Australia Tel: 1300 369 359; www.travelclinic.com. The Australian National Association of Medical Practices has 22 practices throughout Australia and offers travel-health guidance and practical support. Each clinic has access to the latest information on outbreaks and disease prevention, and provides health reports tailored to meet individual needs. Every customer receives a copy of a 56-page *Traveller's Pocket Medical Guide*. This booklet contains vital health information, including the International Certificate of Vaccination and fits into the passport wallet.

The Travel Doctor (TMVC) Tel: 1300 65 88 44; www.tmvc.com.au. This company was established in 1987 and is now one of the largest individual suppliers of travel medicine services in the world. It has 29 dedicated clinics covering most major cities in Australia and New Zealand, plus a growing number of associates internationally, including North America, Europe, Africa and Asia.

USA

Alamo Medical Group 1505 St Alphonsus Way, Alamo, California CA 94507; tel: (925) 837 4225; fax: (925) 838 5775; email: travldoc@earthlink.net. This place has a good list of pre-travel vaccinations and a registered yellow-fever vaccine centre. Also specialises in post-travel care, with medical diagnostics via an on-site laboratory.

Mount Sinai School of Medicine 5 East 98th St, 11th floor, New York NY 10029; tel: (212) 241 7468; fax: (212) 876 1109; email: alejandra.gurtman@mssm.edu

Centers for Disease Control 1600 Clifton Rd, Atlanta, GA 30333; tel: 877 FYI TRIP; fax: 800 311 3435; www.cdc.gov/travel. This central pool of travel information in America publishes the invaluable *Health Information for International Travel*. The website contains country-specific travel health information plus visitors' tips and destination advice.

Passport Health Tel: 1 888 499 PASS (7277) for locations; tel: (410) 727 0556 for advice; fax: (410) 727 0696; www.passporthealthUSA.com. There is an ever-increasing number of Passport Health travel clinics in the US, in 22 states at the last count (Arizona, Michigan, California, Missouri, Colorado, New Jersey, Connecticut, New York, Delaware, North Carolina, Florida, Ohio, Georgia, Pennsylvania, Illinois, Texas, Iowa, Virginia, Kansas,

Washington DC, Maryland and Wisconsin). Each provides full pre-travel vaccination service, leaflets and destination reports and is an official yellow fever centre. Health centres are in .

Rest of World

International Association for Medical Assistance to Travelers (IAMAT) This non-profit organisation provides a list of English-speaking doctors in a number of destinations overseas. Visit www.iamat.org, email info@iamat.com or contact the following individual member offices:

Canada 40 Regal Rd, Guelph, Ontario N1K 1B5; tel: 519 836 0102; fax: 519 836 3412
USA 417 Center St, Lewiston, NY 14092; tel: 716 754 4883
New Zealand PO Box 5049, Christchurch 5. Postal enquires only.
Switzerland 57 chemin des Voirets, 1212 Grand-Lancy, Geneva. Postal enquiries only.

First-aid kit

No visitor to Panama who plans to travel away from Panama City should be without a first-aid kit, especially if they are heading to the islands or the jungle. While medical facilities in the capital may be well equipped and close at hand, the situation elsewhere is very different. Panama's most picturesque islands and rainforests are only accessible by boat or small plane. A spell of poor weather or a spot of engine trouble renders these destinations inaccessible for hours, if not days, well away from the nearest medical centre. Regional health facilities vary in standard but there is a clinic and a hospital in every city nation wide. Most are woefully under-funded but very well staffed by medics determined to provide the best service possible, albeit without frills.

A first-aid kit in Panama should contain all the basics for travel anywhere in the world. Adjust the quantities of individual items to reflect conditions and availability of replacement items (eg: pack additional mosquito repellent). Other suggestions as follows:

- antiseptic wash
- blister patches
- bandages and plasters
- sachets of rehydration mix
- painkillers
- anti-fungal cream
- travel-sickness tablets
- lots of mosquito repellent
- antibiotics
- cold-cure sachets
- throat lozenges
- eye and ear drops
- indigestion tablets
- iodine or alcohol wipes
- your own prescription medicine

In Panama
Medical facilities

Panama's regional facilities vary in quality and remain short of cash and equipment, despite increased investment. Many Panamanian doctors completed their medical training in America and speak good English as a result and most towns have a hospital or a large 24-hour clinic. Panama's finest medical establishments are in the capital where standards are generally excellent. The Hospital Nacional (tel: 207 8100;

fax: 207 8337; email: mercado@hospitalnacional.com; www.hospitalnacional.com) in Panama City is widely regarded as one of the best. Established in 1973 it attends to an average of 500 patients each day and has a blood bank and radiology, cardiology, neurology, maternity, A&E and rehabilitation departments. Centró Médico Paitilla (tel: 265 8800; fax: 265 8861; email: cmp@pty.com), Panama's top private clinic, has 170 beds and 300 staff and is a Royal Crown of Excellence award-winner.

Drinking the water

Panama is the only country in Latin America where the water is good enough to drink straight from the tap. Waiters look genuinely offended by requests for the bottled variety in restaurants such is the pride in Panama's high water standards. The exception to the rule is in the Bocas del Toro Province, where water is obtained from a rudimentary mains system prone to failure. Here water quality varies dramatically each day and while locals swear that it is fine to drink, the discoloration can be bad enough to stain clothing – a turn-off for most visitors.

Some medical problems
Malaria

This parasitic infection is transmitted to humans by mosquitoes and is the biggest risk to health for travellers in the tropics. Fatalities worldwide reach up to two million people each year, and while no prophylactic drug will prevent the disease, there are several available that will significantly reduce your chances of acquiring it. Malaria is especially dangerous in pregnancy, so women travellers should always seek advice before travelling if pregnant. In Panama there remains a relatively low malaria risk in the remote areas of the Darién, Chiriquí and Bocas del Toro. Those who plan to spend time in these provinces are advised take anti-malarial medication as a precautionary measure. The current malaria prophylaxis recommended is chloroquine west of the canal and chloroquine and proguanil if you are travelling east of the canal. Medication should ideally be taken from one week before to four weeks after your visit. No drug is 100% effective so travellers should remain vigilant for symptoms for up to 12 months after returning home. Symptoms range from flu-like effects to a fever, including aches, chills, sweats and fatigue.

Dengue fever

Panama has a few hundred annual reported instances of dengue fever, a viral disease carried by the Aedes mosquito – the same mosquito that transmits yellow fever. This mosquito is unusual in that it bites during the day time, unlike malarial mosquitoes that bite from dusk till dawn. There is no known prophylactic available for dengue and preventative action should be taken to repel mosquitoes to avoid exposure. The Darién Province poses the greatest risk but there have been recent reported incidences in Bocas del Toro. Travellers should wear plenty of mosquito repellent and specialist mosquito-guard clothing here at all times. Symptoms vary but include chills, sweats, fever and a rash with severe backache and pain behind the eyes. There is no treatment for dengue fever apart from plenty of rest, lots of fluids and painkillers. Aspirin should not be taken. Travellers who fear they may have contracted the disease should seek immediate medical help, as dengue can be fatal especially if you have had Dengue before.

Hantavirus pulmonary syndrome (HPS)

Hantavirus was first discovered in Panama in 1999 but by 2004 alone at least 50 cases had been reported, nine of them fatal. HPS is found in rodents and is not usually contracted by direct contact but from hantavirus particles in saliva, urine and droppings. When these particles dry out and become airborne they become a danger to human health as once inhaled they cause infection. Early symptoms can occur at 5–21 days after infection and almost always include fever, fatigue and aching muscles (usually in the back, shoulders and/or thighs). Other early symptoms may include headaches, dizziness, chills and abdominal discomfort (such as vomiting, nausea and/or diarrhoea). Untreated cases of HPS are almost always fatal. However, treatment before the disease progresses to acute respiratory distress greatly increases the chances of survival.

Cholera

This disease is caused by an infection of the intestine resulting in severe diarrhoea. It is transmitted via contaminated food or water containing faecal material from people already infected. Cholera can be treated with antibiotics and is rarely severe in healthy immunocompetent travellers. However, as there is now an effective oral vaccine (Dukoral) available in the UK, it may be recommended for those who are deemed more at risk of severe disease or for those who are travelling long term and are likely to be in areas where sanitation is poor. For adults and children six years and over the vaccine consists of two doses taken at least one week and not more than six weeks apart. The second dose should be taken at least one week before entering the area. Consult your doctor or a reputable Travel Clinic for up-to-date advice.

Leishmaniasis

Panama has no fewer than 80 different species of sand fly and five of them are carriers of the leishmaniasis parasite. An infected sand fly bites its victim, allowing the parasite to enter the body, where it stays for anything up to six months without symptoms. Eventually the parasite creates a sore, which often begins as a pimple before swelling in size. Sores of up to 2.5cm in diameter are not uncommon and these often weep to develop a crusty surface. It is possible to treat leishmaniasis successfully via a series of injections.

Yellow fever

If you are entering Panama from an area of the world where yellow fever is a risk, ie: certain countries in South America or Sub-Saharan Africa, you will almost certainly need to provide proof of vaccination.

The risk in Panama itself is minimal (but a risk nonetheless) and only relevant to those travelling in the jungle in Chepo Darién or San Blas. Fatality is higher than 60% in non-immunised adults. Women who are pregnant should seek medical advice, as the vaccination itself is not without risk.

Chagas' disease

Spread by 'kissing bugs' (otherwise known as Triatomine bugs) commonly found in the cracks and crevices of poorly constructed housing, Chagas' disease is not considered severe in the early stage of infection but can cause death, particularly in infants. Chronic symptoms are rare but can develop some 20 years after infection, decreasing the average life expectancy by an average of nine years by weakening the immune system. Blood tests can determine infection but to minimise the risk avoid sleeping in thatch-and-mud housing and use insecticides to reduce the risk of transmission. Acute symptoms only occur in about one per cent of cases and chronic Chagas' is uncommon in Panama. There is currently no vaccine or recommended drug available to prevent the disease.

Insect repellent

While instances of malaria, dengue fever, Chagas' disease and yellow fever are not that common in Panama, they do exist. Insects transmit each of these diseases so avoiding contact with carriers is one of the most important health precautions you can take. Packing plenty of insect repellent is essential when visiting Panama. A brand that contains at least 50% DEET (*N,N-diethyl-meta-toluamide*) is advisable wherever you are in Panama, an even higher concentration if you are especially prone to bites.

Protect the skin by wearing trousers and long-sleeved shirts, after dark and in the rainforest. Mosquitoes bite mainly at night, from dusk till dawn, and generally fly at well below head height. However, it is important to remain vigilant to ensure exposed areas of skin are fully protected during daytime, as there are plenty of other biting insects that are out in force during daylight hours. Also remember that the Aedes mosquito that carries Dengue Fever fly during the daytime. DEET can irritate the skin and is not suitable for every skin type. Avoid excessive use of strong repellent, as it can be strong enough to dissolve plastic, as my dear departed flip-flops will testify. Applying a weaker mix to skin and using a stronger repellent to spray clothes is a sensible solution, allowing less exposure to toxicity.

Rabies

Many animal species can be infected with this fatal viral infection, including dogs, cats and monkeys. Any bite scratch or lick over an open wound from an animal in Panama should be thoroughly cleaned immediately, using soap and hot water to scrub the area before wiping it with an alcohol or iodine solution. This will stop the rabies virus entering the body and will guard against secondary wound infections, such as tetanus. Panama's vampire bats pose another rabies risk and are found in large numbers in many provinces. Many travellers are unaware that a bat has bitten them until they spot small spots of blood on the extremities of their head or feet after camping outdoors. Those that think they have been exposed to rabies should seek medical attention immediately. Travellers without immunisation that are bitten will need both RIG (rabies immunoglobulin) and a full course of injections. This will prevent the onset of rabies symptoms but can be expensive (RIG alone can cost around USD 800 a dose excluding the cost of the six or seven doses of vaccine needed). Pre-exposure vaccination is a sensible precaution for travellers who plan to visit remote areas, as mortality rates are high. Furthermore if by taking at least two doses of rabies vaccine before exposure then you won't need the expensive RIG and the number of post exposure doses of vaccine will be reduced.

Traveller's diarrhoea (TD)

The medical world disagrees about the causes of TD. Some say that it is due to a contaminant, probably in water and possibly in food, while others say that travel itself and a change of diet are the causes. Certainly the latter seems to be supported by the fact that visitors to the UK or US from the Third World often fall ill when they arrive, despite the disparities in the levels of hygiene. However, one thing is agreed – if you travel you are certain to get it sooner or later; it is just a matter of time. TD is unpleasant, with symptoms that vary in severity from person to person. Generally symptoms will settle within 48 hours and should not require treatment beyond replacing lost fluids and salts and sugar as outlined below. Any blood or slime in the stool or a fever should alert you to the fact that antibiotics are required. Likewise if the TD fails to settle with basic replacement therapy medical help should be sought.

With the exception of Bocas del Toro (see *Drinking the water*) Panama has good, clear water that is safe to drink from the tap. Travellers that still prefer to stick to the bottled varieties will find these stocked in most shops and restaurants. The widespread availability of good-quality drinking water significantly reduces, but does not eradicate, instances of TD in Panama. While there is no foolproof method of avoidance, common sense should prevail when it comes to eating and drinking. Opt for freshly cooked food served in a clean environment rather than street stalls surrounded by dogs and flies. Eat where the locals eat and order a traditional staple rather than a culinary oddity prepared with tourists in mind that may have been hanging around for a while.

Medical advice for the treatment of TD is largely that of rest and plenty of liquids. The most dangerous side effect is dehydration and care should be taken to replace lost body salts. Avoiding food for 24–48 hours can help speed recovery. Refraining from alcohol and caffeine for several days will also help prevent cramping.

HIV/AIDS

Panama is currently ranked 19th in the world on a per-capita basis for HIV/Aids (or SIDA as it is known in Spanish) with the fourth-highest rate of HIV infection in Latin America. Latest figures suggest that the state is currently caring for 8,000 AIDS orphans with just 5,753 AIDS cases officially reported in Panama since September 1984 (4,277 of them resulting in death). However, the total of infected people in Panama is estimated at being closer to 40,000 (2000). Poor health care provisions gave Panama a slow start in tackling its AIDS problem and little would have been achieved without PROBIDSIDA (tel: 225 9119; email: Probidsida@hotmail.com; www.worldaidsday.org), the only AIDS campaign group in Panama. It organises a high-profile 'Walk for Life' through the capital on World Aids Day.

Snake-bite

Many Panamanians will readily admit to being more frightened of snakes than anything else. Much of the country's ancient mythology centres on tales of killer serpents, fuelling a paranoia that can be unnerving for visitors. The balanced view is that reported incidents of snake-bites remain relatively few and far between. Those visitors that are unlucky enough to be in the wrong place at the wrong time should also be aware that even venomous snakes do not always inject poison. Another little-known fact is that most snake-bite victims make a full recovery without treatment.

Panama has 130 species of snake but only 20 or so are venomous. The most widely feared by far is the fer de lance (*Bothrops asper*), which grows to a maximum of 2.5m. It has an irritable disposition, ready to strike with little provocation, and with a dangerous bite. The venom of this species is haemorrhagic, causing internal bleeding and tissue destruction. Visitors are extremely unlikely to encounter a venomous snake, let alone be bitten by one, but wearing boots and watching your step are sensible precautions, especially when walking in rainforest after dark. Those that are bitten should try to make a note of any of the snake's identifying characteristics. The snake is likely to be one of Panama's non-venomous varieties, so while it is wise to fear the worst, there is no immediate cause to panic. Do not apply a tourniquet or attempt to open the wound as both pose more danger to the victim than the bite itself. Stay calm, taking care to subject the bitten area to the minimum amount of trauma. Seek medical assistance at the nearest hospital. Most medical centres hold a stock of anti-venom.

Sharks and marine life

The waters of Panama are rich in marine life and even the most inexperienced divers will encounter barracudas, manta rays and nurse sharks. However, even seasoned scuba divers and snorkellers will admit that it is rare to see large species of shark with any frequency. Travellers that plan to spend plenty of time on the coast or in the rivers should wear footwear (an old pair of trainers will do) to protect the soles of their feet. Stingrays are common along several stretches of water and lie submerged under the sand, inflicting severe pain if stepped on. Fish spines can also been venomous so tread carefully, especially in shallow water.

Ticks (garrapatas)

These tiny arachnids are experts in getting inside clothing unnoticed, penetrating buttoned jackets and long sleeves to transmit a variety of unpleasant infections. Removing a tick quickly and in one piece will significantly reduce the chances of disease transmission, so it is important to check yourself after camping or walking in the forest. Ticks attach themselves by burying their jaws into the skin, so care should be taken to work your finger and thumb as close to the mouth as possible to help prevent the jaws from breaking off. Apply steady, even pressure to pull the tick slowly upward at right angles to the skin. This can be painful, but care should be taken not to twist, squeeze or puncture the tick, to avoid leaving the mouth parts in the skin. Once the tick has been removed, place it in a jar of alcohol (Panama's national liquor, Seco, is ideal) to kill it before disinfecting the wound. Seek medical attention if the wound becomes red or if you experience a rash or fever.

Sun and heat

The reported incidence of skin cancer continues to soar worldwide, as the number of pale-skinned travellers who expose themselves more and more to the sun escalates. Melanoma is responsible for nearly three-quarters of all skin cancer deaths and is increasing in frequency. Unlike other skin growths it is always malignant and caused by DNA cell changes. The most common cause of DNA damage is ultraviolet radiation from sunlight, and Caucasians are 20 times more likely to develop melanoma than those with darker skin. In simple terms the fairer the skin the more susceptible the individual, and people with a large number of moles or freckles are at increased risk. Covering up with loose, baggy clothes and applying plenty of sun-cream will help protect you. Wear a hat when possible and keep out of the harsh midday sun. Those that are determined to sunbathe should apply an adequate sun lotion with protective SPF and build up exposure time gently from a starting point of 15–20 minutes a day. If you overdo the sunshine and begin to feel the effects of heatstroke it is important to drink plenty of fluids. Rest in the shade and keep the body cool with wet towels.

Fungal infections

Moisture encourages fungal infections to thrive and these are more common in hot, tropical climates. Infections are generally concentrated around the groin area, between the toes and on the scalp and are more likely to occur where the body is warm and damp. Wearing loose-fitting clothes in natural fabrics that breathe and avoiding artificial fibres, especially in socks and underwear, will help.

Natural health

Using medicinal plants in the everyday treatment of illnesses is common practice in Panama. Medicinal herbs are widely available at public markets, many cultivated for centuries by Panama's indigenous groups. Rural communities seek treatment from a *curandero* (an ancient tribal healer) and each ethnic group has its own medicinal knowledge and beliefs. There are numerous curanderos in Panama, despite being officially prohibited by law. Because of its prevalence in Panamanian society there have been moves over the years to incorporate traditional medicine into modern primary health care. In the late 1990s the Center for Pharmacognostic Research of Panamanian Flora (CIFLORPAN) and the Panamanian Ministry of Health agreed that the use of medicinal plants would form a part of the training of future health professionals.

Practitioners of non-native holistic and complimentary medicine are scarce in Panama City. A sizeable Chinese population means that traditional Chinese medicine is readily available. Acupuncture and reflexology practitioners can be found in several Chinese-owned medicine shops, although these are unregulated.

A good source of information on tropical botanical medicine in Panama is the website www.ars-grin.gov/~ngrlsb/, a herbal database that stems from the collective activities of US physicians and botanists. The CRC Handbook of Alternative Cash Crops for the Tropics and The Amazonian Ethnobotanical Dictionary: The Green Pharmacy by James A. Duke PhD, are also worthwhile reads. Both are available free on request through USAID (US Aid for International Development).

CIFLORPAN University Mall, Panama City 10767; tel: 269 7655/269 ext. 489; fax: 269 7655/264; email: ciflorp1@ancon.up.ac.pa

USAID Information Center, Ronald Reagan Building, Washington, DC 20523-1000; tel: (202) 712 4810; fax: (202) 216 3524; www.usaid.gov

SAFETY

Tourist-orientated crimes are uncommon in Panama. However, they do happen and as with travelling anywhere in the world, common sense should apply. Certain areas of Panama City are hotbeds of criminal activity, especially in the districts of Chorillo and Calidonia. Thefts and muggings here are common and often involve unsuspecting visitors who have wandered into the area in error. Despite an ongoing restoration and clean-up programme, Panama City's old quarter, Casco Viejo (San Félipe), can be dangerous for lone travellers after dark. While isolated incidents of muggings at gunpoint grab the headlines, it is pickpockets and bag-snatchers that are the biggest threat to tourists. This tends to be opportunist and prompted by negligence. Leave a purse on a table in clear view, an unattended rucksack in a busy bar, or a video camera in the car and you're likely to come unstuck. Crime has increased in Bocas del Toro in recent years and lone female travellers should exercise caution in Bocas Town after dark. Attacks are rare, but do happen, generally alcohol-fuelled and in the unlit backstreets late at night. The arrival of rich Westerners in the archipelago hell-bent on buying up the land has also seen incidences of theft rise. Paraded wealth equals fair game to some islanders and care should be taken with valuables when camping or on the beach. Much is written about Panama's second city, Colón, and most of it is bad. Believe it; Colón is a dangerous place to walk, even in daylight. Tourists stick out like sore thumbs in this decaying community, providing an all-too tempting target to a criminal element that Panamanians from elsewhere are keen to avoid.

However, crime is not endemic in Panama and tales of good Samaritans are found in abundance. A man ran several hundred metres from a shabby cantina in Boquete to return a wallet left at the checkout. It contained at least US$500, small change to its absent-minded American owner, but more than a month's salary to the middle-aged *campesino*.

It is worth collating the following in an envelope and keeping it safe during your trip. This can help in the event that you are a victim of crime.

- A photocopy of your passport
- A photocopy of your travel insurance document
- Contact and claims information for your insurance provider
- A list of your travellers' cheque serial numbers
- A note of your airline ticket number
- Your credit card numbers
- Your bank account numbers
- A set of emergency numbers in Panama (eg: police, British Consulate)

Festivals and elections

Panamanians are passionate about politics, especially in the run-up to a presidential campaign. Canvassing is heightened by rallies, marches and banner waving, and as emotions run high incidents of crowd violence occur. While these outbursts are more a result of alcohol and frustration rather than a concerted organised effort to run riot, they can still prove dangerous. Tourists are advised to stay away from political meetings and marches during election time. The next presidential election in Panama is scheduled for May 2009. The online English-language newspaper, the *Panama News* (Apartado 55-0927, Estafeta Paitilla, Panama City; tel: 632 6343; email: editor@thePanamanews.com; www.thePanamanews.com) often carries details of forthcoming political events.

Women travellers

There is some disparity between how Panamanian society views its domestic female population and women from other countries. Women are well respected in Panama, holding several senior positions in government and leading many of the country's big businesses. Panama also boasts the proud distinction of being the first Latin American country to elect a female president (see *Chapter 1, Government and politics*). However, despite this liberated view, most Panamanians will admit they consider foreign women, especially those from America, differently to those from their own country; a view largely based on how they see women portrayed in imported Tinsel Town movies and cable TV. That many Panamanian men hold this view can be a nuisance to foreign female travellers, who tend to attract more unwanted attention than local women. Most Panamanian men back off pretty easily once faced with total uninterest, and as a lone female traveller the worst I've encountered is a pest. Wolf whistles and a wink or two are part of the culture in Panama. Getting upset about this is pointless; it's what the local women put up with so don't be surprised if you're treated to this Latino flirtation technique too. To minimise attention, dress conservatively (no Britney Spears-style crop tops or miniskirts), avoid eye contact and look like you mean business.

Drugs

Cocaine is pretty easy to come by in Panama City, despite a strict zero-tolerance law (tougher than in the US, Europe and Australia) and various anti-drug measures implemented by the government. The waters, once patrolled by American military and coastguards, are now woefully under-policed. As a result, shipments arrive frequently from Colombia, often via Kuna Yala, and there is a growing drug problem in Panama. Marijuana is also commonly found and there are an increasing number of heroin users in Panama City. Walk through certain streets in the capital, stroll down Main Street in Bocas del Toro or enter a bar in

MAKING THE BEST OF YOUR TRAVEL PHOTOGRAPHS
Nick Garbutt and John R Jones
Subject, composition and lighting

As a general rule, if it doesn't look good through the viewfinder, it will never look good as a picture. Don't take photographs for the sake of taking them; film is far too expensive. Be patient and wait until the image looks right.

People

There's nothing like a wonderful face to stimulate interest. Travelling to remote corners of the world provides the opportunity for exotic photographs of colourful minorities, intriguing lifestyles and special evocative shots which capture the very essence of a culture. A superb photograph should have an instant gut impact and be capable of saying more than a thousand words.

Photographing people is never easy and more often than not it requires a fair share of luck. Zooming in on that special moment which says it all requires sharp instinct, conditioned photographic eyes and the ability to handle light both aesthetically and technically.

- If you want to take a portrait shot, it is best to ask first. This is especially important in Kuna Yala where photography is controlled on a permission-only basis. All indigenous groups are likely to request a fee, which is paid directly to the individual (see *Customs and etiquette*). Snappers should note that all photography, however casual, is strictly policed by Kuna Indians and a very dim view is taken of failure to respect this sensitive law.
- Focus on the eyes of your subject
- The best portraits are obtained in the early morning and late evening light. In harsh light, photograph without flash in the shadows.
- Respect people's wishes and customs. Remember that, in some countries, candid snooping can lead to serious trouble.
- Never photograph military subjects unless you have definite permission.

Wildlife

There is no mystique to wildlife photography. The secret is getting into the right place at the right time and then knowing what to do. Look for striking poses, aspects of behaviour and distinctive features. Try not only to take pictures of the species itself, but also to illustrate it within the context of its environment. Alternatively, focus in close on a characteristic which can be emphasised.

- The eyes are the most important part of an animal – focus on these.
- Look at the surroundings – there is nothing worse than a distracting twig or highlighted leaf lurking in the background. Artificial light is no substitute for natural light, and should be used judiciously.
- At camera-to-subject distances of less than a metre, apertures between f16 and f32 are necessary to ensure adequate depth of field. This means using flash to provide enough light – use one or two small flashguns to illuminate the subject from the side.

Landscapes

Good landscape photography is all about good light and capturing mood. Generally the first and last two hours of daylight are best, or when peculiar climatic conditions add drama or emphasise distinctive features. Never place the horizon in the centre – in your mind's eye divide the frame into thirds and either exaggerate the land or the sky.

Equipment

Keep things simple. Cameras which are light, reliable and simple will reduce hassle. High humidity in many tropical places, in particular rainforests, can play havoc with electronics. For keen photographers, a single-lens reflex (SLR) camera should be at the heart of your outfit. Remember you are buying into a whole photographic system, so look for a model with the option of a range of different lenses and other accessories. Compact cameras are generally excellent, but because of restricted focal ranges they have severe limitations for wildlife.

Always choose the best lens you can afford – the type of lens will be dictated by the subject and the type of photograph you wish to take. For people, it should ideally have a focal length of 90 or 105mm; for candid photographs, a 70–210 zoom lens is ideal. If you are not intimidated by getting in close, buy one with a macro facility, which will allow close focusing.

For wildlife, a lens of at least 300mm is necessary to produce a reasonable image size of mammals and birds. For birds in particular, even longer lenses like 400mm or 500mm are sometimes needed. Optics of this size should always be held on a tripod, or a beanbag if shooting from a vehicle. Macro lenses of 55mm and 105mm cover most subjects and these create images up to half life size. To enlarge further, extension tubes are required. In low light, lenses with very fast apertures help (but unfortunately are very expensive).

For most landscapes and scenic photographs, try using a medium telephoto lens (100–300mm) to pick out the interesting aspects of the vista and compress the perspective. In tight situations, for example inside forests, wide-angle lenses (ie: 35mm or less) are ideal. These lenses are also an excellent alternative for close ups, as they offer the facility of being able to show the subject within the context of its environment.

Film

Film speed (ISO number) indicates the sensitivity of the film to light. The lower the number, the less sensitive the film, but the better quality the final image. For general print film, ISO 100 or 200 fit the bill perfectly; under weak light conditions use a faster film (ISO 200 or 400). If you are using transparencies just for lectures then again ISO 100 or 200 film is fine. However, if you want to get your work published, the superior quality of ISO 25 to 100 film is best. Try to keep your film cool – it should never be left in direct sunlight (film bought in developing countries is often outdated and badly stored). Fast film (ISO 800 and above) should not pass through X-ray machines.

Different types of film work best for different situations. For natural subjects, where greens are a feature, Fujicolour Reala (prints) and Fujichrome Velvia and Provia (transparencies) cannot be bettered. For people shots, try Kodachrome 64 for its warmth, mellowness and superb gentle gradation of contrast; reliable skin tones can also be recorded with Fuji Astia 100. If you want to jazz up your portraits, use Fuji Velvia (50 ISO) or Provia (100 ISO), although if cost is your priority, stick to process-paid Fuji films such as Sensia 11.

Nick Garbutt is a previous winner in the 'BBC Wildlife' Photographer of the Year competition. John R Jones is a travel photographer specialising in minority people.

Colón and you are certain to be offered something, unless you look like a narcotics agent, a nun or a missionary.

Defendants caught with even a small amount of illegal drugs face prison, often spending years locked up before the case is eventually brought to trial. Conviction is almost a foregone conclusion and many Panamanian lawyers refuse to accept a drugs case because the outcome is inevitable.

WHAT TO TAKE

The old travel adage 'pack half the clothes you think you need and at least twice the money' is pretty apt for Panama. It is rarely cold, so unless you plan to climb to the top of Volcán Barú (Panama's highest peak) keep clothing pretty light. Choose items that can cope with the climate. Sunshine can give way to a downpour at a moment's notice so denim is best avoided unless you want to walk around all day clad in a sponge. Travelling light may not seem an easy prospect in a country with such a range of terrain and activities. Yet even those visitors that plan to do everything – scuba diving, hiking, camping in the rainforest and island hopping by boat on the Caribbean – will quickly appreciate the benefits of a single rucksack in Panama. Strict weight restrictions apply on all domestic flights with excess charged after the standard 11.3kg limit. Buses and taxis (especially the shared variety found in Bocas de Toro) are also pretty tight on space. If, like me, you refuse to be parted from your backpack during transit, then you'll be glad you kept your luggage to a minimum. Attempting to board a crowded bus in Panama during rush hour with an oversized bag is impractical at best. It may also result in the driver insisting that it is stored out of sight in the boot. Oh, and don't forget to pack a Spanish phrase book.

Jungle equipment

If your trip to Panama involves time in the jungle, pack the following:

* Strong boots with drainage holes
* Lightweight hiking boots
* Two pairs of cotton–polypropylene/nylon socks
* Two pairs of wool-blend socks
* A pair of washable pumps/plimsolls/daps
* Waterproof air-inflated sleeping mattress
* Plenty of mosquito repellent (pump-spray and lotion, 50% DEET minimum)
* Waterproof poncho/ jacket
* Lightweight trousers (specialist quick-dry ventilated make, eg: Rohan)
* Lightweight shorts (specialist quick-dry ventilated make, eg: Rohan)
* Quick-dry blanket (specialist make, eg: Rohan), thick for highland/light for lowland

Luggage

Most visitors will find a single piece of easily transportable luggage and a daypack is perfectly adequate in Panama. The new style of combination luggage, twinning backpack carry features with an upright pull/push wheels/handle and a detachable daypack, is ideal. It is smart enough for city hotels that may have a backpacker prejudice yet backpack enough to be innocuous elsewhere.

Clothing

The coolest parts of Panama are found in the highlands of Chiriquí. The air, crisp and cool, can chill at times with sub-alpine scrubland on the upper slopes, shrouded in cloud cover and damp mists. These areas are rarely dry, just less wet, and visitors that plan to climb or camp on Volcán Barú will need a fleece jacket, waterproofs and warm clothing. At 3,475m (11,400ft) the peak is renowned for its cold temperatures and hypothermia is a real risk to climbers who tackle it unprepared. Silk micro-knit underwear, available in camp and outdoor supply shops, is invaluable; roll it up into a tiny ball to provide a good 'just in case' option should temperatures drop. Elsewhere in Panama most travellers will find that they can get by on a couple of pairs of shorts, two or three T-shirts, a hat, swimming gear and a long-sleeved shirt and trousers. A lightweight waterproof or plastic poncho is a good idea as are a pair of easily washable lightweight trousers. Rubber-soled shoes are great for hopping on and off boats. Also a pair of hiking boots for the tougher treks and a pair of trainers for walking.

Camping equipment

Pack a lightweight tent with plenty of ventilation and a separate rain fly; a length of strong nylon chord, invaluable as a clothesline; a nest of aluminium cooking pots, a lighter and a box of waterproof matches; a small multi-fuel stove; compass, a first-aid kit, torch, sunscreen, insect repellent, spare batteries; 3-in-1 camping utensils; bottled water, toilet paper, a small container of soap and a scouring pad. Pack a sleeping bag designed for tropical conditions, a sheet or sarong and a lightweight hammock.

Miscellaneous

Be sure to pack a decent first-aid kit that mirrors your environment (see *First-aid kit*) and includes your usual medication. Tampons are harder to find than press-on towels in Panama, so pack a decent supply if you prefer to use these. Bring a spare pair of contact lenses or glasses (and a spare prescription), a travel plug that has a US-style connector, and a healthy supply of plasters. A mask or snorkel is a good idea as rental options in some regions are few and far between. A torch is essential (much of Panama is unlit); also a spare stock of batteries; a candle and a box of good quality waterproof matches; spare camera film and memory cards; a handful of safety pins; a travel sewing kit and spare plastic carrier bag and cotton buds (great for all manner of things). A tiny MW/FM radio picks up hundreds of great local music channels.

FURTHER INFORMATION

Travellers in Panama will find good sources of visitor information thin on the ground. Websites tend to be sponsored by commercial concerns that have a vested interest and have been created with a list-ticking tourist in mind. Instituto Panameño de Turismo (IPAT), the government tourist bureau, offers little practical help but does have an English-language website: www.visitPanama.com. Its sole achievement in recent years seems to have been a range of glossy literature that tells visitors nothing. That each major town has an IPAT office is encouraging (this wasn't the case a couple of years ago), but these tend to be swish affairs that are devoid of leaflets and staffed mainly by people whose approach to tourism is bureaucratic rather than impassioned. Open 09.00–16.00 Monday to Friday and occasionally Saturday mornings.

Tour options are growing with new start-ups almost every month. The monthly tourist newspaper *The Visitor* and the quarterly *Panama Focus* booklet are both distributed throughout Panama and are free. Each contains the usual tourist offerings and list accommodation indiscriminately.

IPAT Centro de Convenciones ATLAPA, Vía Israel, Panama City; tel: 226 7000 (Panama) or call toll free tel: 1 800 231 0568 (US and Canada)

Panamanian consular offices
Australia
PO Box 31, Bardwell Park, Sydney, NSW 2207; tel: (02) 9567 2347; fax: (02) 9567 1539; email: panaconsul.Sydney@bigpond.com.au

Canada
1425 René Lévesque Bd West, Suite 504, Montréal, Quebec H3G 1T7; tel: (514) 874 1929; fax: (514) 874 1947

881 Saint Clair Av West, Toronto, Ontario M6C 1C4; tel: (416) 651 2350; fax: (416) 651 3141

112 West Pender St, Suite 407, Vancouver, British Colombia V6E 2S1; tel: (604) 682 6128; fax: (604) 682 0528

UK
Panama House, 40 Hertford St, London W1J 7SH; tel: 020 7409 2255; fax: 020 7495 0412; email: veronica@panaconsul.co.uk; www.panaconsul.com

USA
1212 Av of the Americas, 6th Floor, New York, NY 10036; tel: (212) 840 2450; fax: (212) 840 2469; www.nyconsul.com

2801 Ponce De Leon Bd, Coral Gables, FL 33134; tel: (305) 447 3700; fax (305) 371 2907; email: Cohenmanuel@aol.com

124 Chestnut St, Philadelphia, PA 19106; tel: (215) 574 2994; fax: (215) 625 4876; email: cgralpmaph@mesn.com

870 Market St, Flood Building Suite 551–553, San Francisco, CA 94102; tel: (415) 391 4268 or (415) 221 5699 or (415) 221 4773; fax: (415) 391 4269; email: oese@msn.com

208 Glenview Dr, San Francisco, California 94131; tel: (415) 648 3164

225 Str Tulip, Courtyard, Suite 5, San Juan 00926-5950, Puerto Rico; tel: (787) 789 2003; email: conpapr@microjuris.com

Century Ughting 1325 SO, Beretania St, Honolulu, Hawaii; tel: (808) 521 5043

24 Greenway, Plaza Suite 1307, Houston, TX 77046; tel: (713) 622 4451 or 4459; fax: (713) 622 4468, email: panama1@winstarmail.com; www.conpahouston.com

13302 Barryknoll Lane, Houston, TX 77079; tel.: (713) 461 4802; fax: (713) 461 7455

3137 West Ball R Suite 104, Anaheik, Los Angeles, CA 92804; tel; (714) 816 1809, email: panamadaly@aol.com

1324 World Trade Center # 2 Canal St, New Orleans, Louisiana 70130; tel: (504) 525 3459; fax: (504) 524 8960, email: consul@consulateofpanama.com; www.consulateofpanama.com

1101 Channelside Drive #279, Tampa, FL 33602; tel: (813) 831 6685; fax. (813) 254 3492

22 Fox Run-East Sandiwich, Massachusetts 02537; tel/fax: (508) 888 7311

ACCOMMODATION
Vast areas of Panama, including some medium-sized towns, have no accommodation for tourists at all. This is changing – and fast – but meanwhile options are often limited. Standards, and prices, also vary enormously from region to region with no discernable grading system. Many of my favourite places to stay in Panama are inexpensive hostels and this guide contains a good number of accommodation choices for travellers on a budget. However, as a lone female traveller I invariably choose where to stay on the basis of safety. I'll gladly put budgetary constraints on the backburner to avoid a red light district and for a night in a room with a lock. Hotels listed in the guide reflect this preference and many are mid-range options.

Pricier places have also been included on the basis that they offer travellers something much more than just an overnight stay. Somewhere exceptional; a place that inspires travellers like me to scrimp and save for a few days to justify the budgetary blowout. Don't be fooled by the price tag, these 'luxury' options rarely come with any top-notch frills. Most don't have hot water (something that isn't high on my list of priorities but I have lost count of the number of fellow travellers that consider this essential) and the nuisance of mosquitoes and sandflies still exists. There is, after all, no such thing as a better class of bug.

Finding a hotel in Panama during public holidays is notoriously difficult, with many rooms pre-booked two years in advance for Carnaval. Reserving a hotel can be ridiculously simple (if it has email, a phone and a fax) or painfully frustrating (no phone at all) but a growing number of mid-range options are accepting fax and phone booking with a credit card. Few budget options are easy to organise in advance. Some require pre-payment but not by credit card. A small independent Panamanian tour operator will often make the booking for you. The fee is nominal (5–10%) and it is usually favourable compared with a bank transfer charge. As a rule, Panamanian hotel owners are a cynical bunch, unconvinced by verbal bookings and only reassured by a deposit. Reservations are often deemed 'provisional' until payment is made. If rooms are in short supply then try to check in early. Generally speaking it isn't possible to reconfirm too much.

Many of Panama's inexpensive hotels have bathrooms with cold water only (fine for the lowlands but chilly in the highlands). Rooms provide what you'd expect from a place offering a 'bed for the night': functional accommodation (usually the floor is a plaster screed or tile) that includes a bed with sheets, a light, a ceiling fan and a place to hang clothes. Rooms can be small, dark and hot. Ask to see it first and if it looks OK switch on the fan to check that it works.

Although there is some evidence of a sea change in Panama, paying for a hotel with a credit card often incurs a surcharge. Many hoteliers accept only cash, and even then in low denomination notes due to a widespread paranoia concerning counterfeiting. Only large city hotels are prepared to accept notes higher than a US$20–US$50 – and even then it is at a push.

PUSH-BUTTON HOTELS

Most, but not all, of Panama's roadside accommodation with 'motel' in the name are what Panamanians call 'pushes' or 'push buttons', sex hotels with hourly rates. These are big business in Panama for very practical reasons. Most families live in large numbers under one roof and few have any privacy, even after marriage. With fewer than three million people, Panama also has many of the characteristics of a small town, and it is difficult to conduct an extra-marital affair or engage in a romantic liaison without news spreading from community to community via a network of relations and old friends. A push button allows for some secrecy.

The highest density of push buttons is along the Interamericana but they are found throughout the country, even in the smallest towns. It costs as little as US$15 for two hours in a modern, air-conditioned room, complete with a television and shower. Many have glitzy names like 'Vegas', 'Flamingo' or 'Shangri-La' and have garage doors as frontage not a lobby. Guests drive into one with open doors and push the 'puerta' button on the wall. This activates the door-closure mechanism, allows access to the room, and a set period of privacy ensues.

It goes without saying that no guidebook author can personally stay in every hotel it lists. I have, however, paid particular attention to the information, observations, comments and testimonials of travellers I have met. I have also endeavoured to take a peek at as many of the hotels listed as has been humanly possible. I estimate that I've stayed at or visited at least 75% of the hotels listed overall and prices quoted generally do not include taxes. Most hotels quote their room rates this way but some are offered inclusive, so it is worth double-checking.

Basic camping facilities are offered by most of the national parks (US$5) and on private land in most provinces (US$5–7). Pitch a tent on a waterfront dock for US$1 in Bocas del Toro. Camp on the beach in Kuna Yala or park a camper van in Santa Clara. Other options include a homestay in Colón; a private island in the Las Perlas archipelago; a cabaña in Coclé; an Indian village in Darién; and a houseboat on the Caribbean coast.

Needless to say, prices will change, hotels will close, chains will merge and new places will open. For a list of registered accommodation in Panama contact IPAT, the Panamanian Tourist Board (Centro de Convenciones ATLAPA, Vía Israel, Panama City; tel: 226 7000 or call toll-free from the US or Canada tel: 1 800 231 0568; www.visitPanama.com). It doesn't include every place in Panama, just those that are willing to pay a 10% government tax.

Note All prices listed in this guide are for double rooms unless specified. As a rule of thumb a single room is generally 75% of the price of a double, although this doesn't always apply. It is common for most Panamanian mid-range hotels to offer a number of special-rate packages. Often these include breakfast and/or dinner. These packages represent great value, but vary from week to week and month to month. They are therefore not listed in this book. Hotels in Panama adhere to no particular recognisable quality standard so each is best judged on its merits.

EATING AND DRINKING
Food

Panamanians love their food, enjoying it in a straightforward no-nonsense sort of way, rather than with overblown gusto. Standards are good countrywide, from the slick eateries in Panama City to the cantinas of the central provinces, although menus are generally simple, the food basic and the choices few. Fish, meat, chicken, rice and plantains are pretty much standard fare and eating on a budget is easy. Every Panamanian town, however small, has a decent handful of no-frills diners. Most offer a *'comida corriente'* – a lunch plate priced at between US$1.20 and US$3.00 – a shoestring traveller's delight. This tends to comprise a choice of beef (*bistec*), chicken (*pollo*) and fish (*pescado*), sometimes pork (*puerco*) and goat (*chivo*). Panamanian specialities include *sancocho,* a peppery chicken and vegetable soup that originates from the central provinces; *ceviche*, sea bass (*corvine*) or shellfish, chopped raw onion and hot chilli peppers (*aji chombra*) marinated in lemon juice; *empanadas,* deep-fried corn patties filled with minced meat. Dishes that are big on meat are often simply listed as *carne* (meat). Vegetarian dishes are thin on the ground outside of the capital, with Panama's large numbers of Chinese restaurants the best option for those keen to eat meat-free.

Just like its language, Panama's gastronomy reflects its ethnic diversity, mixing Latin American staples, such as rice and beans, with West Indian flavours and adding some European, Chinese and Indian touches just for good measure. Recipes vary from community to community and even standard dishes aren't standard in Panama. Some provinces add pizzazz and others take it out. Order a bowl of ceviche in Bocas del Toro and it will taste entirely different to that served in Boquete, simply because its people are different. Flavours are subtle and rarely spicy, as Panamanians prefer to add hot sauce (*salsa piquante*) to taste. In a restaurant this can be home-made in a bowl or in a bottle straight from the supermarket and varies dramatically in strength.

Panama's cuisine owes a further debt to its water, which is good enough to drink straight from the tap. Travellers are spared mealtime dilemmas and fears of contamination, as washed salads, fresh fruit and iced drinks offer relatively little threat. Another boon is Panama's bountiful natural store-cupboard, a landscape rich in fresh produce. Lobster, langoustines, snapper, octopus, shrimp and crab are found on the coastlines while in the highlands, lowlands and central provinces oranges, strawberries, coconuts, lemons, limes, bananas, papayas, pineapples, mangoes, coffee, onions, potatoes, carrots and broccoli grow. Also dairy herds, cattle ranches, pig and poultry farms, rice fields and sugarcane plantations.

Drink

Panama's gustatory pleasures extend to its beverages offering travellers the widest range of domestic brand beer in Central America, lots of tropical fruit juices (typically used for milk shakes), rum and seco, another sugarcane liquor and the national drink.

Four national beers, Soberana, Panama, Balboa and Atlas, are light in flavour and come ice-cold and served with wedges of lemon or lime if you ask. Expect to pay 50c in a local cantina, US$1.50 each in a swish hotel bar and US$1 as the norm. Supermarkets run regular four-for-a-dollar deals. Buy straight from the distributor in Bocas del Toro and get 24 bottles for just US$7.50 (plus a deposit of US$2.40 for the case).

Panama's national liquor 'seco' is the drink of the working man in the rural provinces more than that of the city. Clear, harsh and potent, it is often served *con leche* (with milk), an acquired taste. No visit to Panama is complete without a taster, just for the experience. Another rural tipple of the central provinces is a lethal palm wine (*vino de palma*) made from fermented sap. As there aren't any Panamanian wines Chilean imports are most commonly found but only in the popular tourist

---

SECO: THE NATION'S FAVOURITE

In 1908 a young Spaniard, Don José Varela Blanco, arrived in Panama. He settled in the Pese valley of Herrera, where he founded the country's first sugar mill. It was not until 30 years later that three of his sons proposed he make alcohol from the distilled sugarcane juice. The idea proved a success and after much perfecting, the new spirit was christened Seco Herrerano. This new business venture was named Hermanos Varela (Varela Brothers), a company which today is run by a third generation of Varelas (see *Herrera Province* chapter)

Seco, Panama's national drink, is still produced in the Pese valley, and is known throughout the country by the nickname '*seite letras*' due to the seven letters of Herrera. Seco is as the name suggests (*seco* is Spanish for dry) and has an almost neutral flavour that some consider harsh. Panamanians will insist that sampling this spirit is a must. It is traditionally mixed with milk, but if the thought of a *seco con leche* turns your stomach, seco and Coca Cola is a refreshing alternative to rum. With an alcohol volume of 35% and a price tag of less than US$5 a litre, seco is the cheapest liquor in the country and is renowned as the *boracho's* (drunk's) favourite for this reason.

areas. White and red are often both served chilled. Expect to pay US$2.50 as the norm for a glass of Chilean table wine (red or white) in most places, US$4 in the priciest tourist spots.

Panamanian coffee is good, rich and flavoursome with several local brands to choose from. Due to Panama's large population of Chinese, tea is also widely available. Fruit juices are served sugared, unless specified, with an option of *con agua* (with water) or *con leche* (with milk). Panama's excellent tap water is served as standard with meals in restaurants throughout the country, except in the Bocas del Toro Province where water quality is poor.

BUDGETING

Panama remains an affordable option for travellers in Central America, despite rising prices, and the cost of living is significantly lower than in both Belize and Costa Rica. The average annual wage in Panama is less than US$3,500 and day-to-day living is inexpensive. Food, drink and transportation are exceptional value. Panama's traditional lunch plate (*comida corriente*) costs less than US$3.00, a beer 75c–US$1, cross-town taxi ride US$2 and a seven-hour bus journey US$12.

Accommodation is generally affordable but varies enormously in price, a headache for travellers on a budget. Allowing US$40 per day should cover it to balance out the splurges with the US$6-a-night great deals. Arrive preparing to rough it for camping at US$1, dorm beds for US$10 and hammocks on the beach for free. For more comfort opt for a family-run pensión at US$20 or a mid-range hotel at US$40. Both often include breakfast and sometimes internet, especially in Panama City.

Visiting Bocas del Toro can put a strain on a shoestring budget, but is easily doable on limited funds with planning. Travellers that arrive from Costa Rica to escape its inflated resort price tags will find Bocas prices pleasing – just. Thinking of it as a displaced part of the Caribbean, rather than part of Central America, goes a long way in making the archipelago feel like more of a bargain. (True, it is more expensive than the central provinces but it's a far cry from the Bahamas.)

Of course, how much you spend in Panama depends on what you do, where you stay and the style in which you do it. For food and drink allow a cost-per-day of US$10–15, excessive in some regions but realistic in others. In Volcán (see *Chiriquí Province* chapter) a two-course lunch of *sancocho* soup, fried fish, rice, plantains and frijoles costs US$2 a head. In Bocas del Toro it would be closer to US$8 each, maybe US$5 in Herrera and Colón.

Other than food, drink and accommodation, allow a decent budget for transportation. Taxis and buses are great value but few journeys through Panama's squiggle-shaped landmass avoid flights and boats. Then there are guides, trips, excursions and activities such as rafting, birding or fishing. A 50-minute flight from Panama City to Bocas del Toro costs US$57.75, a bus from Panama City to David US$15, car hire US$40 and bicycle hire US$2.20 per hour. A knowledgeable guide, a worthwhile expense in Panama's dense jungle regions, charges from US$50–120 per day.

MONEY

In 1904 the United States dollar became the official legal currency in Panama, bringing a national economic stability that remains the envy of Latin America. The Panamanian monetary unit, the balboa, is par valued with the dollar and the two are completely interchangeable. Prices are expressed in either balboas (B/.) – for reasons of nationalistic pride – dollars (US$) or both. Panamanian coins are the same value, size and material as US coinage. Both are used, including the 1, 5, 10,

25 and 50 centesimos. One hundred centesimos are equal to US$1, or B/.1 if you prefer. Panama has no paper money of its own, only US dollars.

Travellers' cheques and credit cards
In theory US-dollar travellers' cheques and major credit cards are widely accepted in Panama, although the reality is they are unwelcome outside of Panama City. Few hotels, restaurants and shops accept anything other than cash in the provinces. Using a credit card often incurs a 2.5% charge and banks rarely cash US-dollar travellers' cheques without charging 1%. Withdrawing cash with a credit card remains a headache for amounts less than US$1,000. For a hassle-free trip the advice is to stick with cash.

Cash and credit cards
Despite its status as an international banking hub Panama remains by and large a cash society. Although there are some early signs of this changing, travellers should not rely on a credit card but on cash transactions, ensuring they have ready cash or access to money-changing facilities. Large dollar bills are troublesome in Panama due to a long-standing problem with counterfeiting. Most small businesses refuse to accept notes higher than US$20. Even large enterprises may ask for payment in notes below US$50, preferring bundles of US$10 to any other option. In the central regions, where a three-course meal can cost US$3.50 and a taxi is a dollar, it is essential to carry a healthy supply of US$1 and US$5 notes. Some 90% of travellers report problems with authorisation when attempting to use their credit cards in Panama. Forewarn the holding bank ahead of a visit, as it is notoriously difficult to resolve problems once there.

Banks and ATMs
Finding a bank and an ATM is not difficult in Panama. More than 150 international banks have branches throughout the country making cash withdrawal a breeze. ATMs represent banks from most major countries although the Banco Nacional de Panama has the greatest number. Most Panamanian banks charge a US$3 fee for each ATM transaction and daily withdrawal limits vary enormously from bank to bank. Banco Nacional de Panama allows transactions of US$500 per day from 75% of its branches, although the remainder permit just US$200 for no obvious reason. Banking hours in Panama vary but the majority are open Monday to Friday from 08.00 to 15.00. Some offer a limited service on a Saturday, generally until lunchtime.

Tipping and haggling
Although tipping is not customary in Panama, gratuities have become more prevalent in tourist areas as the number of international visitors swells. Tipping was unheard of in Bocas del Toro and Boquete until just a few years ago but is now standard practice. However, while a 10% gratuity is customary in some of Panama City's pricier restaurants, it is not necessary elsewhere. Taxi drivers do not expect to be tipped, but most passengers round up the fare. Hotel porters are the exception and are reliant on tips. In Panama US$1 or US$2 is sufficient, depending on the number of bags.

Taxes
A hotel tax of 10% is automatically added to your room rate. It is occasionally shown as all-inclusive so this is worth double-checking if you are on a budget. Hotel prices in this book are listed without tax. A goods tax of 5% is added to

products and services, except food and medicines. When you exit Panama an International Departure Duty is levied at US$20, payable in the airport.

SHOPPING

Panama is proud of its traditional handicrafts sold at regional markets, Indian villages, artisan centres, fiestas and department stores. Stalls of baskets, *molas* and jewellery often line the roadside in rural areas, including the approach road to El Vale and the airport road in Bocas Town.

Molas

Panama's most famous handicraft is the Kuna mola, an elaborate appliqué dress panel produced by the womenfolk of Kuna Yala. Brightly coloured inlaid fabrics form intricate designs depicting Kuna belief systems, dreams and culture. Traditional mola designs often centre on turtles, fish and birds or are geometric in style. Molas are widely available throughout Panama, not just in Kuna Yala. Prices start at US$10 but expect to pay US$20–25 for the best-quality designs.

Cigars

Panama's only remaining cigar factory is the privately owned Joyas De Panama in the Coclé Province. Tours aren't just for cigar aficionados and allow visitors to witness every stage of the cigar-making process, which is entirely non-automated. Everything is done by hand, from the grading of the tobacco leaves to hand rolling and packing the final product. Just three people are employed at Joyas De Panama producing thousands of cigars each week from local tobacco plants grown from Cuban seed. **Panoramic Panama** (tel/fax: 314 1417; email: enquiry@panoramicPanama.com; www.panoramicPanama.com), a small independent tour operator based in Panama City, organises tours there. Due to demand it has also launched a mail order service for export cigar orders.

Hats

The interior towns of Ocú and Penonomé are famous for their superior Panama hats. Handmade, using local materials in time-honoured fashion, hats are crafted to the highest standards, and so tightly woven they are 100% watertight. Buy them from stalls in Penonomé or find them in Gran Morrison department stores in Panama City. The luxurious Figali Center (dubbed the 'Harrods of Panama City') has a range of top-notch Panamanian hats with hefty prices to match.

Carvings and baskets

The Emberá Indians produce some beautiful woven baskets, most of which are exported to the US. However, it is possible for visitors to find them in handicraft markets or by visiting an Emberá settlement via a specially organised tour. This tribe is also deft at woodcarving, producing life-sized pieces of extraordinary quality using *cocobolo*, a rich tropical hardwood. They also painstakingly carve intricate pieces, most commonly iguanas, crocodiles or sea turtle, from the tiny *tagua* nut.

Polleras

This elaborate outfit of Spanish origin is handmade in Guararé and the villages and towns in the Las Tablas region. It consists of a highly embroidered skirt with an off-the-shoulder blouson top with two woollen pom-poms, and layers of lace edging and petticoats. A distinctive beaded combed headdress is worn with the outfit, along with an impressive array of jewellery. Almost every woman and man in and around Guararé is involved in making polleras, spending anything up to 18 months on each outfit, which sells for a price well in excess of US$1,000.

ARTS AND ENTERTAINMENT

The art scene in Panama is as diverse as its cultural make-up. Listen to the music, visit an exhibition of contemporary art or study the photography and you will undoubtedly find plenty of clues to the country's fusion of ethnic origins.

Photography

There are several photographers of note in Panama, including Stuart GR Warner W from America and David Short from England. However, it is two female Panama-born photographers, Sandra Eleta and Iraida Icaza, who have made the most significant impact on the international scene.

Sandra Eleta

Eleta is best renowned for her striking portraits of Panama's Afro-Panamanian population. Her book *Portobelo Fotografías de Panamá* has made her one of the most important photographers in the country and she has exhibited worldwide, based from her home in Portobelo.

Iraida Icaza

Born in Panama in 1952 Iraida Icaza is a seasoned exhibitor whose work has been shown at the Rhode Island School of Design; the Museum of Contemporary Art in Panama; Picture Photo Space in Osaka, Japan; Women in the Arts in Tegucigalpa, Honduras; the Art Museum of the Americas in Washington, DC; and the Recoleta Cultural Center in Buenos Aires, Argentina. Her first solo exhibition was at the Panamanian Institute of Art in 1978. Icaza represented Panama in the Havana Biennial in 1986 and now lives and works in New York.

David Short

British-born and UK-based photographer David Short (tel: 01462 450045 and 07974 728244; www.davidshortphotography.com) visited Panama for the first time in 1999. Struck by its photographic qualities, he set to work capturing the place and its peoples, creating one of the largest photography portfolios of Panama in the world. His limited-edition black-and-white and colour prints are becoming increasingly collectable in America. Short continues to contribute to travel guides, leisure magazines and newspapers in the UK and internationally, including the *Sunday Times*.

Stuart GR Warner W

Warner is renowned for his touching human portraits of the indigenous Indian tribes of Panama, such as the Wounaan weavers of the Darién. He has also photographed Panama's teak forests and diverse natural habitats using few professional add-ons, such as camera filters or artificial light.

Painting

Panama's largest art exhibition is held every two years at the Museo de Arte Contemperaneo (MAC) (www.macPanama.org) in Panama City, usually for a one-month period at the end of October or November. However, there is a sizeable permanent collection on display at the MAC as well as a number of visiting exhibitions. Visitors will find that the museum is much more than just a gallery. Regular art workshops, informal lectures by local and international artists and a wide variety of other cultural activities take place daily and there are many ongoing initiatives for artistic children and teenagers.

The Panamanian Art Institute (PANARTE), the focus of artistic activity in Panama since 1962, founded the Museo de Arte Contemperaneo in 1983. Today it remains the only private contemporary art museum in Panama; the permanent collection consists of works donated by the artists who have exhibited in the gallery since its founding. It comprises paintings by both Panamanian and foreign artists, as well as sculpture, photographs and graphic art displays. Famous contemporary painters in Panama include Antonio Alvarado, Julio Zachrisson, Tabo Toral and Teresa Icaza.

Music

Like many of its Latin American neighbours Panama's music is its lifeblood. Switch a radio on, enter a bar, jump in a taxi or take a stroll along even the most innocuous side street, and you are certain to be entertained by salsa, Latin American jazz, reggae, calypso and *musica tipica,* Panama's traditional music from the provinces.

Panamanian musicians Sammy and Sandra Sandoval and the Plumas Negras are worshipped in Panama as are merengue groups and singers Tito Rojas, Gilberto Santa Rosa, La Máquina and Los Ilegales. Few things stir up Panamanians like salsa, and Rubén Blades is considered a national hero. At the forefront of popularising salsa music since the 1950s, Blades established himself as a musical powerhouse during the '70s and early '80s, carving a career as a songwriter and composer of film soundtracks and making his debut as an actor in *The Last Fight* in 1982. However, it was not until he appeared in the semi-autobiographical docudrama *Crossover Dreams* in 1985, which he co-wrote and starred in, that Blades hit super-stardom. Today few people can equal his profile in Panama; he is as instantly recognisable as Michael Jackson and as adored as Doris Day. He even ran for president in 1994, polling a very respectable third place and gaining more than 20% of the vote. In September 2004 Blades achieved his ambition of a place in government and became Panama's Minister for Tourism at the request of his good friend Martin Torrijos, the country's newly elected president.

In Panama City music bars and live salsa music are in good supply in and around the old quarter, Casco Viejo. Check out the *Panama News*, *The Visitor* or the Sunday supplement of *La Prensa* for details of special events – or simply keep your ear to the ground. The strains of salsa music are sure to be heard from a doorway sooner or later when the dance clubs spring to life.

Throughout Panama music is an important part of Carnaval and festivals in the form of marching bands, processions and dancers. Bocas del Toro is famous for its party sounds, pumped loud through a sound system of epic proportions. Carnaval pulsates with sounds of the Caribbean, salsa and Panamanian folkloric music, as the islands enter 24-hour music mode. Local band, the Bastimentos Beach Boys, is legendary in the archipelago, entertaining crowds of partygoers with high-energy calypso music and fast-becoming a famous Bocas institution. For more information on Panama's *musica tipica* contact Panama Tipico (tel: 266 5234; email: marino@Panamatipico.com; www.Panamatipico.com). The dedicated online celebration of Panama's accordion-based folk music provides a chance to listen, learn and buy.

MEDIA AND COMMUNICATIONS
Telephone

The country code for Panama is 507. There are no city codes although at the time of writing, the first number of each existing seven-digit phone number provides a clue as to its region (Bocas del Toro 7, Chiriquí 7, Coclé 9, Colón 4, Herrera 9, Los Santos 9, Panama City 2, Veraguas 9). Mobile phone numbers are currently prefixed with the number 6. There are very few toll-free and no premium rate numbers in Panama. All domestic calls in Panama are regarded as local.

There are over 500,000 fixed telephone lines in Panama, one of the highest teledensity rates in Latin America. The Panamanian phone system is a reliable one thanks to the efforts of Cable & Wireless, which bought Panama's state-run phone company Intel in 1997. It promised to install a payphone in every single community in Panama that had more than 250 residents, a pledge it fulfilled by 2000. More than 10,000 telephones later and almost every city or town has a C&W building. Phone cards (*tarjetas*) can be purchased here for the distinctive blue and white public payphones and are required by at least 50% of payphones nationwide (US$5, US$10 and US$20). Payphones that accept cash take both US and Panamanian coinage. C&W's monopoly in Panama ended in 2003 when all fixed-line telecom services in Panama became open to competition. At the time of writing Cable and Wireless and BellSouth have exclusive concessionary rights to Panama's cellular phone service until 2007.

As competition increases in Panama call rates are steadily falling. At the time of writing, local calls to anywhere in the country can be made from a payphone at a cost of 15c for three minutes. International calls can be made from most C&W payphones as International Direct Dialling (IDD) is widely installed. Using one of the many special-rate tarjetas is often the least expensive way to call. Discounted rates currently apply between 22.00 and 07.00 seven days a week.

Travellers can also visit a C&W or BellSouth office to have calls placed for them between 08.30 and 16.00. Many internet cafés offer this service too, but rates vary significantly from region to region. Operators can assist with international calls, but these are often very expensive.

Making calls from a hotel room carries a minimum charge for a three-minute duration and also incurs a connection fee before billing at a premium per minute rate. To make an international call from Panama use the prefix 0, then dial the country code + area code + local number. For example: to call the US dial 0 + 1 + area code + local number. To the UK dial 0 + 44 + area code + local number and to Hong Kong dial 0 + 852 + area code + local number.

Useful numbers

Police	104
Fire	103
Ambulance	103
Directory assistance	102
International operator	106

Mobile-phone hire

Hiring a pay-as-you-go mobile phone in Panama can make life easier for travellers. In 1997 there were fewer than 17,000 people with a mobile phone in Panama. Today the figure exceeds 450,000 and is expected to more than double by 2006. While the C&W and BellSouth service does not extend to many of Panama's remote areas, it is generally good elsewhere. Crediting a phone is simple using payment cards that are easily available nationwide in US$5, US$10 and US$20 denominations. Hire a Nokia phone from Panoramic Panama (tel/fax: 314 1417; email: enquiry@panoramicPanama.com; www.panoramicPanama.com) and it comes fully charged with a credit and a mains charger. Rates vary with long-term discounts available; collect from and return to a Panama City address.

Fax, email and the internet

There are internet cafés on practically every street corner in every town in Panama, many offering additional services such as fax, post, stationery supplies, printing and photocopying. A large number also offer phone services including international calls. Some IPAT (Panamanian Tourist Board) offices offer free (or discounted) internet use to visitors, although facilities and opening times vary from region to region. Many Cable & Wireless offices also offer internet access and in Panama City most major hotels provide unlimited use to guests on a free-of-charge basis. This practice is becoming increasingly common outside of the capital, mainly by a few larger chains.

Newspapers

Panama's press is heavily politicised and makes little effort to disguise the fact. The Spanish-language *La Prensa* is the most widely circulated and is published daily. Other major Spanish-language dailies include *El Panama America* and *Critica*, *La Estrella de Panama*, *El Siglo* and *Primera Plana*. English-language news is also available in Panama. *The Miami Herald International Edition* is sold countrywide and the *International Herald Tribune* is also available in larger supermarkets in Panama City.

The Panama News, once available in paper format, is now a purely online news resource. It pulls no punches, is factual and unbiased, and is compiled intelligently, but not without passion, by editor Erick Jackson. Tourist sheet, *The Visitor* is published in both English and Spanish specifically for foreign visitors. It is available free countrywide in hotels, airports and popular tourist hotspots, profiles various destinations and activities and lists forthcoming events.

News online

The following offer online news facilities. Some are better than others and a few of the Spanish-language sites offer English translations. Most have front-page news as standard and an archive facility:

La Prensa www.prensa.com
Critica www.critica.com.pa
El Panama America www.elPanamaamerica.terra.com.pa
El Siglo www.elsiglo.com
La Estrella de Panama www.estrelladePanama.com
Miami Herald International www.miami.com
Panama News www.thePanamanews.com

Radio and TV

There are literally hundreds of radio stations in Panama, most FM and almost all run commercially. Very few are talk radio and news channels although some of Panama's many music stations do broadcast regular news bulletins. Visitors that carry a portable radio in their backpack will hear a range of broadcasts, from the have-a-go bedroom broadcasts of local radio to the slick professionalism of large-city stations. Some of the most popular stations for salsa include 97.1 and 102.1. For Latin rock try 93.9, and 88.9 is a pretty good Latin jazz station. At 88.1 is a reggae stalwart and no trip to Panama is complete without a spot of traditional Panamanian music, on 94.5. It is also possible to pick up the BBC World Service and Voice of America.

Cable TV is found throughout Panama and is standard in many larger hotels and bars. On terrestrial TV there are a handful of commercial channels and a couple of public broadcast channels, largely dominated by sport, soaps, movies and situation comedy. American football (NFL), basketball (NBA) and baseball (MLB) games are aired on Panamanian TV. Fixtures from the Spanish and Latin American soccer leagues are also often shown, as are those from the British Premiership, to a lesser extent, in some of Panama City's sports bars.

Mail

There is a post office in every town in Panama, open 07.00–18.00 Monday–Friday and 07.00–15.00 Saturday, although this can vary. Some larger hotels in Panama City sell stamps but this is unheard of away from the capital. A postcard to the UK requires a 40c stamp, 25c to the US, and will take between five and ten days to arrive.

Travellers in Panama can use a poste restante mail address to receive mail at any post office. Mail is held for 30 days and the service is free. Letters should be addressed as follows:

YOUR NAME
Post Restante
Entega General
TOWN
PROVINCE
Republica de Panama.

Collecting mail requires a photo ID and it is not possible to collect mail addressed to other people (so ask your friends and family use the name on your passport not a family nickname).

EMBASSY AND CONSULATE OFFICES
Panamanian embassies and consulates worldwide

Austria Botschaftskanzlei, Elisabethstrasse 4/5/4/10, A-1010 Vienna; tel: (01) 587 23 47; fax: (01) 586 30 80

Belgium Louisalaan 390–392, 1050 Brussels; tel: (02) 649 07 29; fax: (02) 648 92 16; email: Panama@antrasite.be

Bolivia Calle Julio Patiño, 1526, Calacoto zona Sur (entre calle 21 y 22), 678 La Paz; tel: (02) 795 276; fax: (02) 797 280; email: empanbol@ceibo.entelnet.bo

Brazil SHIS, QI 11, Conjunto 11, Casa 18, Lago Sul 71-620-115; tel: (61) 248 7309; fax: (61) 248 2834; email: emPanama@nettur.com.br

Canada 130 Albert St, Suite 300, Ottawa K1P 5G4; tel: (613) 236 7177; fax: (613) 236 5775; email: Pancanem@travel-net.com

France 145 Av de Suffren, 75015 Paris; tel: (01) 45 66 42 44; fax: (01) 45 67 99 43; email: panaemba@worldnet.fr

Germany Lutzowstrasse 1D, 53173 Bonn; tel: (228) 36 1036/36 1037; fax: (228) 36 3558

Italy Viaje Regina Margherite No 239, 4, INT. II 00198 Rome; tel: (06) 4425 2173; fax: (06) 4425 2237

Spain Claudio Coello 86, 1- 28006, Madrid; tel: (91) 576 5001/576 7668; fax: (91) 576 7161; email: panaemba@teleline.es

UK Panama House, 40 Hertford St, London W1J 7SH; tel: 020 7409 2255; fax: 020 7493 4499; email: shipping@panaconsul.co.uk; www.panaconsul.com

USA 2862 McGill Terrace NW, Washington, DC 20008; tel: (202) 483 1407

CUSTOMS

Visitors may bring up to 200 cigarettes and three bottles of liquor into Panama tax-free. Attempting to depart with products made from endangered species, such as turtle shell or ocelot skin, will result in a hefty fine and almost certainly a prison sentence.

BUSINESS HOURS

Although business hours in Panama are supposed to be pretty standard countrywide, there are regional variances. However, government offices are generally open 08.00–16.00 or 16.30 and do not close for lunch. Banks are open 08.30–13.00 Monday–Thursday and 08.30–15.00 on Friday, with a limited Saturday service of 08.30–12.00 or 13.00 in some regions. Shops tend to open at 09.00 or 10.00 until 18.00 or 19.00 Monday to Saturday.

HIGHLIGHTS

Visitors will soon find that there is a *lot* to see and do in Panama, a country with a rare mix of outstanding natural beauty, modern infrastructure, good roads, clean water and year-round warm weather. It's a land rich in history and few tourists, with plenty of wide open spaces, wildlife, rivers and dense jungle for adventurous travellers to explore. More than a third of Panama is protected land and its national parks offer some of the greatest biodiversity on the planet. No visitor to Panama should leave without experiencing these vast pockets of countryside, many of which contain puma, jaguar, waterfalls, rainforest, rivers, wetlands and caves and hundreds of species of endemic and migratory birds.

Parque Internacional La Amistad (International Park La Amistad) Some 407,000ha established in 1988. UNESCO heritage site since 1990, shared by Panama and Costa Rica (see *Chiriquí Province* chapter).

Parque Nacional Volcán Barú (Volcán Barú National Park) Established in 1976 on Panama's Pacific slope. Some 14,322ha contain Panama's highest peak, the dormant Volcano Barú at 3,474m (see *Chiriquí Province* chapter).

Parque Nacional Cerro Hoya (Cerro Hoya National Park) 32,557ha of coastline, volcanic rocks and mountains, established in 1985 (see *Veraguas Province* chapter).

Parque Nacional Sarigua (Sarigua National Park) 8,000ha established in 1985 on the Pacific costal strip between the Río Santa Maria and Río Parita (see *Herrera Province* chapter).

Parque Nacional Omar Torrijos (El Copé) (Omar Torris National Park) Established in 1986 above the continental divide. Highest peak 1,314m above sea level (see *Coclé Province* chapter).

Parque Nacional Chagres (Chagres National Park) 129,000ha of forests, lakes and mangroves that produce almost half the water to work the Panama Canal and support 50% of the needs of Panama and Colón (see *Panama Province* chapter).

Parque Nacional Soberanía (Soberanía National Park) 19,341ha straddling Panama and Colón provinces, established in 1980, bordered to the west by the Panama Canal (see *Panama Province* chapter).

Parque Nacional Camino de Cruces (Camino de Cruces National Park) 4,590ha bordered by Soberanía National Park to the north and the Metropolitan National Park to the south, parallel to the Panama Canal. Established 1992 (see *Panama Province* chapter).

Parque Nacional Altos de Campaña (Altos de Campaña National Park) Panama's first national park (established in 1966) comprises 4,925ha containing 198 tree species and 342 plant species (see *Panama Province* chapter).

Parque Nacional Coiba (Coiba National Park) Designated a national park in 1991, a 270,125ha cluster of islands containing 216,543ha of marine habitat (see *Veraguas Province* chapter).

Parque Nacional Marino Golfo de Chiriquí (Chiriquí Gulf Marine Park) 14,740ha established in 1994 comprising marine habitat and islands in the Gulf of Chiriquí on the Pacific Coast (see *Chiriquí Province* chapter).

Parque Nacional Marino Isla Bastimentos (Bastimentos Marine Park) 11,596ha of this 13,226ha park is marine habitat, established in 1988 on Bastimentos Island (see *Bocas del Toro Province* chapter).

Parque Nacional Portobelo (Portobelo National Park) Established in 1976, UNESCO site since 1980, 35,929ha of coasts, lowlands and highlands (see *Colón Province* chapter).

Parque Nacional Darién The largest park in Panama at 579,000ha. UNESCO site (since 1981) and Biosphere Reserve (since 1982) containing large expanses of primary rainforest (see *Darién Province* chapter).

Humedal Lagunas de Volcán Accessible from David or Volcán, the lagoons of this 143ha wetland area are the highest marsh ecosystem in Panama (Chiriquí Province).

Refugio de Vida Silvestre Playa de La Barqueta Agrícola Home to many nesting birds and sea turtles, these 5,935ha of mangroves and beaches are a protected site (Chiriquí Province).

Humedal de San-San Pond Sak Home to four species of sea turtle, this 16,125ha stretch of wetland, swamps and beaches is accessed from Changuinola (Bocas del Toro Province).

Parque Nacional Marino Golfo de Chiriquí Five species of sea turtle nest here as does the scarlet macaw. Access is from Boca Chica (14,740ha, Chiriquí Province).

Reserva Forestal Fortuna The wet climate of this mountainous forest reserve makes it an ideal home for the 70 amphibians and reptiles and 1,136 plant species recorded here and plays an important role in the Fortuna hydro-electric plant. Access is an hour's drive from David (19,500ha, Chiriquí Province).

Parque Nacional Marina Isla Bastimentos Home to over 200 species of tropical fish, this park conserves marine and coastal ecosystems (coral reefs, mangrove swamps, white-sand beaches etc). Access is from Bocas del Taro town on Isla Colón (13,235ha split between Isla Bastimentos and Bocas del Toro Province).

Refugio de Vida Silvestre Playa Boca Vieja From May to September witness the mass of sea turtles arriving to lay their eggs on the beach (3,740ha, Chiriquí Province).

Area Natural Recreativa Salto de Las Palmas A natural recreation area with picturesque waterfall and swimming pool (reachable via a 100m walk up a fairly steep incline) (1ha, Veraguas Province).

Humedal El Golfo de Montijo Popular stop-off point for many species of water birds migrating south (89,452ha, Veraguas Province).

Reserva Forestal La Laguna de La Yeguada This forest reserve lacks most of its original native trees with thousands of government-planted pine trees taking their place (7,090ha, Veraguas Province).

Reserva Forestal El Montuoso Unfortunately this forest reserve has suffered much at the hands of illegal felling (10,375ha, Herrera Province).

Monumento Natural de Los Pozos de Calobre This natural monument provides viewing access to *Los Pozos* (hot thermal springs) (3.5ha, Veraguas Province).

Reserva Forestal La Tronosa This reserve protects the headwaters and hydrographic basin of the Río Tonosí (20,579ha, Los Santos Province).

Refugio de Vida Silvestre Cenegón del Mangle Coastal reserve and roosting site for an abundance of migratory birds pretty much year-round (776ha, Herrera Province).

Refugio de Vida Silvestre Isla de Cañas Important nesting site for sea turtles, with many thousands returning to its beaches each year (25,453ha, Los Santos Province).

Refugio de Vida Silvestre Peñón de la Honda The Peñón (rock) is the nesting ground for thousands of birds (notably a number of the egret family) and forms the main feature at this reserve, along with mangrove swamps, beaches and thermal waters (3,900ha, Los Santos Province).

Refugio de Vida Silvestre Isla Iguana Be warned, the refuge was previously used for target practice by the US Navy and unexploded bombs do still turn up occasionally! A popular nesting site for sea turtles and water birds (53ha, Los Santos Province).

Monumento Natural Isala Barro Colarado Home to tropical forest brimming with all manner of wildlife, this monument is run by the Smithsonian Tropical Research Institute and is open to visitors (5,346ha, Panama Province).

Area Recreativa Lago Gatún Home to tropical forest, with good fishing opportunities in the reservoir (348ha, Colón province).

Refugio de Vida Silvestre Islas Taboga y Urabá Nesting site of brown pelicans, amongst others. Access is from Panama City (258ha, Panama Province).

Parque Natural Metropolitano Home to more than 250 species of bird and 40 species of mammal, this 265ha park is on the doorstep of Panama City and offers fantastic views of the surrounding area (Panama Province).

Area Silvestre de Narganá This birders' paradise is administered by the Kuna people, with blackcrowned antpitta, speckled antshrike and red-throated caracara waiting to be spotted (98,999ha, Comarca de San Blas).

Reserva Forestal Canglón Another victim of felling, this reserve still boasts lowland tropical forests that are worthy of a visit (31,650ha, Darién Province).

Corredor Biológico de la Serranía de Bagre This 'biological corridor' enables thousands of migratory species easy access between Parque Nacional Darién and Reserva Natural Punta Patiño in search of food (31,275ha, Darién Province).

Reserva Hidologica Serrania Filo del Tallo This forest reserve has remained virtually untouched, despite widespread felling in northern Darién Province (24,722ha, Darién Province).

SPORTS
Events
Panama Marathon www.marathonPanama.com. Held every August on the Amador Causeway, Panama City.

Annual Cayaco Race www.cayucorace.org. Held each May in Gamboa, Panama City.

Clubs, associations, federations
Panamanian Skydiving Club www.Panamafreefall.com

Panamanian Baseball Federation (Federación Panameña de Béisbol) Tel: 225 3381, 225 6544; fax: 264 9280, 225 6544; www.internationalbaseball.org/Panama.htm

Panama Football (Futbol de Panama) http://come.to/futboldePanama

Panama Mountain Biking (Clube de Ciclismo de Montana) www.boaPanama.com

Panama Basketball Federation (Federación Panameña de Baloncesto) Tel: 225 9177; fax: 225 9179; www.fepaba.com

Panama Boxing www.lomejordelboxeo.com

Panamanian Surfing Association (Associación Panameña de Surf) Tel: 229 3720; fax: 260 0744; email: apsradical@hotmail.com

Surfing in Panama
Due to its location, squeezed between the Pacific and Caribbean oceans, Panama offers some of the best waves in Central America. Professionals and wave hunters from all corners of the globe converge in Panama to sample the surf.

Santa Catalina is classed as one of the best areas for waves in Central America. Located on the Pacific coast of Veraguas, the attraction is a year-round swell that can reach 25ft. There are numerous surfing locations offshore, including Punta Brava, Punta Roca, Cebaco and Coiba islands. Booties are recommended here due to razor-edge volcanic reef. Another popular spot is **Venao**, in Los Santos, as international competitions take place here. Further west along the coast is **Cambutal**, a great spot for left and right breaks. Cambutal usually guarantees deserted shores, perfect for those who like to surf uninterrupted. However, it is

Previous page Al Natural eco resort, Isla Bastimentos (DS)

Above and right Many of the buildings of Panama City's Old Quarter, Casco Viejo (San Felipe), have been restored to their former glory (DS)

Above Just 97 out of 1,000 Panamanians own a car (DS)

somewhat off the beaten track and you may need 4WD transport. The nearest town is Tonosi, 22km inland. There may be surf camps in the area, so ask other surfers before you go.

Waves in Panama City can get up to around 7ft hollows; try **playas Las Bovedas, Panama Vieja** and **Mojon**. But just an hour east of the city, **playas Teta** and **Río Del Mar** are far more attractive to visiting surfers. The islands of **Morro Negrito**, off the Chiriquí coast, are great for advanced surfers: right and left breaks on either side of the island. Boat transport is necessary.

The **Bocas del Toro archipelago** has a number of surfing spots of varying-size waves and both reef and beach break, making it perfect for both beginners and advanced surfers. Additionally, the recent Bocas tourist boom has brought new surfing facilities to the area – mainly due to surfers who can't bring themselves to leave. So it's a good place to restock wax supplies and meet other like-minded people. However, this also means in high surf season (November to April) you will have to share waves.

Waves average 4–7ft and surround three main islands. **Isla Colón** has several spots along the ocean side: **Paunch**, **Dumper** and **La Curva** are all reef breaks, the latter two are heavy left- and right-handers, with fast barrels. Further up the island at **Bluff Beach** you will find fast round peaks that can rise to colossal barrels in high season. Undercurrents at Bluff can be incredibly strong and there is a deep shelf that can cause riptides, so it is not ideal for beginners. **Isla Carenero** hosts left-hand peaks and endless tubes over vicious coral reefs and the beach break on **Isla Bastimentos** hosts long right-handers. Bastimentos is also home to **Silverback**, a well-renowned wave in surf circles – I have seen surfers shake in anticipation! You will need at least a 7ft board for this; there are usually boards to rent around the town if yours doesn't size up.

Roughly 55km east of Colón on the Atlantic is the small island of **Isla Grande** (which translates as Big Island). The waters here are stunning, crystal clear and turquoise between the reef; it is where Panama really becomes Caribbean. This tiny island hosts one of the most unfailing waves in the country, 7ft face.

Due to Panama's location there are numerous chances to find waves that aren't on the map. Listen to any surfer who lives in Panama and you will hear them boasting of hidden spots, or certain crests off remote islands they've discovered. The best way to get the most from Panama's surf is to hook up with professionals in the area who offer tours, for the simple reasons that they have transport and, being surfers, they will be as enthusiastic as you are to find the swells.

Travelling around Panama with a board is much like anywhere else. Flying in and out of Panama will most likely incur a charge on the transit of your board, which will vary between airlines. Costs in internal flights should depend on the weight of your total luggage combined, rather than a set price for a board. This depends on the length of your flight, but can be 25–60c per extra pound. Buses may not charge you, unless the trip is crowded and they have a lot of other luggage to fit in. On large buses, your board will be loaded in the understow with everyone else's luggage; on smaller buses, it will be strung to the roof.

FESTIVALS

For Christmas and Easter public holidays visit www.visitPanama.com.

January 6	Wise Men Day (Dia De Reyes)
January 9	Martyrs' Day (Día De Los Mártires)
February	Carnaval (Tuesday before Ash Wednesday)
November 2	All Saints' Day

November 3	Independence Day (from Colombia)
November 4	Flag Day (Día De La Bandera)
November 10	First Cry of Independence from Villa De Los Santos
November 28	Independence Day (from Spain)

Regional celebrations
Dates many vary; check www.visitPanama.com.

January 8–18	Feria de las Flores y el Café, Boquete, Chiriquí
January 14–18	Feria Agropecuaria de Tanara, Chepo, Panama
January 15–20	Feria de San Sebastián de Ocú, Ocú, Herrera
January 21–February 1	Feria de La Chorrera, La Chorrera, Panama
January 27–February 3	Feria de la Candelaria, Bugaba, Chiriquí
January 29–February 1	Feria de la Naranja, Churuquita, Coclé
January 29–February 1	Feria de Santa Fé, Veraguas
February 11–16	Feria de Veraguas en Soná, Soná, Veraguas
December 17–19	Feria de Penonomé, Coclé
March 4–7	Feria de Santa Fé, Darién
March 11–21	Feria de Internacional de San José, David, Chiriquí
March 19–21	Feria de La Chitra en Calobre, Veraguas
April 7–11	Feria de la Orquídea Boquete, Chiriquí
March 25–April 4	Feria Nacional de Colón, Colón
April 15–25	Feria Internacional de Azuero, Los Santos
May 13–16	Feria de Capira en Villa del Rosario, Panama
September 15–19	Feria del Mar, Bocas del Toro
October 16–19	Feria de Río Tigre, Kuna Yala
December 10–14	Feria de Tierras Altas, Volcán, Chiriquí

GIVING SOMETHING BACK
There are lots of ways that travellers to Panama can help the country and its people, even during a short visit. Numerous volunteering possibilities exist and a large number of local charities and community projects are in serious need of resources.

Two notices on a pin-board in Bocas del Toro sum up just what's required in Panama. The first reads: 'Our community is very poor and lacking the minimum conditions to have an adequate way of life. If you are interested to help in the matters of water, electricity, health, sewage, education, trash or production, please email **Fundación Promar** at promarbocas@yahoo.com. We are an environmental organisation that can help you to find the right way to do it, through a number of different programs. Please help.'

The second plea relates to **turtle conservation** and reads: 'Bored in your city??? We urgently need your help. Come and join our project and spend a week or more on a secluded Caribbean beach, getting back to nature while doing your bit for the protection and conservation of sea turtles. INTERESTED??? For more information contact: bocas_del_toro@hotmail.com. Our Planet and our grandsons will thank us.'

Other projects in need of help include those run by the **Foundation for the Children of Darién** (www.darien.org.pa), a non-profit organisation founded in April 1990. For 15 years it has worked to raise the standards of health, shelter and education in Darién's poorest communities, and it welcomes volunteers (both medical and non-medical) on several of its schemes throughout the province.

The Institute for Tropical Ecology and Conservation's popular volunteer programmes in Panama (1023 SW 2nd Avenue, Gainesville, FL 32601; tel: (352) 367 9128; fax: (352) 367 0610; email: ConservationProgram@itec-edu.org;

www.itec-edu.org) are heavily oversubscribed and require an application 12-months in advance. Work includes local education and community projects working with children and adults. The children's program includes lectures and seminars that teach basic ecology and conservation ethics. Adult education is directed towards providing employment alternatives. These include the training of local nature, turtle, and dive guides, the promotion of sustainable land use and promotion of folk art. A dozen ITEC programmes generally accept an intake of three volunteers who are fluent in English and Spanish.

Year-round volunteer positions crop up at the **Smithsonian Tropical Research Institute**'s 18 sites in Panama in scientific, educational and administrative disciplines (tel: 212 8031; fax: 212 8148; email: bilgraya@tivoli.si.edu; www.stri.org). Projects require a minimum one-week commitment and can be applied for by contacting the Office of Education.

SOS Children's Villages has been working in Panama since the beginning of the 1980s, creating permanent homes for abandoned and orphaned children. It now has three projects in Panama City, David and Penonomé that require practical help in a wide variety of ways. Sponsorship, project support, donations or individual contributions of time and materials are all welcomed. Details of volunteer work can be obtained from **SOS – Kinderdorf International** (Billrothstrasse 22, A-1190 Vienna, Austria; tel: +43 (1) 368 6678; fax: +43(1) 369 8918; email: info@sos-childrensvillages.org).

Despite a much-needed shipment of donated equipment from an American expatriate in 2003, the **hospital** in **Bocas del Toro** (tel: 757 9201) remains in desperate need of basic items. Doctors have issued a plea for paper for heart monitoring machines, disposable gloves and masks. Also for dispensing equipment.

ConserVA (tel: 693 8213; email: mariobernalg@hotmail.com) in El Valle is appealing for sponsorship for a wide range of conservation programmes with local schoolchildren. It is also fundraising to finance the purchase of land for a privately owned reserve. Spanish-speakers are also sought to help run school sessions.

Turtle Volunteer Panama in Bocas de Toro (contact Christina Ordinez, tel: 757 9962; email: turtlevolPanama@yahoo.com) is seeking volunteers to help with night patrol, tagging and monitoring. Stamina and commitment is required as the job involves walking beaches throughout the night and accommodation is basic. Training in how to tag, count eggs and record characteristics is provided. One week is the minimum required from volunteers but you can stay for as long as you want and anyone can apply. Season runs from March to June. US$100 per week for food and accommodation, US$16 fee for entrance to the national park.

Weekend volunteers are welcome on conservation projects run by the **Organization for Development of Sustainable Ecotourism** (ODESEN) (tel: 658 5042), an organisation that provides practical support to the Naso Indian communities on the Bocas del Toro mainland. It often requires Spanish-speaking volunteers on educational and health projects.

Francisco Delgado (tel: 996 1725; email: Delgado.Francisco@hotmail.com) (see *Herrera Province* chapter), one of Panama's most respected ornthologists and a Professor at Santiago University, is appealing for help in conserving the red macaw. The birds are killed for their feathers, which are used to create a mask used by festival dancers. In a bid to reduce the need for hunting Delgado has set up a 'bank' of donated macaw feathers on a reuse basis against a deposit to bona fide dancers. Donated feathers can be sent to Susan Armitage in the UK at Tyr Ywen Farm, Mamhilad, Pontypool, Gwent NP4 8TT.

Chocolate made from the beans at the **Punta Gallinazo Organic Cacao Farm** on the coastal mainland of the Bocas del Toro archipelago is famous throughout Panama. The farm has fallen into disrepair but is being rebuilt by volunteers under a Sustainable Land Stewardship International (email: slsi@cwnet.com) programme. The objective is to get production under way to produce enough cocoa to pay for local workers to maintain it. The project will also plant local hardwoods throughout the forest so that harvesting is not detrimental to the sustainability of the soil. Another SLSI programme is under way at the **Isla Solarte Biological Reserve**, which has a year-round intake of volunteers on its sustainable land projects.

Golden frog

Part Two

The Guide

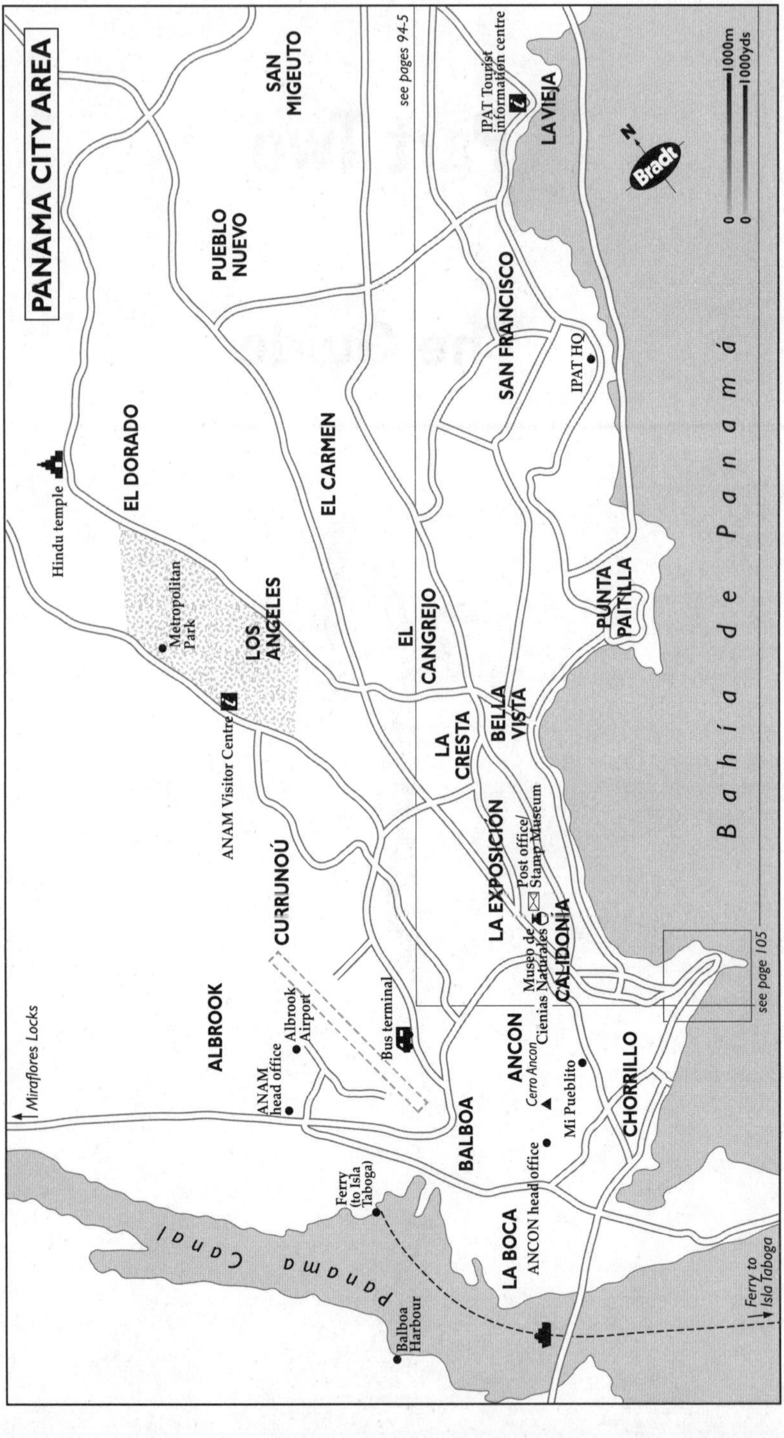
PANAMA CITY AREA
SAN MIGEUTO
PUEBLO NUEVO
see pages 94-5
IPAT Tourist information centre
LA VIEJA
N
Bradt
0 1000m
0 1000yds
SAN FRANCISCO
IPAT HQ
EL DORADO
Hindu temple
EL CARMEN
Metropolitan Park
LOS ANGELES
EL CANGREJO
PUNTA PAITILLA
LA CRESTA
BELLA VISTA
ANAM Visitor Centre
CURRUNOÚ
LA EXPOSICIÓN
Post office/ Stamp Museum
Museo de Cienias Naturales
CALIDONIA
see page 105
Bahía de Panamá
ALBROOK
Albrook Airport
Bus terminal
ANAM head office
ANCON
Cerro Ancon
Mi Pueblito
CHORRILLO
BALBOA
Miraflores Locks
Ferry (to Isla Taboga)
LA BOCA
ANCON head office
Panama Canal
Balboa Harbour
Ferry to Isla Taboga

Panama City

Boasting a striking oceanfront setting on a backdrop of sloping hills, Panama City is the only Central American capital city on the Pacific; a metropolis of contrary character and stark acute disparities. Often referred to as 'three cities in one,' an accurate description, the charming faded façades of the colonial old quarter share few similarities with the futuristic billion-dollar financial district whose skyline wouldn't look out of place in New York. Then there are the remnants of the original Panama City that today lie close to the shoreline in piles of crumbled rock. These forlorn ruins are all that remain of Old Panama (*La Vieja*), after Henry Morgan and his band of buccaneers left the 16th-century Spanish settlement devastated by fire.

A fine collection of restaurants and cafés could rival many cities in Europe, while yachts, harbours, promenades and bridges give Panama City a real Miami feel. Museums, monuments and colonial churches rub shoulders with neon-lit bars and bumper-to-bumper traffic. Prosperity and poverty are in constant collision here and glitzy boutiques sit at the edge of some of the worst slums in the city. Emaciated street kids breathe in exhaust fumes from Porsches and soft-top BMWs, while Indian stallholders sell dollar trinkets under offices of high finance.

Yet, one of Panama City's most remarkable qualities is its close proximity to the natural world. Sloth, monkey, toucan and agouti inhabit many urban districts where 500 birds have been spotted in just one day. Waterfalls, leafy trails, puma tracks and the harpy eagle are all close at hand here, while in the jungle to the north of the city Emberá Indians in loincloths still spear fish in crocodile-infested mangrove forests just 60 minutes from a Gucci store.

HISTORY

The strategic location of the original Spanish settlement known as Panama played a vital role in its prosperity and the city gained strength and influence to become a powerful force. It was founded in 1519 on the site of a small Indian fishing village by Spaniard Pedro Arias de Ávilla and quickly became a prime deposit for plundered gold from the Pacific Spanish colonies. Panama's riches were a source of envy and the city fast became a target of attack. In 1671 it was destroyed after a bloody assault by Welsh buccaneer Henry Morgan, who ransacked the city with an army of 1,200 men, leaving it in ruins and engulfed by fire. In 1674, three years after the attack, Panama was reborn, 7km along the shoreline in a spot known today as San Felipe (or Casco Viejo as it's more popularly known, meaning Old Compound). The new city occupied a vantage point on a small neck of land bounded by the sea on three sides and separated from the mainland by a moat. The founders of New Panama ensured it was fortified by watchtowers atop a vast stone wall with a protected gateway that restricted access.

A-Z OF PANAMA CITY DISTRICTS

24 de diciembre	Chorrillo	Pueblo Nuevo
Alcalde Diaz	Curundu	Río Abajo
Ancon	Juan Diaz	San Felipe (Casco Viejo)
Bella Vista	Mañanita	San Francisco
Bethaia	Pacora	San Martin
Calidonia	Parque Lefevre	Santa Ana
Chilibre	Pedregal	Tocumen

The city was built to survive attack but was never actually tested until the US invasion in 1989. As a result much of Casco Viejo remains much as it did more than 300 years ago and to stroll through parts of the old quarter is to journey back in time.

ORIENTATION

Maps of Panama badly serve visitors who will be lucky to find even a couple of accurate maps of Panama City let alone the country as a whole. Even those used by Panama's census bureau (generally considered to be some of the best but not available to the public) are littered with inaccuracies. Expect spelling mistakes and misplaced roads as standard, use each map as a guide only, employ a healthy amount of scepticism and ignore anything that doesn't look right.

Panama's capital city stretches along the Pacific coastline with Panama Bay to the south; the canal to the west; the ancient ruins of Old Panama (La Vieja) to the east; and acres of protected forested areas to the north. Cross-country buses and internal flights arrive and depart at the main transport terminal and domestic airport, Albrook, about 3km from the centre. International flights are served by Tocumen International Airport 30km northeast of the city. Two expressways bypass city traffic to allow more efficient travel to and from both airports and have eased city congestion considerably: Corredor Norte connects the Curundu district with the toll road to Colón. Corredor Sud links the Paitilla district with Tocumen International Airport.

Panama City itself is divided into 21 districts with **Bella Vista** at its geographic heart, home to gleaming finance houses, bank HQs and a number of embassy buildings. For many the spiritual heart is **Casco Viejo** (also known as San Felipe), a historic neighbourhood in the southwest of the city that has undergone some recent restoration with pleasing results. Colonial architecture and balconied, narrow cobbled streets offer a glimpse of the district's former glory. This is where Panama was reborn after Henry Morgan sacked the original settlement and today Casco Viejo is one of the most charming areas of the city. From here the Avenida Central cuts through **Santa Ana** and **Calidonia,** the main shopping areas for local Panamanians and home to a stretch of stores known as 'El Central'. The residential district of **La Exposition** is poor, grubby and soulless but from here the Avenida Central leads into Bella Vista and beyond. It becomes Vía España at **El Cangrejo** in the east of the city and forms a length of plazas, malls, department stores and supermarkets as one of the busiest streets in Panama City.

TOURIST INFORMATION

Panama's main tourist board (IPAT, Instituto Panameño de Turismo) office is located in the Centro Atlapa on Vía Israel (tel: 226 7000; fax: 226 4849). A dedicated tourist information line (tel: 226 3544; email: infotur@ns.ipat.gob.pa) promises to deal with enquiries promptly yet several visitors report better response when using the main number. Open 08.00 to 18.00 daily. Other IPAT offices can be found at La Vieja and inside Tocumen International Airport. Panama's state-run environment agency, ANAM (Autoridad Nacional del Ambiente) (Building 804, Albrook Panama; tel: 315 0855/315 0990; email: anam@anam.gob.pa; www.anam.gob.pa), can provide details of regional offices, national parks, wildlife reserves, conservation areas, camping and ranger station accommodation. It also has a limited number of maps and leaflets. Open 08.00 to 16.00 Monday to Friday.

EMBASSIES AND CONSULATES

Canada World Trade Centre, Galeria Comerical, Piso 1, Calle 53-E, Urbanización Marbella, Panama City; tel: 264 9731; fax: 263 8083; email: panam@dfait-maeci.gc.ca; www.dfait-maeci.gc.ca

France Plaza de Francia, Las Bovedas, San Felipe, AP 0816 07945, Zona 1, Panama City; tel: 228 7824/7835/8290; telex: 030 229 14100; fax: 228 7852/228 0387/617 4348; email: ambafran@pan.gbm.net; www.ambafrance-pa.org

Germany Edificio World Trade, Piso 20, Calle 53, Urbanización Marbella, Panama City; mailing address: Embajada de la República Federal de Alemania, Apdo, 0832-0536 World Trade Centre; tel: 263 7733/263 7991/264 1147/263 4677; fax: 223 6664; email: germPanama@cwp.net.pa; www.Panama.diplo.de

Greece Antiguo Edificio NCR, Av Manuel Espinosa Batista, Panama City; tel: 263 0932

Italy Av Balboa 25, Panama City; tel: 225 8948; fax: 227 4906

Israel Calle Manuel M Icaza 12, Panama City; tel: 264 8022

Japan Calle 50 y 60 E, Obarrio, Apartado Postal No 1411, Panama City 1; tel: 263 6155; fax: 263 6019

Netherlands Condominio Tower Plaza, Piso 1, Calles 50 y Beatriz M, Cabal, Panama City; mailing address: Apartado 815, Panama 9a; tel: 264 7257; fax: 264 7257; email: consuladonl@cwPanama.net

Spain Frente al Parque Porras, Calle 33 Y Av Perú, Panama City; tel: 227 5122; fax: 264 3458

Switzerland Calle Victoria Y Calle Primera, Entrada Barriada Miraflores, Vía Boyd Roosevelt, Apartado 499, PA-Panama 9a; tel: 269 4018

UK Tower Swiss Bank, Calle 53 (Apartado 889), Zona 1, Panama City; tel: 269 0866; fax: 223 1730; email: britemb@cwPanama.net

USA Building 520, Clayton, Panama City; mailing address from US: American Embassy, Unit 0945, APO AA 34002; mailing address from elsewhere: Embajada de los Estados Unidos, Apartado 0816-02561, Zona 5, Panama City; tel: 207 7000; email: usembisc@cwp.net.pa; www.Panama.usembassy.gov

Australia There is no Australian Embassy or Consulate in Panama. For consular assistance contact the bureau in Mexico: Australian Embassy, Ruben Dario 55, Col. Polanco, CP 11560, Mexico DF MEXICO; tel: (52 55) 1101 2200; fax: (52 55) 5203 8431; email: embaustmex@yahoo.com.mx. The British Embassy in Panama City may be able to provide assistance to Australian travellers in emergencies (see above). The Australian Department of Foreign Affairs and Trade offers an online registration service for travellers in Panama (www.orao.dfat.gov.au and complete the traveller information form). The detail provided is used to trace travellers in an emergency, whether it be a natural disaster, civil disturbance or a family emergency. Australian travellers can check the website: www.dfat.gov.au/zw-cgi/view/Advice/General for travel advice.

GETTING THERE
By air
All international flights to Panama arrive in Panama City are there are frequent schedules from North, Central and South America and much of the Caribbean.

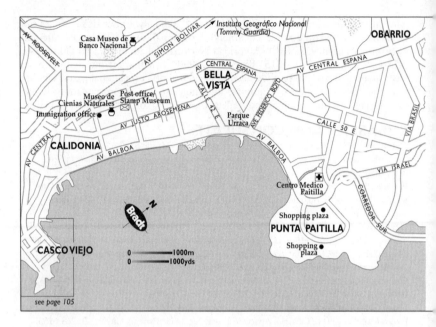

The main connection point for North America is Miami, but there are also flights out of Houston, New York, Washington DC, Dallas and Los Angeles. At the time of writing there are no direct flights from Europe (see *Chapter 2, Getting there*).

Panama's domestic market is in a constant state of flux as new airlines come and go six national carriers become three. Many old flights are still publicised, so for clarity, the former Aerotaxi scheduled service to Kuna Yala is now operated by Aeroperlas, while Ansa, who flew to the Darién and Chitré, closed in 2004. Aviatour has also ceased trading. That leaves **Aeroperlas** (tel: 315 7500; www.aeroperlas.com), **Mapiex Aero** (tel: 315 088; www.aero.com.pa) and **Turismo Aereo** (tel: 315 0279). Aeroperlas is Panama's largest domestic airline and flies from Panama City to David, Bocas del Toro, Kuna Yala, Darién, Contadora and Colón. Mapiex serves David and Bocas del Toro while Turismo Aereo opened in 2004 to launch a Panama City schedule to Kuna Yala, Darién, Contadora and Chitré.

By bus

Buses to and from San José link Panama City efficiently with Costa Rica. **Panaline** (tel: 262 1618; San José office tel: +506 258 0022) and **Tica Bus** (tel: 314 6385; San José office tel: +506 221 8954; www.ticabus.com) charge a similar amount (approximately US$20–25 each way) and depart daily. The journey takes about 14–15 hours in a comfortable 52-seater bus with air conditioning.

GETTING AROUND
Airport transfers

Buses and taxis both serve Tocumen International Airport 30km northeast of the centre of Panama. Buses leave twice hourly from the transport terminal (Terminal Nacional de Transporte) but opt for the route via Corredor Sur (one hour, 70c) to avoid a crowded two-hour journey with dozens of stops en route. A taxi to the airport from Viá España will cost about US$20. To transfer from

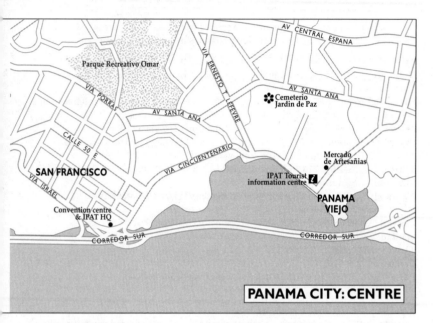

PANAMA CITY: CENTRE

the airport either pick up a taxi from the Transportes Turístico desk (around US$20) or ask for a *collectivo* (a minivan) if travelling in a group of up to eight at US$8–10 per person. Albrook Airport (less commonly known as Marcos A Gelabert) is Panama City's domestic flight facility and is located on the southern outskirts. It's easily accessible from the centre of the city by taxi (US$5 or less) and is also served by a regular bus schedule from the transport terminal.

By taxi
Taxis are everywhere in Panama City and what's more they're cheap and safe. Cars aren't metered but they do abide by a legislated fare structure that is calculated by zones. Each taxi displays a list of charges but expect to pay US$2 for a short ride that crosses just a couple of zones and a maximum of US$5 to cross the city. Travellers on a budget should avoid the large unmarked taxis that serve many of the hotels in the city, many of which charge US$20+ for a journey that would normally cost US$4–5. In the event of a taxi famine (late at night or between noon and 14.00) call a radio taxi. There's a full list in the local telephone directory, but America (tel: 223 7694), El Parador (tel: 238 9111), Latino (tel: 226 7313) and Unico (tel: 221 4074) each offer a comparable service.

By bus
Panama's multi-coloured painted buses (Diablo Rojo) look great but are not the most efficient way to get around the city. If time isn't an issue and you don't mind standing in cramped conditions then these moving pieces of art are a great Panamanian experience – and cheap at 25c a ride.

Car rental
A number of major car rental companies as well as several small independents operate in Panama City. Opt for a 4WD vehicle if heading away from the city, commonly referred to as a *doble* but people will know what you mean when asked

for a *cuatro por cuatro*. Some car hire branches have desks at the airport as well as in the city centre. Many also have booking facilities in some of the city's major hotels.

Avis Tel: 278 9444 (city)/ 238 4037 and 4056 (Tocumen)/315 0434 (Albrook)
Dollar Tel: 270 0355 (city); email: dollar@motoresdelaguardia.com/tel: 238 4069 (Tocumen)/tel: 315 0201 (Albrook)
Hertz Tel: 264 1111 (City); email: HertzPanama@centralamerica.com/tel: toll free from US or Canada 1 888 535 8832/1 800 948 3770 or 238 4081 (Tocumen)
Alamo Tel: 236 5777; fax: 236 2698; www.alamo.com (Tocumen & City)
Budget Car Rental Tel: 263 8777 (City)/238 4056 (Tocumen)/ 315 0434 (Albrook); email: reservaciones@budgetPanama.com; www.budget.com
Thrifty Tel: 264 2613/214 7677 (City)/264 2613/238 4955 (Tocumen)/264 2613/315 0143 (Albrook); www.thrifty-pa.com
National Tel: 265 2222 (City)/238 4144 (Tocumen)/315 0416 (Albrook); email: reservaciones@nationalPanama.com
Central Tel: 223 5165 (city)/230 0447 (Tocumen); email: gcentral@sinfo.net
Shellane's tel: 265 3932
Tico's tel: 229 5257
Barriga tel: 238 4495
Payless tel: 222 1887; fax: 221 2691 (city); www.paylesscarrental.com

By bicycle

Cycling in the city and on the Interamericana is not without danger, but plenty of adventurous visitors choose to see Panama this way. Mountain bikes can be rented from Bicycle Moses (tel: 211 3671) on the Causeway (next to Pencas

DIABLOS ROJOS

Panama City's main form of local transport is provided by old US school buses as you have never seen them before. They are known locally as *diablos rojos* (red devils), a name they have earned by their fearsome reputation. Drivers are notorious in Panama for racing each other so do not be surprised if the bus you're in revs up next to a fellow driver. Reportedly bought from the States after being deemed un-roadworthy, a subsequent lack of finds in Panama can make these buses alarming. Rebuilt engines and modified exhausts create monsters that speed along spewing out black smoke, popping and banging, just short of deafening. Nevertheless, a great number are the prize possessions of those who own and drive them and are painted and adorned as such. Designs vary but expect coloured neon tubes framing spoilers, door and window frames, and elaborate murals relating to anything from the driver's girlfriend to Jesus Christ, and singing conductors. The interior of the bus is even better and can be decked out in feather boas, flashing fairy lights and even disco glitter-balls. Loud Panamanian reggae has been outlawed due to customers missing their stops, but is still played regardless on most city routes.

Diablo rojo drivers need to make a certain amount of money per day to pay bus owners, after which the 25c fares constitute their wages – hence the singing conductors to round up punters. In 2001 a fare increase from 15c caused student riots in the city. A current rumour that the price may rise again has been greeted with dismay by the locals. Plans to phase out these rolling showpieces of airbrushed folk-art in favour of conventional vehicles have also drawn criticism.

restaurant). Costs vary but start at US$2.10 per hour with special daily and weekly rates. Open 10.00 to 19.00 weekdays and 07.00 to 19.00 weekends. Also Tony's Bike Rental on the Causeway (next to the restaurant Mi Ranchito) and from Panama Adventure Bike (tel: 676 4023; fax: 360 2073; email: Panamaadventurebike@hotmail.com) which offers bike hire and runs cycle tours seven days a week around the city.

By motorbike and scooter
Scooters can be rented from Churro's Express next to Tony's Bike Rental and Mi Ranchito restaurant on the Causeway. Rates vary according to the model but expect to pay US$20 per hour with prices for full-day and weekly rental.

By helicopter
Excursions and chartered flights can be booked through Helix Craft Corporation (tel: 269 4028/315 0153; fax: 269 4032; email: helix@helixcraft.com; www.helixcraft.com). Seasonal prices are posted on the website but expect to pay around US$595 per hour for two. Helipan (tel: 315 0452; www.helipan.com) offers a number of set tour packages along the Canal, to Taboga Island and across Panama City as well as tailored options. It also flies countrywide to innumerable destinations (islands, beaches, rivers, mountains and remote locations) and offers an 'at short notice' service for travellers unable to pre-book. It's cheaper at US$210 per hour for two passengers, US$420 for three passengers and US$650 for four passengers.

By charter plane
As you'd imagine this option doesn't come cheap but is a fall back when flights are overbooked or for emergency dashes. Both Arrendamientos Aereos (tel: 315 0478) and Aero Ejecutivo (tel: 315 0439/0279) fly from Albrook. Helix Craft (tel: 315 0153) also fly chartered planes from here to all over Panama and fly one-way (1½ hours) to Chitré for US$551.25. Helipan (tel: 315 0452) have a Cessna 172 for three passengers that can fly anywhere in Panama at a rate of US$150 per hour.

By boat
Passenger ferries between Panama City and Isla Taboga depart from Pier 18 on Balboa Harbour. Yachts can be chartered from the Panama Yacht Club (tel: 314 0904/616 2408; email: Commodore@Panamayachtclub.com; www.Panamayachtclub.com) at Fort Amador Marina for trips to the islands or around Panama Bay.

By train
Panama's only stretch of railway links Panama City with Colón and cuts through spectacular countryside at a sedate speed along the length of the Canal. It passes Gamboa and Barro Colorado and even crosses small islands in the midst of the canal and is a scenic route that allows for wildlife spotting whilst soaking up the views. The line fell into disrepair during the 1980s but was magnificently restored in 2002. Today the Panama Canal Railway Co (tel: 317 6070; fax: 317 6061; email: info@panarail.com; www.panarail.com) has rescued the 145-year-old transcontinental railroad and a historic train transports visitors along the 76.5km track. It departs Monday to Friday at 07.15 from Corozal Passenger Station at the Old Canal commissary (a US$2.75 taxi ride from Panama City centre) and returns at 17.15. The journey takes just under one hour and costs US$20 one-way and US$35 return (see *Colón Province* chapter).

WHERE TO STAY

There are more than a hundred hotels in Panama City plus innumerable backstreet hostels. Unless your visit coincides with Carnaval it's unlikely that you'll encounter a shortage of accommodation in Panama City, especially at weekends. However, this is no reason for complacency. Booking is advisable, even if it's not always necessary, especially if you're choosy about where you stay. New hotels are springing up all over Panama City, which can only be good news for travellers there. Fierce competition between hoteliers means that visitors get more for their dollar in Panama City than in other parts of the country – so don't be surprised to find a mid-range hotel with mod cons is the same price as a leaky hut in El Valle. Options range from a monastic cubicle at US$6 a night to an opulent suite for a four-figure fee and the tourist board predicts that the number of beds on offer in Panama City will rise by 25% by 2008 with a positive impact on prices.

Note As a lone female traveller I am judicious when it comes to choosing accommodation, wherever I am in the world (*see Chapter 2, Accommodation*). On the basis of safety and not frills, I opt to avoid the dozens of budget hotels in the La Exposición district when I'm in Panama City. I also stay away from the red light district. As a consequence my listing doesn't contain details of many of the city's dirt-cheap options if location renders them dangerous. Most safe options are upper-budget and mid-range, offering good levels of personal security at the expense of rock-bottom price. For those unconcerned (or without other options) La Exposicíon has a string of pensiónes along Calle 30 and Calle 33 with rooms for less than US$10.

La Estancia Tel: 314 1417/651 6232; email: stay@bedandbreakfastPanama.com; www.bedandbreakfastPanama.com. This ranks as one of the finest proper B&Bs in Panama. Visitors who want to stay out of the hubbub of the city will find peace and tranquillity here in a leafy lane in the upper foothills of Cerro Ancon (5 minutes from Albrook Airport) with superb views of the Bridge of the Americas. Expect to see monkey, umpteen birds, sloth and agouti in the surrounding vegetation. Cool and airy, stylish rooms are well equipped (some with balconies) and there's a laundry room, grand piano, reading room and free internet use for guests. Tours, transfers and onward tickets can also be organised. US$45 for a double, US$75 for an apartment suite with kitchen, bathroom, lounge, cable TV and phone (2 people) plus US$15 for a third person.

Voyager International Hostel Corner of Vía España and Calle Ricardo Ariatel; tel: Abdiel 260 5913/223 3687/636 3443; email: hostelpm@cableonda.net; www.geocities.com/voyagerih. The most popular backpacker hangout in the city. There's a laundry, 30 minutes' free internet access and a communal kitchen. Breakfast is included. The owner, Abdiel, will collect guests from the airport for US$12. Its dorm beds are US$9 and singles with a private bathroom US$15.

Hostel La Casa de Carmen (8 rooms) Tel: 263 4366; email: lacasadecarmen@cableonda.net; www.lacasadecarmen.com. This is a great little find and boasts a central location just a few minutes walk from Exedra Books and bustling Vía España. It has 8 colour-themed single, double and triple bedrooms with or without private bathrooms as well as a small apartment for longer stays and a dorm with beds at backpacker rates, which includes a Continental breakfast. There's a communal area stuffed with books and magazines in a multitude of languages as well as a TV, a computer with internet access, a shared kitchen, a laundry room, safety deposit boxes, barbecue terrace and private parking. Panamanian lunch and dinner served on request. Rates are from US$20 per double. Visit their website for current pricing.

Hotel Montreal Vía España; tel: 263 4422; fax: 263 7951. For this location and rooms

WHERE TO STAY 99

at under US$30 you could do worse than the Hotel Montreal. Be warned through: rooms vary in quality and while some are a delight, others are truly gloomy, so ask to see a few. Cable TV, air conditioning, hot-water bathroom and minibar plus a rooftop pool and restaurant. US$22.00 single, US$27.50 double and US$33.00 triple.

Hotel Marparaíso (70 rooms) Calle 34 Este; tel/fax: 227 6767. Another competitive option is the 6-storey Hotel Marparaiso. With cable TV, air conditioning and a hot-water bathroom plus a restaurant and bar. US$25 single or double.

The Albrook Inn (30 rooms) Tel: 315 1789; fax: 315 1975; email: ventas@albrookinnPanama.com.pa; www.albrookinnPanama.com.pa. Five minutes from the domestic airport and transport terminal and 15 minutes from Amador, nestled in a sleepy location surrounded by greenery. The rooms are motel style and comfortably furnished with air conditioning, hot-water bathrooms, telephones and cable TV. An on-site spa offers reflexology, massage and yoga. Rooms from US$28 single, US$32 double and US$60 suite, including breakfast, with online booking available.

Hotel El Parador (80 rooms) Tel: 214 4586/3587; fax: 214 4589; email: hparador@cableonda.net. The hotel opened in January 2003 and is located in the financial district a 10-minute walk from Vía España. While it won't win any prizes for glamour, rooms are sensibly priced with good amenities that include air conditioning, cable TV, safe deposit boxes and a rooftop swimming pool. A restaurant serves traditional Panamanian meals with an international twist from dawn until dusk with room service available. Credit cards accepted. A good option at US$30 single, US$40–50 double and US$60 triple or family room, including breakfast.

Casco Viejo Properties Casco Viejo; tel: 262 6813; web www.cascoviejoproperties.com. A recent, much needed addition to Panama's old town, CVP rents newly renovated historic apartments by the night, week or longer. One-, two- and three-bedroom apartments are available, which all include maid service, kitchens, laundry, high speed internet, cable and air conditioning. Features including rooftop ocean views, and balconyies overlooking the lively Plaza Bolivar. CVP can also help with transportation, tours and further accommodation. Prices start at US$85 per night, breakfast is included and special rates are available for long-term stays.

Plaza Paitilla Inn (252 rooms) Punta Paitilla; tel: 269 1122/223 1470; email: ppinn@sinfo.net; www.plazapaitillainn.com. Close to the Multicentro shopping plaza, which is home to a multiplex cinema, boutiques, restaurants and supermarkets. The hotel has a circular pool, business centre, restaurant, coffee shop, 2 bars, hairdressers, safety deposit boxes and a nightclub as well as glorious views across the bay. It may look a little pricey but rates are US$45 single or double with even lower prices off-season.

Hotel Marbella Calle D, El Cangrejo; tel: 263 2220; fax: 263 3622: email: hmarbella@cableonda.net. Was one of Panama City's best-kept secrets but is now a firm favourite with backpackers, Canal buffs and budget conscious businessmen alike. With cable TV, phone, air conditioning and a decent restaurant and bar, it's sensibly priced at US$38 single and US$44 double.

Hotel California Calle 43 Este; tel: 263 7736; fax: 264 6144, email: info@hotel-california.ws. Clean and comfortable with private bathrooms, TV, telephone, restaurant and bar. US$20 single, US$33 double and US$38 triple.

Hotel Herrera (tel: 228 8994) and the **Hotel Colón** (tel: 228 8506/8510) are good bases from which to explore Casco Viejo. The former is badly in need of some TLC with rooms but is good value at US$10 for a fan-cooled single and US$13–15 for a double with air conditioning. The latter is on the outer edges of the old quarter but is easily the nicest. It was built to house Canal workers and was once called Hotel Corcó after its builder, Spanish immigrant José Corcó. Its 46 rooms are cool and airy but vary in quality so ask to see a couple. US$11 for a single with shared bathroom, US$13.20–15.40 for a double with private bathroom room.

Hotel Continental (360 rooms) Vía España; tel: 263 9999; fax: 269 4559; email: reserves@hotelsriande.com; www.hotelsriande.com. Promotes special deals online, such as a double room with breakfast for US$75. This makes it the cheapest 5-star hotel in Panama City with a pool, free internet, gym, restaurant, piano bar and casino. It's also a prime place to stay during Carnaval. Advertised rates are US$110 double and US$90 single but is often considerably cheaper if you turn up and it's not full.

WHERE TO EAT

There are far too many great places to eat in Panama City to be able to mention even half the restaurants worth trying. Eating out is easy with lots of choice and plenty of good-value options, be they Chinese, Italian, Peruvian, Lebanese or Panamanian staples. Concentrations of eateries can be found in Bella Vista and Amador (see *Amador Causeway*) but it is possible to find good restaurants citywide.

Few seafood restaurants in the city can beat the **Restaurant Mercado del Marisco** (tel: 262 8879) on Avenida Balboa for value and freshness. It's a casual place with few airs and graces set atop Panama's seafood market and serves up big plates of shrimp (US$5), octopus (US$7), mussels (US$7), lobster (from US$10), sea bass (US$6.50) and red snapper (US$6) from Monday to Saturday 06.00 to 22.00. Prices are even keener at the **El Rincón Tableño**, a no-frills open-air Panamanian diner where sopa de carne is US$1 and shredded beef and rice is US$2.50. The **El Trapiche**, next to the La Vieja ruins, has a few pricey items aimed at tourists but is famous with the locals for its tamales at US$3.95. Open 08.00–23.00, **Jimmy's** on Calle Manuel María Icaza (tel: 223 1523) is close to the financial centre and is popular with a mixed crowd who adore its friendly service, low prices and fantastic grilled octopus. It's open every day with tables inside and out.

The **Café de Asis** in Casco Viejo (tel: 262 9304) is one the Panama's hippest little meeting places and occupies a glorious old balconied building overlooking the Independence Plaza. It is famous for its potent secret-recipe sangria, fine rum, ceviche (US$5.50) and cool blood-red stucco décor. **Golosinas** on Calle Ricardo Arias (tel: 269 6237) is similarly stylish and comprises a fish restaurant and music club in a reclaimed site that is half underground. Lourdes de Ward who also owns the magnificent Casa de Lourdes in El Valle runs this place and offers a superb menu that isn't overpriced despite a clientele of foreign dignitaries.

Few restaurants in the world serve meat like **Martín Fierro** and this place in the El Cangrejo district near El Panama Hotel is a haven for anyone that loves top-notch steak (US$9–18), open noon–1.00 and 18.00–23.00 Monday to Saturday and 12.00–21.30 on Sunday. The **Trattoria de America** (tel: 223 7734) serves great Italian dishes in style on Calle 57. Menu prices are US$5.50–20 but are a fraction of the price if you order take-away from its sister kiosk on Calle 56.

TGI Friday's (tel: 211 4500) at the Country Inn and Suites on Amador Causeway serves just what you'd expect but offers spectacular views of the Panama Canal and the Bridge of the Americas and is a great place to enjoy a sunset margarita. **Pizzeria Sorrento** on Calle Ricardo Arias is a great find and serves excellent ten-inch pizza cooked in a wood-fired oven for US$3–5 from 11.30 to 23.00 Tuesday to Saturday.

The lowest-priced Mexican food in town is at **La Mexacanita** on Calle 53 and also on Avenida 4 Sur near to Calle Uruguay. The décor is basic but the menu is vast with nothing over US$6. A trio of tacos made to order is just US$3 and a plate of nachos US$2.75.

Cafeteria Manolo on the corner of Calle 49 B Oeste and Calle D is a popular haunt with tourists, shoppers and businessmen. It has inside and outdoors seating and a menu of almost 100 items, including 25 sandwiches and umpteen pasta, salad and seafood dishes that cost US$4–8. A man-sized breakfast is great value at US$3.50. Open 06.00 to 02.00.

There are plenty of Chinese food outlets in town but few cheaper than the **Restaurante Fu Yuan** (tel: 223 8002). Find it on Calle 55 just off Via España opposite the side door of the Hotel Panama. Big portions in classic Chinatown style at US$2–5; open daily 09.00–14.00.

Panama's only veggie diner is a backpacker's delight and found at the base of Calle Ricardo Arias, close to the Voyager International Hostel. **Restaurante Vegetariano Mireya** (tel: 269 1876) offers a simple, cafeteria-style selection of cheap veggie concoctions at US$1.25 per portion. Open Monday to Friday 06.00–20.00, Saturday 06.00–18.00.

Another bargain feed can be had at any of the **Niko's** restaurants in town. There were five at last count, including one Vía España and one at the city bus terminal. Each serves good Greek snack food at excellent prices, including *gyros* (grilled meat) for US$3 and steak for US$3.50; open 24 hours a day.

ENTERTAINMENT

Although *La Prensa*'s superb arts and entertainment supplement 'Talingo' has ceased publication, its replacement, '**Mosaico**', covers much of the subject matter as its predecessor. The website remains www.talingo.com and is a valuable resource for anyone keen to discover Panama's highbrow arts scene. For details of mainstream events and live concerts pick up a copy of *The Visitor*, a bimonthly English language tourist news-sheet that is freely available in hotels, airports, restaurants and shops throughout the city. There's also a great What's On section at www.thePanamanews.com.

There are dozens of cinemas, plenty of casinos and numerous nightclubs that spring to life at midnight. Many of the jazz and salsa bars clustered around the Casco Viejo district look pretty innocuous by day but are jam-packed and hot

CATWALK CONTROVERSY

Stunning Panamanian, Justine Pasek, was crowned Miss Universe by Donald Trump (who jointly owns the age-old show with NBC Television) in September 2002. Panama hosted the contest the following year on June 3 2003 at the newly built Figali Convention Centre on the Amador Causeway, a building that cost US$10 million to complete and stands on the site of an ex-US military base. Much to the delight of the locals, participating beauty queens were paraded around the country. Miss Dominican Republic, Amelia Vega, went on to win.

The Panamanian government paid US$9 million to host the awards but, being broadcast live to an estimated 600 million viewers in 150 countries, thought it good value for the publicity the country would receive. Many local Panamanians disagreed. As the ceremony began, thousands flocked to the Figali to demonstrate their displeasure, maintaining the money should have been spent on the nation's poor. Furthermore, a number of labour unions chose the same moment to protest the government's proposal to privatise the social security system. Justine is the first Panamanian Miss Universe, which prompted calls of support from neighbouring Latin American countries. She has used her status to contribute support to, among other charities, the Panamanian AIDS awareness organisation PROBIDSIDA.

and sweaty by 22.00. There's more thriving nightlife on the Amador Causeway with a cosmopolitan café scene, neon-lit sports bars and a couple of decent cocktail lounges. The lavish gold-turreted Figali Centre, built to host the Miss Universe contest in 2003, stages a year-round calendar of conventions, concerts, sports events and performances. Panama's first Miss Universe, Justine Pasek, thrust her homeland into the limelight in a show that was broadcast live to an estimated 600 million viewers in 150 countries, at a cost of US$9 million (see *Catwalk Controversy*). Similarly the Atlapa Convention Centre, Panama's premier venue, has the Red Hot Chilli Peppers, Christina Aguilera and Luciano Pavarotti to its name.

The city's most popular folkloric dance show is staged at Restaurante Tinajas (tel: 269 3840/263 7890) on Calle 51 in Bella Vista, which has a menu packed with Panamanian seafood specialities for US$7–9. The restaurant opened 20 years ago and shows are very popular. Book a table for Tuesday, Thursday, Friday or Saturday night and allow for a US$5 cover charge. *Mi Pueblito* also stage traditional dance shows, usually at 18.00 at the weekends, while there's live Cuban music at the Hotel Plaza Paitilla Inn on Vía Italia at Avenida Churchill for a US$10 entrance fee on a Tuesday and Saturday. Head to Pizza Pioloa for tango each Thursday at 21.00 and the Take Five Bar and La Bovedas for jazz. Author Nights at Exedra Books (tel: 264 4252; www.exedrabooks.com) on the corner of Vía Brasil and Vía España attract some high-profile guests and a mixed crowd of literati, students and backpackers while Café de Asis hosts regular 'open mike' nights for budding poets and musicians.

A full list of classical concerts, comedy productions and theatrical performances in Panama City can be found at www.talingo.com. Panama's only English-speaking theatre group, the Theatre Guild of Ancon, stages productions year-round (tel: 212 0060; email: guildofancon@hotmail.com). Oddball fringe theatre troupe Ovegra Negra (Black Sheep) can be seen at Alianza Francesa Panameña (tel: 223 5792) at certain points throughout the year, while the Teatro Nacional (tel: 262 3525) stages a wide range of performances from Cuban saxophonists to classical drama.

SHOPPING

More than 20 shopping malls in Panama City are being added to each year. There are also long stretches of shops along Gran Vía and Avenida Central. Department stores, jewellery shops and electrical superstores sell their goods at a fraction of the cost of those in Europe or the US, while a decent handful of local markets provide visitors plenty of Panamanian colour.

Regional **handicrafts** can be found in any one of the Gran Morrison department stores in the city and for those who haven't picked up a mola, basket, ceramic or woodcarving during their travels around Panama this is a decent fallback – albeit at a price that's 25% more. A better option is the Balboa Artisans market, where visitors get a chance to bargain hunt and haggle. It is housed in a historical building in the former American Canal Zone and has a variety of handicraft stalls and artisan knick-knacks. Getting there is easy by taxi (simply ask the driver to take you to *'la antigua YMCA en Balboa'*). A 10–15-minute drive from the centre will cost no more than US$2–3. Molas sell for US$15–30 at Flory Salzman Molas on Calle 49 N Oeste, at each Gran Morrison and on the Kuna stalls in and around Casco Viejo. Find them also at a number of small artisan markets dotted around the city including Mercado de Buhonesrías y Artesanías, behind the Reina Torres de Araúz Museum; at *Mi Pueblito* at the foot of Cerro Ancón; and at the Mercado Nacional de Artesanías adjacent to the La Vieja ruins.

For bargain Colombian sapphire or emerald **jewellery** (30% less than in the US and up to 50% less than the UK) head for Panama's most reputable jeweller, Joyeria La Huaca next to the Continental Hotel. Los Pueblos, a huge shopping complex just ten minutes from Tocumen International Airport, contains dozens of speciality stores with goods at budget prices. Rivalling Miami in appeal with Latin Americans with their eye on a bargain, Los Pueblos is an easy visit on a journey to or from the airport, but allow at least an hour for browsing. The Flamenco Shopping Plaza is another popular place to pick up all manner of souvenirs, handicrafts and cut-price designer goods. It's also home to Reprosa (tel: 271 0033; fax: 271 0672; email: info@reprosa.com), Panama's famous handicraft store, which stocks a unique range of jewellery inspired by Panamanian culture depicting flora and fauna themes.

To purchase works by many of Panama's most celebrated **artists** visit Galería Arteconsult on Avenida 2 Sur, Legacy Fine Art in the Centro Comercial Balboa on Avenida Balboa and Galería y Enmarcado Habitante on Calle Uruguay. More unique finds are awaiting discovery at Colecciones, a moderately priced arts and crafts shop with quality items made throughout Central and South America. A visit to Figali, the Harrods of Panama, is only worthwhile if you're dressed to impress and have a budget to match.

OTHER PRACTICALITIES

The **Immigration and Naturalisation** office (Migración y Naturalización) in Panama City is found on Avenida Cuba at Calle 29 Este in La; tel: 227 1448; fax: 227 1227.

There are several large **post offices** in Panama City and many large hotels offer basic postal services, such as stamps and mailing. The largest and best-equipped post office is on the ground floor of the Plaza Concordia, opposite a big Gran Morrison department store on Vía España. It's open 07.00–17.30 on weekdays and 07.00–16.30 on Saturday.

Panama City has experienced an **internet** boom in recent years and many hotels and backpacker haunts offer free guest use. A growing number of new Internet cafés open (and close) each month but at the time of writing the Transfernet Café in the Plaza Concordia on Vía España is popular with travellers at US$2 per hour. Find it opposite a large Gran Morrison department store, open 12 hours a day (10.00–22.00) Monday to Saturday, closing 21.00 on Sunday. Another place to pick up emails is the McInternet Café at the McDonald's on Vía España, which offers free use with certain meal options; open 06.30–23.00 seven days a week.

Public **telephones** are everywhere in Panama City and most have international dial. For less street noise visit the Cable and Wireless office (tel: 269 3933) on Vía España in Plaza Concordia, open 07.30 to 17.00 on weekdays and 07.30 to 14.30 on Saturday. Phone cards are on sale everywhere and are a good option, as pay phones often don't provide change. Find them in supermarkets, pharmacies and airports or buy them from street vendors throughout the city.

Several good places sell **guidebooks**, **maps** and **English-language publications** (including magazines) in Panama City. All of the Gran Morrison department stores carry a good selection of travel guides, novels and magazines, although some have a larger range than others. Librería Argosy (tel: 223 5344) on Vía Argentina close to the junction with Vía España has a great range of books in a variety of European languages, including English. Librería Cultural Panameña (tel: 223 6267) on Vía España has a good range of literary classics while few bookstores come close to Exedra Books (tel: 264 4252; www.exedrabooks.com) for choice, which holds a great stock of travel guidebooks for Panama, Central America and beyond. Located on the corner of Vía Brasil and Vía España.

Almost every hotel and backpacker hangout has a **laundry** facility or is within easy reach of a *lavamático*. Competition is fierce and as a result prices in Panama City are some of the lowest in the country. Even some of the swankiest hotels don't charge the earth for a handful of laundered items while lavamaticos citywide offer a same-day service at 75c per load. Add another 75c to dry it and a small fee for detergent (usually 20–30c).

Generally speaking **medical services** in Panama City are of a high standard. Many, such as Centro Medico Paitilla (Calle 53; tel: 263 8800), employ physicians that have been trained in the US and have perfect English. Each embassy and consulate office has a list of recommended specialists (see *Embassies and consulates*). In the event of a medical emergency call an ambulance on tel: 227 4142. One of Panama City's best **dentists** is Dr Charles A. Garcia (tel: 264 4380/3348; fax: 223 5834; mobile : 627 7471; email: garciadentist@hotmail.com), a graduate of St Louis University School of Dentistry in Missouri. He spent 31 years working for the US Government and adheres to all US standards of sterilisation, infection and quality control. He is also a dab-hand at dental insurance claim forms (a useful thing to know) and is located at Galerias Balboa (office 27) on the corner of Avenida Balboa and Aquilino de La Guardia streets.

More than 100 **banks** have branches throughout Panama and the city has more than 200 ATMs at ABN Amor, Banco Atlantico, Banco Continental, Banco del Istmo, Banco do Brasil, Banco Exterior, Banco General, Banco Internacional de Costa Rica, Banco Nacional de Panama, Banco Panameno de la Vivienda, BANCOLAT, BANEXPO, BankBoston, Banque Nationale de Paris, Bipan, Caja de Ahorros, Citibank, Credicorp Bank, HSBC, MetroBank, Multicredit, PanaBank, Pribanco and TowerBank. Business hours vary as do ATM withdrawal limits (see *Money*) but more and more ATMs are allowing credit card cash withdrawals. For ATM locations visit www.visa.com/pd/atm, a site that identifies 24-hour and branch cashpoints in all major Panamanian towns.

Changing foreign currency in Panama can be headache so shouldn't be relied upon. Change as much as possible before entering the country as few **currency exchange** bureaus (*casas de cambio*) exist in Panama, and those that do are based in Panama City. Panacambio on the ground floor of the Plaza Regency Building on Vía España is one of the most efficient; open 09.00–18.00 Monday–Saturday.

Emergency
The emergency telephone numbers in Panama City are:

Ambulance	227 4142
Fire	103
Police	104
Drugs (Medic)	226 0000

WHAT TO SEE AND DO
Casco Viejo (San Felipe)
Once a neighbourhood of doorway drunks worked by beggars in daylight and targeted by pickpockets after dark, today Casco Viejo is fast up-and-coming. A stroll under painted wooden balconies, along cobbled streets and past handsome colonial buildings provides a real glimpse into Panama's yesteryear, when this was the city's most affluent neighbourhood and the nation's capital. Much of the architecture that was once left to fade and wither is undergoing a transformation as Casco Viejo is painstakingly restored – with excellent results. Strong demand from many of

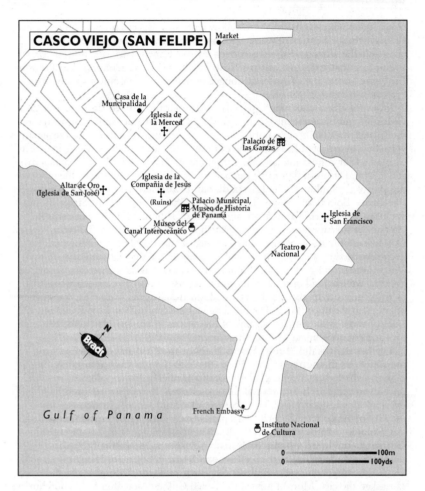

CASCO VIEJO (SAN FELIPE)

Market

Casa de la Muncipalidad

Iglesia de la Merced

Palacio de las Garzas

Iglesia de la Compañia de Jesús

Altar de Oro (Iglesia de San José)

(Ruins)

Palacio Municipal, Museo de Historia de Panamá

Museo del Canal Interoceánico

Iglesia de San Francisco

Teatro Nacional

N

Gulf of Panama

French Embassy

Instituto Nacional de Cultura

0 ━━━━━ 100m
0 ━━━━━ 100yds

Panama's elite is fast turning the district into one of the country's most fashionable pieces of real estate (see *Appendix 2*), and those offered a chance to see the interior of these beautiful buildings should grab it with both hands. Vaulted ceilings, stucco walls and tiled floors look out to delicate wrought-iron balconies through vast arched lead windows. Somehow it seems fitting that the architecture overlooking the Plaza de la Independencia is now proudly magnificent. Further government funding is earmarked for the remaining dingy ramshackle side streets, none of which should currently be walked alone after dark.

Walking Casco Viejo

Casco Viejo's beguiling rendered frontages and flower-filled ironwork encourage many visitors to sightsee the area on foot. Start from the southern tip of the peninsula at the **Paseo de las Bóvedas** (Promenade of the Vaults) and walk to the Parque Santa Ana to take in palaces, parks and museums and spectacular harbourside views. Paseo de las Bóvedas, a protective walkway built by the Spanish that runs along the top of the sea wall, is a natural starting point. The **Plaza de Francia** is dedicated to the 22,000 Canal workers from France, Martinique and

Guadaloupe who lost their lives to yellow fever and a special monument to Carlos J Finlay whose scientific research eradicated the disease. Stone inscriptions on the plaza tell the story of the construction of the Canal. They are overlooked by **Panama's Institute of Culture** (Instituto Nacional de Cultura), the **French Embassy** and a row of restored dungeons that are now home to an upmarket French bistro and art gallery.

From the plaza walk along Avenida A to reach the **Museo de Arte Religiso Colonial** and the remnants of the **Iglesia y Convento de Santo Domingo** on the corner of Calle 3. Turn north and you'll reach the **Ministerio de Gobierno y Justica** ahead of the **Teatro Nacional.** The latter, built in 1907, has been earmarked for restoration and has a magnificent interior of elaborate chandeliers and gold and crimson décor that can be viewed with permission from the office to the side of the building. The **Iglesia de San Francisco** is adjacent and overlooks the Parque Bolívar and is was here, in a schoolhouse, that activist Simon Bolívar attempted to form a Latin American union of nations in 1826. His struggle to liberate Latin America from the Spanish achieved success in Ecuador, Peru, Colombia, Bolivia, Venezuela and Panama. Today his heroic endeavours have been rewarded by an iconic status and he is honoured throughout Latin America. The nearby presidential palace, **Palacio de las Garzas**, is a fine white balconied building with a grand pillared entrance and recessed foyer. The name means Palace of the Herons after the birds that parade in the doorway below the president's quarters on the upper floor. The building was built in 1673 and renovated in 1922 and contains lavish murals, dozens of historic portraits, marble floors, Moorish tiles and columns inlaid with mother of pearl.

Further along is the **Muelle Fiscal** (harbour and port) and the market, while to the south lies the heart of Casco Viejo, the **Plaza de la Independencia**. It was here that the Panamanian declaration of independence from Colombia was made on November 3 1903 and several fine historic and beautifully restored buildings overlook this historic plaza. The **Museo del Canal Interoceánico** is housed in the HQ of the doomed French Canal project near to the faded **Hotel Central** and the **Palacio Municipal** (City Hall). The crumbling ruins of the **Iglesia y Convento del la Compañia de Jesús** can be seen to the south of the plaza, while the **Iglesia de San José** to the west is home to the famous **Golden Altar** (*Altar de Oro*), the only item successfully salvaged after Henry Morgan and his men ransacked the city. Morgan missed the fabled Golden Altar after local churchmen painted it black to avoid detection and when questioned about its whereabouts the local priest convinced Morgan that the altar before him was made of wood, not gold. Morgan demanded to know what had happened to the 'other altar' and was told that an earlier pirate had beaten him to it. The priest even managed to get the privateer to donate money to fund a replacement altar, causing Morgan to remark: 'I don't know why, but I think you are more of a pirate than I am.'

West of here is the **Parque Herrera**, a leafy meeting place for street vendors and passers-by where shoeshine boys and lotto-ticket touts ply their trade. Leave Casco Viejo along Avenida Central to reach the **Parque Santa Ana** and the **Iglesia de Santa Ana**. This signifies the beginning of the Santa Ana district where there is a strong Chinese population and many tea shops, medicine stores and Chinese restaurants.

La Vieja

The remnants of Old Panama (Panama La Vieja) are found at the eastern edge of the city and are a rather pitiful memento of Henry Morgan's devastating attack in 1671. Panama had no fortifications at the time and was unable to defend itself against an onslaught of 1,200 men, despite being offered some protection by a border of sea and boggy marshland. The Spanish panicked and abandoned their stronghold in an attempt to see off the insurgence on the outskirts of the town. The first round of musket fire destroyed the Spanish defence and within hours Morgan had control of the city. As Panama fell its riches were plundered and no building was safe. The first European settlement on the Pacific had prospered from its gateway position, routing gold bullion from Peru to Europe and dealing in silks and spices from the Orient. Some 5,000 houses, 200 mansions, 200 warehouses, 8 convents, dozens of churches and a grand cathedral were ransacked along with the Panama mint. Little more than scarred buildings and rubble remained once Morgan and his men had departed and the area was allowed to fall into disrepair until a protection order was granted in 1976. Sadly this was a case of 'too little to late' and today Panama La Vieja is overrun by an expanse of ramshackle resident housing that overshadows the ruins of the ancient metropolis. The most impressive structures remaining are the belltowered cathedral and the Bishop's House.

To the right of the ruins is the **National Artisans Market** (Mercado Nacional de Artesanias), which stocks a good range of Panamanian handicrafts. Open daily 09.00 to 18.00. Also **La Trapiche Restaurant** (see *Where to eat*).

Panama La Vieja Visitor Centre and Museum
The newly completed visitor centre and museum occupies a scenic waterfront spot with plenty of parking and a small taxi rank close to the IPAT information bureau. Visitor information is scant although there is a leaflet that provides some historic background to La Vieja. A better source of information is the museum and exhibition on the second storey, which has a large-scale model of the original site as well as artefacts unearthed in and around La Vieja. A boutique sells guidebooks, souvenirs and handicrafts plus a few traveller essentials like camera film and suntan lotion. Open 08.30 to 16.30 Monday to Saturday.

Amador Causeway
The Calzada de Amador lies at the Pacific entrance to the Panama Canal and extends 2km from the mainland to four small offshore islands: Naos, Culebra, Perico and Flamingo (also known as Flamenco). Once used as docking spots for Spanish galleons laden with treasure stolen from the Incan Empire, Amador became Fort Grant in 1913 to provide a powerful US defence complex at the entrance to the Canal. Using rocks and earth removed during the Canal construction the American military built a road connecting the three islands. A former secret tunnel and command post carved deep into the rock is still evident on Flamingo, which was used as a strategic base for anti-invasion planning.

Today Amador is one of Panama City's most cosmopolitan hangouts with a thriving café scene on a backdrop that is positively Miamiesque. A pristine palm-lined road runs the entire length of the causeway edged by a cycle path that teems with bikes, rollerbladers, joggers and power walkers overlooking the bay. Sunday afternoon families, shoppers and an international yachting crowd gather here. It is also a venue for live music and has a vibrant nightlife scene. Panama's interactive biodiversity museum, the Bridge of Life at Amador (scheduled for opening on the causeway at the time of writing), will further raise the profile of Amador in the city. The project, which has been jointly managed by the Smithsonian Research Institute, University of Panama and the Interoceanic Regional Authority (ARI), features an extraordinary multi-coloured building designed by renowned international architect Frank O Gehry. An urban botanical garden of lawn, trees and wild natural parkland will contain 287 species of indigenous plants, and the museum is widely predicted to become one of Panama's biggest attractions.

Of the islands **Naos** is renowned for its beach life, and for a US$5 fee visitors can relax on some of the cleanest sand in the province. On **Culebra** a Marine Exhibition Centre (tel: 212 8000) run by the Smithsonian Institute is open 14.00–17.00 Tuesday to Friday and 10.00–17.00 at weekends and housed in a building was once used by General Manuel Noriega for entertaining. Visitors can watch films on Panama's marine ecology and view exhibits of coral, shell, starfish and sea urchin. Six aquariums contain marine life from the Caribbean and Pacific with one devoted to large species of lobster. Entry is for a suggested donation of US$1 adults, 50c children under age 12. **Perico** has several charming restaurants and cocktail bars including Mi Ranchito, while **Flamingo** is the place to lunch, party and shop. Swish cafés and stylish plazas overlook gleaming million-dollar yachts on a backdrop of city skyscrapers. The Fuerte Amador Resort and Marina opened in 2002 to much acclaim, adding an international boat show to the Flamingo events calendar as well as a casino, a shopping mall and a five-star hotel. The mall contains a dozen restaurants, bars and cocktail lounges plus 20 stores that range from cigars to leather goods.

Getting there and around
Amador Causeway is well served by taxis and a ride from the centre of the city will cost no more than US$3–4. Getting around is pleasant on foot with great views and a cooling breeze. Hire bikes and skates from Moses, next to the Pencas restaurant (tel: 211 3671; US$2.10 per hour; open 10.00 to 19.00 weekdays and 07.00 to 19.00 weekends), or from Tony's Bike Rental next to the restaurant Mi Ranchito (from US$2 per hour). Scooters can be hired from Churro's Express next to Mi Ranchito. Rates vary but expect to pay US$20 per hour with discounts for full-day and weekly rental.

Where to stay
The 98-room **Country Inn and Suites** (tel: 211 4500; fax: 211 4501; www.Panamacanalcountry.com/amador) offers nine apartment suites (with lounge, dining room and kitchen), four master suites, and 40 standard suites with air conditioning and cable TV (sleep two to four), pool, superb views, free newspaper and breakfast and data ports in all rooms. Ask for the corporate rate (US$89) for a US$20 discount.

Accommodation at the upmarket **Fuerte Amador Resort & Marina** (tel: 314 0908; fax: 314 0932; email: info@fuerteamador.com: www.fuerteamador.com) has yet to open at the time of writing but looks pricey. Visit their website for an update.

Where to eat
Amador is choc-a-block with places to eat and drink and many restaurants have views across the bay. Most open at 12.00 and stay open until late. **Mi Ranchito** on Perico Island (tel: 228 0116) is one of the few that serves typical Panamanian food. Specialities include garlic shrimp with rice (US$7) and sea bass (US$9) with tables in a relaxed outdoor setting with views of the bay. For a great Cuban menu head to **Restaurante Taberna Habana Rumba** on Flamingo. It's close to **Pencas** (tel: 211 3671) which serves a mix of national dishes, pizza, salads and steak, and **Café Barko** (tel: 314 0000; fax: 314 0002) another popular outdoor diner. Nearby **Bucanero´s**, **Crepes & Waffles**, **Bolero** and **Café Santé** all serve snacks and light bites while **Ancla Sport Bar, Iemanja, Karnak, El Antro, Alcatráz,**

Cocktail Station and **Traffic Island** each serve cocktails and beer. For coffee, cakes and ice-cream head to **Freezy Cones, Tropical Twist** or **Il Cappuccino**. The **Mundo Acuático Coastway** (tel: 266 9920) and **Turiscentro La Playita de Amador** are both renowned for seafood and specialise in octopus, squid and lobster dishes for US$7–14.

Mi Pueblito
This re-creation of three traditional Panamanian villages may be a contrived attraction aimed at the tourist dollar yet it isn't as awful as it could be. *Mi Pueblito* (My Lovely Village) sits in the foothills of Cerro Ancón on the western side of the city and has a certain charm. It was the brainchild of Mayin Correa, a former mayor of Panama City and contains full-sized replicas of different villages of Panamanian ethnicity with a rural settlement from the central provinces plus an Antillean and Indian community setting. Each includes a traditional eatery that serves speciality dishes. There is also a row of fine craft shops that sell artefacts from all over the country. Open 11.30–23.30 Tuesday to Saturday and 10.00–22.00 on Sunday; entrance US$1.

Museums
Despite suffering from a severe shortage of state funding, Panama's museums are well cared for and diverse. This is due to the tireless efforts of dedicated individuals rather than the Government, and many of Panama's great institutions are indebted to benefactors and campaigning anthropologists. In Panama City there are museums devoted to the canal, religious art, natural history and Panamanian ecology. Most charge a US$1 entry and offer English-speaking guides on a tip basis.

Museo Antropológico Reina Torres de Araúz Avenida Central, Panama City; tel: 212 3089. Housed in the former main railway station, this absorbing collection of pre-Columbian artefacts gives visitors a wonderful insight into life in Panama before the Spanish invasion. Open 09.00–16.00 Tue–Sun; US$2.

Museo del Canal Interoceánico (aka **Panama Canal Museum**) Casco Viejo, Panama City; tel: 211 1650. Housed in an impressive French colonial building, this museum is a must-see for anyone keen to get the full low-down on the history of the Canal. Tours in English are available but must be booked at least six hours in advance. Open 09.30–17.30 Tue–Sun; US$2.

Casa-Museo del Banco Nacional Avenida Cuba, Panama City; tel: 225 0640. Display of currency circulated in Panama since the 16th century plus stamps and postal items. Open 08.00–12.30 and 13.30–16.00 Tue–Fri, 07.30–noon Sat; free admission.

Museo de Ciencias Naturales Avenida Cuba, Panama City; tel: 2250645, Panama city's equivalent of the natural history museum with an impressive taxidermy display. Open 09.00–16.00 Tue–Sat and 09.00–13.00 Sun; US$1/25c adults/kids.

Museo de Arte Contemporáneo Ancon district, Panama City; tel: 262 8012/3380. Host of the renowned Bienal de Arte (month-long art exhibition) this privately owned museum has some fine works by Latin American artists, and has housed some good temporary exhibitions, but the rest of the permanent display leaves much to the imagination. Open 09.00–16.00 weekdays and 09.00–noon Sat; free admission.

Museo de Arte Religioso Colonial Casco Viejo; tel: 228 2897, Panama City. Housed in the chapel of the Iglesia y Convento de Santo Domingo, this museum contains many sacred paintings and artefacts from the colonial era. Open 09.00–16.15 Tue–Sat; US$1.

Museo de Historia de Panama Casco Viejo, Panama City; tel: 228-6231. Lacklustre exhibits of Panamanian history. Open 08.30–15.30 weekdays; US$1.

Parque Natural Metropolitano

Protecting a dense 107ha area of hilly forest in the north of the city limits, the Metropolitan Natural Park is just a 10–15-minute car journey from the centre. Bordered to the west and the north by Camino de la Amistad and on the south and east by one of the city's highway bypasses, Corredor Norte, it is hard to imagine another city with such an easily accessible rural expanse, which can here be reached via Avenida Juan Pablo II. The road runs out from the city and straight through the park, passing a visitors centre (tel: 232 5516/5552) where rangers offer guided hikes, maps and leaflets. Two main hiking trails, the Nature and the Tití Monkey, join to form one large sweeping loop, offering unrivalled views over Panama City, Panama Bay, the Canal and out to Miraflores Locks via several observation points at the top of the hill. Much of the land has remained largely undisturbed for the last 80 years, during which time it has been managed from abandoned pasture to secondary dry, deciduous, lowland forest over 35m in height.

The Smithsonian Tropical Research Institute (STRI) uses the park as a project site to study the ecological make-up of the forest canopy. Subsequently paths through the park are well maintained, well signed and easy to navigate and weave through orchid ground cover and cedar forests covered in butterflies. The STRI station erected a canopy crane in the park in January 1995 to enable scientists to study the ecosystem at treetop level. The tropical semi-deciduous forest is home to more than 250 recorded bird species, including the yellow warbler and lance-tailed manakin, while fish, shrimp and turtles inhabit the River Curundu on the park's eastern flank. Other wildlife species include iguana, bats, tortoise, white-tailed deer, sloth and anteater, making this a city park quite unlike any other in Latin America.

A visitor centre is located 50m north of the park entrance and is open 08.00–16.00 daily (tel: 232 5516/5552) and has maps and information leaflets for a US$1 entrance fee. Park rangers can also provide slide shows and one-hour guided tours for US$5 per group of four or five. For details on the Smithsonian Tropical Research Institute project in the Natural Metropolitan Park visit www.stri.org or tel: 212 8000. The Panama Audubon Society (PAS) holds a monthly meeting at the visitor centre on the second Thursday of each month 19.00 to 21.00. The PAS (tel: 224 9371; fax: 224 4740; email: info@Panamaaudubon.org; www.Panamaaudubon.org) often has guest speakers and welcomes visitors interested in finding out more about the birds of Panama.

A taxi to the park entrance gate will cost no more than US$5 from the city centre. It's a 10–15-minute journey (40 minutes if you cycle) on the Avenida Juan Pablo II.

City tours

Sightseeing in and around Panama City is easily organised through dozens of tour companies that range from independent botanical guides to history tours by coach.

The Panamanian Tourist Board (IPAT) may be able to provide details of tour operators in the city although it's likely that your hotel or hostel pin-board will be a better source of information. Almost all Panama City tour companies offer the following:

City/Canal tour (approx 4 hours)
This tour includes a visit to the ruins of Panama La Vieja, Casco Viejo, the Amador Causeway and various points of interest in and around the city with a stop at Miraflores Locks to see the Canal in operation. This is an ideal option for those with limited time in Panama City.

Panama Canal Transit
This takes approximately 8 hours or 5½ hours for a partial transit and is an unbeatable way to witness the Canal locks up-close with partial transits on Saturdays only and full transits once a month. Travel by boat through all three lock systems past dredgers widening the Galliard Cut and exotic birds and wild life on Gatún Lake. Breakfast and lunch included.

Pipeline Road birdwatching (full day)
International birders flock to Pipeline Road, a 17km forested trail inside Soberanía National Park. This ecological tour takes in some of the most important areas of the Pacific rainforest to observe birds, butterflies and wildlife and lush tropical vegetation.

Emberá Indian Village / Chagres River (full day)
Take a motorised Indian cayuco across Lake Alajuela and enjoy the natural beauty of the tropical rainforest. Visit an Emberá Indian community and experience the culture and traditions of this indigenous rainforest community. Sample a typical Emberá lunch, visit waterfalls and explore the Emberá medicinal herb garden with spectacular jungle views and birdlife along the river.

El Valle and Pacific beaches (full day)
Picturesque El Valle lies nestled in the crater of a giant extinct volcano and has many well-defined walking trails that lead into the hills around the valley. The town is also famous for its weekend market when local Indians bring fruit, vegetables, flowers and handicrafts from surrounding villages. The tour also includes a trip to Santa Clara beach with an option to visit Panama's last remaining cigar factory where hundreds of hand-rolled Cubans are made each day and sold at great prices.

Gamboa rainforest (approx 5 hours)
Cruise on Gatún Lake passing large ships transiting the Panama Canal. Journey past jungle-flanked riverbanks in search of birds, sloth and monkey with a short walk in the jungle to discover flora and fauna. Another five-hour tour option to Gamboa offers a trek through the rainforest to a summit observation tower that allows breathtaking panoramic views across Soberanía National Park, the Chagres River and over transiting ships in the Panama Canal. The descent is by aerial tram via the Butterfly House, Orchid Exhibit and Serpentarium and concludes with a boat trip along the Chagres River and Gatún Lake.

Language courses
The Canadian-owned **Spanish Learning Centre** on Vía Argentina (tel: 213 3121/697 3863; email: info@spanishPanama.com; www.spanishPanama.com)

comes highly recommended and offers flexible learning schedules for all levels. It runs two- to four-day crash courses in survival Spanish and offers students homestay with Panamanian families. A full list of courses and fees can be found on the website but expect to pay US$199 per week for one-to-one tuition. The **Language & International Relations Institute** (ILERI) in Avenida Amistad (tel/fax: 260 4424; email: ilery@sinfo.net) runs programmes of five-day, four-hour study in groups of four students or less. Costs vary but run at around US$300 per week for 20 hours of tuition plus lodging and meals or US$200 for the study only. The **PanUSA Centre** (Centro Panameño Estadounidense) (tel: 232 6660/7291; fax: 232 7292; email: panusa@sinfo.net) on Avenida Roosevelt is a member of the Institute of International Education (www.iie.org) and offers structured four-week courses that consist of two hours study a day for four days a week. Prices are US$200–250. Details for Panama's fourth language school, **Spanish by the Sea**, can be found in the *Bocas del Toro Province* chapter.

Special events and festivals

Panama City's Carnaval celebration is one of the biggest in the world, beginning with a coronation ceremony to honour the elected queen and attendants and culminating in about 100 hours of wild, abandoned merriment. Carnaval, which takes place during the four days that precede Ash Wednesday, signifies state-endorsed madness and soon Vía España is packed with crowds of partying Panamanians hell-bent on making the most of it. It's loud, brash and highly charged with street vendors, performers, dancers and parades engulfed in music from a booming PA system. The party peaks on Shrove Tuesday when the biggest and most elaborate procession hits the streets and a crocodile of brightly decorated floats edges slowly through the city. All manner of groups enter the parade, from staid Canal Zone employees and political figures to scantily clad transvestites, most of which party until daybreak. As the sun comes up a sardine is buried in the sand in Panama Bay, a gesture that denotes the end of Carnaval and signifies the cessation of worldly pleasures ahead of the Lenten season.

Holy Ghost orchid

Panama Province

As the second-largest province and most populous in the country, the 11,887km² landscape of the Panama Province is as diverse as its people. Divided into 11 districts – Arrijan, Balboa, Capira, Chame, Chepo, Chiman, Chorrera, Panama, San Carlos, San Miguelito and Taboga – the region boasts mist-shrouded mountains, thick forests and dozens of white-, tan- and black-sand beaches. It borders Kuna Yala (San Blas) and the wilds of Darién to the east, Colón and Coclé to the west, the Pacific Ocean to the south and is home to the majestic Panama Canal. More than a hundred islands sit in its gaze, from the flower-filled vacation haven of Taboga to the unnamed castaway atolls in the Archipélago Las Perlas. Urban concentrations edge vast expanses of dense protected jungle containing Indian villages, waterfalls and rivers. Metropolitan parks, reserves and refuges are home to numerous wildlife species just a short distance from the hubbub of the capital.

PANAMA CANAL

> There will be no more fences, no more signs blocking our entrance. The canal is ours and may God bless it.
>
> President Mireya Moscoso, 1999

> This indeed is an historic occasion, perhaps one of the most significant that has occurred in this hemisphere. It is not only as important to understand what has gone on in the past, to understand the present circumstances where we've just delivered officially the Canal to Panama, but also to lay the groundwork for the future.
>
> Former US President Jimmy Carter, 1999

On December 31 1999 ownership of this great engineering marvel and the 17km-wide enclave surrounding it was handed over to the Panamanians (see *Chapter 1, History of the Panama Canal*), signifying a new era for the isthmus. Today vacated US bases are being transformed into new hi-tech industries, institutes and tourism facilities. For many of Panama's 3.1 million inhabitants, the handover marked the moment of true independence.

How it works

A transit from the Atlantic to the Pacific sails through Bahía Limón, located near Colón City, along a 10km approach channel. A canal pilot boards and manages the entire transit and is helped to control and manoeuvre the vessel as it enters

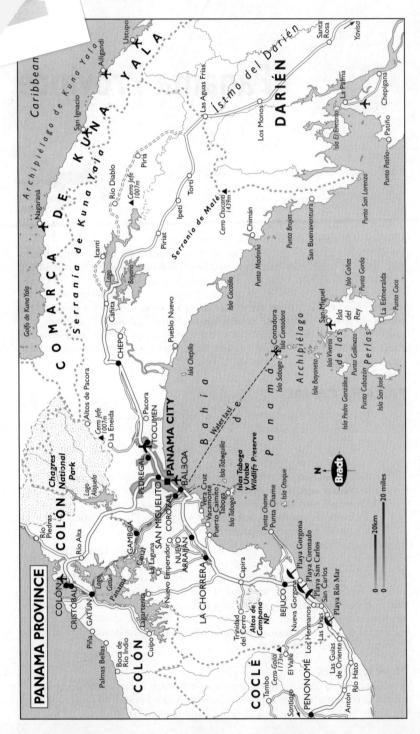

PANAMA PROVINCE

the locks by electric locomotives, known as mules, which run on tracks on each side of the canal walls. Lake Gatún has three tiered locks and each door weighs 750 tonnes. Lock chambers are 350m long and 33.5m wide, with a depth of 34m. These dimensions fit most vessels, but some commercial super tankers, US Navy super-carriers, and the renowned *Queen Mary* exceed this and cannot currently transit the Panama Canal, although there is much talk of widening it. Inside the first chamber, steel gates are closed behind the vessel and valves open to allow water from Gatún to fill the area. Once the water level meets that of the water in the second chamber, the gates in front are opened and the ship can pass. The same process is used to raise the ship to meet the level of Lake Gatún, 26m above sea level.

Lake Gatún covers 262km² and was created by the construction of the Gatún Dam, an 18 million m³ earth dam, to the west of the locks that block the Chagres River at its mouth. Until 1936, Gatún was the largest artificial lake in the world.

For 35km the ship passes exquisite, protected rainforest that is vital to regulate water systems around the canal and to protect Panama's extensive biodiversity. The rainforest of Chagres National Park produces over 40% of the water used for the operation of the canal as well as drinking water for both Panama City and Colón (50% of the country's population).

Before reaching the Pedro Miguel Locks, a ship will pass through the famous Gaillard (or Culebra) Cut, the narrowest part of the canal. This 13km-long channel is named after David DuBose Gaillard, who engineered its construction. It lies between Gold Hill on the east and Contractors' Hill on the west and was widened in 2001 to provide space for two-way traffic; 23.2 million m³ of dry material and 12 million m³ of underwater material were removed in the procedure. The vessel is lowered 9m at the Pedro Miguel Lock to the level of the Miraflores Lake, from where it is just 2.5km to Miraflores Locks. Miraflores has two sets of locks that lower the vessel to the Pacific Ocean.

Once out of the canal, the pilot leaves the vessel to travel under the Bridge of the Americas, past Balboa and out to sea. It takes eight to ten hours and 52 million gallons of water for each vessel to transit the canal.

Future changes

The number of PANAMÁX (the largest vessels that can fit through the canal) is rising. Dimensions are 294m long, 30m wide with 30m draft (depth of vessel) and by 2010 it is estimated that more than one-third of transiting ships will be PANAMÁX. Today the proportion is a quarter. Studies are being undertaken with a view to adding a third, wider Canal lane. This would greatly increase Canal revenue although concerns remain over the environmental impact of this expansion.

In June 2004 Panama announced plans for an anti-terrorism unit whose biggest mission will be to protect the canal from attack by militants seeking to disrupt the global economy. The unit is expected to collect intelligence on possible terror threats throughout the country, and will also investigate money laundering, arms trafficking and the drug trade. 'Panama needs to protect itself from terrorism, and it needs to protect its canal' said a foreign ministry official on condition of anonymity. Panama's government has stepped up security since the September 11 2001 attacks on the United States. Global security experts say the Canal is probably a medium-risk site, not among the most vulnerable worldwide but still attractive as a target given its importance to world commerce.

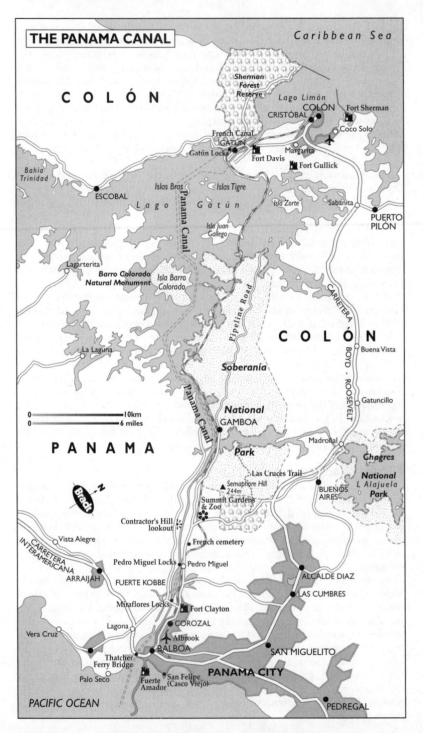

THE PANAMA CANAL

Caribbean Sea

C O L Ó N

Sherman Forest Reserve

Lago Limón

COLÓN

Fort Sherman

CRISTÓBAL

Coco Solo

French Canal
GATÚN

Margarita

Gatún Locks

Fort Davis

Fort Gullick

Bahía Trinidad

Islas Bras

Islas Tigre

Isla Zorte

Sabanita

ESCOBAL

L a g o

G a t ú n

PUERTO PILÓN

Isla Juan Gallego

Lagarterita

Barro Colorado Natural Monument

Isla Barro Colorado

Buena Vista

C O L Ó N

La Laguna

Pipeline Road

Soberanía

Gatuncillo

National

GAMBOA

P A N A M A

Madroñal

Park

Las Cruces Trail

Chagres

National L Alajuela Park

Semaphore Hill 244m

BUENOS AIRES

Summit Gardens & Zoo

Contractor's Hill lookout

French cemetery

Vista Alegre

Pedro Miguel Locks

Pedro Miguel

ALCALDE DIAZ

CARRETERA INTERAMERICANA

ARRAIJAH

FUERTE KOBBE

LAS CUMBRES

Miraflores Locks

Fort Clayton

Vera Cruz

Lagona

COROZAL

Albrook

SAN MIGUELITO

BALBOA

Thatcher Ferry Bridge

Palo Seco

Fuerte Amador

San Felipe (Casco Viejo)

PANAMA CITY

PACIFIC OCEAN

PEDREGAL

0   10km
0   6 miles

Panama Canal

Panama Canal

CARRETERA BOYD - ROOSEVELT

Canal facts

- The Panama Canal is approximately 80km long and links the Atlantic and Pacific Ocean
- It took the US project team ten years to complete using a workforce of 75,000
- It uses a system of locks that raise ships 26m from sea level to the level of Gatún Lake
- Each set of locks is named after the town where it was built: Gatún on the Atlantic and Pedro Miguel and Miraflores on the Pacific side
- Each lock chamber is 33.53m wide x 304.8m long and holds about 2.7 million m³ of water
- The maximum dimensions of ships that can transit are 32.3m in beam and 294.1m in length
- The water used to raise and lower vessels through each set of locks comes from Gatún Lake by gravity
- Calubra Cut is the narrowest stretch of the Canal. It extends 12.6km from the northern end of Pedro Miguel Locks to the southern flank of Gatún Lake and is 152m wide.
- Some 13,000–14,000 vessels use the Canal each year.
- Nearly 4.5% of global sea-going trade passes through the waterway linking the Atlantic and Pacific oceans
- The Canal has a workforce of 9,000 and operates 24 hours a day, 365 days a year
- It costs US$150m per year for basic canal maintenance alone
- Ships transit the Canal on a toll basis. The amount charged depends on size and capacity of the vessel and whether it is ballast or laden
- In 1928 Richard Halliburton paid US$0.36 to swim the canal, the lowest ever transit price paid.
- The Panama Canal uses only fresh water. This is supplied from the Panama Watershed, which has a surface of 552,761ha.
- A boat travelling from New York to San Francisco saves 7,872 miles by using the Panama Canal instead of going around Cape Horn.

Visiting the canal
Miraflores Lock
Little prepares visitors for scale of the Canal locks and the colossal tankers and ships that transit. Miraflores Lock has the most accessible viewing point and is also the nearest to Panama City. An observation platform allows great views up-close with bilingual guides that provide a running commentary when ships are in transit. Miraflores Visitor Centre opened in December 2003 as part of Panama's centennial celebrations at a cost of US$6 million. A US$10 entrance fee for the centre seems hefty but is forgotten once inside when four exhibition halls cover the history of the canal in detail, with information on watershed conservation, statistics, a topographical model and simulator as well as a pilot's view of the canal. A short documentary film in English and Spanish completes the experience. A couple of fast-food cafés are near the viewing platforms over the lock. Also located in the building is the prestigious Restaurant and Bar Miraflores, where scenes from the movie *The Tailor of Panama* were shot. Expect to pay US$6-plus for grilled meat, fish, salads and pasta.

Getting there
Buses leave regularly from Plaza Cinco de Mayo and cost around 70c one-way. Taxis from the city cost around US$5 one-way (bargaining should encourage a driver to wait).

Gatún Locks

While the Gatún Locks may lack an exciting visitor centre it is still worth a visit if passing through on the road to or from Colón. An elevated platform gives superb views of passing ships plus the entrance channel as well as the docks and shipyards of Cristóbal and surrounding tropical forest. There are no tour guides at Gatún but a bilingual commentary is provided over a loudspeaker. Visitors are also permitted to walk across the low bridge in front of the first chamber as long as photographs aren't taken. This is spectacular especially if there is a boat waiting to transit below.

Roughly a mile from the locks is the **Gatún Dam**; simply cross the locks and follow the road to the left. There are no tourist facilities here and the area is restricted, but a pedestrian viewing walkway on the bridge overlooks the front of the dam. During the rainy season, water needs to be siphoned through these colossal gates to maintain the correct level of Lake Gatún. Due to the size of the dam gates, and the size of the lake behind them, the sight of water gushing on this scale is mesmerising. In fact, viewers are prohibited from standing on or around the bridge during the process, and a siren is sounded before the gates are opened. In the absence of a guide the security guards are usually happy to answer visitor questions.

Getting there

Gatún Locks are a short drive from Colón bus or train station. A taxi from Colón should cost US$5 one-way but groups of four may be offered a ride on a mini-tour basis for which the driver will attempt to charge US$40 for a return trip. A bus from Colón is 75c (it will have Costa Abajo on the front). Visitors should be aware of a threat of mugging in and around Colón bus station (see *Colón Province* chapter) and most consider a taxi to be a safer and preferable option. Arriving by bus will also mean a possible one-hour wait for a return ride if the gates are closed for transiting vessels.

Pedro Miguel Locks

People tend to head to Pedro Miguel Locks to avoid the US$10 entrance fee at the Visitor Centre at Miraflores. Located 2km or so on from Miraflores (a little extra in taxi fares) it is here that ships pass at the highest level of the canal in Lake Gatún. Although there is only one lock chamber here, visitors can watch vessels drop 9.5m to Lake Miraflores (and, conversely, see ships rise from Miraflores to Lake Gatún). However, viewing at Pedro Miguel lacks the close-up access you get at Miraflores.

SUMMIT BOTANICAL GARDENS AND ZOO

Founded by the Americans in 1923 to introduce new tropical plant species into Panama via propagation and dissemination, the Summit Botanical Gardens (tel: 232 4854) are today home to over 15,000 different species. Picturesque marked trails take visitors through the 250ha park with signs that list the origins of the plants they contain. The park also has a zoo of endemic Central American wildlife, including tapir, jaguar, macaw, caiman and otter. The top attraction is the harpy eagle compound, which opened in 1998 to facilitate a breeding programme. Panama's national bird is the largest and most powerful bird of prey on the planet and the project, supported by the Peregrine Foundation, is a bid to save the magnificent harpy eagle from extinction. Open 08.00–6.00 daily, admission 25c. For details on the conservation efforts of the Peregrine Foundation in Panama visit www.peregrinefund.org.

Getting there

The gardens are a 25-minute drive from Panama City 10km past the Milaflores Locks. Regular buses depart from the city's bus terminal and are the same vehicles that go to Gamboa. A taxi will cost US$10 one way.

PARQUE NACIONAL SOBERANÍA

Straddling both Colón and Panama provinces, the 19,341ha Soberanía National Park contains one of Panama's legendary birding spots, accessed by most visitors via Panama City. Few stretches of tropical rainforest are so easily explored and numerous hiking trails, river stretches and lake expanses present visitors with plenty of options. Established in 1980, its ecosystem is essential to the efficiency of the canal (see *Panama Canal*), edging the canal's eastern bank and the peaceful backwaters of Lake Gatùn with a landscape of undulating hills and hummocks and rugged terrain. Cerro Calabaza forms the park's highest point at 85m (279ft) above sea level. The forest is magnificent with cotton, cuipo and oak trees and innumerable lianas, epiphytes and orchids. Insect and wild plum support 525 species of bird with forest tracts that contain 1,300 recorded plants including several endemic species. The park is also home to more than 100 mammal species, 79 species of reptiles, 55 amphibians and 36 species of freshwater fish and is an important site for conservations studies. A map of trails and a park information leaflet are available from the ANAM office (tel: 276 6370). Fishing is permitted on the Chagres River and Lake Gatún and while jaguar, white-tailed deer, agouti, raccoon, cotton-topped tamarin monkey, night monkey, caiman, snake, toad, frog and herds of collared peccaries inhabit the Soberanía National Park, it is for birds that it is most renowned. The sheer volume of sightings attracts thousands of amateur and professional ornithologists from across the world. The 30-minute **El Charco Trail** heads towards Gamboa and passes through paths rich in avifauna over pools of crystal-clear water. However, **Pipeline Road** is a firm favourite with birders and nature enthusiasts due to its high yield of wildlife diversity. It forms part of the **Oleoducto Trail** and is the venue for the Panama Audubon Society's famous Christmas bird count, which has produced record figures for umpteen consecutive years (an incredible 525 species were sighted in 24 hours in 1996). Birders can expect to see crested eagle, white-bellied antbirds, black-bellied wrens, keel-billed toucans, buff-throated woodcreepers, golden-collared manakins, red-lored amazon, black-cheeked woodpecker, black-breasted puffbird, broad-billed motmot, blue cotinga, purple-throated fruitcrow, masked tytira, violaceous trogon, fascinated antshrike, shining honeycreeper and a great array of migrants (during the North American winter months) as well as congregations of howler monkeys in the first 75–100m of the trail. Cleared in World War II when a pipeline was built along the Canal as a precautionary measure, the trail was designed to transport fuel from one ocean to the other in the event the waterway was obstructed. Today the road built to enable maintenance of the pipeline provides excellent access to primary rainforests within the park. Dozens of guides offer trips to Pipeline Road but engaging one who isn't an avifauna expert is a wasted opportunity, even for those who aren't diehard birders (see *Guides*).

Getting there

The park is a 25km drive from Panama City centre and served by numerous tour companies and day-trip excursions. A taxi will cost about US$20 one-way. ANAM can provide advice on transport from its regional HQ in Panama City (tel: 229 7885; fax: 229 7879) or the national park offices (tel: 229 7885).

Where to stay

The ANAM ranger station has a handful of beds available at US$5 per night. Accommodation is basic with no food or bedding provided. It's also possible to camp in the park overnight. Contact ANAM on tel: 276 6370 for details.

Canopy Tower

This former US Air Force radar tower sits high atop a hill and boasts spectacular views over a rainforest canopy in a beautiful spot in Soberanía National Park. Built in 1965 as part of the Canal defences, this cylindrical structure became a base for Drug Enforcement Officers in 1988, tracking narcotic shipments from South America. In 1996, in compliance with the Carter–Torrijos Treaties, the tower and the 14ha site on Semiphore Hill was transferred to Panama ownership. Bought by Raúl Arias de Para, a nature-loving Panamanian businessman, it was transformed into a rainforest and wildlife observation centre, complete with fan-cooled rooms and rooftop viewing platform.

The location of Canopy Tower, amidst acres of unspoilt bird-rich forest, has been a huge hit with international wildlife enthusiasts. Accommodation is functional but comfortable and on the ground floor and upper level a host of posters, exhibition boards, magazines and books provides plenty of information on the surrounding flora and fauna. Chestnut-backed, bicoloured, dusky, ocelated and spotted antbird abound here as well as checker-throated and dot-winged antwren; western slaty and fascinated antshrike; red-throated tanager and broad-billed motmot. However, even non-birders wax lyrical about Canopy Tower and its 360° views. Certainly few guests aren't tempted by the shrieks, trills and squeaks of the surrounding forest, and heading off to explore the leafy trails with binoculars in hand is part of the Canopy Tower experience.

Rooms at Canopy Tower (tel: 264 5720/ 263 2784 or 214 9724; email: birding@canopytower.com; www.canopytower.com) are at treetop level, no more than 12m from birds and howler monkeys. A two-night all inclusive package – including entrance to Soberanía National Park, lodging, meals and two guided forest walks – ranges from US$100 to US$200 depending on the season.

Additional tours and guiding can be booked on an à la carte basis (full list on their website). Standard tour packages include a five-hour guided rainforest hike starting at dawn (US$75), lunch on the viewing platform watching birds of prey and ships on the Culebra Cut (4.5 hours, US$75); and singing frogs, screeching owls, bats, night monkeys and innumerable arthropods at dusk (US$85)

Getting there

It's a 45-minute drive from Panama City, one hour from Tocumen International Airport or about 15 minutes from Albrook. Drivers should take the Gaillard Highway towards Miraflores Lock and continue through Pedro Miguel Locks to the town of Paraíso. Keep going under a railway bridge before taking an immediate left turn. Park offices are on the right. Continue on for about a mile, taking the second road to the right once past the entrance to Summit Gardens. Follow the Canopy Tower signs for a further mile; US$25–30 by taxi from the city centre, US$10–15 from Albrook.

PARQUE NACIONAL CAMINO DE CRUCES

The Camino de Cruces National Park covers 4,590ha just 25 minutes from the city centre. Its name means the 'Way of Crossings' and many of the old trails were used by the Spanish to transport gold from Peru, Baja California and Chile to Panama City. Some of the old pathways still contain patches of original cobbling and many routes have been restored.

Established in 1992 and bordered by the Soberanía National Park to the north and the Metropolitan Natural Park to the south, the park forms a protective corridor along the eastern bank of the Panama Canal. Characteristic dewy tropical forest on gently rolling terrain is renown for magnificent palms, oak and cotton trees that are a riot of colour in April and May. Wildlife includes iguana, crested eagle, three-toed sloth, titi monkey, pheasant cuckoo, red and green macaw, red brocket deer, white-tailed deer and agouti. Trails are well defined and maps can be collected from the ANAM visitor centre (tel: 229 7885) at the entrance of the park or from the HQ in Panama City (tel: 229 7885; fax: 229 7875). ANAM can also organise guides and can advise on transport.

Getting there
The park is located 15km from the centre of Panama City as is easily accessible via car on the road to Gamboa. A taxi from the city will cost US$10 one-way.

GAMBOA RAINFOREST RESORT
Unless you have money to burn and like formula-driven tourism, the Gamboa Rainforest Resort (tel: 314 9000; fax: 314 9020; email: reservation@ gamboaresort.com) is unlikely to appeal. However, the 300-room purpose-built resort receives plenty of positive press in Panama and appears on practically every tour schedule in town. Popular with American families and very geared up for this market, as a place to stay it is grossly overpriced with an approach to tourism that borders on the tacky. What the resort does have to offer, however, is a superb location with commanding views across the magnificent vine-tangled River Chagres and rainforest beyond. An impressive menu of guest tour packages takes in every key attraction – but at a price. If cost isn't prohibitive or time is short (the tour schedule packs in lots for visitors) then it may be worth a look. At the resort itself there's a snake house, a butterfly farm and an aquarium. The model Emberá Indian village leaves something to be desired as do room rates at US$200-plus per night.

ISLA BARRO COLORADO
Formed when the River Chagres was dammed to create Lake Gatún, this 1,500ha island lies in the middle of the lake and is managed by the Smithsonian Tropical Research Institute (STRI) (Visitor Office; tel: 212 8026; fax: 212 814; email: visitstri@tivoli.si.edu; www.stri.org or call into the HQ at Tupper Building on Avenida Roosevelt). As a primary site for the scientific study of lowland moist tropical forest since 1923, the island forms the centrepiece of the 5,600ha Barro Colorado Nature Monument (BCNM) protected under the 1940 Convention for Nature Protection in the Western hemisphere. Nature Monuments are defined to give strict protection to 'regions, objects, or living species of flora or fauna of aesthetic, historic or scientific interest', a convention ratified by Panama in 1972. In 1979, under the Torrijos–Carter Treaty, Barro Colorado was declared a Nature Monument under these terms. In addition to the island, the neighbouring mainland peninsulas of Buena Vista, Frijoles, Peña Blanca, Gigante and Bohio were incorporated in the Nature Monument, making the total area of the BCNM 4,856ha.

Once strictly off-limits to visitors, today a restricted number of people are allowed on to the island if accompanied by a guide sanctioned by the STRI. Day trips from Panama City can be arranged through Ancon Expeditions, which is affiliated with Panama's National Association for the Conservation of Nature (AEP), or with the STRI direct. The trip involves a delightful 45-minute boat journey along the Canal from the small town of Gamboa through vegetation teeming with howler monkey and toucan. Home to 1,316 plant species, 381 bird species and 102 mammal species, the island contains 60km of well-maintained marked trails that wind through the most spectacular unspoilt rainforest. Pre-planning is essential to visit Barro Colorado as STRI require plenty of notice and available dates are limited. Trips last four to six hours (depending on the weather) and lunch is included in the price of US$70 for foreign visitors and US$40 for foreign students (ID required). Prepayment by credit card is usual.

Getting there
Ancon Expeditions and the STRI Visitor Office will organise transport as part of your visit, which involves meeting a boatman in the village of Gamboa 38km from Panama City. Boats leave at 07.15 on Tuesday, Wednesday and Friday and 08.00 at weekends. Arriving in plenty of time is essential as the launch transports scientific staff to the island and will rarely wait for latecomers. Visitors are not permitted without STRI authorisation.

PARQUE NACIONAL CHAGRES
More than 40% of the water required to keep the Canal fully functioning is produced in this 129,000ha park, which also supplies drinking water to Panama City and Colon, home to 50% of Panama's population. Terrain at Chagres National Park veers from lush valleys, gushing rivers and streams to soaring peaks, with Cerro Jefe its highest point at 1,007m above sea level. Other peaks include Cerro Bruja (974m), Cerro Brewster (899m) and Cerro Azúl (771m) and these steep ridges and their foothills are popular birding haunts. The landscape is rugged and windswept with rare elfin forests and unmade roads. Endangered species native to the park include jaguars, mantled howler monkeys, tapir and anteaters with recorded sightings of more than 500 species of bird, including the harpy eagle. A debt-for-nature swap by the US government with Panama under the Tropical Forest Conservation Act awarded Chagres National Park additional funding in 2003 in return for a US$10m debt payment reduction over 14 years. This commits the Panamanian government to funding conservation projects to the same tune over the period, ensuring the protection and preservation of Chagres River Basin, which was dammed in 1914. Surrounded by important species of epiphyte, moss, orchid and fern, it is the only river in the world to flow into two oceans. Otter, caiman, crocodiles and 59 fish species inhabit the river and there have been sightings of the rare Tacarcuna bush tanager in the park environs that had previously only been recorded in the Darién.

Getting there
One of the easiest access points to the Chagres National Park by road is at Cerro Azúl via the Interamericana 40km from Panama City. Poor signs make a map essential – pick one up from the ANAM office in Panama City before leaving (tel: 229 7885). Roads to Cerro Azúl and Cerro Jefe are much improved but still require a 4WD. ANAM, who manage the park, can advise on transport, guides and trails and it is also possible to enter the park by boat along the River Chagres. Contact the park administration office on tel: 229 7885. A bus from Panama City takes two hours and departs from 24 de Diciembre bus depot for 85c. For Casa de Campo ask the driver to drop you at Las Nubes.

Where to stay
An ANAM station at Cerro Azúl offers pitches for campers for US$5, including use of kitchen and showers but no food. Bring your own tent and plenty of mosquito repellent (tel: 229 7885). One of the few guesthouses to serve Cerro

Azúl and Cerro Jefe area is **La Posada de Ferhisse** (tel: 297 0197), a typical Panamanian inn with six comfortable rooms with private hot-water bathrooms, TV and phone. It also has a restaurant (open 09.00 to 22.00) and a pool and is US$40 a night for a room that sleeps four. Another one to try is the **Hostal Casa De Campo** (tel: 297 0067) where eight rooms and three budget cabins start at US$10 per night with an outdoor Jacuzzi, swimming pool, spa, home-cooked food and birdwatching hikes in Cerro Azúl. There are charming hillside wooden cabins (US$40) and tents (US$15 for two nights) at the **Cabañas 4X4 Country Inn** (tel: 226 7616) and rustic cabañas at the **Cabañas Turismaru** and **Cabañas y Finca Nicolaise** for US$10 per night (no phone, just look for the road signs).

ISLA TABOGA

Isla Taboga, Panama's self-proclaimed 'Capital of Summer' is the largest of several tiny atolls that lie 17km to the south of Panama City. Its colourful history is rich in maritime adventure but today the boats that dock on this picturesque island are packed with day-tripping escapees fleeing the heat of the city. A laidback community markets itself as a haven of tranquillity; a successful, if questionable campaign that has boosted visitor figures to up to 1,000 per day. 'Come to Isla Taboga where there are no cars, no consumer price tags and no push and shove', urges the tourist board, promising forested trails, sandy coves, pineapple trees and flora-filled gardens fanned by year-round trade winds.

History

Just a small Indian fishing community in 1514 at the time of Conquistador invasion, this pretty 230ha island is the site of Spanish settlement San Pedro, built around a church that bears its name. Locals claim Iglesia San Pedro is the second- oldest church in the northern hemisphere, founded by Padre Hernando de Luque in 1524. The Padre, Dean of Panama Cathedral, blessed ships that set sail from Taboga to plunder the Inca Empire. In his honour Taboganos have named the crystalline pool in the highest point on the island, Picacho del Vigia, as the 'Bishop's Pool'.

Welsh buccaneer Henry Morgan and Francis Drake both ransacked Taboga in the 16th century. Morgan sent his pirates there after the sacking of Panama City and local legend is steeped in tales of buried treasure on the beach. Indeed in 1998, during the construction of a medical centre, some 1,000 17th-century silver coins were unearthed here, and locals remain convinced there is more hidden in the sands.

In the mid 18th century Isla Taboga became the port of choice for Panama City and the mainland due to depth of the water on the island's northern shoreline. Hundreds of Irish workers arrived to man the supply base for the Pacific Steamship Navigation Company. Gold seekers from California also discovered Isla Taboga at about this time, and a trace of Anglo-Saxon names can still be seen on tombstones in the island's cemetery today.

In 1887 Isla Taboga became the home of the post-impressionist French painter Paul Gauguin, who set sail for the island after a short stint on the fated French Canal project. Building a studio from which to paint Gauguin eventually sailed to Tahiti where some of his most acclaimed works of art reflected life on Isla Taboga.

Isla Taboga played an important support role to the Panama Canal construction workers. A French-built 50-bedroom retreat for workers was built in the 1880s at a cost of US$400,000, which the US project took over in 1905 as a respite centre for exhausted labourers. In January 1915 the building became the Hotel Aspinwall, a vacation resort for Canal employees and their families. During World War II Aspinwall became an internment camp for German prisoners but was back at the heart of Tabogan social life at the end of 1945.

Fishing piers and lobster pots give Isla Taboga a quaint seaside-town feel. Most visitors arrive to hike the trails, smell the flowers and enjoy the beach. A couple of hotels, a handful of restaurants and some decent beach bars offer peaceful views across the Bay of Panama.

Getting there and around

Two ferry operators serve Isla Taboga from Panama City and depart from Pier 19 in the Balboa district. **El Calypso** (tel: 232 6687) has two boats, the *Calypso Queen* and the *Calypso Princess*. Both have shaded decks and travel at a leisurely pace on a journey that is designed for views. The trip takes 1¼ hours for US$5 one-way or US$8 for the round trip and departs Monday to Saturday 08.30, returning at 16.00, with two crossings on Sunday at 07.45 and 10.30, returning at 15.00 and 17.45. **Expresso del Pacifico** (tel: 261 0350; email: willifu@cableonda.et) is faster at just 35 minutes for the same price, with three weekend sailings (08.00, 10.00 and 16.00, returning 09.15, 15.00 and 17.00) and two on weekdays (08.30 and 14.30, returning at 09.45 and 15.45).

There are no roads on Isla Taboga but exploring the island is pretty straightforward on foot although trail quality varies. Supplement hiking with boat trips to see the entire island. Boatmen can be hired for US$10–20 per day from the pier.

Where to stay

There are about a dozen places to stay on the island but not all publish their prices; however, the 60-room beachfront **Hotel Taboga** (tel: 264 6096; email: htaboga@sinfo.net) has tennis courts and pool with rooms at US$60–80. Taboga's newest inn, **Hotel Vereda Tropical** (tel: 250 2154), sits on a hillside overlooking Playa Honda with lovely double rooms for US$65.00 per night. The **Kool Youth Hostel** (tel: 690 2545; email: luisveron@hotmail.com) is an offshoot of the Voyager Hostel in Panama City and is a comfortable backpacker joint close to the pier and within easy reach of the beach; free breakfast, communal kitchen, a book exchange, bike and snorkel rental plus a well-used backpacker bulletin board, from US$10.

Others without published prices at the time of writing include **Uva's Guesthouse** (tel: 250 2140 and ask for Yolanda, Uva's daughter) which is owned and run by one of the five people on Isla Taboga aged over 100, and offers double rooms with shared bathrooms and great home cooking in more of a homestay than a B&B. **Casa Roeder** (tel: 250 2208; email: veredatropicalhotel@hotmail.com) is available for rent per night, week or month and can accommodate five easily. The **Casa Brower** apartment (tel: 602 4796) can accommodate seven people with microwave, TV, and stereo system and air conditioning; and eight suites at **Chu Apartments** (tel: 250 2034) sleep up to six people and are clean but rustic with shared balconies overlooking the ocean .

Tourist information

In the absence of a tourist bureau the ANAM office to the east of the pier is a good source of information, especially for those keen to hike the island. A community website launched in 2004 and is worth checking out for hotels and history – www.taboga.Panamanow.com.

What to see and do

To the left of the pier a 5km trail leads to the top of the island, passing the **Iglesia San Pedro** and the **cemetery,** where overgrown graves bear the names of early arrivals. A 16th-century wooden cross, the **Cerro de la Cruz,** denotes the founding of the island on a pathway of wild hibiscus, oleander, jasmine and bougainvillea. Rugged wooded hiking trails lead to **US military bunkers** where vistas are of city, ocean and shoreline. Several **beaches** lie within easy reach of the ferry dock. Many visitors choose to pay the Hotel Taboga a US$5 fee to use its changing rooms and showers, and the beach has a **watersports** rental shop with hammocks, snorkel gear, kayaks and paddleboats. Head to the west of the island for caves that are rumoured to contain buried treasure where on a good day divers can expect to see snapper, lobster, octopus, eels and World War II remnants. A natural habitat for one of the largest breeding colonies of brown pelicans in the world, a **wildlife refuge** protects much of Isla Taboga, home to 100,000 birds at its peak. Vast areas of mangrove host feeding turtles while the surrounding lowlands are renowned for their large butterfly and frog populations.

There's an ANAM ranger station at the east of the ferry dock (tel: 250 2082), where staff can advise on guides, maps and trails to reach the island's ecological highlights. Open 08.00 to 16.00.

ARCHIPÉLAGO LAS PERLAS

This picturesque cluster of 220 islands and unnamed atolls comprises plenty of wildlife, jungle and sandy beaches, but very few humans. Less than a handful of the islands are inhabited, and even then the population is sparse, and it is little wonder that these deserted rugged, sandy islets were picked as the venue for TV reality series *Survivor*. The largest of the group is Isla del Rey at 240km², an island in the south that has a population of 500 descendants of slaves from the pearl-diving days. Isla San José is next at 45.3km² and Isla Pedro González 14.9km², before Isla Viveros (6.6 km²) and Isla Caña (3.2km²). Few visitors are able to visit islands other than Isla Contadora (1.2km²), Isla Saboga (2.96km²), Isla Casaya (2.75km²), Isla Casayeta (0.46km²) and Isla San José. John Wayne liked the archipelago's castaway feel so much he bought an island called Taborcillo as a private retreat. Since then many others have followed in his footsteps and today most of the pinprick-sized islets and atolls have been sold off to the highest bidders. Others are simply too inaccessible for most visitors and remain off limits to both boat and private plane.

Isla Contadora

As the closest in proximity to Panama City, the small island of Contadora is the most visited and developed and was once a major headquarters for the lucrative pearl-diving industry. The name, meaning 'accountant', reflects these affluent times but today it is tourism, not pearls, that brings Contadora prosperity. Despite being just 1.2km² in size, Contadora is served by daily flights to and from the capital. Thirteen sandy beaches are evenly spread and include Playa Suecas in the south, Panama's only nudist beach. Playa Larga is the largest stretch of sand and also the most crowded, sitting in a protected cove in the southeast of the island. One of the least visited is Playa Cacique while Playa Ejectiva is renowned for a former resident, the Shah of Iran. Most southern beaches are quiet and secluded and swathed in magnificent primary forest.

While nearly all of Contadora's tourist facilities are located in the north it is not difficult to traverse the island in 15 minutes on a hired quad bike. Most visitors arrive in Contadora with taking it easy in mind but for those that seek more than beach life there are numerous fishing charters, dive operators and forested trails to explore. **Las Perlas Sailing** (tel/fax: 250 4214) offers more than the name implies and has quad bikes for hire (US$20 per hour), guided jet-ski marine safaris (US$75 per hour), parasailing (US$50) and snorkelling trips as well as full- and half-day sailing tours (US$75). A trip on **Jayson's Glass Bottom Boat** (tel: 624 5126) is a fun way to see puffer fish, parrot fish, sea turtles and sharks and is captained by a Jamaican boatman with hundreds of tales to tell. The 90-minute tour also provides

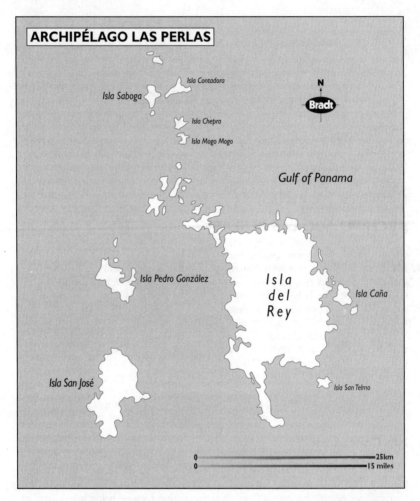

plenty of information on the marine ecology and details the five coral fields and their inhabitants such as damselfish, moray eels and white-tip reef sharks for US$20 per person. **Salvatore Fishing** (tel/fax: 250 4109) run half- and full-day fishing trips from US$50 per person. It also rents boats for US$200 for a half-day and organises snorkel tours and island hops on requests from US$30. **Sailing with Max** (tel: 250 4118; fax: 250 4118; email: maxiten@cwp.net.pa) is another good option with umpteen fishing, whale-watching and snorkel excursions from US$50. For landlubbers there is the nine-hole par three **Contadora Golf Course** or two-hour **walking trails** that are rich in birds and exotic wildflowers.

Getting there and around

Contadora is served by daily Aeroperlas flights from Panama City (tel: 315 7500; fax: 315 7580; email: iflyap@aeroperlas.com; www.aeroperlas.com) at US$29.40 for a one-way ticket and US$58.80 return. Flights depart Panama City at 08.45 and 17.00 Monday to Friday with a weekend schedule of 08.00, 08.50, 09.40 and 17.00 on Saturday; and 15.50, 16.40 and 17.30 on Sunday.

'SURVIVOR'

The numerous untouched islands, islets and atolls that surround the Panamanian mainland make the country a natural venue for a game of Robinson Crusoe-style endurance. Using the slogan 'outwit, outplay and outlast!' TV reality-show *Survivor* was born and several series later the programme is synonymous with Panama. The isthmus has welcomed contestants from the UK, France, Italy, USA, Russia and Argentina and worked with film crews from across the world. The premise of the game is survival and around 25 individuals are divided into two teams who are then 'cast away' on different islands with limited food supplies. Various challenges test strength and endurance, ranging from eating bugs and eyeballs to standing on a water-submerged post for 24 hours. Each week, the two teams attend a tribal council where participants must vote one of their team off the island. Competition is fierce, the tactics ugly and the conditions hot and sweaty. Group tension is fraught and the experience lasts about a month, by which time the remaining participants can't wait to wave goodbye to their competitors – or their paradise island. For avid fans, however, numerous websites have been created, the biggest of which is www.survivalfever.com.

Bocas del Toro archipelago was once *Survivor*'s primary location, although recent US productions and *Gestrandet* (the German edition) chose to film in Las Perlas. This stunning cluster of islands in the Pacific looks like the future venue of choice, after rumours that US film crews felt that Bocas del Toro was too small. Filming has taken place on Isla Contadora, Mogo Mogo and Chapera when Panama's National Maritime Service was hired to stop ships and vessels from coming within a nautical mile of the islands.

Today *Survivor* is one of America's most popular programmes although there is local dispute in Panama over the benefits to its host nation. While it may help to generate tourism (an estimated 21 million viewers watched the US Pearl Islands show) there is discontent regarding the environmental impact of the games as visitors exploring Cayos Zapatilla in Bocas del Toro have found discarded remnants from past games. Indeed the once splendid tribal council voting platform now lies rotting on the farthest stretch of the Bastimentos shoreline and while the buzz surrounding the filming of *Survivor* is entertaining it can cause limitations. Visitors who arrive in an area whilst the game is in progress are likely to be turned away. Others may be requested to contribute as an extra when most would prefer to create a *Survivor* experience of their own. For details of filming in Panama visit www.cbs.com/primetime and click on to Survivor.

Getting around is pretty easy on foot (it can be fully walked in two hours). Quad bikes can be hired from Las Perlas Sailing for US$20 per hour (tel/fax: 250 4214) and Casa del Sol B&B for US$25 for the day (tel: 250 4212; email: skytoxin@bigfoot.com). Boats can be rented from Salvatore Fishing (tel/fax: 250 4109) and both Las Perlas Sailing and Salvatore offer island hops and beach transfers.

Where to stay

The **Casa del Sol** (tel: 250 4212; email: skytoxin@bigfoot.com) is a charming single-storey B&B that is run by German couple, Kitty and Spoon Loeffler. A great breakfast is included in the rate of US$40 for a single and US$50 for a double and rooms come with private hot-water bathrooms. Transfers, spa treatments, tours and

Gulf of Panama

ISLA CONTADORA

0 ━━━━━ 500m
0 ━━━━━ 500yds

other services also, see www.Panama-isla-contadora.com for details. The sprawling **Contadora Resort** (tel: 250 4033; fax: 250 4000; email: reservas@hotelcontadora.com; www.hotelcontadora.com) specialises in all-inclusive package deals with rates that vary throughout the season. Rack rates are US$80 but guests rarely pay that much for a spot that is right on Playa Largo. The Colombian-owned **Hotel Punta Galéon** (tel: 250 4134; www.puntagaleon.com) is a pricier option with 50 top-notch rooms in a resort setting on the coastline at US$100–150 per night. The **Villa Romantica** boasts a superb spot in Playa Cacique (tel: 250 406; email: contadora@villa-romantica.com) and offers nine rooms and a penthouse with mural walls and ocean views for top prices. Not so at the **Cabañas de Contadora** (tel: 250 4214) where four self-contained apartments with a fridge and microwave start at US$50 for double occupancy, including breakfast.

Where to eat

The **Refresqueria y Bar Anglina** is renowned throughout Panama as once having been owned by American singer-songwriter Michael Bolton. Sold in 2000, today the menu has Panamanian specialities but is mainly pizza and burgers at keen prices favoured by backpackers, open 08.00–22.00 daily. Another menu of cheap eats can be found at **Restaurante Sagitario** with shrimp and rice, and fried fish at under US$5.50. Upmarket **Restaurante Gerald's** (tel: 250 4061) has prices to match but serves superb fish (US$9–14) and lobster (US$25) dishes; open for lunch and dinner.

SAN JOSÉ

This beautiful 45.3km² private island is dominated by thick rainforest cover with rushing rivers and waterfalls hidden beyond its primitive trails. A well-maintained 100km road criss-crosses in parts, rising through small valleys and bridging fords to make light of traversing the island. Large areas of San José remain completely unexplored due to the convenience of this trail. Dense jungle flanks edge more than 50 sandy coves and at least ten rivers to form a natural habitat untroubled by human disturbance.

At the clifftop **Hacienda del Mar**, the island's only development, guests have the entire island to themselves. Uninterrupted ocean views are magnificent; the jungle backdrop positively primeval; and the luxury of space allows full days of exploration without seeing, or hearing, another person. Gently sloping verdant hills peak at 135m in the north of the island with a coastline that is cragged and irregular. Several streams flow into the ocean, providing a rich food source for many species of saltwater and brackish fish species. Fertile soil produces an abundance of arboreal species, with coconut palms and wild sugarcane found along the shoreline as well as endemic plant species. A riddle of year-round natural springs serves to irrigate the landscape, with waterfalls up to a height of 18m and a number of dank mossy caves. San José's population of 3,000 wild pigs is one of the largest in Panama and deer, crocodile, iguana, agouti and more than 100 species of birds inhabit the island's untamed habitat.

Considered among the best deep-sea fishing grounds in Panama, the waters of San José are particularly rich in game fish. Some 16 black marlin world records are held here and marlin, sailfish, tuna, dolphin, wahoo, amberjack, cobera, red snapper, corvine, mackerel, turtles, lobster, shrimp, giant oysters, clams and mussels have been sighted along with several species of shark.

The Hacienda del Mar (tel: 269 6634/269 6613; fax: 264 1787; email info@haciendadelmar.net (Panama) or tel: toll free 1 866 HDELMAR or 1 866 433 5627 in the US; fax: (305) 233 9933; email: mzima@bellsouth.net) is the brainchild of George Novey, the former president of Panama's biggest domestic airline, Aeroperlas. He bought the island from its former owner, Al Tupper, after poor health forced the Tupperware magnate to sell. Today a main building overlooks a clifftop spring-water swimming pool and 14 cabins set in tropical gardens. Novey and his family run the hotel, which has a restaurant, bar and a small boutique. Furnishings from Mexico and décor from Guatemala see no expense spared on detail, yet the ambience is relaxed and unfussy with ocean views that are nothing short of stunning.

Nesting turtles descend on the beaches of San José and in a bid to ensure a better survival rate the hotel runs a Sea Turtle Conservation Program. More than 100 turtles are raised in the hatchery each year and guests are invited to participate in the annual release into the wild. Humpback whales pass the island on a migratory path and good clear sightings are not uncommon from San José's beaches.

Tours delve into the most remote spots on the island on foot, by bike, canoe, kayak or on quad bike. A nightly wildlife safari seeks out white brocket deer, wild boars, dwarf anteater, snake and owl. Canoes and kayaks can also be hired to venture into the mangroves and sport fishing and river fishing arranged on request. Cabins aren't cheap but a US$250 cabin sleeps four, a larger cabin at US$350 sleeps up to six. Rates include a hearty breakfast and the hotel will arrange the chartered flight from Panama's Albrook Airport.

Getting there

The cost of a 30-minute flight by private plane is US$60, departing Panama's domestic airport at 08.50 and 17.00 and returning from San José at 09.20 and 17.35. An alternative is a two-hour boat journey.

ISLA DEL REY

Until recent years the population of Isla del Rey has been a stable 500, or thereabouts, a population of descendants from slaves from the days of pearl diving. However, at the time of writing, a major development on a 100ha site is slated to open, comprising a five-star hotel, marina and residential villas. Isla del Rey shows all the signs of becoming a future centre for tourism activities with interest from dive schools, fishing tours and other commercial operators. Planned features at Kingfisher Bay include beachfront accommodation, spa, casino and yacht club. For an update visit www.kingfisherbay.net

The islands of **Isla Saboga, Isla Casaya** and **Isla Casayeta** can be reached by boat from Isla Contadora and are some of the outcrop isles used by CBS for *Survivor*. The small Indian fishing village of Saboga lies about 1km west of Contadora and was the main source of manpower for set-building on the 2003 series. During filming vessels are banned from coming within a nautical 1½ miles of the tiny neighbouring islands of Bartolome, Mogo Mogo and Gibraleon. Lesser restrictions have been placed on incursions around the western part of Saboga and the islands and islets of Chapera, Boyarena, Bolano, Membrillo and Casaya. These islands are popular with yachts and island cruisers who skirt the coastline in search of snorkelling spots.

EASTERN PANAMA PROVINCE

The land that cushions the 26km of Interamericana that stretches from Panama City to reach the Darién Gap forms the Eastern Province. Growing increasingly desolate beyond the urban sprawl of Panama City, it passes few points of interest once it has left the town of Chepo behind. Once the terminus of the Interamericana it is still regarded by many Panamanians as a border town, and a bureaucratic checkpoint on Chepo's eastern outskirts does little to alter this perception.

Chepo

Panama's border town until the 1960s, the town of Chepo still retains the air of a place that travellers pass through. A river-mouth location once made it a popular launch for canoes into the Darién, but today it is a meeting point for birding and fishing tours heading to Lake Bayano. Petrol stations, grocery stores and a vehicle repair shop are here, but no accommodation for travellers on the move. An hourly bus from Panama City takes about 1½ hours to Chepo and costs less than US$1.50.

Burbayor Lodge Nusagandi

The turn-off for the town of Nusagandi is about 16km from Chepo on the approach to the town of El Llano on the Interamericana. It lies within the Area Silvestre de Narganá wildlife reserve created by the Kuna conservation group PEMASKY. Basic lodge accommodation is located about 17km on. The refuge lies in the eastern foothills of Panama City on the border with the Comarca de Kuna Yala, and has been rated as one of the top ten areas in the world by Smithsonian scientists in terms of abundance of flora and fauna. It needs a 4WD to visit (the roads resemble porridge) but is worth the effort to reach the magnificent bird-rich primary forest beyond. The Kuna General Congress created this reserve to protect its outer edges from being eroded by the type of creeping deforestation suffered by the Darién. Funding by the MacArthur Foundation and the WWF helped the Kuna construct a two-story wooden lodge with dormitory accommodation and a shower block. Several trails have been created, including the Kuna Medicinal Forest Trail (*Ina Igar*). The forest is home to large numbers of howler monkeys and muddy paths that lead to three waterfalls deep within the jungle. Trails offer one- to three-hour hikes where visitors can see speckled antshrike, black-crowned antpitta and various species of tanager. The lodge is way off the beaten track along some truly terrible roads and is often overlooked as a result. Beds need to be pre-booked (tel: 264 1697; www.burbayar.com) and cost US$114 for the first night, US$70 per night for longer stays.

Getting there
Turn off the Interamericana 16km after Chepo and follow the road for 15km. Do not be tempted to try this in anything other than a 4WD, as the road is truly appalling.

The town of **El Llano** has a couple of simple restaurants, a bar, a public phone and a vehicle repair shop, which you might need after braving the road to Nusagandi. **Cañita** boasts a similar set of amenities with at least three places to eat for less than US$3. Some 15km from Cañita is **Lake Bayano**, Panama's largest inland body of water and a paradise for birders. This manmade lake was created by the damming of the River Bayano and is the site of an important hydro-electric project. Today flower-filled hedgerows and secondary forest are home to black antshrike, red-billed scythebill, one-coloured becard and white-eared conebill.

The drive-through towns of **Ipetí**, **Tortí** and **Higueronal** each have grocery stores, pay phones, petrol stations and a handful of simple eateries. Tortí, 12km on from Impetí, is the only place with overnight accommodation. None is clearly signed, none has telephones and most are pretty grim. The exception is the **Hospedaje Tortí**, which has 20 fan-cooled rooms with shared bathrooms at US$5 per night.

WESTERN PANAMA PROVINCE
Panama's Western Province is more populated than the barren eastern flank, with an endless succession of small coastal communities stretching from Playa Leona to Playa Corona. It's nicest sandy stretch is shared with its neighbour, the Coclé Province, and these popular beaches are a weekend retreat for carloads of stressed-out urbanites.

La Chorrera
Boasting all the amenities you'd expect from the most populous town in the Western Province, the town of La Chorrera has plenty of supermarkets, a couple of banks and an endless succession of payphones. Most passers-by whiz past en route to the beaches or the capital, pausing only to refuel or grab something to eat. Many key amenities are located on the highway, which makes it even more convenient for travellers keen to avoid the town environs altogether.

Parque Nacional Altos de Campana
The first national park in Panama, Altos de Campana was created in 1966 and occupies 4,925ha on the western slope of the Canal to form part of its basin. The landscape encompasses part of the El Valle volcanic expanse and boasts dramatic peaks and lava fields. It rises to a peak of 850m (2,789ft) above sea level from an altitude of 400m and is a mix of woodlands and deforested rolling grasslands. While illegal logging has threatened wildlife habitat in recent years the mouth of the River Chame remains populated with birdlife. More than 500 plant and tree species, including moss, orchids, bromeliads and epiphytes, and some 36 species of mammal, inhabit the park environs. Two-toed sloth, crab-eating raccoon and three-toed sloth

have been sighted along with 298 species of bird, both endemic and migratory. Expect to see kite, violet-bellied hummingbird, bronze-tailed plumlesteer and orange-bellied trogon, also 62 amphibian and 86 reptile species including the rare frog, atelopus zeteki, salamander, gecko, snake, giant frog and spiny toad.

One key well-maintained trail, **Sendero La Cruz**, winds up through the park to provide a challenging one-hour trek. The path is jointly managed by ANAM and Panama University and is the most common route and in good repair. **Cerro La Cruz** is a rougher trail with magnificent views and leads to join the forest-covered **Cerro Campana** to reach the park's highest point (1,007m). This tricky trail requires plenty of stamina (and a decent pair of boots) but the views at the top are just reward. On a clear day the vistas stretch for 297km out to black and green peaks shrouded in mist and dark brooding crags. From the top a pleasing one-hour downhill trek returns to the road to join the less arduous **Sendero Panama** (1.5km) and **Sendero Podocarpus** (1km) trails. Each is well signed and maps, wildlife booklets and trail information can be picked up from the park ranger station (tel: 244 0092) between 08.00 and 16.00.

Getting there

All buses that head west from Panama City on the Interamericana will drop off passengers at the turn-off for the park (US$1.50). Look out for a bright blue bus stop and a green and yellow 'ANAM' sign about 25km southwest of La Chorrera on a stretch of road known locally as Loma Capana. The main entrance and ranger station are 6km up a steep dirt track after an initial stretch of neat paving suddenly ends without warning. On a dry day there'll be a handful of fruit and vegetable stalls on the verge here. If it's wet even the mightiest 4WD vehicle has a struggle to ascend this track. Drivers should be prepared for a boneshaker of a journey whatever the weather. At best expect dust and rocks; at worst a river of mud.

Where to stay

The park has **six refugios** (basic, covered areas) and several camping options (US$5 per night), which ANAM rangers will point out on arrival. The closest refugio is 15-minutes from the start of the trails and has no beds, but a dry roof and toilets. Simply let the rangers know that you want to stay there and it'll be opened up for your arrival. Another option is **Richard's Place** (tel: 601 2882), an old house on a hillside with amazing views. It's owned by an eccentric American expatriate who has more tales than teeth and is happy for guests to turn up on his doorstep between 08.00 and 20.00. Look for the large white house, a good 15-minute drive past the start of the trails. Ignore the sign that says 'No Estoy' (meaning 'I'm not here') – you are, well almost. The sign for Richard's Place is just a mile or two further. Rooms in this quirky abode offer varying standards of comfort. It's less B&B and more oddball hideaway but travellers in search of a place with character will find a certain charm in Richard's piles of old newspapers, broken radio equipment and shelves of dusty collectables. Rates are US$20 per night for a room that sleeps four to six, less for longer stays. Camping is a good option at US$5 for person. Large groups can hire the whole place out (ten bedrooms can sleep 20–25 people comfortably) for US$120.

PUNTA CHAME

Because of its lack of amenities and off-the-beaten-track location the tiny coastal town of Punta Chame tends to be overlooked by tourists. From Panama City it's the first beach after crossing the mountains of La Campana about 14km

Above The Kuna become adept at handling a dugout canoe (*ulu*) at a young age in Kula Yala, where it remains the only method of transport and crucial to their fishing economy (DS)

Left Tree frog (CT)

Below left Red-lored Amazon parrot (CT)

Below right Bird of paradise flower, *Heliconia* sp. (CT)

Above The crowd-free waters of Punta Vieja (Old Point), Isla Bastimentos (DS)

Right Punta Caracol eco resort near Isla Colón (DS)

Below Waterfront of Old Bank, Isla Bastimentos (DS)

from the turn-off from the national park. The town itself comprises just one road on a needle-thin peninsula. The beach is lovely: wild, sandy and fringed with palms; and apart from a scattering of sea birds, Playa Chame is almost always deserted. In high tide the water reaches a primitive rocky sea defence while at low tide there is evidence of stingrays on the shoreline. The sand here is some of the cleanest in Panama but is in danger of being eroded by frequent sand-dredging activities. Raiding the beach by barge has become the norm for construction projects in Panama City and is seriously threatening the future of this glorious sandy strip.

Waters to the north of a concentration of flower-filled mangroves are popular with windsurfers from **Punta Chame Windsurfing (PCW)** (email: puntachamewindsurf@cableonda.net). The windsurfing season runs from December to April and PCW organise tours, tuition and kitesurfing and windsurfing programmes from an office next to the **Hotel Punta Chame** (tel: 240 5498/263 6590), which has rustic four-person cabins for US$55. Punta Chame is also used as the launch point for boatmen who run trips out past Isla Taborcillo (aka John Wayne Island). The actor bought the island as a vacation retreat and the locals have endless tales to share. One tells of the island's mini town, sheriff station and buildings built on the theme of American Cowboy. Another tells of John Wayne and his drinking buddy, former Panamanian president General Omar Torrijos. Punta Chame is also home to the **Friends of the Sea Turtles Foundation** (FATMAR, Fundación Amigos de las Tortugas), a local conservation group established by brother and sister Ramon and Vilma Morales. This save-and-release project was launched in 1998 to stem the decline in numbers and is located on the right-hand side of the entrance to the town. A series of hatcheries and conservation efforts are entirely self-funded and supported by a local rock band that organises fundraising concerts. To boost finances FATMAR has built some cabins close to the hatcheries. Each of the **Morales Cabañas** sleeps two to four at US$30 per night (no phone, just call in).

Getting there
Turnoff for Punta Chame from the Interamericana immediately east of Bejuco, a tiny hamlet 13km west of the Parque National Altos de Campana turning, a good 45-minute drive from Panama City. Get a bus heading west to drop you at the Bejuco turn-off to catch one to Punta Chame (hourly from 06.00 to 17.00 for US$1).

PACIFIC COAST
A succession of beaches runs from the southern end of Punta Chame along a 40km stretch of Pacific coastline shared between the Panama Province and Coclé Province. Playa Corona denotes the boundary and lies at the end of a glorious stretch of sand. Most beaches are signed by turn-offs on the Interamericana and can be easily reached by car or by a US$2–3 taxi from the bus stop on the highway. All are pretty similar, well maintained with clean sand and an absence of rubbish and driftwood. The coastline is popular with surfers and weekending families from Panama City.

The first, **Playa Gorgona**, is a long, arched black-sand beach surrounded by shrub land. Several places to stay include the **Hotel Club Gorgona Resort** (tel: 240 6520; fax: 222 0766), which has doubles at US$40, quadruples at US$60 and a suite for six at US$80; **Cabañas de Playa Gorgona** (tel: 240 6160) with rooms at US$40–50; **Cabañas Villanita** (tel: 240 5314) at US$45–60; and **Cabañas Rancho Bonito** (tel: 240 6513) at US$40–80.

Upscale **Playa Coronado** follows and an affluent neighbourhood of holiday homes on a pleasant salt-and-pepper beach. **Coronada Hotel and Resort** (tel:

CONTROVERSAL COWBOY

Brusque, uncompromising professional Hollywood cowboy, John Wayne, first visited Panama when filming *Rio Bravo* in the 1950s. He continued to vacation on the isthmus until his death in 1979, but much like his private life, Wayne's relationship with Panama was stormy. The release of *Rio Bravo* in April 1959 was overshadowed by accusations from the Panamanian government that Wayne was politically involved with rebel leader, Roberto Arias, to the tune of US$500,000. His response was a no-nonsense denial that pulled no punches, a trademark style that gained Wayne some notoriety. In the last decades of his career, Wayne became feared for his outspoken views. He was targeted for hate mail from the right wing after he supported President Carter's espousal of the Panama Canal treaties, despite being traditionally conservative. John Wayne was a great drinking and fishing buddy of General Omar Torrijos the Panamanian dictator at the time. He adored spending time on his private island Taborcillo, parting with it only on death.

240 4444; fax: 240 4380; www.coronadoresort.com) is a dominant feature and consists of 100 stylish rooms for US$165–350 a night, complete with tennis court, golf course, spa, swimming pool, half a dozen restaurants and bar.

Playa San Carlos is a paler sand beach located 10km west of the turn-off for Coronado, a 2km walk from the Interamericana (or a US$1.50 taxi). A laidback community of fishermen who often mend their nets on the beach, the place has a relaxed feel and comprises a couple of small resorts, two or three small restaurants, a surf shack, volleyball nets and a hotel on the beach. The **Bay View Hotel** (tel: 240 9621; web www.waystogo.net) boasts a superb location overlooking the ocean with comfortable cabins close to the beach (US$45–59.50) while an elevated open-sided restaurant offers great views across the sands. The food is good, with a menu of Pan-American favourites, including red snapper (US$7), sea bass (US$6.50), Cuban sandwich (US$5), jumbo hotdog (US$3) and garlic octopus (US$8).

Just 2km west is the surfing beach of **Playa Río Mar**, which has a couple of good little hotels and beach bars and a great seafood restaurant. The **Hotel Playa Río Mar** (tel: 240 8027; fax: 264 2272) is packed with weekenders from Friday to Sunday but is a beachfront haven on weekdays when rooms are 50% cheaper; US$35–40 for a double. Expect big helpings of good seafood for US$7–12, including sea bass in garlic for US$10 and octopus in tomato sauce for US$9.

Playa Corona sits on the provincial border with the Coclé Province 5km from the turn-off from the Playa Río Mar. To avoid missing the turn, look out for a sign heralding the **Hotel Playa Corona** (tel: 240 8037; fax: 264 0872). At the time of writing conflicting reports abound about the future of the Hotel Playa Corona, but the **Cabañas Guicci Resort** (tel: 261 9944; fax: 240 8926; email: guicciresort@hotmail.com) is a viable alternative. Six cabins for two to four people are priced at US$40, close to the swimming pool. The road from the Interamericana leads to a strip of sand edging shallow lapping waves where the water is safe enough for swimming and a small palm-fringed beach is exceptionally clean.

Details of neighbouring Pacific beaches of Santa Clara, Farallón and Playa Blanca can be found in the *Coclé Province* chapter.

Coclé Province

Panama's most visited central region produces more salt and sugar than any other province. It also has more Panamanian presidents to its name, a source of great pride to its people. Yet most visit Coclé for its coastline, mountains and culture; the hat sellers of Penonomé and hand-rolled cigars of La Pintada; Natá's fine church building; the lush green countryside of El Valle; and its colourful Indian-run markets.

Wild orchids (including Panama's national bloom Espíritu Santo), pre-Columbian carvings, waterfalls and tobacco plants dot the landscape in the province, where in the beautiful Chiguirí Arriba area a formation of dramatic cloud-topped peaks towers above countryside rich in wildlife and scenic trails. Further along the Cordillera Central in the National Park Omar Torrijos in El Copé a rugged road navigable only by 4WD leads to some of the most picturesque forests in Panama.

Coclé's coastal stretches west of El Valle range from small speckled beaches to vast silver sands. Manuel Noriega's deserted holiday home and Panama's biggest vacation resort are both found in Farallón while the pretty palm-fringed beach of Santa Clara has a quiet no-frills feel. Salt flats and tidal pools in the dusty Aguadulce attract seals and dozens of species of bird, including the American avocet and black-necked stilt.

PENONOMÉ

This inland town sits right at the province's centre and was founded in 1581 as a *reducción de Indios* to house displaced indigenous Indians forcibly resettled to work the land. Penonomé was named in honour of Indian chieftain Nomé who was executed there by the Spaniards. After Henry Morgan destroyed Panama City in 1671 Penonomé deputised as the capital until a replacement city (now Casco Viejo) was built. Today Penonomé is a lively place filled with good basic amenities that serve a prosperous agricultural community well. One of Panama's most famous presidents, Arnulfo Arias, was born there. He served three terms before his death in 1988 and was the husband of the first female president in Panama and Central America, Mireya Moscoso.

While there isn't much for the tourist to see in Penonomé the town makes a decent base from which to explore the region. Architecturally a mishmash of fast-food outlets, handsome government buildings and a rather unspectacular cathedral, the streets around the market bustle with trading *campesinos* (farmers), market stalls, bars, cafés and cantinas. From a traveller's perspective Penonomé has pretty much everything. There's a medical centre, dentist, laundry (from 50c, Monday to Friday 08.00–18.00), police station, at least three pharmacies, two banks (both with ATM)

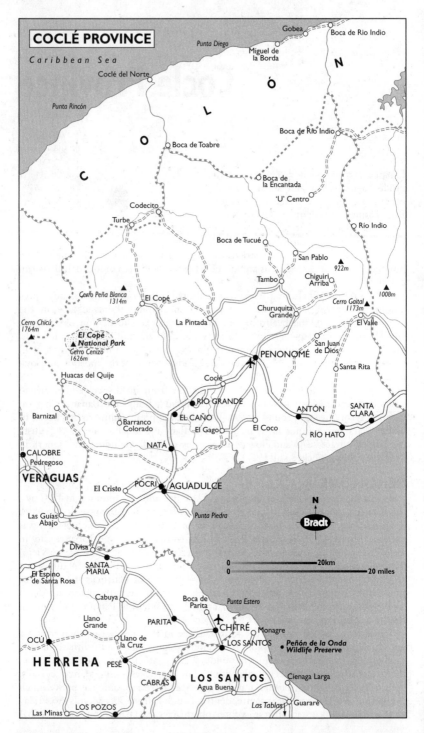

COCLÉ PROVINCE

Caribbean Sea

Gobea
Boca de Rio Indio
Punta Diego
Miguel de la Borda

Coclé del Norte

Punta Rincón

Boca de Río Indio

Boca de Toabre

Boca de la Encantada
'U' Centro

Codecito

Turbe

Boca de Tucué
Río Indio

San Pablo
922m

Tambo
Chiguiri Arriba
1008m

Cerro Peña Blanca 1314m
El Copé

Churuquita Grande
Cerro Gaital 1173m

Cerro Chicú 1764m
La Pintada
El Valle

El Copé National Park
Cerro Cenizo 1626m

San Juan de Dios

PENONOMÉ
Santa Rita

Huacas del Quije

Coclé

Ola

RÍO GRANDE
ANTÓN
SANTA CLARA

Barnizal
Barranco Colorado
EL CAÑO
El Coco

El Gago
RÍO HATO

CALOBRE
Pedregoso
NATÁ

VERAGUAS
El Cristo
POCRI
AGUADULCE

Las Guías Abajo
Punta Piedra

N
Bradt

Divisa
0 ___ 20km
0 ___ 20 miles

El Espino de Santa Rosa
SANTA MARÍA

Cabuya

Boca de Parita
Punta Estero

Llano Grande
PARITA
CHITRÉ
Monagre

OCÚ
Llano de la Cruz
LOS SANTOS
Peñón de la Onda Wildlife Preserve

HERRERA
PESÉ

CABRAS
LOS SANTOS
Cienaga Larga

Agua Buena

Las Minas
LOS POZOS
Las Tablas
Guararé

SOMBREROS PINTADOS: PANAMA'S HAT

Despite its name, the Panama hat (traditionally associated with movie gangsters and cigar-toting millionaires) in fact originated in Ecuador. These soft, cream-coloured hats became known as Panamas during the Canal construction when they proved invaluable in protecting labourers from the intense tropical sun. Panama's own style of hand-woven hat is traditionally crafted in the central provinces but widely available countrywide. A hat can take between 15 days and a month to make and can be so tightly woven it can actually be watertight. Made from palm fibres from the toquilla plant, these hats have become part of Panama's national dress for traditional dance. While women dress in a white lace pollera and wear hundreds of tiny pearls in their hair, men wear a plain cream-coloured shirt and trousers with a handcrafted Panamanian hat. Tipping the brim up is the common style but how it is worn varies from province to province. Panama's hat lacks the flexibility of its Ecuadorean counterpart but the varied patterns make them uniquely Panamanian. Hats are white with black or brown decorative stripes around the rim, patterned according to the area in which each is made. More and more local crafts are now designed with tourists in mind and visitors are just as likely to find one with 'Panama' woven along the side as find a mola sporting images of the Canal. Prices range from US$10 to US$1,000. The pricier models have a silk-like quality and the concentric rings of the weave are hardly visible.

and lots of cheap restaurants. The post office behind the church is open 08.00–17.00 Monday to Saturday and there's a great little market that sets up shop at 04.30 each day. On the outskirts of town there are a number of service stations, vehicle repair shops, hotels and restaurants plus a succession of fruit stalls and hat vendors at the roadside. Famous for its *Sombreros Pintados* (Panama hats) the craftsmen of Penonomé and its surrounds are respected throughout the country for their skill. Intricate hand-woven palm fibres create a variety of styles that are sold in stores and markets all over Panama and worn with great national pride.

Getting there and around

Regular buses link Penonomé with Panama City and arrive from the capital at the bus terminal every 15 minutes or so. Each also drops off and picks up passengers opposite the Hotel Dos Continentes. Getting around the town centre is easy enough on foot and those that need to reach the outskirts of Penonomé can simply flag down a bus as it passes. This is easy given that the town is neatly divided by the Interamericana and there are no shortages of taxis in and around the town. The best places to pick one up are by the central plaza and the Esso garage on the edge of town. Drivers should be vigilant along the Interamericana after dark as local farmers often transport crops unlit on horseback or by cattle-drawn wagon. Several collisions of this type were reported in 2003, some involving tourists.

Where to stay

The **Hotel la Pradera** (tel: 991 0106; fax: 991 0911; email: hotelpradera@cwPanama.net) opened in 2003, a distinctive cream and terracotta building opposite the rice mill on the Interamericana on the outskirts of town. The bar (El Chute) and restaurant are both keenly priced. Each room has air conditioning, TV and a private hot-water bathroom; US$26.40 for a single,

US$35.20 for a double; there is also a swimming pool. Another favourite is the **Hotel Dos Continentes** (tel: 997 9325; fax: 997 9390) opposite the bus terminal, whose restaurant is packed at breakfast (US$4). Lunch and dinner are also good value (sandwiches at US$3–4, steaks US$5.50 and soup US$2.50). Each of the 60-odd rooms has a hot-water private bathroom, air conditioning, and TV. Singles are US$25, doubles US$27.50–30. The Chinese-owned and run **Hotel & Suites Guacamaya** (tel: 991 0117; fax: 991 1010; email: hguacamaya@cwPanama.net; www.hotelsuitesguacamaya@pma.net) on the Interamericana is a vast yellow and white building set back behind a car park. The restaurant serves superb Chinese food (US$4–10). Rooms start at US$22 and overlook some of Penonomé's hat stalls. At the time of writing the **Hotel Fuentes** is just about to open on the edge of town but no details are known (tel: 991 0508). Accommodation at the friendly **Residencial El Paisa** (tel: 997 9242) on the square is cramped and basic but great value at US$7.50–8.50 per person. Other budget options include the **Estrella Roja** a couple of streets behind the square and **Los Piños** on the outskirts of town on the Interamericana. Neither has telephones; both have rooms at US$7–15.

Where to eat
Penonomé has a number of great little local restaurants, fast-food joints and takeaways. **Restaurante Las Tinajas** serves some of the best Panamanian food in the town and is packed at lunchtime serving buffet-style dishes with few items over US$2. Equally busy local is the **Parrillada El Gigante** on the Interamericana (everything under US$3) while the **Chinese Restaurant** (tel: 991 0117) at the Hotel & Suites Guacamaya opposite the hospital has a superb menu with generous set lunches for under US$6.

What to see
The only tourist attraction in Penonomé is the **museum** located opposite the small covered market. The sad-looking rather run-down building is worth a visit for its few good pieces of pre-Columbian ceramic and colonial religious artefacts. Open Tuesday to Saturday 09.00–12.30 then 13.30–16.00, Sunday 09.00–13.00 (US$1 per person).

Festivals
Penonomé is almost as famous for its festivities as it is for its hats. Carnaval is a big event here and brings most of the town's 16,000 residents out for each of the four days leading up to Ash Wednesday. Dances, masks, processions and parades are more colourful and elaborate in Penonomé than in many provinces with celebrations that have lots of pizzazz. Equally popular is the patron saint festival celebrated with vigour over two days in December. Festivities begin with mass followed by a procession through the streets and culminate in a non-stop 48-hour party outside of the church.

Shopping
Penonomé's public market sets up before daylight at 04.30 and closes mid-afternoon. It's a worthwhile browse and mainly sells fruit, vegetables and plants with some other food-stalls, hat vendors and occasionally other Panamanian handicrafts.

LA PINTADA
Lying 10km northwest of Penonomé the village of La Pintada is reached by a road that begins next to the police station on the main square, and winds up through rolling farmland worked by campesinos with machetes. The hills beyond come

fully into view on the approach to La Pintada and offer some unsigned, poorly maintained sloping trails navigable by a 4WD, or on foot during the dry season. Children from the village offer guided walks through the woods for US$1. Most visitors to La Pintada's cigar factory need to ask the way at the shop (red building in the centre) or from local guide Isabel Reina Quiro at the handicraft market (see *Tours and Guides*). Both are happy to act as La Pintada's unofficial tourist office and as well as providing first-class directions also organise cycle hire and hiking.

For a cold drink, a snack and some handicraft shopping call into the **Mercado de Artesanías La Pintada** (tel: 983 0313, open 09.00–16.00) adjacent to the football pitch. Apart from handmade pots and knick-knacks the market has a large range of Penonomé-made hats. Local guide Isabel Reina Quiro (email: reina08pa@yahoo.com or ask for her at the counter) works in the market and is a hat aficionado, taking visitors out to the palms that line the building to demonstrate the picking, drying and weaving process. She is also a keen walker and cyclist and offers guided trips around La Pintada complete with bike hire. Next door a good little Creole–Panamanian restaurant serves great snacks, light bites and ice-cold beers. The **Restaurante Onani** is open 09.00–16.00 and serves chicken, rice and beans for US$4.

According to the locals there were once three cigar factories in the Penonomé area. Today just one remains – the last such facility in Panama. To reach **Joyas de Panama** (tel: 692 2582/634 4437), follow the road southeastwards from the market past Café Coclé on your right. Take the part-grass part-stone track that lies just beyond it and follow it for about 1km to an elevated position on a steep slope surrounded by teak and acacia trees. Look hard between the trees for a corrugated tin-roofed building with a big wooden door with a note on it that lets visitors know they've arrived. Thankfully Joyas de Panama hasn't glammed itself up for the tourists and this gritty hive of activity is just as it has always been. Three workers hand-roll cigars all day at bench tables battered by use in a leaf-strewn workshop without fancy gadgets or machinery. That owner Miriam Padilla is passionate about cigars is evident on arrival, when she gathers up a handful and proudly tells of how the business is more than profit alone. She employed a workforce of more than 60 until 2002 but downsized when the factory began to bring less pleasure and more stress. Today Miriam remains fully immersed in the company she started in 1982 and has 2ha of tobacco plants of Cuban seed. Most of the cigars produced by Joyas de Panama are for domestic consumption although a growing number are being sold to individual export customers worldwide. Prices are competitive and Padilla, who smokes them herself, describes her hand-rolled, hand-cut, hand-pressed cigars as having 'Cuban appeal'. Tours are free and photographers will spot some great potential shots when the cigar-makers are in full swing. A box of 25 of the finest cigars in a wooden presentation case costs US$50 but others are US$1 each sold loose. The only way to mail order worldwide is via **Panoramic Panama** (tel: 314 1417; email: enquiry@panoramicPanama.com; web:www.panoramicPanama.com).

PARQUE NACIONAL OMAR TORRIJOS

Coclé's large expanse of cloud forest spans 6,000ha and sits almost at the geographical centre of Panama. It may not be the most accessible national park but it is one of the most beautiful, offering a tentacle of well-maintained trails through cool highland forest on the Pacific side and a muggier stretch of forest to the Caribbean. Established in 1986 to protect the hydrographic basins of the Bermejo and Marta rivers on the Pacific slope and the Blanco, Guabal and Lajas rivers on the Caribbean slope, the forest is wild, untroubled and rich in wildlife.

A trail system probes into high dense-forested areas to allow incredible views. Rivers, puddles and streams are key breeding sites for Panama's endangered golden

PANAMA'S PETROGLYPHS

There are hundreds of petroglyphs in Panama's central regions. Walk along a stream or take a hike across a field and there's a strong likelihood that you will not be far from one of these strange ancient stone carvings. Finding them is another matter. Many stand weathered in moss-covered anonymity but ask any farm worker or field hand if they've seen one and you'll get a positive response.

Nobody is sure when etching rocks began in Panama. Nor is it certain why. Was the culture that produced this art destroyed by the Spanish Conquest, or were petroglyphs created by an ancient civilisation that rose and fell before the white men came? The evidence is far from conclusive. The petroglyphs in Panama vary in size but in their original state prior to damage and erosion are likely to have been vast chunks of rock. Some sizeable stones remain: large grey masses riddled with hieroglyphics; an indelible inscription of history that has yet to be truly deciphered by archaeologists. Many believe that petroglyphs are a form of map, a theory that is supported by the fact that most etchings have been found on boulders that face water, ancient Panama's principal navigational route.

Other theories are that petroglyphs were used to commemorate festivities and spiritual events. Indeed several comparisons have been drawn between them and the hieroglyphics in Mayan culture. Circular symbols appear to depict the sun and symmetrical characters have been likened to the rain and the earth. Swirls and loops join to form animal shapes and alligators and monkeys are common narratives. Studies have revealed that almost all of the larger carved boulders have craters and channels suitable for blood drainage, giving rise to speculation that they were used for sacrifice. Many petroglyphs have heat cracks thought to be the result of ceremonial fires lit on or around them.

This collection of large ancient stones includes carvings on a boulder the size of a small house. Ask the locals of the meanings of these pre-Columbian etched squiggles and spirals and they'll shrug and point to the skies. Considerable speculation remains about the origins of the petroglyphs. Some look like maps, others like a form of prayer from an ancient belief-system whose meanings are

frog and thickets of vegetation contain rubber plants, orchids and giant ferns. Immaculate antbird, golden-olive woodpecker, white-throated shrike-tanager, red-fronted parrotlet and redheaded barbet have been sighted and puma, American jaguar and tapir maintain a small, but diminishing presence.

The park was named in honour of Panama's populist leader Major General Omar Torrijos, whose illegitimate son, Martin, was elected to office in 2004. The gung-ho general, famous for flying to remote parts of the country in poor weather, crashed in El Copé during a thunderstorm in 1983. A couple of years before his death the general had 'adopted' El Copé, visiting the area on numerous occasions and sponsoring social and economic community projects. Today the National Park Omar Torrijos (El Copé) is his legacy and one that is well cared for. Collaboration between ANAM, US Peace Corps workers and student ecological group Panama Verde has created a trail system that is second to none in the country. Paths lead to lookouts that offer sure-fire views of both oceans. The approach road is a struggle, even in the dry season with a monster 4WD, yet the bumps are worth braving.

An ANAM ranger station is located at the entrance of the park and is open 06.00–20.00. Visitors are charged US$3 (US$5 to camp overnight) and rangers will guide for a tip (tel: 997 90899). For the most dramatic view of both oceans ask for directions to a remote mountain trail. On a clear day it is possible to see farmers lost. According to Neville A Harte, author of *Panorama of Panama Petroglyphs* (1960) and a zealous petroglyph hunter in Panama, many of the carved stones in the central regions have been discovered with coins wedged into cracks and crevices. The coinage is modern as opposed to ancient lending credibility to Harte's suggestion that some communities in the interior regions regard the boulders as more than just large stones. His early findings indicate that gifts of money to petroglyphs are made to bring good luck and fortune. Harte discovered 280 petroglyphs in the central provinces, often travelling by horseback and dugout canoe to access those in remote areas. The stone carvings in La Pintada are some of the largest in Panama including the vast 'Piedra Pintada' (Painted Rock). Of the many symbols yet to be officially deciphered by archaeologists on the isthmus is a drawing that is believed to be a map of the area created by early settlers.

The first Panamanian petroglyph was discovered in 1898 and 55 years later only two others had been found. Discovering more was just the challenge that amateur archaeologist Neville A Harte sought. British-born Harte developed a fascination for archaeology during his childhood after unearthing Roman coins on an ancient site in England before his move to Panama in adulthood to work in the Canal Zone. In 1953 Harte's seven-year search for petroglyphs ensued and it wasn't long before he became renowned throughout Panama for his dedication to the cause. He relied on instinct to lead him to the stones, discovering several buried deep in earth and others in thick vegetation and covered in weeds and vines. He spent up to three days cleaning each petroglyph before carefully outlining each etched design using white chalk. Harte then studied each carving, the boulder and its surroundings, photographing and documenting them in painstaking detail. He was astonished to find that there was no variation in the depth or width of inscriptions on any of the petroglyphs he studied. Each was precisely $1/4$ inch deep and $5/8$ inch wide – an exact measurement that indicated identical tools were used in each carving. Harte spent US$12,000 of his own money on the project between 1953 and 1960.

leading their donkey trains up on the peak of the trail. In the area that surrounds the lookout there are also trails that lead to hidden valleys, waterfalls and wild rivers, many undiscovered by visitors.

Getting there

Reaching this national park requires a 4WD as the five-mile approach road is like a moon crater. First take the turn-off on the Interamericana 18km west of Penonomé and follow the road (and the occasional sign) for 32km. The road is beautifully paved for the first 25km or so but deteriorates alarmingly. Pass the sleepy town of El Copé, set in a deep bowl riddled by a stream, and along the dirt road banked by steep slopes. The entrance and the ranger station are about 7km on.

Where to stay

ANAM has a cabin for use by walkers, birders and visitors to the park that want to stay overnight. It sleeps ten, has bunk beds and basic amenities (US$5 per person, bring sheets). Visitors can also camp in the park for US$5 per night (tel: 997 7538; fax: 997 9077).

Although the **Posada Ecológica** (tel: 983 8900; email contacto@ posadaecologica.com or reservas@posadaecologica.com; www.posadaecologica.com)

in Chiguiri Arriba is a bit of a drive from El Copé it is highly recommended for visitors keen to explore rural Coclé. The journey is a scenic one that winds up a picturesque route into the mountains 45 minutes northeast of Penonomé past cattle fields, pretty villages and up into the gods. While the hotel is nice enough it is the million-dollar views and surrounding countryside that makes the place really appealing. Few settings are as spectacular, atop a verdant summit of sweet-smelling herb gardens overlooking sweeping valleys and soaring cloud-topped peaks.

Surrounding gardens are a botanical delight, attracting dozens of species of birds and butterflies and containing a wide range of plants. A number of trails lead from the lodge out to waterfalls, mountain ledges and woodlands. One path winds through an area of thick vegetation past a lagoon full of tilapia and carp and out into a small forest scattered with orchids. The trail then continues out to a well, said to contain water of curative qualities. Local villagers douse themselves in the water and drink it to maintain good health. It's a strange blue colour due to its high content of copper, magnesium, sodium, potassium and iron, but not unpleasant.

Mule trails stretch from the hotel three hours north to the Valley of Antón, climbing part of the Gaital hill and crossing rivers and reforested hills. Narrow leafy paths enter golden frog habitat also home to three-toed sloth, night monkey, deer and armadillo. Other more arduous trails climb and fall past ancient rock formations and waterfalls, skirting hillsides populated by toucan, hummingbird and numerous butterflies. Take a two-hour trail through the small town of Chiguirí Arriba to the 30-metre waterfall (el Tavidá) where a rocky pool has clean ice-cold water good enough to drink close to a cluster of petroglyph stone carvings.

Room rates vary but range from US$20 Sunday to Thursday for a single to US$75 for a top-notch double with all the trimmings (the choice of former president Mireya Moscoso); mineral and mud spa therapies (US$20–40); restaurant (US$8–12), also a bar.

Around Posada Ecológica

A short walk left of the Posada's main gates leads to a small village of tiny Ngöbe Buglé wood-and-thatch houses. Seasonal land workers that eke out a living from a small number of chickens on the roadside, the community uses woven baskets as coops to keep single chickens. Each basket is elevated to waist height by a wooden stake set in the ground, or is attached to the wall of the house, allowing eggs to be easily released from the bottom. Campers who pitch their tents overnight in nearby woods can buy fresh eggs from the village for breakfast each morning. Ask permission before camping and pay US$2–5 each per night, using the nearby creek for water.

NATÁ

This quiet colonial town is one of Panama's oldest European settlements and comes steeped in tales of gold plunder and slavery. Named after a local Indian chief who was forced to surrender to the Spanish, today the town of Natá is known throughout Panama for its fine church, which dates back to 1522 and is one of the oldest in Latin America. The **Iglesia de Natá** has been well preserved and the building's elegant colonial façade is a fitting entrée to the interior. An altar adorned by ornate Indian-inspired columns depicting winged serpents, fruit, angels and plants is showcased by pine, cedar and hardwood. Visitors that find the building locked should attract the attention of residents in the houses opposite. Someone generally emerges promptly with a key and usually a story or two. During a restoration project in 1995 workers found the remains of three people buried under the floor. Nobody knows who they were and why they were lain there but rumours persist in Natá about further skeletons in the church.

NEW ERA FOR NATÁ

Until 2003 almost everyone in Natá worked within the sugarcane industry. The Nestlé refinery on the edge of town was the major employer, providing locals with long-term year-round contracts at its condensed milk production plant. However, in 2002 Nestlé announced the closure of the plant, citing high sugar and milk prices as the reason for falling exports. At the time of writing Natá is still reeling from the shock, fearful for its future, given that its prosperity and Nestlé were inextricably linked. It is difficult to envisage how the town is going to thrive without the stability the company offered it. Since the announcement the annual sugarcane harvest has been a more sedate affair. Convoys of overloaded vehicles still congest the roadways from January to March but Natá has the air of a town in limbo.

Getting there and around

Natá is located just off the Interamericana and is easily reached by any of the buses that pass along this stretch of highway. The drop-off point is a ten-minute drive from the centre of Natá but it is pretty well served by a local taxi that is parked close by. If he's not in his car the driver is in the nearby café, Restaurante Vega. It's US$1 per person or a 20-minute walk into town, where it is easy to get around on foot.

Where to stay and eat

There are a couple of places to pick up snacks and drinks on the Interamericana near the **Restaurante Vega**. The restaurant serves good, cheap local dishes for less than US$4, including soup at US$1.50 and seafood rice at US$3. A small grocery store and a kiosk are open 08.00–18.00 in the town but the only place to stay is the **Rey David** (tel: 993 5149) on the Interamericana, which comes with good reports at US$23–25 for a comfortable double with air conditioning.

What to see

Only two archaeological sites in Panama are open to the general public and the best is located 8km from the north of Natá about 3km from the town of El Caño. The **Archaeological Park El Caño** contains a large burial site and the five skeletons that were unearthed there in the 1920s remain there for visitors to discover today. The land that surrounds the excavation spot contains a number of stone columns that have been gathered from neighbouring fields and moved into one orderly line-up. The museum promises much but is a real disappointment, housing a tiny collection of pottery pieces, arrowheads and carved stones that are believed to date back to 1500. Unfortunately, the original excavation by an unscrupulous American archaeologist resulted in many of the truly great finds being packed up and shipped back to his homeland. Today this trend continues as this style of pottery becomes more collectable. Foreign buyers are prepared to pay big bucks for a globular or semi-globular pot with a short neck and a slightly flared rim believed to have been used as a vessel in funeral ceremonies. At the time of writing an art dealer in Beverley Hills has a small pre-Columbian terracotta pot from Coclé up for sale at US$8,000. With prices like this it is little wonder that archaeological plunder continues and makes expanding the collection at the museum an uphill struggle. Open 09.00–16.00 Tuesday to Friday and 09.00–13.00 on Sunday, closed Monday. Admission US$1. In the absence of a bus service grab a taxi to El Caño from Natá (US$10–15). The turn-off for the town on the Interamericana is clearly signed but the 3km muddy track can be tricky to navigate in the rainy season.

HISTORY FOR SALE

Panama's National Institute of Culture (INAC) is charged with managing – and recovering – Panama's historical artefacts, but has a poor reputation for caretaking these ancient treasures. Dollar signs and bureaucracy have made it all too easy for Panama's historic collection to slowly disappear. INAC employees have been implicated in numerous thefts from Panama's museums and archaeological sites. The foolish acts of poorly paid opportunists? Not so, it seems, as many have been employees in the upper echelons of senior management.

In 2003 the Judicial Technical Police (PTJ) raided a number of businesses in Panama City, finding 300 pre-Columbian looted ceramic pieces, some of them more than 2,000 years old. Dozens of INAC staff were implicated but only a handful were charged. Several statues were stolen from El Caño in recent years in what appeared to be an inside job. Press reports alleging that the stolen antiquities were driven away from the museum in an INAC car remain unsubstantiated, but make grim reading nonetheless. UNESCO's principal non-governmental adviser, ICOMOS (the International Council on Monuments and Sites), warned Panama that a 'lack of interest and apathy' and 'culture of egoism' put the nation's historic artefacts at risk. In a report submitted to the Moscoso administration it criticised negligence in creating a clear, defined and stable policy in respect to historic sites and said this was causing 'a deterioration of Panama's heritage'.

Festivals

A big event in Natá is the annual Tomato Festival, which brings the crowds in mid-April each year to celebrate the harvest.

AGUADULCE

The stretch of Interamericana that leads in and out of the town of Aguadulce 10km south of Natá is a hive of activity as the end of the dry season approaches. Trucks laden with freshly harvested cane reeds cough and splutter along the dusty highway, crossing over the bridge that straddles the Río Santa Clara scattering dried leaves along the route. Aguadulce (meaning sweet water, a combination of *agua* and *dulce*) is home to several large refineries yet the town isn't just renown for its sugar. Panama's shrimp aquaculture began there in 1974 with the opening of Agromarina de Panama's 34ha facility. Thirty years on, and several shrimp farms later, the country's annual cultured shrimp production exceeds 6,100 tonnes. As cultivated tank and pond production aren't subject to the regulations that govern taking shrimp from the wild, Aguaducle is unaffected by Panama's annual 60-day moratorium. This bodes well for the town's famous jumbo shrimp, which is served in restaurants throughout Panama, and found on every decent Aguadulcean menu.

Another part of the town's agricultural history closed after loosing a fierce price war with Colombian producers in 1999. The salt works of Aguadulce were once the largest in Panama. Today the salt flats that lie south of the town are bereft of workers, but popular with wildlife enthusiasts due to its seabirds and sea lions.

Getting there and around

Aguadulce is 185km west of Panama City, 250km east of David and 10km south of Natá just off the Interamericana. Buses serve Aguadulce from Panama City (three hours, US$4.70) arriving at a stop on the highway just over 1km from the centre of town. The route into the centre along Avenida Rafael Estevez is a prime spot for taxis and at US$1 most arrivals opt for this rather than a hot walk along one of Aguadulce's sun-baked roads. Taxis around town are plentiful (US$1–2). Lots park by the town or sit bumper-to-bumper outside the hospital gates.

Where to stay
There are plenty of modest places to stay in and around Aguadulce from US$10-a-night hostels with cold water and a fan to decent hotel rooms with all mod cons.

The **Hotel Carisabel** (tel: 997 3800; fax: 997 3802) in the centre of town has a bar that hosts regular karaoke parties, a decent restaurant (see *Where to eat*) and a pool. Twenty or so modern, comfortable rooms have air conditioning, TV and private hot-water bathrooms; US$25 for a single, US$30 double and US$35 triple. The **Hotel Sarita** (tel: 997 4437) is a good-value option with 40 rooms that offer a choice of air conditioning and hot water or ceiling fan and cold water. The latter is fine and great value at US$10 for a single/US$12 double; others US$16–23 for a double with TV. There are similar options at the 30-room **Hotel Interamericano** (tel: 997 4363; fax: 997 4975) located on the edge of town close to the bus stop on the Interamericana. The hotel has a great restaurant (see *Where to eat*), a swimming pool and a lively bar and all rooms have hot-water bathrooms and TV (US$26 for air conditioning/US$20 with fan). **The Hotel Plaza (**tel: 986 0788; fax: 997 2888) is also located on the Interamericana and is good value at US$16.50 for a single, US$18.70 for a double and US$20 triple. Both the **Pensión Crystal** (tel: 997 6170) and the **Aguadulce Pensión** (tel: 997 6678) have a number of basic but comfortable rooms at backpacker rates.

Where to eat
There are plenty of places to eat in Aguadulce. Most are along the arterials that lead to and from the central square. **Los Faroles** opens for breakfast, lunch and dinner and is located opposite the church. It serves good-quality local Panamanian dishes from US$4 but is better known for its great pizza (US$2–12). The restaurant has air conditioning but there are also tables outdoors. The **Espiga** is a street-front bakery with outside seating where freshly baked breads, tortilla and pastries cost as little as 15c. It's tucked away a little but the **La Reina** is pretty good for cheap eats with rice, plantain and beans for US$3, shrimp rice for US$4.50 and fried fish for US$5.50 plus burgers, fried chicken and sandwiches from US$2.50. The **Restaurante Caribe** (next to the Hotel Carisabel) serves four different ceviches for less than US$3.50 each, chicken chow mein for US$4 and beef and seafood dishes from US$6. There's a great lunchtime deal at the restaurant at the **Hotel Interamericano** where a two-course special of soup, salad, rice, beans, beef and fried plantains is just US$2.50 per person. The **Restaurante La Oficina** by the bus stop on the Interamericana is a good little stop-off for cheap local dishes (from US$3). Others worth trying are the **Restaurante Barbacoa Barragán** and its neighbour **Los Portales,** but if it's a decent helping of jumbo shrimp noodles you're after, head to the **Restaurante la Gran Muralla China**. A plate that could easily feed two is just US$7.

There are some good restaurants on the road heading out of the town on the route to the saltpans. **El Gallo** and **Marnathy** are close to the Turis Centro adventure park while the excellent **Restaurante Johnny Tapia** is further along overlooking salt flats and shrimp farms. Señor Tapia is a welcoming, jovial character whose restaurant revels in a good long-standing reputation for great seafood dishes. The simple open-sided building is not much to look at but the service is friendly and the food simple and delicious. Johnny Tapia is an entertaining *marisco* aficionado, so expect jumbo prawn salads, ceviche, fried fish and seafood soup for US$2.50–4. Open Friday to Tuesday from 08.00 for breakfast through lunch and dinner until late.

Nightlife

Aguadulce's four-screen cinema, **Cine Mas** (tel: 997 6829), opened in 2000 and shows the latest releases (English and Spanish) to a packed house every night from 17.00. The **Hotel Carisabel** has a calendar of special events that include regular karaoke parties and live music. For thumping dance music, live bands and a dance floor that is packed to capacity head to the **Magic Place** club. This late-night disco is open Thursday to Saturday and offers free admission to women. Entry for men varies in cost depending on the event. If it's a popular band or party night expect to pay up to US$10, possibly more.

Practicalities

The post office is near to the park (open Monday to Saturday, 08.30–16.30) and all banks in town are on the roads that lead from the park. All have ATMS (open 08.30–14.00 Monday to Thursday, 08.30–15.00 Friday and 09.00–noon Saturday). The Cable & Wireless office has the fastest machines (US$3 for three minutes) so head there to email in a hurry (near the McPato burger joint). It also has payphones outside. Opposite you'll find a one-hour photo-processing lab, several pharmacies, shopping plaza and lots of places to get a haircut. There's a police station (tel: 997 4060), fire brigade (tel: 997 0088) and a recently built hospital (tel: 997 5263) .

What to see

The curious **Salt and Sugar Museum (Museo de la Sal y Azúcar)** in the town square doesn't just house artefacts from the salt and sugar industries. It also has a small assortment of pre-Columbian art and a collection of items from the Colombian civil war. Panamanian fighters played a part in the battles that took place during 1899–1903 and the museum has a number of swords and weaponry plus some uniforms. Much of the art collection consists of ceramics which were found in the fields that surround Aguadulce. Open 09.00–16.00 Monday to Friday, 09.00–noon Saturday (Sundays by appointment); US$1

The **Santa Rosa Sugar Refinery (Ingenio de Azúcar Santa Rosa)** is actually 15km west of the town itself but is a worthwhile trek during the peak months of January–March. During this time the refinery runs six-days a week and 24-hours a day, pausing to rest only on Sunday. All of the harvesting is done by hand as Aguadulce's rocky terrain makes it impossible to automate the process. Knowledgeable guides tell visitors that the average American consumes 30kg of sugar each year and the mill first opened in 1991. Three shifts of workers man the refinery (a workforce of 4,000) during the busy months moving to harvest the shrimp farms at the end of the season. Mulch from the sugar cane is used to fire the boilers and molasses, a by-product of the refinement process, is sold to farmers for animal feed and to rum distilleries. Visitors can also see retired machinery and a replica of the original mill-owner's house nearby. Tours should be pre-booked (tel: 987 8101/8102) at 24 hours' notice; available six days a week 07.00–16.00 Monday to Friday and 07.00–11.00 Saturday.

Those travelling to the mill from Aguadulce will spot the signed turn-off for the mill along the Interamericana on the right-hand side, opposite a service station. Follow the road for a short distance (less than a kilometre) to reach a white gatehouse manned by a security guard who guides visitors to the mill. A taxi from

Aguadulce will cost about US$15 one-way (US$25 for the return trip and the driver waits). All buses that pass along the Interamericana will drop off at the guard's post. It's a 1km walk from there to the refinery along a picturesque tree-lined path.

Salt flats, **marshlands** and **shrimp farms** on the southern side of town are popular with wildlife lovers. These fertile wetlands attract flocks of feeding birds and the tidal ponds and brackish soils are rich in weeds and crustaceans. Sea lions can be seen in the deep saline lakes between rocks and mangroves as well as small amphibious and fish species.

The area, a 10–15-minute drive from the town, is not served by a bus. A taxi (US$10) is one option. Another is the free transportation shuttle that ferries visitors back and forth between a pick-up point at a restaurant opposite the church and **Turis Centro** (tel: 977 3720), a rather naff, but fun, adventure playground. It leaves on request 11.00–23.00 daily to take visitors to the roller-skating rink (rent skates for US$1.50 per day), BMX track (rent bikes for US$1 an hour), volleyball court, lake with paddleboats and kayaks (US$6 an hour) and a decent bar and restaurant.

The prettiest salt flats and famous tideland pools of Aguadulce are 4km on from Turis Centro, past the Restaurant Marnathy and a couple of hundred metres from Johnny Tapia's restaurant. The pools – or *Las Piscinas* as they're known – are manmade craters in the middle of some rocks surrounded by rather murky-looking wet sand. Once the tide is out they are accessible and full of water, allowing visitors to take a dip while soaking up views. This beautiful if desolate spot is home to American avocet and yellow-tilled tern.

Festivals

Aguadulceans like to party, especially during Carnaval (the four days before Ash Wednesday) and during the annual celebrations in mid-October to honour the founding of the town, a three-day festival involvingparades, floats and a lot of music and dancing. An altogether quieter celebration is the Aguadulce patron saint festival in July.

ANTÓN

This sleepy little town is full of surprises, from its breathtaking surrounding countryside to its gay Mardi Gras. Panama's central regions are renowned as a hotbed of conservatism, yet picturesque Antón has earned a reputation Panama-wide for its liberal stance. In a country where homosexuality remains a sackable offence, it was something of a surprise when Panama's gay community gained government permission to host a gay parade in peaceful Antón. Roberto, a 28-year-old hairdresser, was crowned its queen and the town gained extensive media coverage for its gay-friendly attitude. Aside of this recent notoriety Antón is a quiet unassuming town, remarkable only for the splendid scenery that surrounds it. This lush valley at the foot of the Campana Mountains sits amidst sugarcane plantations, cattle ranches and rice fields. A blue and white plaster dolphin welcomes visitors to the town which itself has a bank, a couple of local restaurants, a service station and a grocery store but few urban attractions. Most who pass through have their sights set on the countryside beyond and a well-maintained paved road that loops Antón is popular with mountain bikers and hikers.

Getting there and around

Antón is approximately 25km east of Natá to the north of Penonomé on the Interamericana about 15km from Farallón.

Where to stay and eat

Only a couple of the accommodation options in Antón are worth considering. The 16-room **Pensión Panama** (tel: 239 3163) on the Interamericana has sparsely furnished but comfortable rooms with cold-water bathrooms for US$12. The **Hotel Rivera** opposite (tel: 987 2245) has 30 rooms with air conditioning, TV and private bathrooms at US$20 for a single and US$30 double. A handful of small local restaurants in the centre of town by the square serve standard fare for less than US$5.

Events and festivals

The population of Antón plan all year for their annual folklore festival, Toro Guapo. This three-day celebration takes place in October and begins with mass and culminates in a traditional bullfighting ritual. Dances, floats and palm leaf decorations celebrate cattle. Anón's patron saint festival is another big event, in January (13–16).

RÍO HATO AND FARALLÓN

The stretch of Interamericana that forms the approach road to the town of Río Hato forms the gateway to Coclé's picturesque coastal area. Noriega vacationed in the area and his former holiday home, now derelict and abandoned, forms a forlorn contrast with new real estate springing up along the shoreline. Where the Río Hato ends and Farallón begins is a question of much debate, as the two seem to merge together. Yet while Río Hato is a pretty uneventful small town comprising a couple of small hotels and local restaurants with a bar that doubles as a strip club at weekends, Farallón is home to the largest resort in Panama and is a town Panamanians associate with the good life.

A disused airstrip signifies the road to the Royal Decameron Beach Resort, passing a runway once used by Noriega to deploy his infamous PDF troops (Panamanian Defence Force) throughout Panama. The road and the airfield run parallel into Farallón where a turning leads to Noriega's overgrown vacation home. Windows are broken and tiles smashed and it is only the proliferation of bullet holes that provide a reminder of its past.

An **IPAT tourist office** (look out for the flag pole) is housed in a pristine pink and white building set back behind a neat square of green lawn. It boasts the best stock of relevant leaflets in Coclé and also has a video of the highlights of the area. Open 08.30–16.00, Monday to Friday.

Once past the airfield compound you can safely assume that you're in Farallón, once little more than small cluster of houses but now a stretch of million-dollar holiday homes with security fences. Most Panamanians associate Farallón with the Royal Decameron Beach Resort (see *Where to stay*), a giant complex located about 1km or so from the IPAT office. A security gate beyond a National Car Rental sign is designed to keep anyone out who isn't a holidaymaker. Ordinary folk without an all-inclusive ticket will find the sand just as nice at neighbouring Santa Clara.

Where to stay

The ten-room **Hospedaje Las Delicias** (tel: 993 3718) on the Interamericana 1km west of the turning to Farallón is a good little budget hotel with comfortable beds and a choice of fans or air conditioning (US$US12 or US$15). At the other end of the scale is the sprawling **Royal Decameron Beach Resort** (tel: 993 2255; fax: 993 2254), which caters for all-inclusive holidaymakers from Canada, the US and its Central American neighbours. Rates vary from season to season and are more expensive for foreigners and anyone who hasn't pre-booked. A weekend rate of US$99 per person per night is based on two people for a minimum two-night stay. A single is US$89 per person on a weekday and US$119 over a weekend but new special rates and packages are added frequently. Panamanian nationals pay US$36. Breakfast, buffet lunch, afternoon tea and buffet, à la carte dinner, plus all snacks, cigarettes and drinks are included. Umpteen daily activities (aerobics, dance classes etc) and all non-motorised water sports are also included in the price, such as windsurfing, kayaking boating, snorkelling and sailing. Six restaurants serve Thai, Japanese, steak, Italian, Mediterranean and seafood dishes. Each standard room has two double beds, hot-water bathroom with shower, air conditioning and satellite TV. The hotel has a car rental office, a money exchange service and 24-hour doctor. It also offers mountain bike, 4WD and motorbike hire as well as guided tours throughout the region. The long stretch of silver sand beach is pretty and palm fringed but can be windy. Another downside is that the water is often too rough for swimming and can be prone to jellyfish.

EL VALLE

This fine-looking country town is a popular weekend destination for Panama's outdoor-loving urbanites. Arrival is via an elevated approach road that offers dramatic views across peaks and a forested valley. The town is huddled in the crater of an enormous extinct volcano; a hollow so vast that it is less geologically obvious than it sounds. This 5km concave is one of the largest in the Americas and is dated at least three million years old. Today El Valle is a tranquil place that is blessed with many beautiful natural assets: cool lush woodlands, mountain streams and waterfalls, verdant mountain slopes and a liberal scattering of flowers that far outweighs the number of tourists.

Getting there

Buses to El Valle leave Panama City daily from 07.00 for the 2½-hour trip and a return bus serves day trippers quite well, departing El Valle at 16.00. Buses pick up and drop off along Avenida Central. Almost every tour company in Panama City offers a sightseeing day trip or excursion to El Valle often in conjunction with Coclé's beaches.

Driving to El Valle can take less than two hours on a good day (1½ hours if the roads are empty and the weather clear). Avoid doing the journey on a Friday or Sunday evening unless you're happy to join a long queue of weekenders. Roads are also notorious for traffic police on speed-check patrol. The winding approach road to El Valle from the Interamericana is dotted with tiny Ngöbe Buglé handicraft stalls and signs hawking places to stay. It morphs into Avenida Central and it is along this main arterial that most of the restaurants, cafés and hotels are located.

Getting around

There is no real town centre in El Valle but getting around is simple using the Avenida Central as the backbone and where taxis and guides tout for business all day. A journey to anywhere in El Valle is US$2 by taxi and bikes can be hired from the Hotel Campestre (tel: 983 6146/983 6460) and from a shop a couple doors down from the Don Pepe restaurante. Several places hire out horses (just look out for the signs that say '*Alquilier de Caballos*' and one of the best value is run by Mitzila Espinosa (tel: 646 5813) who owns a small kiosk in El Valle. Choose from half a dozen horses for guided or solo rides (08.00–18.00) at US$3.50 per hour.

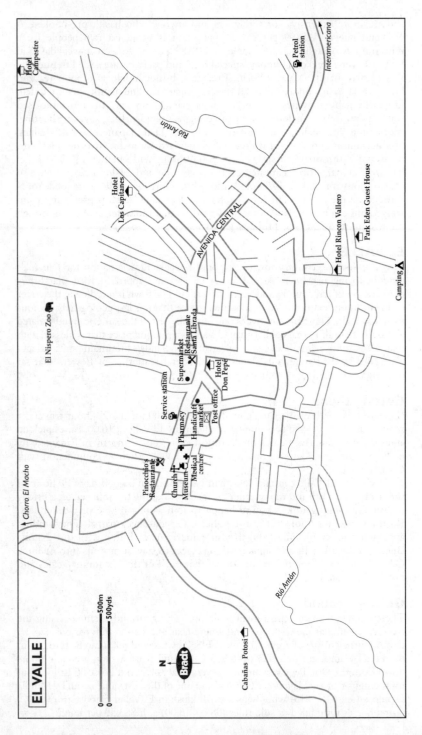

EL VALLE

N

Bradt

500m
500yds
0

Interamericana

Petrol station

Río Antón

Hotel Campestre

Hotel Los Capitanes

AVENIDA CENTRAL

Hotel Rincon Vallero

Park Eden Guest House

Camping

El Níspero Zoo

Chorro El Macho

Service station

Supermarket

Restaurante Santa Librada

Hotel Don Pepe

Pharmacy

Handicraft market

Post office

Pinocchio's Restaurante

Church

Museum

Medical centre

Río Antón

Cabañas Potosí

ESPIRÍTU SANTO

Panama's national flower has a centre that resembles a white dove emerging from the surrounding petals. The likeness is startling. Espíritu santo has been given various epithets over the years including Holy Ghost and White Dove and has so far not been found in any other country. Legend suggests the name stems from Spanish Friars who discovered the tiny flower after their arrival in Panama in the 15th century. They believed the pure white flower with dark red specks on its 'wings' symbolised the white dove of the New Testament. Espíritu santo blooms once a year during the months of August and September and is mainly found in the cool, fresh climes of El Valle de Anton and the Boquete valley.

Where to stay

Prices tend to be a higher in El Valle than in other parts of Coclé, but the town still has its fair share of budget options and a number of places to camp. Visitors that arrive without accommodation will find the IPAT tourist office of limited practical help. A better idea is to look out for the hoardings at the entrance into town. Billboards and road-signs advertise numerous B&Bs. Signs tucked in the hedges point the way to off-the-beaten-track cabañas.

Rooms above the **Restaurante Santa Librada No 1** (tel: 983 6376) on Avenida Central have a private hot-water bathroom and sleep three at US$15–20 a night. The **Cabañas Potosi** at the western end of El Valle has four basic two-bed cabins for US$30 each and plenty of green space for a number of tents. Camping facilities include showers and a toilet and a two-person tent can be supplied on request (US$10) and meals by arrangement (tel: 983 6181; fax: 264 3713). Rooms at the **Hotel Campestre** are also surprisingly good value at US$25. It's the oldest hotel in El Valle close to 'square trees' and several mountain trails. There's an onsite restaurant, a bar and bikes and horses for rent. However, it is the three large cabañas in the grounds that provide the best budget option. Each sleeps four or five and costs US$60. Other accommodation at backpacker rates includes cabins at **Los Mozas Cabañas** (tel: 983 6071), **Cabañas Bambú** (tel: 983 6251), **Hotel Greco** (tel: 983 6149), **Cabañas Giselle** (tel: 983 6507; fax: 983 6604) and the **Motel-Restaurante Nina Delia** (tel: 983 6110). The facilities at El Valle's **Panama Campsite** (tel: 983 6750) on the edge of town are said to be good value at US$10 a night. **Residential El Valle** on Avenida Central has a dozen attractive rooms with cool tiled floors above **Restaurante Santa Librada No 2**. Rates range from US$25 for a double to US$40 for a quadruple and include a TV with cable and a private hot-water bathroom. The **Hotel Don Pepe** (tel: 983 6425; fax: 983 6835) also has 12 comfortable rooms priced at US$35 Monday–Thursday and US$45 Friday–Sunday. The hotel has a TV room and a small laundry where guests can wash and dry a load for US$1. It also has an internet café.

Travellers with an open-ended budget will find that El Valle offers some interesting options. **The Hotel Rincón Vallero** (tel: 983 6175/983 6968; email: rinconvallero@sinfo.net; www.rinconvallero.com) has a lovely garden setting with streams, pools and paved areas and ornamental ponds. There are 14 ground-level rooms that include five spacious suites. Each has air conditioning, hot-water bathroom, telephone and cable TV and a choice of garden or pool views. The hotel's cosy restaurant and cocktail bar are popular hangouts with weekenders from Panama City. Prices start at US$75 for a double room or US$105 for a suite that sleeps four. Five gorgeous rooms at the **Park Eden Hotel** (tel: 983 6167/226

PURE GOLD

The golden frog (*Atelopus zeteki*) is one of Panama's most recognisable cultural symbols. Its image is everywhere, appearing on billboards and websites, and used to market any number of consumer items from calendars to key rings and T-shirts to lottery tickets. Hundreds of commercial enterprises in Panama use the frog as their logo and golden frog bracelet charms are one of Panama's most popular items of jewellery.

Yet this love affair with the golden frog is no modern-day fad. Pre-Columbian indigenous communities revered the species, crafting gold and clay talismans of this iconic amphibian. The frog was considered a symbol of fertility and prosperity and remains the subject of mythological speculation. According to Ngöbe Buglé legend the golden frog transforms into gold when it dies so those seen in possession of a frog during life are said to have good fortune after death.

Visitors to El Valle will need to head to the hills for any hope of spotting Panama's famous frog in its natural habitat. The species is endemic to Coclé but has been on the endangered list for decades and catching a glimpse of this remarkable creature in the wild is pretty rare. However, trekking the mountain paths is a more appealing and preferable prospect than seeing this species in cages in the town.

6849; email: parkeden@cwPanama.net; www.parkeden.com) come with video and cable TV, porch and stoned back terrace. Prices include a full Pan-American breakfast and a hearty afternoon tea. Guests also have full use of barbecue areas and terraces and can rent bikes or book tours through the owners US$65 for a twin and US$120 for a suite. Another appealing B&B is the **Hotel Los Capitanes** (tel: 983 6080; fax: 9836505), which has ten rooms with every conceivable mod con including TV, video, hot-water bathroom and charming décor. There's also a top-notch restaurant and lounge with cable TV. Suites from US$70.

Few places to stay in El Valle are as impressive as the **Crater Valley Spa Resort** (tel: 215 2330/215 2328; email: ventas@crater-valley.com; www.crater valley.com), a grand old building behind a formal stone gated entrance. A lounge area has a small library stacked with travel guides and a vast wall-mounted map of Panama. The spa and yoga, meditation and relaxation classes (US$5 each) are almost as popular as the hotel and attract a mix of guests and ages. The hotel is partnered by PEX (Panama Explorer Club; tel: 983 6939; fax: 983 6243; www.pexclub.com) and offers the best range of adventure tours in El Valle. The gardens are stocked with medicinal plants and herbs used in the in-house tea infusions and spa therapies. Rooms vary so ask to see a few, from US$75 to US$95 including breakfast and use of whirlpool and pool.

Another stylish option is **La Casa de Lourdes** (tel: 983 6450; email: golosinas@cableonda.net) a stunning reproduction of a Tuscan villa that looks like it's been in El Valle for generations. The owners, Edmund and Lourdes de Ward, describe it modestly as an upmarket family hostel, but this beautiful property wouldn't look out of place in a glossy magazine. Handpicked furniture comes from all over Latin America and includes antiques and tiles from Colombia and fabrics from Mexico. A library full of books on Winston Churchill belies Señor de Ward's British ancestry. Guest accommodation is either a cabaña in the grounds, US$195 per night for four persons (or US$150 for two persons) including breakfast or a room in the main house (prices vary). Panamanian

Lourdes de Ward studied Political Science in England before becoming one of Panama City's best-known restaurateurs. The Casa de Lourdes restaurant is open for lunch and dinner and is well worth a splurge.

Where to eat
The **Santa Librada Restaurante No 1** (tel: 983 6376) on Avenida Central serves a good hearty breakfast for US$3. Its sister restaurant, **Santa Librada No 2** is equally recommended and both are open from 07.00 until late and serve standard Panamanian fare. Most dishes are under US$4 and the *sancocho* (chicken soup) and chicken rice (US$3.50) are big in portions and taste. The **Restaurante Don Pepe** also specialises in Panamanian classics with a big menu of seafood and chicken dishes. Most are less than US$8 and the lunchtime special (usually beef and rice) is as little as US$5. Open for breakfast at 07.00 until late. The restaurant and cocktail bar at **Hotel Ricón Vallero** (tel: 983 6175; fax: 983 6968; www.rinconvallero.com) is magical in the evening, when moody lighting reflects on a carp pond in a handsome leafy setting of tiled floors and exposed brickwork. Not as expensive as it looks with dishes at US$8–10. For fast food and cheap pizza try **Pinocchio's** which serve burgers and fried chicken for less than US$4 and a man-sized pizza 'with everything' for less than US$6. El Valle also boasts one of Panama's finest restaurants, **La Casa de Lourdes**, a stylish eatery in a statuesque recreation of a Tuscan villa about 1km from the centre of town. The menu is a fusion of European and Latin American. Soups are US$3.50–5, appetisers US$5.50–6.50 and main courses US$8.50–15; not cheap but a steal for a meal in one of the most celebrated restaurants on the isthmus.

Shopping
El Valle is an important market town for the dozens of indigenous Indian communities in the surrounding mountains. Ngöbe Buglé, Embera, Kuna and Wounaan villagers bring their wares to sell each weekend and the colourful **markets of El Valle** are famous countrywide. Customers come from miles around to buy fruit, flowers, vegetables and handicrafts. Ngöbe Buglé carved woods and soapstone figurines sell for less than US$10, with Embera basketry, beautiful hand-stitched Kuna molas, Panama hats, hammocks, flower pots, wooden furniture, bamboo birdcages, orchids and painted ceramics also available. Bright pink, yellow and violet blooms meet green and red parrots under a sky-blue ceiling. Street vendors also sell rotisserie chicken and freshly grilled sweet corn. Open 08.00 to 18.00 Saturday and Sunday with a smaller fruit and vegetable market throughout the week.

LOS ARBOLES CUADRADOS
There's a wooded area behind the Hotel Campestre where locals insist that there are trees with square trunks. Indeed many are so adamant of their existence that when they sense a hint of disbelief they'll volunteer to show you. The trail that leads to the thicket begins at the right-hand side of the hotel, just behind and to the right of a small building. The trail is signposted and muddy but easily accessible and it's about a five-minute walk to the trees. Are they square? Well, not that this tree-spotter noticed. There was a clump with trunks that showed some subtle signs of flatness. Look for the signs for 'Los Arboles Cuadrados' to check it out for yourself.

Other practicalities

There are a couple of pharmacies, a police station and a 24-hour health clinic on Avenida Central as well as a bank (no ATM at time of writing), grocery store and plenty of shops aimed at tourists. The post office is open 08.00 to 16.00 each weekday and is located behind the market. The IPAT tourism office (tel: 983 6474) is open 08.30–16.30 each day but is a disappointment. The Chinese-owned supermarket, Super Centro Yin Market, in Avenida Central stocks pretty much everything you can think of from safety pins to soft drinks and is open until late.

What to see and do

Tourism is fast rivalling agriculture as El Valle's chief source of income and employment and many of the shops and services in the town cater exclusively to the needs of the visitors. Several local landowners and farmers rent to campers and horseriders and the surrounding landscape is ideal for walkers that don't mind digging around for a trail to follow. IPAT, Panama's tourist agency, opened an office here in 2003 and should at least be able to supply a map. Tourist-savvy hotels in the area are all clued up on the best birding and walking trails. Each place to stay has a number of recommended local guides.

At 600–1,000m above sea level the crater and surrounding slopes and forests are well worth exploring. A riddle of **mountain trails** lead up Cerro Pajita, Cerro Gaital and Cerro Cara Coral to the north to heights of 1000m (3,281ft), while Cerro Iguana and Cerro Guacamayo to the south, Cerro Tagua to the east and La India Dormida to the west are at about 800m (2,625ft). Most have been cleared for pasture except Cerro Gaital and Cerro Pajita and both remain thickly forested and are often shrouded in cloud. In the foothills of Cerro Gaital (behind the Hotel Campestre) El Valle's famous 'square trees' are found (see *Los Arboles Cuadrados*)

El Valle legend centres on a mountain the locals call the Sleeping Indian Girl (*La India Dormida*) and the fable is a tragic one of forbidden love and death. He was a Spanish Conquistador and part of the army that was trying to bring the land under the rule of the king in Madrid. She was the daughter of a local Indian chief who was fighting this invasion. Knowing their love could never be she took her own life. Legend has it she is merely sleeping in the hills and will someday awake and locals insist one of the mountains resembles a girl lying on her back gazing at the skies. Legend aside, La India Dormida is a great place to hike. A muddy trail leads to La Pintada through lush vegetation and past tiny wild orchids. Another winds through rainforest streams, fruit farms and past sugar mills to the crater for breathtaking views before returning past ancient burial grounds.

At the time of writing the only company in El Valle to offer **adventure tours** is the Panama Explorer Club (PEX) (tel: 983 6939; fax: 983 6243; ww.pexclub.com). Hiking, mountain biking and rappelling are offered as packages and one-off tours and it runs training programmes for guides. The company is a member of the International Ecotourism Society and is owned by Californian ecologist Kathryn Herold. Guiding is led by Daniel Burene a former member of the US military with jungle operation and rescue mission training. Guides are experienced extreme sport specialists with equipment that meets high safety standards and the company claims an unblemished safety record during its 15 years in business.

Wet rappelling tours run year round and include a three- to four-hour trip that allows a gentle descent along a beautiful stretch of rainforest under waterfalls into the pool below. The cost is US$20 per person from El Valle, including transportation, guide, equipment and refreshments.

Hiking opportunities are endless and range from a one-hour walk on gentle slopes to a full-day hike on challenging terrain. A four-hour trek through moderately hilly rainforest trails costs US$20 and includes the services of a guide and refreshments.

PEX offer two standard year-round **mountain bike** excursions both around the village and the mountains of the El Valle crater and along rainforest trails. One allows a slower pace to savour the scenery, another is a more exhilarating trip along bumpy dirt roads and rainforest tracks. PEX use high-quality Alpine mountain bikes with 27-speed gearing and front suspension. Prices start at US$10 for two hours and there are few better ways to experience the El Valle countryside.

El Valle is the hometown of one of Panama's most respected **birding and botanical** guides in Panama. Mario Bernal comes highly recommended and is an award-winning naturalist and a passionate environmental campaigner. Bernal is president of Conserva, a conservation group in El Valle, and an ecological adviser to the Panamanian government. His family own Cabañas Potosi at the western end of El Valle and he can be contacted there (tel: 983 6181; fax: 264 3713) or by booking through **Panoramic Panama** (tel: 314 1417; email: enquiry@panoramicPanama.com; www.panoramicPanama.com).

The beautiful **El Chorro Macho** (the Manly Waterfall) is the largest in the region at 80m and is located at the western end of town. It's open 08.00 to 17.00 seven days a week and is an easy 15-minute walk from the centre of El Valle. The entrance to the waterfall is next to the office of the Canopy Adventure (see below) and visitors have a choice of taking a long trail for US$2.00 or a shorter one for US$1.00. Both offer good photographic opportunities especially around the base of the waterfall. This deep pool is a great place to take a dip at US$2 per person and is surrounded by rocks amidst great jungle noises in the middle of a private wildlife refuge.

Another way to take in the vista at El Chorro Macho is via the adjoining **Canopy Adventure** (tel: 983 6547; www.canopytower.com). The experience is difficult to define but is part-sightseeing part-adventure activity using a harness and a hand-held slide suspended from treetop cables. The slide is activated by hand pressure and grip, allowing visitors to move through the rain forest canopy. The cables link several treetop platforms and pass over a stream and waterfalls through forests rich in wildlife. Canadian and Dutch specialists spent seven weeks installing the system and training local guides in its use, while an American husband and wife team of former Peace Corps volunteers spent four months constructing the network of trails through the rainforest. The Canopy Adventure is suitable for all ages and fitness levels but it certainly helps if you're agile and not afraid of heights. It shares the same owners as the highly recommended Canopy Tower in Panama City (see *Panama Province* chapter). Expect to see rubber trees, tarantula nests, ant colonies, three-toed sloth, orchid and countless birds and a glimpse of a blue morpho butterfly. The complete Canopy Adventure tour costs US$40 (with discounts for groups) and US$15 for a three-hour guided walk through the forest. Visitors with limited time should consider pre-booking as queues can be long and capacity is limited.

Dipping in and out of the **Pozos Termales** (thermal springs) in El Valle is a great way to spend an afternoon and at US$1 entrance it's a favourite hangout for travellers on a budget. About half a dozen sunken pools full of thermal water at differing temperatures are said to have curative properties. Alongside, a line of tubs contain cooler volcanic mud rich in natural minerals said to soften and replenish tired skin. Visitors to the pools 'take to the waters' before covering themselves from head to toe in mud. Each pool is linked by stepping stones or a boardwalk and is located at a different elevation amidst rocks and vegetation. It's a popular detoxification ritual with the younger backpacker crowd while older visitors swear by it for arthritis and rheumatism. Bring swimming gear, towels and your own refreshments. The grounds have plenty of shady spots in the leaves in which to read a book or recuperate. Ice-cold showers ensure the worst of the gooey stuff is removed. The covered picnic area has tables and benches and there is a small kiosk, toilets and changing rooms. Open 08.00–17.00 (closed one hour for lunch) seven days a week. Guides are at hand to walk visitors through the gardens and explain the therapeutic benefits of the mud and waters – there's no charge, just tip.

The **El Valle museum** and its collection of religious art is nothing to get excited about. It is open just one day a week (Sunday 10.00–14.00, 25c) but the church that owns it is a more interesting building. This plays host to an annual classical event to honour St. Joseph and has excellent acoustics with numerous international symphonic orchestras visiting as part of an exchange programme organised by Asociación Nacional de Conciertos (www.conciertosPanama.org) each year.

Visitors would do well to ignore all the tourist-office hyperbole concerning **El Nispero**. It may spout eco-tourism and conservation ideals but don't be fooled into parting with dollars on the promise of an ecological experience. El Nispero is a zoo (and a pretty forlorn one at that), the brainchild of two Panamanian businessmen who cultivated the land into an exotic garden in 1978 and filled it with native and non-native wildlife. For US$2.00 visitors can wander through gardens amidst ducks, monkeys, hawks, peacocks, deer, ocelot and turkeys that include several species from Asia. Despite being one of Panama's best plant nurseries other aspects of El Nispero are truly distasteful. A succession of poky cages that house boas and golden frogs in cramped conditions is especially unpleasant. El Nispero's fondness for cages blights the picturesque gardens but while tourists are willing to visit in their droves there are few incentives for change.

SANTA CLARA

The small community of Santa Clara is located just 10km from the beginning of the approach road to El Valle. However, its dry, scorched landscape forms a stark contrast to the lush valley of the crater town. Santa Clara's closest neighbour is Farallón, just 2km further southwest along the coastline, yet this pretty little seaside town is more relaxed than the all-inclusive playground. Comprising little more than a few sun-baked roads lined by clumps of frazzled-looking trees overlooking the shoreline, Santa Clara's rum shacks, beach bars and holiday cabañas are surrounded by brightly coloured bougainvillea. Volleyballers, beachcombers and horseback riders enjoy the sand while fishermen throw a line from the shore. Rent a hammock for US$2, a thatched beach hut for US$5. Use the amenity block (showers and toilets) for US$1 and enjoy a great cocktail for US$4.

Getting there

Numerous buses pass by Santa Clara on the Interamericana and the best option is to jump off at the turning and catch a waiting taxi into town (ask the driver to drop you either at the beach or at the town). The turning to the town leads to the two main hotels and tourist amenities. The beach is less than 2km from the Interamericana turning. A taxi ride in and around Santa Clara costs US$2.

Where to stay and eat

The charming, rustic two-storey cabins at **Las Veraneras** (tel/fax: 993 3313; email: lasveraneras@cwp.net.pa) boast a great location less than 200m from the ocean. Each has a thatched roof and a double bed on the ground floor and an upper single, at US$55. A beach cabin for four people with a TV and fan costs US$40. A larger one for seven or eight is US$110. Camping is great value at US$5 per person to pitch close to the beach. The restaurant at Las Veraneras serves good cheap eats all day from breakfast at 08.00 (US$2) to dinner at 21.00 (US$5–7).

Another great little place is **Las Sirenas** (tel: 993 3235; fax: 993 3597), which has a dozen self-contained suites with bright, modern décor and individual barbecue terraces. Each has a kitchen and lounge area and is a three-minute stroll from the beach; US$80 for two to three persons and US$100 for a cabin for eight.

To find the **Restaurante Jacob** on the outskirts of town look out for the blue swordfish that sit nose-to-nose at the entrance. Shaded outside tables have a steak and seafood menu (and ever so occasionally sushi), it's clean and pleasant but more expensive than some at US$8–14 a dish.

Don't be put off by the need to ask for directions to the impossibly tucked-away **Restaurant Puerte a la Alameda**. The setting is unusual and the food highly recommended at US$8–12 a dish. The restaurant is located in the middle of manicured formal gardens in the grounds of a private mansion house. There are signs from the Interamericana and the turning is on the left-hand side as you approach Santa Clara from El Valle.

Another out-of-town eatery is the **Restaurante Los Camisones**, which boasts a great little elevated plot on the Interamericana surrounded by shrubs, flowers and palm trees. Exceptional Spanish fare lures city dwellers to this small town diner. Find the restaurant on the right-hand side of the road on the journey from El Valle to Santa Clara and expect to spend at least US$12, US$17 with wine.

For snacks and cheap eats head to the **Restaurante La Fogarta**, a cosy open-sided restaurant serving burgers, seafood and sandwiches for US$2.50–4.50. Further along a sandy track is **Pipa's Beach Bar.** Pass by wood-and-thatch huts and look for a big red and white sign to reach it and see the driftwood sign near by. Listen for the reggae music if you're in doubt as it often plays all day. This fun place to be is decked out in funky colours and with great sea views, cold beers and a chilled-out ambience is popular with tourists and locals alike.

158

Herrera Province

This interior province sits in the centre of the Azuero peninsula in a region viewed as a custodian of Panamanian folklore. As Panama's smallest province (2,341km²) it tends to be overlooked by tourists yet what Herrera lacks in dimensions it makes up for in culture and tradition. Nowhere else in Panama is the Spanish legacy so strong or celebrated with a host of Hispanic fiestas that dominate the annual calendar. Fair-skinned people belie European descent and while it has one of the highest population densities in the isthmus few Indian communities exist in the province. Most Herreraens are farmers, distillery workers or herdsmen that work in the rolling savannahs and sun-baked plains. Distinctive local handicrafts include pottery, festival masks, drums and jewellery, while the sleepy town of Ocú has an age-old hat-making tradition. For the spirit of Spain head to the pretty town of Parita for the traditions of Conquistadors and bull-roping fiestas amidst red-roofed Spanish-style houses.

CHITRÉ

Most visitors to Herrera stay in the province's capital Chitré, named in honour of an ancient Indian chief. A bustling fiesta town within easy reach of all major attractions, Chitré has numerous places to stay and eat with plenty of options for those on a budget. Crowds swell over Easter and Carnaval when hotels reach bursting point as people from all over Panama arrive for Herrera's legendary fiestas.

Getting there
By road
The Interamericana joins the Carretera Nacional (also known as the Carretera Central and the National Highway) at the small town of Divisa, the road 36km southeast to Chitré parallel with the coastline.

By air
Twice-daily **Aeroperlas** (tel: 315 7500; fax: 315 7580; email: iflyap@ aeroperlas.com; www.aeroperlas.com) flights connect Panama City with Chitré seven days a week. A weekday service connects Chitré with Colón, David and Contadora. Flights depart Panama City at 07.40 and 16.00 Monday to Saturday (40 minutes, US$35 one-way) with one Sunday departure at 16.15. Chitré's airport is located at the northeast end of town.

By bus
Chitré's busy bus terminal is located 1km south of the town centre, a US$2 taxi ride or a 25c bus journey from a pick-up point behind the square. It serves as a

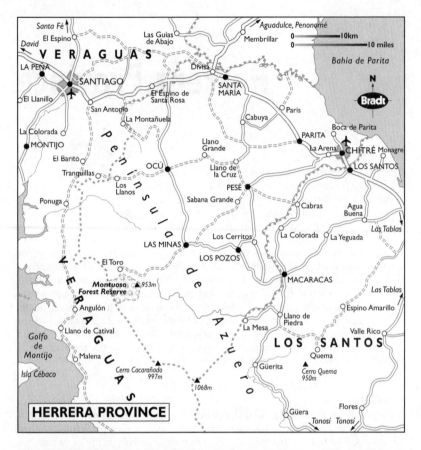

Santa Fé
El Espino
David
Las Guías de Abajo
Aguadulce, Penonomé
Membrillar
0 ————— 10km
0 ————— 10 miles
V E R A G U A S
LA PEÑA
Divisá
Bahía de Parita
SANTIAGO
SANTA MARÍA
N
Bradt
El Llanillo
El Espino de Santa Rosa
Cabuya
Paris
San Antonio
La Montañuela
Boca de Parita
La Colorada
Llano Grande
PARITA
La Arena
CHITRÉ Monagre
MONTIJO
OCÚ
Llano de la Cruz
LOS SANTOS
El Barito
Tranquillas
Los Llanos
PESÉ
Sabana Grande
Cabras
Agua Buena
Ponuga
P e n í n s u l a
Los Cerritos
La Colorada
La Yeguada
Las Tablas
LAS MINAS
LOS POZOS
d e
El Toro
MACARACAS
Las Tablas
Montuoso Forest Reserve
▲953m
A
z
u
e
r
o
Espino Amarillo
Angulón
Llano de Piedra
Llano de Catival
La Mesa
Valle Rico
Golfo de Montijo
V
E
R
A
G
U
A
S
L O S   S A N T O S
Quema
Malena
Güerita
Cerro Quema 950m
Isla Cébaco
Cerro Cacarañado 997m
▲1068m
Güera
Flores
HERRERA PROVINCE
Güera
Tonosí Tonosí

transportation hub for the region and runs frequent services to the rest of the province and beyond. Two private operators offer a daily schedule to and from Panama City with hourly departures 06.00–18.00 at US$6 for the four-hour journey (**Transporte Tuasa** tel: 996 5619 and **Transporte Inazun** tel: 996 1794). Frequent local buses serve Pesé (US$1, 20 minutes), Las Tablas (US$1, 30 minutes), La Arena (25c, 5 minutes) and Playa Agallito (50c, 10 minutes) throughout the day.

By taxi

Lots of good cheap taxis in Chitré are easy to find prowling the main streets and congregating at the edge of the square. Expect a journey around town to cost US$1, US$2 to head to the outskirts.

Where to stay

Three family-run pensións offer the cheapest rooms in town and at the **Pensión Herrerana** (tel: 996 4356) they are basic but clean and have a shared or private cold-water bathroom and fan, US$8–10. The **Pensión Chitré** (Manuel Correa; tel: 996 1856) is the same price and has six singles/doubles of varying size with ceiling fans and cold-water bathrooms. The 15-room **Pensión Central** (Avenida Herrera; tel/fax: 996 1856) just a few doors down from the church is great value at US$10–12 with rooms that have cable TV and hot water.

The **Hotel Versalles** (tel: 996 4422; email reservaciones@hotelversalles.com; www.hotelversalles.com) is a decent if over-bureaucratic roadside hotel with a pool, bar and restaurant. More than 60 rooms have air conditioning, cable TV, telephones and hot-water bathrooms; US$28 for a single and US$38 double. Some are damp so ask to see a few before committing.

The **Hotel Barcelo Guayacanes** (tel: 996 9758; fax: 996 9759) is Chitré's newest option located on Carretera Nacional on the edge of town. Easily the nicest and the most expensive it is not bad value for all mod cons at US$32.73 for a single and US$42.08 double, including a breakfast that seems to never end.

The **Hotel Hawaii** (tel: 966 3534; fax: 996 5330) has 30 comfortable rooms with air conditioning, cable TV, phone and hot-water bathrooms for US$20–35. Twenty nice rooms at the **Santa Rita Hotel** (tel: 996 4610) have hot-water bathrooms and a restaurant, bar, phone and fax service at US$14 for a single with a fan and US$16–25 for singles/doubles with air conditioning.

The **Hotel Hong Kong** (tel: 996 4483) is favoured by the hordes of city dwellers that descend on Chitré during holiday time and is fully booked already at festival time until 2007. Located on the Carretera Nacional with comfortable rooms and guest suites, two swimming pools, a bar and great restaurant (see *Where to eat*). Rates vary throughout the year but expect to pay US$30 for a single or double and US$80–90 for a suite that can sleep five to eight. Despite being sited in the middle of Chitré, past guests say rooms at **Hotel Rex** (tel: 996 6660; fax: 996 4310) aren't subject to late-night noise. Thirty-two have air conditioning, private hot-water bathroom and telephone and the hotel also has a popular restaurant, nightclub and bar. Expect to pay US$17–20 for a single, US$25–30 for a double.

Where to eat

Chitré is famous for its fish, which is exceptionally fresh and astonishingly cheap. In fact most of town's restaurants offer great value for money. Find them in the roads that lead off the square and along the Carretera Nacional on the approach into town.

DKDA's on the outskirts of town serves great Creole food and seafood for less than US$3 according to the locals. For good-quality Panamanian dishes served

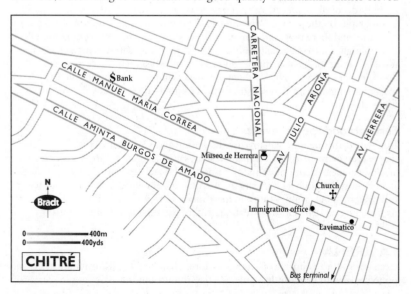

buffet style try **Restaurante La Estrella** opposite the church, which opens early (05.00) and will pack up breakfast for those keen to hit the road; US$3.50–US$4.50. The **Restaurante y Parrillada Vicente** 300m south of the square serves excellent Chinese food at pleasing prices, including three set menus for two at US$5.50 per person. Visit the **Restaurante y Refresqueria Aire Libre** for a great breakfast at outdoor tables (US$2.30) while **Burger Pollo** is a good pit stop for hotdogs and chicken burgers at US$1.50. **Restaurante El Meson** at Hotel Rex serves some pretty good paella for US$5–6 but few places beat the **Restaurante Yully** 100m east of the church for value with Panamanian beef, chicken and rice dishes served buffet style for less than US$1 an item. Open early until 18.00 daily.

Practicalities
There are numerous pharmacies, seven banks (all with ATMs), camera shops and at least half a dozen laundries in the centre of Chitré. Payphones mark practically every intersection and there are plenty of places for a haircut, a decent wet shave (50c) and shoe repair (US$1) just off the square. Chitré is expanding rapidly and new internet cafés seem to be opening up (and closing down) each month. One of the most established, Micro World Systems (tel: 996 1596), has a small air-conditioned office with shop frontage located 400m west of the park; 20 machines at US$1 per hour, open 08.00–21.00 Monday to Saturday. The Thrifty Car rental outlet at the airport (book online and check out special offers at www.thrifty.com) comes recommended and there are several car repair shops and service stations on the Carretera Nacional. Chitré has a police station (tel: 996 4333), ten clinics, a hospital (tel: 996 4444) and a part-time dentist (ask at the hospital) and has a cinema in the centre of town, open every evening from 17.00.

What to see
The **Museo de Herrera** (open 09.00–16.00 Tuesday to Saturday and 09.00–noon Sunday) close to the square opened in June 1984 and is housed in Chitré's old two-storey post office building. Ceramic, folkloric items and artefacts from the archaeological sites of Sarigua and Monagrillo make up most of the collection with several decorative pieces of pottery that date back to the Conquistadors. Photographs on the second floor show local artisans making handicrafts and festival costumes and there is also an exhibit of the costumes themselves, admission US$1.

Although Chitré's elegant 18th-century church **San Juan Bautista** has just a few remaining original features following a refurbishment project in the 1980s, don't let this put you off. Vast stained-glass windows, beautiful polished wood, ornate carvings and an altar section flanked by gold-edged frescos are worth seeing. Open daily.

Festivals and special events
Renowned throughout Panama for its Easter and Carnaval celebrations, Chitré draws crowds from all over Panama each year. Celebrations are lively, involving all-day parades, plenty of drinking, music and water soaking. The Fiesta de San Juan Bautista on June 24 honours the patron saint of Chitré with a religious service followed by mock bullfighting and merriment. On October 19 the town celebrates its founding in 1848 and the streets are full of parading musicians and historic and folkloric pageants.

LA ARENA
Consisting almost entirely of ceramic factories, handicraft stalls, artisan markets and pottery stalls this pretty little hamlet is a five-minute bus ride (25c) or US$2 taxi trip

from Chitré, or a 40-minute walk uphill. Once there, it is possible to watch potters at the wheel at one of the small factory outlets. One of the best places to do this on the basis of friendliness alone is at **Ceramic Calderon** just off the Carretera Nacional. The owner, Angel Calderon, is a genial host who welcomes visitors to his workroom and gives tours of ancient backyard ovens. Since his two children have grown up to become a musician and a teacher, Angel has grown increasingly concerned that his craft faces an uncertain future. To encourage others to take up pottery he runs workshops and offers tuition to locals and tourists interested in learning the art. Angel was 11 when his grandfather taught him how to make ceramics and has been creating traditional pottery in La Arena using a foot-operated wheel for over 50 years. He sells his brightly painted pieces from a small showroom at the front of the workroom seven days a week year-round. He lives with his wife in the adjoining house, so simply knock on the door if the workshop is unattended.

A handful of places serve snacks on a shoestring in La Arena and many outside **cafés** serve food all day. Heated food cabinets on the kerbside are piled with ready-to-eat *tortilla de maize*, *patacones* and grilled *carne,* while two Panamanian kitchens serve rice dishes for under US$4. Kiosks sell cold drinks and beers just along from the row of craft shops. Pots, leather sandals, hammocks and souvenirs can be found at the indoor Venta de Artesania market. Aside from some rather naff tourist trash it also has beaded jewellery from 25c.

The **Empresas San Pablo** is a shop-fronted bakery set back from the road behind a high fence and mature gardens. Visit in the morning for the best selection (it bakes at 04.00) and be spoilt for choice by a range of sweet pastries, cakes, desserts and freshly baked breads (eat in or take away). A small exhibition of local folkloric items and some outdoor seating are in the grounds. Look to the right of the building to see an ancient stone *trapiche* once used in the making of *seco Herrerano,* Panama's potent national drink. Arrive before lunch for a chance of a tour.

Herrera's only **IPAT tourist office** (tel: 974 4532; fax: 966 8040) is located in La Arena and is one of the most useful in the whole of Panama. The pristine apricot-coloured building occupies a conspicuous location on the Carretera Nacional and has a display of exhibition boards dedicated to the heritage and culture of the region on the second floor. The office has more leaflets and information than most (ie: it has some) although the suggested things to see are pretty formula. At the time of writing the office has plans to offer tourists free internet use in a purpose-built internet café in the IPAT building. Open seven days 08.00–16.00.

PLAYA EL AGALLITO

This stretch of sandy mudflat 7km from Chitré consists of banks of silt deposits from the River Parita and River La Villa. Locals helped to create this 'beach' by cutting back the mangroves and today the vegetation that fringes the murky saline pools is ragged and sparse. Most visitors to Playa el Agallito are there for the birdlife, which is nothing short of spectacular pretty much year-round. At low tide the flats are exposed for at least 2km and attract thousands of feeding birds. It's the only place in Panama where the common ground dove is found and hundreds of species have been sighted on the saltpans, including egrets, spoonbills, yellow-crowned amazons, Forster's tern, yellow-billed tern, black-necked stilts, white-winged doves, Wilson's phalarope and stilt sandpipers. Most of the birds are migratory and return to the fertile sands of Playa el Agallito each year.

At high tide the ponds to the east of the mudflats fill with congregations of birdlife and this sheltered spot is an ideal place to view birds en mass. To the north of the mudflats is the Humboldt Ecological Station, run by scientist Francisco

Delgado, an eminent ornithologist and conservationist known in Panama as 'the Professor'. Delgado and his group of students and volunteers have been recording data on birds that visit the Herreranas coast since the 1980s. Most species arrive from California, Vancouver and Anchorage and the Professor manages the monitoring of species and numbers of migratory birds on a month-to-month basis. More than 15,000 birds have been fitted with ID to allow analysis of the bird population. Francisco Delgado discovered the azuero parakeet (*Pyrrhura eisenmann*) in 1979 and it was duly named after Panama's most distinguished native ornithologist, Eugene Eisenmann of the American Museum of Natural History. Projects at the station are collaborations with scientists in America, Canada and Alaska and among the items at the 'Estación Ecologica Alejandro von Homboldt' are migratory route maps and information about the species that pass through Agallito.

Francisco is evangelical about his work and is a part-time lecturer at Santiago University in the neighouring province of Los Santos. He makes no bones about his crusade to educate the population of Panama on environmental issues and hosts a radio show on Radio Reforma (17.00–18.00 Monday to Friday; www.radioreforma.com) and is a regular speaker at seminars, conferences and ecological rallies. He is also campaigning to save the endangered macaw (see *Conservation* and *Giving Something Back*). Birders and conservationists are welcome at the station but should contact Delgado prior to arrival (tel: 996 1725 (home); email: Delgado.Francisco@hotmail.com). Messages can also be left for the Professor at the small café next to the mudflats; ask for Frederico (tel: 996 1820).

Getting there
Playa el Agallito is served by a frequent bus from Chitré between 06.00 and 18.00, which departs from the main bus stop every 30 minutes (50c one-way). A taxi from the square will cost US$3–4, US$2–3 if you travel straight to Playa el Agallito from Chitré Airport.

PARQUE NACIONAL SARIGUA
Visiting the 8,000ha Sarigua National Park can stir up a host of conflicting emotions. Established in 1985, the area is one of complete deforestation; a barren, stripped and desolate place, the result of slash-and-burn and failed agriculture. Cutting down the forest left the ground cruelly exposed to the elements. Wind has removed all traces of soil leaving an expanse of naked terrain that even heavy annual rainfall cannot penetrate. Fissures gouge an amber terrain that the tourist board describe as an exotic 'desert,' yet lateritic soil and cacti give this forlorn place the feel of Death Valley.

However, it's not all doom and gloom at Sarigua National Park, which today serves to remind Panama of the devastating effects of poor land management. Bleak saline scrubland attracts a scattering of gulls where deciduous forest once grew and although wildlife is scarce in this environment, pelicans have been sighted as well as 162 species of migratory bird. Vegetation quite unlike any other in lower Central America consists of prickly pear, acacias and other xeric-adapted trees. A harsh climatic sequence of searing heat and downpours has also unearthed some fascinating archaeological finds and Sarigua is emerging as one the most important pre-Columbian sites in Panama.

Getting there
Sarigua National Park is 10km north of Chitré and like all of Panama's protected areas is managed by government agency ANAM. The ANAM station (tel: 996 8216) is at the edge of the park (open 08.00 to 16.00, entrance is US$3) and

wardens are often able to offer basic accommodation at a lodge at the far end of the park for US$5 per person. The park is well signed from the Carretera Nacional. It is not served by public transport but a taxi from Chitré costs about US$10 (US$20–25 for the round trip and it will wait).

REFUGIO DE VIDA SILVESTRE CENEGÓN DEL MANGLE

Herons nest at this 1,000ha mangrove conservation area close to Parita and the Cenegón del Mangle is prime bird habitat. Manned by an affable park ranger on weekdays (08.00–16.00) who is passionate about marshlands, guided walks are a joy for the price of a small tip. Created in 1980 to protect mangroves in the boggy basin at the edge of the Santa Maria River, the park has boardwalk trails past nesting sites and visitors can also caiman-spot in the mangroves by boat (weekdays and weekends by arrangement). Small natural craters (*Los Positos*, meaning little holes) full of water are used medicinally to treat rheumatism and arthritis. Patients with gastric complaints also ingest these curative waters. According to the ranger, scientists from Panama University studied the water in 1999, and validated its therapeutic benefits and medicinal powers. Several observation points and a viewing tower look out over black and white mangrove species. Expect to see caiman, iguana, duck, roseate spoonbill, yellow-billed cotinga, wood stork and even the elusive jabiru.

Getting there

No bus serves this mangrove conservation site, which is a 45-minute journey north along the Carretera Nacional from Chitré. Drivers should take the turn off to the village of Paris and at the church in the centre take the right fork road. A rough dirt track leads from here with an arrow sign to guide you after 4km. After this it's another 1.9km until the refuge; look for the hut at the entrance. US$20 by taxi from Chitré.

PARITA

Take a stroll around this charming Herrerean town through streets of colonial buildings, just 10km northwest of Chitré but a world away. Pretty Spanish-style houses with scrubbed steps and flower-filled gardens are pleasing on the eye and much of Parita's architecture dates back to at least the 18th century. Some have red-tiled roofs and others ornate porticos and wrought-iron gates. All give Parita the feel of a bygone era. Properties in this sedate little town have become all the rage with Panama's urbanites and prices in Parita look set to boom. However, locals claim that their town is 'less changed' than any other in the province. Folklore, culture and tradition are keenly upheld and the town is home to one of the most magnificent carnivals in Herrera.

Parita resident Denis de Girón lives opposite the church of Santo Domingo. Once a teacher in Parita she has lived in the town for 35 years and has fulfilled the role of unofficial welcoming committee-cum-tourist guide to visitors since her retirement. Señora de Girón is a warm character with plenty of tales to tell. Don't be too surprised if she offers you a meal or a drink if you seek her out, which is highly recommended to those that plan to visit.

What to see
Santo Domingo Church

What sets this church apart from many is a steeple perched above the entrance of the door. Locals say that it is only a matter of time before the doorway caves in but pray hard that it won't. It was built in 1723 and has inlaid mother-of-pearl which townsfolk swear lights up Parita when there is a power cut. Although the building has undergone extensive refurbishment over the years much of its early character remains. Many of the original features have never been cleaned or painted in a bid to limit damage and most of the interior is unaltered. Thick wooden building struts were embedded with funeral casks during the 1800s and an unmarked coffin was discovered in 1972 under a ceremonial table.

Religious artefacts and exhibits housed in a small room in the church building, the **Museum of Religious Colonial Art of the Santo Domingo,** can be viewed by the public Monday to Friday 08.00–16.00. More fascinating, however, is a visit to **Rodriguez-Lopez,** a small workshop opposite, where visitors get the chance to meet the men behind Panama's beautifully restored church altars. The business (next door to Denis de Girón's home) is owned and run by twin brothers José Sergio and Sergio José Lopez and their friend Macario José Rodriguez. Renowned throughout Panama for their knowledge of colonial churches, the trio's specialist skill is in high demand in a country with several hundred fine examples. This, Panama's only such workshop, is a real hive of activity. All three men are more than happy to show visitors around; just call into the workshop between 08.00 and 16.00.

Festivals and events
A rectangular piece of grass next to the church provides the venue for many of Parita's festivals. August 3–6 is when the town's patron saint festival (**Santo Domingo**) begins with mass and is followed by mock bullfights and bull lassoing in the centre. Thousands of people cram into Parita. Terraces become ten people deep with a front-row seat at a premium requiring early arrival to stake a claim at dawn. Parita Day is another big party on August 18. Streets fill with floats, horses and carriages and a procession of marching bands to honour the founding of the town in 1558.

PESÉ
Ask most Panamanians about the sleepy town of Pesé and they will tell you about crucifixion and hard liquor – but don't be alarmed by these satanic-sounding references. For not only is Pesé the birthplace of the nation's favourite tipple, Seco Herrerano, but it is also the venue for an annual re-enactment of Christ's death on the cross. Both have made Pesé a household name in Panama and crowds flock to the religious festival held there on Good Friday. A small town surrounded by acres and acres of sugarcane fields about 20km from La Arena, Pesé is the home of one of the best-known producers of seco, Varela Hermanos. This traditional Panamanian company has a lengthy history in Pesé. Indeed the founder of business, Don José Varela Blanco, also founded the town, arriving in Panama as a young Spanish immigrant in 1908 and building a house on a piece of land he named Pesé. Next he opened a sugar mill, the first in the recently created Republic of Panama, and in the same year the Ingenio San Isidro sugar refinery was born.

The sugar plant was a profitable business and Don José had nine children. In 1936 his older sons, José Manuel, Plinio and Julio asked their father if he'd allow them to start a distillery business, using the sugarcane juice from the Ingenio San Isidro sugar refinery to produce liquor. He agreed and before long the sons were producing seco from a garage adjoining the sugar mill. Before his death Don José bequeathed his business to his children and made them promise that they would maintain the cultivation of sugarcane for liquor production as a family heritage. The company was renamed Varela Hermanos (Varela Brothers) and today, almost a century later, a third generation heads up the business, which has offices in Ecuador, America and Costa Rica and factories in Pesé and Panama City.

Yet despite its great success Varela Hermanos (tel: 217 3111/3727; email: aburgos@varelahermanos.com; www.varelahermanos.com) refuses to abandon

DANGERS ON THE ROAD

Statistically one of the worst weeks to travel through Panama and its Central American neighbours is Holy Week, the traditional Catholic holiday that falls between Palm Sunday and Easter. Fatality figures hit a high over this fiesta-filled holiday period as highways feel the force of a massive surge in inter-city travel and alcohol consumption levels peak. At least 427 people were killed and more than 2,000 injured in Central America during the Holy Week in 2003, according to police and medical reports. El Salvador topped the list with 131 deaths and 1,600 injuries, while Costa Rica and Panama suffered a combined loss of 51 people. Driving accidents in Panama aren't wholly related to alcohol as public consumption is prohibited over the holy weekend and most bars and restaurants are closed. Suicide rates are thought to rise during Holy Week due to the alienation of individuals from their families during this time. Another contributing factor in Panama is the onset of the rainy season and its impact on road conditions. The Easter holiday also coincides with dangerous riptides on the Pacific coast.

the town adored by its founder and the company remains one of the most stable and prosperous Panamanian-owned companies in the country. Visitors are welcome at Varela Hermanos but for a tour of the production facilities it is advisable to let them know in advance. Only sugarcane grown in the Pesé valley (no place has better climatic conditions according to Varela Hermanos) is used in production, which ferments cane juice to an extra-neutral alcohol, before turning it into seco via a special recipe of filters, natural flavourings and sweeteners. An on-site shop stocks seco in every conceivable size and quantity priced from 38c to US$8 and while the Pesé plant mainly produces and bottles Seco Herrerano it has some rum production too. Look for a white two-storey building with brown shutters and a balconied top floor. It's easy to spot, well signed and everyone you ask will know it.

Getting there

A regular bus serves Pesé from Chitré and stops at umpteen places on the way, so be prepared for delays. Advertised as a 20-minute journey it could easily take twice that on a busy day, departing every 20 minutes at US$1 per person.

OCÚ

An old hat-making town now somewhat overshadowed by Penenomé, Ocú's handmade creations are shipped and sold throughout Panama in some of the finest stores in the land. Once a busy place frequented by buyers, traders and haulage companies, modern-day Ocú is quiet backwater town. Now that most of the frenzied hat-buying activity in Panama is concentrated on the Interamericana, the hat-makers of Ocú sell through a co-operative to a distributor. Most sell for US$25–200, depending on the quality, and buying direct is the best way to get a good deal. In Ocú all hat-makers work from home so ask around for directions. Someone will know someone that knows someone…

Getting there

Ocú is 22km from Pesé and is reachable from Chitré by an hourly bus (US$2). The journey takes just over an hour.

Practicalities

There are several family-run hotels in Ocú, including Habitaciones de Juan Pablo (tel: 974 1312) on the outskirts of town. Look out for a flag and sign on the roadside to the left as you approach from the Interamericana. Rooms cost US$10 per night and have a fan, two beds and a bathroom. There are a handful of decent local restaurants, a couple of kiosks selling sweets and drinks, a bank (09.00–15.00 Monday to Friday, 09.00–12.00-noon on Saturday, no ATM), a post office (08.30–16.30 Monday to Friday), a couple of car repair shops, a service station and a laundry.

Festivals and special events

Two famous annual festivals take place in Ocú and both draw visitors from across Panama. The three-day **Festival del Manito** is renowned as Panama's best folklore fiesta and is a showcase for Herrera's culture, traditions and heritage. Every folklore group participates in the festival, dancing in traditional dress and parading through the town. Dates in August vary each year so check with IPAT in La Arena (tel: 974 4532; fax: 966 8040). Ocú's patron saint festival, January 15–20, is another event that draws the crowds and culminates in a burning effigy of St Sebastian.

Los Santos Province

Synonymous with nationalistic fire and strongly upheld traditions, Los Santos forms the third of the central provinces with neighbouring Veraguas and Herrera. A heartland of a folk culture the locals call *cultura típica*, Los Santos and its people are passionate about all things Panamanian. Gutsy festivals draw visitors from the furthest reaches of the isthmus, while Panama's national dress – the ruffled, layered, full-skirted *pollera* – is hand-stitched here and sold countrywide. The exportation of this culture is an important economic sideline for Los Santos, as traditional farming industries struggle on land plagued by drought.

Yet empty beaches and islands mean the province isn't just cowboys and culture, and a growing number of visitors are discovering Los Santos' coastal charms. Wildlife reserve, Isla Iguana, comprises 55ha of unspoilt habitat and a reef that contains 13 of the 20 coral species found in the Eastern Pacific. One of the five most important turtle-nesting sites on the planet, Isla Caña, attracts more than 10,000 turtles to its shores during August and November. The long stretch of coastline between Pedasí and Tonosí has dozens of great surfing and wildlife beaches, and is nicknamed 'the Tuna Coast' for an off-coast congregation of tuna that makes it a favourite with sport-fishermen.

LOS SANTOS TOWN

Villa de Los Santos, the town of the saints, sits on the banks of the River Villa at the province's northern tip. Enter from Chitré and leave the Herrera Province behind at the bridge on a stretch of Carretera Nacional that marks a regional border. Originally named Santa Cruz, the town boasts a heroic and historic past. The first seeds of independence from Spain were sown here and the resulting 1821 declaration earned Villa de Los Santos (or simply 'Los Santos' as it's known by the locals) a lasting honour. Cry of Independence celebrations on November 10 see this quiet town spring to life. Several handsome colonial buildings and a genteel pace make Villa de Los Santos a pleasant base from which to explore southern Herrera or upper Los Santos Province.

Getting there and around

A good, frequent service links Chitré with Los Santos dropping off and picking up at a well-signed bus stop on the Carretera Nacional. A good fleet of local taxis serve the town and its surrounds (US$3 across town). Hail them on the Carretera Nacional or find them parked in the centre of town near the church.

Where to stay and eat

Just two hotels serve Villa de Los Santos and the Hotel La Villa and Hotel Kevin are as different as chalk and cheese. **Hotel La Villa** (tel: 966 9321; fax: 966 8201)

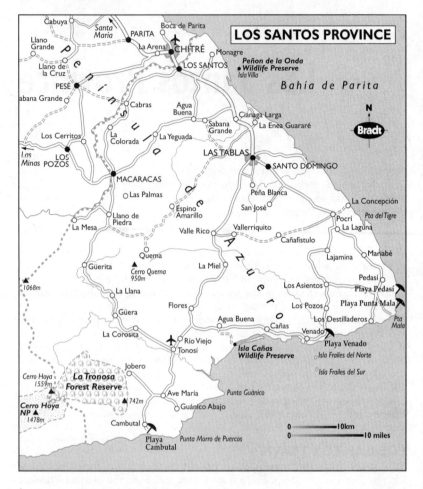

is an old sprawling hotel with a regular domestic holidaying clientele that adore its 38 rooms, pool, restaurant, bar and dark wooden interior. Rooms start at US$32 a night and rise to over US$50 in peak season. Owners are friendly, the restaurant good (open for dinner) but the décor a little on the gloomy side. In contrast **Hotel Kevin** (tel: 966 8276; fax: 966 9000) is a bright, new, modern single-storey motel-style complex with 20 pastel-coloured units set around a lawn. Prices vary throughout the season but start at US$15 for a double, US$19 for a triple and rise to US$30–35 and the little seafood restaurant serves seafood dishes from US$5–9. The owners seem to take pity on cash-strapped backpackers; one German budget traveller had her bill reduced to US$5 a night.

Local tour companies

Guides and tours can be booked at the **IPAT tourism office** (tel: 966 9013; fax: 966 8040; open Monday to Friday 08.30–16.00) beside the park. Check on festival dates here (they vary each year) and pick up a basic list of local hotels. State-owned environment agency **ANAM** (tel: 994 0074; fax: 994 6676) can offer guides for the price of a tip, also permits, transport and ranger accommodation in the conservation refuges in the province. Staff can also advise on the best ways to access and explore the **Peñón de la Onda Wildlife Refuge** located to the east of Villa Los Santos. Designated an area of ecological importance in 1984 this 3,900ha reserve comprises mangroves, beaches, dunes and thermal waters. ANAM has maps and information on how best to access the nesting sites of shore and sea birds. Rangers have sighted blue-footed booby, Audubon's shearwater, Sabine's gull, brown noddy, sooty tern and brown-footed booby. A rare black noddy has also been spotted.

Shopping

Mask-making is an important Los Santos tradition and a frenzy of year-round activity is vital preparation for the colour-packed festivals. Elaborate costumes have kaleidoscopic papier-mâché masks as a focal point, each simulating a dragon or a serpent and replete with coifs of coloured feathers. IPAT can arrange visits to local maskers, all of whom work from home. One of the most accessible and most renowned is Carlos Ivan de Leon, a creator of vivid masks that border on the ghoulish. Used in the famous Dance of the Dirty Devils (*baile de los diablos*), this showpiece of the Corpus Christi festival derives from a Catholic ritual used to teach the principles of good and evil. Masks can be seen in an exhibit at the IPAT office but to buy find Carlos. Each mask takes two weeks to make, sells for US$150+ and is fast becoming collectable in America. Visits are by appointment only (tel: 966 9149) or call into the IPAT office.

Other practicalities

Los Santos has plenty of local amenities, including at least one service station, several supermarkets, a tourist office, pharmacies and a handful of local restaurants and bars. Banks have ATMs and there is also a medical centre, fire service and police station. A laundry (open 08.00–18.00 Monday to Saturday, 09.00–noon Sunday) provides a same-time service for US$1.50 per load.

What to see

While the museum in the centre of Los Santos (**Museo de la Nacionalidad**) looks promising, its collection is meagre. Some exhibits relate to the declaration of independence but most are pieces of pre-Columbian and religious art. However, the building itself is magnificent, a crumbling 18th-century brick-built residence

DISH OF THE CENTRAL PROVINCES

Generations of Panamanians have grown up nourished by *sopa de sancocho*, a thoroughly traditional chicken broth that originates from Panama's rural interior provinces. The traditional recipe for sancocho uses gallina patio (garden-raised chicken), yam, ajo (garlic), culantro (coriander) and seasoning. Nothing else is added. If you find other ingredients in your bowl, say locals from the interior, you are not eating true sancocho. Find bona fide sancocho in *fondas* (tiny local cafés) that cook Panama's traditional comida: rice, beans and fried chicken. Generally served with arroz blanco (white rice) sancocho is believed to be one of Panama's healthiest dishes, able to cure an assortment of ailments, including hangovers. Many regions now have their own varieties, adding practically anything to the cooking pot. Root vegetables such as otoy and yucca are common additions, while the province of Bocas del Toro adds pigs' tails.

DANCE OF THE DIRTY DEVILS

Typical *baile de los diablos* (dance of the dirty devils) costumes consist of red and black trousers (made from strips of cloth sewn together in a chevron pattern), a papier-mâché mask and a headdress made from macaw tail feathers. Children participate using wing feathers, although red plumage is the most highly prized in this deep-rooted provincial tradition that is famous countrywide.

Red macaw are endangered in Panama but a diminishing population remain illegally hunted for feathers, most of which are sold to costume-makers. In a bid to conserve remaining birds, Panamanian professor and ornithological campaigner, Francisco Delgado (see *Playa Agallito, Herrera Province* chapter) issued an impassioned international plea, asking anyone with macaw feathers to send them to him in Panama. Within days thousands of feathers began arriving in parcels, incurring a formidable pile of paperwork and incurring triple-digit postal charges in the process.

Delgado's solution was to provide a 'bank' of reusable feathers available for hire to bona fide dancers of the dance of the dirty devils, thus preventing the need for further culls. Launching an education programme for schoolchildren to promote the use of goose, pheasant and artifical feathers as substitutes, his efforts soon helped depress the scarcity value of macaw plumage, deterring professional hunters. A staggering response saw 4,000 feathers sent from the UK alone. The initiative continues: contact Susan Armitage, Tyr Ywen Farm, Mamhilad, Pontypool, Gwent NP4 8TT, UK; email: susan.armitage@virgin.net.

that was once a prison and schoolhouse and where the Declaration of Independence was signed. Explore the garden for local handicrafts and rusting old farming tools. Open Tuesday to Saturday, 09.00–16.30 and Sunday 09.00–13.00, US$1.

Nearby **Iglesia San Atanasio** took almost a decade to build (1782) but the result is a stunning example of baroque-style architecture with many fine features. A gold-leafed altar adorned with figurines and flanked by carvings is especially well preserved, surrounded by a large religious wooden statue and dozens of artefacts.

Special events and festivals

To honour the signing of the Declaration of Independence from Spain in Los Santos in 1821, the Cry for Independence ceremony is celebrated with gusto on November 10 (or the nearest Saturday to it) each year. Other festivals in Los Santos include Carnaval in February/March (four days before Ash Wednesday), Semana Santa (Holy Week) in April and the Feria de Azuero in April/May. The Fiesta de Corpus Christi is the most spectacular, taking place over a long weekend 40 days after Easter in May/June (check with IPAT for dates) and featuring processions of drum and pipe bands and a re-enactment of a bull hunt led by a flock of running children. The 'bull' is actually a man in a costume with bamboo horns, who hides in the streets and goads the children into chasing him from post to post. Celebrations begin in earnest at dawn when firecrackers are lit and the town square fills with people sharing coffee and bread. Multicoloured folkloric processions follow with the dance of the dirty devils dominating proceedings, as red-and-black-clothed dancers in satanic masks topped with guacamayas (red macaw) feathers run riot through the streets. Next, the dance of the clean devils, an energetic procession of young men clad in outfits made from palm leaves that join the route to the church. Devils wielding pig bladders and feathers and palm leaves fly everywhere, pausing only for a brief interlude for a church service, before resuming the merriment at high-tempo for 24 hours.

Beaches

Both **Monagre** and **El Rompio** serve as Los Santos' city beaches, located 10km from the centre of town and used by fishermen and playing children. El Rompio is the prettier of the two as it is less prone to rubbish and driftwood. Visit from noon to late afternoon to have the dark brown sand to yourself. Seafood served at the adjoining beach restaurant rarely tops US$4. Take a bus from Chitré (US$1) and it passes through Los Santos (50c) to Playa Monagre and El Rompio each hour. A taxi from Chitré will set you back US$7, US$3 from the centre of Los Santos.

Rustic cabins close to the beach come at backpacker rates with few amenities (no phone). A **house rental** ten minutes from Monagre is a good deal for groups looking for a longer stay at US$200 per month (negotiable) (tel: +1 (651) 793 6037 to the US and speak to Danielle or Victor).

VILLA DE LOS SANTOS–GUARARÉ–LAS TABLAS

From Villa de Los Santos to the town of Las Tablas the road winds through cleared pasture dotted with cattle farms. Prior to the slash-and-burn years the land was thickly forested, today the fields are picturesque but bereft of trees, set behind thin hedges and crumbling stone walls. Two small drink-and-snack huts offer little more than soft drinks, sweets and beer. Beyond these, 3km southeast of Los Santos on the Carretera Nacional, there is some of the finest roadside food around at **Kiosco El Ciruelo**. All-day grilled meats are cooked over a smoky wood-fire from a menu where US$2 is the norm. Eat under thatch at square wooden tables set on a dirt floor that is home to pecking chickens and piles of banana leaves. *Tamales* are the speciality here and upwards of 550 a day are sold. This delicious leaf-wrapped snack is made with tomato, garlic, onion, chillies, minced pork and seasoning, and the chef at El Ciruelo does this Los Santos delicacy proud. Open Thursday to Sunday from 06.00 to 22.00.

It is easy to miss the tiny hamlet of **Honda,** a scattering of roadside coconut and *chorizo* stalls, and a few cauldrons of pig fat that sizzle at the edge of the road. The smell is overpowering, a mixture of firewood, garlic, chilli and pork meat, with brick-red loops of sausage strung up from the roof of each stall. Dangling there all day in a bid to lure passing trade, the chorizo found in the central provinces is some of Panama's most tasty. Vendors are happy to chew the fat with visitors and will offer tasting to encourage a sale.

Guararé

A brick-mounted over-sized wooden guitar heralds the entrance to the town of **Guararé,** home to Panama's music festival and a boxing tradition. Named after Guarari, a tribal Indian chief, the town's most distinctive feature is a pretty central plaza with colourful buildings and a handful of bars in neat formation by a museum. Guararé has become virtually indistinguishable from the minuscule communities that edge its borders and El Jobo, Bella Vista, Las Lagunitas, La Guaca, La Pacheca and La Enea are often pre-fixed with the name Guararé as a result. Residents are agricultural workers and the town is renowned for its chicken farms, yet it is World Boxing Champion and Panamanian hero, Roberto Duran (see *Guararé's Most Famous Export*).

Local beaches are Bella Vista and El Puerto and the latter has a highly recommended beachfront seafood restaurant. Shrimp, squid, lobster and whatever has been caught on the day is priced at US$3–4 for most dishes (US$6 for lobster and octopus), less for rice and shrimp dishes that come in a mountainous heap. Both beaches have been subject to extensive illegal sand extraction activities in recent years and bear the battle scars of this abuse and neglect. Visit after a clean-up to find a pretty stretch of grass-fringed sand. Arrive ordinarily and the scene is one of rubbish-strewn sandy patches and plundered dunes.

Getting there and around
Guararé is just off of the Carretera Nacional 20km south of Los Santos. A number of buses pass through the town and will drop off in the centre. Local taxis charge US$2 for a one-way trip to La Enea or to drop off at nearby beaches.

Where to stay and eat
Guararé's one and only hotel is on the Carretera Nacional and rooms at the **Residencial la Mejorana** (tel: 994 5794; fax: 994 5796; email: hotellamejorana@hotmail.com) are inexpensive but can be scarce. Owned by amenable patron Generino Barrios, all 22 comfortable rooms have TV and air conditioning, from US$17.60, with a family suite that sleeps eight for US$77.50.

What to see and do
Music, music and more music is the focus of Guararé's **Feria de la Mejorana**, one of the largest fiestas in Los Santos and held from September 23–27 each year. Thousands from all over Panama (and beyond) attend this celebration of local folk music in honour of the town's patron saint.

Other things to see in Guararé include the **Museo de Manuel F Zarate** (tel: 994 5644; open 08.30–16.00 Tuesday to Saturday, 08.30–noon Sunday; admission 75c). Dedicated to Zárate, a renowned local folklorist, the collection is one of costumes, masks, polleras and cultural artefacts. This is one of Panama's better provincial museums. Visits outside normal opening are by arrangement.

Neighbouring **La Enea** is located to the northeast of the town of Guararé and is renowned throughout Panama for its fine pollera makers. Panama's much-loved national dress is painstakingly made by hand over several months with incredible skill and care. Consisting of two garments – an off-the-shoulder ruffled blouse and a long gathered tiered skirt – each costume requires a dozen metres of fabric and

GUARARÉ'S MOST FAMOUS EXPORT
Roberto Duran, one of the finest world champion boxers, was born in Guararé, on June 16 1951. Holding world titles at four different weights – lightweight (1972–79), welterweight (1980), junior middleweight (1983–84) and middleweight (1989) – Duran is the only boxer to have fought in five different decades. He finally retired in January 2002 aged 52 following a car crash, having achieved a record of 120 professional fights, including 104 wins with an incredible 69 KOs. His wins by knockout place him in an exclusive group of boxers and few international fighters can claim more than 50 KOs. Duran, who remains a hero in Panama and his home town, is nicknamed Manos de Piedra (Hands of Stone). He is rumoured to have knocked out a horse with one punch when aged ten, and is famous for saying, 'There's only one legend – and that's me.'

features intricate needlework. A cluster of beaded hair-combs and half a dozen or so gold chains, earrings and bracelets, is the crowning glory. Two woollen pom-poms (known as *motas*) adorn the neckline and the ensemble is worn with great pride. Girls are often given one in early childhood and then again at puberty, when the costume is made large enough to accommodate any future growth. In La Enea, costumes are made by the womenfolk in workshops in their homes, taking up to a year to complete and selling for as much as US$2,000. Contact the IPAT office (tel: 966 8013) in Los Santos to arrange to meet Panama's pollera makers or simply arrive in La Enea and be prepared to ask around.

Las Tablas
Contrary to popular assumption, it is the town of Las Tablas, not Los Santos town, that is the capital of the province. More a touring base than a place to spend time, the town is well equipped to serve the basic needs of those passing through. In Panama, Las Tablas is a byword for street parties, and the town is famous for its authentic and exuberant festivities. However, aside from this passion for tradition Las Tablas has few conventional tourist attractions, apart from a museum and a fine colonial church.

Almost everything in Las Tablas is a stone's throw from the central plaza and the town is best explored (and best enjoyed) on foot. As the birthplace of triple-term Panamanian president, Belisario Porras, Las Tablas' museum and many local monuments have been named and erected in his honour. Amenities include a barbershop, several pharmacies, at least two banks, a post office, an internet café (**Café Internet** tel: 994 0184; US$1.50 per hour 09.00–20.00 Monday to Saturday) a service station, a car repair shop, two good little hotels and some decent local restaurants. One of the few laundries in Panama that folds and presses is great value at US$1.50 per load; open Monday to Saturday 08.00–17.00.

Getting there and around
Located 30km southeast of Chitré, the Carretera Nacional runs straight into Las Tablas with a twice-hourly bus that connects the two for US$1. Frequent daily departures link Panama City (US$6.50) and Pedasí (US$2). Local taxis serve the town well at US$2 per ride.

Where to stay
While there are plenty of inexpensive places to stay in Las Tablas, some of them are pretty undesirable. Some are used by drunks to sleep off the day's excesses, while others double as brothels. All hotels in Las Tablas are exceptionally noisy during festival and Carnaval time. One of the better places with rooms at budget prices is the **Hotel Manola** (tel: 994 6372; email: hotelmanola@hotmail.com) in the centre of town above a popular restaurant and bar where double rooms with air conditioning, private bathroom, TV and a phone cost US$18. The **Hospedaje Zafiro** (tel/fax: 994 8200) has clean, comfortable double rooms with private bathrooms at US$18 per night and a communal area with balcony that overlooks the central plaza. Others to try include the **Hotel Oria** (tel: 994 6315), an ugly tangerine-coloured building that looks like a garage block but is actually a 12-room hostel with air conditioning, swimming pool and laundry service, with rooms from US$12. Also check out the **Hotel Sol de Pacifico** (tel: 994 1280), which has 31 rooms, two mini-suites and three family suites at varying rates. Expect to pay US$15 for a single room with a shared cold-water bathroom, US$22 for a double room with hot water or US$110 for a suite that sleeps 10–12 people. The **Hotel Las Tablas** (tel: 994 6366; fax: 994 7422), located above the Supermercado Las

Tablas, has clean, comfortable but small double rooms with air conditioning, TV and hot-water bathrooms at US$25.

Where to eat

Eating out in Las Tablas is easy and inexpensive with numerous bakeries, takeaways and small beans-and-rice joints throughout the town. **Restaurante El Caserón** serves the best food in town from a stylish open-side corner spot on the outskirts. It looks pricier than it is and a big menu offers plenty of options, including a plate of shrimp rice big enough for two to share at US$8, and a house special steak and eggs breakfast at US$3.75.

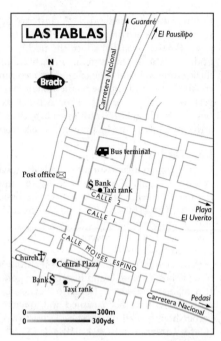

Shopping

The handicraft shop (**Mercado de Artsesanias**) on the Carretera Nacional doesn't hold a great stock but it does have some replica masks, baskets and souvenir items. It's also possible to book guides here and at the time of writing it was hoped that the shop would hold some maps and tourist leaflets in the absence of an IPAT tourist office. Open 08.00–16.00 Monday to Saturday.

What to see

The mud-walled **Museo Belisario Porras** is the former home of Panama's triple-serving president and a monument to his tenure. The liberal leader on the isthmus during Colombia's bloody 1,000-Day War, Porras was elected to three terms (1912–16, 1918–20 and 1920–24) after independence from Colombia was declared. It was during his administration that the Panama Canal opened and Porras gained popular support for his a strong social services bias. He pushed through land reform and built public hospitals and is also credited with many of Panama's most significant bridges, buildings and aqueducts. Porras re-divided the country's regional boundaries during his presidency to create nine provinces from the previous seven. His presidential sash, which is displayed in the museum, has just seven stars as it pre-dates the formation of the Herrera and Los Santos provinces. Find it opposite the central plaza, open 09.00–12.30 and 13.30–16.00 Tuesday to Saturday and 09.00–noon on Sunday; admission 50c.

Nearby the church of **Santa Librada** has many fine baroque features, but it is only the pulpit and walls that date back to 1789 following fire damage in 1950. A gold-leafed altar is painted with murals and decorated with cedar-wood figurines, many of them recent additions. A jigsaw of past and present but a fine building nonetheless, open to the public by request, Monday to Friday 08.00–16.00.

Visitors can also visit the tranquil country estate of Belissario Porras in a picturesque spot in the surrounding countryside. **El Pausílipo** remains much as it did when Porras was in residence and is a modest home in a pretty garden setting. Easily reached by taxi at US$5 for a round trip. Open 09.00–16.00 Tuesday to Saturday and 08.00–noon on Sunday; admission free.

Roads to and around the pretty hamlets of **Santa Domingo**, **La Tiza**, **El Carate**, **Peña Blanca**, **El Cocal**, **El Pedregoso**, **El Muñoz** and **San José** make for a pleasant drive as these typical provincial settlements offer plenty of local colour. Some are prettier than others so if time is short stick to the more picturesque Santa Domingo and San José, which are both renowned for their polleras. Señora Belen de Sánchez (tel: 960 0102) lives in a pink iron-roofed single-storey house in the centre of **Santa Domingo** and is one of the most respected pollera seamstresses outside of La Enea. Ask anyone in the village for directions to meet this pollera-maker of 50 years who welcomes visitors to her home 09.00–16.00 by appointment.

The streets of San José are renowned for their flower-filled gardens and Spanish-style architecture and are home to a community that boasts a strong pollera tradition. Few pollera-makers are as accomplished as Sra Fani Vergara who lists former president Mireya Moscoso as one of her clients; indeed Moscoso wore one of Sra Vergara's creations during the Panamanian centenary celebrations in 2003. Celebrating Flag Day with the presidential party was a great honour for Fani Vergara and the small community of San José, where most residents are involved in making Panama's national dress. Visitors welcome by appointment (tel: 960 9943).

Special events and festivals
While every town in Panama lays claim to the biggest Carnaval celebrations outside of Panama City, Las Tablas' boast is justifiable. Streets fill an endless stream of parades, floats, masks, costumes, musicians and confetti in the biggest display of revelry in the provinces.

PEDASÍ
The 40km stretch of road from Las Tablas to Pedasí runs parallel to the coastline and passes through several small farming communities on the way. Kiosks and fuel are the only roadside features until La Palmas, where quaint local architecture hides a decent internet café, open 08.00–18.00 Monday to Saturday (US$2 per hour). Some 30km or so further and the town of Pedasí beckons, a sleepy little coastal town that is the home town of Panama's first female president, Mireya Moscoso. Few factors thrust communities into the spotlight like a presidential connection and Pedasí has reaped the tourism rewards created by this local girl made good. Dozens of members of the Moscoso clan inhabit Pedasí and each boatman, hotel owner and local guide seems to bear the name. Political commentators made much of Pedasí's infrastructure and amenities and how they came on leaps and bounds during Moscoso's tenure. Today, thanks to generous government funding this humble town is equipped with a gleaming state of the art IPAT tourism centre, an internet café and a private airstrip as well as a road system that has received plenty of TLC. For most visitors Pedasí is a base from which to explore Isla Iguana and the succession of beaches and surf spots that lie to the east. An inexpensive dive shop, local guides and fishing charter serve visitors to Pedasí well and there are good, if basic, small hotels and excellent local restaurants.

Getting there and around
Buses from Las Tablas pass through the centre of Pedasí on their way to and from Isla Caña via Playa Venado. There's at least one per hour; simply hail it southwards or northwards. Pedasí is small enough to explore on foot although many of the surrounding beaches are a taxi ride away. Bikes can be hired from **Dim's Hostal** (tel: 995 2302) at US$3 per hour.

Where to stay
All three places to stay in Pedasí are basic but clean and without hot water. **Dim's Hostal** (tel/fax: 995 2303; email: mirely@iname.com) is a rambling old private house with several tired-looking rooms let on a B&B basis. Sparsely furnished with few frills and no plug points, rooms start at US$20 and include a decent breakfast served under a mango tree. The **Pensión Moscoso** (tel: 995 2203) has 19 rooms in the centre of town priced from US$11 for those with a ceiling fan and from US$17 for air conditioning. Every room at the **Hotel Residencial Pedasí** (tel: 995 2322) has air conditioning and bathrooms at US$17–22, including breakfast.

Where to eat
Although the choice is limited in Pedasí the quality of restaurants is good and both **Restaurante Angela** and **Restaurante Las Delicias** offer typical Panamanian fare, all day from early until 22.00. Expect to pay less than US$3.50 for a big breakfast plate of eggs and steak and US$6 for a chicken and rice dinner. **Restaurante JR** on the outskirts of town is a pricier option and is owned by a chef who serves a French-inspired lunch and dinner menu at US$12–15.

Local tour companies
Guides can be booked through the IPAT office, the ANAM station or by visiting Jeffrey Hopkins at Buzos de Azuero (tel: 995 2405; fax: 995 2412; email: bdazuero@hotmail.com; www.divenfishPanama.com), a no-frills snorkel, fishing and dive shop that doubles as the tourist centre, next to the petrol station, IPAT and ANAM offices. Jeffrey has more leaflets and maps of the area (including Isla Iguana) than the tourism office but it is his tips, practical advice and logistical solutions that make this laidback Californian invaluable. Boatmen used by Buzos de Azuero are registered with the Pedasí Association of Fishermen and Jeffrey knows all of the best ecological, fishing, diving and snorkelling guides in the region. Dubbed the 'Tuna Coast,' local waters are excellent for sport fishing and Jeffrey is a fanatic. Rent masks and flippers for US$10 per day and scuba gear for US$30. Open seven days a week 08.00–17.00 Monday to Friday and 07.00–19.00 at weekends.

Practicalities
Find the bank directly opposite the Hotel Residencial Pedasí at the entrance of town (open Monday to Friday 08.30–15.00, Saturday 08.30–noon) and a laundry (open daily 08.00–16.00, US$1.50) and police station (tel: 995 2122) by the park. Also here are a pharmacy (open 07.00–20.00 Monday to Saturday, 09.00–noon Sunday), and a medical centre (tel: 995 2127). The internet café is located in a suite at the IPAT building (open 08:00 until late).

Pedasí's gleaming new **IPAT Tourism Office** is open 08.30–16.30 Monday to Friday and contains an exhibition of photographs and folkloric artefacts with a limited stock of maps and brochures. For excellent advice on how best to reach the many conservation sites in around Pedasí visit the ANAM office (tel: 995 2134) next to the petrol station, open Monday to Friday 08.00–16.00. Adventure travellers in need of the inside scoop will find Jeffrey Hopkins at **Buzos de Azuero** (see *Local tour companies*) of more practical use than IPAT.

What to see and do
Special events and festivals
June, July and November are big party months in Pedasí when it hosts patron saint festivals on June 29 and November 25, and a fishing tournament at Playa El Arenal on July 16.

The small inland community of **Lajamina** lies 15 minutes northwest of Pedasí and looks every inch the sleepy backwater with its fair share of troubles. However, Lajamina is an extraordinary place with a population keen to escape the cycle of poverty through ensuring the proper education of its young. Economic forces continue to encourage local residents to look outside of Los Santos for a future, so the school in Lajamina has launched a fundraising appeal to finance its classrooms by using local *santeño* culture. The *cantadera* fiesta is aimed squarely at tourists, a big event first held in 2003 that features a *decima* singing competition. The closest thing that Panama has to a blues tradition, the music has a strictly defined beat and tragic lyric of lives and lost loves that border on the hilarious. Due to its financial success, the school hopes to stage the event each June. Check with IPAT for details.

Beaches and surfing

The stretch of coastline that runs from Pedasí southwards to Tonosí has dozens of hidden, unexplored beaches. Many are unnamed and unsigned and are so small the locals view them as insignificant. Yet it is from these tiny sand patches that some of the best surfing waters are found, beginning in the town of Pedasí and ending at the village of Cambutal some 75km away. Pedasí's best beach, **Playa Lagarto** (also known as **Playa Pedasí**), is a ten-minute walk from the town and is unsigned but easily reached via a decent dirt track that is driveable year-round. Open, breezy and with a good number of surrounding trails, the beach is popular with a mixed crowd of fishermen and surfers.

Playa El Toro is located next to Lagarto at the point where the dirt track expires and is another popular beach because of its easy accessibility (you can drive straight on to the sand) although it tends not to be as clean as its neighbour. Nearby **La Garita** is edged by rocks and offers a secluded place to take a dip. Less accessible than El Toro it is reached via a 100m rough trail from the turn-off 3km outside of town. **Playa El Arenal** is where the boats leave for Isla Iguana, a large expanse of tan-coloured sand with an open-sided building that offers the only shade. A short walk from Pedasí **Playa Punta Mala** is a favourite spot with sportfishing fans returning from a day out on the water. Yellowfin tuna up to 18kg, wahoo up to 32kg, rooster fish, cubera snapper and amberjack up to 25kg, sierra to 5kg as well as dorado, black marlin and sailfish have all been caught within 10km of the shore.

Next, **Playa Destiladeros**, a ten-minute drive from Pedasí and a short walk from Punta Mala, is another surfing hangout that is best at medium tide. **Playa Ciruelo** is a 20-minute drive from Pedasí just before Playa Venado and easily spotted from the road. Rarely surfed but raved about by those in the know, reach it by turning off at the shop on the roadside and walk down the hill.

Playa Venado (also spelt **Venao**) is the most famous stretch of beach in Los Santos. Located 30km from Pedasí on a well-signed route, it is Panama's venue for international surfing competitions (including the Billabong Pro), which attracts the surfing elite to this sleepy coastal spot. A 1.5km crescent of soft dark sand is protected by two nubs of land backed by hills and can be camped for free. Rustic tin-roofed beach cabins are the other option at US$16 per night (tel: 995 8107) close to a restaurant that serves up Panamanian surfer fare (beef, rice, beans, French fries and salad from US$3) from dawn. Frequent buses pass through Playa Venado en route to and from Tonosí and Chitré, while a taxi from Pedasí costs US$12–15.

Just 1km along, at the edge of a private home set in tropical gardens, are two charming cabins on a beautiful stretch of beach. Rates at **Playa La Playita** (tel: 996 2225 or contact Angélica Chavex tel: 996 1922) are US$35 Monday to

Thursday and US$50 Friday to Sunday, in a setting where peacocks, monkeys, parrots and geese roam.

The turn-off for **Playa Madrono** is a five-minute drive from the Venado turning but the beach itself is not the most accessible on the stretch. A 30-minute hike leads across fields and rivers. Look out for the signs on the roadside and take a trail across pastureland before following a river that leads to the beach. There are no amenities at Playa Madrona but it is a pleasant place to picnic, camp and enjoy morning waves. The access point to **Playa Raya** is just ten minutes past Playa Venado but also involves a sizeable hike through farmland to reach it. The reward is a beach that is completely secluded, with clean sand and waters full of big manta rays, stingrays and sharks. Turtles nest in season and the beach has plenty of seabirds. Park on the main road by the sign and take the rough trail across the cattle fields for 45 minutes to the sea.

Playa Guánico is about an hour from Venado and easily reached by car from Tonosí. The 16km trip is a US$20 round-trip taxi fare and the sheltered beach has plenty of good camping spots. Get the taxi to travel via the town of Guánico to pick up provisions, as there are no amenities on the beach. Another option is the restaurants in Tonosí who will often pack up food for campers on request. The last beach on the stretch is picturesque **Playa Cambutal** 20km beyond Tonosí and a surfer's delight. Accessible via a muddy track from Tonosí by 4WD or on foot in hiker mode, it lacks any amenities but is a great spot to pitch a tent or hang a hammock.

Isla Iguana Wildlife Refuge

IPAT, ANAM and all local hotel owners will all organise transportation to Isla Iguana, but it is often easier to call into tour and dive company, Buzos de Azuero (see *Local Tour Companies*). Educardo Moscoso (tel: 657 9100), a relative of Panama's former president, is a fountain of knowledge on the history and ecology of the island, and one of region's most learned guides (book through Buzos de Azuero).

Be prepared to hang around for a while whoever organises your transportation, as despite the promise that a boat can be ready immediately, this is optimistic at best. Factor in a good 30–40 minutes and pack plenty of water for the wait. Lone travellers should ask around to share a boat as it costs US$30 (plus US$10 for gasoline), but holds seven people. The departure point is Playa El Arenal, just a five-minute taxi ride (US$2) from the centre of town, where the boat is boarded on the shoreline in water up to 1m deep. Wear easily removable or all-weather footwear and a pair of shorts to avoid getting drenched to the waist.

The journey to Isla Iguana takes 25 minutes and the boat drops visitors off on a white-sand beach close to a newly built visitor centre. It's here that you pay US$3 entrance (US$5 to camp) and pick up leaflets that explain the ecological importance of the reserve. The 55ha Iguana Island Wildlife Refuge sits amidst a 16ha coral formation that comprises 13 of the 20 species of coral found in the Eastern Pacific to a depth of 8m. Established in 1980 in association with the Council for the International of Protection of the Birds (CIPA-Panama), the island offers superb snorkelling and scuba diving with 15ha of shallow snorkel hotspots and an equal area of deep scuba sites. Although much of the coral is dead following the 1982–83 El Niño, 200 fish species and a wide variety of marine life can be found in surrounding waters, including migratory whales, dolphins, sharks and sea turtles. A whale nicknamed 'Crescent' has a curved-shaped piece of dorsal missing, presumed to be the result of a shark attack, and returns each year to the waters of Isla Iguana with her calf.

A congestion of birds on Isla Iguana's elevated ground means that large flocks of frigates, three species of gull and large numbers of oystercatcher are easily sighted.

Two beaches sit on either end of the island, commonly referred to as First and Second but officially Cirial and El Faro. First, the arrival point for visitors is a narrow stretch of silver-white sand, once blighted by tidal driftwood and rubbish. Now cleared daily and home to several thousand crabs, it links to Second Beach via a well-maintained jungle through iguana habitat and across pitch-black rocks to a lighthouse and lofty observation point.

Getting there
The trip from Pedasí to the island takes 25 minutes on a boat booked through the IPAT tourism centre, ANAM, any of the hotel owners in Pedasí or tour and dive company, Buzos de Azuero.

Practicalities
Visitors are advised to trek Isla Iguana with a guide due to the likely presence of a few remaining World War II landmines. Snorkellers and divers should bring their own equipment (see *Pedasí* for rental info) and all visitors should register with ANAM (tel: 995 2734) in Pedasí prior to arrival. Permits are US$3 plus US$5 to camp overnight; bring everything you need, including food and drinking water. A dorm bed at the ANAM ranger station is US$5 per person. Poor weather often prevents boats from crossing to visit Isla Iguana from January to March.

Achotines Laboratory
Visitors can tour research facilities at the Achotines Laboratory (tel: 995 8166 or 995 8282), which include several concrete pools for incubating eggs, rearing larvae and juvenile fish, and for producing algae and rotifers for food. The location of the laboratory is pertinent, in the midst of dynamic marine circulation patterns that result in a wide natural variability of the near-shore habitat, and more than 150 species of fish have been collected in Achotines Bay (including at least ten species of tuna and billfish). The bay contains one of the few mainland coral reefs found on the west coast of Central America and the nearby Frailes Islands are well-known seabird rookeries. Tours are led by scientific staff and available by appointment only, Monday to Thursday. The project is managed by the **Inter-American Tropical Tuna Commission** in California (tel: +1 (858) 546 7100; fax: +1 (858) 546 7133; email: webmaster@iattc.org).

Getting there
Located 30km southwest of Pedasí, the Laboratory is well signed on the roadside. Enter through a large metal gate, which is kept locked unless visitors are expected. Jeffrey Hopkins at Buzos de Azuero organises tours of the facility *(see Local Tour Companies)*.

Isla Caña Wildlife Refuge
Drivers heading to Isla Caña will need eagle eyes to spot the departure point by car, as this poorly marked turn-off is easy to miss on the Carretera Nacional west of the turning for the town of Cañas. Arrivals by bus have a 5km hike from the bus stop along a bumpy dirt track that needs a 4WD during the wet season. Look out for a bus stop and a small ochre road sign that will lead down to a mangrove thicket. Here, unless you're extraordinarily unlucky, a boatman will be waiting. If not, there are three options: waiting for one to turn up; phoning Pedro Perez on the island (tel: 995 8002) to hurry one along; or removing boots and braving snakes and crocodiles (not a threat during low tide) to trudge left along the creek for about 50m to wait in a more obvious spot. Once aboard, the ride is short but spectacular,

passing through gnarled mangroves roots tangled with creepers. Designated an area of ecological importance to protect the 10,000 olive ridley turtles that nest there in August and November each year, Isla Caña is one of only five places in the world that attract such large numbers, the others being in India and Costa Rica. More than 100ha of mangrove and 13km of beach is conserved by ANAM rangers who guide for a tip. Most foreign visitors are automatically assigned a guide to point out nesting sites, hike through jungle trails to camping and snorkelling spots on the beach.

Getting there
Buses run hourly from Macaracas and Tonosí (US$2) from 07.00 to 16.00 each day.

Practicalities
Visitors need to register at the ANAM office in Tonosí or call the ANAM ranger station on the island (tel: 995 8002) ahead of departure. The office can also offer help with transport and accommodation if required. An overnight stay during nesting season is required to see turtles, either staying in one of three rustic cabañas with fans and an outside bathroom at US$10 per person or by camping on the beach (US$5). Entrance is US$3 and boatmen can be organised in the town of Cañas or met at the departure point (daylight hours only). A taxi from Pedasí is US$15 one-way.

Boatmen from Cañas or the dive shop in Pedasí will take visitors out to **Islas Frailes**, two huge chunks of rock in the midst of prime sportfishing territory. Tuna congregate here to reproduce and attract plenty of big predators, including wahoo, hammerhead shark, bull sharks, dolphin and billfish. Most boats anchor just offshore to allow snorkelling, fishing or birding.

To reach the small cattle-rearing community of **Tonosí** take the road 22km west from Cañas into a valley surrounded by mountains. The town has a few shops, a bank and a couple of rudimentary hotels but most visitors passing by stop to eat at **Restaurante El Charcon.** This simple roadside pit stop on a riverbank serves big plates of grilled meat. So huge are the servings that most diners leave plenty of scraps for the caiman that wait expectantly in the murky river alongside.

Similarly **Macaracas** has little to offer other than a good range of amenities and plenty of cowboy charm. Found 55km northwest of Tonosí, the town is distinctive for an open-fronted saddle-making workshop, where freshly oiled leather goods hang from the frontage as apron-clad workers in checked shirts and denim make chaps, saddles and panniers at wooden benches beyond. Owner Obbett Gomez is happy to chat to visitors and has plenty of recommendations on where to stay and eat. Aside from restaurants, banks, a hospital, car parts shop, dentist, pharmacy, bakery, fruit shop and two service stations there is only place to stay. The **Pensíon Lorena** (tel: 995 4181) has 11 rooms located above a pharmacy in the town centre, some with air conditioning, others with a fan at US$12–14 per night.

Veraguas Province

Panama's third-largest province is the only one with both a Pacific and a Caribbean coastline and remains one of the country's least-developed regions with some striking natural features. The lush, green, forested areas of the Caribbean slope are sparsely populated, riddled by fast-flowing rivers and drenched by frequent rainfall. In contrast much of the Pacific slope has been stripped of its original forest, farmed and is home to cattle ranches on dry rolling pasture. Established in 1984, the Cerro Hoya National Park protects much of the remaining forest. At 1,559m Cerro Hoya peak is the highest on the Azuero peninsula, set amidst mahogany, oak and spiny cedar and 900 species of bird. Veraguas is also a Mecca for surfers who swear the 5m waves found at Santa Catalina are some of the finest, and most exhilarating, in the whole of Central America.

Yet one of the most spectacular and unforgettable areas of Veraguas isn't found on the mainland at all. Of the 40 islands in the province Isla Coiba is the biggest (and the largest in Panama) and a national park of extraordinary beauty. Comprising spectacular primeval forests, sparkling rivers, unspoilt sandy coves and the second-largest coral reef in the central and eastern Pacific Ocean, Coiba is one of the largest marine parks in the world. Until 2004 the island was also the home of up to 3,000 of Panama's most notorious criminals. Prisoners held in a remote penal colony on the beach were able to fish, dive, pick coconuts and help out at a park ranger station. Inmates were given the freedom of the island after dark and a more breathtaking setting for incarceration is difficult to imagine.

SANTIAGO

This bustling agricultural commercial hub was founded in 1632 and lies halfway between Panama City and the Costa Rican border to the north of the Azuero peninsula. Split by the Interamericana, Santiago has every on-the-road amenity a traveller could need, from banks, service stations and car repair shops to laundries, supermarkets, restaurant, hotels, car hire and one of the cheapest internet cafés in Panama (US$1 per hour). As the country's fifth most important financial centre Santiago has 14 branches of the 15 banks found on the isthmus, a fact that most Santiagoans can trip of the tongue with ease. Although the town struggles to attract tourism few seek it as keenly as Santiago, which has improved the roads around the town to encourage visitors to stay longer and explore. In 2002 efforts were dealt a blow when Aeroperlas dropped Santiago from its schedule and with no plans to reintroduce the service it remains a road-trip town.

Lines of parked cars obscure the central square, **Placita San Juan de Dios**, during banking hours, but free of traffic this gathering place for the masses is the

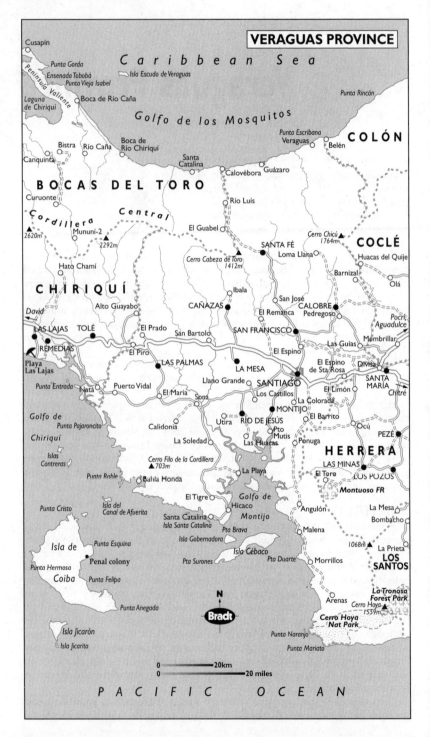

VERAGUAS PROVINCE

BASEBALL CRAZY

Everyone loves a sporting underdog and the province of Veraguas is just that, managing just one National Championship win in baseball since 1944. Fierce rivalry exists between the central region teams but what Veraguas lacks in silverwear it more than makes up for in fanaticism. Despite a fervent crowd the reality is this: it needs three wins to match the province of Los Santos and a miracle to equal Herrera, who have scooped the cup an incredible 13 times.

Federación Panameña de Béisbol Aficionado Estadio Nacional, Av Cerro Patacón, Kilometro 3, Apartado 9664, Zona 4, Panama; tel: 230 4524; fax: 230 4524; email: debeis@cwPanama.net

scene of political rallying and fiestas. Local hero Juan Carlos Torraza brought electricity to Santiago in 1940 and today a park created in his honour contains an ornate rotunda bearing his name. A second tower was added to the adjacent **Santiago Apostal** in 1992 to give it cathedral status, yet much of the original part of this biscuit-coloured structure dates back to 1932. Local residents built the Veraguas Baseball Stadium using donated materials and today it hosts a year-round calendar of fiercely fought league games. Santiago has a cinema (open daily from around about 17.00) a mosque and an under-used airstrip (see *Getting there and around*).

One of the town's most significant buildings is the **Museo Regional de Veraguas**, the former offices of the Colombian police force. Belisario Porras was held here during his battle for Panamanian independence before eventually serving three presidential terms for his country (1912–16, 1918–20 and 1920–24).

A charming green wooden house beyond the square has further political connections as the family home of Santiago's most famous resident, General Omar Torrijos (1972–78). Yet it is **Escuela Normal Juan Demónstenes Arosemena** (known as the 'Normal School') that is Santiago's biggest architectural triumph. Funded by a benefactor after whom the school was named, this important centre for academic studies in the central provinces dates back to 1938. Realising the need for improved educational standards in the interior, Dr Juan Demónstenes Arosemena commissioned the school's construction, much to the displeasure of the Panamanian government who thought Panama City a more appropriate location. Escuela Normal put Santiago on the map and revolutionised learning throughout the central provinces. It remains a centre of academic importance and is currently undergoing a US$10 million restoration programme. Specialists from Cuba and Spain are working on the building's distinctive frontage and visitors are welcome to tour its lower levels. This fine historical monument and its carvings and ornate frescos can be easily seen from the road.

TRES GOLPUS

Santiagoans refer to the trio that is the town hospital, cathedral and cemetery as 'tres golpus'. It means three punches and stems from the pull-no-punches local saying 'If the hospital doesn't cure you then you'll end up on your knees in prayer at church. If praying doesn't help you then you'll end up at the cemetery!'

Getting there and around

Aeroperlas cancelled its daily service between Panama City and Santiago in 2002 and although this was described as being 'an indefinite suspension' there is no sign of the service being reinstated any time soon. To bridge the gap Helixcraft launched a schedule, but this was also dropped in 2003. Buses depart hourly (03.15–21.15) from Panama City bus terminal (tel: 998 4006) and from David (09.00–02.00). Both are US$6. Buses in Santiago serve neighbouring towns well. Taxis are the best way to get around the town itself at US$2 for a cross-town trip.

Where to eat

There are numerous places to eat in and around the centre of Santiago. Locals rave about **Resaturante Kelvin,** a low-key local cantina that serves Panamanian specials for less than US$5 while a **McDonald's** and a **KFC** serve those in need of something polystyrene wrapped. The roomy **Restaurante Tropicalum** is a winner for value sandwiches at lunchtime and cheap eats at dinner and everyone talks of the grilled meat at **El Ranchito Tipico** (US$4). **Mar del Sur** on Avenida Central is one of Santiago's best, serving Peruvian-style seafood dishes for lunch and dinner daily and robust ceviche at US$6–15. **Restaurante Nuevo Quo Vadis** has a menu of man-sized portions of seafood and steak doused in delicious Panama-Mex sauces, US$5–9, while low-key **Restaurante Los Tucanes** on the Interamericana has value specials priced as low as US$3 or US$4, open from lunch until late each day. Food at the Mexican diner at **Hotel La Hacienda** is good and surprisingly reasonable. Expect a full platter of chicken fajitas or a decent slab of steak to come in at under US$10, often with a first or second course included. Open for breakfast at 07.00 until late.

Where to stay

The **Hotel La Hacienda** (tel: 958 8579; fax: 958 8580) on the outskirts of town is a great find and it has fast internet for US$1.50 per hour, a decent Mexican restaurant that's open from 07.00 until late, a small outdoor pool, nice clean comfortable rooms and friendly helpful staff. Open since 2003, a couple of hundred rooms are bright and spotlessly clean. Most staff are tourism students keen to practise their English so the service is excellent. A laundry service Monday to Saturday is US$1 per item and each room has air conditioning, ceiling fans, cable TV, telephone and a private hot-water bathroom. Everything at La Hacienda is Mexican styled, from tiled floors and chunky wooden furniture to terracotta wash on the walls. Expect to pay US$3 for breakfast, US$6–8 for lunch/dinner. Weekend packages are superb value otherwise its US$28 for a single, US$40 double. Cheaper options are **Pensión Central** (tel: 998 6116), **Pensión Santa Monica** (tel: 998 0592) and **Pensión Alessandra** (tel: 998 4508). All have fan-cooled comfortable rooms with shared or private bathrooms at backpacker prices (US$6–18). Rooms are basic at the **Hotel Melior** on Avenida Central but have private bathrooms and TV at US$12 per person. The **Hotel Cion Gi** (tel: 998 2756; fax: 998 7272) is big, dark and uninspiring with rooms to match; US$15 for a single, US$30 for a double with air conditioning or fan. **The Hotel Plaza Gran David** (tel: 998 3433; fax: 998 2553) is better value with 33 comfortable rooms with air conditioning and private bathrooms for US$18–30 and a Chinese restaurant and swimming pool onsite. Rooms at the 60-room **Hotel Piramidal** (tel: 998 3132; fax: 998 5411) may be small but come with air conditioning and cable TV at US$25–35 for a double or quadruple.

Practicalities

Staff at the **IPAT tourist office** jump for joy when asked about Santiago's surrounding countryside and wax lyrical about thermal springs and rocky trails. This enthusiasm is rare in IPAT offices and manager Belgrica de Abadia should be applauded. Find it opposite Super Carnes supermarket, open 08.30–16.00 Monday to Friday (tel: 998 3929; fax: 998 0929). There are internet cafés aplenty in the town centre and a new place next to the IPAT office. ANAM (Panama's environment agency) also has an office here (tel: 998 4271; fax: 998 0615) and can advise on camping, guides and entrance to the region's national parks.

SAN FRANCISCO

Few visitors would know of this innocuous little town if it were not home to one of the oldest examples of fine baroque art. Yet thanks to the **San Francisco de La Montaña** church this sleepy little farming community is renowned throughout Panama and visited by religious pilgrims and art devotees in their droves. It was built in 1727 and features vivid painted frescos in glorious colours that are considered some of the best in the Americas. Lavish carvings and ornate décor have been well preserved and remain tenderly cared for. Vast scriptural images and religious scenes that fuse traditional Catholic depictions with Indian folklore overshadow a spectacular altar. Few other churches in Panama have been so photographed, with good reason.

Find a small waterfall in San Francisco by following a road to the right about 200m beyond the church. **El Chorto del Spiritu Santo** is a five-minute walk from the turning and a great place for a midday dip. Late afternoon the local kids arrive but at all other times it is deserted.

Getting there

San Francisco is about 17km from Santiago on the Interamericana and served by a twice-hourly bus service (US$1) between 07.00 and 18.00. A taxi from Santiago will cost about US$15 round-trip.

SANTA FÉ

The Spaniards founded this charming little town in 1557 and it once formed the heart of Panama's gold mining industry. Today it is fast becoming one of Panama's hiking and birding hotspots and many of the hotels in Santa Fé are actively courting this clientele. Trekking and Hiking specialists, Extreme Panama, run excellent tours here and the town is a venue for conservation workshops and field trips run by the Panama Audubon Society (PAS). Much of the forested mountainous areas of Cerro Tute and Alto de Piedra remain wild, untrodden and rich in birdlife. Hundreds of species have been sighted in Santa Fé, including the great potoo, black-headed saltator, pygmy owl, white-breasted wood wren, crimson-collared ant-tanager, spectacled ant-pitta, wood quail, white-throated thrush, rufous-winged woodpecker, harpy eagle, golden-crowned warbler, red-headed barbet, three-striped warbler, black and white becard, sunbittern, bellbird, white-throated shrike-tanager, yellow-throated bush tanager, russet antshrike, slaty-capped flycatcher, blue-and-gold tanager, lanceolated monklet, bay-headed tanager and silver-throated tanager. The town is also notable for its orchids, which thrive in the cool, verdant surrounding enclaves. Santa Fé is 50km north of Santiago, 35km from San Francisco and nestles under the great continental divide.

Most visitors find that it's more productive (and safer) to use a guide when exploring Santa Fé's dense forested areas. No routes are signed, much like the town itself. Even when the locals point out a trail it doesn't take long to hit a barbed-wire fence or vegetation so thick you need a machete. It is also easy to unknowingly miss out on the best that the Santa Fé area has to offer or, even worse, get horribly and dangerously lost. An excellent area to explore on horseback it is possible to spend a weekend in this sparsely inhabited rugged mountainous expanse without sighting another human being. Most of the dirt tracks that creep through this wilderness require a 4WD.

There are several reputable guides that know the area well (see *Guides*) and who specialise in birding, botanical or adventure tours. Two of the best hiking and trekking **exploration tours** are offered by Extreme Panama (tel: 269 7326; fax: 360 2035; email: info@extremePanama.com; www.extremePanama.com) and ANCON. Extreme Panama's two-day/one-night trip is superb value at US$150 per person, includes all transfers, guides, lodging, meals, refreshments, taxes and insurance, and is led by guides with local knowledge, a head for heights and a natural history bent. Expect to swim under waterfalls, leap across ravines and learn about the birds, vegetation and unique biological components of the forest. Observation points allow great views across the mountain peaks and are a blaze of glowing amber at sunset. A highlight of the trip is a jungle trek at night up through winding trails packed with nocturnal wildlife. Good strong legs are needed for this trip but rewards for effort are high. Local children are often prepared to act as guides as are some of the local nuns according to unsubstantiated reports.

Whoever guides you, physically or spiritually, a trip into the forests that surround Santa Fé should involve exploring **Cerro Tute**. It is reached by a road a few kilometres south of the town but after that point the trail disintegrates to form a maze of crumbling dirt tracks. Despite campaigns Cerro Tute remains largely ignored by Panama's protected land programme and many trails are impassable during the wet season and only semi-clear during the dry. **Alto de Piedra** is more accessible, initially, and reachable by a road at the western end of town. A 5.5km walk from Santa Fé crosses a small cement bridge then a larger new bridge to a gravel path edged to the left with plantations. The Alto de Piedra school building marks 4km and following the road for another kilometre leads to a left fork on the trail to a valley of secondary forest – a prime birding spot. At this point there are two options. One is to continue for 500m or so along the road to find a muddy trail along a stream (another popular location with birders). Another option is to take a right-hand trail past a small house and follow this for several kilometres across three ridges. Locals advise hikers not to attempt this during or after rain – and never by vehicle (although some birders have reported limited success in a pairing of 4WDs equipped with a winch). This stretch of mighty mountainous terrain is excellent explored on horseback (ask at the Santa Fé Hotel for details) with vast expanses of pristine countryside stretching from sleepy Santa Fé to the Caribbean slope. More than 400 species of bird have been sighted as well as deer, sloth, anteaters, tapirs and jaguars.

Getting there and around
There's an hourly bus from Santiago between 07.00 and 16.00 (US$1.50). The journey takes about 1½ hours, but allow plenty of time for delays on this route. A taxi is US$40–45. Getting around Santa Fé is easy on foot and everyone in the town (population 3,000) knows who's who and what's what without the need for road names or signs.

Where to stay and eat
The charming **Hotel Santa Fé** (tel: 954 0941) is a favourite with the birding crowd, as it will serve breakfast at dawn if it's needed. Twenty or so rooms are

CAFÉ EL TUTE
One of the best things to buy in Santa Fé is the local coffee, Café el Tute, which is good and cheap (US$1 a bag) and has an interesting history. Coffee growers who are part of a 30-year-old co-operative, Esperanza de Los Campesinos, produce it and the coffee operation at Café El Tute supports hundreds of indigenous Indian families. A Colombian priest assigned to Santa Fé established the co-operative in the late 1960s. At the time the local coffee-growing industry was controlled by a handful of powerful families (it still is in the rest of Panama) and the campesinos that cultivated the coffee crop were paid with credit at the company store. Esperanza de Los Campesinos evolved from a simple idea. What, the priest wondered, would happen if the campesinos pooled their resources and bought a sack of salt so large that there would be no need to buy from the company store again?

One of the founder members purchased a 100lb sack of salt and carried it up the tortuous winding roads to farmers in the mountains. Thirty years later Café el Tute is the flagship of the co-operative's success. Its survival, despite the murder of the Colombian priest by suspected Panamanian government forces hostile to the co-operative, is a triumph for local farmers and a source of great pride in the community. Coffee is organically grown and produced using traditional methods and is only sold for domestic consumption. The Co-operative Santa Fé is open daily 06.00–20.00.

> **BIRDS, BIRDS, BIRDS !**
> How many birds can visitors see in Santa Fé? Hundreds. Great potoo, black-headed saltator, pygmy owl, white-breasted wood wren, crimson-collared ant-tanager, spectacled ant-pitta, wood quail, white-throated thrush, rufous-winged woodpecker, harpy eagle, golden-crowned warbler, red-headed barbet, three-striped warbler, black and white becard, sunbittern, bellbird, white-throated shrike-tanager, yellow-throated bush tanager, russet antshrike, slaty-capped flycatcher, blue-and-gold tanager, lanceolated monklet, bay-headed tanager and silver-throated tanager have all been spotted. Local orchid collector Bertha de Castellón (tel: 954 0910) is a diehard birder and promises a packed day for enthusiasts keen for a guide. Another good option is Edgar Toribo from Hotel Santa Fé.

clean and well cared for and the hotel has beautiful views across the valley. An edge-of-town location ensures plenty of peace and quiet. Rooms come with air conditioning or fans, US$15–30 (double or triple). Travellers on a shoestring could do worse than the **Hotel Jardin Santafereño,** which occupies a picturesque spot on the very edge of town and has cold-water cabins at US$10. An on-site restaurant serves great budget meals (the chicken is excellent, US$4) and is open early until late.

Other places to eat in the centre of town include the **Restaurante Hermanos Pineda**, the **Cafetería El Popular** and the **Restaurante de la Cooperativa** above the Co-operative shop. All serve chicken, rice and bean dishes for US$3–5 and are open for breakfast, lunch and dinner, apart from the last, which closes at around 19.00.

What to see
Santa Fé orchids
Panamanians visit Santa Fé for its orchids and the town is famous for the residents that cherish this national flower. One of the largest collections of orchids is found in the gardens of Bertha de Castellón (tel: 954 0910). She has more than 250 species, including a pale violet orchid endemic to the hills of Santa Fé. Bertha opens her gardens on a donation basis and is highly knowledgeable about the botanics and birds found in the region. Anyone in town can provide directions to her house, which is signed '**Orquideario y Cultivos**', but callers are asked to phone in advance (09.00–16.00). Bertha is a key figure in the annual orchid display in Santa Fé each August (contact the Santiago IPAT office for dates; tel: 998 3929; fax: 998 0928) and this prestigious adoration of orchids attracts collectors from all over Panama.

LAS PALMAS
This remote mountain town is worth a visit for its waterfall but has little else to offer travellers passing through. It's easily accessible from the Interamericana highway and has a few small shops, a couple of restaurants and church by a town square. There's nowhere to stay in Las Palmas but there is a medical centre which, thanks to a joint donation by American Medical Response (AMR) and MediSend International, is the proud owner of a retired US ambulance. Few towns in the central provinces are so well equipped, a fact worth bearing in mind if you're in a medical fix in northern Veraguas.

The waterfall is tucked away in a hidden gorge at the back of Las Palmas. Take the turn-off from the Interamericana, follow the road for 10km and take the second road into town by the cemetery. A dirt track leads to a fork in the road. Turn right to reach the waterfall along a 1km rough and rocky stretch of road that has recently been improved. The waterfall is beautiful and surrounded by a thinly forested area and a sheltered picnic spot alongside a pool deep enough to swim.

Drivers with time to spare should exit Las Palmas via the old Pan-American Highway. The town has two exit routes and connects with an old section of road that is no longer a part of the highway following a bypass that was added in the 1960s to divert traffic to Santiago. This forgotten back road has some wonderful scenery and is used by a small amount of local traffic. It passes meadows and crosses bridges over flood plains, river valleys and open cattle fields and is highly recommended by cyclists that favour the route from Las Palmas to Soná.

Getting there

The public transport system that serves Las Palmas has been the subject of much debate over the years. However, the town is better served these days from Santiago with several buses daily. These are largely aimed at farm workers and at the time of writing departed at 05.00, 06.00 and 08.00 and 18.30 only. It's a 1½-hour journey from Santiago at a cost of US$2.50. By road Las Palmas is easily accessible 10km from a turning off the Interamericana.

SONÁ

While its more refined neighbours may dismiss this provincial town as a hillbilly backwater, Soná can afford to hold its head high. Several notable diplomats, ambassadors and consulate staff members are proud to call this dusty town home, which is famous for its cantinas and watering holes and has a rather 'wild west' feel. Soná has two budget hotels at backpacker rates, the **Pensión Aguila** (US$15 for a double with air conditioning) and **Pensión Min** (tel: 998 8331) at US$7 for a fan-cooled room. Five buses arrive in Soná from Panama City each day (US$7). The town is also served by a three-times-an-hour regional service from Santiago (US$1.50) from 04.00 to 18.00 daily.

MONTIJO DISTRICT AND WETLANDS

This 80,765ha site covers much of northern Veraguas and is a Ramsar-listed, IUCN-designated area of ecological importance. The make-up is complex, comprising several tiny communities and an area of coastal wetlands, estuarine waters, beaches, mangrove forests, marshes, seasonally flooded grassland, rice paddies and irrigated agricultural land. Two rivers run into the Gulf of Montijo: the San Pedro and the San Paul; and the resulting tidelands, pools and canals attract numerous species of nesting and wintering water birds, including yellow-billed cotinga, pelican and frigate. Various mammals and reptiles inhabit the mudflats, saltpans and flooded grasslands, such as crocodiles and caiman, and the wetlands provide an important gastropod research site. Exact borders are difficult to pinpoint (each IPAT map or local resident has a different definition of what the Montijo district comprises) but it edges the beaches of Malena, Palo Seco, Torio, Los Duartes, Reina and Morrillo and the islands of Coiba, Gobernadora, Cébco, Loenes, Verde and Grande – some of Panama's finest shorelines. These key coastal spots support an important traditional fishing industry and world-class sport fishing. Tours depart daily from Mariato Point and the shoals of wahoo, Pacific sailfish, roosterfish, cubera snapper, yellow-fin tuna, blue-fin trevally, cero mackerel, Peruvian amberjack and dorado attract diehard enthusiasts from all over the world. The IUCN will provide a breakdown of the ecological areas of importance within the Montijo district on request and has a number of online reports and documents for public access (**IUCN Program for Wetlands & Coastal Zones Conservation in Mesoamerica** PO Box 1160-2150, Moravia, Costa Rica; email: nestor.windevoxhel@orma.iucn.org; www.iucn.org).

Fishing in and around the Montijo District

Fishing grounds in the Montijo District are some of the finest on the Pacific coast. The waters off Punta Mariato, Isla Cebaco and Bahía Honda provide excellent deep offshore fishing often within a mile of shore and it's not uncommon to see black marlin and tuna just a few hundred metres from dry land. Locals say the catch of game fish is good throughout the year. Grouper and schooling snapper arrive mid-January and stay until late April and while yellow-fin tuna are evident year-round the record-breakers aren't spotted until late March. Sailfish and wahoo are caught from late April through to early January, while cubera snapper, roosterfish, amberjack and blue-fin trevally are resident year-round.

The **Río Negro Sport Fishing Lodge** (tel: 646 0529; tel: (912) 786 5926 from the US; www.Panamasportsman.com) has three twin-bedded rooms and runs fishing excursions in 26ft and 33ft fibreglass boats. It's serious stuff, but fun with barefoot fishing in fully customised crafts that have been purpose-built by the owners of the lodge. Each boat has a cruising speed of 18–22 knots and plenty of safety features. A typical day on the water starts at daybreak and ends late afternoon and is limited to six anglers. An absence of large fishing boats due to the lack of sheltered anchorage and limited access to fuel has left fish stocks high. Three American retirees, who turned a love of fishing into a thriving business, run the Río Negro Sport Fishing Lodge. Alex Livingston and Billy Boughner are former Canal employees and Tommy Giles is retired from US Military service. Rates vary but range from US$315 per person for group (two minimum) fishing in a 26ft vessel to US$800 for a solo angler in a 33-footer, including a room for the night before and night of each fishing day, meals, local beverages, guide, fishing equipment and tackle. Another option is to stay in a rustic room at **Bungalow Torio** in Montijo town at backpacker rates (tel: 620 3677).

Getting there

From Panama City on the Interamericana take the south turn to Atalaya just before reaching Santiago. It's well signposted and also has a sign that says 'Playa Reina 45 minutes'. Follow the road for about 4km before turning right at a green sign for Ponuga and a blue sign for the beach. Some 20km later the road splits off to the left to Ponuga but stay on the main road that curves to the right that has a green sign for Mariato. Follow this road for 40km and there will be an Accel service station on the left-hand side of the road. Less than 1km on turn right on to the gravel road that is signed for Playa Reina. Continue straight for 3.5km and the lodge is on the right.

SANTA CATALINA
Surfing in the Gulf of Montijo

The costal town of **Santa Catalina** sits in the Gulf of Montijo and is Panama's undisputed surfing Mecca and boasts year-round 5m waves. The town was once a small fishing village but since being discovered by Panamanian surfers like Ricardo Icaza in the early '70s, it is now *the* place for surfers to hangout. Icaza had spent several years scouring Central America for great, uncharted waves and headed to Soná in 1970 on little more than rumour and speculation. With the help of three friends Icaza bashed his way through 60km of bush in search of a collection of fishing huts. When he saw the quality of the white-water off the coast he decided to make Santa Catalina his home and has spent 15 years enjoying this secret surf spot more or less alone.

Icaza opened up the first rudimentary surf camp overlooking the break in 1985 and since the Casablanca Surf Resort opened its doors there's been a steady stream of new surf camps and surfers arriving. Today the secret is out and surfers from all over the world descend on Santa Catalina. Keenly described as 'Hawaiianesque' by the surfing press, much has been written about Santa Catalina's potential as Panama's surfing capital. No doubt this is why an international conglomerate snapped up much of the village and the long stretch of coastline in 2002. The smaller surf shacks still remain but the reality is that bigger surfing resorts will soon dwarf them. Still, at the time of writing Santa Catalina remains a simple place for diehard surfers to hit the waves all day. It is tipped to attract an increasing number of international events and competitions after it staged the Billabong Pro in 2002 and other key Panama Surfing Association (ASP) events in 2003 and 2004.

Getting there and around

The only public transport into Santa Catalina leaves from Soná two times a day, departing at 06.45 and 16.30 at a cost of US$3. Five buses serve Soná from Panama City daily at US$7 a ticket. The town is also served by a regional service from Santiago (US$1.50) from 04.00 to 18.00 daily and drops off at a spot close to Cabañas Rolo (all other accommodation is less than a 1km walk) Look for the signs to the Casablanca Surf Resort and follow the road until it forks. Take the right to the Casablanca and the left for the others.

Where to stay

Few camps offer the versatility of the **Casablanca Surf Resort** (tel: 226 3786; www.casablancasurfresort.com), which offers camping (US$3) plus half a dozen cabañas and a number of double/triple rooms (US$20–30 per person) in a park setting with an on-site restaurant. Accommodation is basic, but clean, and tents are provided. The restaurant serves typical surfers' fare with few menu items more than US$8. The **Punta Brava Surf Camp** (tel: 614 3868; fax: 229 7755; email: info@puntabrava.com; www.puntabrava.com) consists of two lodges overlooking the beach. The main two-storey lodge has three double bedrooms, a kitchen and a restaurant/bar with upstairs and downstairs terraces, cable TV, video, telephone and an internet café. The second lodge is a cluster of five cabins with private bathrooms and air conditioning. Each sleeps up to six people and has plenty of storage space for boards and snorkelling gear. Two boats offer guests plenty of opportunity to island hop and the owners can organise helicopter trips to remote surf spots by prior arrangement. Rates per night vary but it's worth checking for special packages. An eight-day/seven-night full-board stay including transport and surf trips costs US$599 per person for groups of two to three. **Surfers Paradise** (tel: 220 9615) is owned by Brazilian surfer Italo whose son Diego is one of Panama's finest. Five rustic surf shacks boast magnificent views. They're basic but clean (and just US$10 per person) with loft beds at US$5 and breakfast and dinner served on site. The easiest place to find is the tropical multicoloured **Cabañas Rolo** (tel: 998 8600; www.rolocabins.com) as it is on the road into town and well signed by a hand-painted red and white surfboard. Half a dozen fan-cooled cabins are US$7 per person with a shared cold-water bathroom. Breakfast, lunch and dinner are all at backpacker rates.

PUERTO MUTIS

This tiny little port town is a crucial refuelling point for the fishing and cargo boats that pass through and serve Veraguas. A simple and functional place, Puerto Mutis has a couple of waterfront restaurants that pump out Panamanian folk music from dawn until dusk. **Gladys'** is famous for its cheap eats (seafood and rice dishes for US$3) and is a popular hangout with the many visitors that turn up for a boat to Coiba and wait, and wait, and wait.

A small dockside police station is staffed by some of the most helpful officers imaginable. Arrive at Puerto Mutis looking vaguely confused and they'll immediately call one of the few American's that live in town. Tom Yust (or Thomas as they call him) owns and captains Coiba Adventure (www.coibaadventure.com) and knows everyone and everything about Puerto Mutis and the island of Coiba.

Those arriving at the port by car should arrive early to grab the best parking spot in town opposite the police station. Parallel-park tight up against the wall (taking care not to obscure the edifice of the Virgin Mary) and officers will keep an eye on your car during daylight. Just leave a name, passport details and a phone number and return date/information at the police station.

Getting there
Puerto Mutis lies northwest of Santiago and is a 30-minute taxi ride (US$10) from the centre of town.

PARQUE NACIONAL COIBA
The first inhabitants of Coiba were the Cacique Coiba Indians, a nomadic tribe that were ousted in 1560 by the Spanish. It was a brief visit and Coiba lay deserted for centuries until the Panamanian government acquired the island in 1918 and converted it into a penal colony. During the 1970s and 1980s many of Panama's most dangerous criminals were incarcerated on Coiba, housed either in a central cellblock or in prison camps on the beach. In the late 1990s the government announced the closure of the colony and at the time of writing only a handful of prisoners remain, serving out their last few months on an island that once housed 3,000 inmates. The only other buildings on Coiba are a biological station and a few wooden rangers' huts. Visitors can camp close by or stay in a ranger cabin overnight.

The island and its surrounds were designated as a national park in 1991 and ANAM, Panama's environmental agency, manage the 270,125ha site that includes Rancheria, Jicaron, Jicarita, Canal de Afuera, Uva, Contreras, Pajaros and Brincanco islands. Partly funded by the Spanish Agency for International Co-operation (AECI) and the Smithsonian Tropical Research Institute (STRI) it is visited by conservation and scientific organisations from all over the world and has the second-largest coral reef in the Central-Eastern Pacific Ocean. Marine fauna includes hundreds of different fish species as well as 23 whales and dolphin species that habitat its waters year-round. Half a dozen shark species have been sighted, including white-tipped, bull and tiger sharks as well as large numbers of migratory humpback whales. One of the world's largest marine parks it is 80% oceanic, comprising Coiba and 38 other islands off the southwest coast of Veraguas.

Coiba is the largest island in Panama and was part of the mainland until 12,000–18,000 years ago. A land split cast the island adrift, isolating its endemic species in remote segregation away from the impact of the modern world. Today, Coiba is much as it was then. Of the 147 species of birds found on the island, 21 are endemic and the agouti, howler monkey, possum and white-tailed deer on Coiba are wholly unique to the island. Conservative estimates by botanists suggest that 1,450 different plant species grow on Coiba of which fewer than 800 have been identified. There are also two species of crocodile, turtle (four saltwater and two freshwater), six species of iguana (including green

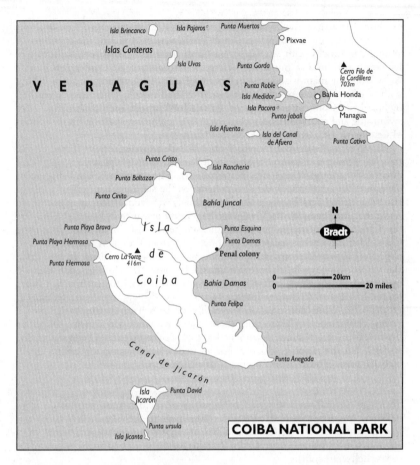

Isla Brincanco
Isla Pajaros
Punta Muertos
Islas Conteras
Pixvae
Isla Uvas
Punta Gorda
▲ Cerro Filo de la Cordillera 703m
V E R A G U A S
Punta Roble
Isla Medidor
Bahía Honda
Isla Pacora
Punta Jabalí
Managua
Isla Afuerita
Isla del Canal de Afuera
Punta Cativo
Punta Cristo
Isla Rancheria
Punta Baltazar
Punta Cinito
Bahía Juncal
N
Isla
Punta Playa Brava
Punta Esquina
Bradt
Punta Playa Hermosa
de
Punta Damas
Cerro La Torre 416m
Penal colony
Punta Hermosa
Coiba
Bahía Damas
0 ━━━━━ 20km
0 ━━━━━ 20 miles
Punta Felipa
Canal de Jicarón
Punta Anegada
Isla Jicarón
Punta David
Punta ursula
Isla Jicanta
COIBA NATIONAL PARK

and black), umpteen frogs, salamander, caiman, 12 species of snake (including fer de lance and coral snakes) and one of the largest populations of nesting scarlet macaws in Panama.

Avoiding hyperbole when discussing the natural beauty of Coiba is not easy. Only streams and marshland break an island almost entirely covered by thick tangles of virgin rainforest. Jagged rocks, palm-fringed silver sands, flower-filled coves and mangrove forests are filled with butterflies, insects, crabs and birdlife and just a short walk through the jungle reveals white-faced monkey, Coiba spinetails, deer and iguana and huge flocks of red parrot. One visitor described it as a 'Noah's Ark of an island' – and that description isn't far wrong.

Three forested hiking trails (two year-round, one only in the dry season) cross the island and pass wetlands, caves, waterfalls and thermal pools up to observation points high on the headlands. Two separate water trails allow exploration by kayak through thick mangrove forests in the north and the south of the island. Sightings of 8ft crocodiles and nesting caiman have been reported as well as a variety of pigeon that was thought to be extinct.

The diving and fishing in and around Coiba is undoubtedly some of best in Panama with exceptional visibility and unbeatable opportunities for underwater photography. Damas Bay is the location of a 135ha reef renown for its extraordinary marine biodiversity. There are only a few species of hard and soft corals but these are found in abundance. This diversity of marine life continues in amongst the rocks with sea horse, pipe fish, frog fish, stargazers, nudibranch, harlequin shrimp and numerous eel species from starry to giant green moray. Away from the main island are neighbouring atolls of outstanding natural beauty with beaches of white pebble, golden sand or shell shingle. These can be reached by boat from Coiba by arrangement with ANAM rangers on the island and offer swimming and snorkelling in pristine waters in complete isolation on the islands of Granito de Oro, Ranchería, Uvas and Contreras.

However, the sanctity of Coiba National Park is under serious threat. At the time of writing a debate is raging about legislation that will have a significant environmental impact on Coiba National Park. The decision by the Panamanian government to close the penal colony heralded the start of 'open season' as far as real estate developers, hoteliers and tourist chiefs were concerned. In an attempt to boost the ailing economy in Veraguas (the poorest province in Panama) Ministers sanctioned tourism development on the southern coast, the area in which the Coiba National Park is located. The move by former President Mireya Moscoso effectively gave the green light for hotel construction on the island. In June 2002 she vetoed previous legislation that afforded Coiba National Park considerable protection and declared that it would be more beneficial to Panama as a more tourist-based area. Today the future of Coiba as an ecological paradise remains in great doubt. While conservationists worldwide launch campaigns to reinstate a better, clearer code of protection, those who have witnessed Coiba's splendour hold their breath. Nothing detrimental to Cobia's ecosystem has been sanctioned so far – but the mood is gloomy. For an update on conservation efforts email: coibaPanama@hotmail.com; www.coibaPanama.com.

Getting there

There are several ways to visit Coiba but all of them require permission from ANAM. A number of tour companies offer trips to the island via a boat from Puerto Mutis or David. Coiba also has an airstrip for chartered flights from Panama City by plane (Charter Pilot Rodolfo Restrepo tel: 613 3058) or helicopter (www.helixcraft.com).

Travelling by boat with ANAM is the cheapest option but requires patience, flexibility and organisation. Usually the journey is shared with maintenance workers and rangers that are assigned to projects on the island. The trip is wholly reliant on the weather and poor conditions can delay or jeopardise this two- to six- hour journey without warning. Allowing for a Plan B contingency is advisable.

First contact ANAM in Santiago (tel: 998 4271) for a permit (US$10 per person) and to beg a ride. Bear in mind that the numbers of visitors to Coiba is restricted and that ANAM does not make the journey each day. Travellers are often to pay fuel costs, an expense but still cheaper than visiting Coiba through a tour operator. Expect to pay US$120–250 per round trip depending on the boat. Organise this well in advance and reconfirm with ANAM at least twice. Meet the rangers at the service station on the portside at Puerto Mutis rather than handing over cash for the fuel as this dispenses with the need to haggle over refunds should the trip be cancelled due to poor conditions.

The journey by boat to Coiba can range from a two-hour sprint to an arduous six-hour slog, depending on the size of the boat, the skill of the captain and the weather. Few boats offer full cover, some none at all, so pack a waterproof and lots of sunscreen, as you are certain to be exposed to the elements.

Where to stay and eat
A handful of rudimentary dormitory-style huts overlooking a small stretch of sandy beach are the only accommodations on Coiba. There's a staff canteen that may help you out with meals but bring food and drinks to be on the safe side. Accommodation is US$10 per night per person and should be booked with ANAM in Santiago (tel: 998 4271). The bedding supplied by ANAM is in short supply (and less than perfect) so bring a sarong or sheet.

Tour operators
The Portobelo-based **Twin Oceans Dive Centre** (see *Colón Province* chapter) (tel: 448 2067/654 1224, email: info@twinoceans.com; www.twinoceans.com) run great four-day dive trips to Coiba for groups of four to ten people. **Scuba Panama** (tel: 261 3841; email: renegomez@cwPanama.net; www.scubaPanama.com) also comes highly recommended for its Coiba excursions. Few sport fishing trips are as well organised as those run by **Coiba Adventure** (tel: 999 8108; email info@coibaadventure.com; www.coibaadventure.com). They're captained by Tom Yust, one of Panama's most respected sports fisherman and offer enthusiasts an all-inclusive no-hassle service. **Ancon Expeditions** (tel: 269 9414; fax: 264 3713; email info@anconexpeditions; www.anconexpeditions.com) organise tailor-made trips to the islands. **National Geographic Expeditions** (PO Box 65265, Washington, DC 20035-5265; tel: toll free in the US on 1 888 966 8687; email: ngexpeditions@nationalgeographic.com; www.nationalgeographic.com) runs highly popular photographic tours to Coiba, while **Ocean Fun Tours** (tel: 227 1532, email oceanfun@sinfo.net) offer snorkelling, fishing, swimming and sightseeing in and around the islands.

Other practicalities
Heat, humidity and plenty of biting insects make packing lots of mosquito spray, water and sunscreen essential. A good pair of boots and a first-aid kit are also good ideas.

PARQUE NACIONAL CERRO HOYA
Straddling the border between Veraguas and Los Santos provinces, the Cerro Hoya National Park covers 32,557ha on the southwestern side of the Azuero peninsula. Established in 1984 to protect the headwaters of the Tonosi, Portobelo and Pavo rivers, it comprises secondary forest on an area once largely cleared for agriculture. The project, managed by ANAM in conjunction with GTZ (Gesellschaft für Technische Zusammenarbeit), a German subcontractor of ECO (the Society for the Assistance of Socio-Ecologic Programs), didn't begin in earnest until the mid- 1990s. Today the park is the largest forested area on the Pacific side of Panama outside of the Darién Province – a remarkable ecological recovery. Lobbyists have put paid to recent moves to claim back the land for cultivation and the future of Cerro Hoya looks good. Panama's most inaccessible national park has much to offer visitors but as it is poorly served by local accommodation, dangerous in the wet season and not reachable by road, it is off limits for most casual travellers.

Those who do venture to this remote forested area will find 30 endemic plant species, waterfalls and gushing rivers. Some 95 recorded bird species include brown-backed dove, azuero parakeet, crested eagle, three-wattled bellbird, rose-throated becard, black hawk, osprey and scarlet macaw. The park has a large population of white-tailed deer and agouti, and is also home to jaguar, ocelot, tapir, several frog species and a number of rare butterfly species. The protected area also

GET OFF MY LAND

Hikers in Veraguas should exercise caution when walking across open fields, as much of the land in the province is privately owned. Cattle ranchers who instigate patrols to ward off poachers and unwanted visitors mean business and foreigners often fall into the category of undesirable visitors. Stick to a path (or follow the line of a hedge) to be on the safe side; shielded by woods is best. Several incidences involving landowners in rural Veraguas involve travellers. A British walker was stopped by a gun-wielding rancher on horseback in a remote location in the province. On this occasion the only intention was to labour a point about trespassing and the walker was unharmed. Other travellers have not been so lucky. An American was shot in the arm whilst walking across open pasture in 2003 and a birder was threatened at knifepoint on private land in 2004.

comprises a stretch of coastline that includes the Restingue Islands, mangrove swamps and coral reefs.

To visit Cerro Hoya fist register at the ANAM office in Santiago or Las Tablas (US$3) where rangers are certain to advise engaging a guide. Enter the park by boat from the nearby coastal village of Cambutal. The two-hour journey will cost about US$70 one-way and deposits visitors at a small coastal settlement just outside the park boundaries. A ranger station allows camping but there are no facilities, although some local residents have been known to offer homestay. An easier route is by bus from Santiago to the village of Arenas where another park ranger station is sited. Staff will arrange transport by boat further down the coast to Restingue to another ANAM outpost at the edge of a pretty beach. Trails lead into the surrounding forest from here but are difficult to navigate. Bring food and plenty of mosquito spray if planning an overnight stay.

Practicalities

Before visiting Cerro Hoya National Park contact ANAM in Los Santos (tel: 994 0074; fax: 994 6676) or the national park offices in Tonosí (tel: 995 8180) or in Restingue (tel: 998 4271) or in Santiago (tel: 998 4271) for transport, permit and guide information.

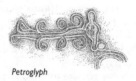

Petroglyph

Chiriquí Province

So proud are the Chiricanos of their province that talk of creating an independent Republic of Chiriquí is a popular, rebel-rousing theme. Dubbed 'Panama's store-cupboard' due to its abundant natural produce, Chiriquí's flower-filled crisp highlands and sultry lowlands are home to the finest agricultural land in Panama. Black volcanic slopes of fertile soil produce bountiful vegetable, fruit and coffee crops, while cattle, pigs and horses graze on lush green pasture. That Chiriquí is also home to Panama's tallest mountains and longest rivers only serves to heighten the pride of its people, who claim their province 'has it all' with just cause.

Visitors will find Chiriquí a province of great rural splendour, from the white-water rapids of Río Chiriquí Viejo and rolling coffee fields of Boquete to the floral villages of Guadalupe and alpine slopes of Volcán Barú with its bubbling mud pools and fumaroles. Most visit Chiriquí to explore 'the great outdoors', and rafting, birding, horseriding, camping and hiking are all accessible pursuits.

THE LOWLANDS

The dusty, dry heat of the Chiriquí lowlands is stifling at times, oppressively steamy and devoid of air. This lack of prevailing winds fails to keep temperatures down and David is hot, humid and sultry year-round, with little respite.

David

The capital of the Chiriquí province is Panama's third most populous city after Panama City and Colón, a crowded commercial hub that is home to 50,000 people. Modern buildings, shops and markets obscure much of the city's colonial past, yet David isn't without character. Roads lined with street stalls and open-fronted thrift shops spill boxes, goods and people out on to the street. Vegetable sellers, ice-cream vendors and shoe stalls all vie for position amidst the crowds. Shoeshine boys ply for trade (25–50c) in Parque Central, one of David's few cool, leafy spots. It's hot, sticky and busied by tooting traffic in streets adorned with sale posters and 50c T-shirt stalls.

With limited classic beauty, David has little to offer in the way of sightseeing, yet few places are better for stocking up on camping and hiking supplies. Equidistant from San José (Costa Rica) and Panama City, it is the main entry point for the Chiriquí highlands; an ideal stop-off for travellers fired with a spirit of adventure but in need of some basic provisions first. Making few concessions to tourism, David's shoppers simply get on with their business, too caught up in the mêlée to notice that a gringo is in town.

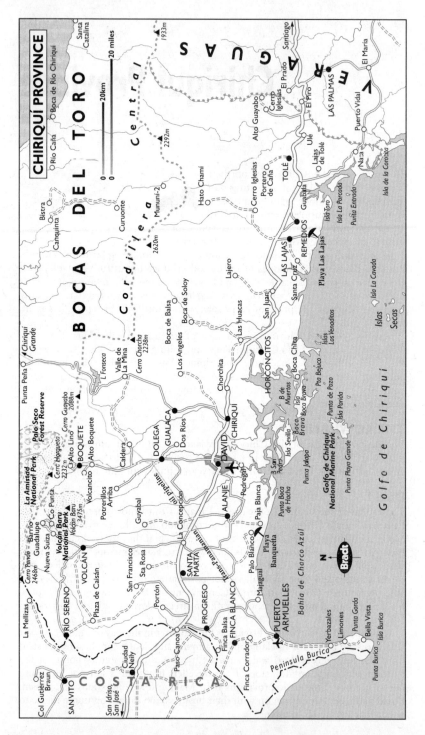

Getting there
By car
The Interamericana bypasses the town to the north, 275km from Panama City, about a six-hour drive.

By air
David is linked by air to Changuinola, Bocas del Toro and Panama City by air Monday to Friday. Aero Mapeix (tel: 315 0888; email: reservaciones@aero.com.pa; www.aero.com.pa) flies from Panama City to David at 06.25, 10.45 and 16.00 Monday to Friday, 07.00, 10.30 and 16.00 Saturday, and 08.00 and 16.00 Sunday. The Aeroperlas schedule is similar (tel: 315 7500; fax: 315 7580; email: iflyap@aeroperlas.com; www.aeroperlas.com) Monday to Friday at 06.30, 10.30 and 16.30, Saturday at 08.05, 10.30 and 15.30, and Sunday at 08.00 and 15.30. Both offer tickets at US$58.80 one-way. Flights from Bocas del Toro and Changuinola are through Aeroperlas Monday to Friday at 10.10 at US$31.50 one-way. David's airport, Aeropuerto Enrique Malek, is about 5km from the city centre (US$2 taxi). It's clean and new with a proficient air-conditioning system and is well served by taxis and hire-car companies.

By bus
David's chaotic bus terminal is about 600m northeast of the centre of town. It serves all of western Panama and runs a great local service. It will also hold luggage, one of the few in Panama that do, for just 50c a day. Buses to Panama City depart every 45 minutes, taking six hours on the express service (US$12) and up to eight on the multi-stop route (US$15).

Getting around
By bus
David's bus depot is one of Panama's busiest and serves Boquete (every 30 minutes), Almirante (every 45 minutes), Cerro Punta (every hour), Panama City (every 45 minutes), Horconcitos (every 4 minutes) and Puerto Armuelles (every 15 minutes) as well as the Costa Rican–Panamanian border town of Paso Canoas (every 15 minutes).

In addition to the schedule that serves the border crossings, Tracopa (tel: 222 5325) also run a direct daily service to San José, Costa Rica. The eight-hour journey departs each morning from the Tracopa office (open 07.00 to 16.00 Monday to Saturday; 07.00 to 11.00 on Sunday) in the centre of David. US$12.50 for a one-way ticket.

By air
Aero Mapeix (tel: 315 0888; email: reservaciones@aero.com.pa; www.aero.com.pa) fly to Panama at 07.35, 12.00 and 17.10 weekdays and 08.15, 11.45 and 17.10 Saturday. Also 09.15 and 17.10 on Sunday. Aeroperlas (tel: 315 7500; fax: 315 7580; email: iflyap@aeroperlas.com; www.aeroperlas.com) fly to Bocas via Changuinola once a day, departing David 08.30 (US$31.50 one-way) and to Panama City daily at 07.00, 11.00 and 17.00 Monday to Friday, 08.30 Saturday and 09.30 Sunday.

By taxi
David is awash with good, cheap taxis that charge US$1 around town and US$2 to the airport.

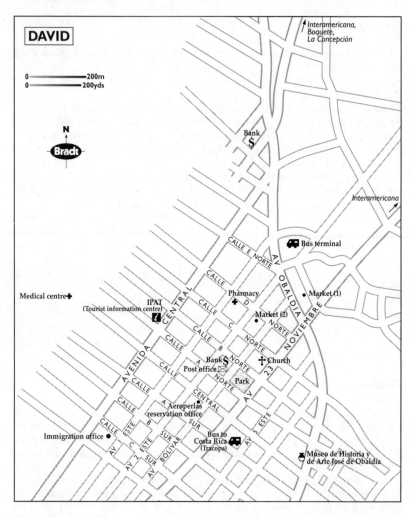

Car rental

Find seven car rental booths at the city's Enrique Malek airport and Avis (tel: 774 7075), Budget (tel: 775 1667), Chiriquí (tel: 774 3464) and Hertz (tel: 775 6828) each has offices in the city.

Where to stay

The Purple House (tel: 774 4059) opened to much acclaim in 2002 and is the only backpacker hostel in the city. Under the banner 'We're purple and proud of it!' it includes free internet access, kitchen, book exchange, luggage storage, cable TV, stereo, video and complimentary breakfast in the dorm rate of US$6.60 per night with rooms from US$17, a US$1 taxi ride from the bus station. The centrally located **Hotel Castilla** (tel: 774 52600; fax: 774 5246) comes highly recommended and has 70 rooms with air conditioning, telephone, private bathroom and cable TV at US$25–35 and US$55 for a suite. A higher price tag, but a good-value option nonetheless, is the 75-room **Gran Hotel Nacional** on Calle Central (tel: 775

2221/2222/2223; fax: 775 7729). This five-star hotel has a pool, restaurant, internet café and casino. All rooms have air conditioning and cable TV, private bathroom and telephone at US$48 single and US$58 double. One of they city's better budget hotels, the **Hotel Iris** (tel: 775 2251; fax: 775 7233) is adjacent to Parque Central with 70 rooms from US$12 for a fan-cooled single, US$15 with air conditioning. Rooms at the family-run **Pensión Clark** (tel: 774 3452) are clean and comfortable, US$8 a night. Rooms at the **Hotel Occidental** (tel: 775 4068; fax: 775 7424) are worn but clean and popular. Each has air conditioning and a private bathroom at US$17, US$21 and US$25 for a single, double and triple respectively.

Where to eat
There are dozens of places to eat in David from Panamanian cantinas and pizzerias to Chinese take-away and chicken wings. Dining on a shoestring is easy here with numerous inexpensive options. Even the five-star hotels have lunchtime specials and buffet deals and the fruit markets, supermarkets and street stalls are good sources of cheap snacks.

The **Gran Hotel Nacional**'s popular weekday all-you-can-eat buffet is great value at US$4.50 per person (US$8.50 to add a bottle of wine) and consists of salads, rice, pizza, pasta, vegetables, soups, seafood, breads, pastries and dessert. Arrive well before noon to get a seat. The restaurant at the **Hotel Occidental** beside the Parque Central serves a mean breakfast of eggs, toast and coffee for US$1 and ham, eggs, sausage and coffee for US$1.75. **Churrasco's Place** on Avenida 2 Este near Calle Central is a popular local lunchtime hangout but serves a menu of inexpensive grilled meats and rice dishes 24 hours a day. **Java Juice** on Calle Obaldía is a pleasant café with bold décor and outdoor and indoor seating. Sandwiches, salads, milk shakes and barbecue chicken are specialities. Open for breakfast, lunch and dinner seven days a week.

The **pizzeria** opposite the Gran Hotel Nacional serves spaghetti dishes, sea bass and steak as well as truly delicious pizza. Two-for-one deals and lunchtime specials offer great-value options and few things on the menu are more than US$7.

Shopping
David's many thrift shops (look for the signs that say *'todos por un dolar'* - everything a dollar) are a great place to pick up replacement T-shirts (five for US$1), boots and trainers (US$2–10) and various items for camping, such as plastic cutlery (50c), bed sheets (US$1) and thermos flasks (US$1), while hardware stores on the outskirts of town stock mallets, rope, tape etc.

Other practicalities
David has everything you'd expect to find in a large city, including dozens of pharmacies, several banks with ATM, lots and lots of public phones, internet cafés, laundries and supermarkets, plus a 24-hour hospital and medical centre on Calle Central. The post office, northeast of the Parque Central, is open 07.00 to 17.30 on weekdays, closing at 16.30 on Saturday (closed Sunday).

Panama's **tourist board**, IPAT, has an office in the centre of David adjacent to the church. It's open weekdays 08.30 to 16.30 (tel: 775 4120) and serves the Chiriquí Province. There are also plans to open up an IPAT internet café for tourists, but no further information is available on this at the time of writing.

The environment agent **ANAM** has an office (tel: 775 7840/3163) close to the airport. It's open 08.00 to 16.00 Monday to Friday and contains lots of information on Chiriquí's national parks and conservation areas. Permits should also be obtained here for camping.

What to see

The only tourist attraction in David itself is a small museum housed in one of the city's few remaining colonial buildings. The **Museo de Historia y de Arte** has a fine collection of archaeological and ethnographical displays, including Indian artefacts that were unearthed around Volcán Barú and photographs of the Panama Canal under construction. The building is quite beautiful and the former home of José de Obaldía, founder of the Chiriquí Province. It dates back to 1880 and retains many of its original features, including several pieces of furniture on the second floor. Admission US$1, open Monday to Saturday 08.30 to 16.30.

Festivals

The city's annual celebration, the **Feria de Dan José de David,** is a big event held to coincide with the patron saint day on March 19. This ten-day fair usually begins on or around the 12th of the month. For exact dates and further info contact the organisers (tel: 775 2128/712/3532; fax: 775 5428; email: fida@feriadedavid.com; www.feriadedavid.com).

La Concepción

Tourists largely ignore this rural farming town just off the Interamericana 30 minutes west of David. Yet its good set of amenities, banks and restaurants make it a pleasant stop-off on the way to Boquete. A working community of market gardeners, shopkeepers and smallholders, La Concepción is every inch the typical friendly Chiricana town. It is also the home of **Concepción Study Theme Tours** (tel/fax: 314 1417; email: Concepciónstudytour@panoramicpanama.com), the brainchild of Panoramic Panama's Gustavo Chan, who grew up in the town. A typical La Concepción home can be rented in full or in part for guests to self-cater allowing access to local people who will 'tutor' in town culture and traditions. Visitors can also brush up on their Spanish in an everyday setting and take part in a range of community projects. The three-bed, two-bathroom property 'Gustaladia' is Gustavo's former family home. It has a laundry, kitchen, tennis courts, garden and terrace, and a spring-fed swimming pool nearby. It's ten minutes from the centre of town where there are banks, restaurants, supermarkets, a bakery, several pharmacies, fruit and vegetable stalls plus a number of fish and meat sellers. US$200 per week, US$600 per month, sleeps six.

Dolega

This small town about 20km north of David en route to Boquete is home to the excellent **Bookmark Secondhand Bookshop** (tel: 776 1688; email: dembook@yahoo.com). Cluttered shelves groan under the weight of travel guides,

METO!

You'll hear the exclamation *meto!* ('mey-toe') all over the Chiriquí Province and this unique Chiricana expression serves a multitude of linguistic purposes. It's often used as 'wow!' or 'get out of here!' in response to an incredible or unbelievable story. Equally it can be used by those nodding in sympathy to a tale of plight as in 'that's terrible' or 'tell me about it'. *Meto* can also be an expletive, an expression of joy, or a rebel-rousing cry. The Chiricanos are famous for their storytelling and tall tales and most would say this funny four-letter word without meaning or context adds to the colour and drama.

classic novels and books on American and Panamanian history. Keen to turn those redundant travel guides into cash? Then pop in to see the cheery hard-of-hearing American expatriate owner, Harold deMun, who has owned the place since 1999 but is originally from New Orleans. Look out for the building on the left-hand side of the road. It's after a succession of small restaurants at the entrance of town. Open 09.00 to 17.00 Tue–Sun.

Paso Canoas
This key border town is the most popular crossing point with Costa Rica (see *Getting there* and *Getting around* for details).

Puerto Armuelles
Home to the Chiriquí baseball stadium (Gloria Barúenses) this portside town was once known as Rabo de Puerco due its pigtail-shaped river. The name was changed to Puerto Armuelles (or 'Puerto' as the locals call it) in 1927 just 12 months before the United Fruit Company (now Chiquita Brands) arrived in town. Heavy investment built the town's infrastructure, founding schools and constructing public utilities and homes. However, in April 1998 after more than 70 years in the town Chiquita Brands laid-off almost 50% of its 4,000 employees, pulling out altogether in 2001. Since then the town has struggled to boost its ailing economic fortunes and many of the town's declining population remains unemployed to this day.

The wooden homes built by United Fruit have a certain charm but Puerto Armuelles is disillusioned, depressed and poverty-stricken. An oil pipeline links the town with Chiriquí Grande in the Bocas del Toro province but brings little prosperity to the townsfolk. Petroterminales de Panama, which owns the duct, closed it in the 1990s when oil companies began to ship petroleum from Alaska's north shore to Japan and Korea instead of the American east coast. It reopened in 2003 to provide a route from Ecuador to the eastern United States and Europe. Few modern petroleum tankers are small enough to fit through the Panama Canal and the ease of piping fuel from ships on one side of the isthmus to ships or storage tanks on the other make the pipeline a viable option. The Panamanian government owns a 40% stake in the pipeline company and the annual contract is estimated to be worth about US$15 million per year, but this is little benefit to the town. A new tuna fish processing plant has offered some employment prospects to the people of Puerto Armuelles but is not without controversy. Environmental protestors, angry that the plant puts the region's fish stocks under serious threat, are campaigning actively for its closure. This followed a damming report of the Moscoso administration and its support of commercial over-fishing in the Chiriquí Gulf (see *Coiba National Park* in the *Veraguas Province* chapter). Most visitors arrive in Puerte Armuelles to catch a boat elsewhere, and while there is little in town for tourists it does provide a gateway to some of the nicest beaches in the area.

Getting there
Puerto Armuelles is located 34km south of the Paso Canoas border crossing on the Peninsula Burica in the Bahía de Charco Azúl.

Where to stay
Within easy reach of Puerto Armuelles, **Pensión Mono Feliz** (email: monofeliz@hotmail.com) means 'Happy Monkey' and there is plenty of tree life in the land in which it sits. A freshwater pool, horses, good surrounding surf and numerous walking trails keep guests busy, including a walk at low tide to Isla Burica, home to numerous sea and shore birds. It's without electricity or telephone

pleasant cabañas near Punta Burica that make a decent base for
rom Puerto Armuelles catch a taxi for US$5 and ask the driver to take
liz Cabañas. Locals may know of it as 'Juancho' so if the driver looks
head towards the tip of the peninsula, and ask a passer by for directions
to Punta Burica on the way. Rates from US$15 per person, US$5 if camping.

Playa Barqueta

Although much of this long, deep sandy beach is earmarked for development, the
planned luxury beach homes sited for construction haven't sold at the rate that was
hoped. So, as the 200-home Barqueta Nice development relies on cash flow
generated from sales off-plan to complete, much of the beach remains untouched
– but not for long. To the east of this stretch of lovely sand is the five-star **Las Olas
Resort** (tel: 772 3619/3000; tel: 800 346 1329 from the US; email:
lasolas@cwpanama.net), which is marketed via a campaign that suggests that 'If
beach worshipping were a religion Las Olas would be a cathedral.' The hotel is
slick, stylish and boasts a breezy location and has restaurants, bars, spas, a gym and
lots of fishing, snorkelling and boating tours. Despite being pitched at the all-
inclusive market it has some good seasonal rates and packages aimed at
independent travellers. The B&B rate can drop as low as US$45 per person per
night: excellent value for five-star facilities and favourably comparable to more
basic accommodation elsewhere in Chiriquí.

Getting there

Playa Barqueta is a 30-minute drive from David via the town of Alanje just off of
the Interamericana. It's a US$20 taxi from David Airport and about US$25–30
from Paso Canoas.

Refugio de Vida Silvestre de Playa La Barqueta Agrícola

Just a wooden gated fence separates this protected coastal stretch from the slick,
shoreline resort of Las Olas. A local environmental group set up a small turtle
hatchery here in 1986 in an effort to conserve this area of sandy beach, mangroves
and wetlands. ANAM, Panama's state-run environmental agency, took over its
management in 1994 when it was officially designated as a nature reserve. Today,
despite being an important protected area of nesting turtles, shore and sea birds,
the land is often disrupted, and nest robbing remains a significant problem. The
5,935ha site attracts a large number of endemic and migratory birds, including the
rare anhinga.

Parque Nacional Marino Golfo de Chiriquí

It takes at least one bus, a 4WD taxi and a boat to reach the Gulf of Chiriquí
National Marine Park but most travellers consider this part of its charm. Some
45km south of David, this 14,470ha site was established in 1994 to protect an area
of 25 islands, 19 coral reefs, and marine waters in the Gulf of Chiriquí. An area of
extensive mangrove swamps lies to the south in the Bahía de los Muertos and this
and the surrounding islands are rich in endemic and migratory bird species.

Known as the Paridas Archipelago, just two islands are populated, Parida and
Paridita, and Santa Catalina, Pulgos, Gàmez, Tintorera, Obispo, Obispone, Los
Pargos, Ahogado, Icacos, Coral de Piedra, Bolaños, Berraco, Bolañitos, San José,
Linarte, Saino, Saintos, Iglesia Mayor, Carey Macho and Carey Hembra are
deserted and vary in size. All are rocky formations less than 100m above sea level
covered in wetlands, coastal plains and thick forest. An average annual rainfall of
2,000–2,500mm supports a number of tree species, such as oak, spiny cedar and

coconut. The beaches attract nesting leatherback and hawksbill turtle, while Isla Bolaños has iguana and frog.

Hiking trails total 12km alone on Boca Brava where more than 275 species of bird has been recorded. Expect to spot tiger heron in the mangrove swamps of Parida and Paridita, also yellow warbler, red-lored amazons, pale-vented pigeons, brown-throated parakeets and orange-chinned parakeets. Large groups of howler monkeys, porcupine, ocelot, sloth, armadillo, wild rabbits, snakes, raccoons and agouti populate the larger islands, while the surrounding coral formations are home to a spectacular range of fish species. The area is renowned for its good snorkelling, diving, surfing and birdwatching and a prevalence of angel kingfish, bicoloured parrotfish and white tipped shark makes it a popular sport fishing region. It's also possible to spot dolphins as well as humpback whales, during the migratory season from September to November.

Getting there

Visitors should head to the ANAM office in the town of Horconcitos (tel: 774 6671; fax: 775 3163) about 38km from David to register and pay a US$3 fee. Rangers can also arrange a boat to the islands (a water taxi from Boca Chica is US$5 person) and provide maps and camping (see *Where to stay*). Two daily buses serve Horconcitos from David (US$1.50) in mid-morning and late afternoon, a service which doesn't suit most travellers as it clashes with tide times in Boca Chica. To reach the launch point earlier in the day jump on any of the dozens of buses that pass the turn-off. Just ask the driver to drop you at Horconcitos junction. Drivers should note that this turning is poorly marked just beyond a rustic restaurant on the right if travelling from David. A taxi into the centre of Horconcitos costs US$2 from the turn-off. The fishing village of Boca Chica is the launch point to the islands. It's 20km from Horconcitos and is US$15 by 4WD taxi along a very poor road.

Where to stay

The **ANAM Ranger Station** on Isla Parida offers basic dormitory accommodation for US$5 per person and camping with few facilities for US$10 a tent. Book at the ANAM office in Horconcitos (tel: 774 6671; fax: 775 3163).

On Punta Bejuco, the **Pacific Bay Resort** (tel: 695 1651; (617) 782 3228 in the US; email: info@pacificbayresort.net; www.pacificbayresort.net) sits in 57ha of land with forest that supports a large bird population and contains numerous native plants. Every effort is made to use renewable resources, such as wind and solar power, and more than 38ha of this plot remain wild and undeveloped. Adventure hikes, snorkelling trips and nature walks are offered to guests from US$5 per person. Rates are US$70 per double room (US$25 per additional person, up to four per room). All meals included.

The **Panama Big Game Fishing Club** (tel: 774 4686/674 4784; (305) 653 2322 in the US; email: biggamepanama@yahoo.com) on Boca Brava is aimed at true sportfishing aficionados. Several three- to six-day fully inclusive packages cost US$1,800–4,500 for one to four people. Non-fishing guests are welcome but only at a price and despite a great location and facilities the US$250 fee and US$250 room rate are steep.

Other smaller accommodation options are springing up in the area at the time of writing. The Panamanian Tourist Board tells me the almost completed **Bungalow Boca Brava** is to be a fine rustic cabin, while a couple of hospedajes are slated to open 2005–06. Visit www.visitpanama.com for an update of Panama's tourist board approved accommodation or ask the ANAM for recommendations on a local level.

CHIRIQUÍ LEGEND

The Chiriquí province is steeped in legend born out of Ngöbe Buglé beliefs. According to one, a lost city of gold is hidden in a remote valley deep in the cloud forest. The Indians believe that their ancestors abandoned the town after it was violently plundered by Spanish pirates and was deemed evil by spiritual leaders. According to the Chiriquí Indians any white-skinned man that arrives in the province in search of gold will hear a charming voice as he approaches the entrance of the ruined city. So irresistible is this soft female tone that the man is powerless to resist, following it further into the forest until he is unable to find his way back. The Chiriquí Indians believe that an untold number men fall foul of the voice, even today.

Another legend tells of a lost tribe of Indios Conejos (meaning Rabbit Tribe), a tribe of white-skinned Indian warriors that grow to a height of only about 1m. So intent are these cave-dwelling hunters on avoiding the modern world that they have magical powers to disorient those who enter their territory.

Tour companies

Panama City-based fishing charters **Panama Fishing and Catching** (tel: 622 0212; www.panamafishingandcatching.com) is US-owned and run, and comes highly recommended. Well-travelled Captain Tony Herndon is adept in Panamanian waters.

Guests staying at the **Big Game Fishing Club** (www.panamabiggamefishingclub. com) (see *Where to stay*) can take advantage of endless sportfishing tour combinations as part of their all-inclusive packages.

Carlos Spragge, a half-British half-Colombian Panamanian resident, runs **Boca Brava Divers** (tel: 721 0930/635 9196; email: bocabravadivers@yahoo.com) on the island. Soft coral, lobster, fish and migrating whales make the waters prime diving territory. Group rates and one-to-one from US$20.

Playa Las Lajas

This is just one of several long, sandy palm-scattered beaches south of the Interamericana, 13km from the turn-off and 62km east of David. A fashionable weekend destination with urbanites the beach is deluged by vast numbers each Sunday. **Las Lajas Beach Resort** (tel: 720 2430/618 7723) is the only place to stay and consists of nine rustic bamboo cabañas just a stone's throw from the beach. US$10 for a single, US$15 for a double with dorm beds at US$7 each and camping at US$5 per tent. A great little restaurant serves up Pan-American food from dawn until dusk with nothing on the menu over US$7.

Getting there

Most of the buses that run up and down the Interamericana will drop off at the turning for Las Lajas on request. It's about an hour's ride from David (US$3) and at the drop-off point you'll need to take a taxi 13km to the beach road (US$5) before a 1km walk to the beach itself.

Futuro Forestal

This 200ha tree farm (tel/fax: 727 0010; email: info@futuroforestal.com; www.futuroforestal.com) at the edge of the town of Las Lajas balances commercial profiteering with a privately funded reforestation project, offering public tours each

Saturday. The reforest is a mixed plantation of six tropical hardwood species on land that was once lush woodlands but suffered at the hands of slash-and-burn activities by cattle farmers. The pasture is now being returned to its natural forested state in a bid to reverse the effects of soil degradation, under a scheme endorsed by the Forest Stewardship Council. Visitors can plant their own tree under a sponsor scheme during a three-hour tour through the forest, which is good value at US$5 per person. There's a cabin in the forest with hammocks and a stream nearby for bathing. There are no other facilities apart from an oil lantern but visitors can stay overnight for US$20 (one person) and US$5 for each additional person.

Getting there
The easiest way to reach the forest is to grab a taxi from Playa Las Lajas (US$5) or the Interamericana (US$3).

Islas Secas
This spectacularly beautiful privately owned archipelago is one of the most breathtaking in Panama. Since snapping it up for a cool six-figure sum in 2002 an American IT guru has taken care to protect its splendour, developing a tiny fraction of just a couple of the islands and installing environmentally friendly cabañas that blend into the jungle. Dozens of white-sand beaches and hidden coves line each shoreline, which are uninhabited apart from leatherback, hawksbill and olive ridley turtles, yellow-billed cotinga, coiba spinetail and scarlet macaw. Each island is unique in size and shape but all have the same basic character of rugged peaks, dense jungle and pristine sands surrounded by warm shallow clear waters. The remote location of Isla Secas has helped in its preservation and the main islands of **Pargo**, **Baracuda**, **Coco** and **Cavada** and ten unnamed atolls contain dozens of wildlife species and rare flora. Waterfalls are found in the forests on Pargo and Baracuda during the wet season, while Coco is renowned for small silver-sand beaches and an abundance of birdlife. Cavada, the largest island, has surrounding waters that teem with fish. Shell-shingle pathways lead to observation points high above the forest with views that extend across the ocean.

Off-boat snorkelling and fishing around the archipelago are superb and offered by a growing number of tour operators. Visiting the individual islands is restricted to guests only – and staying at Islas Secas isn't cheap (Tel: (805) 729 2737 in the US; email: reservations@islassecas.com; www.islassecas.com). Four nights will set you back about US$1,200 (US$1,800 for a week) for a cabaña with ocean view with all meals, drinks (including alcoholic beverages) and several excursions included. Transfers to the archipelago are extra (from Panama City or David).

Getting there
Guests at Islas Secas can take advantage of an arranged transfer from David by boat (US$100) or private plane (US$200) and from Panama City by private plane (US$400). A number of dive tours and fishing trips visit the area departing from the Pedregal Marina in David. These include **Pesca Panama Fishing Charters** (tel: 614 5850; email: pescapanama@aol.com) and **Panama Jet Boat Explorer** (tel: 604 7736; fax: 720 4054/774 2124; email: info@panamajetboatexplorer.com).

Cerro Colorado
About 40km northeast of David you'll find Cerro Colorado, one of the largest copper mines in the world, where deposits were first found in 1932. The decision to mine the site caused outrage and violent demonstrations by Chiriquí's Ngöbe

Buglé communities, culminating in a hunger strike that made the threat to their territory headline news. However, today mining is well under way to excavate an estimated 1.4 million tonnes of copper in Cerro Colorado, and while large-scale mining can promote positive economic change in some regions, the Ngöbe Buglé have seen few benefits. The project continues to be a source of antagonism to the local indigenous community and is not open to tourists (despite much encouragement) largely due to issues of security.

Pozos del Galique

Local legend has it that a dip in these rustic hot-water springs will cure all known ills. Each can accommodate three or four people and are welcome relief to those who've decided to walk the long arduous dirt track to reach them. The poorly marked turn-off for the track is 4km east of the turn-off for Playa Las Lajas and the 3km craterous road beginning 30m west of a small bridge signed 'Galique' is a slog. Drivers should not be tempted to try this trip in anything less than a 4WD vehicle. Pack plenty of drinks, a picnic and some sunscreen and arrive early before it gets too hot.

Tolé

This sprawling rural community is home to one of the largest groups of Ngöbe Buglé Indians in Panama, most of whom live in poverty and are unemployed for much of each year. Most migrating to Chiriquí's highlands find low-paid work coffee picking in season, a short-term answer and a backbreaking one at that. Ngöbe Buglé women can be clearly spotted in the fields in their colourful, hand-stitched dresses called *naguas*. When the women aren't working in the coffee plantations they weave handbags called *chacaras* and baskets made from palms. These are sold on stalls at the roadside throughout Chiriquí or can be bought from the villagers of Tolé direct.

Petroglyphs found in **El Nancito** 5km west of the town are worth a stop-off if you're passing through or fancy a decent hike. The largest, set behind a barbed-wire fence, is carved with distinctive figures and characters. Others have symbols that the locals say depict the gods of the land. The site is about a 3.5km hike uphill from the turn-off for El Nancito on the Interamericana. Walk north until you reach a restaurant called Cantina Oriente and follow a road to the west for less than 100m.

Morro Negrito Surf Camp

This dedicated surfers' resort (email: surferparadise1@cox.net; www.surferparadise.com) is split across two offshore islands, with the combined name of Isla Ensenada, 7km off the mainland some 20km from the town of Tolé. The largest of the islands has accommodation, a restaurant, bar, communal areas and breaks of 2.5m. Those on the neighbouring island (30 minutes by boat) can reach 3.5m high. Guest numbers are limited to 20 at a time with ten breaks to choose from. Established in 1998, the camp also offers a range of watersport and fishing equipment for hire, as well as horses which can be ridden to explore the island. Cabins are rustic with running water and electricity but few frills. Weekly packages include transport from Panama City, a boat from the mainland, food, accommodation and all surfing for US$500 with additional days at US$50. At the time of writing Morro Negrito Surf Camp has plans to add a surf school tutored by Nick Davie from England who has worked professionally at a school in the Canary Islands.

Getting there

Guests are transferred from Panama City by bus (five to six hours) to a port close to the town of Quebrada de Piedra, about 12km from Tolé. A 15-minute boat trip brings surfers out to the island.

THE HIGHLANDS

This picturesque mountainous region of fruit farms, vegetable fields, coffee plantations, dairy herds and thoroughbred stud farms forms a sharp contrast with the sultry lowlands of the province. The air is crisp and cool; the soil dark and volcanic; villages filled with flowers. Street vendors sell strawberry wine, yoghurt and crops from the fields, while clusters of Swiss-style houses with black and white pitched roofs are evidence of a European heritage. Volcán Barú, Panama's highest peak, is scattered with alpine wildflowers. Hiking to reach the summit is the ultimate highland camping trip.

Boquete

It may be just 38km north of David but Boquete seems like another world: green, misty, lush and beautiful, nestled among forested mountains in a picturesque valley setting. After sunny midday highs the air is prone to a refreshing drizzle and cool evenings can chill at times, a stark contrast to David's year-round steaminess. Clear rivers, gushing streams and first-class mountain trails make Boquete a fine place for hikers and birders. Hotels, cabañas, hostels and camping offer visitors plenty of options, and the town and its environs are easily explored on foot. Juicy naval oranges and coffee have brought Boquete fame, as has its scenery, which is undoubtedly some of Panama's finest.

Getting there and around

Buses from David depart every half an hour from 06.00 to 21.00, US$1.20 (1 hour). Cars can be rented from David and a taxi will charge US$35 for the 45-minute journey. Driving from Panama City to Boquete will take seven hours in good weather.

The centre of town is easily navigable on foot and has one main road that runs north to south, the Avenida Central. Cheap local buses serve the immediate area for 50c from the central plaza. Taxis are in reasonable supply at US$2 for a local trip. Views are best enjoyed on horseback or bike. Rent a mountain bike from Panama Rafters (tel: 720 2712), half day US$7 and full day US$12; hire a horse from Eduardo Cano (tel: 720 1750) for US$7 per hour.

Where to stay

There is no shortage of accommodation in Boquete as foreign landowners and locals clamber to make the most of the tourism boom. At least half a dozen new places opened 2003–04 with several more on the cards for 2005. Visitors are well catered for as a result with budget hostels, camping, cabañas and mid-range hotels.

Work is well under way on the **Panama Rafters Lodge** on a 5.5ha site on the Río Chiriquí Viejo, the first specialist hotel for kayakers and rafters in the country. The land, once deforested cattle pasture, has been replanted with over 2,000 trees. The lodge is scheduled to open by the end of 2005. (tel: 720 2712; www.panamarafters.com or call into Panama Rafters for details). The German owners of the cabañas at **Isla Verde** (tel: 720 2533; email: islaverde@chiriqui.com) have paid great attention to detail. The result is six modern, bright and comfortable two-storey cabins with ground-floor and mezzanine double beds, fully fitted kitchens and beautiful gardens. Located in a quiet neighbourhood on the edge of town, three of them sleep six people (US$65) and three sleep four (US$50).

Cabañas La Vía Lactea (tel: 720 2376; email: info@lavialactea.biz; www.lavialactea.biz) 2km from the centre of town was completed at the end of 2003 and sits on the banks of the Río Palo Alto. Each of the ten well-equipped hexagonal cabins is built to a high specification with daily, weekly and monthly rates and discounts for long stays. Each can accommodate two to four persons, US$50–65 for double occupancy plus US$10 for each extra person, with laundry, internet and tour reservations on-site.

Another out-of-town cluster of cabins, **Momentum** (tel: 720 4385; email: info@momentum-panama.com; www.momentum-panama.com), has five fully equipped with kitchens, queen beds and sofa beds at US$60 per night for two people (additional room guests at US$15 each), with discounts for a week and B&B options at US$45 per double and US$35 single.

Rooms at **Valle Primavera Hospedaje** (tel: 720 2881; email: valleprimavera@yahoo.com) are comfortable and spacious with private hot-water bathrooms at US$35 for three persons, US$40 for four, near the Pizzeria Salvatore.

Four two-storey cabins at **Cabañas Sabrin** (tel: 774 2164/720 2374; email: administracion@cabanassabrin.com; www.cabanassabrin.com) are ten minutes' walk from the centre, with fully fitted kitchens, balconies and terraces, TV and park views at US$66.

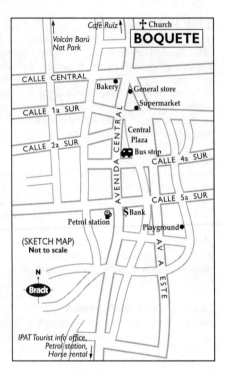

The distinctive castle-shaped **Hotel y Cabañas Fundadores** (tel: 720 1298; fax: 720 1034; email: hotfundland@cwpanama.net) has 40 double, triple and quadruple rooms and cabins from US$30–65 each.

Campers can pitch in the grounds of **Pensión Topaz** (tel: 720 1005, email: schoeb@chiriqui.com) for US$5 per couple with tent and US$7 per couple, tent provided, also rooms from US$18. Another camping option is **La Montaña y el Valle – The Coffee Estate Inn** (tel/fax: 720 2211; email: information@coffeeestateinn.com; www.coffeeestateinn.com) but only during the dry season (January to March) at US$7 per couple with own tent, pre-booking essential. Luxurious rooms at La Montaña come at a price, US$90 per double plus US$35 for each additional person.

Owners Priscilla and Rodrigo Marciacq at **Villa Marita's Lodge** (tel: 720 2165; email: villamarita@cwpanama.net) have seven beautiful cabins and a lodge that offers breathtaking views over coffee farms and mountain slopes, at US$50 for a double (US$10 for additional persons) plus US$4 per person for a huge buffet breakfast. The **Hostal Boquete** (tel: 720 25730) is great value, located east of the park with comfortable rooms and private bathrooms for US$10 (single) and US$16 (double) – ask for a river view. Feedback on the six rooms at **Hostal Palacios** (tel: 720 1653) is mixed so ask to view one first, US$10 (single) and US$15 (double). Others with rooms at backpacker rates include **Pensión Virginia** (tel: 720 1260), **Hostal Las Mercedes** (tel: 624 0350) and **Pensión Marilós** (tel: 720 1380). More expensive, but still good value at US$30 for a double, is the **Hotel Rebequet** (tel/fax: 720 1365) with nine pleasant rooms with fridge and TV plus communal kitchen facilities.

At the northern end of town the flag-adorned **Hotel Panamonte** (tel: 720 1327; fax: 720 2055) is popular with birders and naturalists due to its close proximity to quetzal habitat. It's run by a third-generation European–Panamanian family and has rooms from US$60 and is famous for feeding guests well from a gourmet kitchen. **Villas Lorena** (tel: 720 1848) beside the Río Caldera is popular with long-term stays due to its generous discounts and seasonal packages. Split-level suites start at US$40 for a double.

The **Residencial Campestre Los Pinos** (tel: 775 1521; fax: 774 6536; email: lospinos75@hotmail.com; http://lospinos.tripod.com) has fully furnished and equipped apartments with various daily, weekly and monthly rates and camping (US$7 per person).

Where to eat

New restaurants are opening at a rapid rate in Boquete and the town has numerous inexpensive options and a growing range of international and local cuisine to choose from.

Top for value is the **El Sabrosón** on Avenida Central, a simple Panamanian diner with a big menu of all-day dishes under US$3. **Café Punto de Encentro** serves a good breakfast 07.00 to noon in a simple garden setting for less than US$4, while sandwiches start at US$1 at **Restaurante Mary**, open early until late. Italian pasta and pizza dishes at **Pizzeria La Volcánica** on Avenida Central are good and reasonably priced at around US$6, although **Salvatore's** just has the edge for its outdoor seating. **Tacos y Tacos** is a good little Mexican cantina and is cheaper than **La Casona Mexicana** on Avenida Central. Food at the quirky **La Folklorica Restaurante** is impossible to fault. A varied menu offers everything from salad (75c) and shrimp and rice dishes (US$5), to steak sandwiches (from US$2.50), pastas (US$3.50) and fillet mignon with all the trimmings (US$6.50), served amidst a cacophony of Panamanian artefacts, marionettes and fairy lights. The **Bistro Boquete** on Avenida Central is a temple for backpackers desperate for American staples, serving big plates of nachos, burgers, steak and chicken caesars to the sound of soft rock. Similarly the US-owned **Santa Fé Bar & Grill**, which serves all-day Tex-Mex complete with cable sports and US import beers.

Some 2km out of town, next to the Cabañas La Vía Lactea, the hacienda-style **Palo Alto Restaurante**, opened in 2003 to rave reviews but is let down by service that is painfully slow. Picnickers should head to the **Garden Panaderia y Dulceria** for pastries, cakes and breads that are cheap and delicious. A great partner to these are the fruit jams sold at **Conservas de Antaño**, one of Panama's finest jam-makers located near to the park.

Eating on a budget? A sack of 100 oranges is just US$2 in Boquete and local cheese farms, dairies, ham and sausage makers, jam and wine producers and market gardeners all sell their produce locally at trade prices, making it the cheapest place for fresh (and usually organic) food in Panama.

Tour operators

American-owned kayak and rafting specialist **Panama Rafters** (tel: 720 2712; email: reservations@panamarafters.com) comes highly recommended for its standards of safety and local knowledge. The company uses guides trained in CPR, water rescue and first aid who carry cell phones and US-standard medical kits. Four main runs are offered of varying degrees of difficulty (see *Rafting in Panama*). The Class 4 Jaguar Run is for a minimum of two people aged 14–65 and runs December to May and June to early December, groups of four at US$90.00 per person. Both the Puma and the Caison runs have a four-person minimum (aged over 18) and are multi-day trips for experienced rafters only, Class 5s with a take-out at 30km. Both run May to January only and are prone to change and delay due to high water. Guides pack enough provisions for one/two extra days just in case they are forced to wait for levels to drop; three-day trip US$385 per person, two-day trip US$285 per person. All trips are eligible for group discounts for eight people or more. Shuttle services, guided and non-guided kayaking and kayak rentals available. Also kayak classes from beginner to expert level: US$275 for three-day beginner course and US$90 per day for intermediate and expert, including all equipment and lunch.

As well as horse rental, Eduardo Cano (tel: 720 1750) also offers guided **horseriding tours** on a small group or individual basis from US$7 per hour.

Boquete Mountain Cruisers (tel: 720 4697/627 8829; email: boquetecruisers@hotmail.com) offers customised guided options and has a large menu of full-day and half-day standard tours in a classic 1978 Toyota Land Cruiser. Costs are reasonable (from US$20 per person) for a minimum of two and maximum of eight.

Practicalities

Over recent years Boquete has become increasingly geared up for tourism. A growing expatriate community and numerous foreign-owned businesses continue to leave their mark, and Tex-Mex burger bars and American diners are springing up alongside the Panamanian cantinas. Boquete is a small town that serves travellers well, with a bank, post office, several international payphones, a couple of pharmacies, laundry and an internet café, plus some decent supermarkets, petrol stations and a 24-hour medical centre.

Most of the Panamanian **tourist board** (IPAT) offices are housed in the finest looking buildings in town – and Boquete is no exception. Yet, despite its swish interior and gorgeous, sweeping views, the office has little of practical use to travellers, apart from a decent adjoining coffee bar. Just like the town of El Valle, the best information on hotels and restaurants in Boquete is found on the streets. Look out for the billboards and road signs on the approach road into town.

What to see and do

The heart of Boquete's appeal is its picturesque setting, which offers accessible walking, hiking and birding trails and tranquil country strolls. Pass rocky crags sprouting waterfalls and mossy ravines surrounded by steep banks of palms, shrubs, creepers, and stone walls. Hot springs, petroglyphs and gauged rocks of cut-glass precision look out to verdant valleys, poinsettia fields and wildflower hedgerows. Hillsides of forget-me-nots, orchids, aroids, bromeliads, roses and lilies hide makeshift signs that read 'se venden plantas' (plants for sale).

However, no trip to Boquete is complete without a visit to a coffee producer. **Casa Ruiz** (tel: 720 1392; fax: 720 1292; email: info@caferuiz.com; www.caferuiz.com) runs the slickest tours, offering a 45-minute 'taster' (US$4) and a full three-hour tour of the entire operation, from picking and roasting to processing and packing (09.00–12.00, US$14). Founded in 1983, the company won the 'Coffee World Cup in 2001', according to Casa Ruiz's charming tour guide, Carlos Antonio Jurado. It buys beans from 650 local farmers as well as harvesting 14 Casa Ruiz plantations containing 100-year-old trees, employing hundreds of Ngöbe Buglé pickers during October to March and paying US$1 for a five-gallon drum of beans. The price of coffee is dropping as international production soars. In 1997 a kilo could fetch US$8 but today US$1.85 would be considered a good exchange. Some 90% of Casa Ruiz coffee is exported to Europe and the US for roasting to local taste and own branding. The balance is roasted for the domestic market and sold under the Casa Ruiz brand in supermarkets throughout Panama. Find it on the main road about 500m north of the centre of town.

The largest coffee-production plant in Panama is also located in Boquete, in a shabby blue and white factory signed **Café Suttón** ten minutes outside the town. It lacks the glamorous good looks of Casa Ruiz but is a great budget option with free, guided tours between 09.00 and 18.00. Catch a bus from Boquete for Bajo Mono and ask to be dropped off en route (US$1).

Another option is the beautiful **La Torcaza Estate** (tel: 771 4087; www.estatecoffee.com), a large, family-run plantation a few kilometres outside of town. Owned by brothers Peter, Maico, Carl and Ricardo Janson, the farm is located at an altitude of 1,350m on the southwest slopes of Volcán Barú. The relatively level terrain allows the coffee cherry to ripen evenly, resulting in more consistent bean quality and density. The Jansons manage the 130ha farm on an organic basis using natural micro-organisms, a mulch of coffee pulp and careful weeding by hand rather than chemical pesticides. They also breed thoroughbred horses. Visitors are welcome seven days a week, but it's advisable to phone first. Tours are on foot, by 4WD or on horseback; US$10 per person..

A sign at the entrance of **Jardin Santa Marta** says *'Mi Jardin Es Su Jardin'* (my garden is your garden) and this magnificent, quirky, private garden is located at the rear of a family home. Owned by the octogenarian former owner of Panama's electric company, Gonzalo González, the Jardin Santa Marta has become a fixture on Boquete's sightseeing trail since throwing its gates open in 1995. Neat, formal gardens give way to plastic flamingos, painted cows and oversized flowerpots. Spiral staircases lead to underground carp ponds and paved areas of multicoloured stone. González is a collector of rare and wonderful plants and the gardens are a riot of colour year-round. The garden is open 09.00 to 18.00, 365 days a year and is free to visitors, who should respect the owner's request of parking on the street and staying away from the house.

Although the idea of a **castle** in Boquete sounds ancient and grand, the one on the Bajo Mono road dates back only to 1970, and was only finished in part. It overlooks the Río Caldera, set back behind a bridge, but was never fully completed due to severe flooding in 1972. The continued threat of water damage has rendered this oddity uninhabitable and its creator Pepe Serracin has abandoned the project as a result.

Everything at **El Explorador** is made from recycled materials, from the light fittings to the plant pots, and this café and gardens is full of eclectic bric-a-brac. Reach it on foot via a 45-minute climb from the town centre for fresh breads, pastries and coffee. Open only at weekends from 09.00 to 18.00 with a US$1 entry fee for the gardens.

Local guides and hikes
Popular local guide **Feliciano González** (tel: 624 9940/632 8645; email: felicianogonzalez255@hotmail.com or leave a message at the Panama Rafters office) knows plenty of great birding spots ('quetzals guaranteed!') and is a veteran of all the local hiking trails. Fearless Feliciano has seen bookings double since rescuing two American backpackers from a charging bull in 2003. However, his prices remain as keen as the man himself with a six-hour hike at US$20 per person

Canadian-born **Danny Poirier** (tel: 626 9354; email: poirierdanny2000@yahoo.com), a seasoned hiker and Boquete resident, runs year-round hiking tours in and around the town for US$35–40 and is also highly

RAPIDS AND RAFTING IN CHIRIQUÍ

Visitors who come to Panama looking for good rivers find *great* rivers and there are more than 450 warm-water stretches begging to be discovered on the isthmus. Most are impossible to get to – but not in Chiriquí. Here the rivers are easily accessible. Only one, the Río Chiriquí Viejo, can be run all year but this stretch just happens to be one of the most exciting and most beautiful in Central America.

Although Panama hasn't had a high rafting profile most rafters are convinced it's only a matter of time before the secret is out. More and more people are visiting Chiriquí specifically for the great rafting and kayaking, and the great thing about the province is that every river can be run in a kayak, although the heavy rains in September, October and November mean these months are reserved for experts. Another fantastic characteristic is Chiriquí's variety of rivers with Class 2, Class 3 and Class 4 (that rise to 5 and 6) providing a challenge for every level. Visitors are coming to Chiriquí from the US, Europe, Asia and Australia to see what all the fuss is about. Even Costa Ricans, who have great rivers of their own, have checked out Chiriquí and liked what they've seen. I think it's fair to say the word is out on Panama's rafting.

The longest run is a three-day trip that starts just outside of Volcán. This section has been dubbed 'The Puma' since a large male was spotted on a rocky ledge right above the water. It's a thrilling ride that is full of challenge and only active adventurous types should tackle it: ideally experienced rafters and kayakers or those with a good standard of fitness who want to have one of the most exciting trips of their lives. Walking out to the river takes several hours and is an adventure in itself. Once there it's a case of no turning back! The lower section of the river is called The Caison, another Class 5 run that we consider our two-day trip. The take-out is only five miles from the start and is another one that would be hard to walk away from. The Jaguar section is a full-day Class 4 that runs for most of the year. It's a popular 16km stretch that teems with wildlife and crosses waterfalls, canyons and 73 rapids. When the water is high (usually June to December) it's easily a good Class 5 run and can be a Class 6 during the months of October and November. For a half-day taster session The Harpia section is ideal. It runs 8km along a gentle stretch, suitable for those aged 7 to 70.

The rating system here is pretty standard and ranks runs from Class 1, the easiest, to Class 6, the most difficult. This system is not an exact science and weather can be an influence in causing the class to alter. As water levels change so do the rapids; some become easier and others more difficult; and many rapids become more technical in shallow depths.

US-born Kevin Mellinger runs white-water rafting trips, kayaking tours and offers kayaking tuition from his base in Boquete (see Tours, Panama Rafters). A veteran white-water rafter, Mellinger knows the Chiriquí rafting and kayaking scene and the thrills of Río Chiriquí Viejo better than most.

recommended. Local guide **Santiago Chago** (known simply as Chago) (tel: 626 2200) is renowned for his birdcalls. Indeed so confident is Chago of attracting quetzals during each tour that he promises visitors a part-refund on their fee (US$50 per group) in the event that none is sighted .

The following trails are common to both Feliciano González and Danny Poirier and are challenging hikes that range from three to eight hours. Guide advisable.

Hot Springs of Caldera Trail Five to six hours of moderate difficultly along a scenic trail to curative water pool near the town of Caldera.

Parque Internacional La Amistad Six to eight hours along challenging hiking trails in prime quetzal habitat to the top of the continental divide for views of the Atlantic and Pacific oceans.

Waterfall Trail Five to six hours of mainly moderate walking that includes a one-hour difficult uphill stretch through canyons and rivers to waterfalls.

Walking Boquete Three to four hours of moderate walking on the outskirts of town along country trails through basalt formations to waterfalls and rivers.

Volcán Baru Trail Full 3,478m ascent with overnight camping (see *Parque Nacional Volcán Barú*).

Local walks are numerous but a short one-hour option is a climbing road that leads out of the town to the neighbouring village of **Jaramillo**, past the park and up into the coffee plantations. Look out for the waterfalls around the corner from Conservas de Antaña (see *Where to eat*) on the left-hand side of the road and the colourful sugarcane, banana and orange trees and avocado fields that flank the route in a patchwork formation. The road is quiet and offers breathtaking valley views at its summit across Boquete. Look north to the continental divide and northwest to Volcán Barú. Once at Jaramillo, take a left fork for a 40-minute descent into town or carry on for a two-hour continuation along a leafy trail popular with horseriders and birders.

Fiestas and special events
The flower-filled Parque de Las Mardes is the venue for Boquete's popular festival, the Feria de las Flores y del Café (Flower and Coffee Fair) held in January each year.

Volcancito
This small hillside community above Boquete is home to a decent restaurant and a handful of good hotels. It's impossible to miss the **Café Restaurant Mozart y Petit Hotel** (tel/fax: 720 3764) as it's decorated in murals, painted yellow and blue, and adorned with fairy lights. The friendly German-Peruvian artist owner works on large canvasses in the main house, and is also an accomplished chef renowned for her fusion of Asian, South American and European cuisine. Regular artisan markets are held of invited painters, sculptors and jewellery makers. Two cabañas boast extraordinary views out to the Pacific across organic fruit and vegetable gardens, from US$15 for single, US$19.80–26.40 double and US$33 for triple occupancy. There's also a rental house option for one to six persons. This two-bed two-bath house has a kitchen, lounge with sofa beds and big outside terrace for US$55 to US$95 per night. A breakfast, lunch and dinner menu at US$2.50–6 is great value with monthly themed gastronomy nights (tel: 720 3764/646 1577).

La Estancia (tel: 720 4260) is a small family resort with basic but comfortable rooms, a swimming pool and restaurant tucked away on the hillside. The nearby **Trattoria Villa Floriencia** is actually the kitchen at the back of a private home that serves excellent Italian food at weekends. A US$10–15 menu is pricier than most but comes highly recommended. Look for green wrought-iron gates and a small sign in the hedgerows.

Finca La Suiza

About 4km north of Los Planes to the east of Boquete in the Talamanca Mountains, Finca La Suiza (tel: 615 3774; email: afinis@chiriqui.com) is a real find for hikers and birders who crave peace and quiet. Owned by Herbert Brullmann and Monika Kohler, and set in 200ha of forested trails, the lodge consists of three charming twin rooms with a communal lounge with fireplace. Travellers have raved about the setting, the waterfall hiking trails and birding. A highlight is a 5½-hour jungle walk in highland cloud forest on a trail that is open year-round. Others are closed on the wettest months, June, September and October. The entire trail system can be accessed by guests for a one-off US$8 fee (non-guests can use it for a US$8 per-day fee). Rooms are great value at US$28 for a single, US$36 for a double and US$8 for an extra bed. The Finca is 1km from the road, which is served by bus (just ask to be dropped off at the entrance) but the gate is open only 07.00 to 10.00, so call to arrange luggage transfer ahead of arrival.

Parque Nacional Volcán Barú

Panama's only volcano has been dormant for over 600 years but visitors will find that it is not without activity. Steaming fumaroles, mineral crusts and bubbling mud pools can be seen at the top, a strenuous six- to eight-hour hike via two cloud-shrouded trails. Volcán Barú sits within a 14,322ha park that was established in 1977. At its heart is Panama's highest peak, soaring over 3,475m to afford amazing views of both the Pacific Ocean and the Caribbean. Large areas of agriculture in Boquete and Cerro Punta are supported by the fertile volcanic soils of western Panama's most dominant geographical feature. The region produces more than 50% of Panama's fruit and vegetables and trees, bushes and flowering alpine scrubs grace Volcán Barú's lower and upper slopes.

At 3,478m the summit is a gruelling full-day hike with great camping spots and wildlife-spotting opportunities. The volcano has seven craters and is home to raccoon, puma, wild rabbits, tapirs and numerous species of birds, including quetzals from January to May. Trails lead up from two entrance points to the west and east of the volcano. The eastern trail from Boquete is the less demanding and is reached by a paved road from the centre of town. Driving to the summit itself is along a rough and rocky road and requires a 4WD vehicle and a winch. Those keen to do the round trip in one day set off on this trail by 05.00. They reach the top by 11.00 for a couple of hours at the summit before a five-hour descent. Those that plan to camp also get an early start to make the most of the clearest views. The gruelling Cerro Punta trail takes a good eight hours, requiring an early start and camping overnight before a next-day seven-hour descent (see *Cerro Punta*). The beginning sections of either trail are excellent for viewing quetzals. The forest then becomes more dwarfed until it is little more than scrubland at the summit. This scattered scrub is where the volcano junco, a rare greyish bird with a pink beak and bright orange eyes, can be sighted.

Practicalities

Hikers in the know mark their path with red or orange waterproof tape bought from a hardware store in Boquete. There are no facilities at all en route so visitors should pack plenty of water, food and an emergency kit (first aid, torch etc) and exercise care if hiking alone. Massive climate changes arise from the lower slopes to mid-altitude and the summit. It may be hot and sweaty in the foothills but it is much, much cooler at the top. Pack a waterproof jacket (the cloud cover is often a damp grey mist) and blanket as a just-in-case measure; be sure to opt for a thermal sleeping bag if camping overnight.

The Boquete entrance of the park is accessible by 4WD taxi and beyond an ANAM ranger station a trail has a long steel pipe running along its left side. There's a sign that reads 'Proyecto de Riego' (but the ANAM rangers will point this out). Like all ANAM-managed protected areas a US$3 fee applies, although this is sometimes waived for no known reason at Volcán Barú. After descent, the easiest way to get back to Boquete is to begin the 50-minute walk back into town. Turn left at the first main road you reach until you each the road that leads into Boquete. The bus service begins here and one passes every 15 minutes or so. Taxis also ply for trade along this stretch.

Guides

A fit, wiry 20-year old called **Danis** takes individual and small groups out fishing and hiking in the highlands. He also arranges Sherpa for ascents on Volcán Barú to enable travellers the luxury of not being weighed down with backpacks full of video or photographic equipment, water and camping supplies. Danis is a volunteer firefighter during the dry season and tackles bushfires on Barú so knows it well. To contact him ask around in Paso Ancho or leave a message in the kiosk.

Paso Ancho

Drivers travelling on the approach road to Paso Ancho may experience a strange phenomenon by putting their car into neutral at the bottom of the small climb. The spot is 200m from a blue bus stop on the right-hand side of the road (opposite the old entrance to Volcán Barú). A strange magnetic force that the locals attribute to the volcano, slowly but surely pulls the vehicle up to the brow of the hill.

The town of Paso Ancho is about 3km from Volcán and is surrounded by coffee fields and smallholdings. It has supermarkets, laundry services, an internet café and a handful of restaurants, including **La Luna**, a good and cheap Chinese restaurant on the Cerro Punta road, and a place favoured by travellers eating on a shoestring budget.

The **Las Plumas Guesthouse** (tel: 771 5541 or 5542; email: veerdeda@yahoo.com; www.las-plumas.com) sits on the outskirts of Paso Ancho 1,600m above sea level and boasts extraordinary mountain views. The guest room is actually a beautifully appointed single-storey building in the expansive gardens of a private home and has a lounge, kitchen, two bedrooms, hot-water bathroom, cable TV and private terrace. There's also an internet connection for laptops and a mobile phone for hire on request. Few hosts are more accommodating than Ann-Marie and Dirk de Veer, a super couple from Holland who have travelled extensively worldwide. Las Plumas is a good self-catering base from which to explore the highlands. It sleeps four at US$60 per night, US$210 per week and US$450 per month

Volcán

Nestled in the flanks of the majestic Volcán Barú is the small town of Volcán, the first notable stop-off on the road from Concepción 30km from the Interamericana turn-off. What gives this sleepy little town its charm is difficult to pinpoint. Maybe it's the quiet, unassuming but friendly people or the restaurants that serve great lunches for less than US$2 a head. Spending time here is simple and pleasant, and the decent local amenities such as the internet café at the Hotel Don Tava (75c per hour) make it a beneficial en route stop-off too.

Getting there and around

Frequent buses link David and Volcán, dropping passengers off throughout the town and picking up at the Shell petrol station on Avenida Central. The approach by road from Concepción is well signed and leads to a fork in the road. The left fork leads to the border town of Río Sereno 45km from Volcán; the right leads to Cerro Punto 16km further on.

Once there, taxis are the best bet (US$1 around town) or hail a bus passing through for 25c.

Local tour companies

A roadside 'Turismo Ecologico' sign points the way to the **Highland Adventure** office (tel: 771 4413/685 1682). Tour packages include mountain biking, rappelling, kayaking, climbing and hiking for about US$30 per person.

Where to stay

A rural spot 1km outside of Volcán is home to the delightful **Cerro Bruja** (tel: 629 5604), owned by local artist and enthusiastic patron, Patricia Miranda Allen. Surrounded by herb gardens, strawberries, flowering hedgerows and blackberry bushes this charming B&B lies beyond an unmade track and is something of a local secret, offering two self-contained cabañas and a charming open restaurant with pleasant leafy views. Numerous birds inhabit this picturesque spot (75 species spotted in one day) and only organic cuisine is served in a restaurant that operates on a reservation basis, opening on demand for breakfast, lunch and dinner (closed throughout October). B&B is US$45 for a double cabaña and guests can camp beyond gardens of dill, fennel, thyme and basil for US$5 each (own tent).

The **Motel California** (tel: 771 4272) on the road out to Río Sereno consists of 23 rustic cabins with private hot-water bathrooms at US$25 per night. The **Hotel Dos Ríos** (tel: 771 4271; fax: 771 5794), a pleasant wooden building overlooking the mountains, has 24 rooms at US$50 each, while the **Hotel y Restaurante Don Tavo** (tel/fax: 771 5144) has 16 comfortable rooms with private bathrooms at US$25 each. Others to try include **Cabañas Valle de la Luna** (tel: 771 4225), **Cabañas Las Nonas** (tel: 771 4284), **Hostal Luz** (tel/fax: 771 5643), **Hostal Llano Lindo** (tel: 771 4027), **Cabañas Dr Esquivel** (tel: 771 4770; fax: 774 4492) and **Complejo Turiatico El Oasis Place** (tel: 771 4644/5261). The last is a complex of 27 cheap rooms (US$12–16) and a lively bar that cranks up its music on a Friday and Saturday night.

Where to eat

No visit to Volcán is complete without a visit to **Restaurante Lorena**, a Chiricana eatery whose glamorous owner wears all-day eveningwear and adores Panamanian soap operas. A great-value US$2 lunchtime special is a fish or chicken dish with rice and beans. Outside and indoor seating. Another great place, although pricier, is the **Restaurante y Pizzeria Biga**, opposite the Accel petrol station. A pasta and pizza menu changes weekly and the food comes highly recommended. Expect to pay US$5 for spaghetti and US$7 for a pizza. The coffee and desserts are great too. Breakfast, lunch and dinner at the **Restaurante Hotel Dos Ríos** are good and reasonably priced but the place is frequently empty and lacks in atmosphere. Sandwiches and salads are less than US$3, chicken, fish and grilled meat US$4.50–8. The menu at the **Hotel y Restaurante Don Tavo** on Avenida Central boasts a good broad mix of dishes, from steak and soup to pasta and pizza and Panamanian specials, generally under US$6.

Others include **Restaurante Mary's Pizzeria**, **Restaurante Ana Francis y Don Toño** and Greek-influenced **Café Restaurante Acropolis**, also **Restaurante Coca-Cola**, **Pepsi Café & Restaurante**, **Café Volcán** and **Liang**, a Chinese Pan-American diner serving chow mein, burgers, rice and beans, and fries. **Café Gladys y Gladys** serves local dishes, shakes and coffee and **Castrejon Cafeteria** fast food and take-away. For breads, pastries and deserts the **Panaderia Dulceria y Cafeteria** is a great little find (opposite the police station), while the **Del Pacifico** and **Café El Rodeo** both come highly recommended for their fish and seafood dishes, US$4–8.

Shopping
For fine quality etchings on crystal and glass and hand-carved wood visit the studio of artist José la Cruz González about 3km outside of town. **Arte Cruz Volcán Artesania en Madera** (tel: 623 0313) welcomes visitors seven days a week 08.00 to 17.30 and the Italy-trained artist is happy to provide demonstrations. The **weekend market** at the Sen Benito schoolhouse generates income for the upkeep of the school. A shipment of seconds from America means there is plenty of sportswear, sunglasses and trainers. The market also has a handicraft stall and sells a variety of household items.

Other practicalities
Volcán has at least a dozen good, cheap restaurants, a police station, two petrol stations, a vehicle repair centre, three supermarkets and two internet cafés (the Don Tavo charges 75c per hour, the Volcánet Café (tel: 771 5482; email: Volcanet_place@hotmail.com; open 08.00 to 22.00) is 5c more but has a full business centre and also places international calls.

What to see
A collection of pre-Columbian petroglyphs has been the life's work of a family who live about 5km outside of town. **Barriles**, a private home, has a small museum and exhibition centre set in flower-filled gardens dotted with dozens of carved stones and boulders. The petroglyphs vary in size and origin and have been catalogued and studied by the family in great depth. Two trails lead through the garden with guided walks for a nominal donation. Open 09.00 to 16.30 each day (a US$3 taxi from the town).

The **Lagunas de Volcán** is the highest lake system in Panama about 5km from the centre of Volcán. The 131ha site became protected in 1994 and today the two picturesque lakes edged by virgin forest and flowering hedges are rich in birdlife. At 1,240m it's a beautiful location for birding, with Volcán Barú as a backdrop and cool, leafy lakeside observation points well out of the sun. Expect to see flycatchers, antbirds, tanagers and pale-billed woodpeckers at the water's edge, possibly also the rare rose-throated becard. The Lagunas are easily reached by car; simply follow the signs from the centre of Volcán. A taxi costs US$4 or US$7 round-trip.

The thermal pools (**Los Pozos Thermal**) on the road to Río Sereno are an effort to reach and require a 4WD but are generally deserted as a result. The turning is easy to miss and comes after a sharp left-hand bend beyond a large steel bridge about 30 minutes from Volcán. Look for an orange sign and a stone road marker and take a sharp second turning on the right up a rough, climbing track. Cross a small bridge, ignoring a right fork, and continue with the slow, cumbersome drive for about 20 minutes. The rough halfway point is a wooden gate on the left and a grey wooden house set back from the road. The climb continues past a farmyard on the left before descending to a sharp bend in the road. Ignore all forks to the right and continue with another couple of climbs and descents until you reach a PRIVADO sign. Turn left, just past a right fork, and park here (this is sometimes signed in dry season) and the pools are about 50m along to the left of the riverbank surrounded by rocks, with forest to the left and rapids to the right. There are no facilities here so bring plenty of water and pack a picnic.

The waterfalls at **Cuesta de Piedra** are barely visible from the road and are contained within land owned by an electricity company that rarely grants access without permission from HQ. However, it's possible to get a decent view by sneaking down an unmade slate path that edges the land by the side of an abandoned bodega. Climb across the rock pools for a terrifying view high above the waterfall. Reach Cuesta de Piedra on the road from Volcán to David, following the signs towards the town and parking by a small bridge close by (look for the electricity board signs).

Bambito

The small town of Bambito has a handful of amenities and a hotel of the same name but is little more than a short stretch of road with a few buildings either side. **Venta de Truchas**, a trout farm opposite the Hotel Bambito, promises fishermen that it is impossible to leave empty handed. Thousands of fish live in the waters, which are so full they look like a heavy trout soup. River trout aren't native to Panama but since being introduced in 1925 on the advice of a US official the population has flourished. Today the rivers in Chiriquí boast a healthy trout population but those that don't want to catch it, but do want to eat it, can buy it fresh (cooked or uncooked) in Bambito each day. Open 07.00 to 16.00 with fishing at US$2.50 (own rod) and US$5 including rod rental. Fish sold at US$2.60 per pound plus an extra US$5 for cooking.

Where to stay and eat

Just along from the trout farm, **Cabañas Kucikas** (tel: 771 4245/269 0623, (512) 396 0769 from the US; email: info@cabañaskucikas.com; www.cabañaskucikas.com) has 18 cabins located on a 36ha riverside site. Each has a kitchen and a hot-water bathroom, and sleeps two to ten people. Rates vary but start at US$60 per night. The **Hostal Cielito Sur B&B** (tel: 771 2038; www.cielitosur.com) is 3km from the centre of Bambito, in the tiny, forested hamlet of Nueva Suiza (New Switzerland), a cluster of alpine houses that will have you yearning for cowbells and yodelling. Owned by Janet and Glen Lee, a former US military man, all four large cabañas sleep three to five and range from US$60 to US$70 per night. The **Hotel Bambito** (tel: 771 4265; fax: 771 4207) has all the facilities you'd expect from a four-star resort, including pool, sauna, tennis courts and restaurant with rooms and suites that start at US$125 per night. The **Hotel Manantial Spa & Resort** (tel: 772 4245; fax: 264 3972) (formerly the Bambito Forest Resort) is reopening at the time of writing and looks top-notch after a costly refurbishment and a change of ownership, something that is sure to be reflected in the rates.

Cerro Punta

Views from this picturesque small town 7km from Bambito encompass verdant sloping valleys, market gardens and the misty peaks of Volcán Barú. Renowned throughout Panama for its plant nurseries, fruit stalls and cattle herds, Cerro Punta attracts visitors keen to explore its rural delights and spot quetzals from January to April.

Getting there and around

A regular bus serves Cerro Punta from David and terminates in Guadalupe. It takes 2½ hours, runs every 10–15 minutes and stops at Volcán and Bambito along the way. Local 4WD taxis offer a reasonable service between villages although many visitors rely on hotel transportation to the hiking trails. Many local hotels also have bike hire or rent out horses by the hour.

Where to stay and eat
Rooms at the **Hotel Cerro Punta** (tel: 771 2020) cost US$30 each and all ten have private bathrooms but are a little worn and tired in places. The restaurant is good and inexpensive with a varied menu from US$5.50. A cheaper and more basic option is **Pensión Eterna Primavera** (tel: 775 3860), a five-room hostel with cold- and hot-water rooms that are overpriced at US$12.50 per person. Seafood dishes at **La Canelita** are served on purple-painted bench tables and priced at US$3–9. The family-run **Yardira Restaurante** opens at dawn for breakfast and serves traditional Panamanian fare until late evening, with few items over US$3. Another all-day option is the turquoise and white-fronted **Restaurante Cerra Punta,** which has a simple menu of inexpensive dishes and hearty breakfasts for US$2.

Local tour companies
A number of freelance guides work from the Los Quetzales Lodge & Spa in neighbouring Guadalupe, including Ito Santa Maria, a 24-year-old local who has guided since he was twelve. He holds a certificate from IPAT, Panama's tourist board, and knows the area inside out for hiking, birding, horseriding and Ngöbe Buglé cultural trips. He also organises tailored excursions and can be contacted via Los Quetzales (see *Guadalupe*).

Shopping
Local Cerra Punta produce is sold in abundance from roadside stalls and nurseries. Strawberry yoghurts, fresh strawberries and fruit milkshakes are delicious at **Frescha El Parkente,** while at the **Jardin Mary** plants, shrubs and seedlings are sold with an adjoining café selling ice-cream and coffee. Opposite the nursery a row of canvas-covered roadside stalls sell fruit **jam and marmalade** 08.00 to 16.00, while nearby booths sell freshly picked **vegetables and fruit** year-round.

Other practicalities
Cerro Punta has its own fire station, a couple of small supermarkets (stocking cooking gas, dry snacks and canned goods), a service station and a vehicle repair shop.

Guadalupe
It's difficult not to take Guadalupe to your heart, as this tiny end-of-the-road flower-filled village 3km from Cerro Punta is a testament to neighbourhood pride. A colourful succession of humble houses is festooned from top to bottom in seasonal blooms. Planters, baskets and flowerpots adorn each frontage and several flat roofs have been laid to grass and sewn with a hotpotch of wildflowers. The ambience is tranquil and the setting picturesque and locals are all too eager to answer questions on this plant or that. Signs that read 'Esteemed visitors please enjoy our garden' politely ask visitors to refrain from picking its flora and direct them to a street stall offering posies for US$1.

Where to stay
Without a shadow of a doubt the lofty **Los Quetzales Lodge & Spa** (tel: 771 2291/2182; fax: 771 2226; email: stay@losquetzales.com; www.losquetzales.com) is one of Panama's best-known places to stay. One of the reasons for this is the vast

BIRDS, BIRDS, BIRDS II

Guadalupe, Cerro Punta and the area surrounding Los Quetzales Lodge & Spa is renowned for its world-class birding. More than a 100 species have been recorded at the lodge itself by visiting enthusiasts and it has become a favoured retreat for ornithologists, biologists and zoologists who are keen to study the avian diversity.

Multiple daily sightings of quetzals are comonplace in the environs during the nesting season, January to May. During the rest of the year it is still possible to sight them every two to four days using local Ngöbe Buglé guides who are experts at imitating bird calls. The area is also home to ten species of hummingbird and a significant amount of indigenous birdlife. Sightings of great currasows, black guams, black-faced solitaires, collared redstarts, and yellow-thighed finches are numerous with an ornithological list that includes buff-fronted quail, green violet-ear, white-throated mountain gem, prong-billed barbet, hairy woodpecker, ruddy treerunner, buffy tuftedcheek, spot-crowned woodcreeper, silvery-fronted tapaculo, mountain elaenia, common tufted flycatcher, yellowish flycatcher, barred becard, black-capped flycatcher, ochraceous wren, black-faced solitaire, mountain thrush, black-and-yellow silky-flycatcher, yellow-winged vireo, flame-throated warbler, black-throated green warbler, Wilson's warbler, collared redstart, sooty-capped bush-tanager, large-footed finch and slaty flowerpiercer. As one amateur birder put it: 'I wasn't even trying, but still managed to chalk up over 50 sightings of different species in one day. Just imagine how many I'd have seen if I'd been more serious.'

network of road signs that publicise it at regular intervals along the Interamericana. Another is its high-profile owner, Carlos Alfaro, a local environmentalist who made headline news in Panama for his vocal opposition to the Cerro Punta to Boquete road (see *End of the road?*).

Accommodation at Los Quetzales comprises ten rooms and one suite in the main lodge, a ten-bed dormitory for budget travellers and three cabañas in the cloud forest. Rates range from US$12 per person (dorm bed) to US$55 66 for a single/double room and US$82.50–93.50 for suites that sleep three to eight. Numerous seasonal packages are offered, inclusive of meals, tours and transport. Food served in the restaurant uses produce from the local organic gardens, trout farm and bakery. There's also a reading room with internet, laundry service, games room and bar. An onsite spa offers foor rubs and massage. Visa, Mastercard and American Express accepted.

The spa, situated in a 350ha private reserve, right smack bang in the heart of a magnificent highland cloud forest, is perfect for those looking for immersion. It's a real retreat, 20-minutes from the main lodge by 4WD, a good 30-minute hike or a 15-minute ride on horseback (US$125–150).

At over 2,000m above sea level the Los Quetzales Preserve is part of Volcán Barú National Park, a protected primary rainforest since 1976. Parque Nacional Volcán Barú edges the 407,000ha Parque Internacional La Amistad, which straddles Costa Rica and Panama, and the 350ha reserve was founded via private funding in 1968. Guests at the lodge can either do their own thing or book a local Ngöbe Buglé guide to hike through the forest. Numerous trails, most of them well maintained, lead from Guadalupe, including several that wind through the Los Quatzales Preserve and out into the rest of Barú.

Trails and tours from the lodge

Local hiking and horseback trails Ten trails offer different degrees of difficulty through primary cloud forest led by a knowledgable Ngöbe Buglé guide. The paths cross through prime birding territory rich in local flora and fauna and cross streams and waterfalls. The guide will also track prints left by mountain lions, ocelots and tapirs (from 30 minutes to four hours).

Hiking from Cerro Punta to Boquete This guided expedition takes hikers over the dormant Volcán Barú and down into the town of Boquete, passing through spectacular scenery along a trail that takes about six hours to complete. Overnight stay, return bus/car journey an option. Tour free to lodge guests.

Eight-day hike to the Atlantic Ocean An adventurous option for those who aren't afraid of roughing it and are fit enough for a rugged expedition. Involves a week of sleeping in tents, trudging through mud, climbing mountain summits and descending in slippery conditions. Yet those who have the stamina and spirit will experience a trip that very few non-Ngöbe Buglé have made. The trail passes through remote Indian villages through undisturbed habitat along rivers by cayuco to the banana plantation town of Changuinola.

Cultural excursions Visit local organic gardens to learn about medicinal plants and their healing properties from indigenous experts. Be the guest at the home of a Ngöbe Buglé family to exchange cultural knowledge and learn about the local community.

Cross-border trips to Costa Rica After a 1½-hour drive to Costa Rica visit the Wilson Botanical Gardens located in San Vito and stay overnight (or longer) in the rainforest on the Osa peninsula. Day trip, one to two nights or longer.

Finca Dracula

Although the name suggests something more sinister, Finca Dracula (tel: 771 2223) is actually an orchid sanctuary, named in honor of Panama's *Telipogo vampirus* species. This collection of 1,200 orchid species is a seven-minute walk from the Los Quetzales Lodge, set in gardens of indigenous plants and trees. Owner Andres Maduro has over 100 *Telipogo vampirus*, a handsome plant that thrives in the cool highland soils and which decorates these lush botanical gardens. Other species are propagated here and nurtured in a nursery, including several that are threatened with extinction. Its success has given Finca Dracula prominence throughout Central and South America, and it is thought to be one of the the largest collections of *Telipogo* in the world. Visitors are welcome at Finca Dracula for a US$5 contribution to running costs and will receive a two-hour guided tour from an orchid specialist in return. Numbers are limited to groups of six unless by prior arrangement. This is an informative tour aimed at budding horticulturists. Visitors are asked to call ahead of arrival; open 09.00 to 17.00.

Getting there

Guadalupe is a 1½-hour bus journey from Río Serena, the Costa Rica border town and a 2½-hour trip by bus from David. Guests at Los Quetzales can take advantage of a transfer from David Airport. The drive from David to Guadalupe takes less than 1½ hours.

Parque Internacional La Amistad

This 407,000ha national park straddles the Costa Rican–Panamanian border and is split with even acreage in both countries. Las Nubes, a tiny village near to Cerro

END OF THE ROAD?

When President Moscoso announced her intention to transform a rough hiking path linking Cerro Punta and Guadalupe to Boquete into a fully-fledged road, wildlife lovers throughout the world gasped in disbelief. For the trail, Sendero de los Quetzales ('Path of the Quetzals'), winds through 144ha of Panama's Volcán Barú National Park and is one of the best places on the planet to see this rare and spectacular bird. An estimated 300 to 400 endangered quetzal breeding pairs are thought to inhabit the park, holding out against their number-one enemy – forest devastation.

Since Moscoso's announcement a broad alliance of activists and concerned citizens have been campaigning to stop the road, citing untold destruction of quetzal nests, seed trees on which the quetzals depend upon for food, as well as the improved access it would provide for poachers, illegal loggers and other habitat-destroying activities. This fierce opposition made headline news, bringing a Panamanian environmental issue to the fore in a country usually more concerned with economics. ANCON, Panama's foremost privately funded environmental advocacy groups described the Panamanian protest as a 'watershed crusade', yet in the face of this strong public opposition Moscoso continued to dismiss counter-proposals with less environmental impact as economically unviable.

In December 2002 she awarded the US$4.6 million construction contract to a firm of her choice without the stipulated review and public comment processes. ANCON responded with a lawsuit; the government countered by changing the regulations governing Volcán Barú National Park; and press

Punta, is one of three access points in Panama. Another is in Guadalupe close to the Los Quetzales Lodge. There is also one in Wekso in the Bocas del Toro province on the Caribbean side (see *Bocas del Toro Province* chapter).

Three scenic trails lead from the ranger station at the Las Nubes entrance: a winding 1.5km climb up to the Mirador la Nevera observation point at 2,500m; the 2.1km Sendero El Retoño trail, rich in avifauna; and the 1.7km path to the La Cascada path that leads to a beautiful waterfall, passing several lofty lookout points and breathtaking views on the way. The park's extraordinary biodiversity supports a sizeable wildlife population, including more than 100 species of mammals such as howler monkey, black-handed spider monkey, night monkey, tapir, squirrel, shrew and five species of cat. Birders delight in spotting quetzal, umbrella bird and bellbird, whose distinctive shrill call is heard along the El Rentoño trail. Ninety-one amphibian species, 400 birds and 61 reptiles occupy this habitat, including mountain salamander, arlequin frog and spiny toad. Look out for coral snakes underfoot on some of the reddish trail stretches.

Where to stay

ANAM, Panama's state-run environment agency, offers 16 bunk beds in its **ranger station** at US$5 per night (pre-booking advised, tel: 775 7840/3163). Facilities are pretty basic but the location is rather special. Bring bedding, food and plenty of water, and a tent to camp at US$5 per night.

Los Quetzales Lodge & Spa also has three cabins, **Cabañas Los Quetzales**, tucked away inside the park (see *Guadalupe, Where to stay*). Each has a terrace at canopy level and is decked out with feeders that attract numerous hummingbirds. Those that like the jungle on their doorstep with enjoy the allegations surfaced about the possible motives for Moscoso's zeal to get the project underway. Some alleged that her prime concern was maximising the sale price of real estate she owned along the route. These accusations, once vehemently denied, were countered by claims that the anti-road activists had ulterior motives and were protesting using underhand tactics.

Today, despite the protests, the road appears to be a done deal, although construction scheduled for January 2003 has been stalled by local environment group the Integrated Foundation for the Department of Cerro Punta (FUNDICCEP, Cerro Punta, Chiriquí, Panama; tel: 771 2171; fax: 771 2171; email: amiscond@chiriqui.com). The forested footpath remains an environmental battleground as activists march against state-deployed bulldozers and the fate of Volcán Barú and its colourful quetzals hangs in the balance. Who knows the real reason why the road became a matter of extreme urgency (Moscoso awarded the project national emergency status in 2002) but if it had been routed further down the hill the habitat of the endangered quetzal would be spared, and deforested cow pastures and scrubland used in its place. Visitors to Chiriquí should expect to find Boquete linked with Cerro Punta as per Moscoso's wishes. The byway carves through a stretch of forest described as 'one of the most ecologically sensitive areas' by the University of Panama Centre for Biotic Studies. Although known as the Cerro Punta to Boquete road it actually begins in Guadalupe by the Los Quetzales Lodge. The project is lamented by the Panama Audubon Society for the untold damage it will cause to the threatened and resplendent quetzal, just one of over 100 bird species recorded in the area.

immersion the cabins allow. Few settings are so seemingly remote yet are just a 30-minute hike from the village or 20 minutes by 4WD vehicle (US$5 from Guadalupe).

Where to eat
At the entrance to the park, at the edge of the village of Las Nubes, is the **Restaurante Asaela**, which opened mid-2003. It has indoor and outdoor seating and a great-value menu of local fare. Expect a lunchtime special using local organic produce to cost as little as US$1.50. Set up by the Asociación Agroecoturística La Amistad to help raise funds for local conservation initiatives, the restaurant is open from 07.00 to 19.00 and is popular with locals and tourists alike.

Río Sereno
The fork that heads west from the entrance of Volcán leads to the Costa Rican border 45km away. This scenic road is a joy to travel by bus as it weaves through coffee plantations, cattle fields and past stud farms, rivers and forest thickets containing thermal pools (see *What to see, Volcán*). It's not possible to cross this border by car. (For details on the border town see the *Practical Information* chapter.)

La Reserva Forestal Fortuna
Benefiting from little direct human disturbance and an altitude of 1,500m, the 19,500ha is blessed with a wet, cool climate and glorious fauna and flora. It was created in 1976 to protect the hydrographic river basin of Lago Fortuna, an artificial lake used for the generation of electrical energy, and has the highest registered precipitation in the country at 8,000mm per year. Today the reserve offers visitors

HORSE COUNTRY

Chiriquí, the land of rolling hills and grassy fields, is truly Panama's horse country. Getting about is still common using horses as transport, either ridden bareback or pulling a cart. Unsurprisingly, Panama's road laws have been created with horses in mind.

Hit a horse with a car in daylight and it's your fault, regardless. If it's being ridden at the time the driver of the car is also totally liable for all costs that ensue from injury or death. Hit a horse by car after 18.00 and the law deems the rider is liable, as it's illegal to ride a horse after this time on any of Panama's roads. Hit a horse without a rider by car during the day and it's the owner's fault as the law says that all horses should be kept under proper control.

who are prepared to pre-plan excellent access to a vast and largely unspoiled wilderness containing more than 1,200 species of plants.

ANAM, the national environmental authority, and an electrical generation company, EGE Fortuna SA (www.fortuna.com.pa), share the management of the Fortuna Reserve and offer scientific facilities to the Smithsonian Tropical Research Institute (STRI). The focus for STRI researchers has been a ten-year study of tree frogs following the discovery of large numbers dead or dying in the interior of the park. The cause, a rare fungus found only in Central America, continues to be monitored in a habitat that is also home to dozens of bird species, including rufous-browed tyrannulet, sulphur-winged parakeet, mixed flocks of tanager, emerald, bay-headed, silver-throated and tawny-capped euphonia, and rare yellow-green finch. Projects also include impact studies on the building of the Edwin Fabrega Dam across the upper Chiriquí River, and the construction of an oil pipeline and highway from the Pacific coast across the Fortuna catchment to Chiriquí Grande on the Caribbean coast.

An STRI visitor centre welcomes visitors by appointment (tel: 212 8000/8148; email: visitSTRI@tivoli.si.edu). Accommodation also exists in the reserve and although designed for visiting scientists is made available for overnight visitors on occasions by prior arrangement. Multiple trails lead from the lodge into the forest surrounding Fortuna Lake where the fauna and flora is particularly magnificent. An ANAM office (tel: 775 3163; fax: 775 3163) at the entrance to the reserve is manned from 08.00 to 16.30, or thereabouts.

In February 2004 ANAM rejected a second application by Generadora Electrica de Panama (GEPSA) to build and operate a windmill farm in part of the Fortuna Forest Reserve. The proposal was opposed because of the deforestation required to site the windmills and the erosion of prime bird habitats on the Chiriquí Ridge.

Getting there

For further information on visiting the Fortuna Reserve contact the Smithsonian Tropical Research Institute (Roosevelt Av, Building 401, Tupper Balboa, Ancon, Panama; tel: 212 800; fax: 212 8148; email: visitSTRI@tivoli.si.edu) or ANAM Chiriquí regional HQ (tel: 775 3163; fax: 775 3163).

Above Posada Ecológica, Chiguiri Arriba (DS)

Left and below Workers hand-roll cigars at Panama's only surviving cigar factory, Joyas de Panama, in La Pintada, Coclé Province (DS)

Above Street vendors and foodstalls dot the roadsides of Bocas Town, Isla Colón (DS)

Above right and below Old Bank's on-the-water gas station (DS)

Bocas del Toro Province

On the country's northwest flank, the
Province of Bocas del Toro (or simply
'Bocas' as it's known by the locals) is a
wholly unique slice of Panama, culturally,
geologically and botanically. Lying on the sloping
terrain of the Talamanca and Central Mountains,
the province is bordered by the Caribbean Sea to the north, Veraguas Province
to the east, Chiriquí Province to the south and Costa Rica to the west. Its
population of 90,000 of diverse ethnic mix comprises descendants of banana and
Canal workers from Africa, Colombia, Jamaica and the French Antilles; four
indigenous Indian tribes; and a burgeoning expatriate community fresh from
Europe and North America. Low-lying coastal areas, forests and islands boast an
eclectic synthesis of cultures where ancestral lines are blurred. This
extraordinary mix of peoples owes its fusion to history and prosperity, from the
visiting Spanish fleets and French Huguenot settlers of the 17th century; the
arrival of black slaves and banana workers in the 19th century; and the 21st-
century real estate boom.

Today's interminable number of sub-communities and mini-cultures in Bocas
brings a unique mix of gastronomy, music and language to the province. More
English speakers are found on the archipelago than anywhere else in Panama,
while the indigenous Indians use Ngabere, Spanish or Guari-Guari. An influx of
holiday-homers has brought a new era of internationalism to Bocas and 50
different nationalities were tallied in the province in 2003. Such a trans-national
character can be a surprise to travellers fresh from the eastern provinces that step
from ancient customs into a funky laidback tourist haven, complete with tropical
rum shacks and a take-us-as-we-are culture.

As many of its traditional industries dwindle, tourism has become increasingly
vital to Bocas del Toro. Yet while discovery by international travellers may be a
recent event, the appeal of this craggy stretch of coastline and its gorgeous outlying
islands is far from new. Panamanians countrywide have holidayed here for
generations and so far soaring prices have done little to dampen their ardour. Palm-
fringed and separated from Jamaica by nothing but water, the Caribbean coastline
of Bocas del Toro and its strange ethnicity may just as well be an overseas
destination.

THE ARCHIPELAGO

Although it comprises hundreds of atolls and coralline keys, it is six large palm-
forested islands that dominate the archipelago of Bocas del Toro. Isla Colón
(61km²), Isla Popa (53km²), Isla Bastimentos (51km²), Isla Cristóbal (37km²), Cayo
de Agua (16km²) and Isla Solarte (8km²) form a cluster amidst peninsulas in a vast
mouth-shaped bay, surrounded by dozens of unnamed islets. Those that are

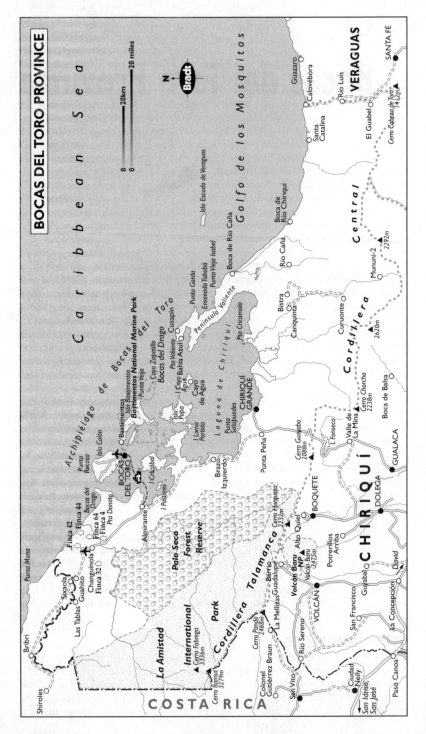

TALK THE TALK

No province in Panama boasts a rural trans-national culture like that of Bocas del Toro, home to 50 nationalities and dozens of languages and dialects. The archipelago's indigenous Indians use Ngabere and locals speak Spanish or Guari-Guari, a distinct Creole tongue unique to the province that mixes English with Spanish. More English speakers are found here than anywhere else in Panama and holiday-home owners from North America and Europe have added to the verbal stew. Anglicising place names, in whole or in part, has created a hybrid Pan-Am (locals call it Span-glish) language, adding Americanisms to the rich local language, already a hotpotch of influences, and one that is changing at a rapid pace.

Panamanian phrases and slang

Whappin'?	What's happening (Bocas Caribbean)
Q sopa?	What's up? What's happening?
Q lo q?	What's up?
Bien pritti	Cool
Vaina	Literally means 'thing' but is used frequently in conversation, ie: 'y vaina' at the end of sentences where it refers to nothing (like 'and that' slang)
Voy polante	I'm going (from *para adalante*)
Mopri	Friend, (from *primo*, cousin, cut up and swapped round).
Chuletta	Literally 'pork chops', used to express disbelief.
Como assi?	Used as 'What do you mean?'
Arranque	Last drink (when you intend to have many more) or party (*vamos a aranque*)
Un palo	US$1

named share many different titles, a potential source of great confusion to visitors reliant on maps and hearsay. Isla Colón, capital of the archipelago, is often simply referred to as Bocas. Coral Cay, a tiny islet renowned for the stunning array of marine life that surrounds it, is often called Crawl Cay, while Isla Solarte, another popular snorkel spot, is also known as Cayo Nancy. The archipelago's trans-national culture has played its part in the confusion, adding Anglicised place names, in whole or in part, to create a hybrid language of Americanisms and local speak. 'Main Street' and 'the Main Drag' are commonly used and you're just as likely to hear Bocas (Bock-as) pronounced with an American drawl (Bowe-cus).

Although home to Bocas del Toro Airport, Isla Colón had few roads until recently, a slow-paced community where pedestrians, street dogs and the occasional municipal truck used hot, dirt tracks. However, things are changing in Bocas – and no more so that on Isla Colón. Thanks to the expatriate influx a host of gas-guzzling MPVs rule the roads on Isla Colón, roaring from A to B in a cloud of dust in preference to a ten-minute walk.

The island of Bastimentos, the archipelago's 'second town', is also undergoing immense change. Although Isla Colón is home to most of the hotels, bars and restaurants, Isla Bastimentos is attracting its fair share of new resorts, with more planned development in the pipeline.

Hailed as an 'investor's paradise' by the American money press in the late 1990s, Bocas del Toro had soon aroused the curiosity of foreign buyers in search of the next big thing. Today, less than a decade on, the landscape is undergoing great

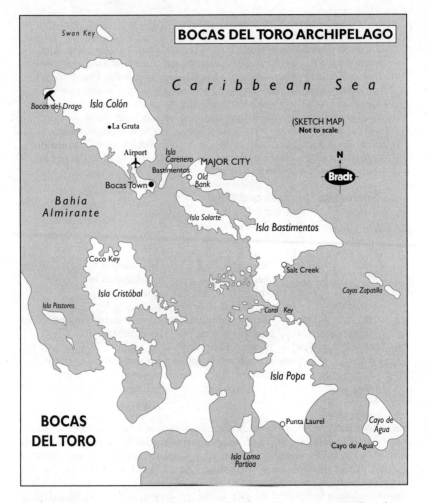

change, especially in Bocas Town, where uninterrupted views out to sea have been replaced with waterfront bars, dive shops and restaurants, and a number of holiday apartments have been built. Away from the town, the region remains largely unspoilt. Many outer islands are totally untouched and uninhabited, while others are sparsely populated by Ngöbe Buglé communities who live as they did generations ago. Visitors don't need to travel far from the crowds of Isla Colón to find complete solitude in jungle that remains wholly undisturbed. Vast wild swathes of vine-tangled rainforest and marshlands are home to an exciting array of wildlife, an inviting prospect for naturalists, hikers and botanists. The snorkelling, diving, boating and fishing around the islands are some of the finest in Panama.

Bocas del Toro attracts independent travellers and remains devoid of mass tourism. Rustic wooden B&Bs and small low-key hotels discourage big-vacation crowding and even in its peak months the province is relatively free of congestion. The absence of large hotels and big resorts gives the province a casual feel and most places to stay offer convenience, comfort and charm as opposed to five-star frills. Bocas del Toro appeals to an easy-going crowd of travellers who favour adventure over luxury and trimmings. Most are barefoot champions of leisure keen to explore the great outdoors in a setting that combines the Wild West with the Caribbean and offers plenty of colourful character. No visit to the archipelago is complete without spotting its unique strawberry-coloured frog. Panama's first marine park on Isla Bastimentos is also an important nature reserve for rare Caribbean wildlife species.

ISLA COLÓN

Most visitors to Bocas del Toro arrive at Isla Colón on a domestic flight from Panama City, flying low over dense emerald forests and orange rivers into Bocas del Toro Airport. Isla Colón is the commercial hub of the archipelago and by far the most visited, populated and developed of all the islands. The airport, located on the outskirts of town, is a ten-minute walk from the centre. Arrive on the morning flight and a pleasant cooling breeze blesses the stroll. Arrive on a hot and humid Bocas afternoon and it presents more of a struggle, especially if weighed down with luggage.

Taxis head to the airport to meet each flight and are used to supplement the public transport system on a shared 'hail and stop' basis. If there isn't one free at the airport start walking towards town. One will pass by sooner or later and will toot a horn staccato-style if it has a spare seat. Just a couple of years ago there were only five taxis in Bocas so getting a ride was very hit and miss. It often meant sharing a pick-up truck with a crate of fruit, even livestock, but that situation is much changed. Today dozens of taxis serve this small dusty town. Journeys are short and less about distance and more to do with avoiding the heat.

A close-knit lazy-paced town that comprises shoulder-to-shoulder wooden architecture, Bocas is vaguely reminiscent of a cowboy town. New development has added a handful of gleaming boutiques yet Bocas remains the domain of independent travellers and good local amenities make it an ideal base from which to explore the archipelago. Most enjoy hanging out in Bocas for a few days, catching water taxis to explore the palm-scattered islands and diving the surrounding coral reefs. Waterfront restaurants form the heart of the town – for the views as much as the food. Few places are better for swapping stories with fellow travellers, looking out across the bay and out to islands with sunset views.

WET AND WETTER

Ask the locals what the climate is like in Bocas and they will tell you of two distinct seasons – wet and wetter. Hot, sticky and sunny it may be but Bocas is also blessed with more than its fair share of rain. While there are fewer downpours during September, October and March, it is still not uncommon to experience a shower or two at least once a week. Serious rainfall generally occurs overnight and presents few problems for visitors. However, those who do get caught in a daytime downpour will find it a full-on drenching affair. Be warned: it can happen in an instant, with few obvious telltale signs. In a flash the heavens have opened, emptying the streets at the first splash of rainfall until the torrent shows promise of a let-up. Rain in Bocas can stop just as quickly as it starts but a waterproof jacket is essential even in the so-called dry season. Residents welcome the rain in this region which is also prone to drought. High levels of precipitation mean fresh supplies of water, verdant rainforest canopies and abundant vegetation, and after a dry spell a downpour is positively blissful.

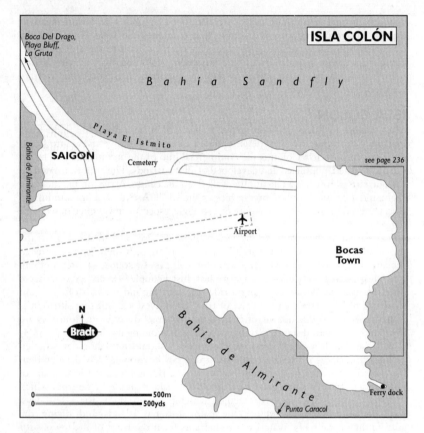

ISLA COLÓN

Boca Del Drago,
Playa Bluff,
La Gruta

B a h í a   S a n d f l y

P l a y a El Istmito

SAIGON   Cemetery

Bahía de Almirante

see page 236

Airport

**Bocas
Town**

N

Bradt

B a h í a   d e   A l m i r a n t e

0 ▬▬▬▬▬ 500m
0 ▬▬▬▬▬ 500yds

Ferry dock

Punta Caracol

Getting there

Getting to Isla Colón is straightforward by boat or by plane with a regular daily service for both.

By air

Aeroperlas (tel: 757 9341 for the airport) runs a daily flight schedule from Panama City to Bocas (see *Panama City* chapter for flight information) with two flights a day to Panama City from Bocas, departing at 09.00 and 14.30 Monday to Friday. On Saturday there's a single flight at 08.40 and one on Sunday at 09.25. The journey time is just short of an hour at US$57.75 one-way (simply double for a return ticket). Aero Mapiex (tel: 757 9841 for the airport) also has a daily schedule to Panama City from Bocas with a twice-a-day flight Monday to Friday at 08.30 and 15.30, two flights on Saturday at 08.00 and 14.30 and a single Sunday flight at 17.00. The ticket price is the same as Aeroperlas. Mapiex and Aeroperlas both fly to Changuinola on the mainland and Aeroperlas also offers a daily service to David from Bocas del Toro at 09.40 Monday to Friday for a single fare of US$31.50.

Aeroperlas (main booking office) tel: 315 7500; fax: 315 7580; email: iflyap@aeroperlas.com; www.aeroperlas.com
Aero Mapiex (main booking office) tel/fax: 315 0888; email: reservaciones@aero.com.pa; www.aero.com.pa

By sea

Catch a water taxi in Almirante on the mainland to travel to Isla Colón by boat. Two companies offer a regular daily schedule (with few discernable differences) and leave hourly, or thereabouts, from 06.30 to 18.30, charging US$3 for the 35-minute journey. Despite having covered roofs it is usual for passengers to get damp from sea spray in windy conditions. Pack a waterproof as a 'just in case' measure as the roof also provides limited shelter from the rain. No need to book, just turn up ten minutes ahead of departure and join the queue. Boats leave from Bocas Town centre at the **Expreso Taxi 25** office (Calle 1, Isla Colón; tel: 757 9062) and **Bocas Marine Tours** (Calle 3, Isla Colón; tel/fax: 757 9033; email: info@bocasmarinetours.com; www.bocasmarinetours.com).

Visitors travelling to Bocas del Toro from Costa Rica via the Sixaola–Guabito border can catch a water taxi directly from Changuinola. This one-hour journey is one of the most scenic routes into Bocas, travelling along wetlands, through jungle and pastures across along the Changuinola Canal. The boat taxi leaves from Finca 63, a five-minute drive from Changuinola town centre. A taxi from the bus station should cost no more than US$1, but those on a shoestring budget can opt for a minibus at 50c and this also runs between the boat and the bus station.

Getting around

Bocas is a small town that is easily navigable on foot. Most visitors walk it end to end several times a day to get from A to B, supplemented by taxis and bicycle hire. The road layout is a rough grid system that is easy to master. Most streets share both local and American names, the hub being Calle 3 (or Main Street or 3rd Street as it is commonly known). Most hotels, bars, shops and tourist essentials are located along Calle 3 and this is where Parque Simon Bolivar is located, the heart of Bocas life. Taxis serve the town for 50c per person from dawn until dusk. They become a scarcity after 21.00 and at lunchtime, noon–13.00. Bicycle hire is cheap and easy (US$1–2 per hour) with scooters from US$20 per day and rent-a-wreck-style cars from US$40. A bus service to Boca del Drago departs from the park every 90 minutes. See the schedule in hotels and any of the internet cafés on Calle 3.

Street vendor **Señor Camilo** (tel: 647 5557) parks his van full of bikes and motorbikes for hire next to the Golden Grill restaurant and also rents out surfboards at US$8 per day. Scooters are US$30 a day and bikes US$1 per hour. There is also a single car available at US$40 per day. Open seven days a week, 08.00–18.00.

Bikes at **Bocas Action Tours** in Calle 3 cost US$8 to hire for a day. The company also rents out jet skis for US$75 per hour (US$40 for 30 minutes) – a pricey option and one that's not popular with those that share growing safety concerns about water traffic in the bay.

A big range of hire bikes can be found at **Casa Amarillo**, the yellow house (as the name suggests) opposite Posada Los Delphines on the corner of Avenida G and Calle 5. Hourly hire is US$1 and daily US$8. Also snorkel equipment at US$5 a day and surfboard hire (enquire for rates).

Where to stay

Hospedaje Heike (7 rooms) Calle 3, Isla Colón; tel: 757 9708; email: hospedajeheike@yahoo.com. This excellent little hostel has comfortable rooms that are clean and affordable, right in the centre of town. Rooms have shared bathrooms, 1 or 2 beds (extra on request) and mosquito nets and there is also a small communal kitchen. Rooms at the back of the property are US$8 single and US$15 double, US$16 with balcony. Breakfast is served in the downstairs restaurant where a plate of eggs plus fruit and

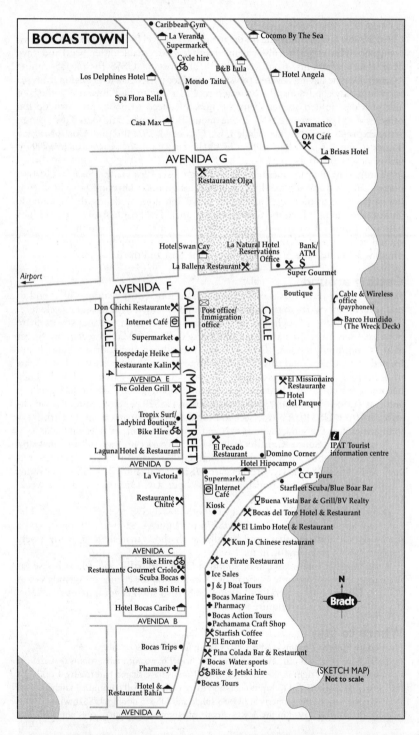

BOCAS TOWN

Caribbean Gym
La Veranda
Supermarket
Cocomo By The Sea
Cycle hire
B&B Lula
Hotel Angela
Los Delphines Hotel
Mondo Taitu
Spa Flora Bella
Casa Max
Lavamatico
OM Café
La Brisas Hotel
AVENIDA G
Restaurante Olga
Hotel Swan Cay
La Natural Hotel
Reservations
Office
Bank/
ATM
La Ballena Restaurant
Super Gourmet
Airport
AVENIDA F
Boutique
Cable & Wireless
office
(payphones)
Don Chichi Restaurante
Post office/
Immigration
office
Barco Hundido
(The Wreck Deck)
Internet Café
Supermarket
Hospedaje Heike
Restaurante Kalin
AVENIDA E
The Golden Grill
El Missionairo
Restaurante
Hotel
del Parque
Tropix Surf/
Ladybird Boutique
Bike Hire
Laguna Hotel & Restaurant
El Pecado
Restaurant
IPAT Tourist
information centre
AVENIDA D
La Victoria
Domino Corner
Hotel Hipocampo
Supermarket
Internet
Café
CCP Tours
Starfleet Scuba/Blue Boar Bar
Restaurante
Chitré
Kiosk
Buena Vista Bar & Grill/BV Realty
Bocas del Toro Hotel & Restaurant
El Limbo Hotel & Restaurant
Kun Ja Chinese restaurant
AVENIDA C
Bike Hire
Restaurante Gourmet Criolo
Scuba Bocas
Artesanias Bri Bri
Hotel Bocas Caribe
AVENIDA B
Le Pirate Restaurant
Ice Sales
J & J Boat Tours
Bocas Marine Tours
Pharmacy
Bocas Action Tours
Pachamama Craft Shop
Starfish Coffee
El Encanto Bar
Pina Colada Bar & Restaurant
Bocas Water sports
Bike & Jetski hire
Bocas Tours
N
Bradt
Bocas Trips
Pharmacy
Hotel &
Restaurant Bahía
AVENIDA A
(SKETCH MAP)
Not to scale

CALLE 3 (MAIN STREET)
CALLE 2
CALLE 4

coffee will set you back US$3.50. The hostel doesn't accept credit cards or travellers' cheques and there is no reservation system. Turn up early to stand a chance of snapping up one of these popular low-budget rooms.

Hospedaje Sagitarius (16 rooms) Calle 4, Isla Colón; tel: 757 9211. This is another good-value option for visitors that want to stay close to the town centre. Each of the rooms has private hot-water bathrooms with colour TV, air conditioning and ceiling fans in a quiet location a few minutes' walk to restaurants, shops and bars. Priced from US$17 for a double room.

Hotel Hipocampo (9 rooms) Calle 1, Isla Colón; tel: 757 9073/674 1167; email: hotelhipocampo@yahoo.com; www.bocas.com/hipocampo.htm. Since reopening in 2004 under the management of affable local businessman Caleb Porta the Hipocampo has been given a new lease of life. It is far from fancy, but is an affordable option for a prime spot in town. Nine rooms are small but comfortable and have private bathrooms, air conditioning and TV. The 4 downstairs rooms have cold water only, priced at US$20 single, US$25 double and US$30 triple. Upstairs rooms have hot-water bathrooms and are US$5 more. Find it opposite the Hotel Bocas del Toro and Buena Vista Grill & Deli. Only cash accepted.

Hotel Calaluna (7 rooms) Calle 5; tel: 757 9066; email: calaluna@cwp.net.pa. Owned by Alberto e Marcella, patron of Alberto's restaurant, and newly opened at the time of writing. Two triple rooms, 4 doubles and a suite for 4–5 people (2 bedrooms, kitchen, lounge, private balcony) each have hot water and air conditioning and there's a private bar and small pizzeria. Rates are US$30–35 per person for a single, US$35–40 double, US$40–45 triple and US$85 suite. This includes complimentary tea and coffee and internet.

Casa Amarillo Corner of Av G and Calle 5. Run by a well-established and friendly ex-pat couple that have recently converted their bright yellow-painted house to offer clean and comfortable rooms with cable TV and air conditioning. A penchant for keeping caged parrots makes the balcony a depressing sight; US$30–35

Spanish by the Sea Tel/fax: 757 9518; email: Spanishbythesea@hotmail.com; www.spanishbythesea.com. This Spanish study school lets out rooms to non-students when it isn't full. Rooms are basic but comfortable and have ceiling fans, communal kitchen and a shared bathroom. The owners speak Dutch, German, French and English and the atmosphere is relaxed. US$6 per person per night.

Suite Hotel Costes (6 suites) Calle 1, tel: 757 9442/9591; email: info@suitehotelcostes.com; www.suitehotelcosts.com. Newly built in 2004, Suite Hotel Costes has added an individual touch to each room with hand-painted murals. As the name suggests, all rooms are suites and include a mini-fridge, cable TV, hot-water shower and safe box. The two upstairs front rooms overlook the park and can be hired together as one large apartment. Prices range from US$60 to US$70 and include breakfast. There is a peaceful and private afternoon and early evening bar on the back terrace.

Mondo Taitu (2 dorms, 8 doubles, 2 singles) Av G; tel: 507 757 9425, www.mondotaitu.com. A long-established backpacker hostel with a lively ambience, the bright yellow Mondo Taitu building is original and rustic with a relaxed close-knit vibe that makes it a great place for travellers to meet. Communal use of kitchen, hot water showers, surfboard rental (and sale) and advice on surf conditions in the area are all on offer. Additionally, the only cocktail lounge in Bocas del Toro is situated here (see *Where to Eat and Drink*, *Nightlife*). Dorm prices are US$7 and US$8 per person for quadruples and doubles respectively. Doubles are US$16 and there is also a tree house with bath, from US$30.

Hospedaje Emanuel (4 rooms) Av G, Isla Colón; tel: 757 9958. Four triple rooms offer good-value accommodation at US$8 per person. Only one has air conditioning and all have cold-water bathrooms but each room has a ceiling fan.

Hotel Dos Palmas (8 rooms) Av Sur, Isla Colón; tel: 757 9906. This great-value hotel is situated entirely over water with hammocks and tables and chairs on a wonderful sea-view porch. Each room has a private hot-water bathroom and a ceiling fan and 6 also have air conditioning. The latter are priced at US$30, others at US$24.

Hotel Casa Max (11 rooms) Av G, Isla Colón; tel: 757 9120; email: casa1max@hotmail.com; http://casamax.netfirms.com. This striking 2-storey wooden Caribbean building is located next to Posada Los Delphines and is run by a Dutch couple. It has English-, Dutch- and Spanish-speaking staff, bright, cheerful rooms and en-suite hot-water bathrooms. Spotless rooms are excellent value at US$18 single, US$20 double and US$30 triple, including a coffee and fresh fruit breakfast.

Hotel Angela (12 rooms) Av H Norte, Isla Colón; tel/fax: 757 9813; email: Claudio@hotelangela.com; www.hotelangela.com. Once a cheap and cheerful backpacker hostel, the Hotel Ángela has been painstakingly refurbished since 2001 by Claudio Talley, the Angela's softly spoken attentive patron. Twelve individually decorated no-smoking rooms come with air conditioning, private hot-water bathrooms and beds with orthopaedic mattresses. Double rooms are priced between US$35 and US$55 per night (the latter with a balcony), triples at US$50–60 (the latter also with a balcony) and quadruple at US$60–65. All prices include a hearty tropical breakfast served in the hotel's open-sided waterfront Restaurant O'er the Sea. A spacious self-contained balconied suite with whirlpool bath and uninterrupted ocean views is priced at US$175.00 per night. Credit cards accepted.

Hotel La Veranda Av G, Isla Colón; tel/fax: 757 9211; email: laveranda@cwPanama.net; http/laverandaPanama.tripod.com. This vintage-style Caribbean guesthouse in Bocas del Toro has hardwood floors, antique furniture, Kuna wall hangings and leafy verandas. It is located just a few hundred yards from the Posada Los Delphines, just one block from the sea, and has a fully equipped communal kitchen. All rooms are non-smoking and have mosquito netting and a ceiling fan, priced from US$49. Optional air conditioning is offered but at additional cost.

Bahía del Sol Saigon Bay, Isla Colón; tel: 757 9060/628 3954; email: info@bocasbahiadelsol.com; www.bocasbahiadelsol.com. This out-of-town hotel is on the road to Boca de Drago, a 15–20-minute walk from the centre of Bocas. Buses run along this route every 90 minutes and taxis provide an all-day hail-on-stop service for 50c per person. Double rooms start at US$50 per night (third person charged at US$25 extra) with a master suite at US$100 complete with private patio. Owner Steve Jones provides meals on demand. A Continental breakfast of fresh fruits, local breads, tea and coffee is included in the room rate with tours, bike hire and mobile phone rental on request.

La Estrella de Bocas Calle I, Isla Colón; tel: 757 9011/680-6880; email: feryleriz@yahoo.com. This apartment-hotel has an attractive burnt-orange-coloured frontage adorned with Spanish painted tiles and black wrought ironwork, located opposite the local jail. Spacious apartments are big enough for 4–6 people and boast tiled floors, air conditioning, cable TV, private bathroom, kitchenette, lounge and breakfast bar. Rooms at US$30–40 and apartments US$50–100.

Hospedaje E&L (aka EyL) Tel: 675 5693. This little hospedaje above the Bocas Trips office is co-owned by Ligia, the owner of Bocas Trips, and her friend Emeline (hence the name). This affordable option costs as little as US$6 (most expensive is US$20) and has a small kitchen and laundry but rooms can suffer from late-night noise from the adjacent El Encanto bar.

Hotel Las Brisas (40 rooms) Calle 3, Isla Colón; tel: 757 9248/9247/9555. This large, rather mediocre-looking hotel is located on a tight bend at the northern end of Main Street close to the marvellous OM Café. Rooms are keenly priced and in peak season getting a room here is almost impossible. Brisas has three different blocks, the cheapest located in a white-painted wooden building over looking the Main Street, with rooms at just US$10 for a double, basic but including hot-water shower. Prices in the main block, situated on the

water, and a newly built block with ocean views, range from US$15 to US$75. All rooms are en suite, and have cable TV, air conditioning and a couple have kitchenette facilities.
Hotel Del Parque (8 rooms) tel: 757 9008; email: delparque35@hotmail.com. This small family-run hotel, located in a leafy garden behind the Park, is very homely. Polished wooden floors are spotlessly clean (follow the lead of the owner and remove your shoes before entering) and rugs, flowers and pin-boards give it a comfy feel with a great breezy terrace. Doubles US$33 and triples US$37, including morning fresh fruit and coffee.

Hotel Bahía Calle 3, Isla Colón; tel: 757 9626/676 4669; fax: 757 9692; email: hotelbahia@cwPanama.net; www.bocas.com/bahia.htm. This grand old Bocatorian landmark celebrates its 100th anniversary in 2005. Once home to the United Fruit Company, three consulate offices and the Tropical Radio & Telegraph Station, this handsome building became the Hotel Bahía in 1968. Today the architecture, imposing façade and classic interior retain many of its original features, thanks to the dedication of owner and Bocas local José (Tito) Thomas. Explore the lobby and you'll see a large safe that dates back to 1905 and once contained the wages of banana workers in the archipelago. High ceilings and large windows give this hotel a spacious feel and rooms have a ceiling fan or air conditioning and cable TV. Rates vary but expect to pay US$55 triple room in high season (US$49.50 in low) and US$49.50 double in high season (US$44 in low). Single occupancy starts at US$38.50, add US$10 for an extra bed, and ask about discounted rates for longer stays. Mastercard and Visa accepted.

The Bocas Inn (7 rooms) tel: 757 9226; email: info@anconexpeditions.com; www.anconexpeditions.com. This B&B is managed by Ancon Expeditions, a sister operation of Panama's largest private conservation group. Most guests, but not all, stay here to make the most of ANCON's excellent tours, which can be arranged direct with the lodge. Pre-book if you specifically want one of Panama's top naturalist guides. Comfortable rooms have air conditioning and a private bathroom. Also restaurant, sun deck, hammocks and bar; US$45–65 a room.

Cocomo On the Sea Tel: 757 9259; email: cocomoonsea@cwPanama.net. At the moment 'The Cocomo', as most people know it, has just 4 double rooms, furnished in breezy Bocatorian-style. However, such is demand, owner Donald Ruscher is considering adding another two, which is great news for travellers that like lovely small-scale hotels that are big on hospitality. Daisy (she of big smile) books tours, sorts out guests and helps get luggage from A to B. Sea views, hammocks, wind chimes and a relaxed ambience prevail. US$45–65 per night, including breakfast. Booking strongly recommended. Credit cards accepted.

Posada Los Delphines (10 rooms) Av G; tel: 757 9963; fax: 757 9075; email: posadalosdelfines@posadalosdelfines.com; www.posadalosdelfines.com. Los Delphines shares the same Italian owners as the Hotel Laguna and is run admirably by Maribel González. Wooden-floored rooms are spacious, comfortable and spotlessly clean with private hot-water bathroom, air conditioning and cable TV, just 5 minutes' walk from the centre. The town's only spa, Bella Flora, is also located here and the hotel's terrace café serves Italian ice-cream, breakfast and a good range of light-bites, hotdogs and beers from 07.00 each day. US$45–50 double, US$55 triple and US$60 junior suite.

Hotel El Limbo (16 rooms) Calle 1, Isla Colón; tel: 757 9062; email: ellimbo@hotmail.com; www.ellimbo.com. Guests who book a room in advance over the internet at El Limbo qualify for a special rate – and at this hotel you'll almost certainly need to book. Great sea views and the only air-conditioned hotel lobby in town with rooms with private bathroom, cable TV and air conditioning, bar-deck on the water, built using 12 different types of local wood in true Antillean architectural style. Eight standard rooms without balcony US$65, 4 with city view, US$85, 4 with ocean view US$105.00, additional beds US$15. Visa, Master Card and American Express accepted.

Lula's B&B (6 rooms) tel: 0800 544 1097 (toll free)/757 9057; email: lulabocas@msn.com; www.lulabb.com. This pretty family-owned and operated hotel adjacent to Cocomo on the Sea has charming second-floor rooms with air conditioning, fans and private hot-water bathrooms. Double rooms US$42, triples US$47, including breakfast.

Pensión Bocas Caribe Calle 3, Isla Colón. The Bocas Caribe doesn't have a telephone so travellers in search of room just turn up on spec. Rooms are basic but are popular with backpackers on a budget at US$5–6 a person.

Hotel Laguna (16 rooms) Calle 3, Isla Colón; tel: 757 9091; fax: 757 9092; email: hlaguna@cwp.net.pa. The Hotel Laguna is located right in the heart of Bocas Town and has the same owners as the Posada Los Delphines. Sixteen rooms and one suite (with kitchenette) are small, but clean and comfortable with private bathroom, telephone, TV and air conditioning. From US$45 per night for a double. Credit cards accepted.

Hotel Swan's Cay (46 rooms) Calle 3, Isla Colón; tel: 757 9090/9316; fax: 757 9027; email: swanscayisla@cwp.net.pa; www.swanscayhotel.com. Rooms at Swan's Cay range from standard to superior and de luxe with suites that come with a whirlpool bath; pool, sundeck, terraces and leafy gardens. It's renowned as Bocas Town's most luxurious option and comes priced accordingly, at US$66 single, US$77.50 double, US$98 triple and US$110–200 suite. Credit cards accepted.

Hotel Bocas del Toro (10 rooms) Calle 2, Isla Colón; tel: 757 9018/689 2684 or (34) 935 892 902 (Spanish office); email: h_bocasdeltoro@hotmail.com; www.bocas.com/hbocas.htm. An impressive Bocatorian building that contains a smart but rather soulless hotel in the centre of town. Rooms have air conditioning, hot water and TV and the hotel offers an ever-changing range of seasonal accommodation packages for 1–4 people that include meals, and it is the restaurant most guests rave about (a table right out on the water offers one of the prettiest dining spots in town). US$52 double (or single), a triple US$76 and quadruple US$99. Credit cards accepted.

Hotelito del Mar (5 rooms) Av 1, opposite IPAT; tel: 757 9861/638 2220; email: tashmoo@cwPanama.net. This hotel was brand new at the time of writing, so the entire place was spotless, with state of the art air conditioning and cable TV in each room. Situated in a very convenient spot right in the heart of town, Hotelito comes with a charming lady owner, Sally Ramirez, who is quite devoted to Bocas. Prices range from US$45–60.

The following hostels are unknown to the author (but might be the finds of the decade): the **Hospedaje La Sirenita** (tel: 757 9372; US$15 per double room), the **Hospedaje Kalaus** (tel: 757 9432; US$16 per double room), **Hospedaje Dixon** (tel: 757 9542; US$12 per double room) and **Hotel Scarlett** (tel: 757 9290; US$20 per room). **Hospedaje Maritza** (tel: 757 8446; email: maritzacontreras28@hotmail.com) opposite Barco Hundido (the Wreck Deck) has a couple of decent fan-cooled rooms decorated in vibrant pink priced from US$14.

Homestays
Homestays in Bocas are becoming big business, which is great news for travellers keen to immerse themselves in local culture. None advertise, so ask around. A room in a house of a local fisherman costs about US$12 per person for lodging and breakfast, with a morning spear fishing part of the deal.

Camping
At the time of writing it is possible to rent a small pitch on a wooden dock on the water for US$1 a night, a popular backpacker option with those looking to stay in Bocas for several weeks. Just turn up at Avenida Norte and ask the locals to point you in the right direction.

A small campsite in Boca de Drago has pitches for US$5 a night (tel: 774 3168). Several private landowners also rent out small areas of their grounds during peak season, most without facilities. A waterfront spot on Bastimentos, five minutes by boat from Red Frog Beach, is US$3 per person per night plus US$3 for breakfast (email: brs@dial.pipex.com). Camp at Bluffs Beach for US$3 per person per night (US$12 to include all meals) close to the surf and nesting turtles April–September. Just turn up (plenty of room) or email: cgrisini@hotmail.com.

Renting a pad in Bocas

Before 2002 it was almost impossible to find a property to rent in Bocas. Today, the real estate boom in the archipelago has sprouted a growing rental, which is great news for visitors looking for a long-term option. Demand currently exceeds supply and prices are high as a result, but as the market opens up increased competition will mean lower rates. Locally owned rental properties are a less expensive option and are often let for 10% of the rent charged by foreign owners. These tend to be advertised by word of mouth, so ask around the local bars and restaurants to see what's about. All owners are all too happy to accept bookings for longer stays, offering significant discounts to those that plan to stick around.

Houseboat www.bocashouseboats.com. Live literally on the water in a 35ft houseboat. Sleeps 4–6 people with upper, front and rear sun deck. Fully equipped kitchen with oven, fridge and microwave; US$1,200 per week with reduced rates for long-term bookings.

Tropical Suites (16 rooms) Tel/fax: 757 9081; email: bocaslasolas@cwPanama.net; web:www.tropical-suites.com. Brand-new complex of 16 serviced apartments that is so pristine and polished it dazzles. Six fully furnished suites have sea views and 10 overlook the town with access controlled via a 24-hour security desk and CCTV. Kitchen, cable TV, hot-water bathroom, at US$35–50 per night and from US$1,000 per month. They also offer a sectioned-off area in the water behind the hotel for safe swimming.

Central Apartment Email: susanagg1@yahoo.co.uk. Fully renovated self-contained rental apartment in the same building as the Hospedaje Heike. Comfortably furnished with hot water in kitchen and bathroom, air conditioning in lounge and bedroom, ceiling fan and cable TV in each room. Sleeps 4, at US$60 per night, US$250 per week with discounts for longer stays.

Waterfront Apartment Email: brs@dial.pipex.com. This large 1-bedroom self-contained apartment is part of a large home in Bahía Honda, Bastimentos. It has a fully equipped kitchen, bathroom and double bedroom in an elevated quiet location on a hillside overlooking fields, mangroves and open water. Ten minutes from Bocas Town by boat. US$50 a night (sleeps 2), US$320 per week, US$1,200 per month (long-term discounts).

Beachfront Home Email: TisaL@aol.com. This fully furnished two-bedroom beachfront home on Isla Carenero has a boat dock, bathroom, fully equipped kitchen, lounge and a deck dining area with hammocks and great views. Fans and air conditioning, long-term monthly rent of US$1,500.

Island Life Tel: 757 9522. A rare opportunity to rent a fully refurbished single-storey home in the heart of Bastimentos Town. The property was modernised by Bastimentos resident Mr Jordan at the end of 2003 and is situated right on the central pathway (the 'Main Street'). Close to shops, restaurants and beaches with a fully equipped kitchen; US$300 per month.

Bocatarian Waterfront Home Email: Bocasproperties@planet-save.com. Three-bedroom waterfront house, simple and rustic in local style with local wood and bamboo. Large open deck and kitchen, 2 bathrooms; 5 minutes from beach. Six-month rental US$550 per month; weekly US$250; single month US$750.

Bluff Beach House Email: Bocasproperties@planet-save.com. Three-storey beachfront house amidst sand beaches 4 miles from Bocas Town. First floor sleeps 6, US$600 per month (6-month minimum), weekly US$300, US$1,000 for a single month. Ground floor sleeps 2, US$375 per month (6-month minimum), US$250 weekly; US$600 single month. **Ismito Beach House** Email: Bocasproperties@planet-save.com. Two-bedroom beachfront home with kitchen, bathroom, and deck with beach and ocean views. US$800 per month (6-month minimum), weekly US$500; US$1,500 for a single month.

Where to eat and drink

For a small town Bocas has a lot of great places to eat. Hanging out in a waterfront restaurant or beach bar is an important part of the Bocas experience and visitors will soon find that they are spoilt for choice. Most are located on Calle 3 but don't let this confine you. Countless cafés, delis and diners are springing up all over town and few places offer better value for money than Bocas' innocuous backstreet eateries. The town's transnational character ensures it boasts every conceivable style of cuisine, from tipico Panamanian to Tex-Mex, Chinese, Italian and fast food. Seafood is Bocas' culinary backbone, freshly caught and cooked simply with a Caribbean twist.

At the **Restaurant Kalin** in Calle 3 opposite the park, good local Bocatorian fare is served at a relaxed pace. Most, like the fish and rice, are less than US$5 and served at tables outside.

Buffet-style **Don Chicho** in Calle 3 serves big helpings of OK Panamanian dishes all under US$3, also chichas (fruit drinks) for 35c and home-made cakes and sweet breads. A favourite with locals and backpackers alike, it's open early until late.

Everybody who eats at **El Pecado** seems to rave about the menu and booking a table there is easier said than done. Located next on Calle 3, cosy balcony tables overlook the park and the liveliest part of town. Full most nights, which speaks volumes about the Asian–Panamanian fusion food served here. Homemade hummus and warm Johnny cakes (local bread made with fresh coconut milk) are delicious. Open for early evening drinks and dinner. Closed Mondays.

Stroll south on Calle 3 past the Hotel Bahía to find **El Ultimo Refugio** tucked away in Avenida Sur (tel: 640 1878). This is a great place over the water, mellow and moody with a tropical menu of seafood, meat and chicken dishes. Choose from red snapper with olive oil and oregano (US$7), oriental chicken in curry sauce with coconut and peanuts (US$7) and prime fillet steak in a tropical sweet pineapple, green pepper and onion sauce (US$8). Open daily for dinner only from 17.30.

The entrance to the **Piña Colada** waterfront bar and restaurant midway along Calle 3 is via a scruffy side-door that is easy to overlook. Great views and good cocktails (from US$3.50) are popular with surfers and boaters and while the food is a bit hit and miss the punters don't seem to mind.

The **Restaurant Bahía** at the hotel of the same name at the southern end of Calle 3 reopened in 2003 to rave reviews. The menu, a mix of Caribbean and Italian dishes, includes pasta, lobster, risotto and fish, great pizzas, with a breakfast for US$3.

The seafood at waterfront restaurant **Le Pirate** in Calle 3 (next to Transparente Tours) is popular with locals and tourists alike. Dishes include octopus (US$8), lobster (US$12), squid (US$6), shrimp (US$6), snapper (US$5) and crab (US$6–8) served with coconut rice, beans, patacones and salad, with a great-value lunchtime special for US$3.50.

The **Liki Tiki** (Playa El Istmito; email: likitikitoo@yahoo.com) opened in 2003 and has quickly become one of the most popular places to eat and drink in Bocas. Relaxed people run this laidback place that appeals to a mixed crowd that enjoy a

'No shirt, no shoes, no problem' attitude. Lunchtime nachos lead to evening Happy Hour (see *Nightlife*) and great Caribbean-cum-Mexican food until 22.00. A sophisticated menu has a beach-bum twist: open at weekends only in low season.

At the time of writing **La Ballena** (tel: 757 9089) doesn't open for breakfast any more, a pity as they were top-notch for value and quantity. Both the lunch and dinner menu are tempting but the service can be iffy. While Ballena prides itself on good cuisine, a starchy atmosphere is very un-Bocas and US$8 for a Greek salad isn't inexpensive. An adjoining wine bar has a cellar of European vintages (with wine tasting each evening). Open 11.00 for lunch and from 17.30 for dinner.

Another pricier option is the cute and colourful **Cocina del Mar**, run by a Californian couple and located over Starfleet Scuba. This recently established seafood restaurant offers wonderful views over the water, but has suffered from mixed reviews over high prices and stingy portions. Open 17.00–22.00.

The restaurant Da Claudio at the **Hotel Laguna** has an Italian dinner menu and a terrace café that serves breakfast. Food is good but the tables are a magnet for flies and the service can be painfully slow. At dusk the bar is the perfect spot for people-watching, the flies have gone by then and the bar stocks 20 different beers.

For a decent meal on a budget head to **La Chitre** on Calle 3, a great little place in the centre of town that charges US$3.50 for a plateful and US$1 for an ice-cold beer.

Restaurante Olga doesn't look much but backpackers swear by the inexpensive meals (less than US$3) served from a kiosk on a triangular piece of scrubland at the northern end of Calle 3 – opposite Las Brisas Hotel.

For the best cup of coffee in town head to the **Starfish Coffee Shop** in Calle 3, next to Pachamama, which serves a breakfast of waffles and pastries from 08.00 Tuesday–Saturday and coffee, deserts and cakes each afternoon between 15.00 and 18.30. Open Sunday 08.00–12.30 then 16.00–18.00. Closed Monday.

Unashamed gringo hangout (and proud of it) the **Buena Vista Bar & Deli** serves plates of burgers, hot chicken sandwiches, nachos and fries in generous portions. Cable TV shows, sport or CNN all day while customers discuss real estate, boating conditions and the state of the American economy. The food is good and available as take-away and those without an appetite for fillet steak and BLTs can order a bean-dip starter (US$3) and a sundowner. The speciality, a weighty margarita fuerte (US$4, 3oz Cuervo Gold, triple sec and fresh lime) is limited to three per person with good reason.

EL HOMBRE DEL AVIÓN

He is rarely seen during daylight and is known simply as 'the aeroplane guy' but this resident of Isla Colón doesn't fly planes, he makes them, entirely out of rubbish. Models range in size but can be as big as 2m. Each is painstakingly crafted from salvaged scrap paper, food packaging and tin cans and incorporates intricate operational parts. He favours Panamanian aircraft above all others and most models are replicas of Aeroperlas aeroplanes, usually a Short 360. They are not made for sale and the owner refuses to part with them, although visitors often attempt to persuade him otherwise. A few, rather elderly examples of his work are suspended from the roof struts in the bar at the Hotel Angela. Visitors keen to view more recent works stand a good chance by being on Main Street at dusk. This is when the aeroplane guy 'road tests' his latest triumph, attaching a piece of string before dragging it along the centre of the road at speed to check moving parts.

Fast-food freaks should head to the **Golden Grill** opposite the park, on Main Street for round-the-clock hamburgers, fried chicken and hotdogs for less than a couple of dollars.

A far nicer burger restaurant with great ocean views is **Bumpers Bar and Grill**, located on Calle 1 close to Barco Hundido. A small, relaxed place that offers full cooked breakfasts, burgers and grills as you would expect, and a killer home-made hot sauce that is only for the brave. Prices don't quite match the Golden Grill but are reasonable, and friendly staff are happy to adapt the menu to please. Open from breakfast till late.

The restaurant at the **Swan's Cay Hotel** caters for another budget entirely and serves well-prepared Italian dishes including pasta, risotto and pizzas, while **Alberto's** on Calle 5 (tel: 757 9066; fax: 757 9315) serves traditional Italian pizza and pasta at easy prices every day (except Sunday), 17.00–23.00.

Sandwiches, milkshakes and smoothies are good at the **Bocas Internet Café** on Calle 3. There are a couple of tables outside if it's jam-packed with emailers inside.

Although largely ignored by tourists, those in the know agree that **El Kiosko Misionario** is a great little find. Everything on the menu is less than US$4. Find it behind the park; eat in or take away.

For handmade Italian ice-cream head to the **Arco Iris Café** at Los Delphines, which also serves club sandwiches, burgers, nachos, salads, tropical fruit shakes and hotdogs, from US$3.

The only Chinese restaurant in the archipelago is next to Le Pirate. Portion sizes are vast at **Restaurante Kun Ja** and so is the menu. Eat in on the waterfront deck to encounter the restaurant's resident pelican, or take-away for a quiet life. Good value at US$2–4 a dish.

For top-notch Indian food head to the diminutive **OM Café** on Avenida G. The menu is as small as the restaurant itself, which makes ordering a breeze. Curry dishes are tame by international standards so ask the staff to pep things up if you like yours fiery. Open for dinner at 18.00 (US$5–7 for a main dish) and for breakfast 08.00–noon. US$4 for home-made granola, yoghurt and fruits, hot bagels and Indian milkshakes.

THE BOCAS SUNSET

Everyone waxes lyrical about the sunsets in Bocas – and justifiably so. Each one is different, ranging in hue from a bright tangerine flame or a ruby-red glow to a pale amethyst smoulder with vibrant violet splashes. Those with decent camera skills – or some good luck – can leave Bocas with some spectacular shots. At least two companies run sunset tours including the small boat co-operative, Boatmen United (tel: 757 9760; email: boterosbocas@yahoo.com). On a larger scale, but equally as enjoyable, is the Sunset Cruise by Transparente Tours (Calle 1; tel: 626 1902/664 9206). It picks up from Le Pirate and The Reef at 18.30 and heads out towards Bastimentos to maximise the views. The price of US$25 per person includes a seafood supper and drinks (beer, wine and soft drinks), an enjoyable extravagance with superb photographic possibilities. Pre-booking is essential for this tour, as it doesn't run unless it has more than six passengers. The pontoon boat can accommodate up to ten people and is fully equipped with a marine radio, life jackets and navigation lights, returning to Bocas Town at about 21.00.

An outside table at the **Restaurant Hotel Bocas del Toro** boasts one of the prettiest spots to eat on the waterfront in Bocas Town. A big international menu has plenty of European touches with numerous daily specials from US$6–12.

Nearby at **El Limbo** the breakfast (US$4), lunch (US$5), dinner (US$7) and cocktails (from US$3.50) are served at outside tables overlooking the water. An excellent chef whips up a mixed menu and all of it is good. Avoid the strawberry vodka unless you plan to do nothing all day. It comes in a bucket-sized measure and is delicious – but potent.

Food is consistently good at **Restaurant O'er the Sea** at Hotel Angela with lobster, shrimp, conch, calamari and fish specialities and an excellent fillet mignon. Organic pork, salads and oriental dishes and umpteen Caribbean favourites. Turn up for a drink, a meal and sunset views from 18.00.

Nightlife

Every night at 21.00 a siren sounds in town, denoting the time from when it is against the law to be without ID. This Panamanian anti-crime initiative amuses the locals, who say the 15 minutes of nightly rain some time between 20.45 and 21.15 is enough to set your watch by.

The most popular late-night tourist hangout in town is **Barco Hundido,** an open-sided unassuming looking bar with a thatched roof that is better known as the Wreck Deck. Its popularity and late hours are no coincidence. While other bars wind down at 22.00 or 23.00, the Wreck Deck prepares to party, attracting a mixed clientele that ranges from backpackers to boating forty-somethings hell-bent on salsa dancing. Pass by during daylight and the bar looks innocuous, shielded from the road by a wooden gate with just a sign to mark the spot. Visit again after dark (it opens at around 19.00) and it's a different story as boardwalks, a dance floor and barstools prepare to take the strain. The Wreck Deck overhangs the sea close to where a sunken banana boat lies submerged – hence the name. Midnight swimming is not uncommon – but watch your feet on the rusty wreck!

Apart from a great menu (see *Where to Eat*) the triangular bamboo-and-palm **Liki Tiki Restaurant & Bar** (Playa El Istmito; tel: likitikitoo@yahoo.com) has a bar (made from huge chunks of rock) that springs to life at happy hour. To the sound of salsa and American rock with regular live calypso music Barman Marlin whips up great cocktails that pull in the crowds.

With an outstanding reputation as a chill out spot – with music to match – and a rustically stylish bamboo terrace, **Precision Tropical Cocktails** at **Mondo Taitu** (Avenida G) is run by London-trained Panamanian cocktail barman, Rica. An endless array of exotic drinks is created, from passion-fruit margaritas to lemongrass martinis, and Rica even makes his own fresh coconut cream for coladas. Don't leave the island without sampling Rica's own creation, the Naturalito. Open from 18:00 till late, closed Tuesdays.

Located next to El Encanto on Calle 3, **Piña Colada** has to compete with its neighbour's incredibly loud sound system and therefore is more enjoyable early evening before El Encanto gets going. A large place, with some great tables over the water, it's a great spot to watch the sun drop with a Panama beer.

Bar July, next to Liki Tiki on Playa El Istmito, is a local bar on the beach, with excellent prices and small hall for local events.

The crowd at **El Encanto** is almost entirely Bocatorian and this dilapidated over-the-water dance hall plays its music deafeningly loud. A big-drinking, fist-fighting, salsa-dancing place that has pool hall at the front of the building and live music some weekends.

Local tour operators
Boating and fishing

Two marinas serve Bocas del Toro and an increasing number of international boating enthusiasts choose to arrive in the archipelago under their own steam. Numerous companies offer chartered boat tours, fishing trips and pontoon hire. Some also offer tuition, a godsend for first-timers in Bocas who plan to take to the waves.

The first marina built in Bocas is located at the Careening Cay Resort on Isla Carenero, a five-minute boat journey from Isla Colón. **Marina Carenero** (tel/fax: 757 9242; email: marcar@cwp.net.pa; www.careeningcay.com) has 26 slips for boats up to 60ft in length as well as all the facilities you'd expect. A second marina was completed in 2002. The **Bocas Yacht Club & Marina** (tel: 757 9800; fax: 757 9801; email: bocasyachtclub@yahoo.com; www.bocasmarina.com) is a state of the art facility that can cope with 100 vessels of up to 100ft in length. Visit their website for an entry map in printable format, a crucial tool for boats that plan to sail between the islands. The sailing fraternity in Bocas is served by a marine store on Calle 3, **Rukel SA** (tel: 757 9939; email: rubenchaw@cwp.net.pa). It carries a decent stock of outboard engines and marine hardware and is a registered Yamaha distributor.

There are some great waters for sport fishing in and around the archipelago. Visitors that had fished with any seriousness reported large numbers of billfish, yellow fin and big eye tuna and red snapper (reports of 40lb). Mackerel is good year-round as is wahoo (reports of 90lb). Dorado is plentiful and there is also a bountiful supply of king fish, blue marlin and grouper (20lb seems to be the accepted norm). Bocas is also a haven for tarpon and fisherman report large numbers year-round of 50–80lb.

Boatmen United Tel: 757 9760; email: boterosbocas@yahoo.com. This collective of half a dozen local Panamanian boatmen offers a wide range of daily half-day and full-day group boat tours around the islands. Most stop at the most popular snorkelling spots, including Hospital Point, Red Frog Beach and Dolphin Bay and also offer sport fishing, tube skiing, surfing, rainforest hikes and wildlife tours, from US$15 per person. They also arrange special trips, including night snorkelling, romantic evening cruises and sunrise dolphin-spotting tours.

Drago Adventures Tel: 698 2555 (Panama), 410 666 2514(US office), email: dragoadventures@yahoo.com. This specialist fishing operation is run by American couple Mark and Lisa Rush, using either a Pro Sports 2860WA Mirage 28ft Catamaran (three persons plus crew) at US$500 per day plus fuel or a Mirage II 18ft (two persons plus crew) at a rate of US$250 per day, both plus fuel. Drinks, ice and refreshments are included. Guests can stay in a purpose-built lodge for US$80 a night (half price for children under 12) for B&B and dinner. Breakfast is a hearty plate of eggs, a jug of Panamanian coffee and fresh juice. Dinner is whatever you catch that day or choose from a menu of lobster, shrimp, fresh fruits and salads.

Bocas Charters Tel: 676 9968; email: bocascharter@hotmail.com. This specialist deep-sea-fishing and spear-fishing operator is confident that most people will get a nibble from dorado, Spanish mackerel, kingfish or red snapper. Rates include a qualified captain and fuel with half-day tours at US$225.00 and full-day from US$360.00. The company will also arrange food and drink on request for an additional charge. It also rents out a 12ft fibreglass 15 HP at US$25 per hour, or US$150 per day. Only cash or US travellers' cheques accepted.

Catamaran Sailing Adventures Calle 3; tel: 637 9064/757 9710; email: movida@cwPanama.net web; www.bocas.com/operaciones/movida. CSA offers 2 standard daily sailing packages and any number of tailor-made fishing trips and overnight excursions to

Cayos Zapatilla, Tobobe and Cusapin. It also runs 3–7-day learn-to-sail courses tutored by licensed captain Marcell Schmitt. Daily tours leave at 09.30 and return at 16.45 and include snorkelling, swimming and dolphin spotting. Each also allows the opportunity to swim inside mangroves amongst barracudas, snappers and sardines – great for those with an underwater camera. Every attempt is made to spot a nurse shark, often close to Coral Cay. Day tours cost US$25 per person, including lunch, snorkel gear and fishing rods. Only cash payment is accepted but it's a good idea to pre-book by telephone or email or call into the office.

Captain Christian's Boat Tours Tel: 638 2220/620 5130; email: info@ccboattours.com. Local character Captain Christian has a 24ft Panga Boat that can accommodate 16 people at a squeeze. It has cushioned seats and a cover – essential when boating in Bocas. While he offers all the usual Bocas water-tour staples it is worth paying a little extra for one of his customised specials. Christian has good local knowledge of Swan's Cay, Cayos Zapatilla, Boca Torrito, Boca del Drago and Red Frog beach.

Del Toro Surf Tel: 607 8962; email: deltorosurf@yahoo.com.ar. This small specialist operator set up in 1995 to help surfers find the sought-after secret surfing spots of Bocas. Tailor-made group and individual tours take surfers by boat to perfect waves in and around Carenero, Playa Bluff, Puss Point and Old Point. The company also offers a number of combination packages, such as surf & dive, surf & snorkel and surf & languages. It can arrange accommodation, book tours and also offers surfing tuition.

Transparente Tours Tel: 757 9915/626 1902; email: transparentetour@hotmail.com. Simply turn up at the office in Calle 3 at 09.00 to join one of several daily tours, priced at US$15, or thereabouts. A guide, snorkelling gear and an icebox for drinks are included and each boat has a cover, a marine radio for emergencies and a driver who knows the archipelago like the back of his hand. Tours leave at 09.30 and return at about 16.30, 7-days a week. All of Bocas del Toro's most popular tourist spots are covered and offer a mixed bag of snorkelling, swimming and sightseeing. Most include a pleasant stroll to Red Frog Beach through a half-mile cleared jungle track for an hour or so on the sand. The most popular standard daily tour takes in Dolphin Bay, Crawl Cay, Red Frog Beach and Hospital Point. Other options include Cayos Zapatillas, Old Point, Bastimentos Village, Boca del Drago, Conch Point and Swan's Cay. The fishing tour comes highly recommended, a full day on the water in the Soropta Channel for an all-inclusive price of US$400. There's a freshwater shower on this 40ft vessel with tackle, bait, drinks and an icebox for your catch of the day. Sister company, J&J Boats, is housed in the same cream wooden building. It provides scheduled and on-demand water taxis out to the other islands, from US$1 to Isla Carenero to US$10 to Red Frog Beach.

Bocas Action Tours Tel: 757 9610. Small company that runs boat tours and snorkelling trips between 08.00 and 19.00 to Dolphin Bay and Hospital Point (US$15 per person) and Boca del Drago (US$15 per person). Also group trips (minimum 4 persons) to Bird Island (Swan's Cay) for US$60 and to Cayos Zapatilla for US$80. Children half price.

Bocas Marine Tours Tel/fax: 757 9033; email: info@bocasmarinetours.com; web: www.bocasmarinetours.com. Scheduled services to Changuinola (US$7 return), Almirante (US$3 one-way) and Boca de Drago (US$2.50, one-way), 7 days a week. Also tailor-made boat trips and water taxi service.

Bocas Trips Tel/fax: 757 9206; email: Bocastrips@hotmail.com. This efficient one-stop tour shop in Calle 3 is owned by personable Bocas local, Ligia Smith Lange. Ligia (who also co-owns Hospedaje E&L, see *Where to stay*) is a dab-hand at putting together island hops and regional tours and can also find accommodation when everyone insists they are full. Daily trips include snorkelling, fishing, birdwatching and horseriding. Ligia plans to offer a domestic flight-booking service and a greater number of tours for 2005.

Pontoon Boat Hire Tel: 624 8075 or leave a message at Transparente Tours. Bocas resident Chi Chi hires out his great pontoon boat from just US$350 a week. He also offers daily and monthly rates.

Scuba tours

Starfleet Scuba Tel/fax: 757 9630; email: scubastar@hotmail.com; www.explorePanama.com/starfleet.htm. Starfleet Scuba was established in Bocas in 1995 and comes highly recommended. Full- and half-day PADI courses, snorkelling and scuba trips are offered in small groups. Divemasters have a good reputation for high standards of safety and staff are PADI-qualified, licensed boat captains and run trips year-round 7-days a week. Prices are reasonable too. A regular 2-tank dive, including all equipment and a PADI Divemaster costs US$50 per person. A 3-day PADI open-water course is US$205 and includes all equipment, lunch and a PADI certificate. Multi-lingual staff can provide tuition in English, Spanish, Dutch and German with course manuals in 7 languages.

DIVING IN BOCAS DEL TORO
Captain Joanne of Starfleet Scuba

What's so special about diving in the archipelago of Bocas del Toro? There are at least 74 of the 79 known varieties of coral in the Caribbean (stag and brain coral are some of the more spectacular) and over 300 different sponges (from huge purple vases to tiny orange and green fingers). There is a myriad of small creatures within these areas. Fish-cleaning stations, nudibranches, delicate anemones, elusive seahorses and colourful brittle stars provide so much for both scuba and snorkel divers to see.

Year-round warm water (26–29°C, mostly 29°) and calm areas make this a top place for coral and wildlife aficionados. It is also a comfortable place to dive for cold-weather natives keen to complete their open-water dives in warm water after doing theory and pool work at home (Brrr!). During the trade winds season from about mid-November to March, diving is mostly within the lagoon area where coral and sponges particularly abound. Underwater sites around these islands reveal a vast array of tropical fish, from french, grey and queen angels, hogfish, spotted drums, parrotfish and triggerfish to nurse sharks, spotted eagle rays, moray eels, crustaceans and more. Lucky divers will even get to see the more unusual batfish, toadfish and other stonefish. During calmer times of the year (September, October and usually May and on many other occasions between April and November) diving trips go outside the lagoon area to the following sites:

Tiger Rock
For more experienced divers, with stronger currents, deeper dives, bigger fish and lobsters, sharks and fantastic coral, sponges and smaller creatures.

Dolphin and Wash Rocks
Easy diving with rock pinnacles, overhangs, plenty of fish including big midnight blue parrotfish and nurse sharks, dive-through caverns and more.

Shashay
Shallow and easy, with a multitude of fish, wonderful overhangs and garden atmosphere.

La Gruta Polo
Great coral at snorkel depths with fun canyons, caverns and dive-throughs for scuba divers.

Scuba Bocas Tel: 757 9550. PADI dive school located opposite Bocas Marine Tours offering a good range of standard group and individual tuition packages and a dive trips. Also customised options.

Bocas Water Sports Tel: 757 9541; email: bws@bocaswatersports.com. Bocas Water Sports serve all the usual tourist, diving and snorkelling spots at US$60 per person for diving and US$15 per person for snorkelling. A 2-dive trip is US$50, a 1-dive US$40 and a night dive (18.30–20.30) US$50. Also kayaking, waterskiing and scuba diving and PADI instruction (US$65–200). Water-skiing (US$45 per hour) can work out expensive but half-day and full-day rates make a more competitive option in perfect conditions. Single and double self-draining kayaks come complete with extra-lightweight paddles. Book by the hour at US$3 single and US$4 double or for a half-day for US$10 and US$12.

Adventure tours

Cocomo Adventure Tours Tel/fax: 757 9259; email: cocomoonsea@cwPanama.net. Affable American Donald Ruscher, owner of the delightful B&B Cocomo on the Sea, launched this tailor-made tour company in 2004 after a succession of guests bemoaned the fact that no tour took them off the beaten track. Adventure-loving Ruscher didn't need much more encouragement than that and today offers a number of tour itineraries that encompass jungle hikes through virgin rainforest, river journeys by canoe, visits to remote Indian villages and plenty of wildlife to satisfy those that yearn to experience 'undiscovered Bocas'. Ruscher is also a keen amateur photographer and has a portfolio of stunning underwater shots of coral reefs. Ask him nicely and he may take you to one of the prime snorkel spots he's discovered – quite unlike any other.

Ancon Expeditions Tel: 269 9415; email: info@anconexpeditions.com; www.anconexpeditions.com. ANCON, the privately owned National Association for the Conservation of Nature, has played a pioneering role in Panamanian conservation, fundraising to purchase large areas of rainforest for preservation. Today these areas are accessible to tourists via Ancon Expeditions and its excellent guides. A number of fixed itinerary trips over several days are offered as well as shorter on-demand excursions. Travellers in Bocas can find out more about tours in and around the archipelago by visiting the local office at the Hotel Bocas Inn, an Ancon lodge. Prices vary depending on itinerary (and there are plenty of options to choose from) but for a package that includes meals, accommodation and day tours expect to pay from US$100 per person.

Odesen Tours Tel: 658 5042; email: eliseovargasgarcia@yahoo.com; www.bocas.com/odesen. This local organisation was established to develop sustainable eco-tourism in the Teribe (Naso) Indian communities and supports the preservation of local natural resources and cultural traditions within local tribes in Bocas del Toro. Day tours leave from Changuinola so visitors need to get a water taxi from Bocas bright and early to pick up the boat. One of the most popular tours is a visit to a Teribe community. Each 8-hour tour needs to be booked in advance and requires at least two people to run. It is charged per boat at US$30 for each boat plus US$10 for a guide and US$25 for a traditional dance demonstration. A day trekking in the Wekso jungle costs from US$2 to US$4 per person plus US$10–20 for a boat. Part of the experience is a journey along the spectacular vine-tangled Teribe River. Overnight accommodation is offered at US$8–12 per person with breakfast, lunch and dinner at US$2.50-4. Bookings can be made in person at the Bocas Aventuras offices.

Bocas Aventuras Tel: 737 9367/620 6670; email: bocasaventuras@yahoo.com. This company offers a comprehensive set of tour services, from hotel bookings and honeymoons to caves and coral reefs – and everything in between. It can also organise local guides and ecological experts to accompany a trip anywhere in the province, including the Teribe Indian project. It also offers standard boat trips to beaches, snorkelling spots and dolphin habitats, priced from US$15.

Horseriding tours

Several companies offer horseriding (*caballos para rentar*) in Bocas with guided tours for less-experienced riders and hourly hire for those that prefer to ride solo. Routes take in a diverse range of terrain along shady countryside paths, jungle trails and across sandy beaches. A number of visitors raved about their experiences with a guide they simply referred to as the Arizonan cowboy (tel: 603 5497). Horses are saddled Western-style with guided tours by the hour, half-day or full day, priced at US$7 per person per hour with discounts for group bookings of up to six riders.

Surfing
Resorts and tours

Rancho Paraiso Tel: 757 9415; email: info@ranchoparaiso.biz; www.ranchoparaiso.biz. Spot-on accommodation for surfers in a quiet location on a wild expanse of beach just yards from the waves. Three double rooms in an octagonal-shaped cane-and-wood pole structure; 2 bathrooms with an outdoor hot- and cold-water shower. Rates are US$120 for a single, US$75 per person for a double and US$65 per person for triple. This includes breakfast, lunch and dinner and transfers. Surfboard hire and tuition available.

Del Toro Surf Tel: 607-8962; email: deltorosurf@yahoo.com.ar; www.bocas.com/operaciones/deltoro/deltoro.htm. Bocas-based specialist tour operator offering guided trips to breaks on Carenero as well as Playa Bluff, Puss Point and Old Point. Local guides, board hire, lodging and tailor-made schedules for every standard of surfer.

Panama Surf Tours Tel: 236 8303/7069, toll free in US tel: 1 800 716 3452; email: info@surfertours.com; www.Panamasurftours.com. Run 8- and 5-day surf tours departing Panama City to Bocas del Toro with luxury, standard and budget accommodation packages priced from US$540 per person.

Surfers who want to pitch a tent close to the surf can do so at Bluffs Beach for US$3 per person per night or US$12 including breakfast, lunch and dinner. Fresh water and home-cooked meals at hand, close to the shoreline and nesting turtles during April–September. This spot rarely gets overcrowded so simply turn up or email: cgrisini@hotmail.com.

Surfboard hire

Plenty of places in Bocas hire out surfboards including **Señor Camilo** (tel: 647 5557) who charges US$8 per day from a van next to the Golden Grill. He's there seven days a week, 08.00–18.00.

Tropix Surf in Calle 3 has a limited range of overpriced boards for sale as well as carry cases, wax and associated surfing paraphernalia. There's also a board with charts, tours and guide information. Open daily 08.30–12.30 and 17.00–21.00.

The **Mondo Taitu** (see *Where to eat and drink*) is a popular hangout with the surf crowd and hire and sell secondhand boards. It's a good place to head in the evening if you're keen to swap stories on the breaks that make the grade, and those that don't.

Cycling in Bocas

Hiring a mountain bike to get around Bocas Town is a good way to get from A to B, but most travellers with a spirit of adventure yearn to explore the interior once they're in the saddle. A dirt road from the outskirts of the town leads to the heart of the island and to the other side. While much of Isla Colón remains thick primary and secondary rainforest some tracks on this 20-mile long and 8-mile wide island are navigable by bike. Most wind bumpily through pasture and past small pueblos of thatched roofed huts. La Gruta (the cave) is located in one such village in the middle of the island, and this is where most mountain bikers head. Another decent ride is to

SURFING IN BOCAS DEL TORO
Kristian Salkovich of Rancho Paraiso Surf Camp

The surf scene is still pretty new here but everybody is excited about the possibilities. Although it is hosting a growing number of competitions, Bocas is still a virgin to the surfing world. Once an entire classroom in an Indian village ran to the beach because they had never seen surfers ride waves before. What's especially exciting is that much of the archipelago's 100 miles of surfable coastline is still waiting to be explored. Many of the finest surf spots in the archipelago remain the secrets of a few local aficionados. Others are yet to be discovered. I arrived in Bocas in the 1990s in search of great waves, saw the great potential and ended up starting a surfing resort. I've surfed every good spot in and around the archipelago and Bluff Beach has some of the most accessible there is.

On Isla Carenero there is a surf spot simply known as Carenero amongst surfers. It has a reef point break with five different peaks and long, rippable waves that can barrel for an eternity and is every bit as good (and dangerous) as The Dump. It gets crowded during peak months because of its close proximity to Bocas Town but is suitable for intermediate and advanced surfers. A continuation of Carenero is Kiddy Corner, a fun surf spot that extends into the adjoining bay. It's smaller, less challenging and suitable for all levels. Another fun spot is nearby Black Rock.

Surf on Bastimentos is less accessible and some spots can offer fickle waves that are tricky to predict but several dedicated surfers have raved about the beach break on First Beach. Others have said that its unpredictable and strong currents make the 20-minute hike to reach the beach not worth the effort. There's another spot on the island known as Coco. It has a long reef break and tube sections and needs a bigger-than-average swell to amount to much. Catch this on a good day and even advanced surfers admit that it can provide a true test of boardmanship. But what most surfers visit Bastimentos for is The Silverback, a much-discussed Hawaiian-style surfing favourite for those that like serious waves, a combination of Backdoor (for its barrel) and Sunset (for its peak). Expect at least 20ft on the biggest swells with long hold-downs in deep water.

Playa Bluff, a challenging 45-minute journey to one of the archipelago's nicest beaches. The ride to Boca del Drago is more gruelling but is doable within two hours (take plenty of water). Both roads are a mixture of dirt, tarmac and gravel and bicycle hire is inexpensive at US$1–2 per hour or US$7–9 for the day (see *Getting around*).

Festivals
Bocas likes to party and in November celebrations go into overload when a succession of local and national festivals dominates two weeks. The increasing internationalism of the province is reflected in its festival calendar and visitors should expect Hallowe'en parties and Thanksgiving dinners to be part of future events in Bocas.

May Day
A national holiday anyway due to the countrywide Workers' Day (*Día del Trabajador*), May Day (May 1) is notable in Bocas del Toro for its maypole dancing in Bastimentos.

Virgen del Carmen
This religious festival on the third Sunday in July sees residents of Bocas Town make a mass pilgrimage to the cave (La Gruta) on the road to Boca del Drago.

Feria del Mar
The Festival of the Sea is a full-on affair, with at least four days of celebrations on El Istmito beach in September (date varies). The main attraction is music, specifically Panamanian reggae, which locals love and groove to well. Grab a beer and watch the locals dance like professionals at any one of the stalls or live music acts. Purpose-built market stalls lay unused all year in readiness for this event, with umpteen jewellery and trinket vendors and a succession of food traders. They name it the International Feria Del Mar de Bocas as it attracts music lovers from neighbouring countries.

Bocas del Toro Day (Día de Bocas del Toro)
This anniversary of the foundation of the province (established 1904), held on November 16, is a big event for every Bocatorian, lasting two days and involving all most everyone in Bocas Town in making decorations for the processions. Day one is children's day and groups and musical bands from schools from surrounding districts assemble in elaborate costumes to parade, sing and dance. The adults lead the procession the following day and much drinking ensues at the local park, drawing thousands of people from all over the province and attended by several government ministers, if not the Panamanian president.

Bastimentos Day (Día de Bastimentos)
Celebrated on November 23 with a parade of drummers, school children and local dignitaries before a non-stop party of music and merriment that lasts well into the night.

Christmas Parade
A magical parade, in mid-December, of children in costumes and processions of colourful floats and a Father Christmas who throws sweets and toys to those who come to watch.

Carnaval
Although the most infamous Carnaval in Panama takes place in Los Santos, Bocas has its own version at the end of February. Relaxed, small-scale but every inch a party, many Panamanians enjoy the laidback Bocas Carnaval time. Decorated floats, brass bands and Carnaval Queens battle out traditional competitions, whilst every resident takes to the town for four days of non-stop partying. In true Panamanian style water trucks are transported to Bocas for the event and locals and tourists dance away hot Carnaval days under fountains of hosed water.

Shopping
Pachamama ('Mother Earth') **Art & Crafts** is next to the Starfish coffee shop. All the wooden carvings, wall hangings, artefacts and baskets in stock are made locally from indigenous materials. Open Tuesday to Saturday 09.00–noon and 13.00–17.00, closed on Sundays and Mondays.

The great little surf shop **Tropix Surf**, in the Ladybird Boutique on Calle 3, has some useful bits and bobs, including a good back catalogue of international surfing magazines. Also surfboards and wax plus a pin-board of surf spots, tours and guide information. Open daily 08.30–12.30 then again 17.00–21.00.

SHOPPING FROM AFAR

Travellers who plan to stay in Bocas for a while (and many do) often bemoan the lack of places that can fix a tent or replace a pair of worn hiking boots. While the number of shops in Bocas has tripled in recent years, camping, hiking and backpacker needs remain poorly served, despite a growing demand. What is stocked locally is imported from elsewhere in Panama with a significant impact on cost. A number of hardware stores have opened up since 2003 to service the construction boom and occasionally carry tent pegs and camp stoves, but little else of use to travellers. Changuinola is a good first option as it has everyday items at normal prices. Aside from this the option is a round trip to David or Panama, a costly excursion for those travelling on a budget. The alternative is a personal shopper, details below.

In **Panama City**, driver and all-round good egg José Luci Saénz (aka 'Bocas Friend'; tel: 222 5150; mobile: 672 2221/614 7811; email: bocasfrog@yahoo.com) will lend a hand with all manner of shopping, delivery, shipping and transportation quandaries. He has been highly recommended by everyone I know that has used him. Each swears by his speed, reliability and trustworthiness. He really will tackle anything and seems to know how to get the right item at the right place in an instant.

David resident Toby (tel/fax: 775 1812; mobile: 607 0279) also comes with good feedback and will undertake any shopping project, big or small, from electrical equipment to clothes and toiletries.

Indian craft stalls in Bocas face a constant battle with local authorities that have attempted on numerous occasions to move them to a sidestreet location. This is sad as these stallholders sell handmade treasures available nowhere else. You can even see molas being stitched as stallholders often sew and thread natural beads while they watch their stalls. Friendly, sweet, happy to bargain. The Kuna molas are especially colourful opposite Hotel Las Brisas at the northern end of town.

The **Garrimarr** on Calle 4 sells a range of leather goods, shell-topped pillboxes, beaded necklaces, bags and bracelets. A range of local handicrafts at **Artesanias Bri Bri** includes handmade bags, Kuna molas and woodcarvings, while **La Victoria** on Calle 3 is a treasure-trove of postcards, tourist knick-knacks and low-priced tie-dye clothing and beach sarongs.

The retail arm of the **Bocas Water Sports** dive shop sells T-shirts, postcards, beach novels and suntan lotion, while creams, lotions and body scrubs at the **Spa Bella Flora** (tel: 757 9086) at Los Delphines are made from local cacao beans, tropical fruits, nuts and plants, including several to soothe sunburn.

The super-rich dark Bocas **chocolate** is made from locally grown organic cocoa beans. It's delicious and sold in two outlets, the Super Gourmet store in the north of the town and a kiosk in the airport.

What to do and see
Museum
This top-floor display of historical facts and figures in the IPAT Building (tel: 757 9642) is more an exhibition than a museum – and a small one at that. However, the screen-printed boards are a worthwhile read with timelines and information on the archipelago and its geological make-up. Efficient air conditioning makes this a pleasant venue on a hot afternoon. Open 08.30–16.30 Monday to Friday.

Caribbean Gym

Locals and tourists frequent this small weights room, open Monday to Saturday 07.00–11.00 and 13.00–22.00. Call at any other time to be greeted by some ferocious-looking dogs on patrol. Tourist membership is from US$2 a day

Spa Flora Bella

Each treatment at the Spa Flora Bella (Los Delphines, Avenida G, Calle 5; tel: 757 9086; email: spaflorabella@yahoo.com; www.spaflorabella.com) has a distinctive tropical theme, from the relaxing Papaya Pleasure and Isla Bonita to the Sweet Almond Nut Scrub. Chocolate therapies use locally grown organic cocoa beans while beer facials use a cooling Panamanian brew. Rubs, scrubs and touch therapies are great for tired limbs, sore feet and sunburn. An orange and coconut foot massage is just the thing after a long walk through the jungle while the Ginger Mint body treatment eases backpackers backache no end. Also hair beading and braiding.

Learning Spanish in Bocas

This Spanish language school has a sister facility in Costa Rica and offers courses that splits study between the two. Classes are limited to four students and led by tutors from a variety of Spanish-speaking nations, often in classrooms outdoors. **Spanish by the Sea** (tel: 757 9518; email: Spanishbythesea@hotmail.com; www.spanishbythesea.com) is located behind the Hotel Bahía and is owned and run by Ins Lommers who also speaks English, Dutch, French and German. Classes follow a step-by-step programme and students are assessed on arrival to gauge their ability accurately. Organised tours, lectures and Caribbean cooking classes are part of the curriculum and students that join between April and October can also volunteer on a sea turtle protection programme. Standard courses range from beginner to advanced. Others specialise in medical and travel Spanish and language skills for children. Priced from US$70 to US$130 per week for two to four hours a day, five days a week, and US$100–190 for five days of individual tuition, with homestays available at US$12 per night, US$6 per person at the school.

Dominoes

A game of dominoes is a serious business in Panama and in Bocas the locals do battle each night. Half a dozen men gather around a small battered table on a small patch of scrubland to the south of the park to play dominoes in a style that is best described as 'fierce'. Rules are complicated and scoring meticulous, managed by a man in a hat who chalks up a tally on a wall. Dominoes are slammed on to a battered table at machine-gun pace. Watch and learn amidst street dogs and scurrying crabs.

Library and book exchanges

The library in Bocas has a limited number of books in English, but is reluctant to loan to tourists, and backpackers report mixed success on trying. A shelf of English-language titles and *National Geographic* magazines is growing slowly thanks to donations. Find it opposite the church on Calle 3. Book exchanges can be found in the Buena Vista Bar & Deli, Mondo Taitu and Bocas Water Sports office. The Hotel Angela also has a decent shelf of well-thumbed novels and guidebooks that is used by visitors from all over the world. The etiquette requires having a drink in the Hotel Angela bar before doing a swap, no real hardship. Time it right and you'll find a Bryson, Elton and Theroux classic in any number of languages.

Open house

Newcomers to Bocas can join the open house event held at **Bocas Yacht Club & Marina** (tel: 757 9800; fax: 757 9801; email: bocasyachtclub@yahoo.com; www.bocasmarina.com) every other Friday. An open invitation to turn up at 16.30 is enjoyed by a mix of short-term visitors, long-staying backpackers and expatriates. Grab a water taxi for US$1 and enjoy a beer for the same in a nice setting on the water. The only stipulation for admission is to bring something for the barbecue.

Bocas Town FC

Arrive on Isla Colón by plane and you may spot the local soccer team in action. It practises on a strip of land close to the airport runway, limbering up to a thunder of aviation engines that renders the whistle temporarily redundant. Matches are publicised through word of mouth alone but tickets are sold more publicly. Sales are brisk so visitors keen to attend a match day should look out for a man with a megaphone in the Park. Hotels sometimes have a fixture list, or ask around in town.

Beaches

Playa El Istmito is the closest beach to Bocas Town, a 'city beach' just a 15-minute walk (or five-minute taxi journey) out of town along Avenida G. Also known as Playa La Cabaña (or Cabaña Beach) this long and thin sandy stretch is a popular Bocatorian hangout with volleyball nets and sunshade cabañas. The Liki Tiki Restaurant & Bar (see *Nightlife*) and local Bar July have put it firmly on the tourist map. Bluff Beach, 7km away, may be prettier and preferred by the purists, but El Istmito is all about fun.

    Isla Colón has numerous small stretches of sandy beach, many unnamed and not served by bus. Most taxi drivers are happy to take visitors to their own particular favourite. These generally include **Punch Beach**, a stretch too dangerous for swimming but good for surfing and **Bluff Beach**, the most attractive sandy stretch on the island. It's located 7km outside of Bocas Town (a 15-minute taxi or picturesque 45-minute bike ride) and is where most surfers head on arrival in Bocas. Though prettier than neighbouring Punch Beach it shares its strong waves and dangerous undercurrents. Bluff is an important nesting site for sea turtles from May to September. Other smaller beaches include **Big Creek** and **Puss Head Point**.

La Gruta

Colonia Santeña, a small village located in the centre of Isla Colón, is named after its founders, early settlers from the province of Los Santos. This migrant community developed the land, breeding cattle and pigs and growing fields of crops. Today most of the fresh meat sold in Bocas is from the sizeable herds and pig farms that surround this tiny settlement. The location of Colonia Santeña, well away from the tourist mêlée, would normally ensure quiet anonymity. Yet thanks to a magnificent cave the village of Colonia Santeña find itself on the tourist map. The cave (La Gruta) has a statue of the Virgin Mary at its entrance, an important focus for worship by a local Catholic congregation. Lush ferns obscure the opening after the rains but step inside to find stalactites, a trickling freshwater creek and thousands of bats. The air is foul, due a thick layer of bat excrement coating every nook and cranny. Don't let this put you off; bats hanging in the shadows from a mighty jagged ceiling are an incredible sight. Should the smell begin to get too much, there is a second, smaller cave that is often overlooked by visitors, but contains fewer bats. The cool, damp limestone rock can be slippery so wear boots or trainers. La Gruta is an important shrine for the residents of Isla Colón; many locals pilgrimage to the cave in honour of the Virgen del Carmen each year in July.

Birding in Bocas

The archipelago boasts an extraordinary number of birds, many of them endemic species. The Panama Audubon Society has recorded sightings of dozens of rare birds in the province and green-breasted mango, snowy cotinga, stub-tailed spadebill, white-tailed kite, uniform crake, purple martin, zone-tailed hawk, olive-throated parakeet, lesser nighthawk and chestnut woodpecker are all recent sightings. In 2003 a growing number of tour operators added Bocas del Toro to their itineraries and a bird lodge and several cabañas aimed at international birders are slated for opening in 2005.

Swan's Cay (also known as Bird Island or Isla de los Pájaros), a bird sanctuary located to the north of Isla Colón, can be reached easily from Boca del Drago. Home to a large number of indigenous and migratory marine birds the island also has a sizeable population of ground nesters. A leeward grotto offers birders plenty of protection, allowing close observation of red-billed tropics and white-crowned pigeons. Brown booby, brown pelican and frigate and numerous gulls and terns can also be easily spotted. Visiting Swan's Cay is by permission and is advisable with a guide. Contact ANAM (tel: 757 9244), Panama's state-run environmental agency, at its office on Calle 1. Open 08.00–12.00 and 13.00–16.00.

Sandpipers, herons, egrets and kingfisher are commonly found in the mangrove forests of the archipelago, while hummingbirds, hawks, doves, parrots, owls, woodpeckers and tanagers are frequently sighted in the forests. Toucans inhabit Isla Popa and during early March and October large flocks of migratory turkey vultures fly over Isla Colón.

Hiking in Bocas

Challenging jungle hikes are a pursuit poorly served by the water-orientated archipelago and its tour operators. While boatmen, fishermen and cayuco owners

PANAMA'S NO 1 BIRDWATCHING GUIDE

Talk to those who have engaged Mario Bernal (tel: 693 8213; email: mariobernalg@hotamail.com) as a guide and a gushing recommendation generally follows. An award-winning naturalist and passionate environmental campaigner, Bernal is widely regarded as one of the finest guides in Panama – if not Central America as a whole. President of ConserVA, a regional conservation group, and an adviser to the Panamanian government on eco-tourism issues, Bernal is renowned as a dedicated and highly knowledgeable birding expert. His limitless energy and enthusiasm for Panama's flora and fauna is contagious and his daily fees are some of the most reasonable in the isthmus, and this lifelong naturalist cites love not money as his prime motivation.

Bernal worked for many years for the Smithsonian Tropical Research Institute and promotes education programmes relating to Panama's fragile ecosystems in schools and colleges. His birding and botanical packages can be booked through ANCON and Panoramic Panama (see *Local tour operators*). Bernal is due to open a specialist birdwatching observation lodge in Bocas del Toro complete with overnight cabañas in late 2005. No further details are available at the time of writing.

are two a penny, landlubbers at home in the jungle seem to be thin on the ground. Trails are rugged, unmade and unsigned and known only by the local guides who are prepared to disembark. Exploration of the less accessible forested areas is best done with a specialist operator, such as Ancon Expeditions or Cocomo Adventure Tours, or a local Indian guide, such as those at Bahía Honda. Many trails remain completely unknown by tourists but as demand for adventure treks increases in Bocas barely a month goes by without news of a great new undiscovered jungle hike. Ask around for a one-to-one guide or contact ANAM for a recommendation. IPAT should have a list of accredited local guides and may even know of some entrepreneurial islanders prepared to have a go.

The following trails aren't challenging but are led by a local guide who knows the jungle well.

The **Trail of the Sloth** begins at the Bahía Honda Ngöbe Buglé village on Isla Bastimentos and can be picked at the village's restaurant or booked through a guide via most major tour operators in Bocas Town. The walk takes about 90 minutes or so along relatively easy water and land trails, the main wildlife attraction is sloth and these are easily spotted. The trail expires at a bat cave and is guided by a local from the village. Part of the trek is by cayuco along a stretch of river to see crocodiles, oropendolas and hawks. Do this at night or sunrise to see whiteface capuchin and spider monkeys.

This easy 15-minute trail through a cleared private forest leads to the white sand and surf of Red Frog Beach. The **Trail of the Red Frog** crosses from the southern to northern coast of Bastimentos under a jungle canopy past ponds of caiman and lilies. Red dart frogs, the most famous residents of the islands, can be seen along the trail.

Most visitors embark on the **Trail of the Salt Creek** on Bastimentos to see Indian huts, learn about medicinal plants and look out for local birdlife. It's another easy but enjoyable walk and takes in Quebrada Salt village and the route to Long Beach.

The two-mile **Trail of Sandubidi** is on Popa Island and runs from Sandubidi village (known as Popa II) through spectacular rainforest. Guides will point out any number of birds, mammals and medicinal plants and will extend this walk for those that want to see more. There is also a mangrove trail close to the village.

If you are heading to Zapatilla then it's worth doing the short, easy walk dubbed 'The Forest Behind the Reef' in the Large Cayos Zapatilla inside the Marine Park. It's an easy walk but is breathtakingly beautiful, through flower-filled jungle and towering ferns.

Other practicalities
Tourist office
Don't be fooled by the impressive-looking IPAT (tel: 757 9642) building in Calle 3. It promises much at first glance but is of little practical help with bare shelves where visitor leaflets and tourism information should be.

ANAM (tel: 757 9244), Panama's state-run environmental agency is located next to Barco Hundido. Call in for details of camping, ranger accommodation and permits to visit Swan's Cay. Open 08.00–12.00 and 13.00–16.00.

Medical
Hospital
Bocas del Toro Hospital (tel: 757 9201) is located on Avenida G on the road to Saigon about a ten-minute walk from the centre of town. It acts as a GPs' surgery, dispensary and treatment centre and deals with every manner of medical need from basic first aid to life-saving surgery.

Herbalist

Natural medicine continues to play a sizeable part in modern-day Panamanian medicine. In Bocas an appointment at **La Ortiga** (tel: 757 5753/625 4843) provides patients with treatment for mind and body, with individually prescribed herbal therapies as well as spiritual guidance. Sessions cost from US$5 a person.

Dentist

A part-time practitioner opens for business every Saturday morning on Calle 3 (southern end).

Pharmacies

There are two pharmacies in Bocas del Toro and both stock a decent range of over-the-counter remedies for common ailments. The Rosa Blanca Pharmacy midway along Calle 3 on the southern stretch is the better of the two, although the adjacent Chen Pharmacy isn't bad.

Laundry

Using the Lavamatico south of the Hotel Angela on Avenida G is a cost-effective way to tackle a rucksack full of laundry, at US$3 for a full load. Leave if for collection later, packed in a black refuse sack with your name pinned on (sack and name tag supplied). Washing is returned un-ironed and tumble-dried, so avoid synthetic fibres. The Laundry El Lorito on Calle 3 offers a similar same-day service as does the Hotel Scarlett on Calle 4.

Groceries

Newly opened Chinese-run **Mercado Super** on Calle 3 opposite Hotel Laguna is fast becoming the grocery store of choice in the town centre. The **Hebesa Supermarket**, an older but well-stocked mini-mart on Avenida G, accepts American Express and has plenty for self-caterers, campers and hikers. The upmarket **Super Gourmet** on Calle 2 (tel: 757 9357; email: labocaloca@cwPanama.net) opened its doors in 2003 to the relief of every expatriate and backpacker who missed Cheddar cheese and Oreos. This mini-supermarket is aimed entirely at foreigners (with prices to match) with all the usual American brands, a cheese and meat counter, and European wines. It's also an outlet for the region's famous dark chocolate made using organic cacao beans. Open Monday to Saturday 10.00–18.00, closed Sunday.

The best place to buy beer for a day on the water, a camping trip or a beach party is at a **drinks wholesale** outlet located next to The Reef restaurant. The place is open 08.30–16.30 Monday to Saturday and for just US$7.50 you get 24 bottles (plus a deposit of US$2.40 for the case). Bulk ice can be bought from the Transparente Tour office in Calle 3.

Media and communications
Newspapers

In the late 19th century the archipelago had three newspapers – today it has none. A daily shipment of *Miami Herald*s and Panamanian nationals arrives on the first flight from Panama City each morning, along with *The Visitor*, Panama's tourist news-sheet.

Banks

The only bank in Bocas is located next to the Super Gourmet store and is open 08.00–14.00 and tends to be crowded as a result. Avoid the queues by arriving before 12.00–14.00 or use the ATM. Also open Saturday 09.00–12.00, closed on Sunday.

Post office

The post office is housed in a large government administration building next to the Park. Its poste restante service is well used and works well as a result. Open 08.30–15.30 Monday–Friday and Saturday 09.00–12.00.

Migration office

This is also in the government building although usually refers foreigner visitors with a visa or passport problem to the main office in Changuinola.

Internet cafés

Bravo Centre Calle 3. Probably the fastest internet connection you will get in Bocas along with international phone calls (rates vary depending on country), mobile phones (for sale or rent), DVDs and books. Internet is US$2 per hour. Opens daily from 09.00 until late.

Bocas Internet Calle 3. Space is tight in this tinted glass building with a dozen or so PCs squashed shoulder-to-shoulder around the room. Despite the squeeze, service is good and staff helpful with a coffee bar and a business services desk that places international calls, sends and receives faxes, photocopies (to A3 size) and prints from floppy discs or CD-roms. A small range of computer consumables and stationery is kept in stock. Open daily from 08.00 until late; US$2 per hour.

Internet Don Chicho Calle 3. This tiny internet café was the first to open in Bocas and many of the half a dozen machines are beginning to show their age. One battle-scarred PC has keys with the characters worn off with use. Cramped conditions make it impossible to pick up emails with any privacy. Also fax, photocopy and international calls. Open daily; US$2 per hour.

IPAT Internet Plaza (Tourism Bureau) Calle 1; tel: 757 9642. Internet connections are painfully slow but at 50c for the first hour (and 75c for the next) it is worth checking out. Expect to queue as just a handful of computers struggle to keep up with demand. But the building has air conditioning, the views are great and the staff friendly. Opens to strict regular business hours 09.00–17.00, Monday to Friday, closed weekends.

Pay phones

Now that Cable & Wireless has installed a payphone in every community in the country with more than 250 residents, Panama has one of the highest teledensity rates in Latin America. Find a number of payphones outside the Bocas C&W building where phone cards can be purchased in US$5, US$10 and US$20 denominations and International Calling Cards offer great rates abroad. Cash phones accept both US and Panamanian coinage and there are plenty of these throughout the archipelago, on the corner of almost each block, in hotels and restaurants and in all key public meeting places, such as the Park.

Emergency

Police Tel: emergency number 104. The police station is located in Calle 1 in the same building as the local jail.

Fire Tel: emergency number 103. The fire station is located on the northern end of Calle 1.

Coastguard At the time of writing there is no coastguard in Bocas, a situation that is far from satisfactory as visitor figures soar. Some small tour operators carry life jackets, life buoys or first aid kits – but not many – while finding boats equipped with marine radios is also rare. So, while the local tourism industry in the archipelago waits for the Panamanian government to implement proper safety controls, it is left to boat operators to deal with difficulties on the water. The death of a tourist while swimming on Isla Bastimentos recently has brought the need for proper coastguard provisions in the archipelago further to the fore.

Further out

Punta Caracol Tel: 612 1088/6767186; email: puntacaracol@puntacaracol.com; www.puntacaracol.com. Stylish architecture, ecological initiatives and a spectacular setting have seen Punta Caracol become one of Panama's most-photographed on-the-water hotels. The brainchild of a Spanish family it opened in 2001, a string of pastel-coloured wooden lodges rising up on poles from the sea. The entire project has been built using traditional building methods. Handcrafted cabins have palm-leaf roofs and are made from native woods, clay, bamboo, wild cane and other indigenous materials. The location is stunning: pristine shallow waters on a mile-long coral reef; on a backdrop of mangrove forest. Uninterrupted views out to sea offer no other distractions than the landscape. Wooden walkways connect each lodge with a large open-sided restaurant and bar adorned with flowering tubs and dugout canoes filled with shrubs. The surrounding waters and mangroves teem with marine life and offer superb snorkelling. Expect to see parrotfish, angelfish, needlefish and manta rays. Also dolphins in calm early morning conditions.

Hard-working brother-and-sister team Piluchy and Luis ask guests to respect the ecological and peaceful character of surrounding natural habitat, installing solar power and wastewater recycling systems in each cabin and asking visitors to leave environmentally incompatible items at home. Rates aren't inexpensive at US$215–240 for a double (US$325–395 for a quad) but include transfers, a hearty breakfast, snorkel and canoe hire, afternoon tea and a 3-course dinner. Credit cards are accepted and booking is highly recommended.

Punta Mangler Eco Resort Tel: 757 9541/595 2665; email: reservas@puntamanglar.com; www.puntamangler.com. This small collection of rustic over-the-water wooden cabañas is built in mangrove forest close to a coral reef over a shallow marine. The diving is good and so are the views, although biting insects can get a little too close for comfort. Two doubles (one with air conditioning and one with a fan), dorm room (4 bunks) and 2 family rooms (4–6 people) all have sea-facing balconies. Dorm beds US$12 per person, cabins at US$30–50 (US$7 additional guests). One-night stay and dive packages from US$70 (2 dives).

BOCA DEL DRAGO

It's possible to walk or cycle to Boca del Drago (mouth of the dragon) but visitors who decide that the winding 16km climb is a bit too much will find it easily accessible by bus, boat or taxi. It's a 30-minute journey by bus for a US$2 per person one-way ticket and the little air-conditioned bus hurtles at speed uphill past fincas and cattle fields, swerving to avoid chickens that really do cross the road.

According to history books, Boca del Drago was the first piece of land trodden by Christopher Columbus in Panama when he arrived from Costa Rica, sailing into what is now known as Admiral Bay (or Caribaro by the Ngöbe Buglé Indians) via a channel that separates the mainland from Isla Colón. Swan Key, a small island within reach of Boca del Drago, attracts large numbers of nesting and migratory birds, including boobies, frigates and pelicans. Visit this bird sanctuary with a guide to avoid disrupting ground-nesting activity (see *Tour operators*) and expect to see several endemic species.

Boca del Drago's Ngöbe Buglé population live along the road to Bocas Town in a collection of two dozen wood-and-thatch huts. Close by, the Institute for Tropical Ecology and Education (ITEC) facility (see *Conservation*) is set amongst coconut palms, banana, lime and breadfruit trees, home to a large population of fruit bats. A small pretty beach and a nearby coral reef can be snorkelled when the waters are calm and clear. A cemetery filled with moss-covered tombstones of early

European settlers is also worth a look and those who have arrived by bike and still have itchy feet will find a couple of rough tracks to explore.

Getting there

Taking a boat taxi is now the easiest ride to Drago, leaving from Taxi Maritimo on Calle 1 at about US$5 return. The bus is an easy option, leaving every 90 minutes or so (two in the morning and two in the afternoon) from the park. An up-to-date bus timetable is posted in most hotels and in the internet café on Calle 3. Another option is to pick up a collectivo taxi, which costs the same as the bus. A regular taxi will charge US$20–25 for a one-way trip – and while you're there it pays to keep an eye on the time. Getting stranded at Bocas del Drago is easy as both boats and buses run to a strict, and limited, schedule. Missing both means finding a taxi – or a long, hot walk back to Bocas Town. A passing water taxi (Changuinola–Bocas) will stop if it sees people waiting on the dock beyond the restaurant. Ask where to wait (ignore the schedule and arrive early just to be sure). Another option is a workers' bus that will pick up tourists for just US$3 if it's got room.

Where to stay

Accommodation options in Boca del Drago are limited and basic and each place comes with mixed reports. **Cabañas Estefani** (tel: 774 3168) and **Casa Nina** (tel: 260 7135) get the thumbs-up for camping (US$5) but rooms are without water at US$18–20 each. A cabaña for up to eight people at US$55 is often without power. The nearby **Drago Mar Beach Resort** (www.dragobeachresort.com) is slated to open at the end of 2004 and plans are pretty impressive: 21 rooms in individual bungalows on 6ha of land and a private beach with pool, spa and sauna, massage rooms, and centre for alternative healing. Expect to pay US$75–200 per night, including breakfast and transfer from Bocas Town.

Where to eat

However, most people visit Boca del Drago simply for a change of scenery. Also to eat lunch at **Yarisnori** (tel: 613 1934/615 5580; email: jamelsv@jhotmail.com), a great little open-sided local restaurant steps from the sand. A seafood menu is cooked local style. Choose from lobster, fried fish, octopus and shrimp served with coconut rice and salad, patacones or breadfruit at US$6–10. The service is leisurely and the food freshly cooked. If you're in a hurry (or there's a group of you) it is worth phoning your order through.

ISLA CARENERO (CAREENING CAY)

This small low-lying island is a stone's throw from Bocas Town, a five-minute (US$1) boat ride across a few hundred metres of water. Its close proximity to Isla Colón has made it popular with investors and the shoreline facing its bigger, brasher neighbour is dotted with waterfront bars and hotels as a result. Early businesses that opened on Isla Carenero found luring visitors away from Bocas Town a challenge. Today, however, a string of decent tourist haunts more than hold their own, appealing to those that seek a quieter pace away from the hustle and bustle. Isla Carenero got its name from the nautical term 'careening', meaning to lean a vessel on its side for cleaning. The island, chosen as a spot for maintenance of the ships under the command of Christopher Columbus in 1502, has a modern-day maritime facility today, a 35-berth marina.

Most visitors head to Isla Carenero to experience the sand and the surf or to enjoy the views and grab a beer at the Buccaneer bar on the water. The island, which has no roads, is navigable on foot via a strip of crumbling concrete path and unmarked sandy trails that fizzle out without warning. There isn't much in the way of sightseeing other than the coastline itself. A walk across the island takes less than two hours, passing Ngöbe Buglé villages and a shoreline of fishing boats and swimming children, dodging rubbish and fruit trees along a crab-ridden trail.

Getting there

Grab a water taxi from the Transparente Tour office for US$1 one-way. To return stand at the end of any of the docks on the island and put your hand in the air, or whistle, and a passing taxi will stop.

Where to stay and eat

Restaurant Las Tortugas 'El Brequero' Tel: 757 9360. This low-key Panamanian waterfront eatery may be uninspiring but it has magnificent views. Mediocre food is by no means terrible with lobster (US$9), octopus (US$7.50) and ceviche (US$3) and seco on tap.

Bernard's Pargo Rojo (6 rooms) Tel: 757 9649. Visitors who enjoy waterfront views, good food and character landlords will adore this place. The patron, an Iranian who went to an English public school, is a real one-off, but visitors who survive his quick wit and clever retorts develop a lasting affection. The menu at Pargo Rojo is one of the most exciting in the archipelago with Asian-, Mediterranean- and Middle Eastern-inspired recipes that are exceptionally good. Choose from a spicy seafood soup (US$4), Greek salad (US$4), Thai fish (coconut, lemongrass and fenugreek) (US$7.50), chicken curry (US$7.50) and Thai pork with curry noodles (US$7.50), each cooked by Bernard personally. He's sure to moan about everything in Bocas (momentarily causing visitors to question why they're there) but there is something highly engaging about Bernard venting his spleen. Open all day, 7 days a week, with dinner at 17.00. Over-the-water rooms are good value, from US$27.50. Each has a private hot-water bathroom, downstairs and loft bedroom that sleeps 3–4, and many budget travellers in Bocas would never dream of staying anywhere else.

Dona Mara (6 rooms) Tel/fax: 757 9551. Owned by a guy called Milford, this family-run B&B and kitchen serves some of the best fried fish on the islands. Nothing on the menu is much more than US$5. Open all day from 08.00 to 23.00. Eat at tables out front alongside a parrot. Rooms are US$35 single, US$45 double and have air conditioning, hot water and local TV – but ask for one with a sea view.

Careening Cay Resort (6 cabins) Tel: 757 9242; email; marcar@cwp.net.pa; www.careeningcay.com. This American-owned cluster of large thatched cabins have been built using native hardwoods and each has hot-water shower, fan and a sheltered porch that overlooks the gardens and the bay. A great R&R spot complete with hammock can be found at the end of an on-the-water boardwalk. Rooms are US$55 per night double occupancy, US$20 for each additional person. The *chitras* (sand flies) are pretty hungry this end of the island so pack some extra insect repellent to be on the safe side. An on-site restaurant, the **Sunset Bar & Grill,** is popular with the boating crowd. Choose from Greek salad (US$5), stir fry (US$10), garlic chicken (US$9) and rib eye steak (US$12) and weekly themed nights Tuesday (Texas BBQ), Wednesday (Mexican) and Thursday (Italian).

The Buccaneer Resort www.buccaneer-resort.com. At the time of writing this mid-budget resort has just been sold to San Cristobal International (SCI) who have announced tentative plans to refurbish and expand it by the summer of 2005. Rumours are circulating that it is to become Panama's first private-member community. For an update visit the website. Here's hoping, however, that its great waterfront bar will stay, as few tourist haunts are as relaxing as the **Bucanner Bar** (tel: 757 9137; email chefchrisruss@msn.com). Boasting a blissful spot with open sea views gazing out to Isla Solarte, it's an easy jaunt from the centre of Bocas Town but a world away from tooting horns and traffic. Americans Jo and Chris run the place with good humour serving plates of fillet steak and mashed potatoes and lots of barbecued favourites. A 2-for-1 happy hour

Monday to Saturday 16.00–18.00 with two beers for a US$1 is popular with a budget travel crowd. On Sunday happy hour actually lasts for 4: 14.00–18.00. The place to be in Bocas for fans of sports TV.

Blue Marlin Resort Tel: 757 9853/620 6388; email: bluemarlin@cwPanama.net. Owned by George Ingenthran from Kansas City and his Panamanian wife. Has lots of natural hardwood detail. Each comfortable room has hot water, air conditioning and ceiling fans as well as a fridge with cooking facilities over the water. Dubbed the Pickled Parrot Rancho. Rates vary throughout the season.

Casa Acuario Chico (4 rooms) Tel/fax: 757 9565; email: joberg1301@cwp.net.pa. Each of the 4 comfortable rooms has air conditioning, with a pocket-sized strip of neighbouring beach and great snorkelling off the dock. Rates are US$65 per double room including breakfast and there is also a kitchen for guest use.

Tierra Verde (7 rooms) Tel: 757 9903; email info@hoteltierraverde.com. Nestling in a coconut grove, the Tierra Verde is close to Carenero break and popular with surfers. Spacious rooms have air conditioning and private hot-water bathrooms with French windows that open on to rainforest from a wraparound terrace. Internet, fax and cable TV. US$45 single, US$50 double and US$55 triple per person including breakfast.

Restaurante Ocean Queen Tel: 757 9360. A great find, and owner González offers a good little seafood menu. Octopus (US$6.50) is exceptionally good as is the crab (US$7) and the lobster (US$10), served on a thatched-roofed deck over the water in a setting that is gloriously peaceful.

ISLA BASTIMENTOS

The kite-shaped isle of Bastimentos is known locally for its vibrant Afro-Caribbean town, Old Bank, with a population of 900 that has shared the island with indigenous communities for almost 100 years. Though just ten minutes

BANANA ISLES

The banana industry began its investment in Bocas de Toro even before Panama gained independence from Colombia, building infrastructure and establishing banana farms on its rugged terrain. Local workers were supplemented by immigrants from the Caribbean and Central American refugees, primarily Nicaraguan. The United Fruit Company, now Chiquita Brands, developed early sanitation systems, established clean water supplies, opened hospitals and developed preventative health care methods to control yellow fever and malaria. New ports and railroads in Panama ensured fruit could be transported from plantations to faraway markets, while the introduction of new shipping methods cut delivery times in half. Effective transportation of this perishable fruit saw exports increase dramatically and soon several enterprises were shipping bananas to the United States. At the beginning of the 20th century Panama Disease, a soil-borne fungus, wiped out thousands of acres of banana crops, forcing the growers to seek land outside of the archipelago to ensure it was clean. The industry was saved but was dealt a further blow in 1991 when an earthquake hit the province followed by a devastating flood. Chiquita suffered losses of US$45 million and Government taxes, wage disputes, industrial working practices and banana wars took their toll on an industry under pressure.

The United Fruit Historical Society Email: united_fruit@yahoo.com; www.unitedfruit.org

264 BOCAS DEL TORO PROVINCE

> ## THE BASTIMENTOS BEACH BOYS
> These local cultural icons of calypso and musica tipica are part of modern-day Bocatorian music legend. Each band member is a Bastimentos islander and a resident of Old Bank and this eight-piece ensemble is at the heart of every celebration on the island. The music, a mix of calypso and Panamanian cumbria has its roots firmly in the West Indies, spawned by the calypsonians of Trinidad who created a heady musical fusion of African and European styles. A band of local legendary stamina, rumour has it that the Bastimentos Beach Boys can jam non-stop for 15 hours, playing a high-energy dance rhythm littered with scandalous lyrics that sees these charismatic calypsonians hero-worshipped among residents for their mischief.

southeast of Isla Colón, there are few similarities, with a language, culture and populace from the banana plantations of the 1800s. Afro-Caribbean predominance gives Bastimentos an air of old Jamaica, where English-Patois is spoken and calypso, soca and reggae pulsate all day long.

Much has changed in Bastimentos since the days of the early *bananeros*. Today islanders farm cattle on the rolling terrain while old-timers reminisce in the Old Bank – Bastimentos Town. Tourism, slower to pick up speed here, is fast becoming Bastimentos' economic future, and the One Love bar and Roots restaurant have given its pecuniary hill-climb a boost. The island's two small Ngöbe Buglé settlements supplement an income from fishing with tourism. Guides introduce visitors to Bastimentos' wild, forested habitats, home to sloth, monkey and crocodile, and a species of strawberry-coloured poison dart frog unique to the area.

Old Bank

This, the largest community on the island, is almost entirely of Afro-Caribbean descent. Although the locals call it a town it has the feel of a pretty coastal village, a length of a hundred or so flower-trimmed wooden zinc roofed houses, neatly divided by a pathway. Floral curtains, flowerpots and curbed doorsteps would be at home in a British hamlet if it weren't for the Day-Glo hues. English speakers have names to match. Meeting 'Mr Marshall' and 'Mr Smith' in the grocery store can take some adjustment, given the preponderance of Spanish just minutes away.

The appeal of Old Bank lies in its colour and interesting characters. It's a place of painted bridges in Rasta shades, rainbow-coloured street signs and quirky house names (there's a place called Beverly's Hills). A mural splashes vibrant colour on a drab, grey wall and reveals who lives where in Old Bank in good humour. Stuck for directions? Then talk to Mr Green (aka Leonard or 'The Doll'), who runs the over-the-water fuel pump and provides an unofficial welcome party with his children at the dock.

In the absence of a tourist office, Rose from the Restaurant Nikka Rosa (see *Where to stay and eat*) is a good guy to talk to. His family have run the place since 1940 and he knows everyone and everything about Bastimentos and its people. Its location in the very centre of Old Bank makes it a popular stop-off with islanders and Rose graciously introduces his guests to every passer-by. Meet the man who farms shrimp using pig excrement, the lead signer of the Bastimentos Beach Boys or the guy who plans to sell hammocks on the beach. Like most islanders, Rose hopes to build up his business and has plans for a free water taxi from Isla Colón to the Nikka Rosa to encourage people to visit. A valuable source of local information he's happy to 'shoot the breeze' with his customers. If he doesn't know the answer to a question he usually knows someone who does and on some occasions will wander off to find them.

Getting there
A water taxi from Bocas Town will cost US$3 to Old Bank or if you plan to eat or drink at Nikka Rosa call Rose for a free taxi.

Beaches
The island has a number of pretty beaches and directions to some are posted on makeshift signs in the town. Although most of the beaches on the northern side are too rough for swimming some can be surfed, and there are some great snorkelling spots both inside and outside the island. Polo's beach (or fourth beach) is good for snorkelling and surfing as waves hit the surrounding reef. The best snorkelling spots are the inside stretches, from Punta Vieja to Coral Cay. Visitors can hire snorkel equipment by the hour from the Hospedaje Silvia in Old Bank (tel: 757 9442).

First Beach (Playa Primera or **Playa Wizard)** is a 20-minute walk from the centre via a lovely little path on the eastern edge of town from the football field. Easy to navigate but boggy in places it climbs past flower-filled gardens and through leafy trails to a sandy beach popular with surfers. The riptides here are strong and the water is not suitable for swimming but those looking for a place to hang a hammock will enjoy its laidback character.

A small path at the end of First Beach leads to **Red Frog Beach (Playa Segunda** or **Second Beach)**, the island's most popular stretch of sand. The walk is unreliable as the trail isn't always accessible, impassable after bad weather and muddy when over-used. Allow an hour to reach Red Frog along a difficult path to navigate with a surfboard. This picturesque stretch of white sand has surfable waves and is edged by woodlands that can also be accessed by boat from Bocas. Passengers are dropped at a jetty at the entrance of a private cut-through, a ten-minute walk along a leafy trail past ponds and over bridges to the edge of the beach (US$1). This is a prime location for spotting the island's unique red frog, a diminutive species after which the beach was named. Past a small reforestation project is the Red Frog Beach Bar, a rectangular wooden open structure shaded by trees. It has suspended swing seating made from rope and planks that matches the rhythm of the waves: a laidback place with few airs and graces serving snacks, fries, cocktails and ice-cold beer.

An innocuous trail at the end of Red Frog Beach leads to **Magic Bay**, a small crescent-shaped cove that is popular with kayakers. At the end of the beach, it is hard to notice the trail, which is muddy and a steep climb. But there is a path that goes over the hill between beaches. There are lots of little red frogs hopping around here, very easy to spot. The trail should only take five minutes or so, and is worth the walk as Third Beach is always deserted. For a longer hike, keep walking along this beach and through another jungle path at the end of it. This is a beautiful walk, but may be a problem in very wet weather. Although parts of this entire stretch of Bastimentos is privately owned, by Panamanian law all beaches whether privately owned or not have to have public right of way. (However, don't be tempted to pick the pineapples and other fruits along the way as this forms the backbone of the locals' livelihood.)

After the jungle track, on to **Playa Polo** (Polo's beach), a stunning sandy stretch with a reef that halos the shoreline, for fantastic snorkelling in languid mini-lagoons that are protected from the waves. Owner Polo, a recluse well known

BASTIMENTOS CULTURAL CENTRE

Established in the 1990s as a local initiative, the aim of the Bastimentos Cultural Centre is to protect the culture and economy of the island. Having realised that foreign buyers had snapped up 80% of local land, islanders faced up to the fact that the time had come to conserve Bastimentos for future generations. Tired of watching lucrative foreign-owned businesses flourish while its fishing and agriculture industries declined, the group encouraged islanders to build businesses, clean up the town and re-enforce community pride, and stressed the importance of land retention. Education programmes advised landowners on the implications of selling land for short-term financial gain after many Indians admitted that they had given away land for free. A commonly held Ngöbe Buglé belief places little capital importance on the land they own, viewing it as 'god given' and to be shared. Today many local people own businesses in Old Bank and the project advises on the negative impacts and positive benefits of growing tourism on the island. 'Competing with foreign capital is not easy,' admits Mark Chavez, who heads the centre. 'Another challenge is attracting healthy groups of tourists that share positive social values.'

throughout the region and fondly regarded as an eccentric, has lived on the beach in a small wooden hut for over 30 years. He offers camping at US$7 a night, including a fresh catch for dinner and hot bread and coffee for breakfast, as well as plenty of outspoken observations. Arriving at Playa Polo by boat requires extra caution along a single channel that only experienced boatmen can recognise.

Another half-hour walk on from Playa Polo leads to **Playa Larga**, one of the most important turtle-nesting sites on the archipelago, therefore deserving of care in nesting season, March to June. This spectacular 14km stretch is part of Panama's first marine park, Parque Nacional Marino Isla Bastimentos. The beach denotes the entrance to the park (see *Parque Nacional Marino Isla Bastimentos*) and access requires ANAM permission and a US$10 fee plus US$5 to camp.

Quebrada Sal (Salt Creek Village)

This small Ngöbe Buglé community in the southeast of the island sits in a mangrove thicket at the end of a narrow canal. Fifty bamboo-and-thatch buildings house fishermen and subsistence farmers and their families with a schoolhouse, small handicraft stall and a football pitch that is a riot of children, dogs and chickens at dusk. A number of walks lead from the outskirts of the Marine Park through forests and wetlands to beaches and reefs and since opening up to tourism several villagers have become part-time guides. In 2004 the community opened a lodge for overnight visitors (tel: 592 5162). Salt Creek is close to Punta Vieja (Old Point), a secluded, beautiful beach nested by turtles. Coral reefs and clear waters make this an enjoyable place to snorkel.

Bahía Honda

This Ngöbe Buglé village (tel: 603 1857; www.bocas.com/indians/bahiahonda.htm) is located in a bay of the same name, a cluster of thatched huts that teeter on the shoreline with a schoolhouse that doubles as a community centre and restaurant for tourists. Villagers fish and subsistence farm but are becoming increasingly reliant on tourism. Guides offer a number of jungle excursions and a handicraft centre sells carvings and baskets. A restaurant serves great chicken and rice dishes (US$6–8) and offers superb views across the bay. Due to the community's fish-recovery programme lobster, conch, octopus and crab aren't on the menu.

Practicalities
Laundry
Located at the Hospedaje Seaview and open Monday to Friday, 08.00–13.00. Costs are US$1.50 for a full load washed and US$1.50 for drying. Drop laundry off at 08.00–11.00 to get it back the same day.

Snorkel hire
The owners of the Hospedaje Silvia hire out snorkel equipment on a per hour basis. Call in to see what they've got or tel: 757 9442. Kayaks and snorkel gear are both available for hire at El Pelicano for US$2 per hour for a kayak and US$5 a day for snorkel equipment. Find it at the very end of town.

Telephone
There's an international pay phone outside the Restaurant Nikka Rosa.

Shops
A small grocery store (look for the mural on the wall) sells fruit, water and canned goods, while the Kiosk AB Maritza stocks cold drinks, snacks and sweets.

Parque Nacional Marino Isla Bastimentos
This 13,000ha marine park was the first in Panama and comprises an area of land that zigzags from Cayos Zapatillas and surrounding waters out to Playa Larga (Long Beach). A belt of land across the interior; mangrove forests to the south; and Buttonwood Cays and Gallego Cays within the conservation area, which extends to the edge of Coral Cay. An important reserve that protects numerous indigenous Caribbean marine life, freshwater fish and wildlife species (such as sloth), the Park is also a critical location for scientific studies by conservation groups worldwide.

The Park is protected and managed by ANAM from a rangers lodge in Cayos Zapatillas, two beautiful islands (defined as major or minor or north and south) on a coral platform that have beautiful white-sand beaches, pristine waters and small shady forests. Named after the zapatilla fruit and also resembling a pair of shoes (*zapatilla* in Spanish), the islands are an important nesting site for leatherback and hawksbill turtles, and used as a study based by scientists almost year-round. Rough waves and thick forest make accessibility difficult, although birders who have made it report a rich diversity of endemic and migratory species. Snorkelling and diving here are unsurpassed by any other spot on the archipelago (see *Diving in Bocas del Toro*) with waters home to bottlenose dolphin, grey angelfish, yellow angelfish, spotted eagle ray, long spine squirrelfish, toadfish, grey snapper, graysby, flounder, yellowhead jawfish, grunt, scrawled filefish, sharptail eel, damselfish, doctorfish, great barracuda, seahorse, spotted drum, lobster, crab, needlefish, trumpetfish and spotted pufferfish. Nurse sharks and large numbers of reptiles and amphibians including frog species, iguana, crocodile and snake inhabit the waters of the Parque Nacional Marino Isla Bastimentos.

Entrance to the park is US$10 payable at the ANAM office in Bocas Town. Camping (US$5) also requires an ANAM permit and rooms at the Ranger Station are in high demand during peak season.

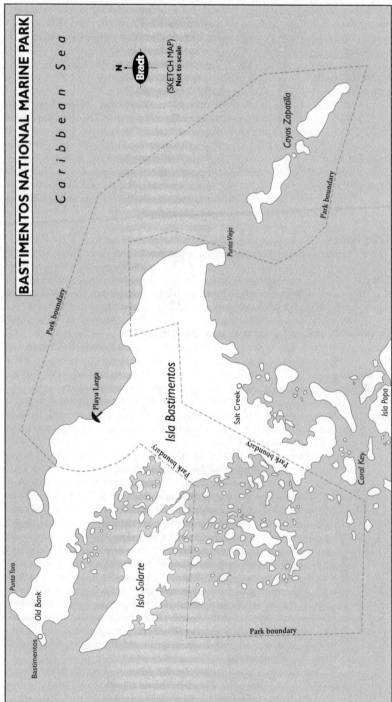

BASTIMENTOS NATIONAL MARINE PARK

Caribbean Sea

(SKETCH MAP)
Not to scale

Cayos Zapatilla

Park boundary

Punta Vieja

Park boundary

Playa Larga

Isla Bastimentos

Salt Creek

Isla Popa

Park boundary

Coral Key

Punta Toro

Old Bank

Isla Solarte

Bastimentos

Park boundary

Where to stay and eat
Old Bank

A concentration of bars, restaurants and inexpensive hotels in Old Bank boasts a laid-back Caribbean feel. Most are on the water or along the town's central path. A handful are located on a scratch of sand close to the waves a five-minute walk from the centre.

Restaurant Nikka Rosa (tel: 624 5641) serves good-value seafood dishes and plates of beans and rice for US$5 in a great spot on the water. Plans also include accommodation for 2005 with rooms at backpacker rates, a 24-hour bar and regular live music plus a free water-taxi service from Bocas Town.

It's considered by many to be the social heart and soul of Old Bank and **Roots Restaurant** rarely disappoints. Co-owner Oscar Powell, a former banana worker with plenty of charm, plays reggae loud and tells tales with plenty of colour. Tasty Creole rice and bean dishes cost less than US$5 and Oscar also guides with a speciality of cave tours (see *Local guides and tours*). Open from 09.00 until late, closed Tuesdays.

The **Tio Tom** (4 rooms) (tel: 757 9831) has four basic rooms over the water, one with a private hot-water bathroom (US$20 per night) and others that share (US$10 per night). Visitors rave about the restaurant for its European classics (US$6–15).

Opposite the Roots Restaurant the **Hospedaje Midland** has a handful of rooms in a handsome two-storey building and a restaurant that serves breakfast, lunch and dinner. Rooms from US$20 per night, menu US$3–7.

Rooms at the **Pensión Black Snapper, Hospedaje Ais' le 'nis, Hospedaje Silvia** (tel: 757 9442) and **Hospedaje Sea View** all come similarly priced at US$10 each as do those at the flower-covered **Hostal Bastimentos (**13 rooms) (tel: 757 9053; www.hostalbastimentos.com), which also has a restaurant and bar that serve cocktails, sandwiches, fruit juices and snacks, plus a kitchen for guests.

Every Monday night is party night at the **Blue Bar** in Old Bank and this Calypso event is fast becoming one of the biggest in the archipelago. Reggae on Saturday and Sunday tends to be a hardcore affair for devotees while Monday attracts a mix of locals and tourists with beers at 50c and barbecue food for US$1.

There are also some basic **cabañas** on the beach trail. They have no fans or air conditioning but do have a cold-water shower. Simply turn up and the owner will appear in order to charge US$10 for a double. **El Jardin del Bambu** is also located on the way to the beach and is US$5 per person for the cheapest room. All are bare and basic and without electricity but are in a decent location.

At the time of writing the **Tree House Hotel & Restaurant** (tel: 507 1701) is still under construction but the plans and location are impressive. Owners Jack and Don Vitale, brothers from Cape Cod, are building a nine-room hotel on a rocky shoreline that is just yards from lapping waves with part of the structure located in the treetops. Each room will be equipped with hot-water shower, mini-fridges and internet for US$20–35 per room. It's close to good surf and the Vitales also plan to offer fishing tours and snorkelling. A restaurant with an international menu will also include a sushi bar. Find it next to Casa del Sol.

The owner at **Restaurant Alvin** is renowned for her fish dishes and is one of the few restaurants that can be relied on to open on a Tuesday; everything under US$5.

Look for the signs in Old Bank that point the way to the **Café One Love.** It's on the way to the beach and serves great-value snacks while Bob Marley classics play all day, as the name suggests.

The sign for the **Casa del Sol** says it's the 'home of breeze' and a coastal location next to the Tree House Hotel & Restaurant ensures just that. Basic rooms overlook crashing waves in a great little spot at the end of a path two minutes from the centre of town; US$10 for a single, US$25 double.

El Pelicano (tel: 757 9830) is owned by a friendly Italian–Panamanian couple who serve great food that combines both influences. Locals rave about the spaghetti and lobster dish and the Creole-style seafood pizza is also highly recommended. Five basic but comfortable rooms, two with shared bathrooms and fans and three with private bathrooms, US$10–15. Open for breakfast 08.00–10.00 and 12.00–21.00 for lunch and dinner. Find it at the very end of town.

Punta Vieja (Old Point)

On the opposite side of the island some 20 minutes by boat from the Old Bank, an eco-lodge in one of the most spectacular beach locations in Bastimentos offers a unique accommodation option.

It's hard to imagine how a hotel could be more intimately connected to the great outdoors than at **Al Natural** (tel: 757 9004/623 2217/640 6935; email: alnaturalbocas@cwPanama.net; www.bocas.com/hoteles/alnatura/alnarate.htm), without doubt one of the finest places to stay in Panama. Stand on the white-sand beach with your back to the sea and you'll face a wall of white-faced monkeys. Stand with the forest behind and you'll look out to a panorama of clear emerald waters with nothing to spoil the view. The concept is simple and uses the natural splendour of the surroundings to its full potential. Five wood-and-thatch elevated bungalows on the beach are open-sided on one wall. The beds, draped in mosquito nets to keep insects at bay, are exposed to the sights, sounds and smells of the shoreline with uninterrupted sea views. Rustles, howls and chirps in the jungle make an overnight stay an experience. Guests are so close to nature here that they can literally reach out and touch it (a fair amount ends up on the mosquito net) from cabañas that overlook a mass of phosphorescent plankton.

Calm clear waters and a beautiful coral reef offer superb snorkelling and masks, kayaks and windsurfing equipment are available free of charge. Each cabaña has a private rainwater shower and solar-powered ceiling fans and lighting. Those that

BLUE MONDAY

Nobody is quite sure of the exact origins of Blue Monday. Some swear that it's a marketing gimmick. Others say it is simply a tradition of Bastimentos' party-loving islanders who feel that the weekends are far too short. Whatever the reason, Blue Monday is now a firmly ensconced Bastimentos custom, the biggest party in the archipelago and a night when the Blue Bar (sepage 000) does big business.

Blue Monday really doesn't begin until the evening, but when it does it is difficult to ignore. The volume on the sound system at the Blue Bar hits maximum and Old Bank begins to pulsate to the sound of reggae, calypso and soca. The music is loud and the place packed by 20.00 when the heat on the dance floor is stifling. Those who aren't hell-bent on drinking Bastimentos dry at 50c a bottle enjoy the music from a distance. A barbecue outside serves grilled chicken and hotdogs for US$1, stopping only when the music does in the early hours, when party-goers make a dash for the boat back to Bocas. Accommodation in Old Bank on a Monday night tends to be in high demand. After a late night of partying few on Bastimentos can work at full capacity, and many businesses have their closed signs out on a Tuesday.

head to Al Natural to become Panama's hippest castaways are a mixed bunch, from TV types and botanists to honeymooners and backpackers that can't think of a better place on which to blow a budget. From US$85 per person for a double room, US$127.50 for a single, including all meals and wine with dinner

Coral Cay (Crawl Cay)

This popular dive and snorkelling site is situated just off the southeast portion of Isla Bastimentos, a 20-minute boat journey from Bocas Town. Shallow, clear waters offer good year-round conditions on a reef that teems with a rainbow of fish. A popular location for underwater photography, the colours at Coral Cay are good and blessed with plenty of light and sand. Expect to see bristletree worms, crabs, anemones and Christmas tree worms, although there tend to be fewer large pelagic fish here than at Hospital Point. Arrive early during peak season as Coral Cay is deluged with tourist boats. The restaurant is superb but is included in every tour company itinerary so tends to be jam-packed. For a peaceful dive visit Coral Cay before noon and after 15:00.

The **Coral Cay Cabañas** (tel: 626 1919/3269; email: cayocoral@hotmail.com; www.bocas.com/coralcay.htm) is a rustic cluster of thatched-roofed cabins that boast a picturesque over-the-water location in a remote spot on the edge of Bastimentos Island National Marine Park. Wooden boardwalks link stilted cabins on the water, a popular location for swimmers that like to jump in from the dock. Three comfortable cabins have shuttered windows and comfortable beds complete with a throw and mosquito net. An on-site seafood restaurant serves great local dishes and a dugout canoe, transfers from Bocas, breakfast and dinner, snorkelling equipment and use of kitchen facilities are included in the room rate of US$75 per person.

Local guides and tours

Over the years **Oscar Powell**, co-owner of Roots Restaurant in Old Bank, has made guided cave tours a speciality. Few people know the complicated routes to the best caves in Bastimentos Marine Park like Powell, who swerves his boat along narrow creeks to avoid submerged trees, pointing out plants and birds along the way. Pass through rivers and mangrove forests, a habitat for heron, sloth and crocodile. The local caves are home to a large population of bats and Powell is knowledgeable about the rock formations that continue to baffle geologists. Reaching the caves requires a good standard of fitness and steady feet and involves plenty of wading through water and climbing rocks covered in slippery bat excrement. The water reaches neck height in some places with deep pools that need to be swum. Low ceilings and high humidity makes this unwise for anyone with claustrophobic tendencies, despite them being some of the largest known caves in Central America. Book a trip to Nivida Cave directly with Oscar at the restaurant or with Bocas Marine Tours (see *Tour operators*)

Everybody in Bastimentos knows **Cabrioli Livingston** (or Livingston as he is known; tel: 757 9388) so if you can't reach him by telephone simply mention his name in any bar in Old Bank and it is likely he'll turn up as if by magic. Livingston's a Bastimentos islander and an enormous hulk of a man who wears a Houston Astros baseball cap and aviator goggles. Imagine a West Indian Santa Claus with a booming belly laugh that announces his arrival before he casts a shadow. Livingston runs tours throughout the archipelago and also works as a 'roadie' (or more accurately a 'boatie') for the Bastimentos Beach Boys.

Basiano (Basil) Powell is a relative of Oscar from Roots and offers a wide range of boat tours to all local snorkelling spots as well as full- and half-day fishing trips at US$110 (three hours) and US$220 (six hours). Visitors eating at the restaurant should mention their tour needs to Oscar so he can book things while the Creole chicken is cooking. Otherwise book at the Hostal Bastimentos (tel: 757 9053; email: reservas@hostalbastimentos.com; www.hostalbastimentos.com).

OTHER ISLANDS

The second-largest island in the archipelago, **Isla Popa,** is home to two Ngöbe Buglé communities, distinguished as Popa 1 and Popa 2. The older settlement is Popa 1, a village of more than 300 people who live in wood-and-thatch homes by a river on the southwest of the island. Hills, dense forest and thick mangroves are the island's key topographical characteristics, the habitat of the only toucans found in the archipelago. Islanders fish the waters and live without electricity and telephone. Most homes have fresh water via an aqueduct fed by an island creek. In 2004 building work started on a medical centre and a communal toilet block to improve sanitation in the village.

The Popa 2 community comprises more than 200 Ngöbe Buglé migrants from Cayo Agua, Popa 1 and Isla Tigre. Although largely sustained by fishing the settlement is gearing itself up for tourism, and a narrow strip of cement pathway that links a small dock to a schoolhouse will soon also lead to a restaurant. Building work is also under way on a cabaña for visitors. A local women's organisation is working on handicrafts to sell in a craft shop. Several villagers plan to offer guide services for walks through the mangrove forests.

The islet of **Cayo Agua** (Water Cay) is located just beyond Popa 1 on Isla Popa, a tiny settlement considered by many Bocatorians to be one of most colourful in the archipelago. Most of the over-the-water wooden houses have been painted with brick-red and sky-blue paint. Villagers are lobster and crab fishermen or cattle farmers on the island's lush pasturelands. Ancient deposits of coral are found in the northwest portion of Cayo Agua that islanders say date back three million years. The island is rarely visited by tourists and is a rewarding place to explore.

The island of **San Cristóbal** tends to be overlooked by most visitors apart from those that visit Bocatorito and beautiful Dolphin Bay. The island's Ngöbe Buglé community is one of the largest in the region, growing cocoa, yucca and rice and farming chicken and pigs. Valle Escondido, a settlement of 200 fishermen, is located at the mouth of a creek and can be accessed by foot or by boat. A trail connecting Valle Escondido to the San Cristóbal community winds through jungle along rugged picturesque paths. In the north of the island, Bocatorito, a smaller Ngöbe Buglé settlement, looks out on a labyrinth of mangrove islets and a calm lagoon known as Dolphin Bay. A quiet spot naturally, it transforms during peak season as an endless succession of crowded tourist boats buzz in and out of the bay. Large shoals of small fish and jellyfish that prefer still waters make this stretch a fertile feeding ground for dolphins and sightings in Dolphin Bay are pretty much guaranteed.

Another good reason to visit Dolphin Bay is the **Centro Turistico Bocatorito,** a rustic restaurant on the water that is open for lunch and dinner. Owner Santos Flore Cabellero has run the place with her family for over five years, cooking fish caught by her brother to perfection (US$7–8). Space is limited and tables are in demand so arrive early at lunchtime to be on the safe side for delicious food and bay views and amidst Santos' flower baskets, the envy of many.

On **Isla Solarte (Nancy Cay)** a Ngöbe Buglé fishing community of 200 lives a simple life without electricity or a telephone system, obtaining its water from a well. Walkers will find a couple of decent trails through the interior of the island leading from the right of the village. Both meander through rainforest that reaches at least 90ft in places. The **Solarte Inn Caribe** (tel: 757 9032; fax: 757 9043; email:

HOSPITAL POINT (PUNTA HOSPITAL)

This jutting tip of land on Isla Solarte is where the United Fruit Company hospital once stood. The footings remain, dating back to 1899, but the building is long gone, decommissioned in 1920 when the facility moved to Almirante. Hospital Point has a rich history and has been owned by former United Fruit research employee, Clyde Stephens (email: bananabyte@aol.com), since 1991. He is the author of *The History of Hospital Point*, a fascinating book that takes an in-depth look at the subject in human terms. Stephens is also an accomplished lecturer in Bocatorian history and author of *Banana People and Other Stories*, a collection of anecdotes and tales of banana-industry culture. Since retiring after 32 years with United Fruit (now Chiquita Brands International) he has worked as a banana consultant and an adviser to small banana producers worldwide on a volunteer basis. Few historians have the depth of knowledge in this field that Clyde does. His keen grasp of the facts and attention to detail makes him a valuable source of historical data. His public lectures are well publicised in Bocas Town and provide a fascinating insight to the islands and its people. Clyde will also oblige history buffs with tours of the old hospital site by prior arrangement.

However, for many visitors Hospital Point means snorkelling, and the shallow reef that lies in the small horseshoe bay under Clyde Stephens' house is one of the most popular spots in the archipelago. A narrow beach has a dusting of sand with woodland beyond and most tour boats drop you here or allow you to jump from the boat 100yd from the shoreline. The Stephens' family own the land and are happy for it to be used by visitors that respect its boundaries. Tales of crowds of tourists descending on their back garden at siesta time abound and understandably this can leave them a little nonplussed.

On a good clear day the snorkelling at Hospital Point is spectacular, but visibility varies and can be disappointing. More than 40 rivers join the sea in the waters around the archipelago, unloading silt from the hillsides during periods of heavy rainfall. The low-lying reef has a rocky peak that gently forms a slope into the maritime channel. The waters are full of lobsters, eels and squid as well as various species of coral. Visitors have also reported sightings of nurse sharks, puffer fish and grouper. Much like Coral Cay this spot is surrounded by a mass of tour boats in high season. Given its close proximity to Bocas Town it tends to be a favourite first or last call in tour operator itineraries. If you're travelling to Hospital Point under your own steam and favour quieter snorkelling conditions then it is well worth giving it a wide berth between 10.00–11.00 and 15.30–16.00.

steve@solarteinn.com; www.solarteinn.com), the island's only hotel, is a 15-minute boat journey from Bocas Town; it's a single-storey wooden building that occupies an elevated position amongst palms and ferns. Surrounded by a 40ft rainforest canopy and fruit tree thicket, the hotel works closely with its Ngöbe Buglé neighbours, buying fish, lobster, fruit and vegetables from the village and employing them as guides. This secluded spot was chosen by TV reality show *Survivor* as the base of evicted participants in the French, Russian and Venezuelan versions, as it is well away from the paparazzi and is comfortable and relaxed.

Guests choose from double, triple or family rooms that all have fans, private bathrooms, blinds and wooden floors. The Rates range from US$65 for a double (US$15 per extra person up to five people) to US$110 per night for a two-room suite (three people) and US$175 per night for a three-room suite (five people). Each includes breakfast of local fruit, omelette, freshly baked muffins and coffee, with internet at US$3 a day. Likeable host Steve Hartwig organises tours, guides, boat rental and will cook dinner on request for US$8 a person.

MAINLAND BOCAS DEL TORO
While the towns on the mainland are nothing special the countryside is nothing short of spectacular in places. Expanses of primeval terrain hide murky orange rivers, black lagoons, boggy swamps and dense mangrove forests that teem with birdlife. Apart from some small Indian settlements much of this jungle region remains as it was in centuries past. Large areas are wild and unexplored, providing an ideal habitat for jaguars and harpy eagles, both of which need vast territories to survive. It was in this beautiful, hostile wilderness that General Manuel Noriega established a hideout in 1990, shielded by trees that soared 80ft high. These towering tangled forests attract birders, adventure travellers and tree climbers seeking the ultimate challenge scaling vast and unidentifiable arboreal species. Yellow-tailed toucans, parrots, snakes, giant spiders and flocks of frigates of pterodactyl size continue to amaze wildlife lovers, while swamplands and mangrove islets hide lilies, frogs and caiman.

La Parque Amistad
The name means 'Friendship' and this 407,000ha national park is a collaboration between Panama and Costa Rica, a UNESCO-inscribed territory (1990) spanning the border between the two countries. This vast protected area comprises the single largest forest in Central America, containing several hundred endemic plant and wildlife species and various communities from three indigenous tribes: the Teribe, the Bribri and the Ngöbe Buglé. No other protected area in Central America contains as many viable populations, species and life zones or has the altitudinal variation of La Amistad. The soaring Talamanca Mountains are estimated to harbour almost 4% of the varieties of terrestrial species on earth; the Panamanian portion contains endemic fish, reptile, amphibian, mammal and bird species with recorded sightings of puma, jaguar and harpy eagles. In Panama the park straddles areas in both Chiriquí and Bocas del Toro provinces.

Although archaeological sites have been reported along all major watercourses, little or no excavation work has been conducted, making the analysis of human history in the Park difficult. Each indigenous community in La Amistad has experienced varying degrees of cultural contact. Most have been settled in the region for 400 years and have retained much of their folklore, language and customs, sustaining their population from a traditional hunting and gathering lifestyle.

Two Panamanian entry points lead into La Amistad and in Bocas del Toro access is possible at Wekso (also Wetso or Wetzo). Reaching this entrance requires a half-hour bus or taxi journey from Changuinola to the tiny riverside settlement of El Selencio where a boat leaves to Wekso along the magnificent Teribe River (45 minutes, US$15 per person or US$40–50 per boat). Indian boatmen usually wait by the river but if not call into the ANAM office to ask the ranger to call a boat by radio. The river trip is spectacular, passing waterfalls through thick jungle on a backdrop of the Talamanca Mountains. Spot lizard, birds, monkey and iguana on the slower, shallower sections, a riverbank of gnarled tangled roots and knotted vines. Endless birds sit in the branches overhead the fast-flowing stretches, the

BOSQUE PROTECTOR PALO SECO

The area of greatest focus for tree climbers is an expanse of primary and secondary rainforest close to the Palo Seco Forest Reserve. Reports of balsa trees under 30 years old but 110ft tall with 5ft-diameter trunks abound and locals swear the rains make trees grow extra big. Canopy and forest floors are dark and foreboding, allowing only flecks of sunlight at the tips of each tree. The sheer diversity of trees is the attraction with as many as 350 species per hectare; most climbers favour the big hymenia, nutmeg and ceiba trees, choosing between drier primary forests and soggy swamps to find these giant species. Conquering a ceiba nicknamed 'The Tree of Pain' has become something of a dare amongst the tree-climbing fraternity. It earned its name from the short, hard spines that grow on the tops of each limb and has a trunk that exceeds 100ft. Tarantulas the size of a human hand and 20-inch eyelash vipers add to the thrill of the climb.

The **Institute for Tropical Ecology & Conservations** (see *Conservation*) in Boca del Drago has lecturers in Tropical Rainforest and Canopy Ecology, and is a good source of information on tree climbing in the province. **Tree Climbers International** is also worth a try. Contact them c/o PO Box 5588, Atlanta, GA 31107, USA; tel: +1 (404) 377 3150; email: tci@treeclimbing.com; www.treeclimbing.com.

habitat of howler and black-handed spider monkey, white-throated capuchin, mountain salamander, glow-throated hummingbird and quetzal.

At Wekso follow the sign for La Amistad and look out for rustic accommodation advertised by the roadside at US$4 a night. A better option is the Teribe village (tel: 658 5042; email: eliseovargasgarcia@yahoo.com; www.bocas.com/odesen/odesen.htm) where local guides help visitors to pick up the hiking trails, from a site formerly known as Pana-Jungla, a military training camp for Noriega's notorious Panamanian Defence Force (PDF). Established in 1983, the camp was renowned for its brutal training regime, incorporating guerrilla-style warfare with jungle-survival techniques. Today only a couple of the old barracks remain on the 125ha site and those have fallen to ruin. Some of walls are adorned with painted poems and propaganda, with determination and perseverance a common theme.

Visitors to the Teribe village can stay in thatched roofed cabañas for US$12 per person (US$8 for large groups) and eat meals in a rustic restaurant for US$2.50–4.

Humedal de San-San Pond Sak (San-San Pond Sak Wetlands)

This important reserve is home to 133 bird species (of which 36 are endangered); 55 species of mammal (of which 24 are under threat); 54 species of reptiles (of which seven are threatened); and 20 species of amphibians plus a large population of marine birds. Woodpeckers, iguana and warblers are commonly found as are a number of snake species and small crocodiles. It is located about three miles north of Changuinola on the edge of a large banana plantation, accessible by 4WD taxi from Changuinola Bus Station. Ask the driver to drop you off as close as it can get and book the return journey for a couple of hours later to avoid being stranded.

First, a word of caution about the mud: the wetlands are very, very boggy and require sure-footedness to emerge unscathed, so don't be surprised to depart with a thick black coating to the ankle. A mile-long boardwalk is the first hurdle, poorly

CHIQUITA IN PANAMA

Chiquita and the people of Panama enjoy a rich history spanning more than 100 years. The first commercial banana business was established there in 1899 and Chiquita is the longest-standing foreign investor in Panama.

The Chiquita banana-producing division in the Bocas del Toro province employs approximately 4,700 people on about 5,900ha of farmland, shipping 15 million boxes of bananas from this division annually (1 box = about 40lb/18kg). In June 2003 the company sold the assets of its banana division on the Pacific coast of Panama at Puerto Armuelles to a co-operative of workers. The company continues to market bananas from this co-op under a ten-year fruit-purchase agreement.

Today Chiquita Brands International (www.chiquita.com) is the major supplier of bananas to Europe and North America, generating US$2.9 billion in revenue in 60 countries on an annualised basis and employing 24,000 staff. It has marketed bananas, the company's best-known product, for more than 100 years, selling 130 million 40lb boxes of bananas a year. Chiquita boasts the No 1 banana market share in the European Union and a No 2 market share in North America, surviving bankruptcy in 2002 and a complete change of leadership to emerge intact.

maintained in places. Narrow low-lying planks are often fully submerged under brackish water, making it difficult to navigate easily, yet the views it allows as it weaves precariously though the jungle are nothing short of thrilling. Thick vegetation is alive with sloth, toucan and monkey, while many the wetlands' reptile population wriggles silently underfoot. The boardwalk expires at the entrance to a beach that is an important nesting site for loggerhead, hawksbill, green and leatherback turtles. Camp here or opt for a bed at the ANAM ranger station for US$5 per person, a place with few facilities other than a toilet but fine for those used to roughing it. The wetlands are internationally recognised within the framework of UNESCO's Man and the Biosphere (MAB) Programme as a terrestrial and coastal ecosystem of importance and has been on the Ramsar List of Wetlands of International Importance since 1993.

The towns of **Chiriquí Grande** and **Almirante** offer tourists little to see or do. Both were once crucial stop-offs on the route from the Interamericana to Costa Rica. However, since the completion of the highway, travellers sail right past to make their border connections. As a result Chiriquí Grande is used only by specific commercial haulage firms today and is a shadow of its former self, a declining population with an ailing local economy.

The port town of Almirante is faring slighter better and today it fulfils an important role as a transportation hub in and out of the province. A grubby portside area has a growing reputation for petty theft and Almirante's amenities are functional but far from plentiful. Ramshackle housing edges streets criss-crossed with railway tracks from when banana transportation hit its heyday. Chiquita Brands International (formerly the United Fruit Company), a significant landowner and employer and one of the largest banana producers in the world, still holds a sizeable stake in the town.

Above Kuna woman, Panama Province (DS)

Right Emberá girl, Panama Province (DS)

Below Convoys of overloaded ox-drawn carts congest roads in the central provinces during the sugarcane harvest at the beginning of the year (DS)

Right Mola seller, Kuna Yala (DS)

Below right Emberá child, Panama Province (DS)

Below left Emberá woman dressed in traditional brightly coloured fabric (DS)

Colón Province

The fourth most populous province in Panama has a rich and colourful history. Once a centre of untold wealth, the towns of Portobelo and Nombre de Dios were used as stores for plundered bullion; Aladdin's caves of gold and silver looted and bound for Spain via the Sendero Las Cruces (Cruces Trail). Both Portobelo and Nombre de Dios were fortified but were repeatedly attacked by disparate bands of buccaneers. Francis Drake's first assault in 1572 saw him leave 'the treasure house of the world' (as he called it) with untold riches. His return, 24 years later, was more brutal and all but destroyed the town (see *Sir Francis Drake*). Drake's death a few weeks later from dysentery brought great shock to his troops. After placing his body in a leaden cask they buried it at sea off Portobelo before sinking his ships at Nombre de Dios as a mark of respect.

In 1671 Welsh buccaneer Henry Morgan seized San Lorenzo (see *Sir Henry Morgan*) and advanced across the isthmus to sack Panama. Portobelo was ransacked twice in the 17th century and destroyed in 1739 by Admiral Edward Vernon. The British fleet of six ships, 2,735 men and 370 pieces of ordnance, entered at dawn on November 21 and took possession of the fortresses, Spanish galleons and 120 infantrymen. Portobelo was left intact when the English left for Jamaica several weeks later. They had held the town, and protected it from renegade Spanish sailors, but left without booty. In 1848 the California gold rush spurred thousands of prospectors to hurry to America's west coast, travelling from the east coast via the isthmus. In 1850–55 the Panama Railroad was built to benefit from these fortune hunters, a project that brought migrant workers from the West Indies and China.

With its ruined forts, battle lines, cannons and ramparts, the Colón province has much to offer visitors that seek a slice of Panama's history. Panama's old gold-rush railway, now beautifully restored, is the best way to arrive, along the length of the Canal. The charming fortified market town and rusting weaponry of Portobelo and moat-ringed Fuerte San Lorenzo on the Río Chagres are two of Panama's most visited spots. The capital of the province, Colón City, is not.

COLÓN CITY

> In all the world there is not, perhaps, now concentrated in a single spot so much swindling and villainy, so much foul disease, such a hideous dung-heap of moral and physical abomination.

British journalist James Anthony Froude in 1886

In fact Froude didn't actually ever visit Colón, but that doesn't seem to matter. His feelings about the city during the French Canal construction in the 1800s mirrored

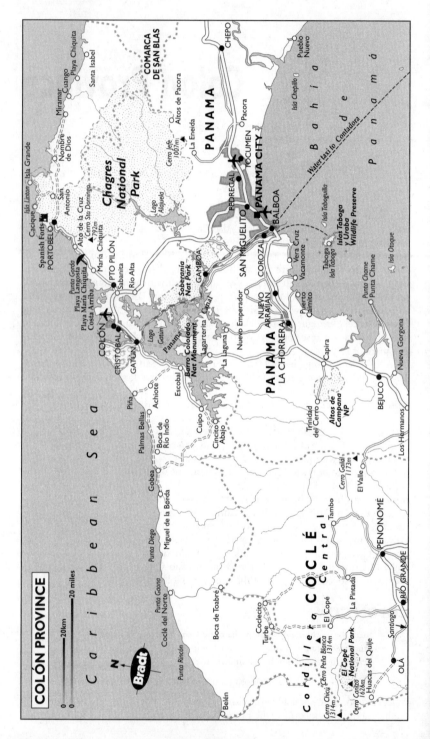

that of his contemporaries and were he to visit today it's unlikely there would be much to alter his account.

Panama's second city on the Atlantic entrance to the Canal represents the dark side of Panama that never makes it into the holiday brochures. Colón bears all the battle scars of long-term economic depression and to most Panamanians its name is a byword for poverty, aggression and urban decay. A population of almost 150,000 are mostly descendants of West Indian Canal workers who live in dilapidated housing in rundown neighbourhoods. Crime is the pecuniary lifeblood in this desperate place, a city that has collapsed, both socially and structurally, and is crushed under the burden of unemployment. Once a city of fine, French-style balconied buildings, today Colón is mostly slum with rubbish-strewn streets that are a no-go area for most outsiders. Crime and unemployment figures are the highest in Panama and Colón's growing drug scene looks set to further spiral the city's interminable decline.

Visitors should exercise extreme caution when visiting the city of Colón. A bag-laden tourist makes an obvious target in this poverty-stricken community – and Panamanians from other provinces make little secret of giving it a wide berth. Those that do decide to travel to Colón should be sure to keep their wits about them. In 2003 a backpacker was mugged at an ATM and a birder robbed at knifepoint for his binoculars – both in daylight. Those arriving by car should lock all doors when driving through the city centre. Visitors by bus should not consider the short walk into town from the station. Take a taxi, even during daylight, and avoid being out on the streets after dark. A sign in the city reading, 'Be nice to tourists they are your source of income', is posted with good intentions. The irony isn't lost, however, on those who have had their wallets swiped.

Around Colón City

The outskirts of Colón are noteworthy for the Colón Free Zone (Zona Libre, CFZ) a tax-free retail area, and Colón 2000, a cruise ship port complete with bars, restaurants and shopping mall. The port in Colón is Panama's busiest and since 1999 the Panamanian tourism authorities have invested heavily in courting the cruise market. Today Colón welcomes a large number of tourists by sea (see *Cruise Passengers*). Most are whisked away to the Colón 2000 visitor park, the Free Zone or taken on tours to Portobelo and San Lorenzo – anywhere that keeps them away from the run-down environs of the city.

Colón Free Trade Zone (CFZ, Zona Libre)

The Colón Free Trade Zone (tel: 445 3229/1033/1559; fax: 445 2165; email: zonalibre@zolicol.org; www.colonfreetradezone.com) is on the itinerary of every cruise ship passenger to Panama. It is also a popular stop-off point for staff aboard Panama's merchant fleet, the largest in the world at 9,355 vessels. Ships buy supplies from traders in the Colón Free Zone, a 400ha compound comprising

---

FARE'S FAIR

Taxi drivers in Colón are an entrepreneurial bunch that now offer round-trip fares. Prices are based on a full car, and rarely adjusted to allow for fewer people, and couples and lone travellers should be prepared to haggle hard. Expect to pay US$40 to Gatún Locks with a stop at Gatún Dam, US$30 to Zona Libra (make sure the driver knows where to take you once inside), US$80 to Fort Lorenzo, US$80 to Portobelo and US$100 to Isla Grande. Even Panama City is doable by taxi for a day trip for US$120 from Colón.

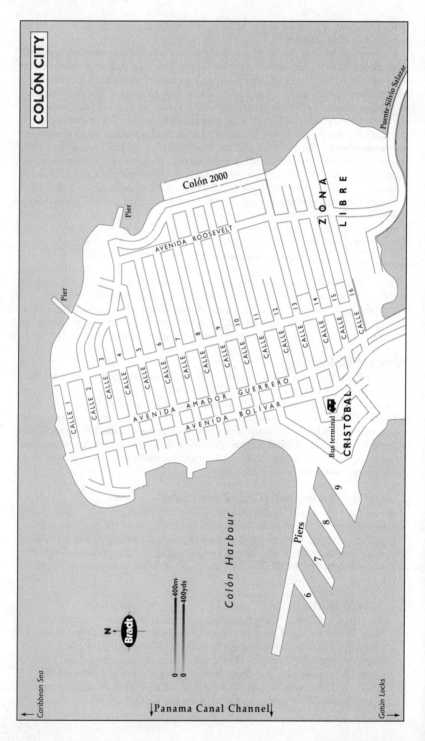

COLÓN CITY

Caribbean Sea

Panama Canal Channel

Gatún Locks

Colón Harbour

Colón 2000

AVENIDA ROOSEVELT

AVENIDA AMADOR GUERRERO

AVENIDA BOLÍVAR

Pier

Pier

Pier

Piers

ZONA LIBRE

CRISTÓBAL

Bus terminal

Puente Silvio Salazar

CALLE 1
CALLE 2
CALLE 3
CALLE 4
CALLE 5
CALLE 6
CALLE 7
CALLE 8
CALLE 9
CALLE 10
CALLE 11
CALLE 12
CALLE 13
CALLE 14
CALLE 15
CALLE 16

6
7
8
9

N

Bradt

0   400m
0   400yds

AWAY FROM THE SHOPS
The CFZ isn't all shopping and tax-free goods. Drive past the Colón Free Zone and the little town of Coco Solo and a right turn leads to a dusty track and mangrove forests. This seldom-used road is best accessed by a 4WD but ranks among the best places to find shorebirds and seabirds in the area. Black-tailed trogon and American pygmy-kingfisher and also significant numbers of boat-billed heron have been sighted. Keel-billed toucans and lineated and crimson-crested woodpeckers are also common to the woodlands in this area (see *Birding in Colón*).

1,600 businesses, bordered by concrete walls. Goods range from utilitarian to luxury in the second-largest free zone in the world after Hong Kong. It may lack the sophistication of its Asian cousin but not for want of trying, and swish billboards promise to deliver designer brands at knockdown prices under the slogan '0% Taxes and 100% Opportunities'.

Since opening in 1953 the CFZ has been a favoured distribution point for trade shipments between Latin and North America and contains an import–export centre with capabilities for commercial bulk handling, warehousing, assembly and trade transhipments. Imports account for US$4.2 billion per annum and exports US$4.9 billion, with Hong Kong, Japan, the United States, Venezuela, Columbia and Ecuador as key trading partners. Representing about 10% of Panama's GNP and employing over 14,000 people the CFZ is served by three ports at the Atlantic entrance of the Panama Canal and one on the Pacific side. It claims to have the best-trained bilingual workforce in Central America and attracts more than 250,000 annual visitors, depositing US$416 million in revenue during 2002.

The Free Zone was created to revive the fortunes of Colón and today in its out-of-town location it forms a sharp contrast to the ragged disorder of the city. Little if any of the Free Zone's annual billion-dollar turnover benefits the crippled financial system of the city. Shops are staffed by employees bussed in from Panama City and profits are shipped out to HQs elsewhere. Few customers spend a dollar outside of the compound yet spend US$250 each on average inside. Cameras and electronic goods are particularly competitively priced at the CFZ. Some of the retail outlets are listed online but a full directory of businesses is available from Focus Publications International (PO Box 6-3287, El Dorado, Republic of Panama).

Colón 2000
Launched in December 2000 just in time for the Christmas rush, Colón 2000 is a cruise-ship port with an adjoining enterprise similar to the CFZ. A village of cut-price designer stores, restaurant, bars and souvenir shops encourages passengers to disembark and part with their cash. A visitor information desk, ATMs, a supermarket and a line of ten telephones provide the basics, while a system of buses and escalators deposit cruisers straight to the shops. In response to safety concerns, a taxi-booking service was launched in 2002 to organise transport for visitors keen to go further afield. Trips are logged with driver registration details and are a fixed price.

Getting there
By bus
Frequent buses connect Panama City with Colón's bus terminal (tel: 441 4044) (US$2, two hours), which serves towns throughout the province (06.30–19.00). A daily service to Portobelo runs hourly 06.30–21.00 (18.00 on a Sunday), US$1.30.

RIVER OR CATTLE THIEF?
Some say Gatún is the name of a river that appears on Spanish maps as early as 1750. Others say that the name comes from *gatunero*, meaning seller of smuggled meat. The latter may be true as the area around Gatún Lake was once a meeting place for cattle thieves keen to sell their spoils.

By car
Travellers who drive to Colón enter the city on two major roads at its southern end, forming the backbone of the grid system that runs to the north. These main avenues (Avenida Amador Guerrero and Avenida Bolívar) expire at the waterfront and have numerically named streets running across them, from Calle 1 at the water's edge to Calle 16 at the southern entrance of town. Several petrol stations are located at the entrance of Colón but drivers should be aware of recent reports of bag snatches at the pumps.

By air
Aeroperlas (tel: 403 1038; www.aeroperlas.com) operate a regular schedule to Colón from Panama City, a 15-minute flight that departs at 08.45 and 17.00 Monday to Thursday, 08.45 only on Friday (US$35.70 one-way).

By train
Panama City–Colón Train
Panama's only stretch of railway connects Panama City with Colón. The Panama Canal Railway Company (PCRC) (tel: 317 6070; fax: 317 6061; email: info@panarail.com; www.panarail.com) is a US-owned joint venture that links the Atlantic and Pacific alongside the Canal, an ocean-to-ocean route that dates back 145 years. After falling into disrepair in 1979 it was eventually restored in 2001. Today it is completely modernised at a cost of US$1.2 million and the 77km railroad provides an efficient transcontinental shipment service, connecting the Canal, the Colón Free Trade Zone and port terminals, to transport passengers and freight. Panama privatised the railroad in 1988 and the Panama Canal Railway Co now owns it. The glorious red and yellow train was bought for US$800,000 from a company in Florida who were using the elevated carriage as an ice-cream cart and the original track was entirely replaced for a smooth ride. Old sections of the railroad have been stolen, bronzed or chromed and sold to dealers for up to US$500. The train travels at a sedate speed along the length of the Canal, passing Gamboa, Barro Colorado and crossing small islands in the midst of it. Spot toucans, monkeys and crocodiles; enjoy a superb view of the canal without paying vast sums to transit it.

The train departs Monday to Friday at 07.15 from Corozal Passenger Station, Old Canal commissary, Panama City (US$2.75 taxi from Panama City centre) and returns 17.15. The journey lasts one hour (US$20 one-way and US$35 return).

Where to stay and eat
Unfortunately Colón is sufficiently unsafe to make the city's many budget hostels a risk. All are located in the roughest neighbourhoods where mugging, violence and gun crime are all a threat, especially to tourists. The same applies to Colón's best (and cheap) Caribbean seafood restaurants. Stick to a hotel with security, good lighting and a restaurant. The following are two of the better options but still leave something to be desired.

The New Washington hotel (124 rooms) Calle 2da. y Bolivar; tel: 441 7133; fax: 441 7397; email: nwh@sinfo.net. Constructed in 1870, Washington House was used for social gatherings for Panama's railroad workers, a grand building that contained a library and billiard room for directors of the company. Due to this history the establishment now calls itself the legendary and famous New Washington Hotel, but much of the grandeur is gone. Rooms appear not to have been touched for years and are in need of complete renovation with a sea-facing patio and garden that are dreary and unloved. Private bathrooms, air conditioning and cable TV. Good on-site restaurant with seafood menu. Single US$38.50, double US$44.00, triple US$49.50, suite US$110–165.

Hotel Carlton (65 rooms) Calle 10; tel: 441 0111; fax: 447 0114. Has comfortable rooms just a short journey from the Free Trade Zone, containing double or triple beds, air conditioning, TV, telephone and hot-water bathroom. It's popular with businessmen and traders visiting the CFZ and has a decent restaurant, a conference room and a laundry service (US$2 per item); US$35 double, US$45 triple.

GATÚN LOCKS

A perfectly positioned viewing point adjacent to the control tower allows visitors to see these vast locks in action. Ships sit in the Lock chambers attached with cables to locomotives that guide them from lock to lock. Lower chambers are entered at sea level before rising to the level of Gatún Lake (26m above sea level) then on to Pedro Miguel and Miraflores Locks 40km away, a vast project that took four years to complete. Each chamber can easily accommodate a ship the size of the *Titanic*. Unprecedented amounts of concrete were poured into steel forms to create the largest chambers in Panama. Each lock is 34m wide by 304m long and was constructed using 3,440,488 cubic metres of concrete seven miles south of Colón.

Getting there

Buses leave from Colón bus terminal hourly (75c) for the 20-minute journey to the Locks. Doing the trip by taxi allows an additional stop-off at the Gatún Dam (this isn't on a bus route) and also spares you from hanging around the bus depot. A round trip to both sights shouldn't cost more than US$40 a trip or US$5 per person.

GATÚN DAM

Constructed to create Gatún Lake, the second-largest artificial body of water in the world, the Gatún Dam was completed in 1912. The spillway, a key component of the Panama Canal, operates at a range of 1.5m above sea level. The Gatún Dam and Gatún Lake are vital to the Canal, enabling ships to sail across most of the isthmus and providing hydro-electric power for the Canal Zone, including the electrical mechanisms of the canal locks. The countryside that surrounds the locks is notable for its birdlife. Turn left immediately after crossing Gatún Locks on a bridge that spans the spillway to enter woodland trails to the right. Other top birding spots are found on the Atlantic side of the Canal. Cross the locks to where the road forks and take the fork right.

FORT DAVIS AND FORT GULICK

These former military bases northeast of Gatún Lake were both handed over to Panama as part of the Carter–Torrijos Treaty of 1977 (see *History of Panama* and *History of the Panama Canal*). Today, despite plans for redevelopment, some of the military buildings have fallen into disrepair. Fort Gulick is the exception (renamed Fort Espinar after a portion of the reserve was transferred to

Panamanian ownership in 1984) and military Building 400 is now a Spanish-owned hotel.

Building 400 was once home to the US Army School of the Americas but is now the most lavish hotel in the province. Each of its 300+ rooms and suites is packed with gleaming five-star amenities and boast pleasing views across Lake Gatún. The building sits on jutting headland at the edge of the lake and is popular with fishing tour groups, birdwatchers and a deluge of tourists en route to the Colón Free Zone. Most CFZ weekenders that decide an overnight stay in Colón City isn't for them end up here and the hotel runs an efficient transportation system back and forth throughout the day. The building dates back to 1949 and is often visited by its former students who seem to approve of the redevelopment. More than 30,000 soldiers from Latin American were trained here over the years, including two of the most notorious figures in modern military history. Former Argentine President Galtieri and El Salvador's Roberto D'Aubuisson are both graduates of the US Army School of the Americas, a fact that hasn't found its way into the glossy hotel brochure.

Where to stay

Melia Panama Canal (300+ rooms) Fuerte Espinar, Cristóbal; tel: 470 1100; fax: 470 1916; email: melia.Panama.canal@solmelia.com; www.solmelia.com. Discounted packages, cut-price offers and booking online can see the price drop significantly, US$75 for double including breakfast.

Davis Suites (10 rooms) Tel: 473 0639; email: davissuites@yahoo.com; http://davis.suites.iwarp.com. This hotel is located on the former site of Fort Davis. The setting is less impressive than that of the Melia but bird-filled mango and palm trees surround the Davies Suites nonetheless. The Colón Duty Free Zone, Colón 2000 and Colón Airport, the Colón Bus Terminal and the Panama Canal Railroad Station are all within easy reach. Each suite sleeps four and has air conditioning, a fully equipped kitchenette, living room with TV and hot-water bathroom. US$55 for double occupancy plus US$10 for each extra guest.

SAN LORENZO FORT

It's about an hour's drive from Colón to San Lorenzo Fort (Fuerte San Lorenzo) along a winding road lined with hedgerows filled with birdlife. Pheasant cuckoos, tanagers and honeycreepers hide amongst bushes in an area renowned for its sightings of plumbeous hawk. San Lorenzo Fort is well signposted and located beyond the former US military base of Sherman (at the time of writing passers-through need to show ID at the entrance to Sherman) about 9km from the checkpoint, open daily 08.00–16.00.

Balanced at the mouth of the Chagres River (Río Chagres) on a peninsula west of the Canal, the fort commands an elevated position overlooking the river and over the bay. Built in 1597 by the Spanish using thick blocks of coralline rock, it is ringed by a moat with moss-covered cannons to the front and much of the ramparts remain well preserved. There is a solitary British-made cannon at the fort, a relic of the plunder, battles and incursions at the fort throughout the 17th and 18th centuries.

Getting there

In the absence of a bus service grab a taxi from Colón to San Lorenzo Fort for about US$20. Drivers should follow the signs to Gatún Lock and follow the road through to the northern entrance gate before heading to Gatún Dam less than a mile away. After crossing the dam the road is well signed to San Lorenzo.

THE SAN LORENZO PROJECT

The Fort forms a part of the San Lorenzo Project (tel: 433 1676; email: sherman@sanlorenzo.org.pa; www.sanlorenzo.org.pa), an ecological conservation scheme that covers an area of protected land that spans 9,632ha. Forests, mangroves, wetlands, rivers and 19km of coastline are managed with participation from the local community and include the site of the Sherman military base. The Fort denotes the northern tip of the Protected Zone and was declared a World Heritage Site by UNESCO in 1981, along with the fortifications of Portobelo. It was also added to the World Monuments Fund List of Endangered Monuments in 1997. Birding and hiking trails lead through some magnificent expanses of rainforest that were used as the site for jungle training by the US Defence Department from 1953 to 1999 as the base of its Jungle Operations Training Battalion.

An important area of biodiversity, the reserve contains at least 12 different kinds of forest, including mangroves, floodable cativo, moist and semi-deciduous as well as other high-humidity ecosystems. Some 600 species of vertebrates have been sighted (a third of the number known to live in Panama), including 430 birds and 81 mammals. Members of the Panama Audubon Society counted 357 species of birds in a single day at the mouth of the Chagres River in 1999 – a record for the Western hemisphere. Jaguars and tapirs can also be found in the area, reflecting the healthy state of the ecosystem despite its relatively small size. The Smithsonian Tropical Research Institute (STRI) has set up a crane in the middle of the San Lorenzo Protected Area to study the forest canopy. It elevates scientists above the trees in a metal gondola to provide access to more than 9,000m^2 of forest.

Two especially good paths – Black Tank and Skunk Hollow – lead from the left of the roadway and allow frequent sightings of pheasant cuckoo, assorted tanagers and honeycreepers and a number of grassland species, including savannah hawk and palm warbler. Good local guides can be booked through ANAM (tel: 442 8348) or CEASPA (Panamanian Centre for Research and Social Action) (tel: 226 6602).

AROUND COLÓN

A succession of tiny settlements lines the coastline west of Colón. Most have a small scrap of beach and a kiosk but few have more. Some are used as refuge dumps and litter blights many of the spots with real potential. The first, **Piña**, is one of the most accessible and those that know it rave about the snorkelling, although the sand is grubby. For great birdlife and monkeys take a winding road out of Piña south to the lakeside village of **Escobal**. The route itself is forested and every fencepost and branch appears to be occupied by a puffbird, trogons, oriole, spot-crowned barbet, black hawk-eagle, rufous-crested coquette, montezuma oropendola, brown-hooded parrot, black-bellied wren and rarities like the grey-cheeked nunlet and white-headed wren. Some good trails enter the forest on the left side and are a haven for bronze-tailed plumeleteer, pygmy antwren and stripe-breasted wren. On a lucky day it is possible to see crested and harpy eagles, sloth and several families of howler monkeys. Raptors favour the tallest spots while woodpeckers prefer fallen trees, and at the entrance to the village hummingbirds feed in flowering shrubs on the left.

CARIBBEAN PINE
This tall skinny tree was introduced to Panama in 1949 and today this fast-growing arboreal dominates large chunks of the landscape in Colón. It thrives in the acidic soil found in the province and grows more rapidly than any native Panamanian species. Yet unlike most non-native species that are introduced deliberately it brings few benefits. Its wood isn't suitable for use as material in construction or manufacturing and its branches aren't a habitat or source of food for birds or wildlife.

Escobal is a distinctive community for two reasons. Firstly it has cleaned up its beaches in a bid to attract tourists. Secondly it has launched a homestay programme (**Escobal Homestay** tel: 434 6020, ask for Bill Everskey or Saturnino), the only such organised project in Panama. Most of Escobal's population are descendants of former Canal and railway workers and the Latino-Afro-Antillean-Panamanian culture is relaxed and friendly. The community is keen to give its fledgling tourism industry a boost, funded by a grant from the US Peace Corps. Choose from a range of private homes or pitch a tent in a garden. Bed, fan and breakfast are assured as standard but other facilities vary from home to home. Local guides offer kayak rental, bike hire and horseriding as well as jungle hikes and fishing. Local co-ordinators welcome advance bookings but it is fine to turn up on spec; from US$10 a night.

On the way to Portobelo
A northeasterly drive to Portobelo from Colón winds along a scenic road that passes villages, fields and coastline. **Puerto Pilón**, a community of West Indian descent, provides a convenient stop-off for passers-by. A laundry is prepared to tackle a full load for US$1.50 in 60 minutes while the car repair shop will mend a puncture in half an hour. An internet café and supermarket are other reasons to park up in Puerte Pilón as is the restaurant that serves an all-day plate for US$1.25.

Pass hibiscus bushes and cattle fields at the far end of Puerto Pilón and a vast social housing development beyond. **Maria Chiquita** is home to a small community of fishermen and farm workers and a beach that shares its name. A kiosk with indoor seating serves inexpensive dishes from early morning. The guy that mans the pumps at the petrol station near to Casa Angel, the local bar, is happy to point out trails along Playa Maria Chiquita. A small tourist centre here (open 08.30–16.00) doesn't have anything of much use. The neighbouring stretch of sand, **Playa Langosta**, is geared up for families and weekenders from Panama City. A small restaurant (everything under US$4) serves food all day and the beach is kept clean for volleyball and beach parties. Arrive by car and there'll be a charge – but not for entry. It's to ensure the guy on the gate keeps an eye on the vehicle and its contents (50c for a half-day or US$1 for all day.)

Sabanitas
Lying roughly equidistant from Colón and Portobelo, the town of Sabanitas, 22km east of Portobelo, is an important local transportation and shopping hub. A jumble of market stalls, kiosks, food-stands and supermarkets forms the centre visited by a constant stream of buses, trucks and taxis.

Sabanitas is the nearest town to the only birding and wildlife lodge in the province, a little-known place set in woodland trails half an hour from Colón City. Guests at the **Sierra Llorona Panama Lodge** (tel: 442 8104; fax: 638 9557;

email: info@sierrallorona.com; www.sierrallorona.com) have recorded sightings of 188 species, including band-tailed barbthroat, bat falcon, blue cotinga, long-tailed tyrant and grey-headed kite as well as different types of osprey, vulture and tinamou. The lodge is set in 81ha that contain an interlocking series of trails with pathways and observation platforms under a canopy of forest. Half-day and full-day birdwatching, guided jungle hikes and night-time wildlife safaris are also offered. The owners are also establishing a butterfly research facility and organic gardens with the support of scientists from the Neo-tropical Panamanian Lepidoptera. Tours US$25–130. US$55 for a double with private bathroom, balcony and hammock, US$48 with shared bathroom.

Getting there
From Colón city take the highway towards Panama City turning left at the sign for Santa Rita Arriba (SRA) just past the town of Sabanitas. The lodge is signed from this point (SLPL). The cost is US$20 by taxi, or book a transfer direct with the lodge at US$5 per person from Colón City and US$15 from Panama City (four person minimum).

PORTOBELO
Christopher Columbus gave the town its name in 1502, calling it 'Puerto Bello' (meaning Beautiful Port) in honour of the picturesque natural harbour. This fortified bayside settlement is 90km from Panama City and 45km from Colón and was once little more than a dozen fishing huts. Today it has a population of 4,000 but is still a quiet, sleepy town that ekes a living from the sea. Many of Portobelo's original footings can still be seen in the town centre. The buildings were made of coral blocks and their ruins form a part of the San Lorenzo Protected Area (see *San Lorenzo Project*). The centre of town has one of the most useful IPAT tourist offices in Panama, staffed by people who really know their stuff. Combined with all-day cafés and restaurants and some decent hotels this makes Portobelo a convenient base from which to explore the surrounding area; a region rich in tall tales about stockpiled Spanish gold.

RESURRECTING DRAKE
Speculation surrounds the move by some members of the Sir Francis Drake Exploration Society (SFDES) (7 Rosewood Avenue, Burnham-on-Sea, Somerset TA8 1HD, UK; tel: 01278 783519; email: sfdsociety@aol.com; www.chantec.co.uk/drake-society) to get Drake's body raised from its watery grave. Rumour has it they want it returned to English shores so he can be laid to rest in Plymouth where he was once a mayor and MP. Expedition leaders claim they can pinpoint the spot, but the project is expected to cost in excess of £500,000. It would need the agreement of the Ministry of Defence and the Panamanian government – and both are thought unlikely. But while some SFDES members are enthusiastic at the prospect of resurrecting Drake, others are not, and this divisive project remains a contentious topic amongst Drake aficionados worldwide.

The Society runs two-week Drake jungle treks in Panama each year to retrace his journey by foot and on horseback. Prices vary but are open to members (£14 in UK, £15 overseas) that include Drake enthusiasts in Panama.

THE CONGO

Portobelo is synonymous with the congo, an expressive tribal dance ritual originated by slaves to poke fun at their colonial Spanish masters. Performers imprison and capture each other with a demand for ransom whilst feigning lunacy through movement and screams. Elsewhere male dancers strut around a woman who gently shakes her hips, swirling long flowing skirts in graceful movements unmoved by all that is going on around her. Any attempts by the men to get close to her are rejected and their approaches are brushed away. The men decorate their clothing with bottles, old radios and just about anything else they can think of, taking turns to dance with the rey and reina (the congo king and queen) in their oversized crowns. Dancers walk and talk backwards, goading each other and blowing whistles as townfolk cheer and clap in the balconies that overlook the square. The ritual continues at a lively pace to music that is spirited and highly rhythmic. Drummers pump out the congo beat and singers carry the tunes in a call-and-response style.

Portobelo's beautiful bay provides plenty of natural defences, a fact that wasn't lost on the Spaniards. Following an attack by Francis Drake, King Félipe II ordered that the Fort at Nombre de Dios be abandoned and a replacement built in Portobelo, 27km miles to the east and offering considerable natural protection and strategic advantage. Initially two forts were built close to the mouth of the bay, San Diego on the southern side and San Félipe on the north. Others were added over the years and the battlements formed a formidable fortification high above the bay. Despite this Portobelo suffered numerous invasions by bandits and the English Navy. In fact the body of Sir Francis Drake lies in a lead coffin at the bottom of the sea just a couple of miles from the Portobelo shoreline, behind the tiny atoll of Drake Island. Drake, who died of dysentery on January 28 1596, was buried at sea by his crew at depth of 129ft. Two wrecks from Drake's fleet, the *Elizabeth* and the *Delight*, are also thought to lie close by, sunk by his men in his honour.

Getting there
An hourly bus from Colón City departs from the bus terminal 04.30–18.00 (US$2.30 one-way). There is not a direct service between Panama City and Portobelo.

Getting around
The town of Portobelo is easily navigable on foot and consists of a sprawl of ramshackle housing along a neat two-lane road. A few taxis operate in and around town but not enough to rely on.

Where to eat
Portobelo's decent local restaurants are near the church. Most serve Creole-style dishes and many for under US$4. **Restaurante Yaci** has fried fish on the menu at US$3.50 at lunchtime, while on the edge of town **Restaurante Gloria** dishes up big helpings of seafood, rice and fried banana for a couple of dollars. There are more restaurants along the approach road to Portobelo near to the Coco Plum. These are open for breakfast, lunch and dinner and all have a superb reputation. One of the best is the **Restaurante La Torre**, an open-sided Colombian-owned stone-built place that has an ever-changing menu. Breakfast costs US$2.75 while

grilled sea bass with garlic is US$6; Colombian sausage and rice US$4.50 and seafood platters for two at US$24 are great dinner options. Scrubbed wooden benches, leafy palms and a cool breeze make it a pleasant spot for lunch, popular with local business owners and tourists on the move.

Festooned with seaside paraphernalia and decked out in tropical colours, and the great little beach resort of **Coco Plum** (tel: 448 2102; email: cocoplumPanama@hotmail.com; www.cocoplumPanama.com) is on the approach road to Portobelo. A slim strip of land runs behind the **Restaurante Las Anclas** down to the water and has brightly painted bungalows and a bar with plenty of seadog character. Both are owned by Alvaro Guzman, a cheerful Colombian who also runs the Happy Tour Company. Views from the restaurant overlook the water from a breezy terrace. Caribbean-Creole food comes served amidst tiled floors, potted palms and bold tropical prints under dangling Panama hats and knick-knacks. Open 08.00–18.00 Monday to Thursday, 08.00–21.00 Friday and Saturday, and 08.00–18.00 Sunday. Breakfast, US$2.50, red snapper and Creole shrimp US$7–10. Huge seashells, buoys and fishing nets adorn the bar on the water close to a stretch of yellow sand and the Twin Oceans Dive School. Crimson-coloured bungalows are decorated with mosaic, shell and kaleidoscopic tropical fish murals and come with a fan and private bathroom – US$35 single, US$45 double, US$55 triple and US$65 quadruple.

Tour companies
None of the dive groups from **Twin Oceans** (tel: 448 2067/654 1224; email: info@twinoceans.com; www.twinoceans.com) leaves the dock without a mobile phone, marine radio and full emergency equipment and everyone that works there is fully PADI trained. A friendly Pennsylvanian woman called Patricia Allen owns this beachfront dive school and like most ex-military types she is pretty exacting. A good menu of dive excursions covers the waters of Colón and also long-distance dive trips to Coiba National Park (see *Veraguas Province* chapter). Patricia offers

EL NAZARENO
In Portobelo they talk about El Nazareno when referring to their icon, a dark-skinned Jesús with delicate facial features honoured in celebrations dating back to the 17th century. According to local legend, Portobelo was besieged by plague in the 1600s, until a wooden statue of the Nazarene was found by fishermen on October 21 and brought ashore. The villagers took this as a Catholic reminder that Jesus Christ is not just a figurative saviour. Today a mass of purple-robed pilgrims arrives in Portobelo on the same date each year to honour the Black Christ.

Everyone is invited to take part in the Black Christ festivities. There's no need to dress in purple (though many do) and it is open to all religions. This party for everyone is one of the high points in Panama's cultural calendar. Hundreds of people arrive in Portobelo on foot on October 21 and dozens of food and drink stalls mark the way. Many walk from the town of Sabanitas and are prepared to do the journey on their knees if necessary. Celebrations begin at dusk and after a formal ceremony the statue is decorated with flowers and candles and carried throughout the city on the shoulders of eight men walking at the unusual gait of two steps forward and one step back. After the statue is returned at midnight, there is dancing, music and feasting until dawn.

PADI courses in French, English and Spanish and Twin Oceans comes recommended for value for money and safety. Sites include a cargo ship and a twin-engine plane, priced at US$30 for an escorted dive (without equipment hire) and US$60 (including hire). Package stays include a seven-nighter at the Coco Plum with full board including five full days of diving (three tanks and weights) and airport transfers from Tocumen International Airport (call for prices). At the time of writing many neighbouring dive centres seem to have closed down. Twin Oceans operate seven days a week, year round.

Coco Plum owner Alvarao Guzman's **Happy Tours** (tel: 264 1338; fax: 223 9444; email: happypty@c-com.net.pa; www.happytours.biz or contact via the Coco Plum resort) offers horseriding and walking tours.

Finnish couple, **Maria and Hecka** (tel: 448 2143), have mounts and routes to suit horseriders of all levels with trails across the mountains and beach rides. Two guys called José and Miguel run **Selv Aventuras** (tel: 651 6568/688 6247/683 5318; email: selvadventuras@hotmail.com; www.geocities.com/selvadventuras) and both are enthusiastic ambassadors of tourism in Portobelo. Leaflets, photographs, booklets with posters publicising local events and tour schedules adorn every wall of their office. Excursions range from genteel 30-minute guided 4WD trips to full-on jungle adventures that last a fortnight. Most tours come with hourly, daily and weekly options and endless itinerary possibilities. Nature trails take in waterfalls and lots of unspoilt countryside inhabited by monkeys, toucans, white hawks. The guys also run camping, hiking and walking weekend trips and organise specific tours for photographic shoots and birders. The office has a little coffee shop and travellers don't seem to be able to rate Selv Aventuras high enough. Open 09.00–16.30 seven days a week

Practicalities

The tourist information centre (IPAT; tel/fax: 448 2200) in the middle of the town is housed in one of Portobelo's finest buildings. It was the home of the wealthiest Spaniard in the Colón Province, Don Idelfonso Rodrieguez and provides a handsome example of the area's fine period architecture. Open 08.30–16.00 daily. The Selv Aventuras office is located at the entrance of town (see *Tour companies),* while the library in the centre of town is the only place with public internet use, open 10.00–15.00 Monday to Friday, US$2 per hour. Several grocery stores and a medical centre (tel: 448 2033) are found near the church. The police station is on the approach road into town, 2km west.

ISLA GRANDE

Weekenders from Panama City adore Isla Grande and a mass exodus on a Friday evening sees cars packed to the hilt with beach gear for the two-hour journey. Once the favoured playground for partying American GIs it is now a destination for lazy R&R. Fewer than 400 people live on the island, almost all of Antillean descent. Plenty of tropical colour abounds and coconut rice and reggae form the staple diet. Fishermen sell their catch of octopus, lobster, crab and shrimp to local restaurants before hanging out on the beach. The watersports are good, so are the bars, and while the sand may not be as spectacular as that of Bocas del Toro the mood is just as mellow.

Some of the best dive sites are located 15 minutes offshore and kayaks, surfboards, snorkel masks and boats can be hired from most hotels. The island has no roads and much of the central terrain is undisturbed forest. The 'town' stretches along a coastal strip that can be walked via a concrete pathway end-to-end in under 20 minutes and is lined with restaurants, bars and street vendors. A second trail cuts across the island through some beautiful forests full of butterflies. This is also concrete but in a poor state of repair and difficult to navigate in places.

Despite its diminutive size at 5km by 2km, hiking through the interior of Isla Grande can present a challenge. Sloping tracts of forest and thick vegetation can hamper penetration. Most local guides tackle their trails with a machete in hand and there are plenty prepared to head up the mountain. Paths of swarming ants and tall palms climb up to the peak that rises out of a coconut grove and offers an almost perfect 360° view of the island over treetops and fields of flowers. The northern side of Isla Grande is more rugged than the south with fewer forest clearings and trails. Some of the finest beaches on Isla Grande with more accessible trails are located on its southern side, where humming birds, butterflies and dozens of crabs inhabit the coastal path. Offshore habitat comprises brain and sheet coral formations, sea fans, staghorns and rods. Snapper, angelfish, parrotfish, trunkfish and damselfish have all been spotted.

A lighthouse on the island was built by the French in 1893 and once contained a lamp designed by Gustav Eiffel. Today it forms part of a display in the lobby of the Canal Museum in Panama City (see *Museums, Panama City* chapter).

Getting there and around
Boats to Isla Grande depart on demand from the tiny waterside village of La Guayra (five minutes, US$1). Simply turn up during daylight hours and a boatman will appear. Buses to La Guayra run from Colón bus terminal every two hours 09.30–18.00 (US$3) and pick up en route at Sabanitas and Portobelo. Buses return from La Guayra daily at 08.00, 09.00 and 13.00. Getting from A to B around the beaches on Isla Grande is easiest by water taxi and these are easy to find at the pier by Super Jackson.

Where to stay and eat
There are plenty of places to stay on the island and it is not difficult for budget travellers to find a bed for the night, unless it is a national holiday. Prices soar during Carnaval but range from US$20 a night for a comfortable but basic double cabin at the **Super Jackson** (tel: 448 2311) to well over US$150 at the **Banana Village Resort** (tel: 263 9766; fax: 264 7556; www.bananaresort.com). Super Jackson is the closest accommodation to the main pier and is handy for water taxis, restaurants and bars. Five rooms have ceiling fans and private bathrooms. The Banana Village Resort is located on the north of island and has a restaurant, bar with a pool table and a swimming pool on a beautiful stretch of beach. Other options include **Cabañas Cholita** (tel: 448 2962) with singles at US$20 and doubles with air conditioning and private bath US$30. Cabañas at **Sister Moon** (tel: 448 2182; www.hotel-sistermoon.com) are spread along the hill 1km east of town, from US$50.

Festivals and events
The population of Isla Grande swells at weekends, on public holidays and during festivals when accommodation comes at a premium. San Juan Bautista is celebrated on June 24 with canoeing and swimming races. The festival of the Virgen del Carmen on July 16 is marked by a land and sea procession, mass and baptisms. Carnaval is celebrated here with great gusto when the locals dance the conga.

NOMBRE DE DIOS
That this settlement of such historical significance should look so inconsequential can be something of a disappointment to visitors expecting more. None of the ruins of the Spanish settlement remains and there are few clues to its affluent and

colourful past. However, Nombre de Dios is not without charm. Ask a local guide to point out sand bank trails that lead to small deserted beaches and coral reefs. Mooch around San Cristobal Bay or enjoy views from the town of forest and mountains. Pale turquoise corals, purple pipe sponges and lavender sea fans up to 1.2m wide have been sighted here, along with large black sea urchins, lots of French, grey and queen angelfish and turtles, nurse sharks and grouper.

The Afro-Caribbean population in this sleepy town is friendly and laidback. A small central plaza in the middle of the town has a hostel, a payphone and a couple of simple fish restaurants alongside. Kuna Yala is less than 30km east along the coastline and fishing boats that cross the border depart from the neighbouring villages of Palmira and Miramar.

Nombre de Dios' newly formed cultural foundation plans to open a museum following the discovery of a shipwreck in its waters. Locals hope that it is Christopher Columbus's *Vizcaina* – and so do historians – yet the museum is not without controversy. Other communities are opposing the museum on the basis that the wreck would be better housed in Portobelo, but most social commentators feel that Nombre de Dios and its hard-pressed community could do with the tourism possibilities it presents.

Getting there and around
Buses to Nombre de Dios depart from the bus terminal in Colón each hour from 06.30–18.00. It's a US$3 fare from the city and can also be picked up at Sabanitas until 16.00. Stay on the bus until it reaches the centre to avoid a long walk into town. There are no taxis in Nombre de Dios.

Where to stay
Visitors have raved about **Jimmy's Caribbean Dive Resort** (tel: 682 9322; www.caribbeanjimmysdiveresort.com), located about 4.5km east of Nombre de Dios. Five cabins sit at the water's edge with first-class views and amenities that are enjoyed by both non-divers and aficionados. Jimmy's offer a wide range of trips and excursions, from jungle camping to horseback riding and fishing trips. The diving is superb here and rates of US$589 for four nights (US$489 for non-divers) include two tanks per day, all meals and transfers from Panama City. A restaurant next door serves great food and hosts banks at the weekend and rumour has it there are plans to add a 15-room motel in late 2005.

Diablos Rojos

Kuna Yala

The autonomous region of Kuna Yala comprises 400 islands and a 230km needle-thin strip of coastline that streches from the Colón Province to Colombia on the Caribbean side. Meaning 'Kuna-land' in *Dulegaya*, the unique language of its people, Kuna Yala has been self-ruled since 1930, when the Panamanian government granted the tribe the right to govern its own land. This followed a Kuna uprising, which began on February 25 1925, and saw the Panamanian police on Tupile and Ukupseni islands violently overthrown. Led by Nele Kantule and Simral Colman, a bloody revolution ensued born out of anger at the forced suppression of Kuna cultural practices. Twenty-two policemen and 20 tribesmen died in the fighting before the autonomous status of the Kuna was secured. The self-ruled region was established in 1938 under the name awarded to it by Spanish Conquistadors. In 1998, to signify independence, the Kuna changed the name of their land to Kuna Yala, although it is still commonly refered to by its former title, Comarca de San Blas. The governmental structure of Kuna Yala is defined in the Carta Organica (of Law 16 of 1953) and ruled by The Kuna General Congress, the region's highest political authority. All communities in the comarca are represented within the Congress, which sits regularly throughout the year. Each has one vote, regardless of population size, cast by a *sahila,* the Kuna spritiual and political chief.

Today much of Kuna Yala's 32,500 population live in the archipelago, a large group of beautiful palm-fringed islands, many of which surpass every travel brochure 'paradise island' cliché. Many have white-sand beaches, some have thatch-and-mud villages, but all are blessed with uncluttered ocean views. Only 40 are inhabited with communities that range in size from 5 to 5,000. Some 9,000 Kuna also live on tribal mainland territory in nine fishing communities along the Caribbean coastline. A further 30,000 live outside the region, a large proportion in Panama City. In 2003 a proposal by a delegation representing Panama's 68 Kuna communities to unite under one rule was rejected by the Moscoso administration. The suggested unification combined Madungandi, Wargandi and the Darién communities of Paya and Pucuro, under the umbrella of a single Kuna national government. The proposal also encompassed the substantial urban communities of Kuna Indians in Panama City, such as Kuna Nega and Arraijan. At present people of Kuna Yala rule themselves and also have voting rights in Panamanian elections as well as two representatives in Panamanian legislature. In 1999 the Kuna voice gained volume when Enrique Garrido, a Kuna-born legislator, became head of Panama's General Assembly.

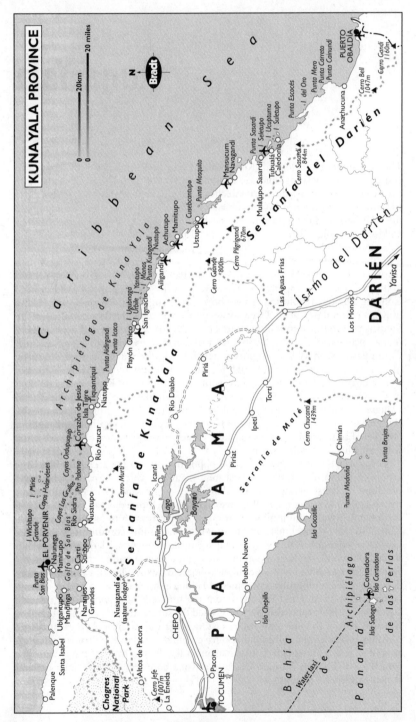

THE ORIGINS OF KUNA YALA

The people of Kuna Yala are believed to be descendents of the Kuna of modern-day Colombia, whose tribes migrated to Darién to escape disease in the Colombian jungle. They are thought to have settled in the Darién in the 1600s in an area known as Amukadiwar where small groups of Kuna still remain today. In the jungles of Darién the Kuna faced various indigenous battles and invaders, fighting with pirates and allying with others in unity against the Spanish. When news reached Darién of the devastation caused to the French Canal project at the hands of malaria and yellow fever in 1884, the Kuna left the mosquito-ridden wilds of the jungle to migrate to a land free of disease. Eventually arriving at clear fertile waters and an abundance of fish, these early settlers were soon joined by others who established communities on the mainland coast and surrounding islands.

Since settling on the archipelago the Kuna have struggled as outsiders in Panama, isolated by culture and location. The last 130 years have been a period of immense change for people that have fought to retain their traditions against a background of economic, discriminatory and political challenge. Declining fish stocks in recent years have caused Kuna Yala to look elsewhere for revenue, and its modern-day economy is becoming increasingly reliant on the exploitation of its culture. Tourism is a contentious issue that is endorsed by some but not all Kuna. Traditionally a barter economy, the sales of mola to tourists is bringing greater cash orientation to the islands, a cause of some social tension. Yet in many respects there are few discernable differences between the people of Kuna Yala and those olden settlements in northern Colombia. Men fish, and hunt wild tapir, agouti, monkey, deer, bird, peccary and iguana using blowguns, spears, bows and arrows and a variety of traps and pits. Women cook on open fires in one-room bamboo-and-thatch huts while children play in the rivers and on the shoreline with coconut husks and palm fronds.

THE KUNA PEOPLE

They call themselves *tule*, meaning 'the people' and the Kuna are born fishermen who are dark-skinned and small in stature with physical characteristics that provide great power and strength. A race of short, broad-backed, small-footed skilful hunters who are highly adept in water, Kuna women, men and children are all practised oarsmen whose only method of transport is dugout canoe (*ulu*). Men set sail to fish at dawn and return at lunchtime with a catch to sell or barter, and lobster diving is *the* choice career in the region. Twin-propped planes descend daily to procure lobster for Panama City's top-notch restaurants, paying the Kuna US$4 a pound. Women, who are equally strong and as powerful as their male counterparts, chop wood, build walls and take care of children and the home. The Kuna's matriachal society sees inheritance pass through its women. Indeed men must live in their mother-in-law's house after marriage to work as an apprentice to their father-in-law. Divorce is uncommon, but not prohibited, the marriage being absolved at the point a husband gathers his clothes and moves out of his in-laws' home.

Family life is important to the Kuna who devote at least three hours together as a unit each day. Most communities are poverty stricken with poor sanitation and the effects of the socio-economic plight of Kuna communities can be seen in employment, nutrition, health and education. At 70%, Kuna Yala has the highest rate of infant malnutrition in the country. Consequently many Kuna are emigrating to Panama City and Colón to find other means to support their families. Daughters are especially prized because they will eventually bring additional manpower into the family. Those with long hair are pre-pubescent and unmarried, those with short hair physically mature and wed. Hair cutting at puberty is one of the most important, and most celebrated, Kuna rituals. Every member of the community is invited to a ceremony that is steeped in tradition. Much food is eaten and drink is drunk, and it is an event that is planned for several years by members of the family (see *Festivals*).

To the Kuna the world is a dual civilisation containing the 'world of spirit' and the 'world of subsistence'. The world of spirit surrounds and resides inside every material thing, underpinning the world of subsistence and giving it power. Spirits respect those who reinforce tradition and so the Kuna respect 'spirit sanctuaries' where these spirits dwell. These sanctuaries are usually on what would be quality agricultural land but because of the Kuna belief, it remains forested and intact. Violation of these sanctuaries would cause the spirits to rise up in rage and bring harm to the community, a principle based on the Earth as the body of the Great Mother who in union with the Great Father gave birth to all plant, animal and human life.

The Great Mother instructs every living thing of its duties. Medicinal plants were informed on their role in curing illnesses and certain animals told they were to be used by Kuna for food. The trees renew their energy by drinking water through their roots. The Great Mother drinks the sap produced by the trees, and this is how she strengthens herself. Trees are Kuna life; they protect them, provide medicine for illnesses, and fruit for the animals. If the land were exploited there would be no culture, no soul. Kuna are taught early in life to take care of Mother Earth, not abuse it. They personalise every element of nature by treating it with respect, flattery, and compromise, as if it were human,.

The Kuna diet consists of what's around them but is largely obtained from the sea. Main staples are fish, plantains, bananas and coconut with some chayote, avocado and mango when in season. *Tuli masi*, a traditional dish of boiled green plantains, fish, coconut and root vegetables, is eaten with salt and lime. Small-scale subsistence farming has added greater year-round variety to the Kuna diet. At festivals and celebrations the Kuna drink *chicha*, a crude fermented sugarcane concoction that stupefies in minutes. Mango juice or coconut water is the soft drink of choice although there is a growing prevalence of fizzy drinks, beer and coffee due to trade with Colombian coconut merchants.

The distinctive dress of the Kuna women comprises a mola (blouse), gold nose- rings, a long skirt, a red and yellow headdress, gold breastplates and colourful long strands of beaded leg wraps (*uini*). A long black line is painted on

THE KUNA MOON CHILD

With the highest rate of albinism in the world, an estimated seven of every 1,000 births in Kuna Yala is a white Indian – a 'Moon Child'. Few Kuna marry outside of their village, but according to the Kuna an albino birth occurs after the pregnant mother is exposed to the moon. In a culture where individualism is frowned upon, the Kuna albino was once treated as inferior by Kuna society. Not so today. The Kuna view the Moon Child as a special person; gifted, strong, born to lead and blessed with confidence.

The life of the albino may not suit all born to it. Unable to bear the rays of the Great Sun, the yellow-haired, pink-eyed, pale-skinned boys are trained in the ways of the Kuna woman. While dark-skinned peers are playing, hunting and fishing, the Moon Children spend their days sitting in the dark cool of the village, sewing molas and making handicrafts with the women folk.

the face from the tip of the nose to the forehead and a woman will adopt this dress after puberty rites when she is properly named. Until this point she is known only by a nickname but after menstruation her position is reinforced in matrilineal Kuna society by a name. This strong female status is further strengthened by the income generated by mola sales, a practice that began in 1945 after a missionary purchased one as a souvenir. Today making molas for tourist revenue represents an important part of the Kuna economy, and one that is wholly reliant on its women.

The Kuna are friendly people who vary in character throughout Kuna Yala. Typically warm, polite and deeply private, they may be gregarious, forthright and welcoming on some islands or shy and suspicious on others. Much of this depends on their exposure to tourism and the behaviour of the visitors they've met *(see Note below)*. Many are keen to connect with foreigners and are curious, candid and engaging. Most want to know what visitors think of Kuna Yala, while other popular questions are 'Are you married?' or 'Where's your husband/wife?' as the matrimonial habits of outsiders are of great fascination to the Kuna (unmarried men in particular).

Others enquire about world events and the global threat of terrorism. Despite isolation the Kuna are well informed on international issues, almost certainly because of their interaction with visitors and their strong political tradition.

Note Sadly, I've witnessed several incidences of blatant disrespect by tourists in Kuna Yala, many fresh off the cruise ships. In each case the cultural sensibilities of the Kuna were ignored, a disregard for values that horrified entire communities. The Kuna response to these incidents has been a further tightening of tourism control, which is bad news for those, like me, who seek greater interaction. Skimpy clothes may be de rigueur in Acapulco but they are alien attire in Kuna Yala. The offence it causes and the image it creates presents the Kuna with an unfavourable picture of the 'outsiders' and breeds cynicism in those once keen to show their homeland to the world.

VISITING KUNA YALA

Each of the 400 islands is privately owned by the communities of Kuna Yala and for reasons of accessibility and language, most visitors book their accommodation through a tour company and arrive by plane from Panama City (see *Getting There*). Almost every arrival needs a transfer from the airstrip to their hotel by boat and as there isn't a formal transport system in Kuna Yala this is often easiest if it is prearranged. Another reason to plan ahead is the limited amount of accommodation. Pre-booking also suits the Kuna style of tourism perfectly as they like to know who's arriving and when. This allows for greater control over visitors, which enables better protection of their land *(see Kuna People)*. At the time of writing none of the nine communities on the mainland is geared up for visits by '*wagas*' (the Kuna word for foreigners) and the archipelago is the focus of visitor activities.

Adventurous travellers used to a high degree of freedom may initially find Kuna Yala restrictive. Kuna see tourists as visitors, there with their permission and by invitation. Subsequently they expect to lead and guide tourists while they fulfil a passive role. They are also a rule-based society managed by a strong code and so governing tourists with 'dos and don'ts' seems entirely natural. Not all 400 islands are open to tourists and several communities remain closed. No restaurants (apart from one or two exceptions and those in hotels), no transport system, no maps or campsites means visitors are almost entirely at the mercy of their hotel owner. In Kuna Yala, getting around and seeing as much as you can (or what you want) relies on the willingness of the staff to sort things out on your behalf – hence the need to book the right hotel.

Every visitor who steps on to any island in Kuna Yala needs to pay a fee to its people, the only possible exception being one that is uninhabited and out of sight. The rate varies from island to island but is between US$3 and US$5, payable to the village elders who may require registration on arrival. Be sure to carry ID for this purpose as well as plenty of US$1 bills, as a dollar fee is payable to the subject of each photograph that you take. The photogenic Kuna and their colourful clothes make striking subjects, but visitors should never take a photo without first gaining permission.

The issue of photography is a sensitive one in Kuna Yala and can lead to some misunderstanding. However, the rule is simple ('no fee no photo') and is rarely wavered. Kuna elders enforced this law after learning that photographs of Kuna Yala were being used for commercial gain without any financial benefit to its people. Today the value of its culture in terms of 'bankability' has been a valuable lesson learned, especially by the many Kuna with a photogenic smile.

Travellers used to snapping away will need to make a significant mental adjustment in Kuna Yala, as the permission-before-photo process makes capturing spontaneous shots virtually impossible. A few staged 'woman holding mola' pictures may be the only ones possible on the basis of budget and etiquette, something even ardent snappers will need to accept. Given their photographable appeal, the Kuna assume every visitor is there to take photos. Those who aren't but have a camera in their luggage should keep it out of sight or run the risk of being suspected of taking pictures dishonestly. The Kuna also feel that it is safe to assume that tourists with a camcorder plan to use it. A charge of at least US$10 can be levied even if they've not seen it in use.

THE ISLANDS

Just how many islands comprise the archipelago is a question of some conjecture. While the tourist office blurb declares that the number is 365 ('one for each day of the year') this figures falls at least 30 short. The Kuna are continually creating manmade islands to accommodate tourism, built from layers of coral and sand and thus allowing the natural islands of Kuna Yala to remain undisturbed. Most of these new islands are just large enough to accommodate a hotel or some cabañas, meaning visitors are often segregated from the Kuna people by some distance with few opportunities to freely interact. Older, larger islands are home to communities of up to 5,000 or have neighbouring islands of Kuna population, thus making intermingling more possible.

El Porvenir

This gateway island to the region is also the capital. Its name means 'the future' but at present it is little more than an airstrip, a small dock, a hotel, a police station, two payphones, a Kuna administration post and a cluster of homes. Most visitors use it as an arrival or departure point if they're not staying at the **El Porvenir Hotel** (tel: 229 9000; fax: 221 1397). This simple 13-room tin-roofed building has triple bedrooms with private cold-water showers for US$30.

Nalunega

In Kuna the name means 'Red Snapper Island' and most of the 400 or so inhabitants of Nalunega are fishing from a dugout canoe before the first sign of light. It's located to the south of El Porvenir and although there's no beach here the island and its shoreline are clean and well maintained, thanks to an army of diligent caretakers who clear driftwood and collect rubble in the employ of the island's hotel. The 29-room **Hotel San Blas** (tel: 262 9812) is one of the busiest in the archipelago and located on the south of the island. Its rustic rooms and sand-floor huts have shared cold-water bathrooms. Room partitions consist of thin bamboo screens and privacy is minimal, so if peace and quiet is essential opt for a beach hut; both are US$35 per person including all meals and a boat trip. There's snorkel rental (US$6) but the over-the-water toilet system of the neighbouring village puts most people off swimming here.

Wichub-Wala
It's renowned for its surrounding snorkelling spots and many of the visitors to Ukuptupu and Nalunega head to Wichub-Wala for a dip. The island is home to the **Kuna Niskua Lodge** (tel: 225 5200) which has a dozen comfortable rooms with shared bathroom for US$40 per person.

Ikuptupu
This small rocky island is a muddle of wooden buildings connected by a series of planked boardwalks. It was once a Smithsonian Tropical Research Institute site; in fact STRI scientists worked on Ukuptupu for over 20 years before finally, and reluctantly, withdrawing in 1998. The research centre is now the island's only hotel, and **Ukuptupu Hotel** (tel: 220 9082) offers 15 basic rooms for US$35 per person, including all meals and transportation. The downside of Ikuptupu is its lack of Kuna inhabitants but it's a good base from which to explore neighbouring communities.

Isla de Los Perros
This small island shares a second name of Achutupu with a large, crowded island further east, but is everything that its namesake is not. The surrounding waters are calm, crystal clear and contain a magnificent reef full of tropical fish. The sand is pale, the views magnificent and peace and quiet abounds. Just one extended Kuna family inhabit little Isla del Los Perros. There aren't hotels or amenities but it's not uncommon for residents to offer food and water to visitors, especially if treated with respect.

Carti Suitupo (Crab Island)
The Carti coastal hamlet is the launch point to the archipelago for those that have entered Kuna Yala by road, and the island of Carti Suitupo is within easy reach of the shore. A favourite port of call for visiting cruise liners, it is hot, polluted and can get ridiculously congested with tourists. Islanders also show all the signs of the influence of tourism on their culture. Carti Suitupo has the greatest density of Western-clothes-wearing Kuna, who don traditional dress the moment a cruise ship weighs anchor. The island has a small folkloric museum and plenty of pushy mola sellers with armfuls of appliqués. The founder of the museum provides bilingual guided tours of the museum and has lots of tales and facts about Kuna mythology and rituals, including burial rites (admission US$1). It's one of the most well-equipped islands in the archipelago, with a radio communication centre, post office, public library, junior school, several grocery shops, bakery, medical centre and a Catholic church. The only hotel in town is **Dormitory Cartí Sugdup**, a rustic hostel with beds for US$8 per night (tel: 299 9002).

Isla Aguja
Though just a dot in the water, Isla Aguja is still worth a visit for its pristine sands flanked by swaying coconut palms. It's not far from Carti Suitupo, is home to half

a dozen people and has cared-for sands and scenery that is gloriously unspoilt. Few places have all the right credentials for a castaway movie but this little atoll comes close.

Río Azúcar

This overcrowded island close to the mainland has been a focal point for US missionaries over recent years and holds services in sweltering heat in a dilapidated little church. A medical centre, a number of payphones, a simple grocery and hardware store are found on the island, amenities that tend to attract the yachting crowd. As the word spreads that there are tourists in town dozens of children appear, each keen to greet the new arrivals with a few practised phrases in English, generally 'Hello', 'Where are you from?' and 'What is your name?' Some sell molas, others pose for pictures, but most are simply enjoying the curiosity show.

Nargana and Corazón de Jesús

A long footbridge links Nargana and Corazón de Jesús, two built-up islands containing tin-roofed concrete buildings. Nargana is an administrative centre, home to a court, jail, bank, police station and airstrip. Corazón de Jesús is a busy commercial and trading hub with a big police presence and a large grocery store.

Isla Tigre

This sleepy island 7km east of Narganá is home to an ordered collection of houses and streets that are swept scrupulously clean. The population goes about its business, chopping coconuts, making rope and cooking fish over an open fire, often pretending not to notice that visitors have arrived. Tourism has been embraced by some residents but rejected by others. Mola sellers are happy to pose for photographs but it's difficult to find others who enjoy the attention.

Kwadule

Consisting entirely of a picturesque wood-and-thatch resort on a silver stretch of sand, the idyllic pinprick island of Kwadule is reserved for the use of guests at the **Kwadule Eco-Lodge**. One of the archipelago's nicest places to stay it has six cabins on stilts with fans, balconies and private bathrooms. A restaurant, bar and hammock deck overlook the water and the lodge is a ten-minute boat trip to the nearest Kuna tribe. Rooms are pricey at US$110 to US$120 for a double but include all meals and snorkel trips to Isla Tigre. Book through Green World Ecological Tours (tel: 269 6313; fax: 269 6309).

Río Sidra and Mamardup

The communities of Río Sidra and Mamardup share an island about 16km east of Cartí Suitupo. They aren't really geared up for tourists as such, most of which arrive to use the payphones or stock up at the grocery store.

Nusatupo

Just a couple of minutes away Nusatupo is similarly rarely visited by anyone other than the adventurous. Rustic **Hotel Kuna Yala** (tel: 315 7520) attracts backpackers who don't mind its basic amenities and a US$40 room rate includes three big meals, unlimited transport and the services of a local guide. The biggest appeal is its close proximity to the coral reefs, wrecks and numerous fish at Cayos Los Grullos, one of Kuna Yala's prime snorkelling spots.

Kuanidup

The swaying palms and low-slung hammocks at **Cabañas Kuanidup** (tel: 227 7661; fax: 227 1396) are every inch the stuff of paradise bliss. The island is half an hour from the airstrip that serves Río Sidra and Mamardup and is home to seven bamboo cabins with thatched roofs on the edge of soft white sand. Each is nothing special, but the location is. It's US$45 per night including all meals, transfers and a daily snorkel trip.

Naranjo Chico (aka Narascandub Pipi)

The sparsely populated 'Little Orange' island is another delight and has a beach of powdery sand, lush vegetation and plenty of tranquil spots to hang a hammock. The **Cabañas Narascandub Pipi** is the only overnight option, consisting of half a dozen thatch-and-bamboo cabins that look like they've been thrown together overnight. Gaping holes in the roof and no electricity won't appeal to everyone especially given the US$50 price tag. That said, the owners are friendly and the meals tasty and generous. There's no phone, but brave souls with excellent Spanish can ring the public payphone on Río Sidra (tel: 299 9007). Most don't and simply turn up via a 30-minute boat ride from the airstrip on the mainland.

Cayos Holandéses (Dutchmen Key)

This beautiful uninhabited island lies about 10km from Río Sidra and Mamardup and is part of Cayos Los Grullos, a cluster of deserted atolls popular with yachters. Sheltered bays and calm waters provide ideal anchorage and Cayos Holandéses is renowned for its fascinating snorkel site and picturesque views. The Wreck Reef contains the remains of several old shipwrecks, some ripped apart by crashing surf and others partly intact. Evidence suggests that numerous vessels have come to grief on the reef 100m north of Holandéses, many of them smuggling goods or drugs from Colombia at night.

Mamitupu

The shoreline of Mamitupu is dotted with dugout canoes full of women and children selling molas and men trading fish and vegetables. It's the home of Pablo Perez, a man who was once married to a British woman and is famous as a result. This failed marriage has awarded Perez unofficial tour-guide status with British visitors, who are taken to his home for a formal introduction. Pablo met and married his former spouse in Panama City but the elders of Mamitupu rejected the marriage. The couple moved to London but Pablo missed his homeland so much he returned to Mamitupu alone. Today he is remarried to a Kuna and has five children. Pablo chats about his ex-wife and London politely before giving visitors a tour of Mamitupu. He's an intelligent and thoughtful host who enjoys the companionship of fellow travellers and tells of life as a boy when he believed the whole world was like Kuna Yala. Today, he says, his experiences have taught him that not every child runs free, fishes for supper and climbs coconut trees.

Isakardup

This picturesque palm-tree island is home to the finest (and priciest) resort in Kuna Yala. The **Sapibenega Kuna Lodge** (tel: 226 9283/8824/676 5548) is also one of the most organised and tourist savvy and, much like the Dolphin Hotel on Uaguitupo, has a website (www.sapibenega.com) and a slick reservation system.

The name Sapibenega represents the Kuna belief in the essence, beginning and end of life, and means a place where all of Earth's life forms are born, and the lodge, whose motto is *napa anmar burba* (meaning 'nature is our life') boasts a suitably idyllic location. Thirteen pleasant individual cabins sleep two to four by the water while an open-sided restaurant serves freshly caught seafood. Solar power and great ventilation ensure a high level of comfort while an enthusiastic owner can't wait to drag guests off on exhilarating jungle hikes. The rate of US$75 per person includes all meals, transfers and a boat trip. Day-long tours and jungle hikes are extra and run from US$10 to US$25.

Playón Chico (Ukupseni)

This charming sprawl of bamboo-and-thatch homes is a popular day-trip destination. Most of the Kuna women have molas to sell and others are readily prepared for scrutiny of their daily life. The population is used to interaction with foreigners as its storm-damaged church is frequented by a group of American missionaries. Juliano, a local lobster fisherman, sells fresh fish and will also take visitors out spear fishing in his dugout for US$10. The island has an airstrip that serves the surrounding islands, including Isakardup and Yandup.

Isla Yandup

This tiny coral-ringed island is close to Playón Chico and has a little beach with calm, crystal-clear waters. The only place to stay is **Cabañas Yandup** (tel: 261 7229), a collection of four rustic cabins crafted by workers from neighbouring islands at US$60 per person including all meals, trips to Playón Chico and airport transfers.

Isla Uaguitupo (Dolphin Island)

A large proportion of visitors to Kuna Yala head to Uuaguitupo to stay at the charming **Dolphin Island Lodge** (tel: 263 7780; email: cdolphin@sinfo.net; www.dolphinlodge.com), owned by amiable host Jeronimo de la Ossa. This popular local character was once involved in Kuna politics and remains an active force in community issues. His daughter, Mariela, runs a non-profit organisation called the Uaguitupu Foundation, and funds a variety of educational, social and cultural projects on the island via income generated by the Lodge. The hotel opened in 1992 and comprises bamboo cabins set on a grassy oceanfront plot edged by palms. Each was upgraded in 2002 to offer hammock terraces, private cold-water showers and environmentally friendly flushing toilets. The Bohio Restaurant, the heart of the Lodge, boasts gorgeous views of lapping waves and fishing boats. It also serves the most delicious seafood (the lobster is superb) in man-sized portions. Guests can take advantage of a full menu of nature tours (including those for ecological research) as well as beach and snorkel trips. Rates vary but start at about US$85 per person and include three generous meals plus a couple of tours and transfers, five minutes from the Achutupu airstrip.

Achutupu

The neighbouring island settlement of Achutupu has an airstrip and plenty of local colour. A small scratch of beach is boat dock, laundry and children's playground while at the communal house of sahilas regular meetings of the village congress discuss community issues. Mola sellers display their wares each afternoon on the outskirts of the village by the beach.

Ustupo (Ustupo Ogobsucum)

This, the largest island in the archipelago, has a population of almost 5,000 and is a crowded, sprawling and noisy community 15km from Uaguitupo. There are few reasons for tourists to visit other than to stock up on supplies. Several grocery stores sell fruit, vegetables, rice and bread plus a number of canned goods from Colombia. There's also a library, school and a police station, where visitors should register as soon as they arrive.

Ailigandi

This densely populated island 35 minutes from Uaguitupo contains lots of political murals and statues and is a living monument to the struggle of Kuna people, Nele Kantule and Simral Colman, and the 1925 revolt. Displays of patriotism abound, from flags and graffiti to badges decorated with proud cultural statements. It's a popular trading post with Colombian merchants who swap jars of Nescafé for bags of coconuts and has a library, a school and several political HQs. The **Hotel Palmera** is the only place to stay on the island and has five rooms above a restaurant with shared cold-water bathrooms for US$10 per person. The owner can be contacted via a couple of payphones (tel: 299 2969/2968 and ask for Bolívar Arango).

San Ignacio de Tupile

Here is a friendly community in a tidy collection of bamboo huts with playing children and green pet parrots in the centre. A grocery store sells plantain, delicious bread, mango and coconut. The community is particularly well organised with at least eight different social committees that look after education, social welfare, health and water. There's also a conservation group and a women's co-operative. Mola sellers congregate on the outskirts of town but don't demonstrate many of the pushy sales techniques found on the larger islands.

Isla Pino (Pine Island)

This beautiful pine-forested island 25km southeast of Ustupo contains a decent jungle trail. It's not a lengthy hike (the island is only about 2km by 1.5km) but the noises and the wildlife make every step thrilling, especially large sleepy boas wrapped around branches.

Mulatupo (Mulatupo Sasardi)

The highly populated but charming island is less visited than many of its neighbours. As a result tourists are viewed as a rare and welcomed treat and greeted by dozens of eager children, who are keen to claim them as their own. The **Herrera Hotel** (no phone) costs US$20 per person and is a very basic affair. It has no running water or functioning toilets and is hot, stuffy and noisy. The local restaurant, **Mi Pueblo**, is much more pleasant, serving delicious fried fish with coconut for US$3.50 and always with a smile.

Puerto Obaldía

This sleepy little portside town is the jumping off point to cross into Colombia, although this option is currently considered prohibitively unsafe due to local guerrilla and paramilitary activity.

ETIQUETTE

Visitors should be mindful that the Kuna are very reserved people who find immodesty offensive and consider it an affront to their culture and beliefs. Clothes worn by visitors should respect these cultural sensibilities (skimpy shorts, bikinis and tops that reveal plenty of flesh have no place in Kuna Yala). Nudity is strictly prohibited and men are asked not to go shirtless. The Kuna also ask that their privacy be respected and that photographs be taken in accordance with Kuna Yala law (see *Visiting Kuna Yala*).

ARTS, CRAFTS AND TRADITIONS

The Kuna are famous for their molas, a traditional handicraft made of brightly coloured layers of cotton fabric appliqué. Tiny, evenly spaced stitches frame each piece of fabric, bits of which are cut back to expose lower layers, which are then sewn together to form a colourful design. Mola means blouse and these designs are actually dress panels and two joined together form the front and back of the Kuna woman's traditional dress. Designs vary today and molas fall into two distinct categories, referred to by the Kuna as 'typico' and 'commerciál'. The former is often a geometric design that depicts the Kuna philosophy that the tangible world depends on the spiritual well-being of Earth. The latter features Kuna flora or fauna and uses a riot of tropical colour. Molas reflect what's around them and popular contemporary culture is creeping into some of the designs generated on the more touristy islands, where Disney characters, Santa Claus and sword-brandishing Teenage Mutant Ninja Turtles can be found. Molas are available in abundance throughout Kuna Yala and sell for US$15 to US$30 depending on quality.

Other Kuna handicrafts include jewellery, basketry and wooden flutes and panpipes played at ritual ceremonies; and the 10–20cm nuchugana wooden figures which are treated as spiritual helpers by the Kuna Indian.

LANGUAGE

Dulegaya (meaning 'people's language') is the unique language of the Kuna people and is an important part of Kuna culture. A vast amount of time is dedicated to talk in Kuna communities because much of its structure is wholly perceived, conceived, organised and controlled by language and speech. The origins of Dulegaya provide an insight into all aspects of Kuna culture and society. Much of the economic, political and social structure is reflected in the language and religion and the ecology forms a large chunk of the language and its roots. Until recently Dulegaya wasn't a written language. As a result written forms differ greatly in the translation from spoken to written word. The letters b, c, t and w are often written as p, k, d and v, while most words have at least three different written variations. Sahila, the Kuna political and spiritual guide, for example, can be written as sakla, sayla or saila. Dulegaya is still by far the dominant language although Spanish is fast becoming a second language. English is only spoken by the small number of people in each Kuna community directly involved in the organisation of tourism.

Visitors that learn a few key Kuna phrases will earn significant respect from a community that is proud of its language. *Kuna Ways of Speaking: An Ethnographic Perspective* by Joel F. Sherzer provides help with basic greetings and plenty of traveller essentials. It's published by Hats Off Books in Arizona (US$16.95) and can be ordered from 610 East Delano Street, Suite 104, Tucson, Arizona 85705 USA; tel: +1 (520) 798 3306; fax: +1 (520) 798 3394; email: info@hatsoffbooks.com.

FESTIVALS AND EVENTS

The Kuna have a custom for every event and happening in their life and these customs are passed on to their children through dances and chants. These events are also documented in their molas. Some of the most important celebrations in this matriarchal society are the puberty rites. As menstruation begins the parents of a girl reaching puberty announce her womanhood to the village, and a two-day festival ensues. A second puberty ceremony follows on from this. Men in the community create a sacred thatched enclosure for the girl, where she lies secluded in a hammock made by her father, for four days. To protect her from evil spirits, she is painted black with jagua, a fruit brought by men from the mainland and taken to the girl. If anyone sees the men the Kuna believe it will cause her children to have birthmarks, so their arrival by canoe is heralded by gunfire. Panpipe flutes are then played when taking the fruit to her on foot. After she is painted, the villagers take turns pouring water over her body to cleanse her as she completes her transition into maturity, while eating a spicy soup. On day four she rejoins her community, has her hair cut short and is bestowed a name during lavish festivities. Up until this point she has been known by a nickname. A *kantule* (*gandule*) or fluteman performs and chants a long list of formal Kuna names, while maracas made from nutshell are shaken. The parents of the girl for whom the ceremony is held choose a new formal name from one of those in the list.

The celebrations are planned and prepared over several years and it is not uncommon for men of the family to hunt for two to three years for sufficient food for their guests. Meat and fish are smoked, char-grilled and stored in sealed vats ready for cooking with coconut, plantain and rice. Chicha, a heady home-made liquor made from fermented sugarcane, is produced in large quantities for liberal consumption, while long loose-wrapped cigars, *war suid*, are passed from guest to guest. The smoke is said to keep spirits at bay. Every member of the community attends the festival and drinks from a series of three different-sized cups at intervals. A large portion of chicha is consumed first at 20.00, followed by two measures at 23.00 and 02.00 that decrease in size. Guests then sleep off the effects for four hours before starting again. From this point the girl wears traditional Kuna dress and is available to marry.

FLORA AND FAUNA

In a country of disappearing rainforests the Kuna Yala is something of an exception. When landless peasants from the interior of Panama began to encroach upon Kuna land, many large areas of lush vegetation became desolate. Deforestation and pollution threatened the Kuna, who saw their trees disappearing and did something about it. Because of their kinship with the natural world the Kuna did not need scientists to tell them the impact of losing forest. The Kuna belief system is one of 'spirit sanctuaries' on forested land and according to the spirits any violation of these sanctuaries will result in harm to the Kuna community. In 1983, the Kuna set aside a vast piece of virgin rainforest for conservation, the first indigenous group in Latin America to do so. The 60,000ha nature reserve, Kuna Park, is managed according to the Kuna spiritual-based respect for nature. Different management zones divide the reserve, and certain activities are allowed in each:

- Nature Zone: only the gathering of medicinal plants is permitted, and sacred sites are respected
- Recovery Zone: degraded natural areas are being left to regenerate
- Marine–Land Cultivation Zone: Kuna live, fish, and grow crops traditionally
- Special Zone: public use, administration of biosphere reserve, and sustainable use of natural resources
- Buffer Zone: located outside of the boundaries of the natural reserve in an area that is under the administration of the government

While largely successful, conservation efforts in Kuna Yala are not without flaws. The Kuna culture is undergoing a dramatic and rapid change. While much of the traditional knowledge that dominates Kuna life remains intact, they have been unable to resist the influence of unplanned commercialism and its adverse environmental consequences. In some of the larger communities, overcrowding and sanitation have become a serious threat to the marine ecosystem. The high demand for fresh seafood from restaurants in Panama City has also led to over-

THE COCONUTS OF KUNA YALA

Until the late 1990s the coconut was the main currency of Kuna Yala, before mola sales soared to become the greatest source of revenue. Soil conditions are perfect for growing sweet-tasting coconuts and in Kuna Yala thousands of plants grow fast and furious. Harvests of 25–30 million coconuts each year are not uncommon and the Kuna use these to barter with Colombian traders in preference to selling them to 'Panama' (as the Kuna refers to it in remote terms). In return, coconut merchants bring jars of Nescafé, canned goods, clothing and fuel to Kuna Yala in large painted wooden schooners that are instantly recognisable.

However, the coconut remains important to the people of Kuna Yala in ways other than currency. Shells are used as bowls, cups and lamps, while the coconut water is drunk; the copra eaten; husk chips used as tools; dried husks and palm stems used as firewood; oil extracted for moisturiser and cooking; palms used for making mats, roofing and partitions; husks woven to make rope and hammocks; brooms made from the frond spines; coconut milk used for cooking; and trees serving as shelter.

fishing and an abuse of marine resources. Management plans for Kuna Park have addressed these but remain woefully underfunded and poorly staffed.

The Kuna themselves realise the importance of protecting their resources and operate important environmental monitoring programmes as well as educational programmes for schools within Kuna Yala. Unlike elsewhere in Panama, the threat of deforestation does not come from inside forces and apart from the tree trunks required to make *ulus*, the essential dugout canoe, the Kuna have little use for hardwood. Bamboo, reeds and palm fronds are used to construct buildings and an absence of large-scale farming means little jungle has been lost to agricultural needs.

TOUR OPERATORS

Panoramic Panama Tel: 314 1417; email: enquiry@panoramicPanama.com; www.panoramicPanama.com. Offers tailor-made camping trips, 2–5-day cultural tours, short birding breaks and snorkelling trips.

Ancon Expeditions Tel: 269 9415; fax: 264 3713; email: info@anconexpeditions.com; www.anconexpeditions.com. Offers a range of specialist tours to Kuna Yala with the services of a natural history guide, including a 3-day/2-night trip and fixed departure programme.

Extreme Adventures Tel: 269 7326; fax: 360 2035; email: info@extremePanama.com; www.extremePanama.com. Offers 2–3-day excursions combining snorkelling, natural history and cultural activities.

San Blas Sailing Tel: 226 2005; fax: 226 8565; email: info@sanblassailing.com; www.sanblassailing.com. Runs highly recommended yachting trips in Kuna Yala. It's the only sailing operator fully endorsed by the Kuna for its understanding of local laws and regulations and was established in the late 1990s to represent several skippers based in Kuna Yala, all of them experienced sailors. Guests fly into Corazon de Jesús from Panama City where a boat transports them to their first anchorage. Fishing is a daily activity (as is dining on the catch) as well as swimming, kayaking, birdwatching, dolphin spotting and snorkelling in a boat with fan-cooled double cabins, equipped with shower. Choice of French, Spanish or English guide.

GETTING THERE
By car/on foot
Reports vary about the trail that leads from Nusagandi to Kuna Yala. According to the Panamanian Tourist Board it's impassable. According to several adventurous souls that have tried it the route is OK during the dry season, January to March. Be prepared for a rough ride through virgin forest to Cartí and don't attempt it in anything other than a robust 4WD with chains. Boatmen in Cartí can provide transport out to the islands.

By air
The islands are served by light aircraft that fly to 11 destinations and land on grassy airstrips, some of which are only accessible in good weather. Most flights require an early start and are particularly prone to delay due to the thick cloud cover above the mountains. Expect a bumpy ride and small seats and if you're the biggest passenger you'll be sat next to the pilot if the plane is full. Most airstrips ask to see ID. The biggest carrier by far is Aeroperlas (tel: 315 7500; www.aeroperlas.com), which serves Kuna Yala via 72 flights a week (see schedule below). Tourismo Aereo (tel: 315 0279) run a limited service that is new at the time of writing.

By boat
This popular region for boaters should only be sailed by experienced yachtsmen as the submerged islands, tricky currents and coral reefs of Kuna Yala are notoriously troublesome to navigate. Those that do attempt it will find the excellent *Cruising Guide*

FLIGHTS TO/FROM PANAMA CITY

To	Depart	Arrive	Schedule	One-way	Round-trip
Ailigandi	06.00	06.55	Daily	US$39.90	US$79.80
Achutupu	06.00	06.55	Daily	US$39.90	US$79.80
Cartí	06.00	06.50	Daily	US$31.50	US$63.00
Corazon de Jesús	06.00	06.30	Daily	US$33.60	US$67.20
Mulatupo	06.00	07.15	Daily	US$45.15	US$90.30
Porvenir	06.00	06.25	Daily	US$31.50	US$63.00
Playon Chico	06.00	06.40	Daily	US$37.80	US$75.60
Puerto Obaldia	06.00	07.00	Thu/Sun	US$52.50	US$105.00
Río Sidra	06.00	06.45	Daily	US$31.50	US$63.00
San Ignacio Tupile	06.00	06.40	Daily	US$37.80	US$75.60
Ustupo	06.00	07.10	Daily	US$39.90	US$79.80

From	Depart	Arrive	Schedule	One-way	Round-trip
Ailigandi	07.05	08.25	Daily	US$39.90	US$79.80
Achutupu	07.05	08.25	Daily	US$39.90	US$79.80
Cartí	07.00	07.25	Daily	US$31.50	US$63.00
Corazon de Jesús	06.40	07.25	Daily	US$33.60	US$67.20
Mulatupo	07.25	08.25	Daily	US$45.15	US$90.30
Porvenir	06.35	07.20	Daily	US$31.50	US$63.00
Playon Chico	06.50	08.25	Daily	US$37.80	US$75.60
Puerto Obaldia	07.15	08.15	Thu/Sun	US$52.50	US$105.00
Río Sidra	06.55	07.20	Daily	US$31.50	US$63.00
San Ignacio Tupile	06.50	08.25	Daily	US$37.80	US$75.60
Ustupo	07.20	08.25	Daily	US$39.90	US$79.80

to the Isthmus of Panama an essential tool. This extraordinary work by Nancy Schwalbe Zydler and her husband Tom details every nautical hazard, current and tide consideration (see *Appendix 1* for details) and every visiting sea dog in Kuna Yala has a salt-sprayed copy. Another option is to let others take the strain (see *Tour operators*).

Those keen to travel by boat in a small group from Colombia to Kuna Yala, without risking a stint as a cargo passenger, can do so from Cartagena for about US$180. Book it through Hans at the Viena hostel on Calle Luna. The trip takes between two and three days and passengers need to bring their own food. The boat disembarks at Porvenir and requires a minimum of five people. It's US$250 for a return trip.

PRACTICALITIES

As a protected area under autonomous rule all tourism activities are controlled (see *Visiting Kuna Yala*). Moving around unguided is difficult; accommodation is limited; and fees to visit each island (US$3–5 each) and to cover photography (US$1 per photo) can soon stack up. Respecting the beliefs and sensibilities of the Kuna is another key consideration (see *Etiquette*) as is an abidance of laws in this land of self-rule. Each community has different laws and tolerances and what is acceptable on one island may be wholly unacceptable on another. Many of the more remote communities may only have seen a handful of foreigners each year – if any. Some will know the latest Britney Spears hit and may have had chips and Coke for their supper. Some communities prohibit alchohol; others are lenient on consumption. So it's important to take advice ahead of visiting each community. There are only a few restaurants in the entire 2,360km^2 region, a reason why there is a prevelance of room rates that include all meals. As a result prices seem high and cutting costs isn't easy, unless you can negotiate a half-board package and are within easy reach of a grocery store. Shops are pretty limited to local fruit and veg and whatever the Colombians bring in, but fresh Kuna bread is delicious and just 10c for a bag. Beer is 25c for a can, a bag of rice is US$1 and fresh fish US$2–3. A rare and simple restaurant on Mulatupo Sasardi, 7km from Isla Pino, serves big meals with a smile for less than US$4 a plate.

Aside from the rustic Kuna hotels (see *The Islands*) the only option is camping, which is frowned upon on some of the islands and can be dangerous if you pick the wrong spot. The chances of running into Colombian drug-runners increases on outer atolls so a good option is to engage a knowledgeable guide. One of the few independent tour operators to offer this service is Panoramic Panama, whose affordable guided camping trips allow travellers to sleep safely on the beach (see *Tour operators*). Added benefits include having someone that can spear fish for supper and also knows where the best snorkelling spots are in the archipelago.

Travellers keen to avoid the crowds should give the island of Carti Suitupo a miss from October to April. Those who don't could find themselves engulfed by 1,000+ rampaging passengers wearing high-cut shorts whilst paying over the odds for Kuna handicrafts and stuffing their faces with pizza.

There are a number of payphones throughout the archipelago and some are subject to a dubious US$1 'tourist tax'. There are also a handful of banks but visitors are advised not to rely on these for smaller denomination notes. Pack loads of US$1 to allow for tips, photographs, payphones and payments to the sahila. As Kuna Yala is hot, humid and without paved paths, road transportation or 24-hour electricity, visitors should also bring plenty of sun lotion and insect spray. A couple of bottles of water is advisable (it is rarely sold) as is a pair of boots or trainers and a torch.

Darién Province

> Or like stout Cortez when with eagle eyes
> He star'd at the Pacific – and all his men
> Looked at each other with a wild surmise –
> Silent, upon a peak in Darién.

In the sonnet 'On First Looking into Chapman's Homer', Keats famously refers to a ground-breaking trek across the inhospitable, tangled jungle of the Darién Province in 1513, when the first European viewed the Pacific Ocean from the New World. Unfortunately Keats confused Vasco Núñez de Balboa, the leader of the expedition, with Hernán Cortez. He should have written 'stout Balboa' rather than 'stout Cortez', and nor did Balboa just stand, 'Silent, upon a peak in Darién.' He waded into the sea in full armour and claimed the ocean for Spain. In 1519 Balboa fell foul of a jealous Spanish grandee sent out as his superior. He was tried on trumped-up charges and beheaded.

For hundreds of years the Darién defied explorers. An unmapped wilderness containing some of the most torturous jungle on the planet, captured in harrowing tales of perilous journeys and human survival. Most famous is that of Isaac Strain in 1854, an ambitious young US Navy lieutenant. His flawed 97-day expedition in Darién pushed his men to the brink of madness as they trudged deeper into the jungle. Physical exhaustion, starvation, cannibalism and flesh-imbedding parasites saw them surrender to despair. Today the Darién is still a relative unknown; fabled worldwide as a great, untamed, primitive wilderness and a lost, uninhabited world that time seems to have forgotten. In part that is not far from the truth although, paradoxically, while Darién contains some of the most unspoilt land in the Americas, it is a region ravaged at the hand of man.

The split is geographical with the worst of the destruction in the north. Until just 20 years ago there were no roads in the Darién. Today the Interamericana cuts through as far as the town of Yaviza 100km from the Colombian border, the only uncompleted piece of the Pan-American Highway connecting North and South America overland. The road into the north of the region has exposed it to loggers, cattle ranchers and migrants from Panama's overcrowded interior provinces that have been able to penetrate the more accessible outer areas. Today the destruction continues; slowly but surely shaving away at the forest, erasing areas of breathtaking beauty and ecological importance now that there's nothing left to plunder in the central regions.

Darién's wild and inaccessible south forms a sharp contrast to the man-ravaged north; the very antithesis of sullied and soiled where inaccessibility has been its salvation. Magnificent, pristine, vine-tangled rivers loop thick bright-green forest containing a staggering array of wildlife in a 576,000ha conservation area of jungle swamp, rocky coves, sandy beaches, waterfalls and mountains. Few places on earth

DARIÉN PROVINCE

PANAMA

COMARCA DE KUNA YALA

San Ignacio
Punta Kuibgandi
Ailigandi
Achutupo
Mamitupo
Ustupo
Punta Mosquito
Piriá
Cerro Grande
800m
Cerro Pilgrigandi
670m
Mansucum
Navagandi
Ipetí
Tortí
Uala
Mulatupo Sasardi
Morti
Punta Sasardi
I Seletupo
Tubuala
Caledonia
I Suletupo
Punta Escocés
I del Oro
Las Aguas Frías
Cerro Chucanti
1439m
Cerro Sasardi
844m
Punta Carreto
Anachucuna
PUERTO
OBALDÍA
I Cabo Tiburón
Los Monos
Santa Fé
Cerro Bell
1047m
Capurganá
Cerro Anachucuna
701m
Quebrada Lino
Arretí
Cerro Gandí
1160m
AKANDÍ
La Quebrada
Meteti
Puerto
Quimba
Santa Rosa
Bajo
Grande
Cerro Armila
1421m
Río Congo
I Iguana
LA PALMA
Canglón
Boca
de Tuquesa
COMARCA EMBERA
No I
(Cemaco District)
Punta San
Lorenzo
Punta Patiño
Patiño
Chepigana
Canglón
Forest Reserve
COLOMBIA
Golfo de
San Miguel
Punta
Garachiné
Taimati
Cerro Tanela
1415m
EL REAL
YAVIZA
Garachiné
Boca de Sábalo
San José
Boca de Cupé
PUERTO INDIO
Balsal
Alto Limón
605m
Cerro Sapo
1145m
Boca de
Trampa
COMARCA
EMBERA No 2
(Sambú District)
Cerro Pirre
1200m
Los Katíos
National
Park
(Colombia)
Mamatí
Caracoles
Darién National Park
Cerro Setetule
1220m
Punta Carreones
Cerro Pirre
1581m
1706m
Marené
1568m
Puerto Piña
Calle Larga
Punta Piña
Jaqué
Co Mangle
470m
Cerro El Crúce
250m
PACIFIC OCEAN
Punta Guayabo Grande
Cocalito
COLOMBIA
CHOCÓ
N
Bradt
Punta Ardita
Jurado
0   20km
0   20 miles
Bahía de
Humboldt
Coredo

Caribbean Sea

Istmo del Darién

Serranía del Darién

Darién National Park

are habitat to such diversity of wildlife species and the birding is ranked with the best in the world. Those keen to add a speckled antshrike to their life list will find the pre-trip planning and preparation worth the hassle. There is also a better chance of seeing a harpy eagle (Panama's national bird) in the Darién than anywhere else in the country, and endemic species such as green-naped tanager, pirre warbler, beautiful treerunner and tacarcuna wood-quail. Four species of macaw, caiman, snakes, giant American crocodile, deer, ocelot, jaguar, anteater, monkey and a host of butterflies, frog and insects inhabit the Darién. Spotting most of these during a three-night/four-day expedition isn't out of the question such is the quality of the habitat in the south.

For visitors the sheer size of the 16,670km² province is daunting as are its vast, impassable expanses and few navigable roads. A hot hazardous climate, unmarked and overgrown trails, and few places to stay make exploration a challenge. Most travellers find the only way to discover its inner reaches is along a hidden riddle of murky river trails that require a dugout canoe, a guide and machete. Long arduous hikes through ankle-deep mud are the norm as are ticks, mosquitoes and heat like Hades. Discovering the Darién is breathtaking, exhilarating, dark, foreboding and tough – but worth it – and a must for any traveller that relishes adventure Amazonian-style. Visit with a professional guide (a naturalist preferably) for an unforgettable jungle trek through some of the finest terrain in the Americas.

CAUTIONARY NOTE

Travelling through certain parts of the Darién remains inadvisable due to the likelihood of spill-over trouble from the Colombian border. The highest risk area is the swathe of swampy jungle that forms the east of the province, known as the Darién Gap, but danger is not confined to this stretch only. Risk exists beyond a line drawn from Punta Carreto in the Comarca de Kuna Yala on the Atlantic coast, through Yaviza in the eastern Darién Province, to Punta Piña on the Pacific coast. Some of this area is unpredictable and much of it far from safe. Continued violence between Colombian paramilitaries and rebel insurgents renders this belt of forest off-limits. Most cross the border into Panama to elude government forces and spill-over fighting, looting and violence can occur without warning, as several travellers have found out to their cost. Reading *The Cloud Garden* (Corgi Adult) by Paul Winder and Tom Hart Dyke provides plenty of food for thought. This haunting real-life story of kidnapping by FARC paramilitaries is a fitting reminder that a trip to Darién can go horribly wrong.

In 2003 Colombia's AUC paramilitary group kidnapped three Americans after attacking the mainly-Kuna Darién villages of Paya and Pucuro. During the assault Indian chiefs were killed with bayonets and their bodies taken into the jungle and planted with landmines to discourage relatives from recovering the remains. Five houses were burned and after villagers fled for safety their homes were looted for food and other valuables. The Americans' Panamanian guide Víctor Alcázar, a veteran of the jungle, managed to escape but suffered bayonet wounds. The kidnappers held the hostages in the Darién Province for seven days before releasing them in Colombia. One of the kidnapped was danger-seeking author Robert Young Pelton, a writer on assignment for *National Geographic Adventure* magazine. Pelton, an adventure enthusiast renowned for his forays into global trouble spots, is the author of four books including, ironically, such titles as *The World's Most Dangerous Places,* a guide to global hotspots, and *Come Back Alive,* a travel advice book billed as 'The Ultimate Guide to Surviving Disasters, Kidnappings, Animal Attacks, and Other Perils of Modern Travel.'

That this danger hasn't dissipated over the years is a bitter blow to Panama's tourism efforts. Opening up the most beautiful jungle on earth would be a boon to a country striving for a bigger chunk of the eco-tourism pie. However, the advice from IPAT (Panamanian Tourist Board) is suitably cautionary. It doesn't warn against visiting altogether (as it did in 1999) but it does recommend travel only with a specialist guide and in a group.

Advice of the British Foreign Office, 2004

> Travel to the Darién province should be conducted only with an organised group and to protected tourist destinations such as Bahía Piña Tourist Resort, usually by air from Panama City. You should not stray from the immediate vicinity of the protected resort areas. Expedition companies based in Panama also sometimes organise expeditions to Darién. Check carefully that police protection is included. The border area with Colombia is particularly dangerous and political and criminal violence in Colombia often spills over into Panama. There are regular incursions by Colombian guerrillas and other armed groups.

Advice of the US State Department, 2004

> US citizens are warned not to travel overland through the eastern area of Darién Province (beyond a line drawn from Punta Carreto in the Comarca de Kuna Yala on the Atlantic coast, through Yaviza in the eastern Darién Province, to Punta Piña on the Pacific coast). This area encompasses parts of the Darién National Park as well as privately owned nature reserves and tourist resorts. While no incidents have occurred at these resorts, US citizens, other foreign nationals and Panamanian citizens have been the victims of violent crime, kidnapping and murder in this area. The Panama–Colombia border area is very dangerous due to the activities of Colombian terrorist groups, drug traffickers and common criminals. Note: The Secretary of State has designated the Revolutionary Armed Forces of Colombia (FARC), the National Liberation Army (ELN) and the United Self-Defense Forces of Colombia (AUC) as Foreign Terrorist Organizations.

Author's note

Heeding the advice of the US State Department means travelling no further east than the town of Yaviza. Indeed following it to the letter means stopping short of the Interamericana terminus by a good 10km. Using the 'imaginary line' to define troubled areas would also make Darién National Park completely off limits – an important point to consider. Always seek the advice and services of an expert guide when travelling in the Darién (see *Guides* in this chapter) and check the foreign office websites for travel updates (www.fco.gov.uk in the UK and www.state.gov in the US). The Darién Gap really is as volatile as it sounds, as many Indian villagers know only too well.

Advice of the Panamanian Tourist Board (IPAT), 2004

> Only certain areas of the Darién pose a safety threat to tourists. We recommend visitors to the province use a specialist guide and travel in a group to ensure their safety.

MAPPING DARIÉN

In a bid to better understand the make-up of the Darién, a congress of Embera, Wounaan and Kuna tribesmen began working with the **Centro de Estudios y Acción Social Panameno** (CEASPA) on a project to map indigenous land use in the Darién in 1993. From May through October of that year a team of two professionally trained cartographers and 23 local surveyors (*encuestadores*) made maps that meticulously depicted the river systems vital to the indigenous peoples. It showed where local communities hunt, fish, farm, cut firewood, gather building materials and collect medicine and indicated the extent of the territory utilised by the indigenous population. It also provided greater insight into the tourism possibilities of the region and helped to demystify much of its vast, remote wilderness. The map of the Darién was completed in March 1994 and has played a crucial role in discussions about the economic and environmental future of the region. It has also helped provide the Congreso Embera–Wounaan–Kuna with a voice to better influence governmental decisions regarding the future of Darién.

PARQUE NACIONAL DARIÉN

The Darién National Park is the largest protected area in Panama and in Central America as a whole, located to the east of Santa Fé and the Gulf of San Miguel. Extending along more than 80% of the Colombian border, this vast conservation area includes part of the Pacific coast and also the Darién, Sapo, Jungurudo and Pirre mountain ranges. The Chucunaque River and the basins of rivers Tuira, Balsas, Sambú and Jaqué fall within the park's boundaries with Cerro Tacarcuna forming the highest elevation at 1,895m above sea level.

Preserved since 1972 after the creation of the 700ha Alto Darién Protected Forest, the Darién National Park was established in 1980 and added to the World Heritage List a year later. In 1983 it was internationally recognised as a Biosphere Reserve under UNESCO's Man and the Biosphere Programme. The park is in a unique geographical position, as it forms a land bridge between Central and South America.

Slow natural erosion caused by tidal impact on the Chucunaque and Tuira rivers has created carved ravines, cuts and gorges and lowland and upland tropical forests contain some of the most remarkable wildlife in Central America. Giant cuipo (*Cavanillesia platanifolia*) trees abound, a species with a bizarre trunk and conspicuous crown and smooth bark, while the wetland forests along the Chucunaque and Tuira rivers are covered by 'cativo' (*Prioria copaifera*) the most utilised species for timber in the region. Wildlife found in the reserve includes bush dog, giant anteater, jaguar, ocelot, capybara (largest rodent in the world), howler monkey, racoon, brown-headed spider monkey, Baird's tapir, agoutis, white-lipped peccary, caiman and American crocodile. Staggering numbers of birds can easily be sighted and some 450 different species have been recorded here, five endemic to the region and 56 that are threatened or endangered, including scarlet browed, tawny crested and lemon spectacled tanagers, white fronted nunbird, grey cheeked nunlet, willets, mangrove black hawk golden-headed quetzals, yellow-green grosbeaks, yellow-collared chlorophonias, beautiful treerunners, varied solitaires, Pirre warblers, Pirre hummingbirds, Pirre bush tanagers, grey and gold tanagers, rufous-breasted Anthrush, sharpbills, black-tipped cotingas and Panama's national bird, the harpy eagle.

Fewer than 1,300 humans live in the reserve comprising two Indian tribes of

DISASTER IN DARIÉN

Scottish colonisation attempts in the Darién in the 17th century were doomed from the start. So what was it that prompted an adventurer from Scotland to build a settlement in the wild ravages of the Panamanian jungle?

Scotland was in a state of crisis at the end of the 17th century. Successive decades of warfare and famine had driven entire communities from the countryside to the cities, where the situation was equally bleak. People were left with little choice but to roam the streets as vagrants until they starved to death or died from disease. Trade had been crippled by England's wars against continental Europe, while Scotland's homegrown industries were suffering decline. This scene of desperate plight was nothing short of a national disaster and it wasn't long before the Scottish realised they needed to plan to revive Scotland's fortunes to avoid the country's total collapse.

A Scottish financial adventurer called William Paterson came up with the answer after meeting a sailor called Lionel Wafer in London through his role as founding director of the Bank of England. Wafer had regaled him with tales of paradise land on the Isthmus of Panama, where friendly Indians lived in a sheltered bay on rich, fertile land in a region called Darién. Patterson returned from the south to announce his plan in Edinburgh, and soon everyone was talking about Scotland as a major broker of trade across the Pacific Ocean.

Paterson seized on the potential of the Darién as a suitable location for a trading colony, offering the lucrative Pacific markets an alternative to the hazardous trip round Cape Horn on the southern tip of South America to reduce both time and costs significantly. A colony in the Darién would take months off of the journey time, with goods ferried across Panama from the Pacific and loaded onto ships in the Atlantic, speeding up trade and making it more reliable. A commission could be charged to merchant ships for the privilege of using the colony. The only obstacle in the way was the Spanish, who currently controlled that part of Panama.

The Darién Venture was a hugely popular idea attracting a massive take-up of subscriptions to the Company of Scotland Trading to Africa and the Indies, founded in June 1695. Considerable opposition came from England who feared the loss of its monopoly on British trade to the Indies, and after successfully lobbying the English Parliament many English investors were forced to withdraw.

Patterson was undaunted and turned to the Scottish people for support, attracting thousands of Scots, both rich and poor, and raising £400,000 in funding within 6 months. Five ships were built for the expedition, the Unicorn, St Andrew, Caledonia, Endeavour and Dolphin, despite efforts by the English authorities to stop them as the Darién Venture began to get underway.

Yet William Patterson and his colleagues were completely unprepared for Panama, thanks to Lionel Wafer's rose-tinted stories. Everyone involved in the project had an unrealistic vision of what lay ahead, packing a cargo of combs and mirrors to sell to the Indians as well as wigs and other useless items to use themselves. Under the command of Captain Robert Pennecuik, the ships set sail

some 1,000 Chocos (the collective term for the Embera and Wounaan) and 250 Kuna. Conserving these indigenous cultures is an important management objective of the park and communities are supported by subsistence agriculture projects and a small amount of tourism. In recent years some of the Embera villages have opened up to visitors and one riverside community offers overnight accommodation by permission of the *cacique* (chief).

from Leith harbour on July 4 1698 with 1,200 settlers aboard, although only he and William Paterson knew of the destination sealed in packages and soon to opened on the open sea. They made landfall at Darién on 2nd November, having lost only 70 people during the voyage.

They set to work building a settlement, soon realising that the land was unsuitable for agriculture and that the Indians in Darién cared little for their cargo of trinkets. The arrival of torrential rains in spring 1699 brought an epidemic of disease, resulting in the deaths of more than 200 colonists by March 1699 – a mortality rate of over ten a day. This desperate situation was worsened by the news that all English ships and colonies were forbidden to trade with the Scots by order of the King. Soon colonists were living in terrible conditions, living on less than a pound of mouldy flour full of maggots a week and growing weaker with each day. Despite food shortages, every man worked from dawn to dusk, their bodies growing macerated due to malnutrition and racked with disease. William Paterson's wife died on that first expedition along with his dreams and then the colony learned that the Spanish were planning to attack the settlers took to the sea in panic, abandoning the settlement to return to Scotland – although just one ship containing 300 passengers arrived in tact.

A second expedition left Scotland in August 1699 knowing nothing about the fate of the first colony and carrying 1,302 settlers on the ships led by *The Rising Sun*. Some 160 died before the arrival of the ships at the abandoned colony, which they set about rebuilding only for the second settlement to fare little better than the first. These fresh arrivals were completely unprepared for the harshness of the Darién territory and were soon faced with a collapse of discipline and rampant disease. They also lived with the constant threat of a Spanish attack and were unsupported by the English colonies, which had been ordered not to come to their aid.

A newly arrived young officer, Captain Alexander Campbell of Fonab, persuaded the colonists to launch a pre-emptive strike against the Spanish forces massing at Toubacanti on the mainland. The attack was successful but only served to inflame the Spanish who under the command of Governor-General Pimiento, launched a massive fleet and forced the colony to surrender in March 1700. Although surviving colonists were permitted to leave aboard their remaining ships, only a handful ever made it back to Scotland and the Darién Venture proved a complete disaster for Scotland and the Scottish morale. Those that did make it back to their homeland became outcasts in their own country, disowned by family and friends as failures to live a life of misery. William Paterson was also forced to defend his actions and died a deeply disillusioned man.

Economically the Venture was devastating, losing £232,884 in life savings of many Scottish people and leaving Scotland incapable of independent rule. Seven years later Scotland conceded to the Act of Union, joining Scotland with England as the junior partner in the united kingdom of Great Britain. England paid off Scotland's debt as part of the deal using an institution to administer the money that went on to become the Royal Bank of Scotland.

Getting there

Reaching the National Park is easiest via a chartered flight at El Real through ANCON that takes you straight to Caña Scientific Station (it has a landing strip for light aircraft with tours booked with Ancon, see *Specialist tours*). Another option is to fly into La Palma and get a boat to El Real and hike to the nearest ranger station (see *Suggested hiking itinerary*). Another possible entry point is Sambú (arrive by boat or by plane and get a canoe along the Sambú River). The Pirre Station can only be reached on foot from El Real (three hours) and is a difficult trail without a guide. ANAM rangers in El Real can supply one for US$20–30 and this is money well spent.

Where to stay
Visitors to Darién National Park can stay in any of the ANAM ranger stations by prior arrangement including those at El Real, Pirre and Cruzamono. Costs are US$5 per person or US$5 to camp and accommodation comprise bunk-bed dorms (bring a sheet) with river bathing or cold-water showers. Lodging at the Ancon station in Caña costs US$90 per day including three meals (tel: 264 8100) but by far the most cost-effective way to stay here is to book a four-day/three-night package that includes everything – flights, guide and all camping equipment, horses and porters. A bed in a cabin at the nature reserve at Punta Patiño (tel: 269 9414) costs from US$10.

Practicalities
Spending time in Darién National Park requires proper planning and considerable preparation. Most visitors engage a specialist guide on the basis of safety, ease and convenience as getting around often involves canoes and unmarked trails. Many guides use horses to transport tents, provisions and backpacks, making long jungle treks less arduous and photography easier. Specialist tour operators also co-ordinate accommodation with the Indian communities and know the safest places to camp. Most expert guides carry a GPS phone for emergencies as well as medical kits, flares etc. Trips are registered with local police and the ANAM office. Veteran Darién also know the territory sufficiently well to spot a potential threat to safety.

ANAM (tel: 299 6373) has an administration office in El Real and ranger stations with overnight accommodation and/or camping at Caña, Pirre Cruzamono and Balsas. Panama's largest private conservation group, ANCON (tel: 264 8100), is located at the Caña Environmental Centre and Scientific Station, where accommodation and tours are offered via Ancon Expeditions (see *Specialist guides*). All visitors to the Park should pack plenty of jungle essentials (see *Chapter 1, Basics*).

COASTAL DARIÉN
La Palma
For a pleasant alternative to the road trip that deposits visitors at Yaviza choose the flight into La Palma, the most populous community in Darién at the mouth of the River Tuira. While there isn't much in the way of sightseeing the town does make a practical point to begin or end a visit; indeed La Palma is always full of fresh arrivals just off the plane or travellers that are hanging around to catch a boat or a flight home. The only bank in the Darién is found here as well as a medical centre, police station, vehicle repair shop, half a dozen bars and hotels, and a line of street food vendors. Pick up a guide here for the Punta Patiño Reserve or local Embera Indian villages, although few are inclined to journey into Darién's interior unless it is on the promise of a very hefty fee.

Getting there
Aeroperlas has a regular schedule to La Palma from Chitré at 07.00 Monday to Friday, and from Panama City 09.00 on Tuesday and Friday and 08.45 on Saturday.

EXCAVATING PRE-COLUMBIAN DARIÉN

The Darién fascinates archaeologists and there have been significant finds in the province. In 2004, a team of British explorers made one of the most exciting discoveries in recent years, unearthing four pre-Columbian sites in the Bahía Piña. The findings by the Scientific Explorer Society (SES) were especially remarkable as they came from an area where none was thought to have existed. Dating from AD500 to AD1000, they included a 5m, 30-tonne boulder covered in petroglyphs, the only one discovered so far in the eastern part of the country. The team's two doctors and a dentist were also able to provide medical aid to Embera and Wounaan Indians in the area. For details of future SES expeditions in Panama contact SES Motcombe, Shaftesbury, Dorset SP7 9PB, UK; tel: 01747 854898; email: base@ses-explore.org; www.ses-explore.org.

Where to stay

La Palma has a number of cheap hotels and a few good little places to eat a decent meal on a shoestring budget. One of the nicest (and cheapest) places to stay is **Pensión Tuira** where 11 basic but comfortable rooms cost US$10–15. Fan-cooled rooms at the family-run **Hotel Biaquira Bagara** have shared or private cold-water bathrooms at US$15–20 per night.

Punta Alegre

This small Afro-Dariénite community shares the same nub of land as Punta Patiño and is located on its northern jut in the Gulf of San Miguel, 8km southwest of La Palma and 19km northwest of Garachiné. The name of the village means 'Happy Point' and its 500 or so people are renowned for their love of music, an African-Latin American mix that plays from dawn until dusk. Fishing huts, a couple of restaurants and a handful of grocery stores are drenched in coastal sounds and drumbeat. The restaurants serve seafood all day and emanate with booming Bullerengue.

Punta Patiño

This 24,300ha nature reserve, a former coconut plantation owned by ANCON and managed by ANAM, contains a 13,805ha Ramsar-listed area of wetland of importance and sits in the Pacific watershed at the mouth of the Tuira River in the Gulf of San Miguel. Visitors arrive either by plane from Panama City or by a combination of foot, horse and canoe from El Real or Yaviza. Protecting dozens of threatened species of flora and fauna including jaguar, crocodile, deer, puma, green iguana and harpy eagle, the reserve contains mangroves, sandy beaches and marshlands that attract nesting pelicans and sea birds. Agriculture scholarships benefit 50 Darién communities, including those in La Palma, Cucunatí, Metetí, Mogue, Cémaco, Sambú and Taimatí. An Environmental Centre displays details of this project and guides can be booked for a number of eco-tourism expeditions throughout the wildlife refuge.

Some 68 species of birds have been recorded at Punta Patiño, four of which are endangered and five under threat. Reptiles include iguana, caiman and crocodile and 15 species of mammals including 12 that are threatened with extinction. Sea turtles have been tagged on Patiño Beach and the site also supports agouti and several species of deer. A large tract of virgin forest and a dense area of mangrove swamp remain largely undisturbed and five species of mangrove, sea grass and an unidentified cactus species thrive

Getting there

The boat journey from La Palma to Punta Patiño is a true delight and follows a route that hugs the shoreline through fishing-boat waters and past the mouth of the mangrove-edged Mogue River. Boats that arrive at Punta Patiño should wait for the ANAM tractor to pull them ashore. It drives out on to the mud flat and picks up arrivals to avoid muddy feet.

Where to stay

Accommodation at **Punta Patiño Lodge** (tel: 269-9414) consists of ten brightly painted cabins nestled in a garden of bougainvillea with magnificent lofty views. Each has two single beds or bunk beds and a shared cold-rainwater shower for US$10 per night.

Garachiné

Located on the southwest curve of Bahía Garachiné, this small fishing community is served by an airport and a decent stretch of road that loops out to Taimatí village, connecting with Sambú Airport on the way. Garachiné provides another entry point into the Darién via the Sambú River and the bay is a popular place for yachts and cruisers to anchor. Boatmen living on the bay-side are a good source of transportation to the Embera community in Playa de Muerto further along the coast to the south. One place to stay in Garachiné has rooms at US$6 per night and a couple of mediocre restaurants are at least open early and late. To book a room contact Gisela de Olmedo via one of the two payphones in the village (tel: 299 6428/6477).

Getting there

Aeroperlas fly to Garachiné from Chitré via Panama City and La Palma 07.00 Tuesday and Friday and from Jacqué Tuesday and Friday at 09.55. There's also a flight from Panama City 09.00 on a Tuesday and Friday via La Palma.

Playa Muerto

Embera at this small coastal community are keen to develop cultural tourism efforts and regularly welcome visitors to its beachfront village.

Spectacular jungle backdrops and a neat collection of wood-and-thatch huts contain overnight accommodation (two separate double rooms at US$8–12 per night including food) and cook Mama Grajales serves up lobsters, fish and chicken with plantains and rice. Dozens of children (there are more than 100 in Playa Muerto) play in the shallow waters on the shoreline and herald the arrival of visitors. An Embera guide is US$20 for a group of four per day. Expect jungle treks, botanical walks and cultural displays of dance, handicrafts and body painting – and don't let the name (Death Beach) put you off.

Getting there

A large motorised canoe will do the journey from Garachiné in 2½ hours or less for US$100 round trip. Boats usually depart in the calm early morning tides and arrive at Playa de Muerto by 09.30.

Sambú

The village of Sambú sits on the Sambú River close to a small runway that serves as a gateway to the Darién interior via the River Sambú. Here it is possible to hire a guide with a motorised dugout canoe for an unforgettable river trip through some truly primeval jungle scenery. Wind past a succession of Embera fishing villages and hunting territory used by tribesmen with blowguns and spears.

Crocodiles bask on riverbanks under a knot of creepers and vines, while scorched vegetation teems with waterfowl and supports jaguars and harpy eagle. Navigating huge mud banks, shallow waters and drifting fallen trees, the route requires a skilful boatman and it is wise to pick one with the most comfortable-looking boat. The journey is long – and very, very hot. Pack enough water, sun block and mosquito spray or find this trip unbearable. Prices vary but expect to pay US$100 for a round trip to **Pavarandó**, the farthest village from Sambú. Add extra for food and lodging (around US$15 per person per day, unless you've brought camping supplies). All guides from Sambú have a network of villagers they call on for some form of lodging but pack a tent to be on the safe side. Allow for the cost of fuel for the return journey, which should be purchased in a drum from Sambú).

Getting there
The two-hour boat ride from La Palma to Sambú will cost US$100–200 depending on how many there are in the party and the size of the boat. Aeroperlas runs scheduled flight services from Chitré via Panama City 07.00 Monday, Wednesday and Friday, from David 07.00 Monday, Wednesday and Friday, and from Panama City via El Real 08.45 Monday, Wednesday and Friday.

Bahía Piña
Ask anyone in Panama about Bahía Piña and they are sure to mention big fish, for this pretty little bay between Jaqué and Punta Piña is renowned for its great sportfishing records. Black marlin, blue marlin, Pacific sailfish, dorado, yellowfin tuna, grouper, roosterfish, snapper and amberjack are all found here and fished by visitors from all over the world just 8–20km offshore. Its calm, fertile waters have broken more International Game Fish Association (IGFA) world records than anywhere else – 170 at the last count.

Enthusiasts with fishing on their mind stay at the Tropic Star Lodge where over 40 world records are held for black, blue and striped marlin and Pacific sailfish. It has also recorded over 23 Junior Angler World Records and attracts a dedicated fishing crowd who book week-long all-inclusive packages at pretty hefty prices.

Getting there
The owners of the Tropic Star (see *Where to stay*) built the local airstrip, which is served by Aeroperlas from Chitré on Tuesday and Thursday at 07.00 and on Saturday 08.00; from Colón on Tuesday and Thursday 08.15; from David on Tuesday and Thursday 07.00; and from Panama City Tuesday, Thursday and Saturday 09.30.

Where to stay
The **Tropic Star Lodge** boasts a sterling reputation and its fair share of Hollywood names as clientele. Following a sportfishing conservation ruling in Panama in August 1997 the Bahía Piña area has a 32km 'non-commercial' fishing zone. Guests at Tropic Star release all billfish (it was awarded the IGFA 1999 award for its conservation efforts) and also practise catch-and-release fishing methods.

Accommodation consists of self-contained cabins and rooms and the resort has an excellent restaurant, a bar and incredible views across the bay. Sitting in several thousand acres of rainforest with waterfalls, birding observation points, silver-sand beach and a coral reef, the property is often booked 12 months ahead so an advance reservation here is essential. Rates vary throughout the year and depend on the size of each party. Expect to pay from US$2,750 per person for a seven-day/six-night stay and US$1,595 per person for a four-day/three-night stay, based on four people. At the request of guests there are no telephones at the Lodge. Bookings and enquiries are handled in Florida; tel: toll free 1 800 682 3424; tel: (407) 423 9931; email bonnie@tropicstar.com; www.tropicstar.com.

Jaqué

A more modest base from which to explore this costal strip is Jaqué, a small community 8km from the Tropic Star, and the last town ahead of the Colombian border region. Colombian refugees who fled across the border to escape fighting paramilitary groups have joined the indigenous Indians of this community, which has no roads, one telephone and very little tourism. Refugees have placed further economic strain on Jaqué and its impoverished residents who have traditionally eked out a living from small-scale agriculture and fishing. A remote location, unpredictable weather and strong currents explain the virtual absence of local trade markets. The addition of a small workshop via a UN funding programme in 2002 gave the community a boost and today local women are taught to sew under a blue fluorescent light at dusk.

While there are no formal amenities for visitors don't let this put you off. The Jaqué community is more resourceful than it may first appear and offers meals and lodging for those prepared to ask around. Several people have raved about a seafood lunch prepared by a woman called Gumi, while Don Pininin is an interesting local character who is worth seeking out. Pininin, a self-taught carpenter, creates amazing drums using balsa logs crafted with a machete and stretched wild pig skin across the top of the wood once it is hollowed out. Another local resident Dona Vicenta has rooms to rent to visitors in her simple home and has hosted visiting dignitaries, missionaries and charity workers.

In December 2003, 80 of the 400 Colombian refugees in Jaqué were repatriated in the first phase of Panama's agreement with Colombia.

Getting there

Jaqué is served by Aeroperlas schedules from El Real on Tuesday, Thursday and Saturday at 10.35; from Chitré via Bahía Piña on Tuesday and Thursday at 07.00; and from Chitré via Bahía Piña on Saturday at 08.00. The flight from Colón departs at 08.15 on Tuesday and Thursday; from Contadorra on Tuesday and Thursday 08.55 and on Saturday at 08.25; and from David on Tuesday and Thursday at 07.00. There's also a flight from Panama City via Bahía Piña on Tuesday and Saturday at 09.30.

THE DARIÉN INTERIOR
Santa Fé

This little town 3km off the Interamericana and approximately 20km from Meteti has a grocery store, bakery, kiosk and a couple of small hotels. The nicest of a grim bunch is the **Honee Kaiba**, where ten rooms with shared and private cold-water bathrooms cost US$8–10 per night. March 4–7 (or thereabouts) is when the town celebrates its annual fiesta, the Feria de Santa Fé. A procession of marching bands and brightly coloured costumes is the most celebrated in the Darién.

Meteti

Most travellers agree that this small roadside town makes a better stopover option than Yaviza. It sits on the Interamericana 50km from its terminus and has several family pensiónes and a handful of friendly restaurants where bus drivers from

Panama City stay before doing the return trip. Bars play loud salsa music, the cantinas serve good cheap food all day and the place has a party feel when drivers congregate and (rather worryingly) decide to drink until dawn. The **Hotel Felicidad** (tel: 299 6188) seems to be the stopover of choice for most travellers passing through and has 30-plus rooms at US$8–15 a night. Light sleepers should bring earplugs as it sits over a noisy bar.

Yaviza

The Interamericana grinds to a halt in Yaviza after whistling through dozens of unsigned communities that comprise a handful of thatch-and-wood huts. Drivers heading to this last Panamanian outpost before the Darién Gap from Panama City should allow at least six or seven hours for the 266km drive. Doable in less after a dry spell, the road is prone to erosion after the rains, and it is not unusual to encounter pot-holes the size of a minivan on its most difficult stretches. Yaviza is a dismal place without soul or character; an end-of-the-road town whose function is little more than a car park and jumping-off point. It's the place where visitors grab a ride or register with the police if they plan to travel into the jungle. It is also home to the final bus stop in Panama. Restaurants, a car repair shop, bar and a ten-room budget hotel half-heartedly serve the tourist, but Metetí makes a more pleasant stop-off. The **Hotel 3 Americas** is faded and uncared for. It has fan-cooled rooms and a communal bathroom at US$8 per night.

El Real

El Real is hot, steamy and all that you may imagine from a frontier jungle town, which Spanish Conquistadors built to provide protection to the transportation of gold from Caña mine. Today it is one of the largest settlements in the Darién and an arrival and departure point for travellers to and from the interior – a ramshackle collection of wooden buildings that has a certain charm. Tables of womenfolk play bingo on the square and the buildings creak in a breeze. Visitors can hire a guide and horses, buy food and water, find a hotel for the night and register with ANAM here. Rooms at the **Hotel El Nazareno** (tel: 228 3673) are grotty with termite-eaten walls that look like they are about to crumble at any minute. Showers are cold- rainwater buckets and the toilets are grim but double rooms are US$8 per night.

Getting there

El Real is served by Aeroperlas schedules from Chitré Monday, Wednesday and Friday at 07.00; from Colón Monday, Wednesday and Friday at 08.15; from David Monday, Wednesday and Friday at 07.00; and from Panama City Monday, Wednesday and Friday at 08.45. There is also a flight from Jaqué at 09.40 on Monday, Wednesday and Friday.

Boca de Cupe

Forming the border control point as the last town to the eastern flank of Darién ahead of the Colombian border region, the town's sandbagged defensive positions and police lookout points reflect a real concern of paramilitary incursions. Boca de Cupe was once home to 16,000 workers that mined gold in Caña but today much of this 19th-century town feels like a ghost town, despite having a population of around 1,000. Most are Afro-Dariénite but the number of Colombian refugees is growing as more and more seek to cross this section of the border under temporary status.

Most visitors arrive here to simply pass through to or from the Ancon station at Caña. A trail from Boca de Cupe has a chequered past and was once (and possibly still is) a favourite route with Colombian rebels. Today it is used frequently by major adventure tours and birdwatching guides to reach Caña and is deemed safe (or as safe as it can ever be) at the time of writing. However, caution is strongly advised. Visitors should register with the authorities in Boca de Cupe but not openly discuss their route with local people. ID is required at the checkpoint where police questioning is usually brusque, understandable given that Colombian guerrillas overran Boca de Cupe in 2003 and patrols remain jumpy.

SPECIALIST WILDLIFE AND ADVENTURE TOURS

Ancon Expeditions PO Box 0832, World Trade Centre, Panama; tel: 269 9415; fax: 264 3713; www.anconexpeditions.com. By far the best tours in Darién are offered by Ancon. Tailor-made and guided travel packages include specialist guide, charter flights into Caña using private airstrip and full back-up support. Ancon guides are renowned for their exceptional quality and trips are well organised with little left to chance. All are natural history experts, scientists, conservationists, birders or botanists. Itineraries offer a good mix of adventure and ecology and guides have superb local knowledge as well as jungle survival techniques.

ECO Circuits Tel: 314 1586/617 6566; fax: (708) 810 9350 (US); email: annie@ecocircuitos.com; www.ecocircuitos.com. Offers organised trips and guided cultural tours in Darién to Embera Indian villages and coastal communities to discover handicrafts, traditional fishing practices and ecological tours of rivers, waterfalls, jungle and medicinal plants.

SPECIALIST GUIDES

For a full list of guides, including those with Darién expertise, refer to *Chapter 2, Guides*. Dozens of travellers to the Darién have recommended **Hernán Arauz,** which is why he is worthy of a special mention. Undoubtedly one of the most accomplished natural history guides in Panama, Arauz arguably knows the Darién like no other. He knows what to do in the event of a peccary charge, an ant swarm and a striking fer de lance and packs a gun, legally. Calm under pressure he comes from a family of explorers and field scientists as the son of Reina Torres de Arauz, Panama's leading anthropologist and Amado Arauz, legendary explorer of the Darién. Hernan is a veteran of trans-Darién expeditions, including the first one transmitted over the internet. He is an avid birder with a Panama bird list of more than 750 species and is able to convey knowledge with enthusiasm and considerable flair. Hernan Arauz leads expeditions for ANCON (see *Specialist wildlife and adventure tours* for details) and is a colleague of **Mario Bernal**, another noteworthy Panamanian natural history guide *(see Chapter 2, Guides)* Recommendations for specialist birding guides can be obtained from the **Panama Audubon Society** tel: 224 9371; fax: 224 4740; email info@Panamaaudubon.org; www.Panamaaudubon.org.

Appendix

FURTHER INFORMATION
Books
Activities and sport

Friar, William *Adventures in Nature: Panama* Avalon Travel Publishing, 2001, 1566912407. Highlights activities for adventure travellers, drawing particular attention to conservation and how you can get involved.

Agnew, Jeremy *Scuba Diver's Travel Companion* Globe Pequot Press, 2003, 0762726687. A general guide to the best dive sites around the world, with a section on Central America.

Archaeology

Lothrop, Samuel K *Coclé: An Archaeological Study of Central Panama* Peabody Museum, Cambridge, 1942. A rare collector's item, on sale from www.bartlebybooks.com. Limited availability.

Art and design

Lothrop, Samuel K *Pre-Columbian designs from Panama: 591 illustrations of Coclé Pottery* Dover Publications, 1976, 0486232328. A collection of stylised gods, men, birds, fish, monkeys, florals and abstracts in a unique Coclé style.

Miller, Tom *The Panama Hat Trail* National Geographic Society, 2001, 0792263863. A humorous journey that charts the making and the marketing of the famous Panama hat. Based mainly in Ecuador, this is an exciting story of capitalism and cultures in collision.

Biography and memoir

De Goodin, Melva Lowe *From Barbados to Panama*, 2001. This book can be purchased through the *Panama News* bookshop: Apartado 55-0927 Estafeta Paitilla, Panama; email: editor@thePanamanews.com; www.thepanamanews.com. This is a bilingual narrative about a Panamanian schoolgirl who sets out to discover her roots. There are several pages of historical photos documenting the construction of the Canal.

Donadio, William *The Thorns of the Rose*, 2002. This book can be purchased through the *Panama News* bookshop: Apartado 55-0927 Estafeta Paitilla, Panama; email: editor@thePanamanews.com; www.thepanamanews.com. This memoir documents the experiences of the European part of the Canal Zone's Silver Roll. It is a valuable insight into US–Panama relationships from a middle-class perspective.

Ford, Peter *Tekkin a Waalk: Along the Miskito Coast* Flamingo, 1993, 0006545122. This is a travel memoir that takes the reader along the Central American coastline, from Belize, through Guatemala, Honduras and Panama. It is a portrayal of a people who live geographically and culturally on the border of two worlds, combining fascinating historical accounts of the Garifuna and Miskito kingdoms and the effects of colonialism throughout the area.

Greene, Graham *Getting to Know the General: The Story of an Involvement* Vintage, 1999, 0099282666. Greene's account of his five-year friendship with Omar Torrijos, ruler of Panama 1968–1981.

Morris, Edmund *Theodore Rex* Random House, 2001, 0812966007. The sequel to *The Rise of Theodore Roosevelt,* this lively biography of the naturalist, adventurer soldier and politician charts his numerous achievements, including the acquisition of the Panama Canal.

Noriega, Manuel and Eisner, Peter *America's Prisoner: The Memoirs of Manuel Noriega* Random House, 1997, 679432272. US prisoner of war Noriega tells his life story and exposes the secrets behind US relations with Panama. Award-winning correspondent Peter Eisner confirms the validity of many of General Noriega's claims.

Sosa, Juan B *In Defiance: The Battle Against General Noriega Fought from Panama's Embassy in Washington* Francis Press, 1999, 0966505115. The memoir of Panama's ambassador to the US who waged a two-year battle against General Noriega to maintain control of the embassy in the name of the constitutional government of his nation.

Children's books

English, Peter *Panama in Pictures* Lerner Publishing Group, 1996, 082251818X. An illustrated introduction to the history, geography, government, people and economy of Panama and the Panama Canal, suitable for children of 9–12 years.

Meachen-Rau, Dana *True Books: Countries – Panama* Children's Press, 1999, 0516211897. An introduction to the geography, people and culture of Panama for kids of 9–12 years old.

Precilla, Maricell E *Mola: Cuna Life Stories and Art* Henry Holt and Company Inc, 1996, 0805038019. An explanation of the Kuna tribe and their art, told through life stories, with vivid illustrations. For children aged seven and up.

Sensier, Danielle *Costumes* Hodder & Stoughton Children's Division, 2003, 0750245255. A good introduction to the clothes of other cultures, including the mola blouses of Panama.

Culture

Howe, James *The Kuna Gathering: Contemporary Village Politics in Panama* Fenestra Books, 2002, 1587361116. A fascinating anthropological study of Kuna village politics.

Howe, James *A People Who Would Not Kneel: Panama, The United States, and San Blas Kuna* Smithsonian Institution Press, 1998, 1560988657. Anthropologist James Howe tells the fascinating story of an indigenous tribe who fought against takeover, and set their own terms to the expanding nations of the Western hemisphere.

Keeler, Clyde E *Secrets of the Cuna Earth Mother: A Contemporary Study of Ancient Religions* Exposition Press, 1960, 0682468150. Provides a useful comparison of the religion and culture of the Kuna with that of the Far East.

Perrin, Michel and Dusinbere, Deke *Magnificent Molas: The Art of the Kuna Indians* Flammarion, 2001, 2080136747. A fascinating collection of more than 300 fabric paintings, made and worn by the women of the Kuna, with useful background to mola art, its origins and meanings.

Salvador, Mari Lynn *The Art of Being Kuna: Layers of Meaning Among the Kuna of Panama* University of California Museum, 1997, 0930741617. An insight into the art, music, culture and values of the Kuna tribe that has helped them to defend and retain their way of life.

Stephens, Clyde *The Banana People: True Stories of the Tropics* This book is print-on-demand from www.dollarbillbooks.com. Adventures in Panama as told by a former researcher at the United Fruit Company, and tales of other banana people.

Tice, Karin E *Kuna Crafts, Gender, and the Global Economy* University of Texas Press, 1995, 0292781377. An analysis of the origins and craft of mola designs and the direct impact of global forces and tourism on local culture.

Ventocilla, Jorge, Herrera, Heraclio and Núñez, Valerio *Plants and Animals in the Life of the Kuna* University of Texas Press, 1995, 029278726X. A study by two Kuna biologists and a Panamanian colleague that analyses Kuna ecology and argues for a positive environmental policy.

Early history

Anderson, C L G *Old Panama and Castilla Del Oro* The Page Company, 1911. A hard-to-find narrative history of the discovery, conquest and colonisation of Panama by the Spanish.

Earle, Peter *The Sack of Panama: Sir Henry Morgan's Adventures on the Spanish Main* Viking Press, 1982, 0670614254. An account of the looting of Panama in 1671 by Welsh pirate Sir Henry Morgan.

Howarth, David A *Panama: Four Hundred Years of Dreams and Cruelty* A readable history of the isthmus from 1513 to 1964.

Economy and aid

Barry, Tom *Roots of Rebellion: Land and Hunger in Central America* Lightning Source Inc, 1987, 0896082873.

Barry, Rachel and Garst, Tom *Feeding the Crisis: US Food Aid and Farm Policy in Central America* Bison Books, 1991, 0803260954. A thoughtful academic analysis of whether the shipments of US aid are feeding the people, or in fact fuelling the crisis.

Fiction

Banks, Iain *Canal Dreams* Abacus, 1990, 034910171X. A political thriller, in which a world-famous cellist from Japan is captured aboard a ship on the Panama Canal.

Galbraith, Douglas *Rising Sun* Pub Group West, 2001, 0802138640. A 17th-century journey to the northern coast of Panama leads to comrade rivalry, disease and misery.

Gilbert, J S *Panama Patchwork: A Treasury of Isthmian Life in Poetry, self published by Canal Zone,* early 1900s. Gilbert worked for the Panama Railroad Company, but died of malaria before this book could be completed. He was known as the poet laureate of the isthmus, and wrote this collection of poems depicting life in the area before the completion of the Canal.

Le Carré, John *The Tailor of Panama* Sceptre, 1999, 0340766549. This spy thriller offers an insight into life and society in Panama, woven around the politics of the American hand-over of the Panama Canal.

Levi, Enrique Jaramillo (ed) *When New Flowers Bloomed* Latin American Literary Review Press, 1991, 0935480471. These short stories by women from Costa Rica and Panama mirror their countries' struggles to overcome poverty and violence.

McCreary, Paul, 'Panama Madness' in his *Panama Madness and Other Bedtime Stories* Xilibris Corporation, 2000, 0738829935. This one isn't for kids. A trademark McCreary with frightening and imaginative characterisations.

McNab, Andy *Last Light,* Simon & Schuster, 2002, 0743406281. Forced into an assassination mission against his will, Nick Stone ends up in Panama, embroiled in a sequence of action-packed events.

Miller, Carlos Ledson *Panama* Xlibris Corporation, 2000, 073880715X, print-on-demand. A fast-paced saga that captures the sweep of Panama's tumultuous history and its search for a national identity.

Geography and ecology

Coates, Anthony *Central America: A Natural and Cultural History* Yale University Press, 1988, 0300068298. An excellent introduction to the geographical, political and cultural development of Central America. The book is the outcome of the Paseo Pantera project, an international conservation effort dedicated to fostering a system of interconnected and protected natural corridors throughout the Central American isthmus.

Darcy, William G and Correa, Mireya D *The Botany and Natural History of Panama* Missouri Botanical Gardens, 1985, 0915279037. Out of print. This collection of research papers contains the results of various experiments including instructions on how to build aerial walkways in rainforest canopies.

Dressler, Robert L *Field Guide to the Orchids of Costa Rica and Panama* Cornell University Press, 1993, 0801481392. This accessible guidebook points out all the main orchid species in the area, and is illustrated with 240 colour photographs and 229 line drawings.

Eisenberg, John F *Mammals of the Neotropics – The Northern Neotropics* University of Chicago Press, 1989, 0226194506. A good introduction to bio-geography, and to the species of mammals found in the neo-tropics, aimed at field researchers and graduate students.

Hilty, Steven *Birds of Tropical America* Chapters Publications, 1996, 1881527565. As opposed to a field guide, Hilty offers a natural history of tropical birdlife, from nesting habits to the structure of the birdlife community, song patterns and migration within the tropics. As such, it is equally as fascinating for the armchair bird enthusiast as for the field birdwatcher.

Hunter, Luke and Andrew, David *Watching Wildlife Central America* Lonely Planet Publications, 2002, 1864500344. From toucans to tapirs and jaguars to jacamars, this innovative all-in-one guide will help you to find and identify Central America's amazing wildlife.

Kricher, John C *A Neotropical Companion: An Introduction to the Animals, Plants, and Ecosystems of the New World Tropics* Princeton University Press, 1999, 0691009740. A readable and thoroughly researched introduction to the South and Central American neo-tropics.

Leigh, Egbert Giles and Ziegler, Christian *A Magic Web: The Tropical Forest of Barro Collerado Island* Oxford University Press, 2002, 0195143280. Inspiring photographs of Barro Collerado Island with clear and authoritative text makes this an ideal coffee-table book.

Reid, Fiona A *A Field Guide to the Mammals of Central America and Southeast Mexico* Oxford University Press USA, 1998, 0195064011. Accounts and range maps for all species of mammals, plus sections on how and where to find the animals. Described as a 'labour of love', this book is very highly regarded by both amateur and professional naturalists.

Ridgley, Robert S and Gwynne, John A Jr *A Guide to the Birds of Panama* Princeton University Press, 1989, 0691025126. A great illustrated field guide to some 1,000 species in this rich and varied (and threatened) region. It is expensive and very much in need of a new edition, but it is still considered to be one of the best field guides to the birds of Panama.

Wheatley, Nigel and Brewer, David *Where to Watch Birds in Central America, Mexico and the Caribbean* Princeton University Press, 2002, 0691095159. A thorough list of bird species in the area, with useful information about accommodation, transport, safety, and when to visit. This book is particularly good in the early stages of planning a trip.

Windsor, Leigh and Rand (eds) *The Ecology of a Tropical Forest: Seasonal Rhythms and Long-Term Changes* Smithsonian Books, 1996, 1560986425 This hard-to-find title summarises research from the tropical forest on Barro Colorado Island, Panama. Although a little dated, it does have an afterword, which runs through ecological findings of the past 15 years.

Health

Dawood, R *Traveller's Health: A Complete Guide to the Hazards of Travel* Oxford University Press, 1987, 0192615629. Helpful advice on how to stay healthy abroad.

Hatt, J *The Tropical Traveller: The Essential Guide to Travel in Hot Countries* Penguin, 1993, 0140165487. This thorough book will answer all your questions from what to pack, to dealing with culture shock.

Robin, M and Dessery, B *The Medical Guide for Third World Travellers* K-W Publications, 1992, 0929894065. A portable medical handbook that will help you to diagnose common illnesses, with advice on prescription medication, first-aid kits, and a list of travel clinics should you contract something more serious. An absolute must for those planning extensive trips.

Wilson Howarth, Jane and Ellis, Dr Matthew *Your Child's Health Abroad: A Manual for Travelling Parents* Bradt Travel Guides, 1998. A reassuring and practical guidebook for those travelling with children, offering advice on how to deal with minor ailments or life-threatening situations.

Young, Dr Isabelle *Healthy Travel: Central and South America* Lonely Planet Publications, 2000, 1864500530. A user-friendly guide to minimising health risks and dealing with problems while on the road.

Language

Eposto, Roberto *Latin American Spanish Phrasebook* Lonely Planet Publications, 2003, 1740591704. A handy pocket-sized phrasebook specifically of Latin American Spanish, and its various dialects throughout the region.

Wegman, Brenda and McVey Gill, Mary *Streetwise Spanish*, McGraw-Hill, 1998, 0844272817.

The Panama Canal

Cadbury, Deborah *Dreams of Iron and Steel* Fourth Estate, 2004, 0007163061. Cadbury recounts the development of seven of the greatest worldwide engineering feats from the mid 19th century, one of which is the creation of the Panama Canal.

Dutemple, Lesley A *The Panama Canal* Lerner Publishing Group, 2003, 0822500795. Drawing from letters, quotes and speeches made by those involved, Dutemple looks at the cause and effect of the building of the Panama Canal from the perspective of the people.

Espino, Ovidio Diaz, *How Wall Street Created a Nation: J P Morgan, Teddy Roosevelt and the Panama Canal* Four Walls Eight Windows, 2003, 1568582668. A readable but perhaps at times over-dramatic telling of the coalition that created the Panama Canal, detailing the financial speculation, fraud and international conspiracy involved.

Friar, William *Portrait of The Panama Canal: From Construction to the Twenty-First Century* Graphic Arts Centre Publishing Company, 2003, 1558687467. A historical synopsis of the Canal that also paints a vivid picture of the life of a child growing up in the Canal Zone.

Keller, Ulrich *The Building of the Panama Canal in Historic Pictures* Dover Publications, 1984, 0486244083. An impressive pictorial account of the building of the canal, that really brings events to life.

Lafeber, Walter *Panama Canal: The Crisis in Historical Perspective* Oxford University Press USA, 1990, 0195059301. Out of print.

Lindsay-Poland, John *Emperors in the Jungle: The Hidden History of the U.S. in Panama* Duke University Press, 2003, 0822330989. Bringing together the very latest research, Lindsay-Poland discloses the full extent of American intervention in Panama, from the 1989 invasion to prolonged chemical-weapons testing, and the huge human and environmental toll of the building of the Canal.

Markun, Patricia Maloney *It's Panama Canal!* Shoe String Press, 1999, 0208024999. Currently out of print, this is an evaluation of the Canal past and present written just before the official hand-over in December 1999. Maloney discusses how she believes ownership of the Panama Canal will affect its people.

McCullough, David *The Path between the Seas: The Creation of the Panama Canal 1870–1914* Simon and Schuster, 1978, 0671244094. An exciting description of all the events and personalities involved in the creation of the Canal which led to revolution, economic crisis and a new Central American Republic.

Politics

Barry, Tom and Lindsay-Poland, John *Inside Panama* Latin American Bureau, 1995, 0911213503. Hard to find. A varied overview of the country's geopolitical position as an international crossroads; the make-up of its government, economy and aid, as well as history and talks of the future.

Dinge, John *Our Man in Panama: How General Noriega Used the United States, and Made Millions in Drugs and Arms* Random House, 1990, 0394549104. Dinge details the relationship between the US and Noriega, with critical emphasis on US involvement in Panamanian affairs.

Dolan, Edward F *Panama and the United States: Their Canal; Their Stormy Years* Franklin Watts Inc. March 1990, 0531109119. A history of Panama's relations with the US, this book contains extensive source notes, with good photos and maps to support the text.

Donnelly, Thomas, Roth, Margaret and Baker, Caleb *Operation Just Cause: The Invasion of Panama* Rowman and Littlefield, 1991, 0669249750. Out of print. Drawing on hundreds of interviews, the authors describe the invasion by 26,000 US troops against the Panama Defence Forces, and the toppling of Manuel Noriega.

Franklin, Jane (Independent Commission of Enquiry) *The US Invasion of Panama: The Truth Behind Operation 'Just Cause'* South End Press, 1994, 0896084078. A controversial and passionate argument against the invasion of Panama in 1989.

Jackson, Eric *Nine Degrees North* (self published) A diverse sampling of six years of articles, photos and cartoons that reflect the many facets of Panama, written by the editor of the *Panama News*. Available from the *Panama News* book shop, Apartado 55-0927 Estafeta Paitilla, Panama; email: editor@thePanamanews.com; www.thepanamanews.com.

Kempe, Frederick *Divorcing the Dictator: America's Bungled Affair with Noriega* Putnam Publishing Group, 1990, 0399135170. A chilling expose of the CIA's involvement in Noriega's rise to power.

Murillo, Luis E *The Noriega Mess: The Drugs, the Canal, and Why America Invaded* Video Books, 1995, 0923444025. This out-of-print title offers some useful answers to why Noreiga was able to reign for so long, and to what extent the US was involved in the drug trade and the manipulation of the media. At 1,000+ pages, it is a long but seemingly unbiased and informative read.

Taw, Jennifer M *Operation Just Cause: Lessons for Operations Other Than War* Rand Corporation, 1996, 0833024051. A discussion of the success of the 1989 invasion of Panama, and what lessons can be learnt for the future.

Weeks, John and Gunson, Phil *Panama: Made in the USA* Latin American Bureau, 1991, 0906156556. An analysis of the invasion of US troops in 1988 and their attempt to topple Noriega; and US–Panama relations since the country's creation in 1903.

Traditional music

Los de Azuero *Traditional Music From Panama* (CD) Nimbus Records, 1999, US Import. This collection of music originates from the still-rural Azuero peninsula of Panama; largely percussive, with African and Afro-Carribbean influences.

Various Artists *Rendezvous in Panama* (CD) Columbia River Entertainment, 1998, US Import. A collection of music from various artists which gives a full flavour of the traditional music of Panama.

Transport

Vipond, Anne *Panama Canal by Cruise Ship: The Complete Guide to Cruising the Panama Canal* Ocean Cruise Guides, 2001, 0969799187. A useful reference source for those specifically interested in the Canal, or planning to travel by it. Good details of various ports, and possible shore excursions.

Zydler, Tom and Zydler, Nancy Schwalbe *The Panama Guide: A Cruising Guide to the Isthmus of Panama* Seaworthy Publications, 2001, 1892399091. The definitive guide to the Isthmus, this book includes specific piloting instructions covering all coastal Panama, its navigable rivers and the famous Canal.

Articles and journals

Friar, William 'Place Names and Their Meanings' in *The Panama Canal Review* Spring 1972
'Early Day Towns Along the Line' in *The Panama American* August 15 1939.
'Lake Villages' in *The Canal Record* December 6 1911.

Maps

Panama Canal Map Treaty Oak, 1995, 188971000X.
Panama Map ITMB Publishing, 2001, 1553413598. Scale: 1:800,000 with inset maps of the region including the Canal (1:400,000) and Panama City, with an index of hotels and services and information about history and places of interest.
The Panama Canal Cruise Map Publishing Co, 1995, 188791000X. Scale: 1:80,000 full-length map of the Canal, with a detailed history, information about the workings of the canal and photographs inset.
Kapp, Capt Kitt S *The Early Maps of Panama up to 1865* K S Publications, 1971.
Lewis, S A *Panama* Treaty Oak, 1996, 8437818109. An indexed road map of the country (scale: 1:1,000,000) with a detailed street map of the city on the reverse. Legends are in Spanish.

Websites

www.businessPanama.com Tips for business travellers and news articles concerning the country's business exploits.
www.canalmuseum.com Geographical information and interesting statistics about the Panama Canal.
www.hri.ca/partners/ccs Spanish-speaking website of the Centre for Social Training in Panama, which aims to promote and defend human rights in Panama.
www.latinamericanbureau.org This is a good place to get hold of political and environmental books on Central America and has a good list of NGOs/voluntary organisations which deal with Panamanian issues.
www.Panamacanalcountry.com A useful alternative to the official tourist website, this has a good list of recommended reading, useful facts and suggested itineraries.
www.Panamainfo.com Lots of useful info on things to see and do in Panama to help you plan your trip.
www.pancanal.com The Panama Canal Commission provides updated info on the Canal today, including toll prices and current press releases, as well as offering an introduction to the Canal's history.
www.sanlorenzo.org.pa The English- and Spanish-language website of the San Lorenzo project, an NGO working for the protection of the forests, wetlands, coasts and rivers of Panama in conjunction with local rural communities.
www.visitPanama.com This is the official website for the Institute of Panamanian Tourism. It is an easily navigable site with facts about the country and some interesting articles.
www.vivaPanama.org Expatriate site for Panamanians in America with excellent links to Panama sites worldwide and full schedule of cultural events and folkloric festivals.
http://earthtrends.wri.org World Resources Institute, 2004. EarthTrends: the Environmental Information Portal.

Appendix 2

FINDING A HOME IN PANAMA

The absence of restrictions on foreign land ownership has seen the numbers of overseas buyers in Panama increase ten-fold since the end of the 1990s. A dollar economy, low cost of living and pleasing year-round climate have made Panama an attractive prospect. If economists are to be believed, the isthmus is about to hit the big time, as holiday-home buyers, investors and retirees continue to discover its charm.

Foreign retirees were the first to snap up real estate in Panama after realising that they were eligible for significant tax benefits under a Pensiónado Programme (see *No 1 with Retirees*). Indeed *CNN Money, International Living* and *Homes Overseas* have each tipped Panama as an emerging international real estate market, while *Modern Maturity*, the world's largest consumer magazine, ranked Panama the fourth-best retirement destination on the planet after Costa del Sol (Spain), Cinque Terre (Italy) and Provence (France).

Prime property hotspots are the Bocas del Toro archipelago on the Caribbean and the highland town of Boquete where boom-time has been led by demand from American and European buyers. Elsewhere the Pacific coast, a favoured destination with Panama's affluent second-homers, has attracted recent Japanese interest. China, with whom Panama maintains excellent relations, is also tipped as a likely future market. A significant number of the country's 1,500+ pinprick islands are now under private ownership. Prices have soared since the TV series *Survivor* (see *Panama Province* chapter) as buyers clamber to find their own deserted castaway isle.

Horror stories abound about buying real estate in Panama. Most involve renegade vendors ripping off naive gringos for six-figure sums. However, in reality, it is unscrupulous foreign developers that are at the centre of most property scandals in Panama. Every boom attracts get-rich-schemers and Panama is no exception.

Sensible purchasers will find that it is more than possible to find a place to call their own on the isthmus without falling foul of deception. Prices are keen, but rising, yet it is still possible to find an entire atoll for under US$40,000, albeit a small one. Eager buyers arriving with this amount in cash should observe caution. It may be small change for foreign property hunters but it represents more than ten years' salary to an average Panamanian (the equivalent of US$368,000 to an American and £251,00 for a Briton).

Panama is slowly becoming more adept in dealing with foreign buyers administratively. Dozens of lawyers, relocation agents and real estate agents actively target the overseas market. The quality can vary as dramatically as the ethics as past buyers will confirm. Logging on can help, as umpteen expatriate websites and chat-rooms offer advice, tips and contacts to spare others pain. *Panama News*, the country's online English-language newspaper, has run exposés on real estate rogues – and there is nothing better than this 'warts and all' stance for hearing it like it is.

Buyers should be aware that there are two types of property in Panama, 'titled' and 'rights of possession' (ROP). Thanks to Panama's bureaucratic tendencies its public registry system is top-notch and as a result problems relating to titled land are rare. ROP wrangles, however, are less straightforward to resolve and can take several years of legal battles and costly solicitors' fees. This type of land is common throughout the Bocas del Toro archipelago as it commonly relates to islands and beachfrontage. Although this is trickier to purchase, it isn't impossible, but buyers should be mindful that most of Panama's high-profile disputes relate to ROP land. Other considerations are visas (see *Chapter 1, Visas and red tape,*) and medical care and whether the property is built on land prone to earthquakes. Residency rules meanwhile are fairly simple and non-bureaucratic. Whilst there are no statutory residency rules as such, an individual is considered resident if he or she is present in Panama for more than 180 days in any single tax year. This has to be officially recognised by the government.

Those thinking of living, working or setting up a business in Panama will find few distinctions between foreigners and nationals under Panamanian law. Personal income tax applies to Panama-sourced income and after personal allowances is levied on a sliding scale up to a maximum of 30% on income over US$200,000 a year. Other taxes include social security contributions, with the employer paying 10.75% of salaries and wages plus a 1.5% educational tax, whilst the employee pays 7.25% plus 1.25%. Real Estate tax is levied on a sliding scale based on an official valuation starting at a rate of 1.4% on the first US$100,000 and rising to 2.1% on value in excess of US$75,000. There is also a form of value added tax on consumer purchases, generally charged at a rate of 5%, although imports, alcohol and tobacco attract a 10% tax.

Real estate tours
Panoramic Panama Tel: 314 1417; e-mail: enquiry@panoramicPanama.com; www.panoramicPanama.com. Dedicated real estate and orientation tours to all known developments in areas around Boquete and Bocas del Toro, for serious buyers, curious investors and those looking to relocate.

Real estate agents
Compañía Inmobíliaría San Félipe Calle 2, San Félipe, Panama City; tel: 228 3808; fax: 228 3864; email: sanfelipe@cwPanama.net; www.sanfelipe.com.pa. Specialist agents for renovated period homes in Panama City's old quarter, Casco Veijo.
Happy Whale Real Estate Edificio Impresoras Central, Av 2, Calle E Sur, PO Box 1026, David, Chiriquí; tel: 774 6190; email: saskia@happywhale.com; web: www.happywhale.com
Tropical Properties Tel: +1 800-390-8818 (US toll free); email: info@tropicalproperties.com; www.islasolarte.com. A master-planned development of properties on Isla Solarte in Bocas del Toro.
Panama Real Estate Las Margaritas Building, Ground Floor, 49th St, El Cangrejo, Panama City; tel: 223 0085; email: Panamarealestate@hotmail.com; www.Panamarealestate.freeservers.com
Big Creek Village Tel: 757 9966; email: info@bigcreekvillage.com; www.bigcreekvillage.com. A planned development of de-luxe beachfront condominiums in Bocas del Toro.
Chiriquí Realty Tel: 771 5531/622 4075; www.chiriquirealty.com
PAN-AM Construction Global Bank Building, Boquete, Chiriquí; tel: 615 6450; email: JohnV@pan-am-construction.com; www.escapetoboquete.com
Bocas Paradise Tel: 633 8050; email: liveyourdream@bocasparadise.com; web: www.bocasparadise.com
Tropical Pathways Email: info@tropicalpathways.com; www.tropicalpathways.com
Boquete Land Auctions Tel: 720 2337; email: boqueteauctions@hotmail.com; http://boquete.ibussinessdot.com
Las Olas Beach Development Playas Barqueta, David; tel: 772 3000; fax: 772 3619; www.lasolasresort.com
Panorama Panama Tel: 223 3648; email: info@panoramaPanama.com; www.panoramaPanama.com

NO I WITH RETIREES

Panama's Pensionado Visa Program has made it a hit with retirees keen to take advantage of the following tax holidays and money-saving discounts:

- Tax exemption to import a car every two years
- Import tax exemption for furniture, appliances and fixtures up to US$10,000
- 50% discount in cinema, cultural and sporting events
- 30% discount on train, bus and boat transportation
- 15% discount on loans made in your name
- 1% reduction on home mortgages for personal use
- 25% reduction on water, telephone and electricity bills
- 20% discount on doctor visits – and more

In order to apply for a residence permit under the Pensionado Programme it is necessary to prove a life pension of a minimum amount of US$500 per month. This should come from a foreign governmental institution, a private company, insurance scheme or private fund from outside of Panama.

Valle Escondido Tel: 507 720 2897; fax: 507 720 1450; email: sales@valleescondido.biz; www.valleescondido.biz. Custom-built homes on a master-planned development in Boquete.
Buena Vista Realty Email: bvrealty@cwp.net.pa; www.bvrealty-Panama.com
Escape Artist http://realestate.escapeartist.com. Online relocation and property sales listing with decent Panama section.
Island Realty Tel/fax: 757 9966; email: grpiii@cwp.net.pa; www.bocasdeltoro.net
Panama MLS Tel: 649 9373; email: info@Panamamls.com; www.Panamamls.com
Hemingway Hideaway Realty Tel: 771 5948; fax: 771 5948; email: hp3xbh@tierrasaltas.net; www.hemingwayhideaway.com

Websites
www.nvmundo.com Property listings for real estate in various regions of Panama.
www.viviun.com Online international property agency with good Panama property listing that has a wide range of different properties in provinces nationwide.
www.Panamarealtor.com Properties and land in Bocas del Toro, Boquete and Panama City,
www.caribpro.com Online listing of properties, islands and land in the Caribbean, which includes lands and properties in Bocas del Toro.
www.Panamadera.com Pacific beachfront properties and reforestation investment programmes.
www.panamaride.com

Relocation agents and information
The Barrington Group Plaza Credicorp Bank, 50th St, 6th Floor, PO Box 833-00034, Panama City; tel: 210 0001; fax: 210 0004; email: info@barringtongroup.com; www.barringtongroup.com
Panama Relocation American Chamber of Commerce Building, Calle Uruguay, Bella Vista, Panama; tel: 270 0687; email: info@Panamarelocation.com; www.Panamarelocation.com
Bocas Relocation Services Email: brs@dial.pipex.com; www.bocasrelocation.com. UK–Bocas relocation team that organises real estate tours, orientation packages, rental properties, schooling, shipping and documentation.

Panama At Your Service http://Panamaatyourservice.com. Relocation and real estate service in Panama, Bocas and Boquete.

Lawyers and legal information
Panama Title & Escrow, Inc Av Ricardo J Alfaro, Sun Towers, 1st Floor, Office #39, Panama City; tel: 236 8303; fax: 236 7150; email: info@Panamatitle.com; www.Panamatitle.com
Panama Legislation www.legalinfo-Panama.com. Lawyers, translators and advisory bodies.
Business Panama www.businessPanama.com. Relocation, legal and tax information.

Expatriate websites and chat rooms
www.escapetoboquete.com
www.2Panama2bocas.com
www.tightcircle.com
www.biviendoinPanama.com
www.americansinPanama.com
www.bocasrelocation.com

Expatriate Associations
American Association of Panama www.amsoc.org

Other resources
Potential buyers in Bocas del Toro should head to the Buena Vista on a Wednesday for the weekly 'Gringo Wednesday' meet-up of expatriates at the Buena Vista Bar & Grill. It's not the same bunch each week, just those that are in Bocas Town shopping for supplies. If you're considering a move to Bocas it's a chance to pick the brains of those that have done it before you. People drift in and out from lunchtime so grab a table at noon.

Mola pattern

Index

Page numbers in bold refer to major entries